STRE... ...S

Nottin...........shire

C000292583

www.philips-maps.co.uk

First published in 1994 by
Philip's, a division of
Octopus Publishing Group Ltd
www.octopusbooks.co.uk
2-4 Heron Quays, London E14 4JP
An Hachette UK Company
www.hachettelivre.co.uk

Third colour edition 2006
Second impression 2009
NOTCA

ISBN 978-1-84907-001-0 (pocket)

© Philip's 2006

Contents

III **Key to map symbols**

IV **Key to map pages**

VI **Route planning**

X **Administrative and Postcode boundaries**

1 **Street maps** at 2⅔ inches to 1 mile

221 **Approach map of Nottingham**

222 **Street map of Nottingham city centre**
at 5⅓ inches to 1 mile

224 **Index** of towns and villages

225 **Index** of streets, hospitals, industrial estates, railway
stations, schools, shopping centres, universities
and places of interest

Digital Data

The exceptionally high-quality mapping found in this atlas is available as digital data in TIFF
format, which is easily convertible to other bitmapped (raster) image formats.

The index is also available in digital form as a standard database table. It contains all the details
found in the printed index together with the National Grid reference for the map square in which
each entry is named.

For further information and to discuss your requirements please contact
victoria.dawbarn@philips-maps.co.uk

Motorway with junction number	
Primary route – dual/single carriageway	
A road – dual/single carriageway	
B road – dual/single carriageway	
Minor road – dual/single carriageway	
Other minor road – dual/single carriageway	
Road under construction	
Tunnel, covered road	
Rural track, private road or narrow road in urban area	
Gate or obstruction to traffic (restrictions may not apply at all times or to all vehicles)	
Path, bridleway, byway open to all traffic, road used as a public path	
Pedestrianised area	
DY7 Postcode boundaries	
County and unitary authority boundaries	
Railway, tunnel, railway under construction	
Tramway, tramway under construction	
Miniature railway	
Railway station	
Walsall	
Private railway station	
South Shields Metro station	
Tram stop, tram stop under construction	
Bus, coach station	

Ambulance station	
Coastguard station	
Fire station	
Police station	
Accident and Emergency entrance to hospital	
H Hospital	
Place of worship	
i Information Centre (open all year)	
Shopping Centre	
P P&R Parking, Park and Ride	
PO Post Office	
Camping site, caravan site	
Golf course	
Picnic site	
Prim Sch Important buildings, schools, colleges, universities and hospitals	
Built up area	
Woods	
River Ouse Tidal water, water name	
Non-tidal water – lake, river, canal or stream	
Lock, weir, tunnel	
Church Non-Roman antiquity	
ROMAN FORT Roman antiquity	
87 Adjoining page indicators and overlap bands	
246 The colour of the arrow and the band indicates the scale of the adjoining or overlapping page (see scales below)	

Acad	Academy	Inst	Institute
Allot Gdns	Allotments	Ct	Law Court
Cemy	Cemetery	L Ctr	Leisure Centre
C Ctr	Civic Centre	LC	Level Crossing
CH	Club House	Liby	Library
Coll	College	Mkt	Market
Crem	Crematorium	Meml	Memorial
Ent	Enterprise	Mon	Monument
Ex H	Exhibition Hall	Mus	Museum
Ind Est	Industrial Estate	Obsy	Observatory
IRB Sta	Inshore Rescue Boat Station	Pal	Royal Palace
		PH	Public House
Recn Gd	Recreation Ground		
Resr	Reservoir		
Ret Pk	Retail Park		
Sch	School		
Sh Ctr	Shopping Centre		
TH	Town Hall/House		
Trad Est	Trading Estate		
Univ	University		
W Twr	Water Tower		
Wks	Works		
YH	Youth Hostel		

■ The small numbers around the edges of the maps identify the 1 kilometre National Grid lines
■ The dark grey border on the inside edge of some pages indicates that the mapping does not continue onto the adjacent page

Railway or bus station building	
Place of interest	
Parkland	

The scale of the maps on the pages numbered in blue is 4.2 cm to 1 km • 2⅔ inches to 1 mile • 1: 23810

0	¼	½	¾	1 mile
0	250m	500m	750m 1 kilometre	

The scale of the maps on pages numbered in red is 8.4 cm to 1 km • 5⅓ inches to 1 mile • 1: 11900

0	220 yards	440 yards	660 yards	½ mile
0	125m	250m	375m ½ kilometre	

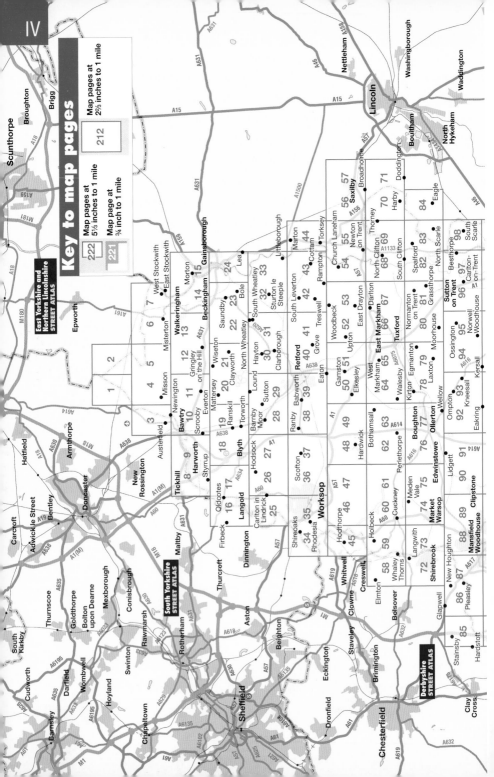

IV

Key to map pages

Map pages at
5½ inches to 1 mile
222

Map page at
¾ inch to 1 mile
221

Map pages at
2⅔ inches to 1 mile
212

East Yorkshire and Northern Lincolnshire STREET ATLAS

South Yorkshire STREET ATLAS

Derbyshire STREET ATLAS

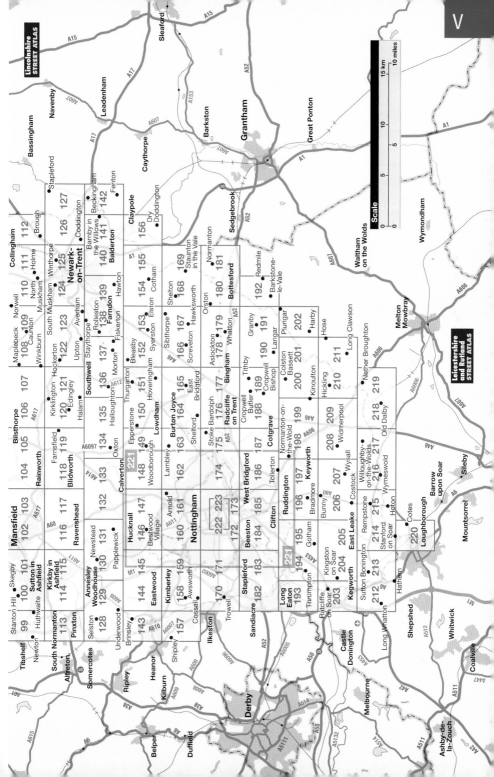

Route planning

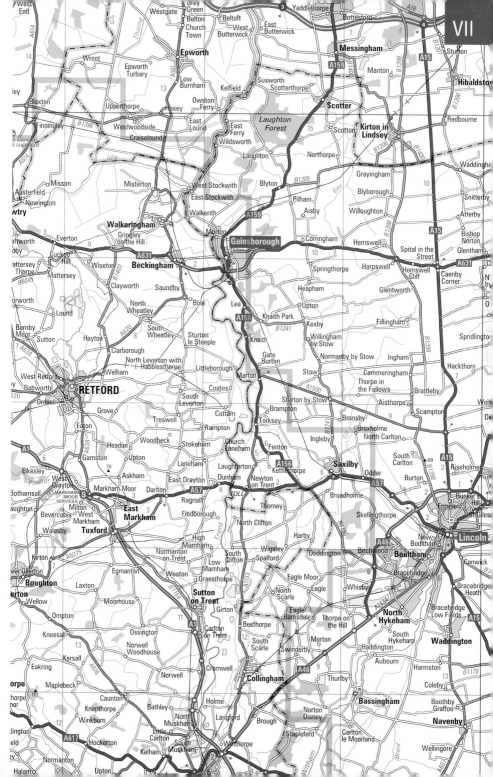

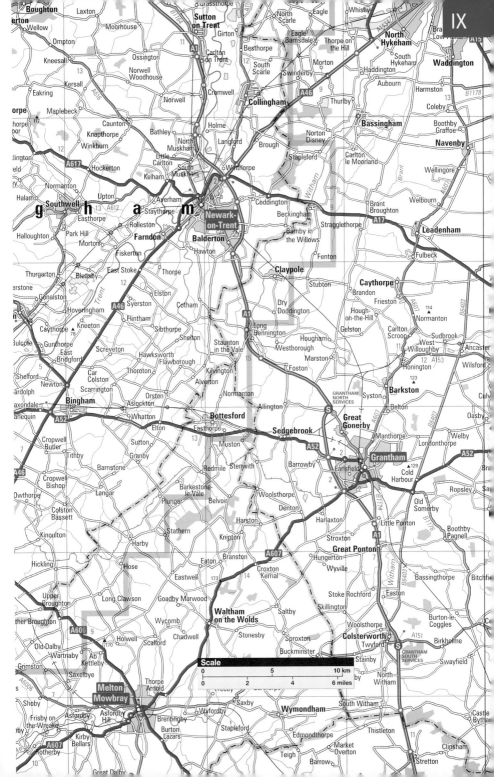

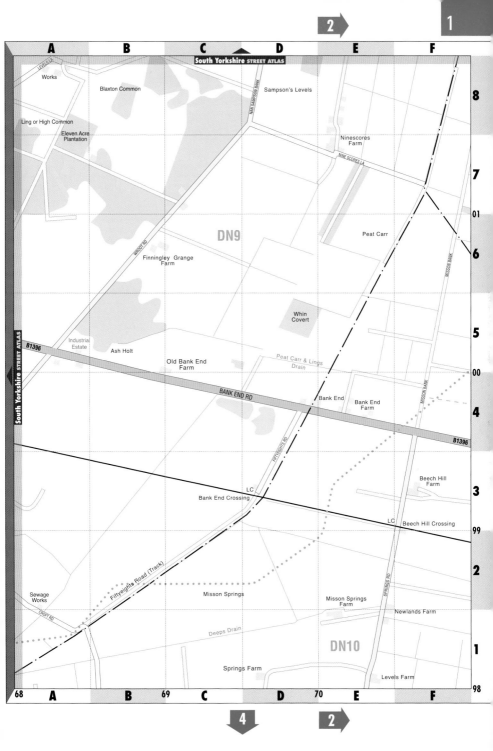

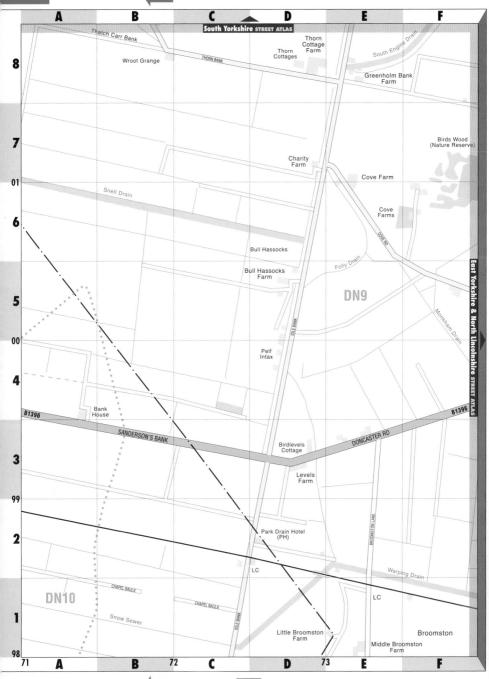
South Yorkshire STREET ATLAS

East Yorkshire & North Lincolnshire STREET ATLAS

Thatch Carr Bank

Thorn Cottage Farm

Thorn Cottages

Wroot Grange

THORN BANK

Greenholm Bank Farm

South Engine Drain

Birds Wood (Nature Reserve)

Charity Farm

Cove Farm

Snell Drain

Cove Farms

Bull Hassocks

Bull Hassocks Farm

Folly Drain

DIE RD

DN9

Monkham Drain

Pelf Intax

DIE BANK

B1396

Bank House

B1396

SANDERSON'S BANK

Birdlevels Cottage

DONCASTER RD

Levels Farm

BROOMSTON LANE

Warping Drain

Park Drain Hotel (PH)

LC

DN10

CHAPEL BAULK

LC

CHAPEL BAULK

DIE BANK

Snow Sewer

Broomston

Little Broomston Farm

Middle Broomston Farm

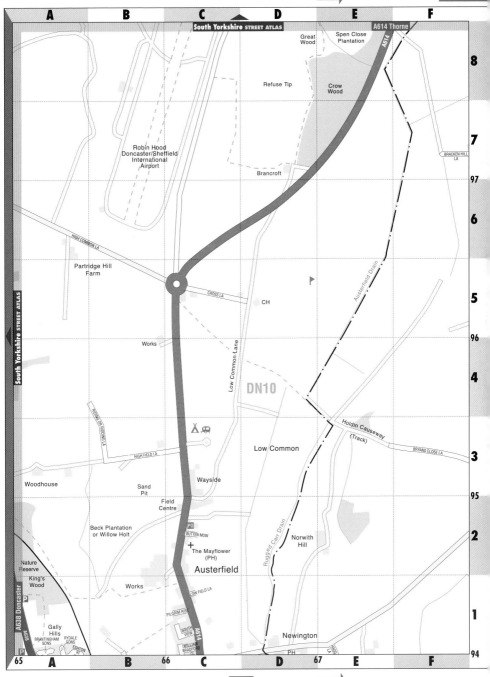

South Yorkshire STREET ATLAS

A614 Thorne

Great Wood

Spen Close Plantation

A614

Refuse Tip

Crow Wood

8

Robin Hood Doncaster/Sheffield International Airport

7

BRACKEN HILL LA

Brancroft

97

HIGH COMMON LA

6

Partridge Hill Farm

CROSS LA

Austerfield Drain

CH

5

Works

96

Low Common Lane

DN10

4

Holdin Causeway

(Track)

BRYANS CLOSE LA

HIGH FIELD LA

Low Common

3

Woodhouse

Sand Pit

Wayside

95

Field Centre

Beck Plantation or Willow Holt

PO

BUTTEN MDW

Norwith Hill

2

Rugged Carr Drain

The Mayflower (PH)

Austerfield

Nature Reserve

King's Wood

Works

LOW FIELD LA

P

A638 Doncaster

A638

PILGRIM RISE

SOUTH VIEW

A614

Newington

1

Gally Hills

BRANTINGHAM GDNS

RYDALE GDNS

ESHTON RI

WILLIAM BRADFORD

PH

94

South Yorkshire STREET ATLAS

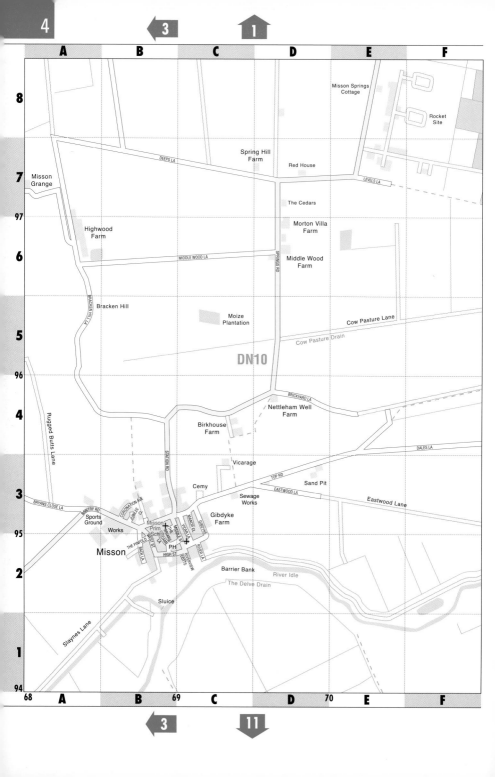

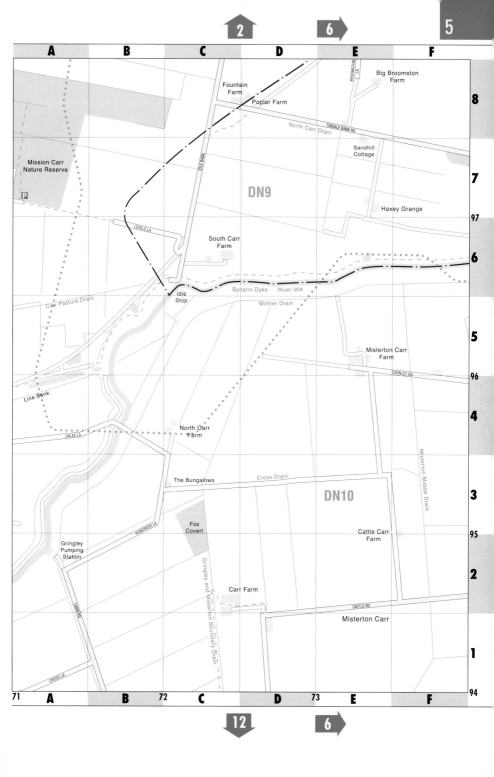

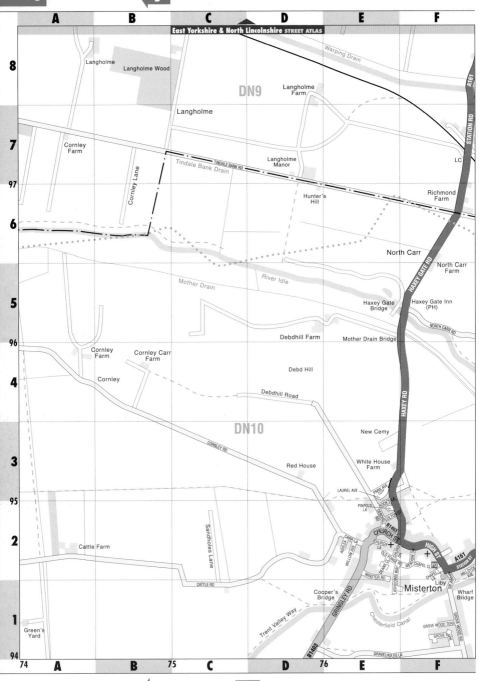

East Yorkshire & North Lincolnshire STREET ATLAS

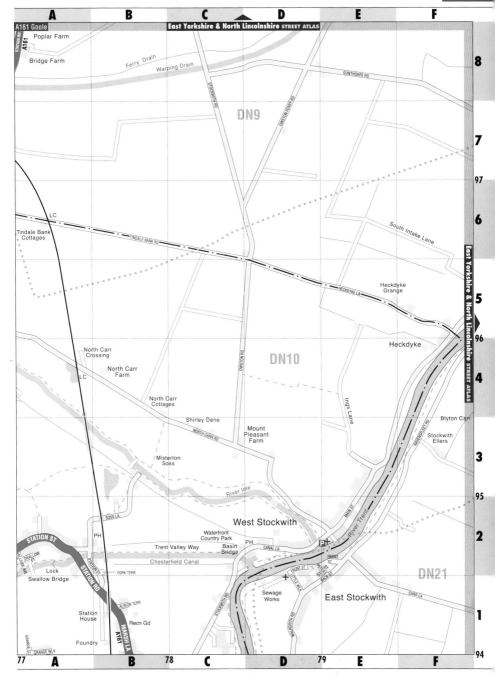

A161 Goole

Poplar Farm

Bridge Farm

Ferry Drain

Warping Drain

GUNTHORPE RD

DN9

8

7

97

LC

Tindale Bank
Cottages

TINDALE BANK RD

South Intake Lane

6

HECKDYKE LA

Heckdyke
Grange

5

96

Heckdyke

North Carr
Crossing

North Carr
Farm

LC

DN10

DARTON RD

4

North Carr
Cottages

Shirley Dene

NORTH CARR RD

Mount
Pleasant
Farm

Ings Lane

RAVENSFLEET RD

Blyton Carr

Stockwith
Ellers

3

Misterton
Soss

River Idle

95

West Stockwith

MAIN ST

River Trent

2

DN21

SOSS LA

Waterfront
Country Park

Trent Valley Way

Basin
Bridge

PH

CANAL LA

FRONT ST

TRENT
ST

STATION ST

PH

Chesterfield Canal

Lock

Swallow Bridge

YORK TERR

ALBION TERR

Station
House

Recn Gd

Foundry

GRANGE WLK
GRANGE AVE

SWALLOW CT

STATION RD

MARSH LA

A161

STOCKWITH RD

Sewage
Works

WALKERITH RD

PACK ST
MOTLEY LA

East Stockwith

CARR LA

1

77

78

79

94

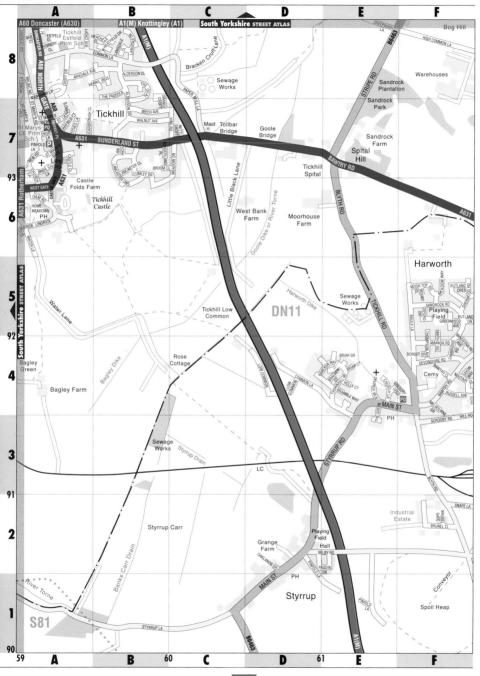

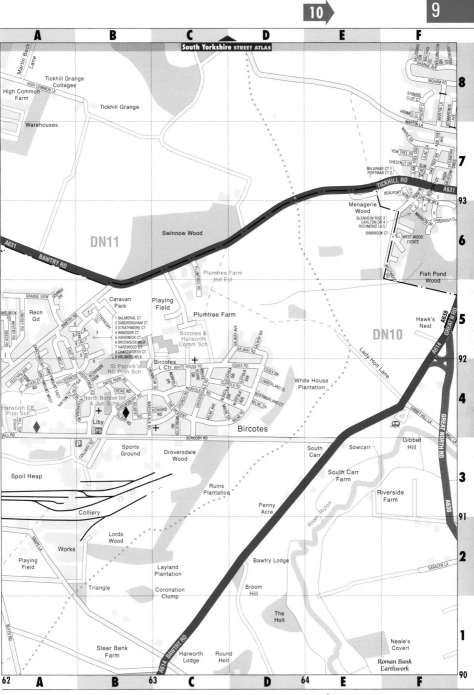

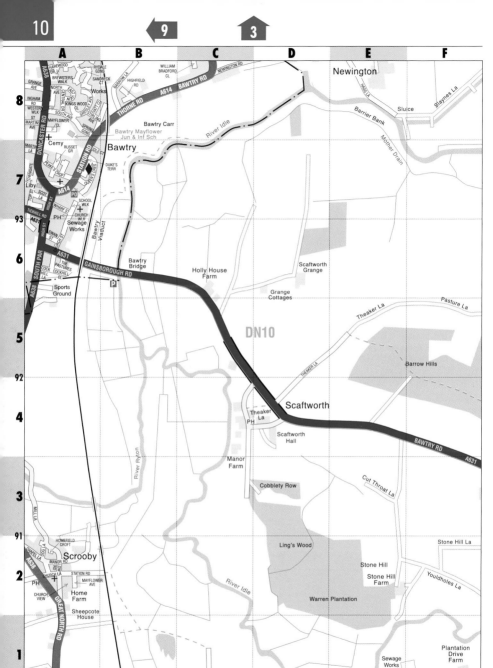

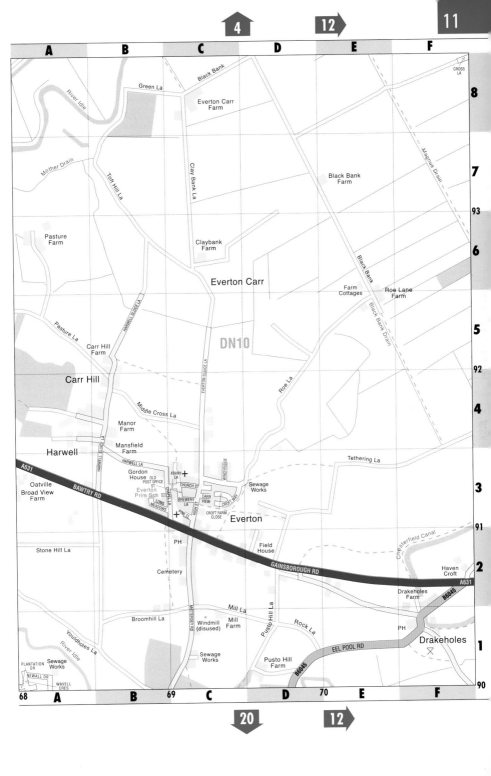

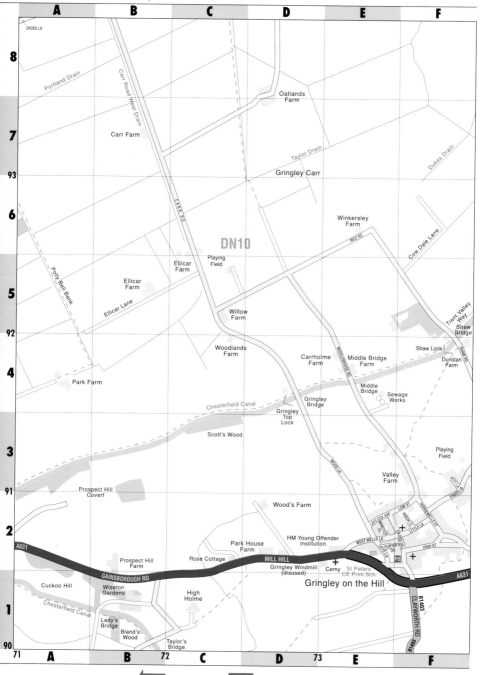

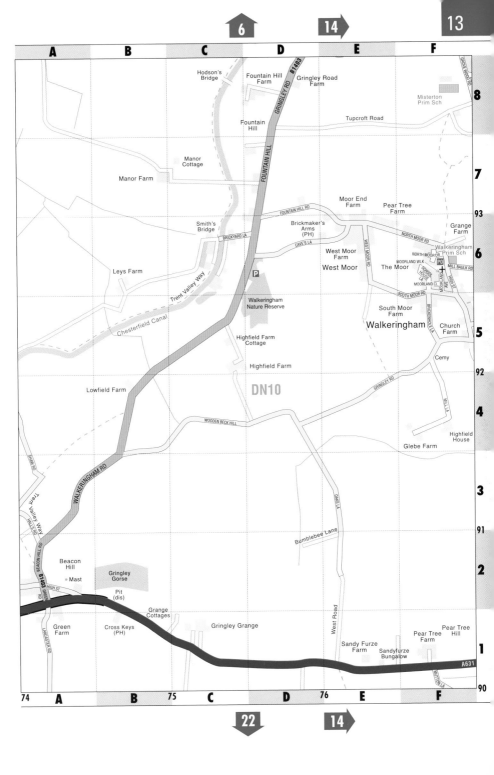

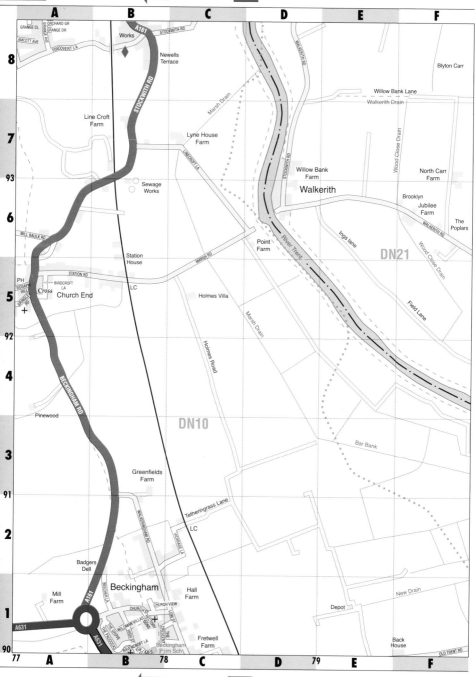

GRANGE GR
ORCHARD GR
GRANGE DR
GRANGE CL
AMCOTT AVE
FOXCOVERT LA

A161
Works
STOCKWITH RD
Newells
Terrace

8

Blyton Carr

Willow Bank Lane

Line Croft
Farm

Walkerith Drain

7

Lyne House
Farm
LIMECROFT LA

Wood Close Drain

93

Willow Bank
Farm

North Carr
Farm

STOCKWITH RD

Sewage
Works

Walkerith

Brooklyn
Jubilee
Farm

6

MILL BAULK RD

The
Poplars

WALKERITH RD

Ings lane

DN21

Point
Farm

Station
House

MARSH RD

River Trent

Wood Close Drain

STATION RD

PH
SIDGATE HILL
BIRDCROFT
LA

LC

Holmes Villa

Field Lane

5

GREENER RD
Cross
Church End

92

Marsh Drain

Holmes Road

4

BECKINGHAM RD

Pinewood

DN10

Bar Bank

3

Greenfields
Farm

91

WALKINGHAM RD

Tetheringrass Lane

LC

2

VICARAGE LA

Badgers
Dell

New Drain

Mill
Farm

BECKER LA

Beckingham

Hall
Farm

Depot

A161

CHURCH ST
CHURCH VIEW
WITHAM VILLAS
THE GROVE
LOW ST
THE
VICARAGE LA
CHURCH VIEW

Back
House

1

A631
THE PADDOCK
RAVENSCROFT LA
THE ELMS
Fretwell
Farm
Beckingham
Prim Sch

OLD TRENT RD

A631

90

77

78

79

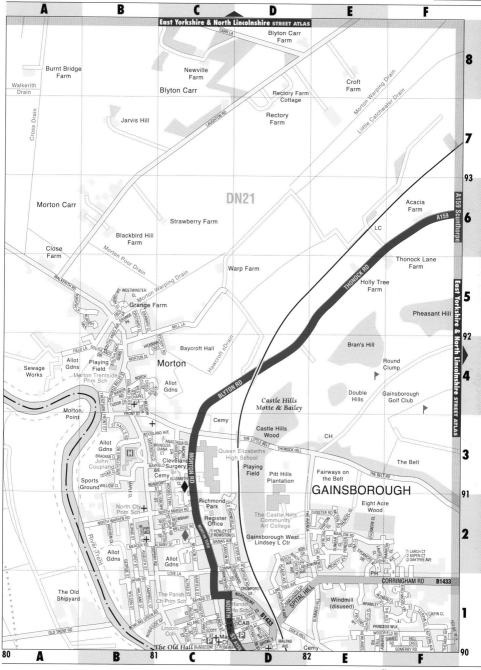

East Yorkshire & North Lincolnshire STREET ATLAS

A159 Scunthorpe

DN21

Blyton Carr Farm

Burnt Bridge Farm

Walkerith Drain

Newville Farm

Croft Farm

Blyton Carr

Rectory Farm Cottage

Jarvis Hill

Rectory Farm

Morton Warping Drain

Little Catchwater Drain

Cross Drain

Acacia Farm

A159

Morton Carr

Strawberry Farm

LC

Blackbird Hill Farm

Thonock Lane Farm

Close Farm

Morton Poor Drain

Warp Farm

Thonock Rd

Holly Tree Farm

Morton Warping Drain

WESTMINSTER CL

Pheasant Hill

Grange Farm

MILL LA

Bran's Hill

Baycroft Hall

Hawcroft sDrain

Round Clump

Sewage Works

Allot Gdns

Playing Field

Morton Trentside Prim Sch

Morton

Blyton Rd

Double Hills

Gainsborough Golf Club

Allot Gdns

Castle Hills Motte & Bailey

Morton Point

Cemy

Castle Hills Wood

CH

The Belt

THE LITTLE BELT

Allot Gdns John Coupland

Woodland Ave

Queen Elizabeths High School

Thonock Hill

Sports Ground

ANASTASIA CL PRINCESS DIANA CT

MAYFIELD AVE

Cleveland Surgery

Cemy

Playing Field

Fairways on the Belt

THE BELT RD

GAINSBOROUGH

Morton Rd

Richmond Park

Pitt Hills Plantation

Eight Acre Wood

North Cty Prim Sch

Register Office

The Castle Hills Community Art College

Gainsborough West Lindsey L Ctr

1 LARCH CT 2 ASPEN CT 3 OAKTREE AVE

Allot Gdns

Allot Gdns

LOVE LA

River Trent

The Old Shipyard

North Beck Rd

Windmill (disused)

CORRINGHAM RD

B1433

SPITAL HILL

PH

The Parish Ch Prim Sch

Lincoln Coll

The Old Hall

MALPAS AVE

Cemy

B1433

PRINCESS AVE

SOMERBY RD

Old Trent Rd

GLADSTONE ST

ROSEWAY

SPITAL TER

COX'S HILL

F1 1 BLACKTHORN CL 2 THE ROWANS 3 FOSSEWAY 4 MAPLE CT 5 THE ALDERS 6 COUPLAND CL

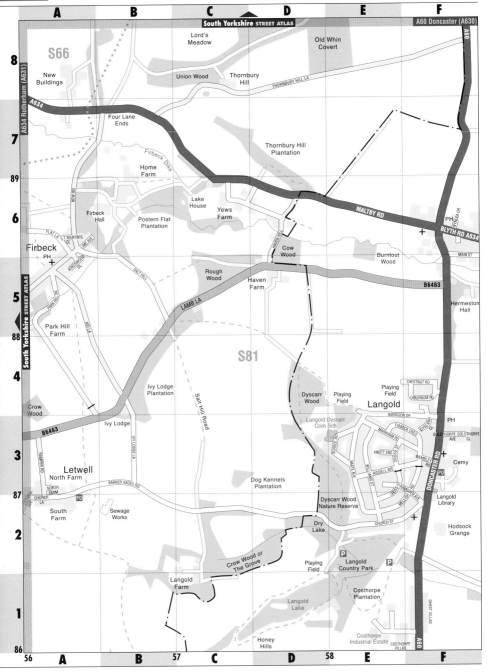

S66

A60 Doncaster (A630)

New Buildings

Lord's Meadow

Old Whin Covert

A634 Rotherham (A631)

Union Wood

Thornbury Hill

THORNBURY HILL LA

Four Lane Ends

A634

Firbeck Dike

Thornbury Hill Plantation

Home Farm

Lake House

Yews Farm

MALTBY RD

Firbeck Hall

Postern Flat Plantation

PH

BLYTH RD A634

Cow Wood

Burntout Wood

MAIN ST

Firbeck

PH

Rough Wood

Haven Farm

B6463

Hermeston Hall

LAMB LA

S81

Park Hill Farm

Ivy Lodge Plantation

Dyscarr Wood

Playing Field

Playing Field

Langold

CHESTNUT RD

LABURNUM RD

HARRISON DR

Crow Wood

Ivy Lodge

Langold Dyscarr Com Sch

FIRBECK CRES

PH

B6463

Salt Hill Road

MARKHAM RD

GOLDTHORPE GOLDTHORPE AVE CL

Letwell

North Farm

BARKER HADES RD

KNOTT END

Cemy

WEMBLEY RD

DONCASTER RD

South Farm

PO

Dog Kennels Plantation

RIDDELL AVE

WHITE AVE

WILLIAM ST

Langold Library

Sewage Works

Dyscarr Wood Nature Reserve

CHURCH ST

Dry Lake

Hodsock Grange

Crow Wood or The Grove

P

Playing Field

P

Langold Country Park

Langold Farm

Langold Lake

Costhorpe Plantation

GHEST VILLAS

Honey Hills

Costhorpe Industrial Estate

COSTHORPE VILLAS

A60

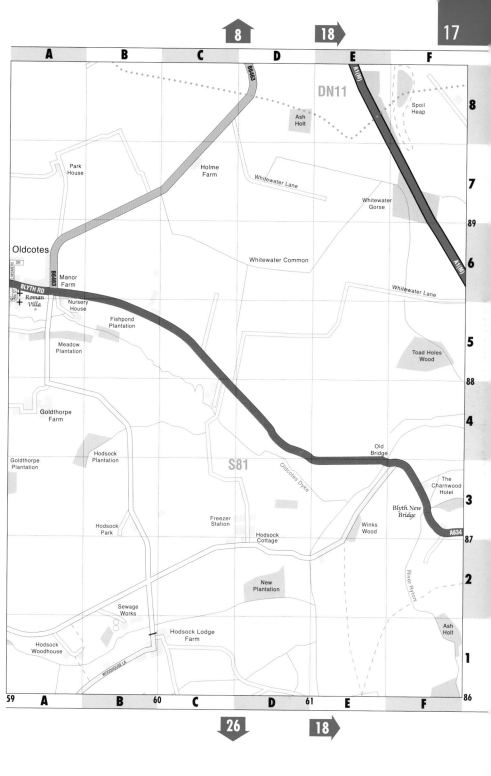

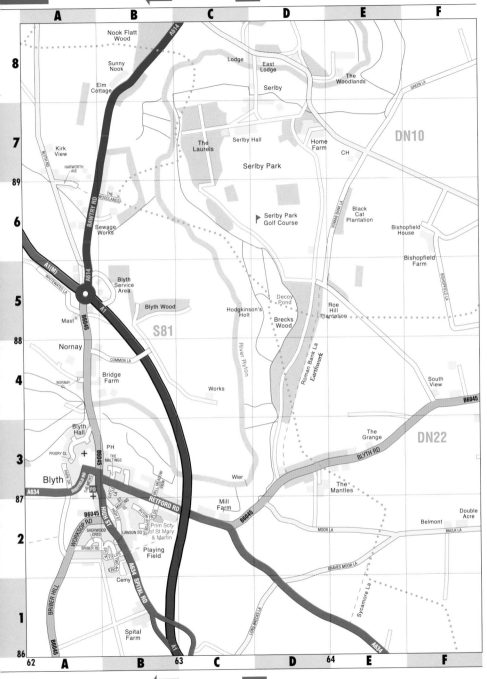

A B C D E F

8

Nook Flatt Wood

Sunny Nook

Elm Cottage

Lodge

East Lodge

Serlby

The Woodlands

GREEN LA

DN10

7

Kirk View

BLYTH RD

HARWORTH AVE

The Laurels

Serlby Hall

Serlby Park

Home Farm

CH

89

THE WOODLANDS

BAWTRY RD

6

A1(M)

WHITEWATES LA

A614

Sewage Works

Serlby Park Golf Course

ROMAN BANK LA

Black Cat Plantation

Bishopfield House

Bishopfield Farm

BISHOPFIELD LA

5

Mast

B6045

A1

Blyth Service Area

Blyth Wood

S81

Hodgkinson's Holt

Decoy Pond

Brecks Wood

Roe Hill Plantation

88

Nornay

COMMON LA

River Ryton

ROMAN BANK LA Earthwork

South View

B6045

4

NORNAY CL

Bridge Farm

Works

DN22

3

Blyth Hall

PRIORY CL

PH

THE MALTINGS

B6045

Wier

The Grange

BLYTH RD

The Mantles

Blyth

A634

SHEFFIELD RD

PO

THE HORSE

RETFORD RD

Mill Farm

B6045

MOOR LA

Belmont

Double Acre

BAULK LA

87

B6045

WORKSOP RD

HIGH ST

ST MARTINS

LITTLE LA

MILL MEADOW VIEW

LAWSON SQ

RYTON CL

Prim Sch of St Mary & Martin

2

SHERWOOD CRES

BRIBER RD

SPITAL

FIELDS

CRES

Playing Field

GRAVES MOOR LA

BRIBER HILL

A634 SPITAL RD

Cemy

A1

Sycamore La

A634

1

B6045

Spital Farm

86

62 A 63 B C 64 D E F

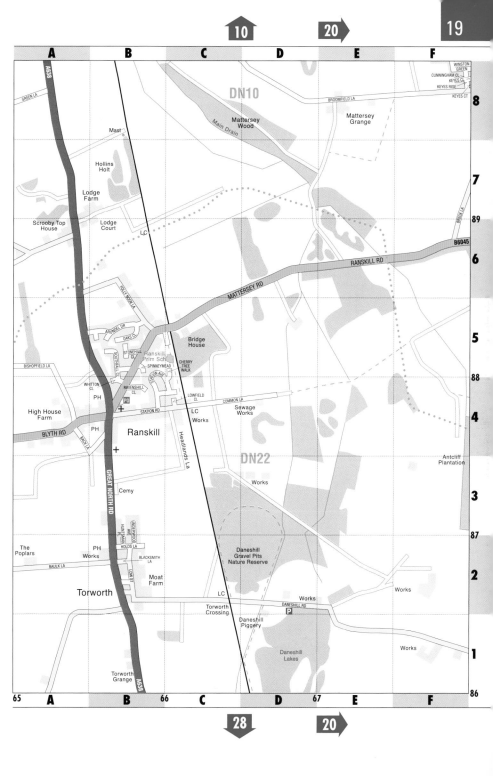

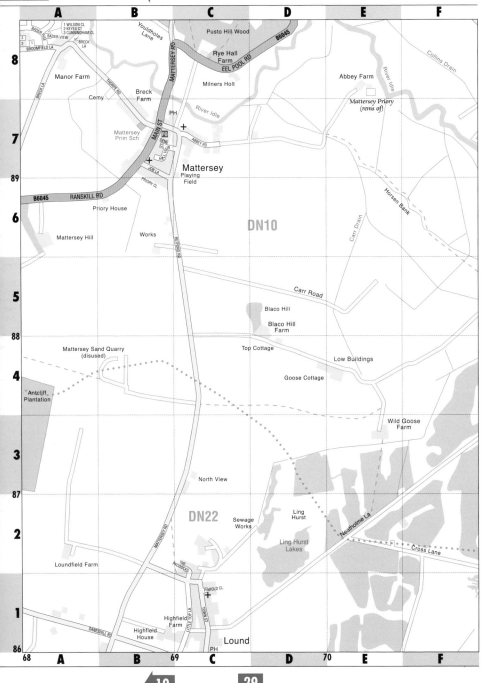

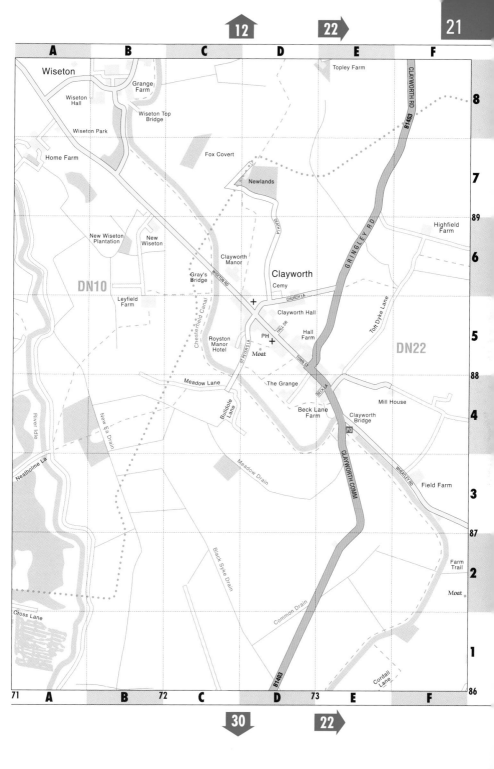

A   B   C   D   E   F

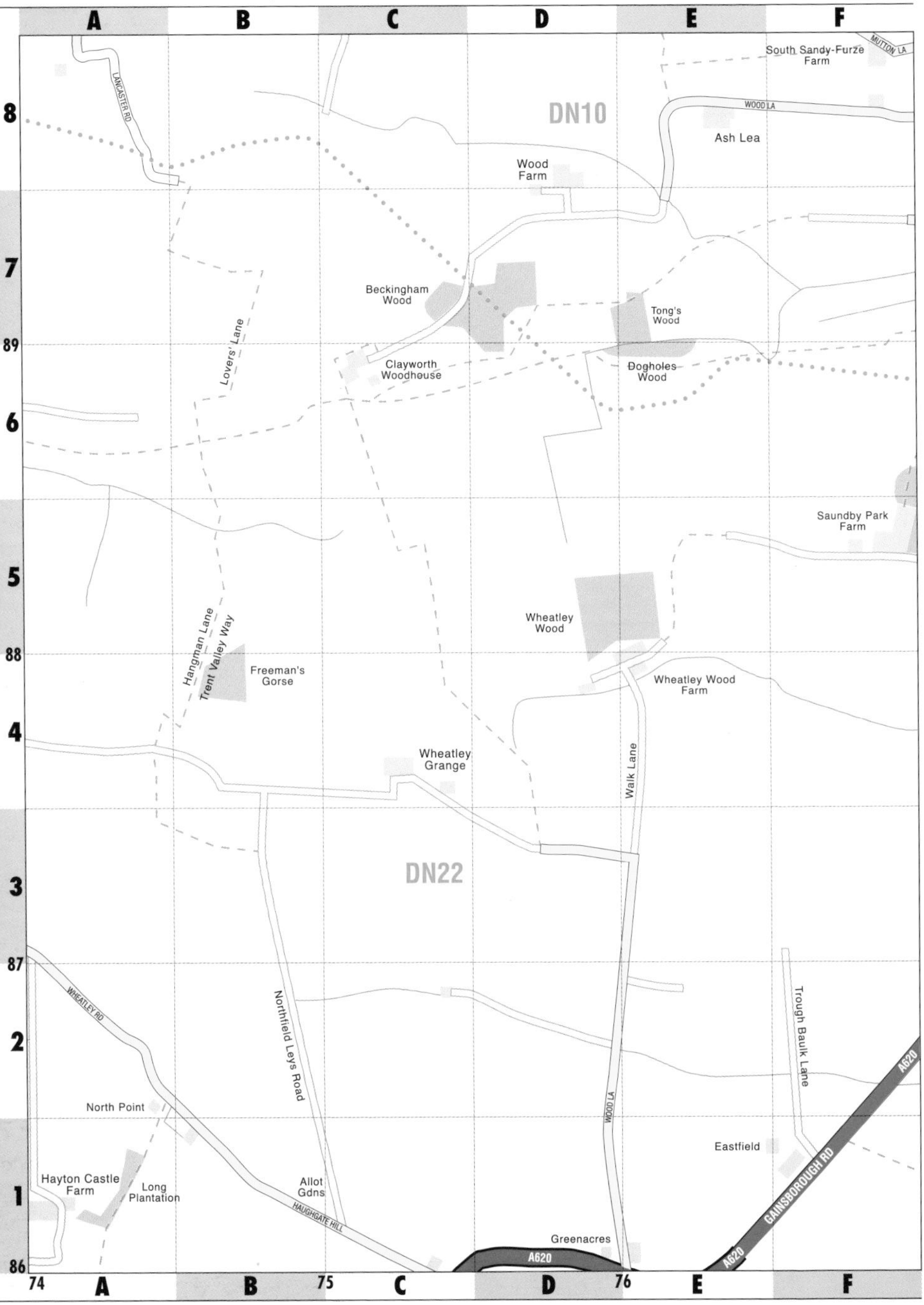

8

DN10

South Sandy-Furze Farm

MUTTON LA

WOOD LA

Ash Lea

Wood Farm

7

Beckingham Wood

Tong's Wood

89

Lovers' Lane

Clayworth Woodhouse

Dogholes Wood

6

LANCASTER RD

Saundby Park Farm

5

Wheatley Wood

88

Hangman Lane

Trent Valley Way

Freeman's Gorse

Wheatley Wood Farm

4

Wheatley Grange

Walk Lane

3

DN22

87

WHEATLEY RD

Northfield Leys Road

Trough Baulk Lane

A620

2

WOOD LN

North Point

Eastfield

GAINSBOROUGH RD

1

Hayton Castle Farm

Long Plantation

Allot Gdns

HAUGHGATE HILL

Greenacres

A620

A620

86

74   A   B   75   C   D   76   E   F

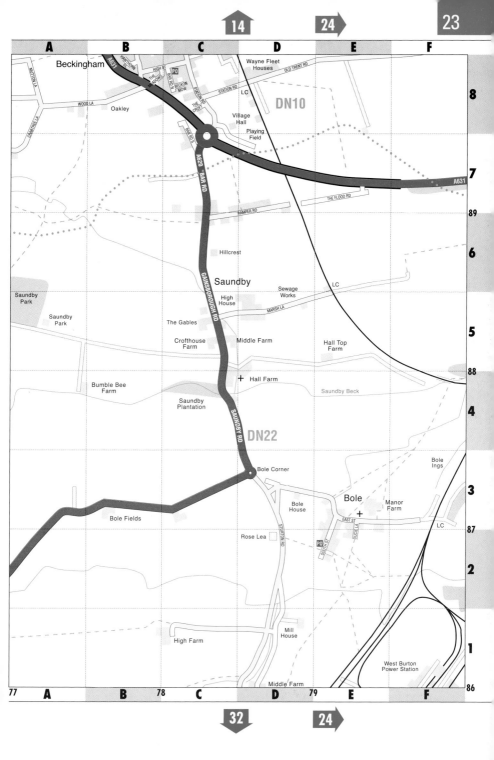

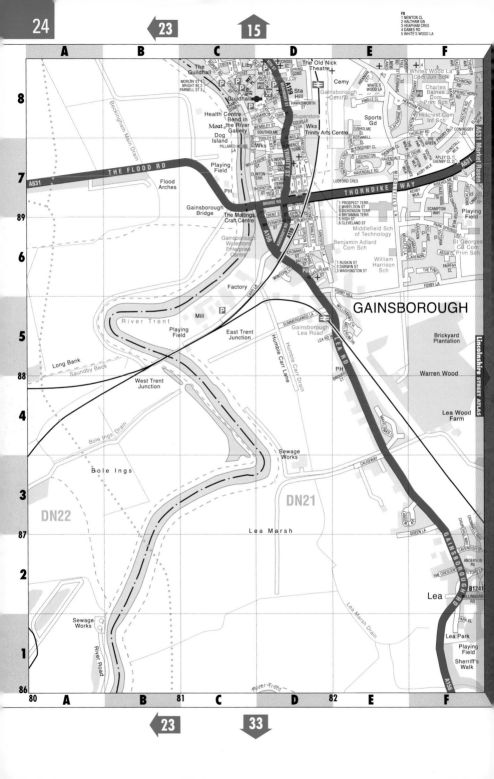

A **B** **C** **D** **E** **F**

South Yorkshire STREET ATLAS

8

Miller Lands

Acorn
Piece

Costhorpe

WEST
VIEW

Langold
Holt

Ingham
Bungalows

Trading
Estate

Woodland
Farm

Buckwood
Farm

PINFOLD DR 1
GREENFIELD WAY 2
HARVEST CL 3
PLOUGH DR 4

PH

7

ROTHERHAM BAULK

CHILTERN WAY 1
PENTLAND DR 2
HAMBLETON CT 3
LOWTHER SQ 4
CLEVELAND CL 5
BEVERLEY WLK 6
CHICHESTER WLK 7
CHEVIOT CT 8
MENDIP CT 9
CANTERBURY WLK 10
LICHFIELD WLK 11
COTSWOLD CT 12

OAK TREE RISE

85

Carlton in Lindrick Liby

OXFORD RD

Kingston Park
Prim Sch

6

Castle
Garden

Wallingwells
Wood

WINDSOR
GDNS

WINDSOR RD

ARUNDEL DR

WARWICK
AVE

Carlton
Wood

Carlton in Lindrick

5

Wallingwells

Wallingwells Hall

S81

Wallingwells Park

Hollin
Hills

Owlands
Wood

The Lawns

84

Carlton Lake

Corn Mill
Farm

The
Ashes

Holme
Wood

South Carlton

4

Field House
Farm

Sewage
Wks

The Bottoms

Owlands Wood Dike

Holme House
Farm

Hardwick
Ashes

3

83

OWDAY LA

Broom
Farm

2

Owday
Wood

Owday
Plantation

Nab's Ashes
Wood

Little Broom
Wood

The
Homestead

Sand Hill
Plantation

Rough
Piece

Whipman
Wood

Cocked Hat
Wood

1

WORKSOP
RD

PEAK HILL
CL

Fox
Covert

Ashes
Wood

Dog Kennel
Plantation

GREENWOOD CL

FOXWOOD CL

BROOM
CL

NUTHATCH
CRES

82

A **B** 57 **C** **D** 58 **E** **F**

56

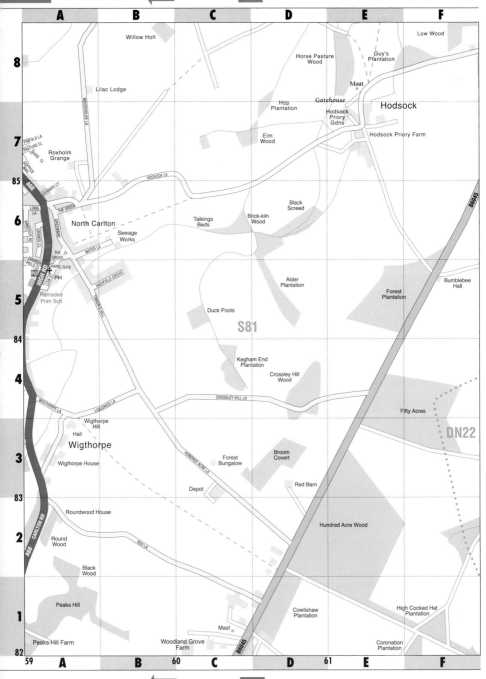

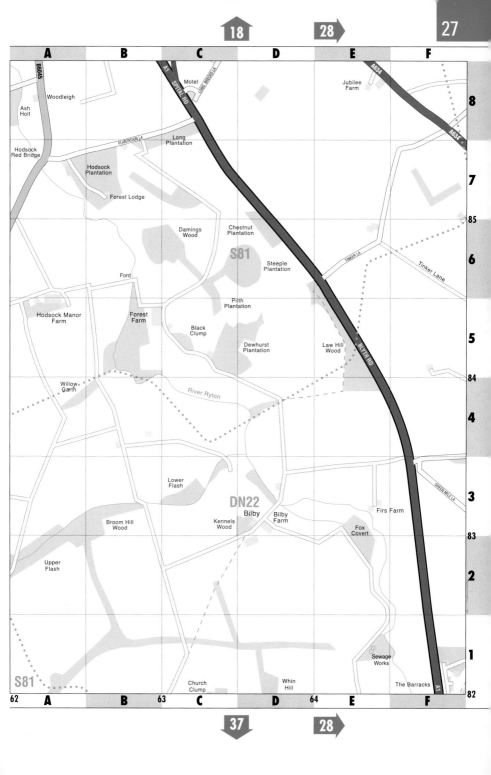

A B C D E F

B6045
Woodleigh
Ash Holt
Hodsock Red Bridge
PLANTATION LA
Long Plantation
Hodsock Plantation
Forest Lodge
Motel
A1
SPITAL RD
LONG BRICKS LA
Jubilee Farm
A634
A634
Damings Wood
Chestnut Plantation
S81
Steeple Plantation
TINKER LA
Tinker Lane
Ford
Pilth Plantation
Hodsock Manor Farm
Forest Farm
Black Clump
Dewhurst Plantation
Law Hill Wood
BLYTH RD
Willow Garth
River Ryton
Lower Flash
DN22
Bilby
Broom Hill Wood
Kennels Wood
Bilby Farm
Firs Farm
Fox Covert
GREEN MILE LA
Upper Flash
S81
Church Clump
Whin Hill
Sewage Works
The Barracks
A1

62 A B 63 C D 64 E F 82

8 7 85 6 5 84 4 3 83 2 1

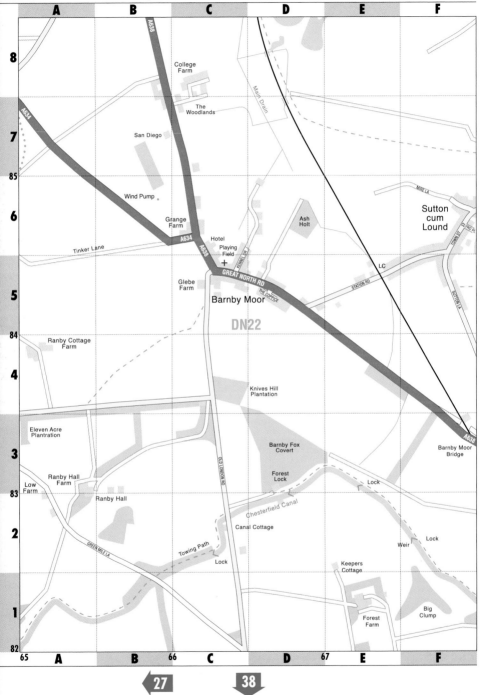

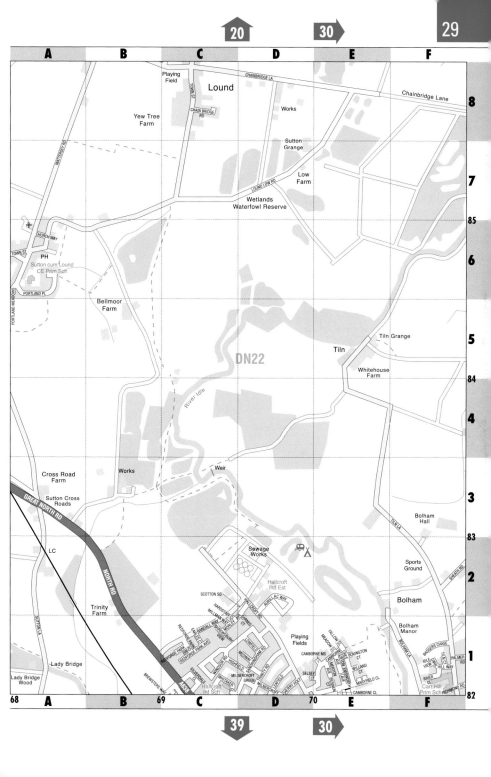

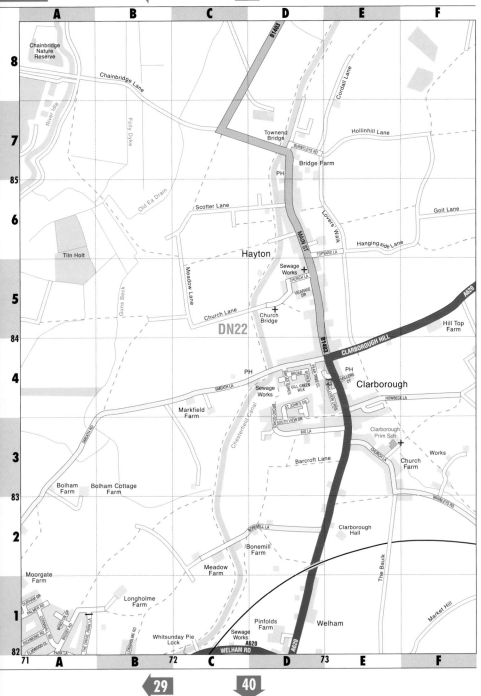

A B C D E F

8 — Chainbridge Nature Reserve

Chainbridge Lane

River Idle

Folly Dyke

7 — Townend Bridge

BURNTLEYS RD

Cordall Lane

Hollinhill Lane

85 — PH

Bridge Farm

Old Ea Drain

6 — Scotter Lane

Lover's Walk

Goit Lane

Hanging side Lane

Tiln Holt

Hayton

MAIN ST

Meadow Lane

Sewage Works

CHURCH LA

TOPYARD LA

5 — Church Lane

VICARAGE DR

Church Bridge

DN22

B1403

CLARBOROUGH HILL

A620

Hill Top Farm

84 —

4 — PH

SMEATH LA

BROAD GORES

Sewage Works

BROAD GORES

GILL GREEN WLK

PEAR TREE CL

GORES

ST JOHN'S DR

SOUTH VIEW DR

BIG LA

PO

MILLERS CT

PH

MILLVIEW CRES

Clarborough

HOWBECK LA

Markfield Farm

SMEATH RD

Clarborough Prim Sch

Works

3 — Barcroft Lane

CHURCH LA

Church Farm

WRINKLEYS RD

83 — Bolham Farm

Bolham Cottage Farm

BONEMILL LA

Clarborough Hall

2 — Bonemill Farm

Meadow Farm

The Baulk

Moorgate Farm

Market Hill

Longholme Farm

1 — DURHAM DR

PALMER RD

RICHMOND RD

WINSTON GR

REGBY RD

COSSINGTON CT

COSSWOOD CL

THE DRIVE

PARK LA

LONGHOLME RD

Pinfolds Farm

Welham

Whitsunday Pie Lock

Sewage Works

A620

82 — ELLWOOD CL

PARK LA

WELHAM RD

71 A 72 B C 73 D E F

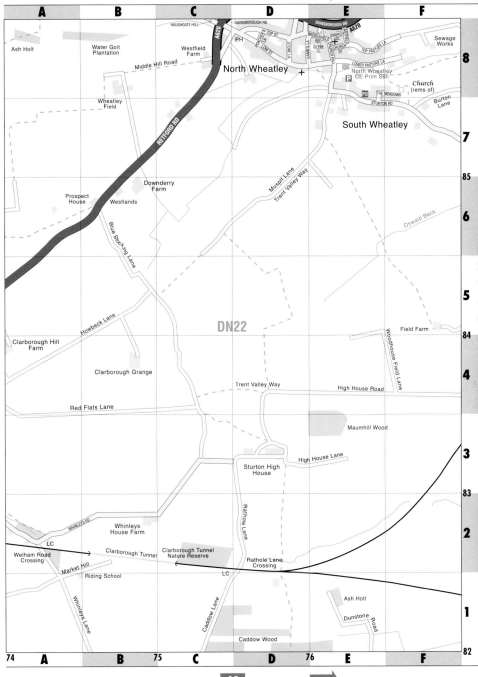

A   B   C   D   E   F

8
85
7
6
5
84
4
83
3
2
82
1

74   75   76

Ash Holt

Water Goit
Plantation

Westfield
Farm

HAUGHGATE HILL

GAINSBOROUGH RD

GAINSBOROUGH RD

A620

PH

Middle Hill Road

North Wheatley

TOP ST
POPLARS RD
STONE LA
LOW ST
ST MARYS ST
MIDDLEFIELD RD
GLEBE
CL
CHURCH
ST
CHURCH
ST
TOP PASTURE LA

LOWER PASTURE LA

North Wheatley
CE Prim Sch

P

Sewage
Works

Church
(rems of)

Burton
Lane

PO

THE MEADOWS

STURTON RD

South Wheatley

Wheatley
Field

RETFORD RD

Downderry
Farm

Prospect
House

Westlands

Blue Stocking Lane

Muspit Lane

Trent Valley Way

Oswald Beck

Howbeck Lane

DN22

Field Farm

Clarborough Hill
Farm

Clarborough Grange

Woodhouse Field Lane

Red Flats Lane

Trent Valley Way

High House Road

Maumhill Wood

Sturton High
House

High House Lane

Whinleys
House Farm

WHINLEYS RD

Rathole Lane

LC

Welham Road
Crossing

Clarborough Tunnel

Clarborough Tunnel
Nature Reserve

Rathole Lane
Crossing

LC

Market Hill

Riding School

Caddow Lane

Ash Holt

Dunstone

Road

Whinleys Lane

Caddow Wood

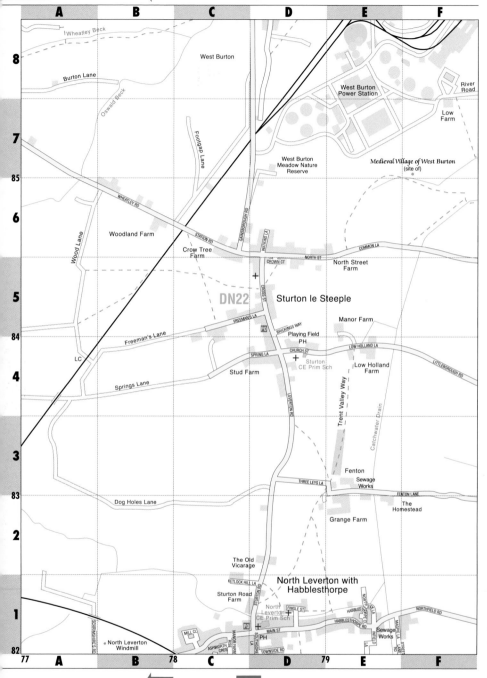

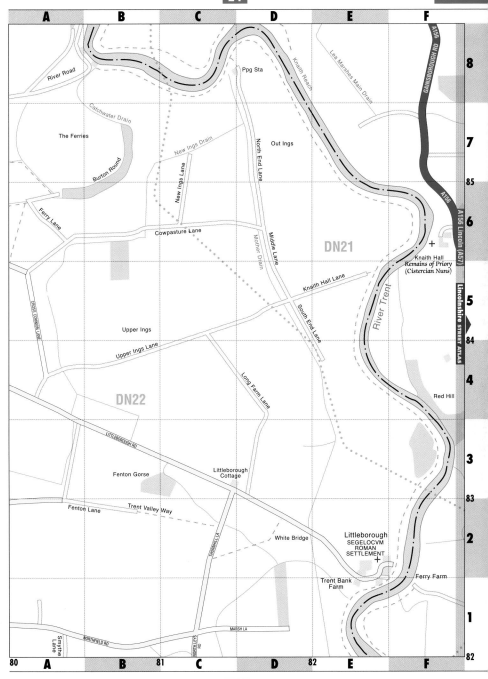

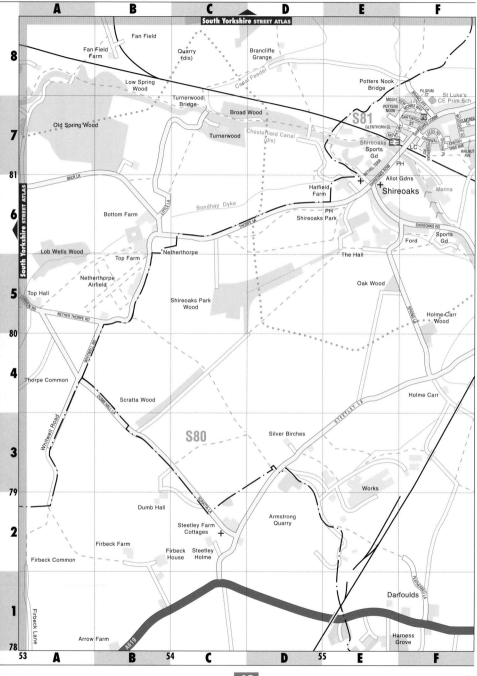

South Yorkshire STREET ATLAS

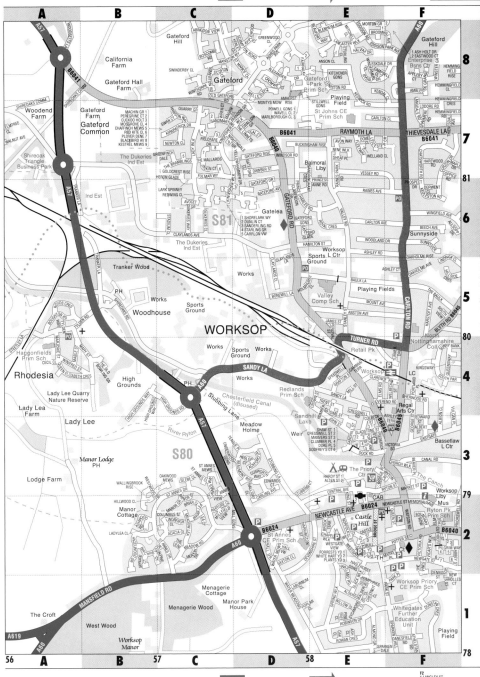

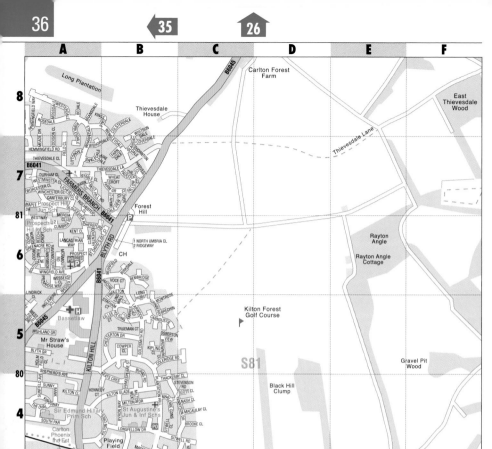

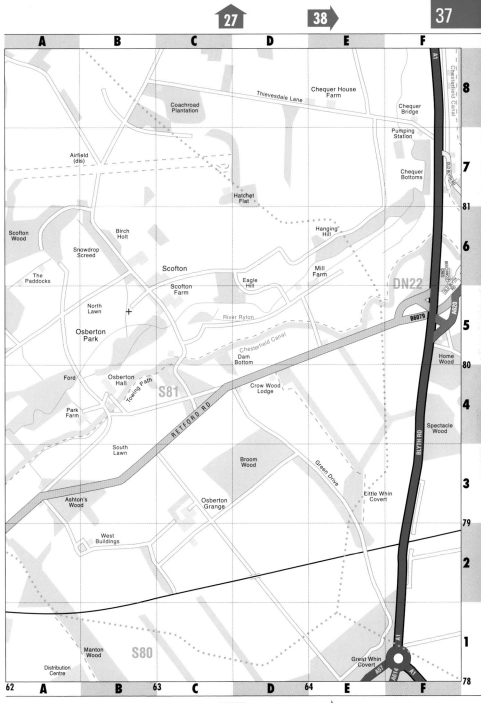

	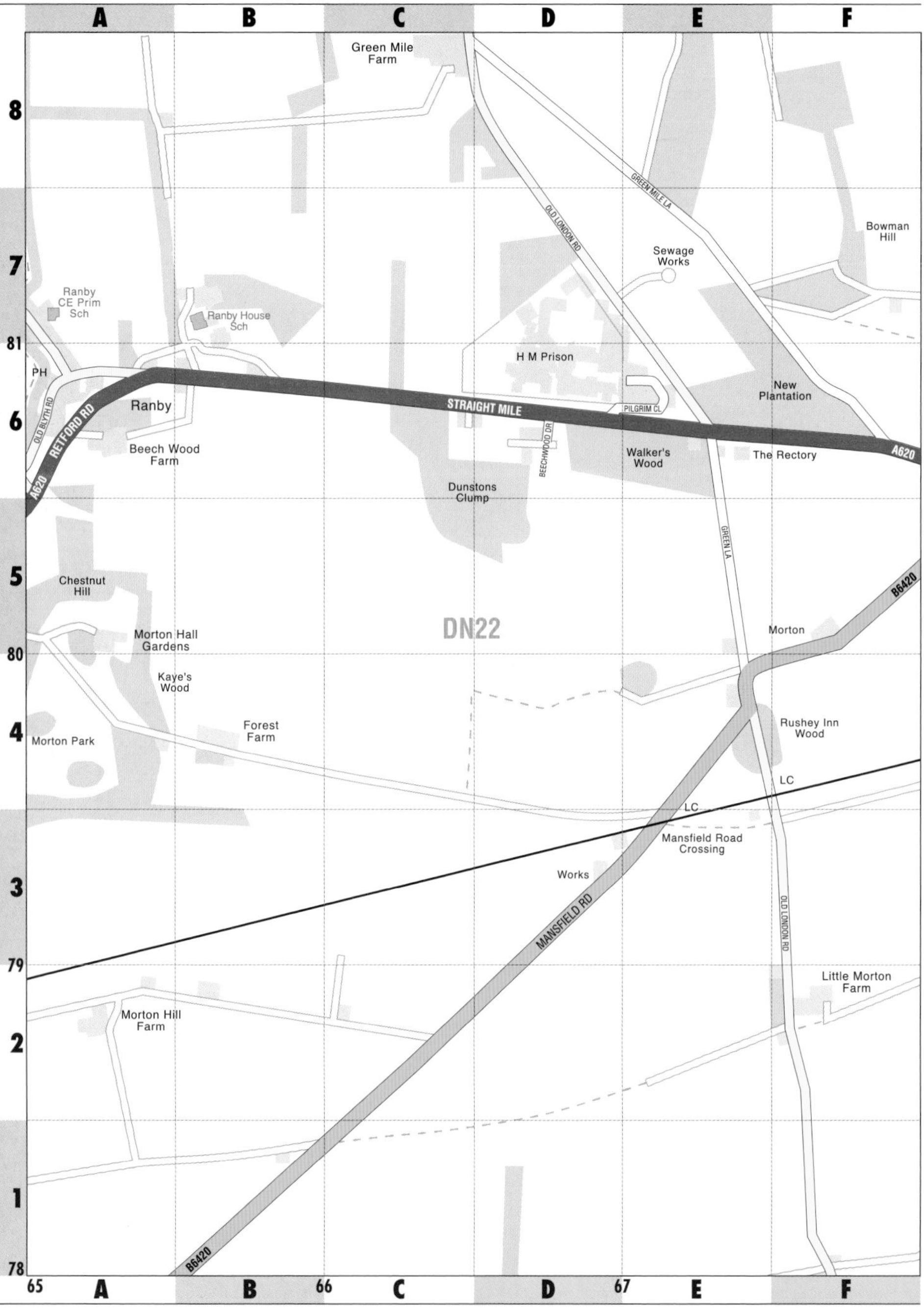 A	B	C	D	E	F

8

Green Mile Farm

Bowman Hill

7

Ranby CE Prim Sch

Ranby House Sch

Sewage Works

OLD LONDON RD

GREEN M LA

81

H M Prison

New Plantation

PH

6

OLD BLYTH RD

RETFORD RD

Ranby

STRAIGHT MILE

PILGRIM CL

The Rectory

A620

Beech Wood Farm

BEECHWOOD DR

Walker's Wood

A620

Dunstons Clump

5

Chestnut Hill

DN22

Morton

B6420

GREEN LA

Morton Hall Gardens

80

Kaye's Wood

Rushey Inn Wood

4

Morton Park

Forest Farm

LC

LC

OLD LONDON RD

Mansfield Road Crossing

3

Works

Little Morton Farm

MANSFIELD RD

79

Morton Hill Farm

2

1

B6420

78

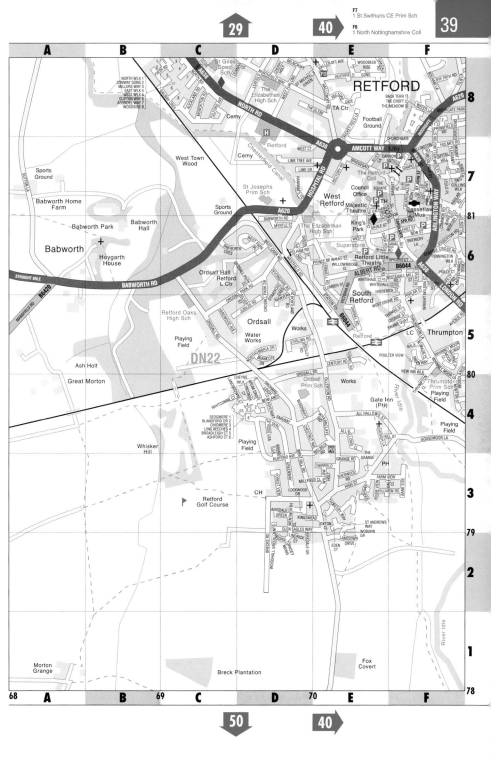

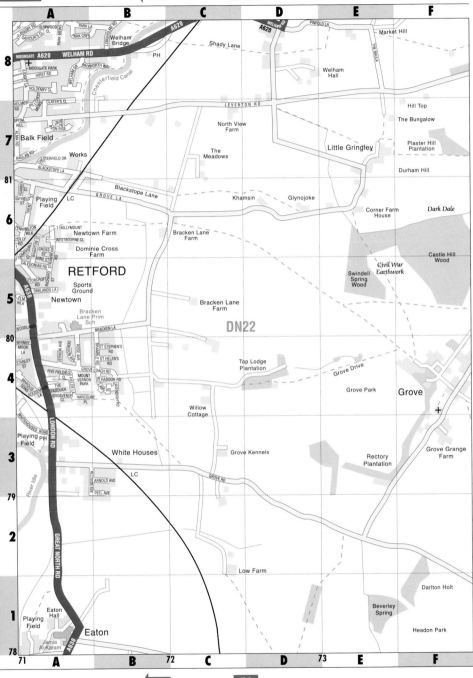

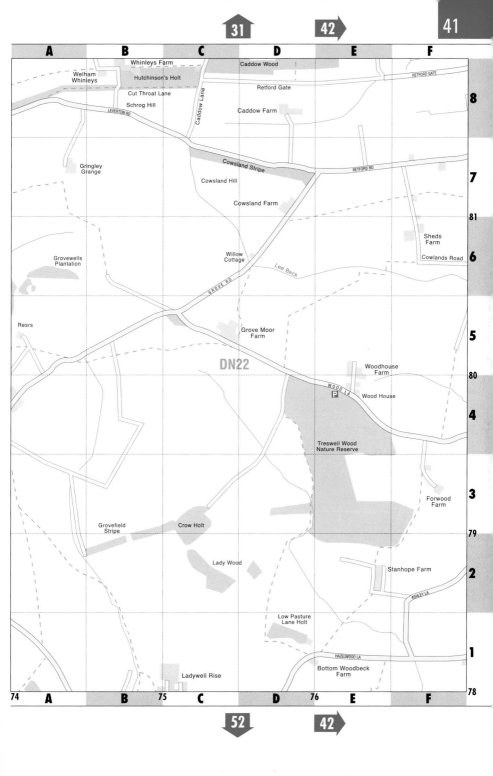

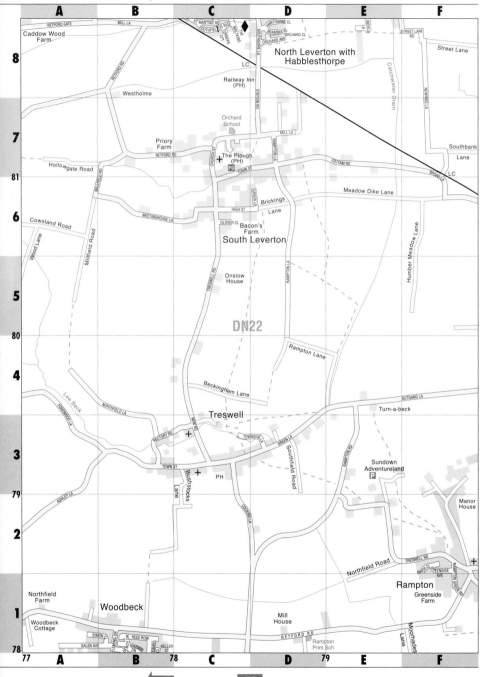

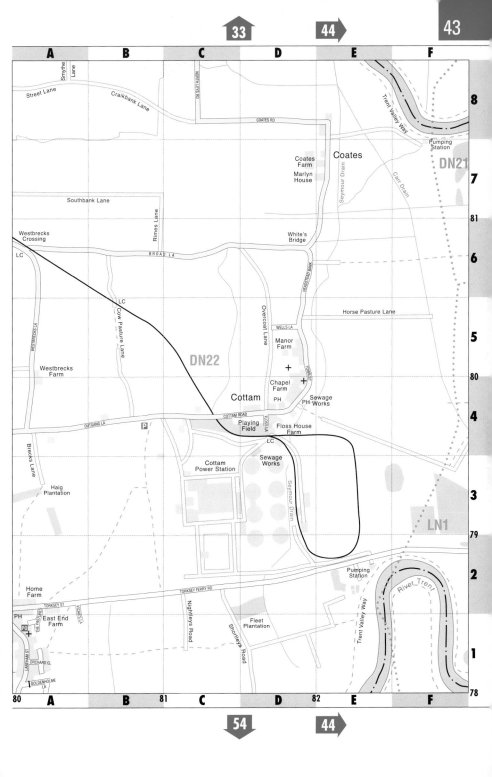

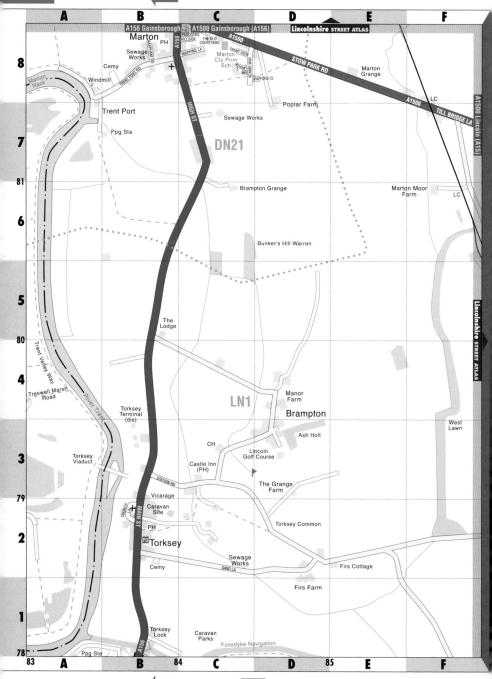

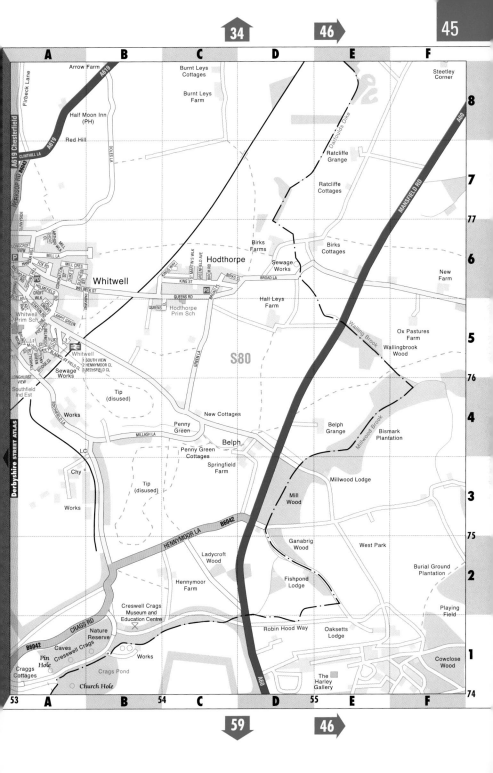

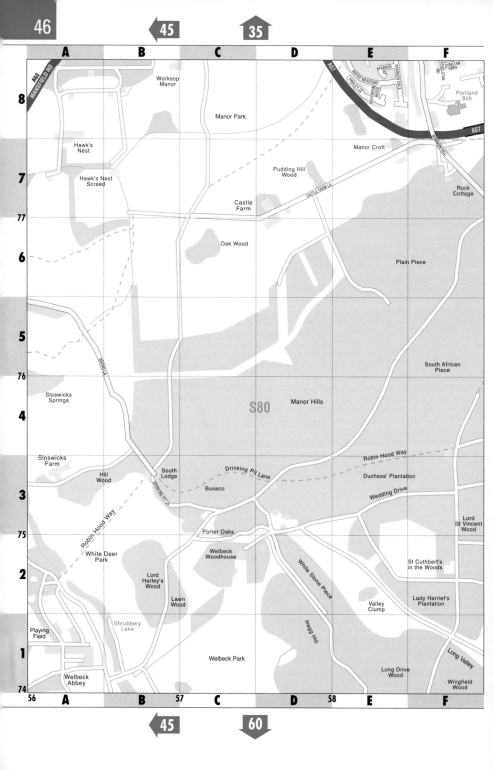

A B C D E F

A57
Distribution Centre
ROEBUCK WAY
Top Wood
Calloughton Wood
A57
A614
WORKSOP RD
A1
Lodge Brake Plantation

8

Manton Plantation
Manton Lodge
Apleyhead Lodge
Apleyhead Wood

7
OLD COACH RD
Coach Road Plantation
Nature Reserve

77
Forest Farm Plantation South
The Birk Rows

6
King Charles's Breck
LIME TREE AVE
Sharp's Hill

Heron Hill Wood
Hardwick Wood
School House
Double Clump

5
S80

76
Osberton Round
West Bridge
BLYTH RD

4
White Pheasant Wood
Hardwick Village
Weir

Robin Hood Way
P
Hardwick Grange
Weir

3
Ash Tree Hill Wood
P
Ford
Ford
Normanton Screed

Clumber Park Country Park

75
Clumber Lake
Tank Wood
Clumber Park Hotel

2
Clumber Lane
P
Boat House Plantation
Cabin Hill Covert
Cabin Hill House

1
New Road
Five Thorns Plantation
Freeboard Lane
Robin Hood Way
A614

74
P
South Lawn

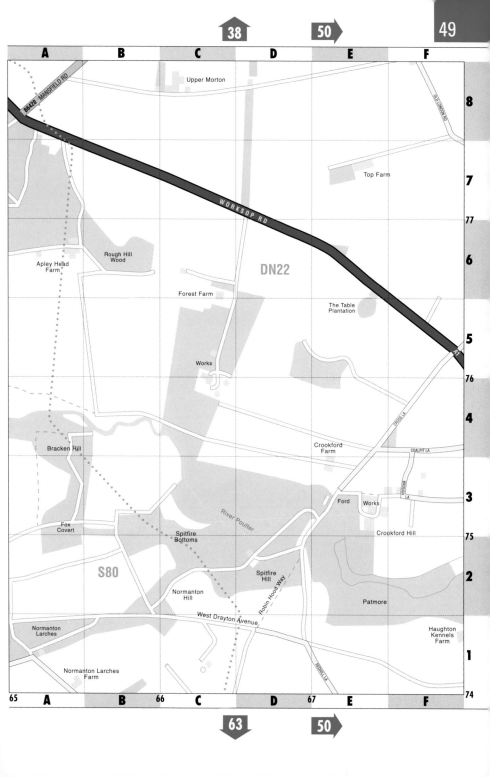

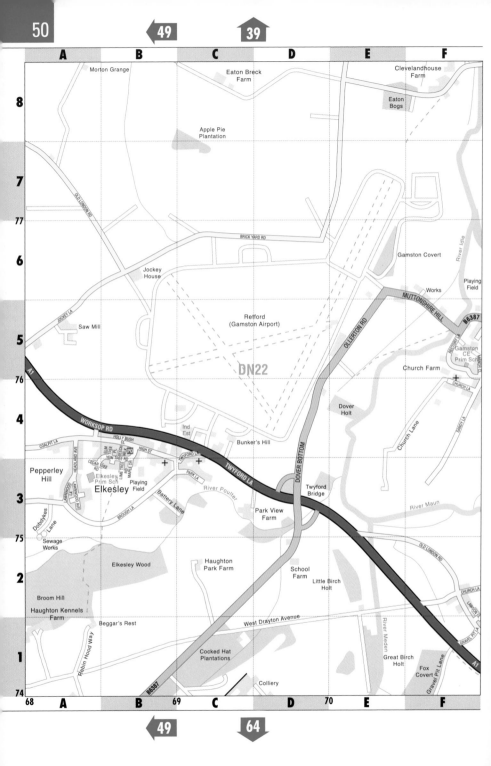

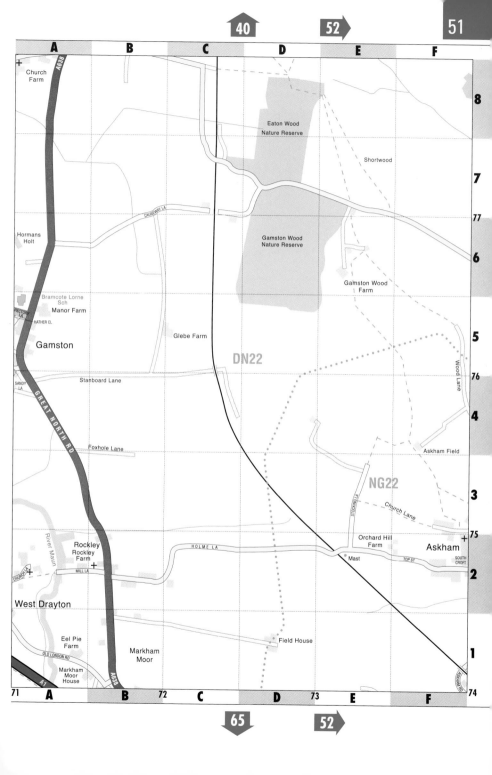

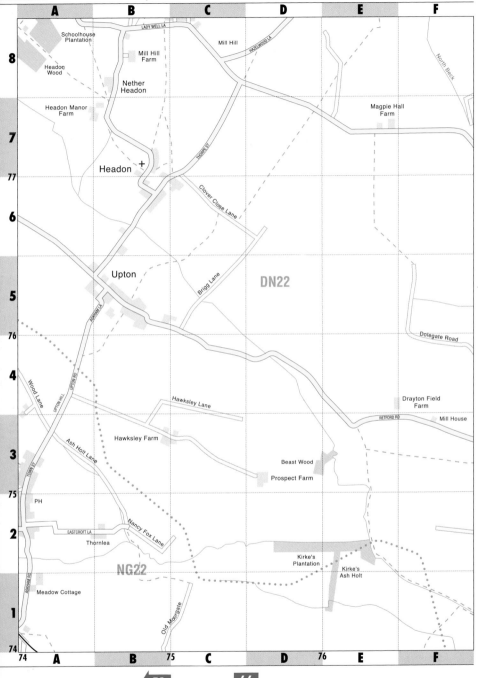

Schoolhouse Plantation

LADY WELL LA

Mill Hill

HAZELWOOD LA

Mill Hill Farm

Headon Wood

Nether Headon

North Beck

Magpie Hall Farm

Headon Manor Farm

THORPE ST.

Headon +

Clover Close Lane

DN22

Upton

Brigg Lane

ASKHAM LA

Dolegate Road

Wood Lane

UPTON HILL

UPTON RD

Hawksley Lane

Drayton Field Farm

RETFORD RD

Mill House

Ash Holt Lane

Hawksley Farm

Beast Wood

TOWN ST.

Prospect Farm

PH

EASTCROFT LA

Nancy Fox Lane

NG22

Thornlea

Kirke's Plantation

Kirke's Ash Holt

ASKHAM RD

Meadow Cottage

Old Moygate

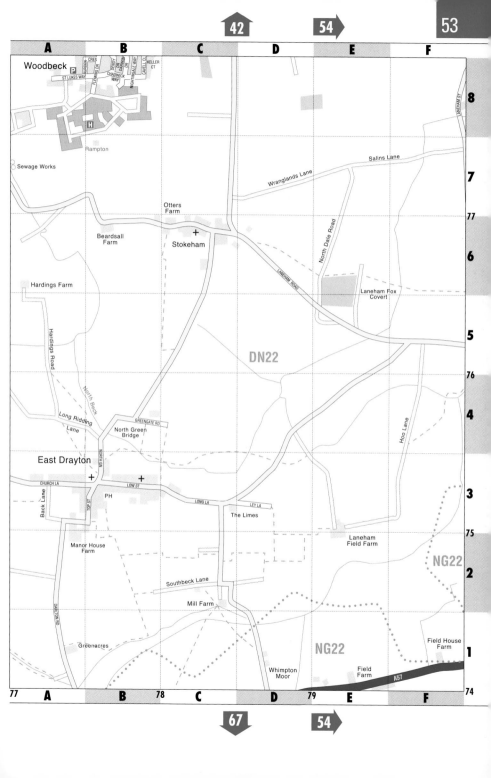

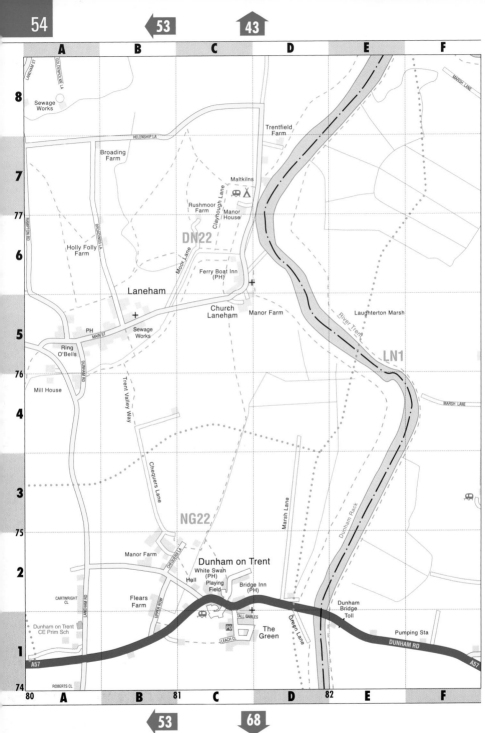

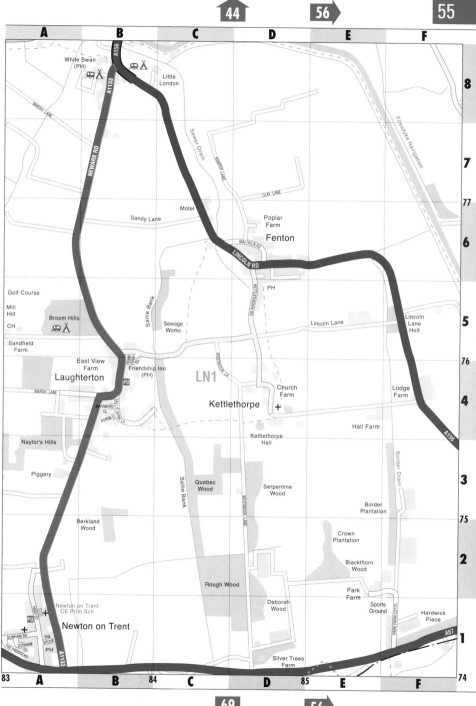

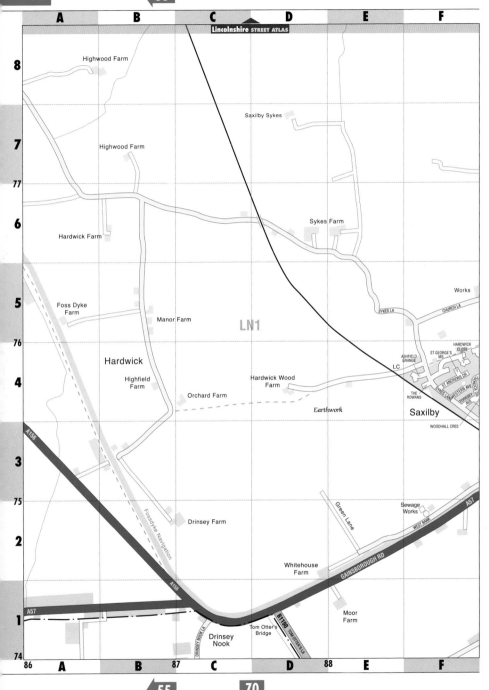

Lincolnshire STREET ATLAS

8

Highwood Farm

7

Highwood Farm

77

6

Saxilby Sykes

Sykes Farm

Hardwick Farm

5

Foss Dyke
Farm

Works

Manor Farm

SYKES LA

CHURCH LA

LN1

76

ASHFIELD
GRANGE

ST GEORGE'S
MS

HARDWICK
CLOSE

LC

ST ANDREWS DRI

Hardwick

4

Highfield
Farm

Hardwick Wood
Farm

THE
ROWANS

SYKES LA
CHESTERFIELD AVE

TURNSBY
DRI

Orchard Farm

Earthwork

Saxilby

WOODHALL CRES

A158

3

75

Green Lane

Sewage
Works

A57

WEST BANK

Drinsey Farm

2

Whitehouse
Farm

GAINSBOROUGH RD

Fossdyke Navigation

A198

Moor
Farm

A57

1

DRINSEY NOOK LA

Tom Otter's
Bridge

B1190

TOM OTTER'S LA

Drinsey
Nook

74

A   B   C   D   E   F

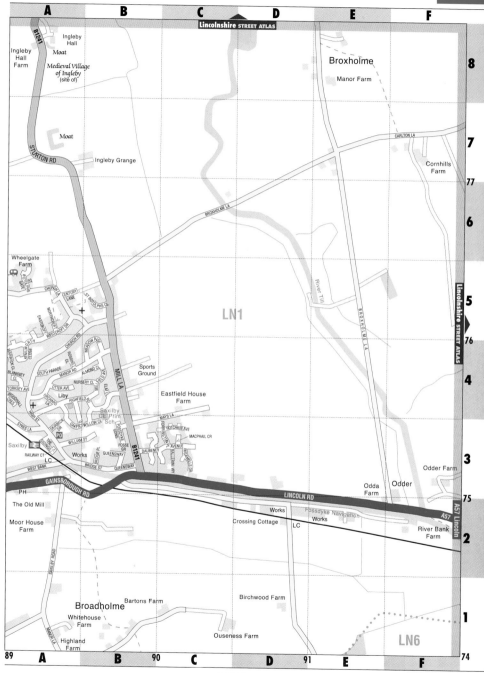

Lincolnshire STREET ATLAS

A B C D E F

8

B1241

Ingleby Hall Farm
Ingleby Hall
Moat
Medieval Village of Ingleby (site of)

Broxholme
Manor Farm

7

77

STURTON RD
Moat
Ingleby Grange

CARLTON LA

Cornhills Farm

6

BROXHOLME LA

River Till

Wheelgate Farm

LN1

5

76

BROXHOLME LA

CHURCH LA
CENTURY LANE
ST BOTS PHS CL
ST PHS GARTH
NORTHGATE
WESTCROFT DR
EASTFIELD CL
GARTH
WADDICK CL
PATRICK ST
BLANKNEY CL
WOODHALL CRES
TORKSEY AVE
SYKES LA
PRIOR ST
SKINNER LA
BRIDGE PL
RAILWAY CT
WEST BANK
MEADOW RISE
ROSEHILL RD
SOUTH PARADE
MANOR RD
ALMOND CL
NURSERY CL
ORCHARD
OTTER AVE
HIGHFIELD RD
ELMS
CARRICK
WILLOW CL
LIME GR
MILL LA
WILLIAM ST
FOSSE GR
DAUBENEY
QUEENSWAY
BRIDGE ST
QUEENSWAY
MACPHAIL CR
MAYS LA
HOTCHKIN AVE
AVENUE
BALDERTON WY
RINGWELL CL
HARDING HL PL

Sports Ground

Eastfield House Farm

Saxilby CE Prim Sch

Liby

4

Saxilby

Works

LC

B1241

3

Odder Farm

Odda Farm
Odder

75

GAINSBOROUGH RD
LINCOLN RD
A57 Lincoln

PH
The Old Mill
Moor House Farm

Works
Crossing Cottage
LC

Fossdyke Navigation
Works

River Bank Farm

2

SAXILBY ROAD

Broadholme
Whitehouse Farm
Highland Farm
Bartons Farm

Birchwood Farm

Ouseness Farm

LN6

1

MANOR LA

74

A B 90 C D 91 E F

89

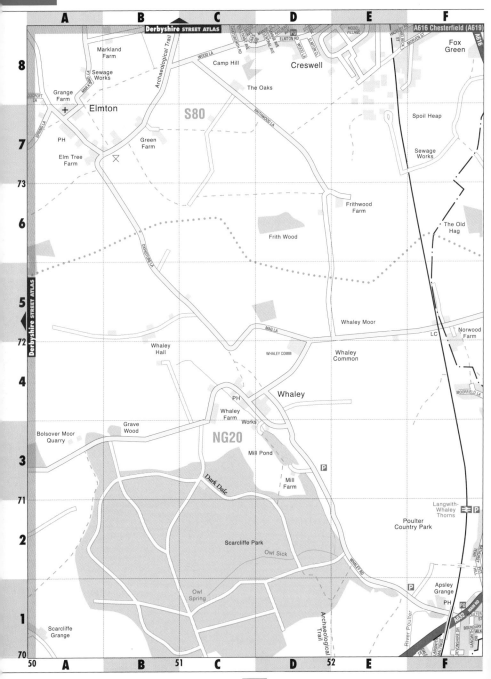

A616 Chesterfield (A619)

Fox Green

Markland Farm

Sewage Works

Camp Hill

Creswell

MODEL VILLAGE

The Oaks

Spoil Heap

Grange Farm

Elmton

S80

Sewage Works

PH

Green Farm

TRITHWOOD LA

Elm Tree Farm

Frithwood Farm

The Old Hag

Frith Wood

Derbyshire STREET ATLAS

Whaley Moor

Norwood Farm

LC

Whaley Hall

MAG LA

WHALEY COMM

Whaley Common

MOORFIELD LA

PH

Whaley

Whaley Farm

Works

Grave Wood

Bolsover Moor Quarry

NG20

Mill Pond

P

Mill Farm

Langwith-Whaley Thorns

P

Dark Dale

Poulter Country Park

Scarcliffe Park

Owl Sick

WHALEY RD

P

Apsley Grange

Owl Spring

PH

PO

Scarcliffe Grange

Archaeological Trail

River Poulter

A632

50   A   B   51   C   D   52   E   F

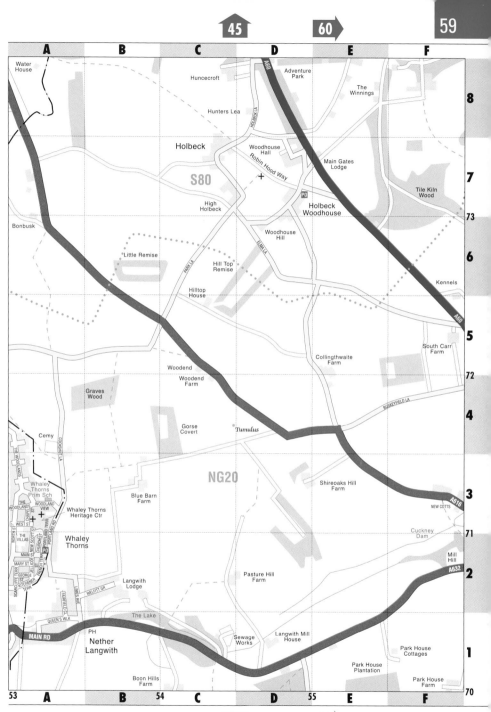

59 46

	A	B	C	D	E	F

8

Sports Ground

The Roses

Wilderness

Landing Stage

S80

Clown Hill Plantation

Wood Barn Plantation

Greendale Oak

Lambing Cabin Clump

Angling Garden Plantation

Moss Hall Plantation

Tichfield Hill

Battlefield Plantation

7

Great Lake

Deer Park

73

Common Piece Plantation

Kennel Plantation

Fox Covert Plantation

6

Robin Hood Way

Park Lodge

Bunker's Hill Plantation

Welbeck Park

Weir

Cat Hills Plantation

Bunker's Hill

Milnthorpe Lodge

Carburton Forge Dam

5

A60

Harvest Dam Hill

Norton

Corunna Lodge

Corunna Hill Plantation

INFIELD LA

River Poulter

Mon

72

BUCKEYFIELD LA

Bentinck Lodge

4

WORKSOP RD

Sewage Works

Battarain Plantation

Cuckney

Bridge House

Motte & Bailey

NORTON LA

Old Mill House

Hatfield Grange

Burn's Breck

Lord Woodstock's Plantation

3

GLOVERS RIVERSIDE CL

A616

CRESWELL RD

MANSFIELD RD

BUDBY RD

PO

Greendale Oak (PH)

OLD MILL LA

NG20

BUDBY RD

A616

Cuckney House

Old Mill House

High Hatfield

Sedan Lodge

71

SCHOOL LA

BAKER LA

A632

LANGWITH RD

A632

Gleadthorpe Breck Plantation

2

A60

Cuckney CE Prim Sch

Sandy Lane

Hatfield Plantation

Presley's Plantation

Welbeck Colliery

1

Spoil Heap

Elkesley Hill

ELKESLEY RD

BUDBY CRES

1 RUFFORD AVE

PORTLAND TERR

HATFIELD AVE

70

A60

Warsop Hill Plantation

NETHERFIELD

| 56 | A | | 57 | C | D | 58 | E | F |

59 74

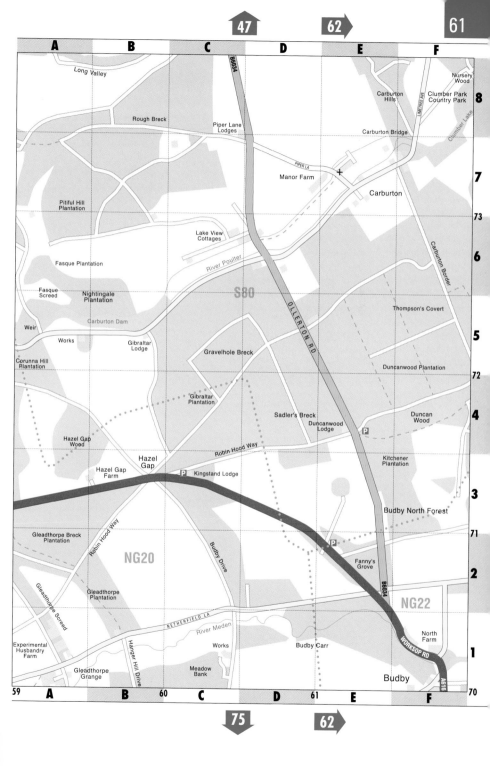

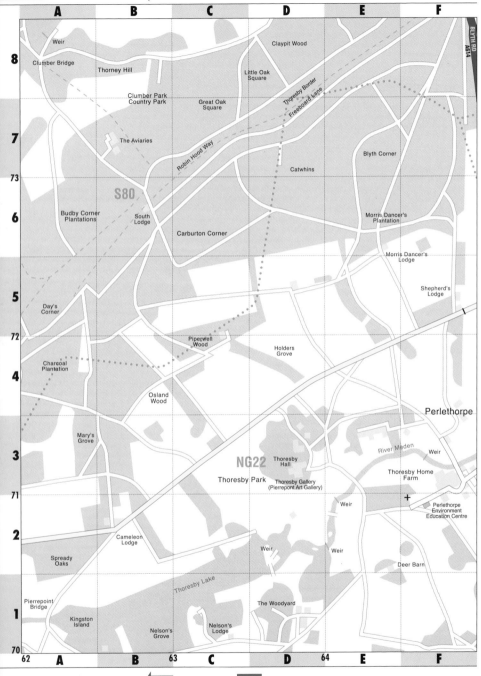

Weir
Clumber Bridge
Thorney Hill
Clumber Park
Country Park
The Aviaries
S80
Budby Corner
Plantations
South
Lodge
Day's
Corner
Charcoal
Plantation
Mary's
Grove
Spready
Oaks
Pierrepoint
Bridge
Kingston
Island

Claypit Wood
Little Oak
Square
Great Oak
Square
Thoresby Border
Freeboard Lane
Robin Hood Way
Catwhins
Carburton Corner
Piperwell
Wood
Osland
Wood
Holders
Grove
Cameleon
Lodge
Thoresby Lake
Nelson's
Grove
Nelson's
Lodge

Blyth Corner
Morris Dancer's
Plantation
Morris Dancer's
Lodge
Shepherd's
Lodge
Perlethorpe
River Meden
Weir
NG22
Thoresby
Hall
Thoresby Park
Thoresby Gallery
(Pierrepont Art Gallery)
Thoresby Home
Farm
Weir
Perlethorpe
Environment
Education Centre
Weir
Weir
Deer Barn
The Woodyard

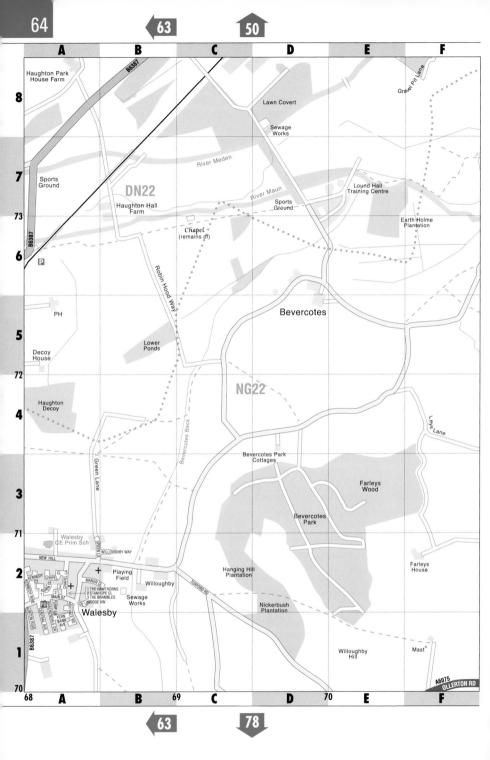

A B C D E F

8

Haughton Park
House Farm

Lawn Covert

Sewage
Works

Gravel Pit Lane

River Meden

7

Sports
Ground

DN22

Haughton Hall
Farm

River Maun

Sports
Ground

Lound Hall
Training Centre

73

Chapel
(remains of)

Earth Holme
Plantation

6

P

B6387

Robin Hood Way

PH

Bevercotes

5

Decoy
House

Lower
Ponds

72

NG22

Haughton
Decoy

4

Bevercotes Beck

Leys Lane

Bevercotes Park
Cottages

Farleys
Wood

3

Green Lane

Bevercotes
Park

Walesby
CE Prim Sch

71

GREEN LN

WILLOUGHBY WAY

Farleys
House

NEW HILL

2

KENNEDY

CL

CHAPEL

Playing
Field

Hanging Hill
Plantation

Willoughby

1 THE HAWTHORNS
2 STANHOPE CL
3 THE BRAMBLES

MAIN ST

KENNETT RISE

ASKHAM

COLERIDGE VW

Sewage
Works

TUXFORD RD

CENTRAL AVE

Walesby

BRITON RISE

FERN
BANK
AVE

Nickerbush
Plantation

Willoughby
Hill

Mast

1

B6387

70

A6075
OLLERTON RD

68 A B 69 C D 70 E F

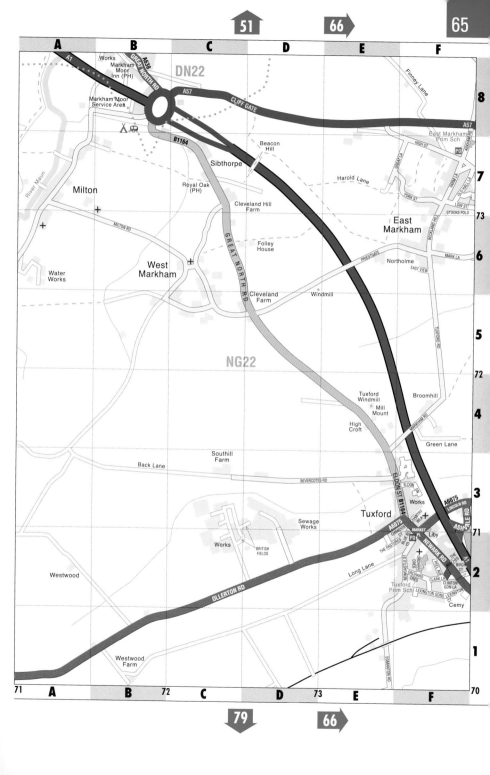

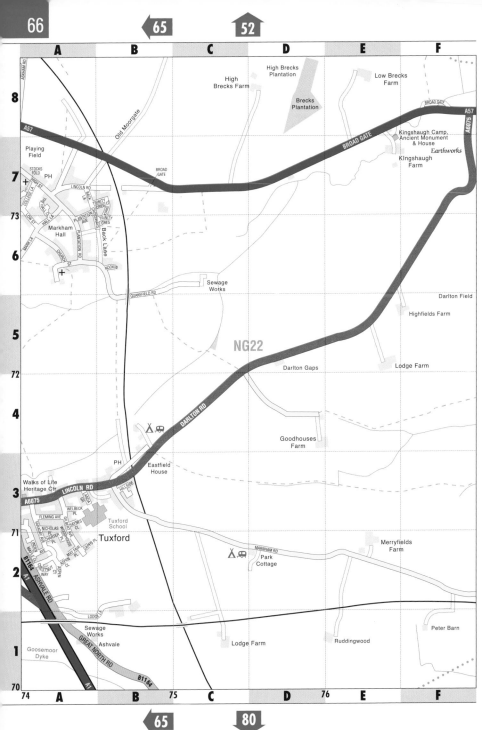

A B C D E F

8

A57

BYRON CL

BROAD GATE

Medieval Village
of Whimpton
(site of)

Darlton

Low Farm

Grange Farm

Farhill Farm

Farhill Lane

Grange Farm

7

73

Field Farm

America Farm

WOODCOATES RD

Vicarage Farm

Fledborough Beck

6

NG22

North Farm

5

Majors Farm

GREEN LA

Top Farm

72

Gibraltar

4

Wells
Farm

Woodcoates

FAR RD

Crabtree Lane

Station
Cottages

3

71

Babbington Springs
Farm

CRABTREE LA

NG23

2

LC

POLLY TAYLOR'S RD

Skegby

SKEGBY RD

1

70

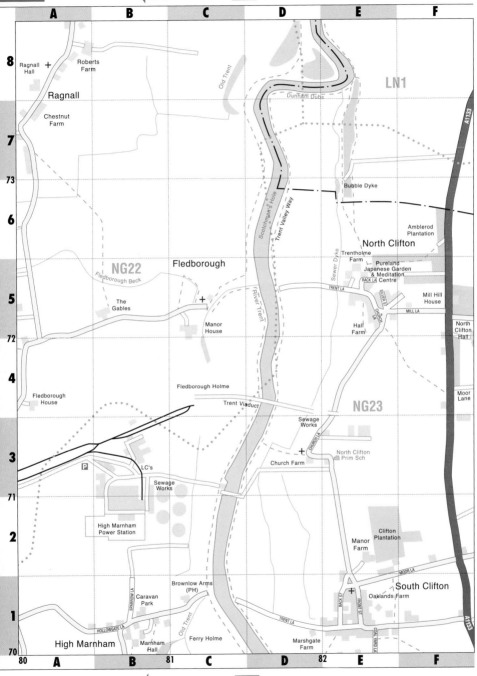

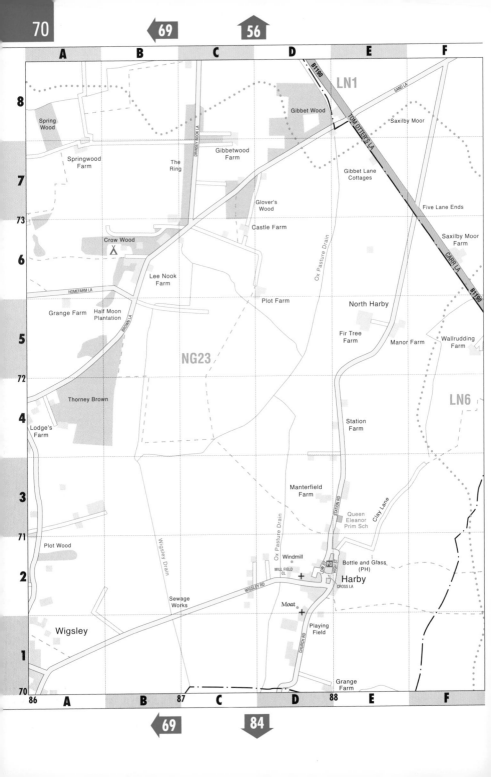

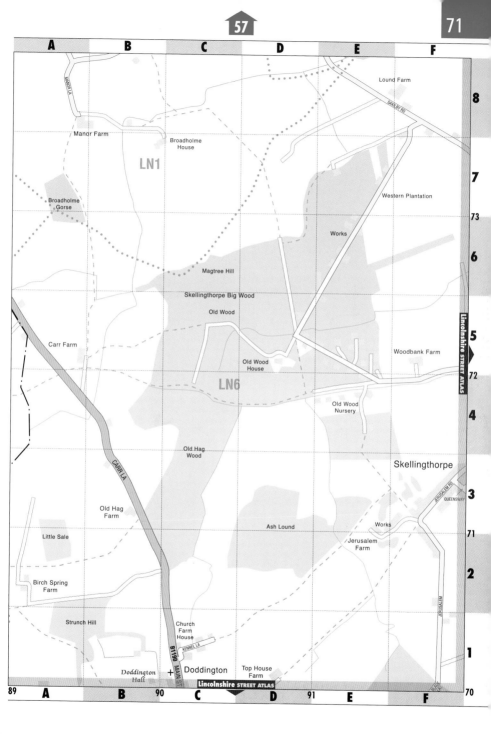

MANOR LA

Lound Farm

SAXILBY RD

8

Manor Farm

Broadholme
House

LN1

7

Western Plantation

73

Broadholme
Gorse

Works

6

Magtree Hill

Skellingthorpe Big Wood

Old Wood

5

Carr Farm

Woodbank Farm

Old Wood
House

72

LN6

Old Wood
Nursery

4

Old Hag
Wood

Skellingthorpe

CARR LA

3

JERUSALEM RD

QUEENSWAY

Old Hag
Farm

Little Sale

Ash Lound

Works

71

Jerusalem
Farm

Birch Spring
Farm

2

JERUSALEM

Strunch Hill

Church
Farm
House

KENNEL LA

Top House
Farm

1

B1190 MAIN ST

Doddington
Hall

Doddington

70

89   A   B   90   C   D   91   E   F

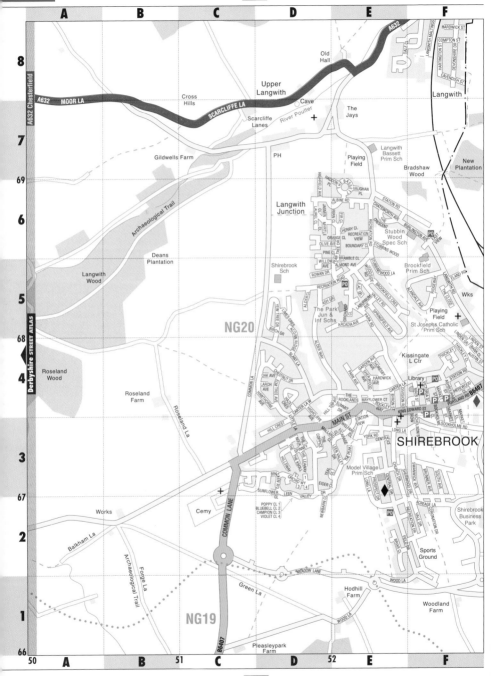

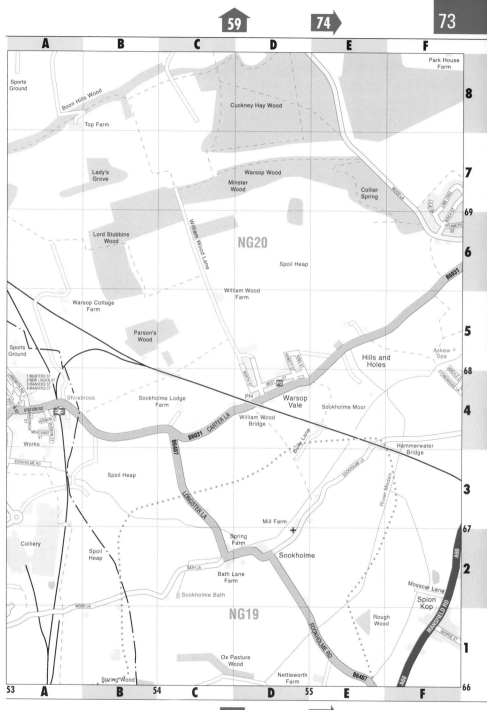

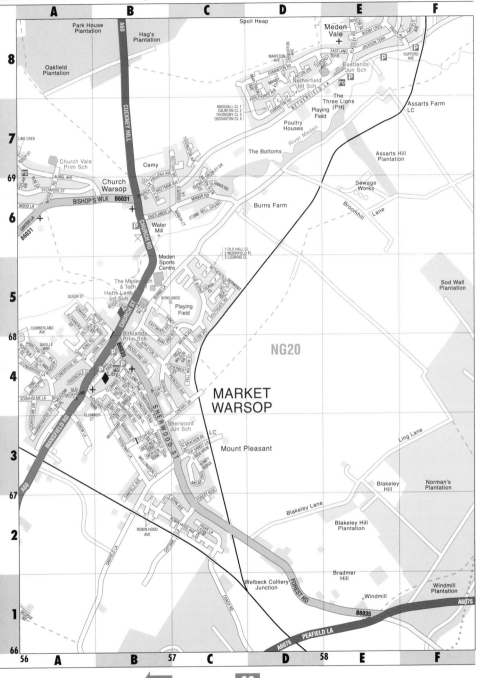

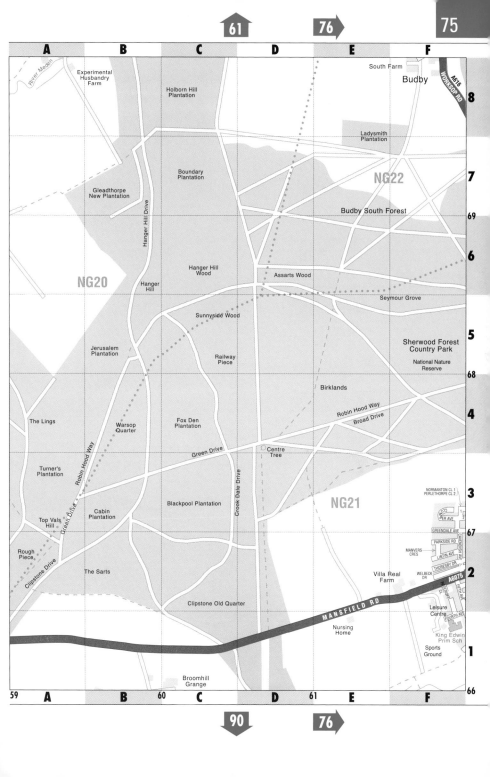

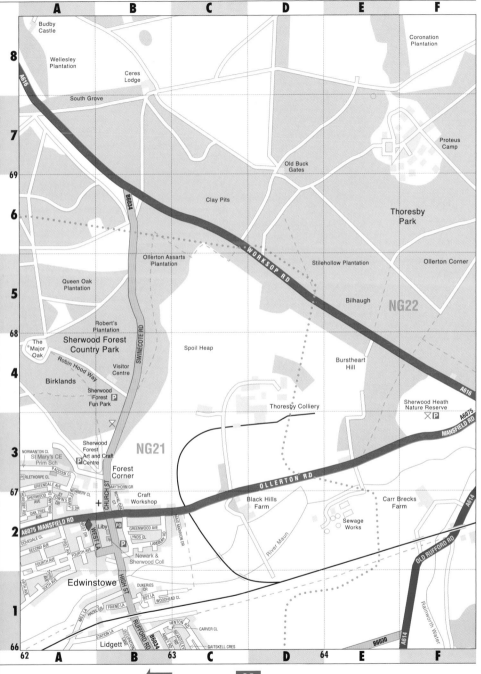

A B C D E F

8
7
69
6
5
68
4
3
67
2
1
66

Budby Castle

Wellesley Plantation

Ceres Lodge

South Grove

Coronation Plantation

Proteus Camp

Old Buck Gates

Clay Pits

Thoresby Park

Ollerton Assarts Plantation

Stilehollow Plantation

Ollerton Corner

NG22

Queen Oak Plantation

Bilhaugh

Robert's Plantation

The Major Oak

Sherwood Forest Country Park

Spoil Heap

Burstheart Hill

Birklands

Robin Hood Way

Visitor Centre

Sherwood Forest Fun Park

Thoresby Colliery

Sherwood Heath Nature Reserve

MANSFIELD RD

A616

A6075

Sherwood Forest Art and Craft Centre

NG21

NORMANTON CL
St Mary's CE Prim Sch

PERLETHORPE CL

GREENDALE AVE

PADDOCK CL

THORESBY AVE

SHERWOOD AVE

OAK TREE AVE

NEWBURY CL

ST EDWIN'S DR

S DR

Forest Corner

MAYTHORN GR

Craft Workshop

OLLERTON RD

Black Hills Farm

Carr Brecks Farm

CHURCH ST

A6075 MANSFIELD RD

Liby

PO

WEST LA

DOVEDALE CL

SECOND AVE

FOURTH AVE

FIRST AVE

THIRD AVE

GREENWOOD AVE

LYNDS CL

LANSBY RD

MARION DR

Newark & Sherwood Coll

River Maun

Sewage Works

OLD RUFFORD RD

A614

Edwinstowe

FIFTH AVE

SIXTH AVE

HIGH ST

DUKERIES CR

BOY LA

WOODHEAD CL

Rainworth Water

MELL LA

HAZEL GR

FRIEND LA

STATION LA

OCCUPATION LANE

RUFFORD RD

B6034

HENTON CL

BEXLEY CL

CARVER CL

GAITSKELL CRES

B6030

A614

Lidgett

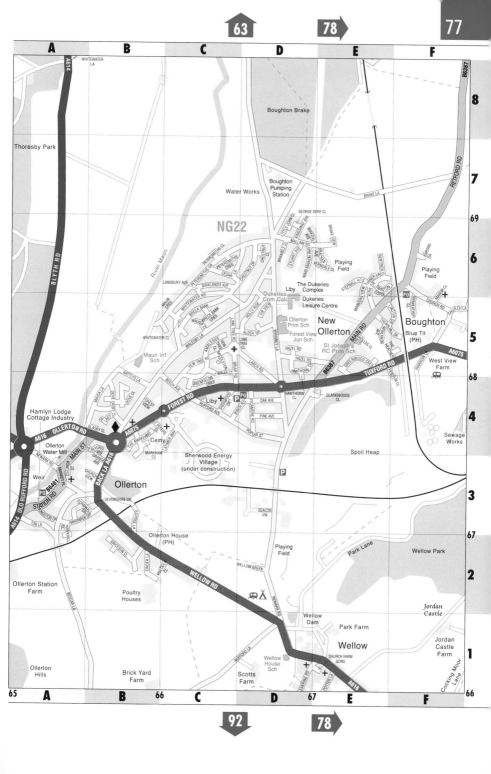

A   B   C   D   E   F

8

Collinridge
Wood

TUXFORD RD

A6075   OLLERTON RD

Priors
Park
Farm

Manor
Farm

7

Pasture Farm
and Victorian
Carriages

PH

Goosemoor Dyke

Hall Farm

RECTORY GDNS

69

SANDFIELD LA.

KIRTON DRIVE

Kirton

Winson
Hill

6

Doncaster
Farm

CHARLOTTE CL.

KIRTON CT.

MAIN ST.

THE FURLOL

ORCHARD LA.

Manor
Farm

PRIMROSE LA.

NG22

Kirton Wood
Nature Reserve

5

A6075

Boughton
Ind Est

68

Cocking Hill
Farm

Brick Works

TRENT RD

MEDEN RD.

BROUGHTON

JOHN BROUGHTON

Marl Pit

Norton
Wood

4

MAUN WAY

Sports
Ground

COCKING HILL

Golden
Hill

West Field

Birkhill
Wood

3

Mounds

Wellow Park

Laxton
Common

67

The Holocaust
Centre

Westwood
Farm

ACRE EDGE RD

Cocking
Moor

2

Jordan Castle
Farm

Cocking Moor La

Ompton
Lodge

SHORTWOOD LA.

1

66

68   A   B   69   C   D   70   E   F

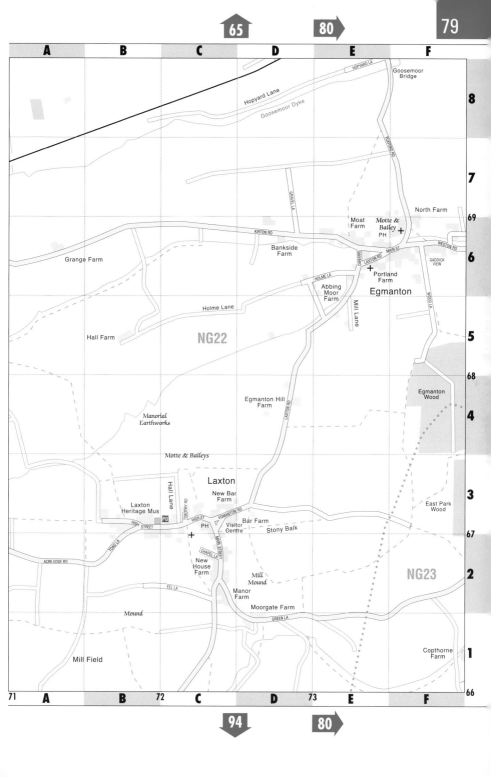

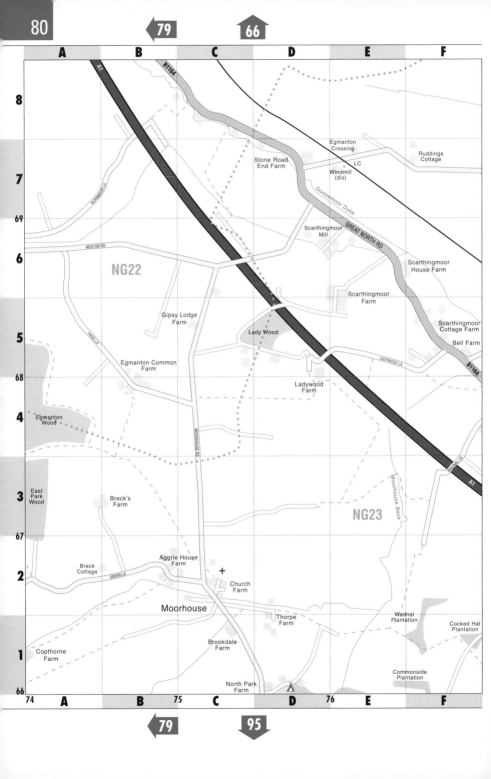

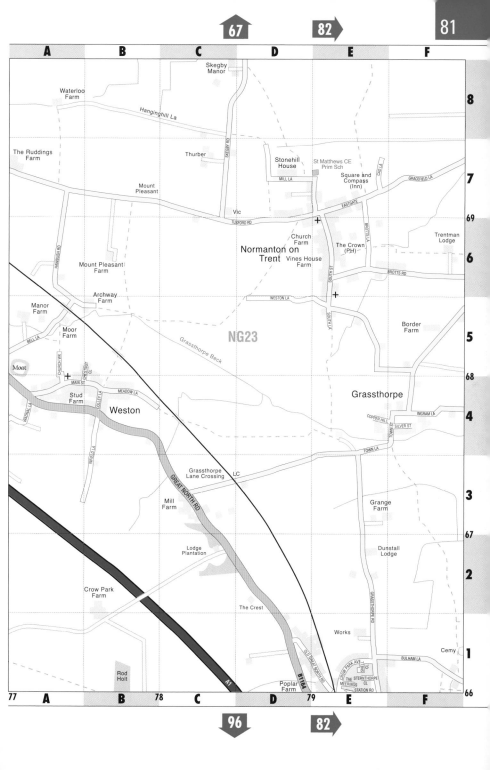

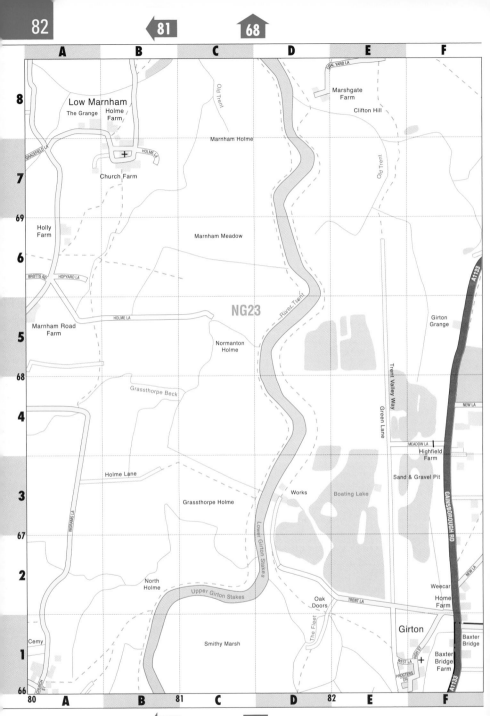

Low Marnham
The Grange
Holme Farm
GRASSFIELD LA
Church Farm
HOLME LA
Holly Farm
BROTTS RD
HOPYARD LA
Marnham Road Farm
HOLME LA
Marnham Holme
Old Trent
Marnham Meadow
NG23
River Trent
Normanton Holme
Girton Grange
Grassthorpe Beck
Old Trent
OAL YARD LA
Marshgate Farm
Clifton Hill
Trent Valley Way
Green Lane
A1133
NEW LA
MEADOW LA
Highfield Farm
Sand & Gravel Pit
GAINSBOROUGH RD
Holme Lane
INGRAMS LA
Grassthorpe Holme
Lower Girton Stakes
Works
Boating Lake
North Holme
Upper Girton Stakes
Oak Doors
TRENT LA
The Fleet
Weecar Home Farm
NEW LA
Girton
Cemy
CHURCH ST
Smithy Marsh
WEST LA
HIGH ST
PROCTERS DR
Baxter Bridge
Baxter Bridge Farm
A1133

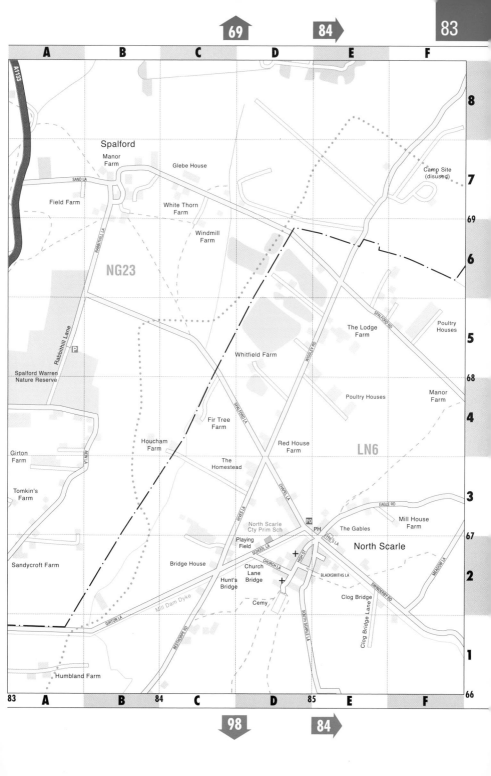

A   B   C   D   E   F

8

Spalford

Manor Farm

Glebe House

Camp Site (disused)

SAND LA

7

Field Farm

White Thorn Farm

69

Windmill Farm

RABBITHILL LA

6

NG23

The Lodge Farm

Poultry Houses

SPALFORD RD

Rabbithill Lane

P

Whitfield Farm

5

WISEL'T RD

Spalford Warren Nature Reserve

68

Poultry Houses

Manor Farm

Fir Tree Farm

SPALFORD LA

4

HINES LA

Girton Farm

Houcham Farm

Red House Farm

LN6

Tomkin's Farm

The Homestead

EAGLE RD

3

Mill House Farm

The Gables

Sandycroft Farm

Bridge House

Playing Field

North Scarle Cty Prim Sch

SCHOOL LA

RD

PH

North Scarle

FYNE'S LA

67

CHURCH LA

Church Lane Bridge

HIGH ST

BLACKSMITHS LA

MEADOW LA

2

Hunt's Bridge

Clog Bridge

SWINDERBY RD

GIRTON LA

Mill Dam Oyke

Cemy

SOUTH SCARLE LA

Clog Bridge Lane

BESTHORPE RD

1

Humbland Farm

66

A1133

HINES LA

83
70

A
B
C
D
E
F
8
7
69
6
5
68
4
3
67
2
1
66
86
87
88
Fir Tree Farm
Swinethorpe
NG23
Middle Farm
Fox Holt
Corner Farm
Wigsley Drain
Cock Pit
Crow Wood
Parson's Wood
Hurn Wood
Old Farm
The Jungle
Large Farm
Woodhouse Farm
Plots Farm
MILL LA
Mill Farm
GREEN LA
Holly Tree Farm
SPALFORD RD
EAGLE MOOR
Eagle Moor
EAGLE RD
Enfield Farm
Westwood Farm
LN6
HILLTOP CL
Fir Tree Farm
Wellands Farm
EAGLE RD
The Poplars
Westwood
SCARLE LA
Eagle Cty Prim Sch
Cherry Farm
PH
MEADOW LA
WILLIAM & HENRY MEWS
CHURCH LA
PO
FALCON CL
Eagle
HIGH ST
Playing Field
New Lane
TANGLEWOOD
MANOR CL
KESTREL RISE
Back Lane
Enfield Farm
THORPE LA
Slack's Hill
Aspen House
Thorpe Lane Farm
JOB'S LA
Eagle Hall High Wood
Eagle Hall High Wood Farm
SWINDERBY RD
BEEHIVE LA
Preston Farm
Lincolnshire STREET ATLAS
Lincolnshire STREET ATLAS

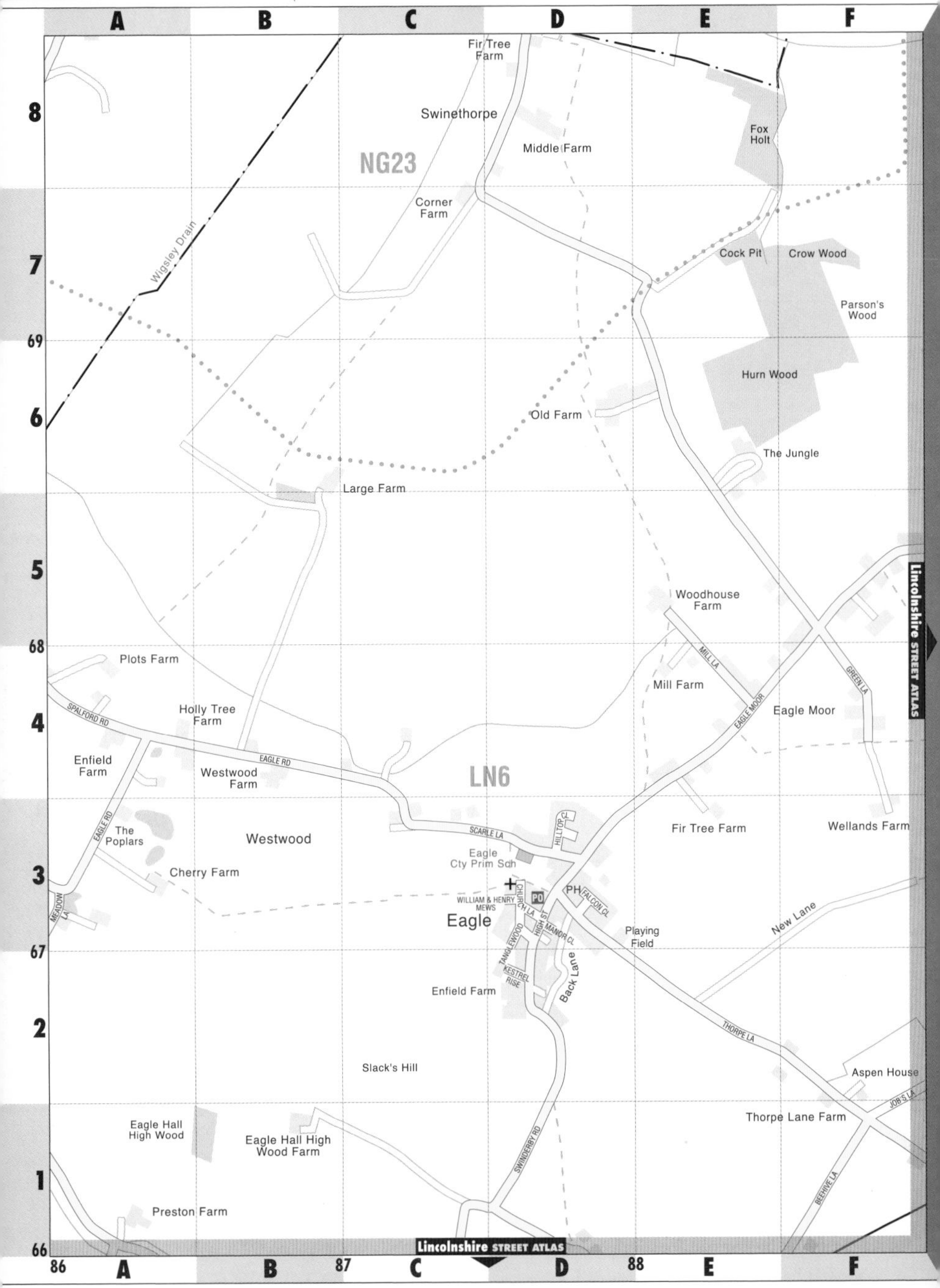

83

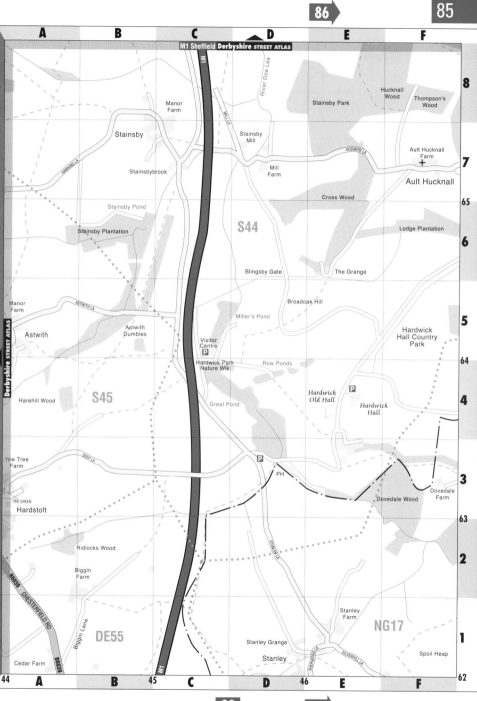

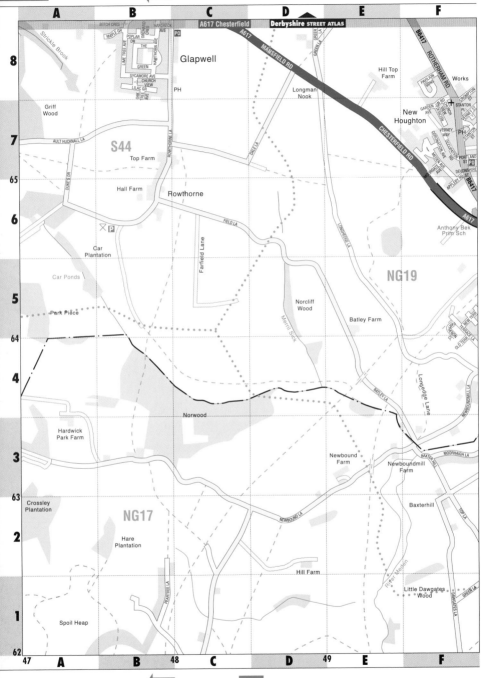

A617 Chesterfield **Derbyshire** STREET ATLAS

Glapwell

S44

BEECH CRES
MAPLE GR
POPLAR
DR
THE
GREEN
SYCAMORE AVE
LILAC GR
CHURCH
VIEW
OAK TREE AVE
HARDWICK
CLOSE
HAWTHORN AVE
LIME TREE AVE
PO
PH

Stickle Brook

Griff Wood

AULT HUCKNALL LA

Top Farm

Hall Farm

Rowthorne

ROWTHORNE LA

DUKE'S DR

FIELD LA

Farfield Lane

Car Plantation

Car Ponds

Park Piece

MANSFIELD RD

A617

Longman Nook

DALE LA

GREEN LA

Hill Top Farm

New Houghton

CHESTERFIELD RD

PAVILION GDNS

GARDEN GR RD
STANTON
ST
CROMPTON
ST
VERNEY
WAY
COCKINGTON LA
MAIN ST
PH
PORTLAND
ST
DEVONSHIRE
ST
APPLEBY RD
PO

B6417
ROTHERHAM RD

Works

Anthony Bek Prim Sch

NG19

Norcliff Wood

Merril Sick

LONGACRES LA

Batley Farm

NEW TERRACE PL
OLD TERRACE PL
CHALLAND RISE

Longedge Lane

NEWBOUNDMILL LA

BATLEY LA

Norwood

Hardwick Park Farm

Newbound Farm

BAXTER HILL

Newboundmill Farm

MOORHAIGH LA

Baxterhill

TOP LA

Crossley Plantation

NG17

Hare Plantation

PEARTREE LA

NEWBOUND LA

Hill Farm

River Meden

Little Dawgates Wood

DAWGATES LA

GREEN LA

Spoil Heap

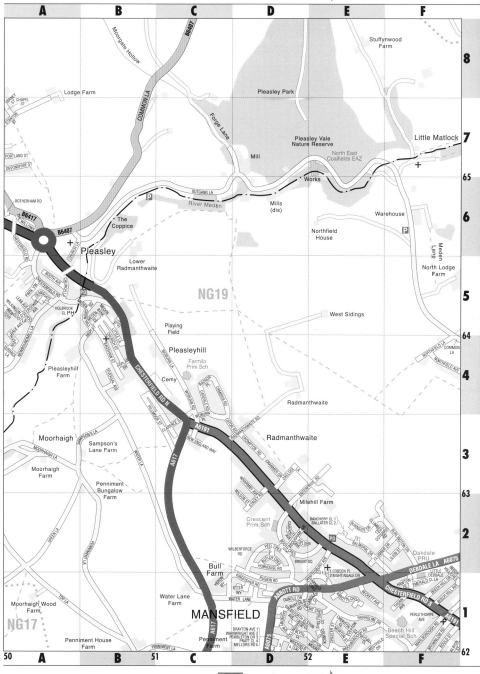

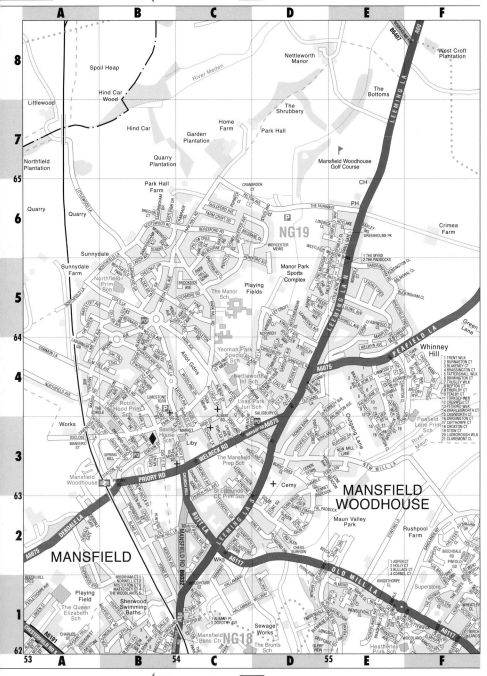

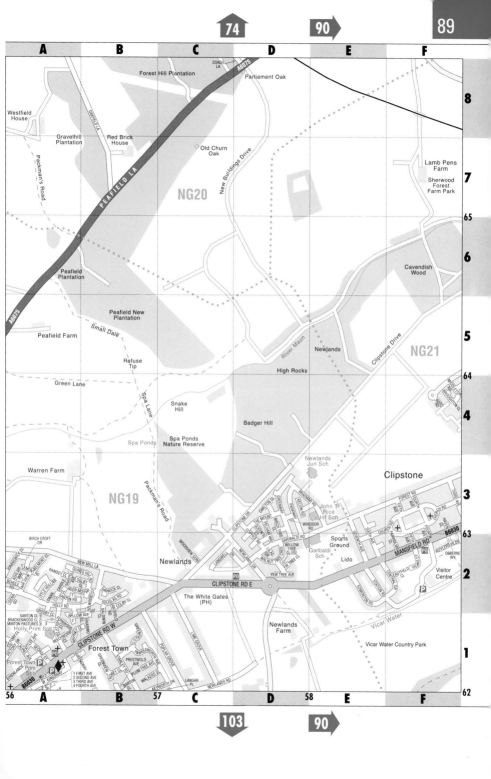

A   B   C   D   E   F

8

Broomhill
Gorse

New Lodge
Plantation

Robin Hood Way

Gorsethorpe

Forge
Bridge

Clipstone
Junction

Halfmoon
Plantation

7

River Maun

Eastfield
Farm

Eastfield
Cottage

Lawn
Hills

65

Clipstone Dr

SQUIRES LA

PH

B6030

6

Cavendish
Lodge

SQUIRES CRES

King John's
Palace
(rems of)

Old
Clipstone

Cavendish
Wood

NG21

MANSFIELD RD

Forest Walks
Cycle Route

Culloden
Farm

5

Intake
Wood

Waterfield
Farm

Lindleys
Plantation

Culloden

Culloden
Plantation

64

BARKER LN

ROCKLEY CL

Vicar Water

P ✕

4

Clipstone

WAY

WOODLAND
CL

DAVIS
CL

SHERWOOD
PL

BAULKER LA

Cemy

HIGHFIELD RD

GREENDALE
CRES

Sherwood Pines
Visitor Centre

Samuel
Barlow
Prim Sch

Library

NORTH CR

THE
CIRCLE

Go Ape!

Forestry
Office

3

CHURCH RD

SECOND
AVE

SOUTH CRES

Forestry
Holdings

Sherwood Pines
Forest Pk

THIRD
AVE

B6030

Colliery

63

Vicar
Pond

Clipstone Forest

2

Spoil
Heap

NG22

1

62

Sherwood Forest
Golf Course

59   A   B   60   C   D   61   E   F

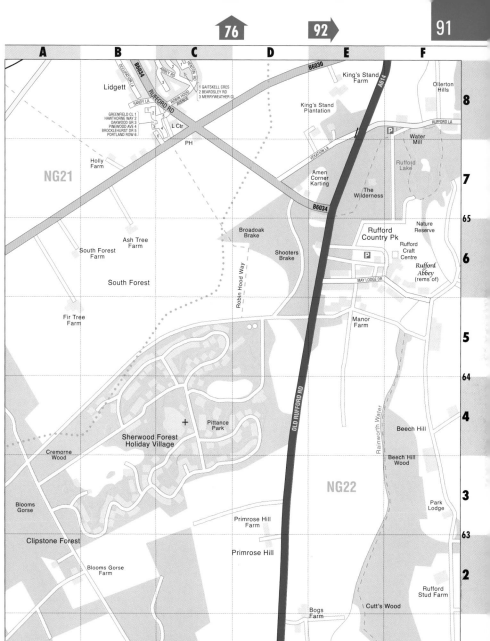

91
77

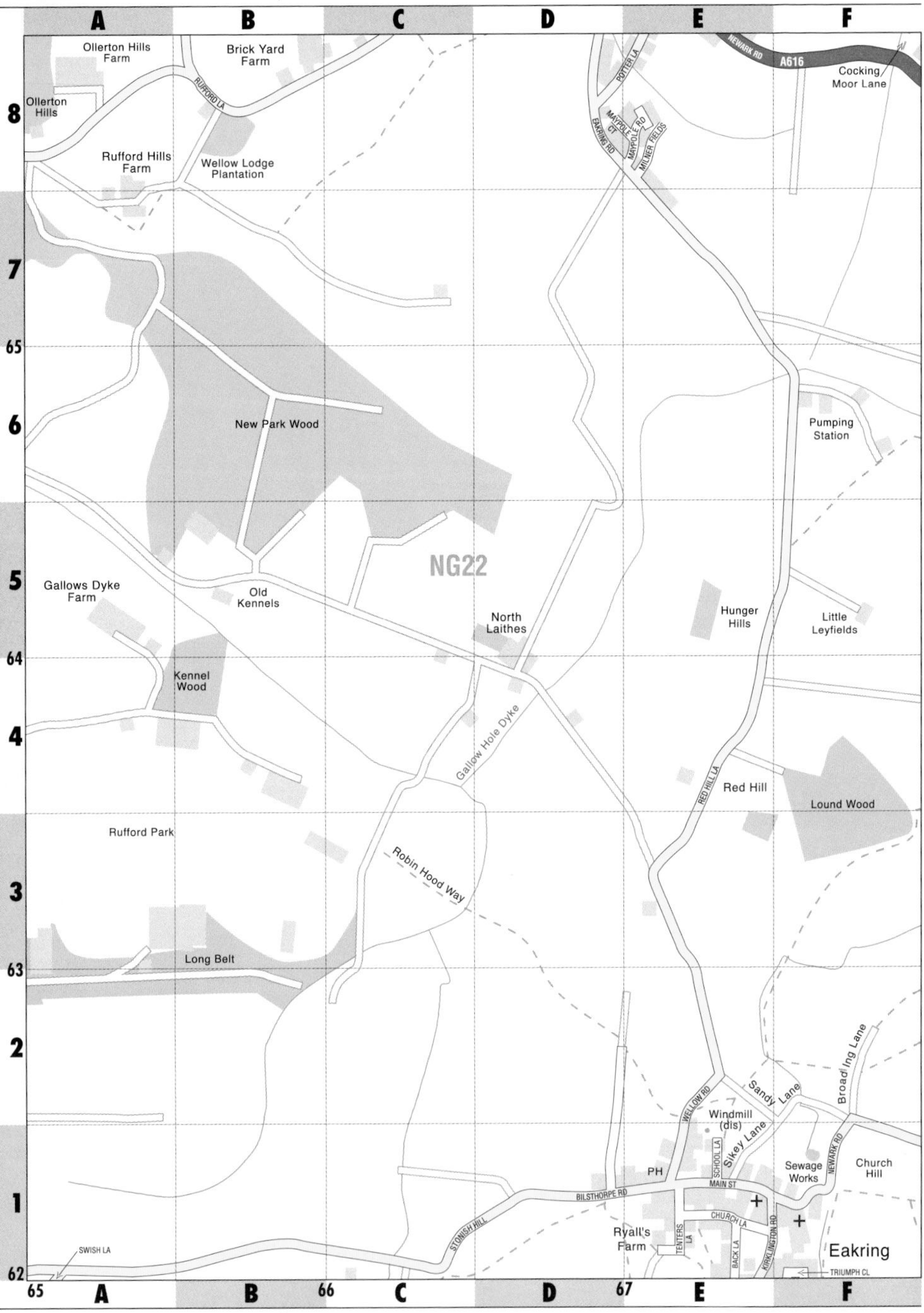

A   B   C   D   E   F

8

Ollerton Hills Farm
Brick Yard Farm
NEWARK RD
A616
Cocking Moor Lane

Ollerton Hills

RUFFORD LA

POTTER LA
EAKRING RD
MAYPOLE RD
MAYPOLE CT
MILLSET FIELDS

Rufford Hills Farm
Wellow Lodge Plantation

7

65

Pumping Station

6

New Park Wood

NG22

5

Gallows Dyke Farm
Old Kennels
North Laithes
Hunger Hills
Little Leyfields

64

Kennel Wood

4

Gallow Hole Dyke
RED HILL A
Red Hill
Lound Wood

Rufford Park

3

Robin Hood Way

63

Long Belt

2

BROADING LANE

WELLOW RD
Sandy Lane
Windmill (dis)
Skegby Lane
NEWARK RD
Church Hill

1

SCHOOL LA
MAIN ST
PH
BILSTHORPE RD
Sewage Works

SWISH LA

STONEY HILL
CHURCH LA
Ryall's Farm
TENTERS LA
BACK LA
KIRKLINGTON RD
Eakring

62

TRIUMPH CL

65   A   B   66   C   D   67   E   F

91
106

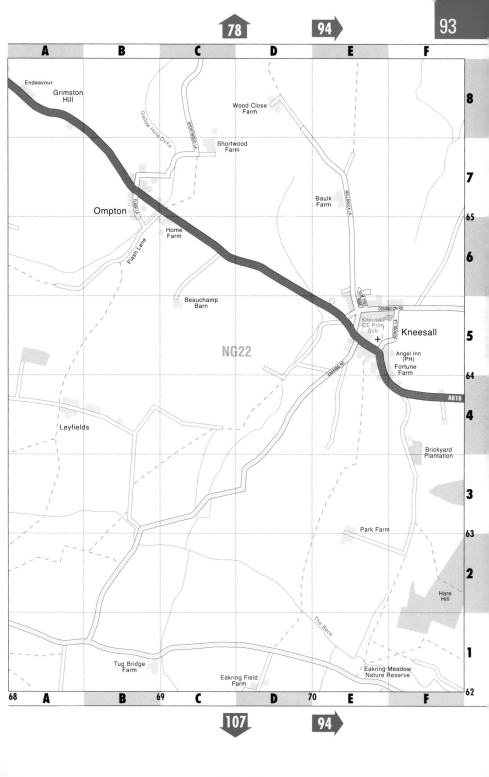

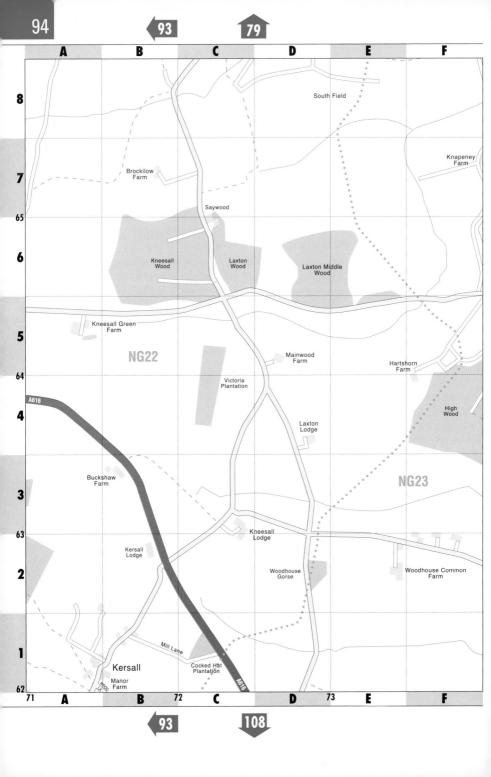

A B C D E F

8 South Field

Knapeney
Farm

7 Brockilow
Farm

Saywood

65

6 Kneesall
Wood
Laxton
Wood
Laxton Middle
Wood

Kneesall Green
Farm

5 NG22
Mainwood
Farm

Hartshorn
Farm

64 Victoria
Plantation

High
Wood

A616

4 Laxton
Lodge

Buckshaw
Farm

3 NG23

63 Kneesall
Lodge

Kersall
Lodge

2 Woodhouse
Gorse
Woodhouse Common
Farm

Mill Lane

1 Kersall
Cocked Hat
Plantation

A616

Manor
Farm

62

71 A B 72 C D 73 E F

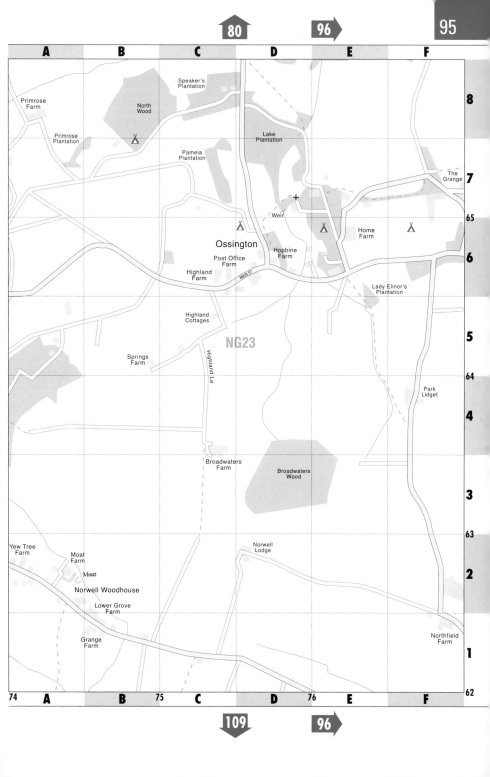

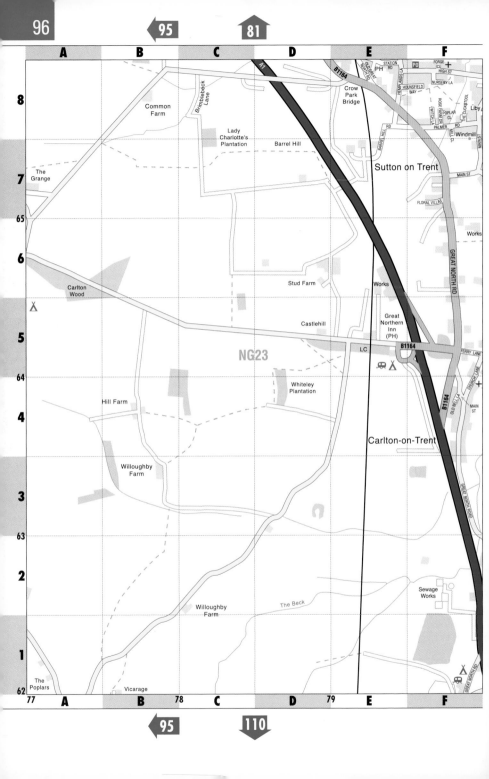

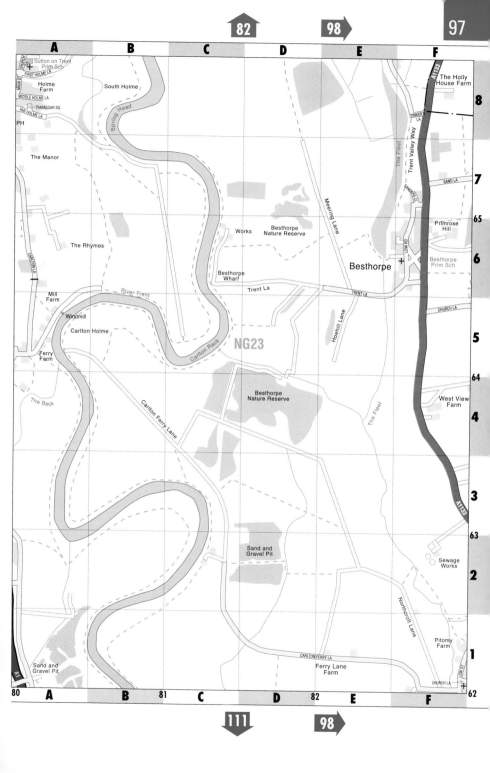

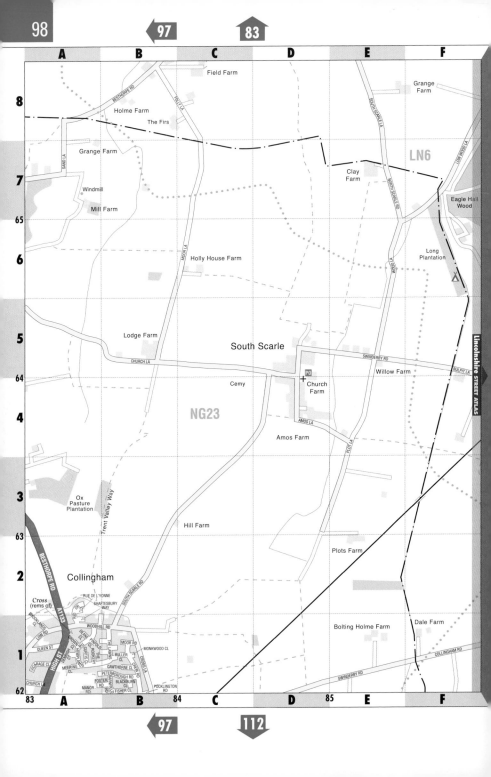

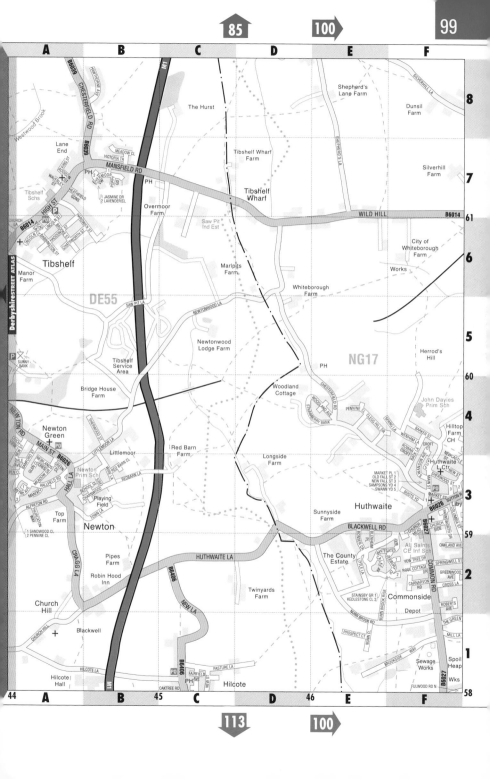

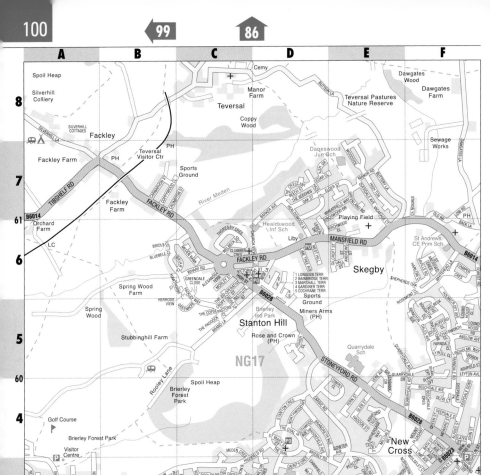

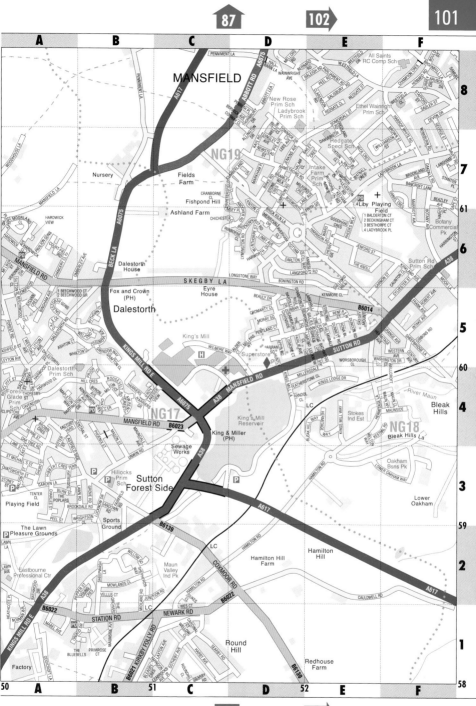

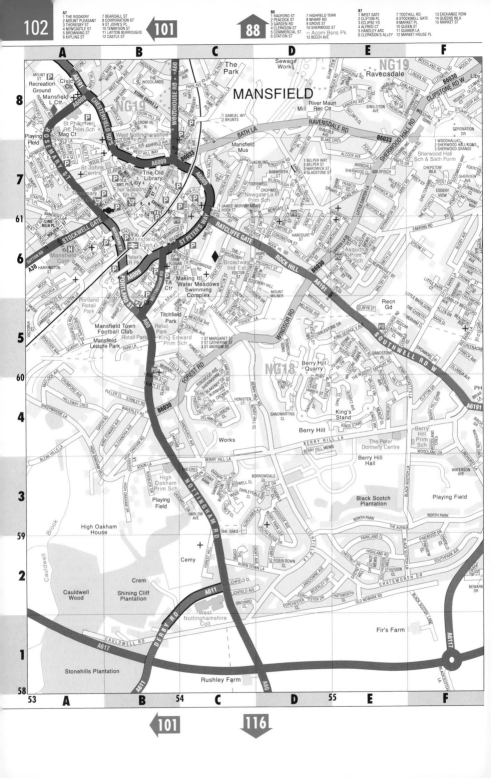

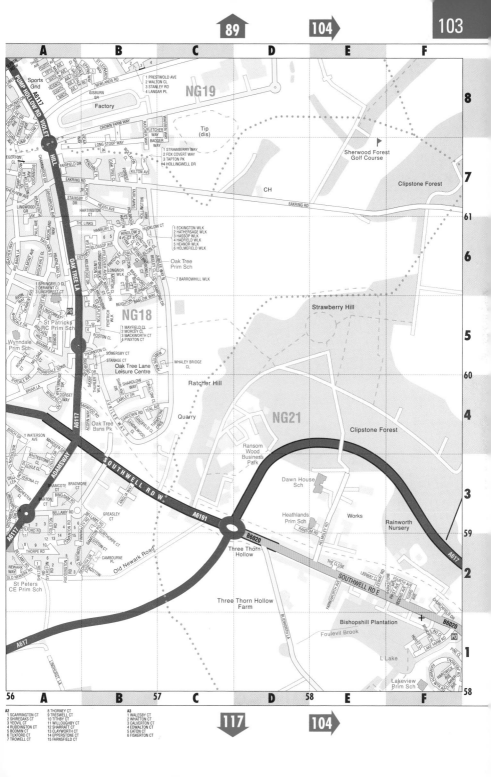

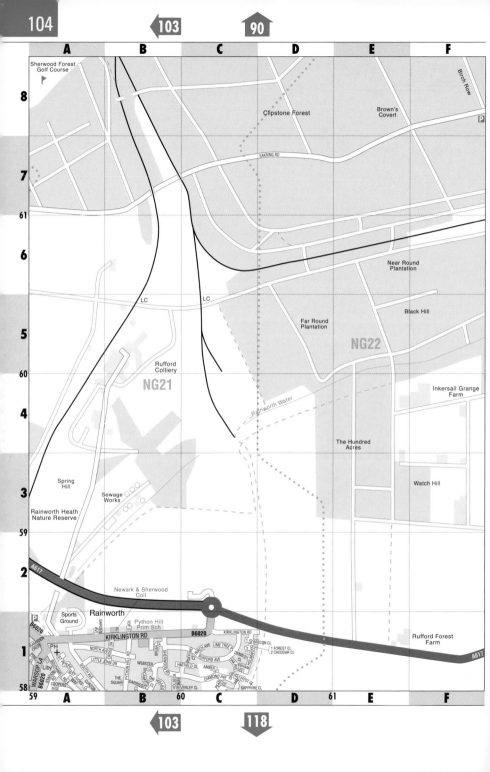

103
90

Sherwood Forest
Golf Course

Clipstone Forest

Brown's
Covert

Birch Row

P

EAKRING RD

Near Round
Plantation

LC

LC

Far Round
Plantation

Black Hill

NG22

Rufford
Colliery

NG21

Inkersall Grange
Farm

Rainworth Water

Spring
Hill

The Hundred
Acres

Sewage
Works

Watch Hill

Rainworth Heath
Nature Reserve

A617

Newark & Sherwood
Coll

Python Hill
Prim Sch

Rufford Forest
Farm

P

Sports
Ground

Rainworth

KIRKLINGTON RD

B6020

KIRKLINGTON RD

A617

B6020

PH

Liby

WARSOP LA

B6020

LITTLE JOHN DR

WEBSTER

BRECON CL

1 FOREST CL
2 CHEDDAR CL

DENBIGH
CL

LIME TREE PL

RUFFORD AVE

HATFIELD DL

AMBER

DIAMOND AVE

BEVERLEY CL

SAPPHIRE CL

THE SQUARE

THE HOLLIES

103
118

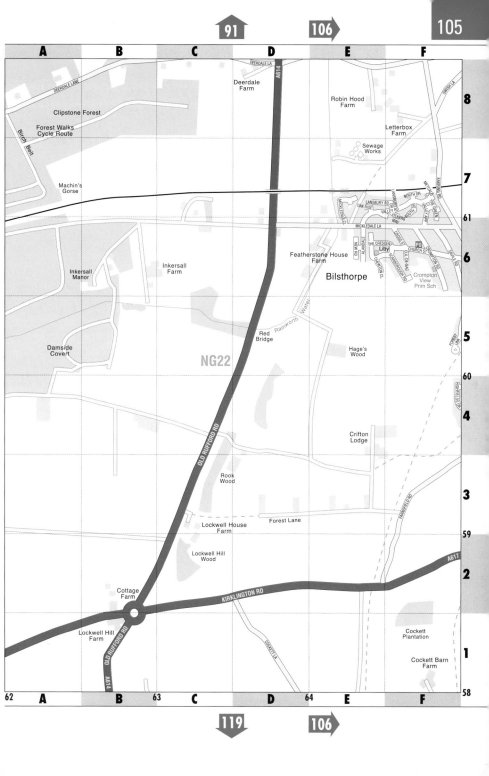

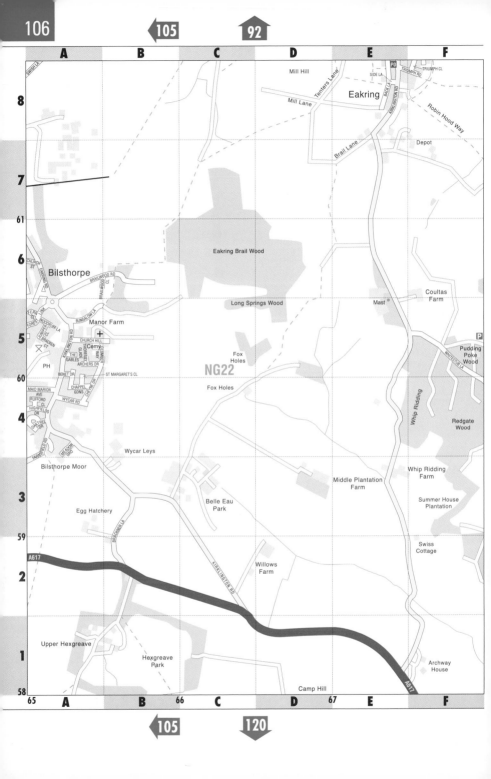

A B C D E F

8

7

61

6

5

60

4

3

59

2

1

58

Swish La

Mill Hill

Tenters Lane

SIDE LA

PO

TRIUMPH RD

TRIUMPH CL

BACK LA

KIRKLINGTON RD

Eakring

Mill Lane

Robin Hood Way

Brail Lane

Depot

Eakring Brail Wood

CHURCH ST

EAKRING RD

Bilsthorpe

BRAILWOOD RD

BRAILWOOD CL

BUNGALOW LA

Long Springs Wood

Mast

Coultas Farm

Manor Farm

FERN CL
STORES
BROOKCLIFF LA
KIRKLINGTON RD

CHURCH HILL

LIMBER GLADE
THORESBY WAY

BRACKEN CT

P

CEM₄

THE GABLES

ST MARGARET'S CL

Fox Holes

Whitesub La

Pudding Poke Wood

PH

BENET DR

CHESTNUT DR

ARCHERS DR

NG22

Fox Holes

Whip Ridding

CHAPPEL GDNS

WYCAR RD

Redgate Wood

MAID MARION AVE
RUFFORD CL
HIGHFIELD DR
OAK TREE DR

LIMEACRE GRO

Wycar Leys

Whip Ridding Farm

FARNSFIELD RD

Bilsthorpe Moor

Middle Plantation Farm

Summer House Plantation

Egg Hatchery

BRACKNER LA

Belle Eau Park

KIRKLINGTON RD

Swiss Cottage

A617

Willows Farm

Upper Hexgreave

Hexgreave Park

Archway House

A617

Camp Hill

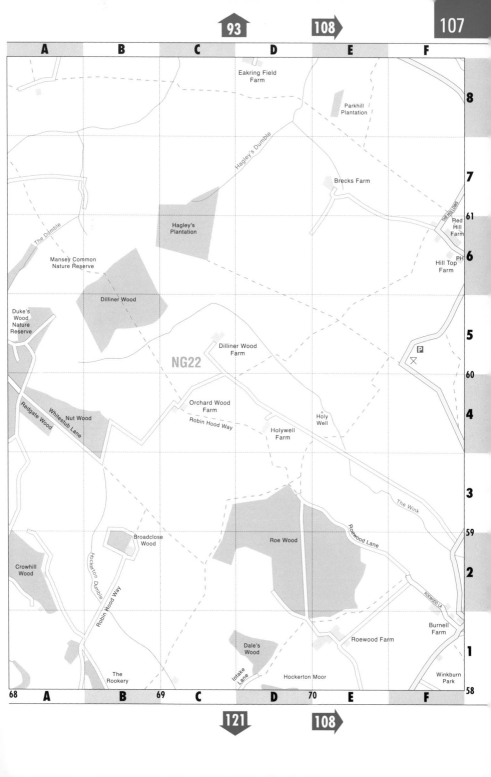

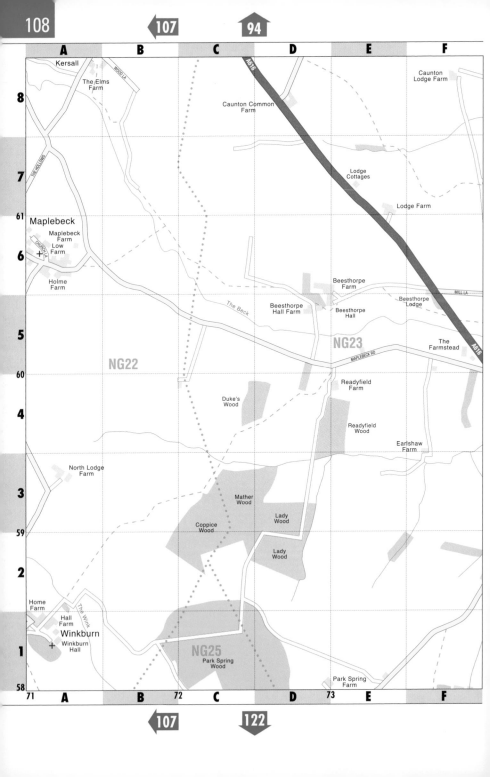

A B C D E F

Kersall

The Elms
Farm

WOOD LA

8

Caunton Common
Farm

Caunton
Lodge Farm

THE HOLLOWS

7

Lodge
Cottages

Lodge Farm

61

Maplebeck

Maplebeck
Farm
Low
Farm

CHURCH LA

6

Holme
Farm

Beesthorpe
Farm

Beesthorpe
Lodge

MILL LA

Beesthorpe
Hall Farm

Beesthorpe
Hall

The Beck

5

NG22

NG23

The
Farmstead

MAPLEBECK RD

A616

60

Readyfield
Farm

Duke's
Wood

4

Readyfield
Wood

Earlshaw
Farm

North Lodge
Farm

3

Mather
Wood

Coppice
Wood

Lady
Wood

59

Lady
Wood

2

Home
Farm

THE WINK

Hall
Farm

Winkburn

Winkburn
Hall

1

NG25

Park Spring
Wood

Park Spring
Farm

58

71 A B 72 C D 73 E F

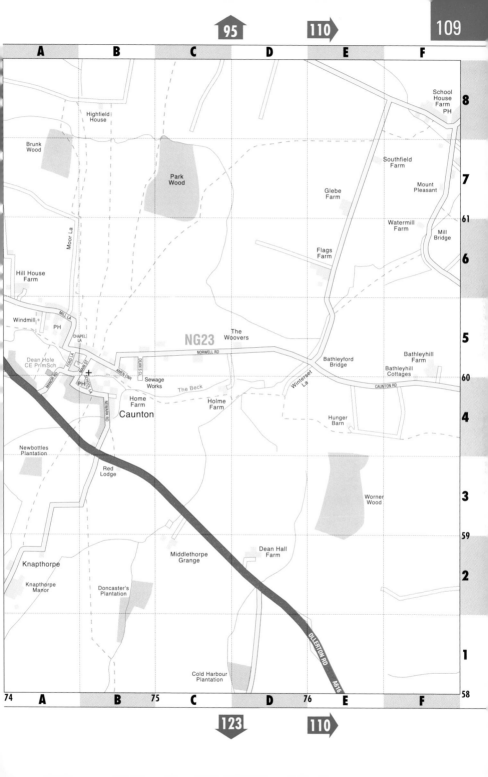

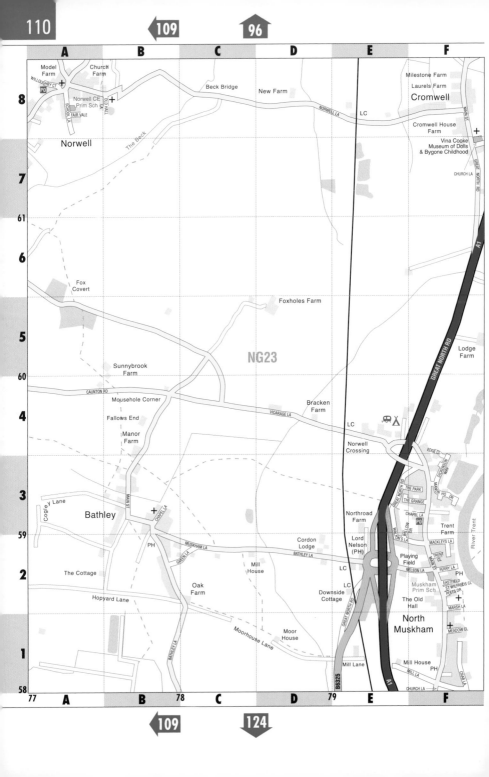

109
96

A **B** **C** **D** **E** **F**

Model Farm
Church Farm
WILLOUGHBY CT
PO
Norwell CE Prim Sch
SCHOOL LA
OLD HALL
FAIR VALE
8
Beck Bridge
New Farm
NORWELL LA
LC
Milestone Farm
Laurels Farm
Cromwell
Cromwell House Farm
Norwell
The Beck
Vina Cooke
Museum of Dolls
& Bygone Childhood
CHURCH LA

7

61

6
Fox Covert

Foxholes Farm

5
Lodge Farm

NG23

GREAT NORTH RD

Sunnybrook Farm
60
CAUNTON RD
Mousehole Corner
VICARAGE LA
Bracken Farm
4
Fallows End
LC
Norwell Crossing
Manor Farm
EDGE CL

3
Cogley Lane
Bathley
CHAPEL LA
MAIN ST
THE PARK
DICKERSON
MANOR HO DR
Northroad Farm
THE GRANGE
CHAPEL LA
PO
Trent Farm

59
PH
MUSKHAM LA
GREEN LA
Cordon Lodge
Lord Nelson (PH)
NELSON CL
MACKLEYS LA
TRENT CL
FERRY LA
PH
2
The Cottage
Mill House
BATHLEY LA
LC
Playing Field
NELSON LA
Muskham Prim Sch
EASTFIELD
ST WILFREDS CL
PEETS DR
The Old Hall
MARSH CL
Oak Farm
LC
Downside Cottage
North Muskham
MEADOW CL

1
Hopyard Lane
BATHLEY LA
Moorhouse Lane
Moor House
GREAT NORTH RD
Mill Lane
Mill House
PH
MILL LA
CHURCH LA
CHAPEL LA

58
B6325
A1
River Trent

77 **A** **B** 78 **C** **D** 79 **E** **F**

109
124

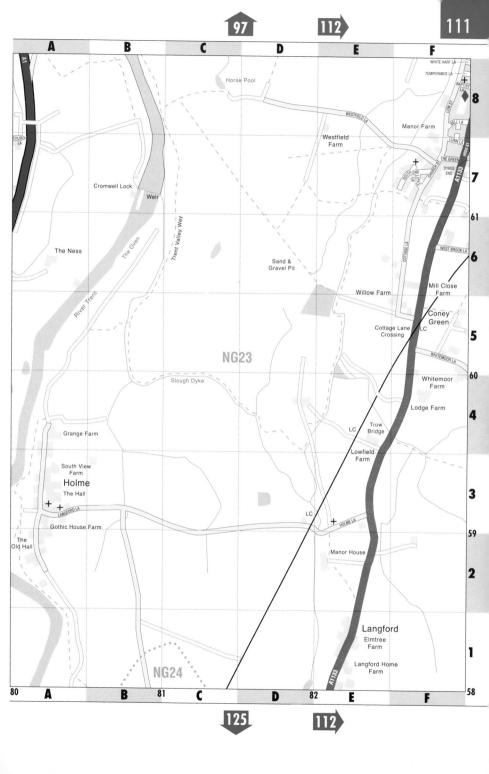

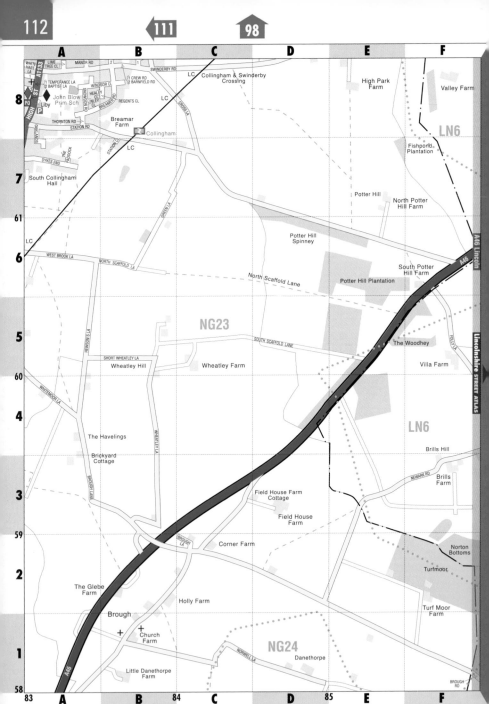

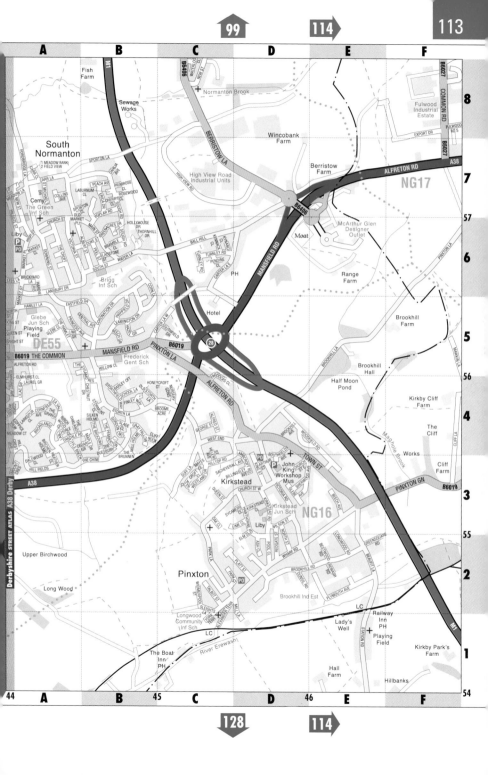

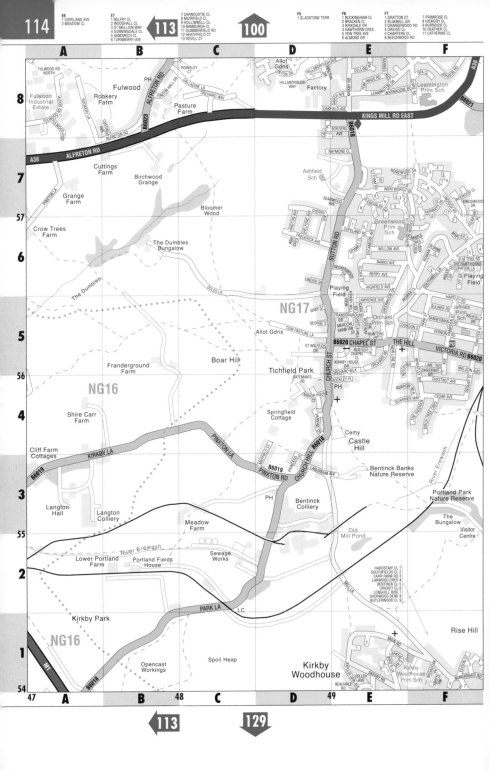

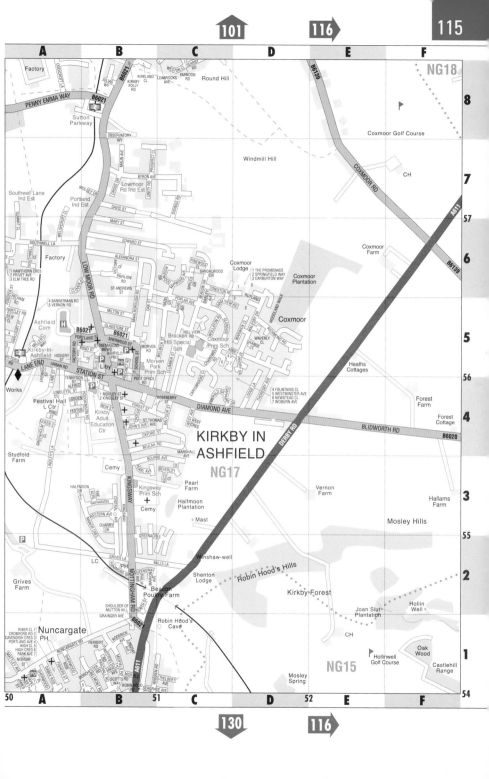

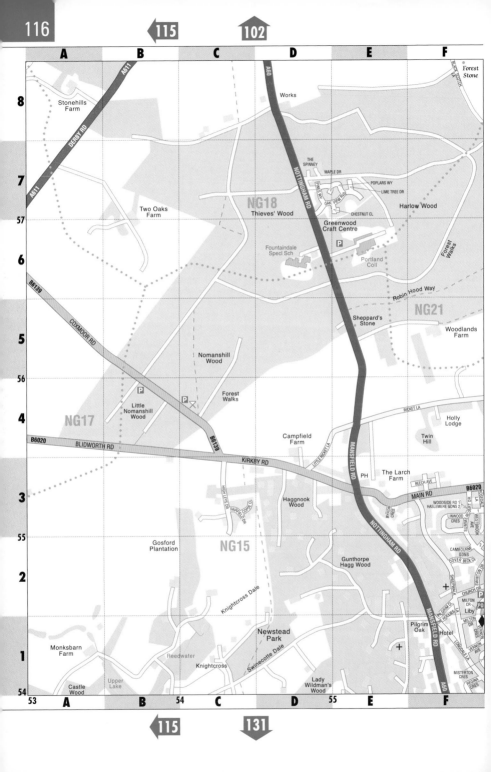

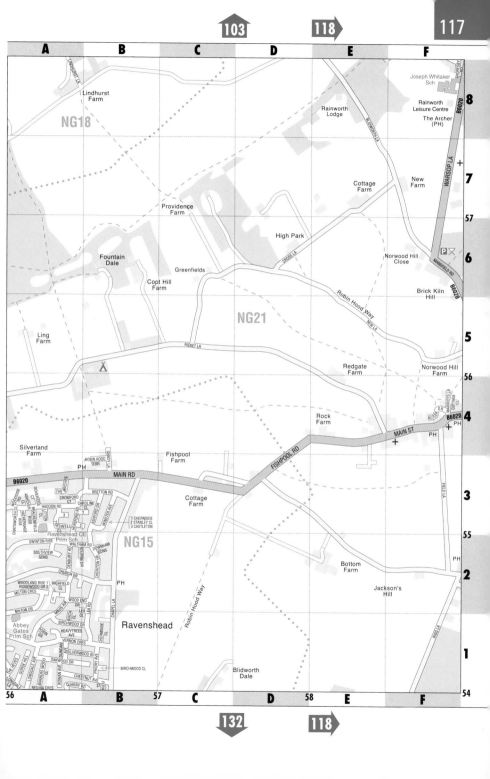

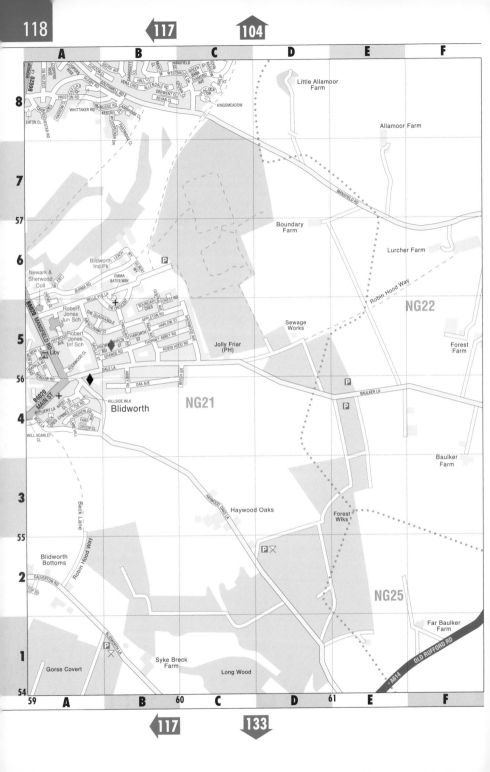

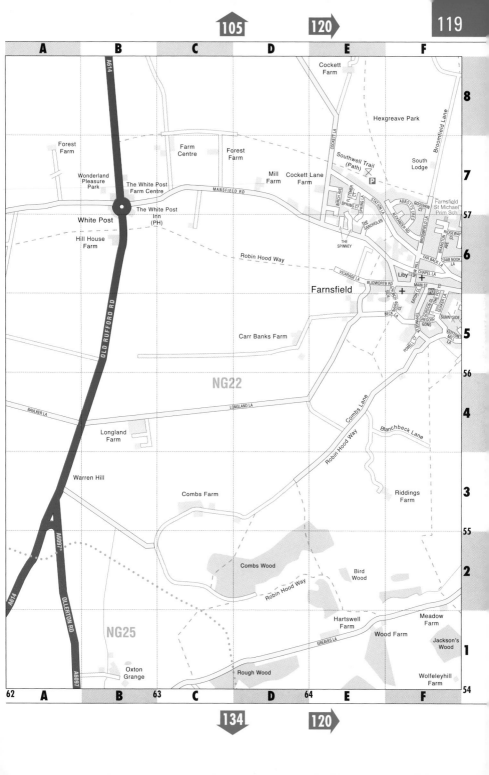

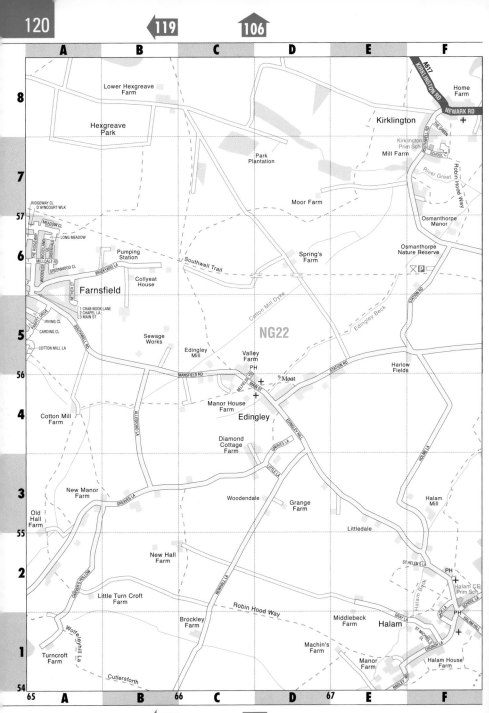

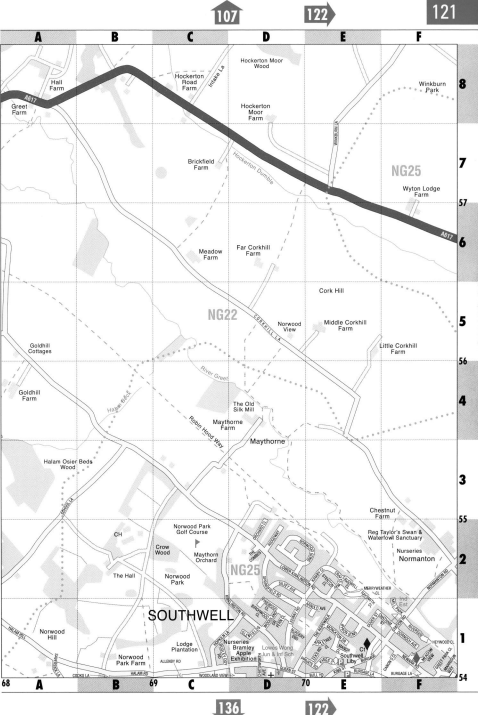

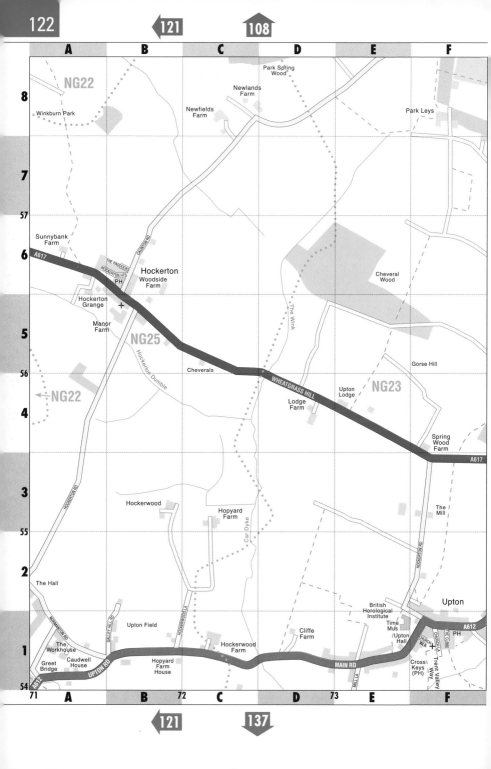

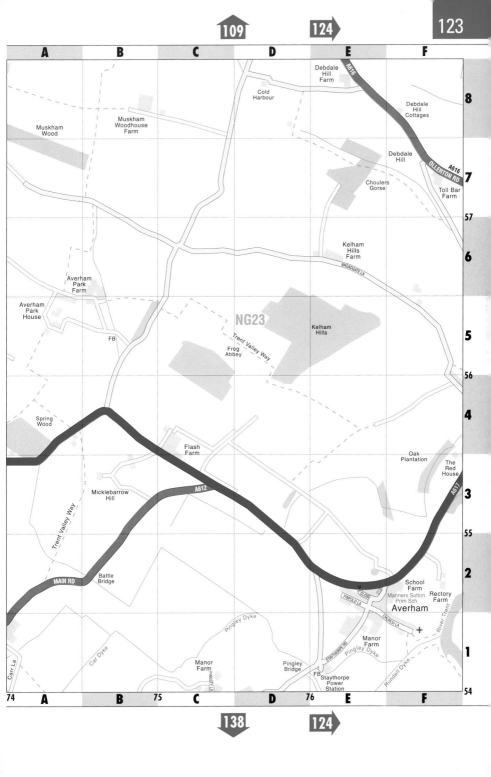

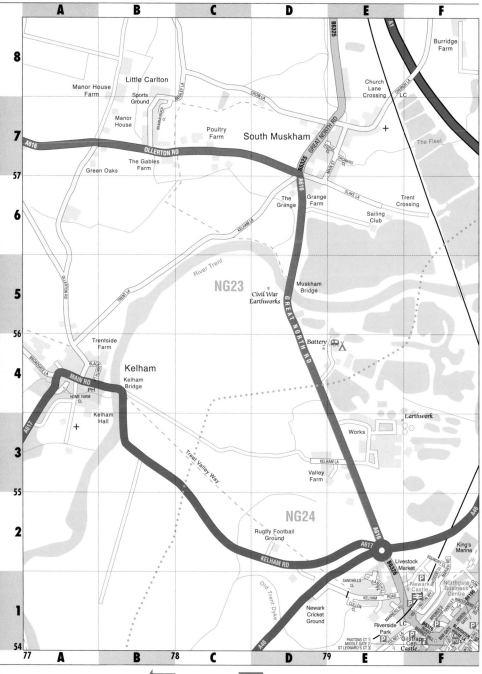

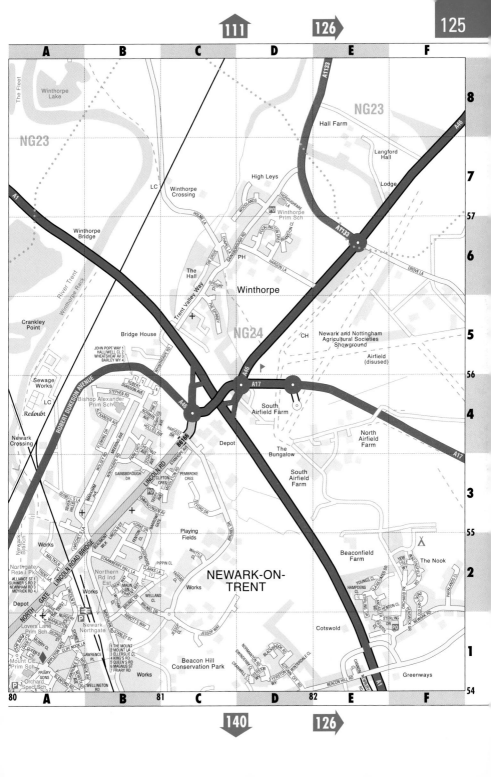

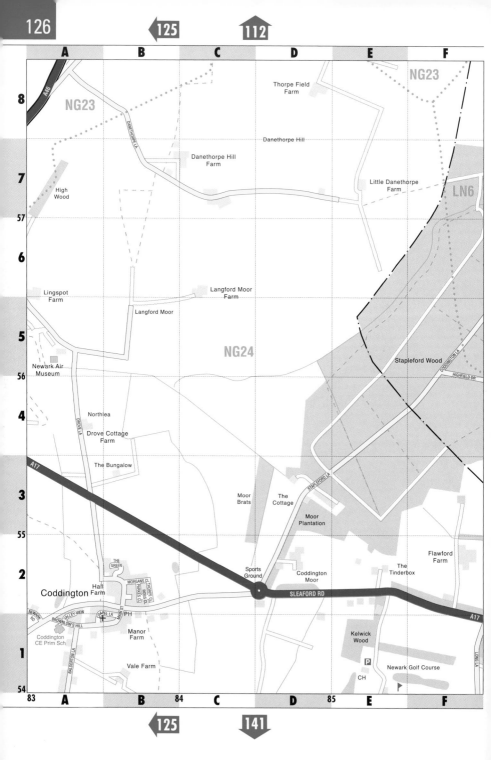

A **B** **C** **D** **E** **F**

8

NG23

NG23

Thorpe Field
Farm

Danethorpe Hill

7

Danethorpe Hill
Farm

High
Wood

Little Danethorpe
Farm

LN6

57

6

Langford Moor
Farm

Lingspot
Farm

Langford Moor

5

NG24

Stapleford Wood

Newark Air
Museum

56

CODDINGTON LA

HIGHFIELD DR

4

Northlea

Drove Cottage
Farm

DROVE LA

3

A17

The Bungalow

Moor
Brats

The
Cottage

Moor
Plantation

STAPLEFORD LA

55

Flawford
Farm

2

THE
GREEN

Sports
Ground

Coddington
Moor

The
Tinderbox

Coddington

Hall
Farm

MORGANS CL

THORPE CL

MOSS CL

PARKES CL

SLEAFORD RD

A17

LONG LA

1

VALLEY VIEW

CHAPEL LA

PH

NEWARK RD

BROWNLOW'S HILL

Manor
Farm

Kelwick
Wood

P

Newark Golf Course

Coddington
CE Prim Sch

BLUE BELL LA

Vale Farm

CH

54

83 **A** **B** 84 **C** **D** 85 **E** **F**

Stapleford Moor

Moor Farm

Pailing's Ride

CODDINGTON LA

Lodge Drive

Forest
Walks

Stapleford Wood

Grange Drive

Stapleford
Grange

HIGHFIELD DR

Highfield
House

Stapleford Moor

Four
Acres

NG24

College
Plantation

Barnby
Manor

A17 SLEAFORD RD

SLEAFORD RD

Rifle
Range

BRECKS LA

THE
PADDOCKS

NORTON RD

The Hall

Church Lane

NEWARK RD

Poplar
Tree Farm

Stapleford

Woodland View

The
Laurels

Moor Lane

BROUGHTON RD

Broughton Clays

Stapleford
House

LN6

The
Elms

CLAY DALE

DANGER AREA

River Witham

Top Covert
Farm

Lincolnshire STREET ATLAS

Top
Covert

DANGER AREA

LN5

DANGER AREA

Youle Dike

Hanley Farm

Whitegate
House

WOODGATE LA

Beckingham
Training Camp

Sewage
Works

A17

8
7
57
6
5
56
4
3
55
2
1
54

A B C D E F

86 87 88

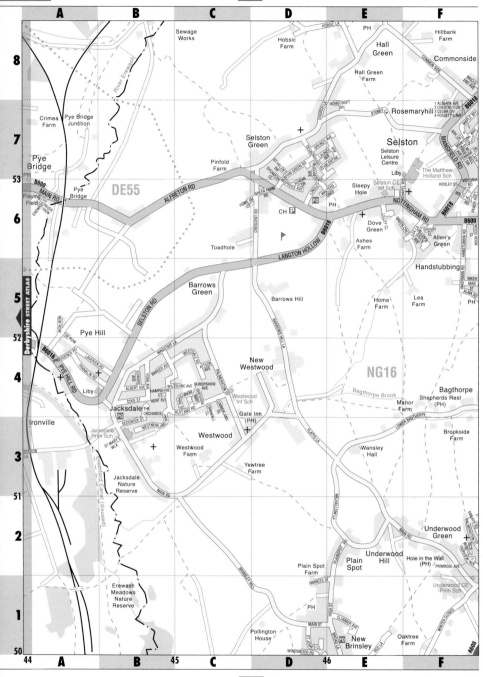

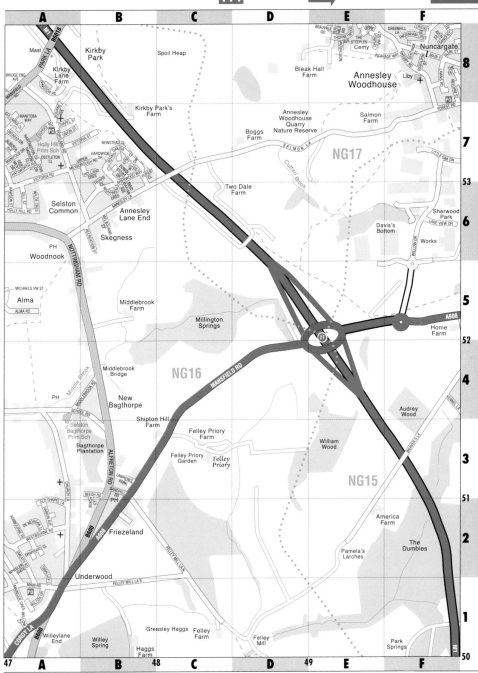

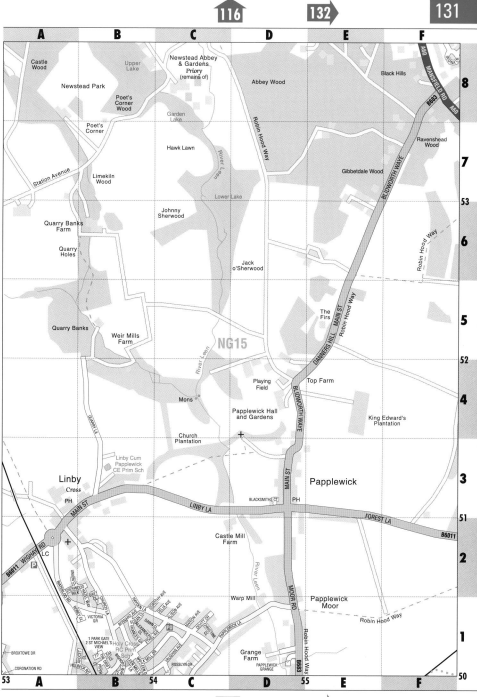

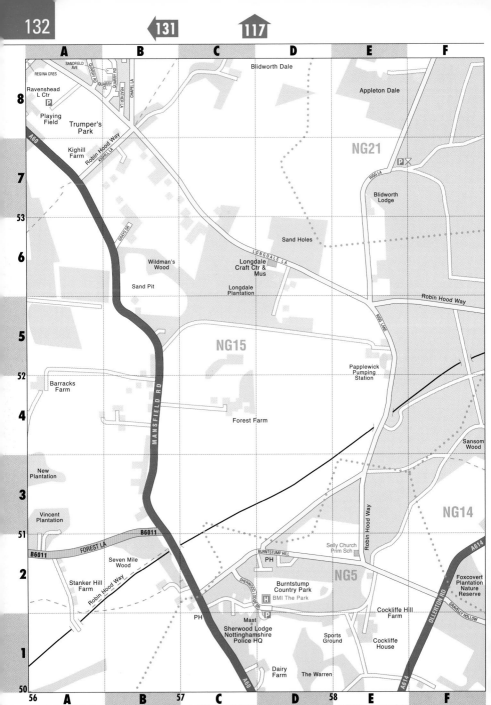

SANDFIELD AVE
REGINA CRES
Ravenshead
L Ctr
Playing
Field
Trumper's
Park
Kighill
Farm
Robin Hood Way
QUARRY RD
QUARRY CL
HEATHER LA
CHAPEL LA
KIGHILL LA

Blidworth Dale

Appleton Dale

NG21

Blidworth
Lodge

RIGG LA

Sand Holes

LONGDALE LA

Wildman's
Wood

Longdale
Craft Ctr &
Mus

Sand Pit

Longdale
Plantation

Robin Hood Way

NG15

RIGG LANE

Papplewick
Pumping
Station

Barracks
Farm

MANSFIELD RD

Forest Farm

Sansom
Wood

New
Plantation

Vincent
Plantation

NG14

B6011

FOREST LA

B6011

Seven Mile
Wood

Stanker Hill
Farm

Robin Hood Way

SHERWOOD LODGE RD

BURNTSTUMP HILL

PH

Burntstump
Country Park

Selly Church
Prim Sch

Robin Hood Way

NG5

A614

OLLERTON RD

Foxcovert
Plantation
Nature
Reserve

BRIDLEY HOLLOW

PH

Mast

Sherwood Lodge
Nottinghamshire
Police HQ

BMI The Park

Cockliffe Hill
Farm

Sports
Ground

Cockliffe
House

A60

Dairy
Farm

The Warren

A614

56 57 58

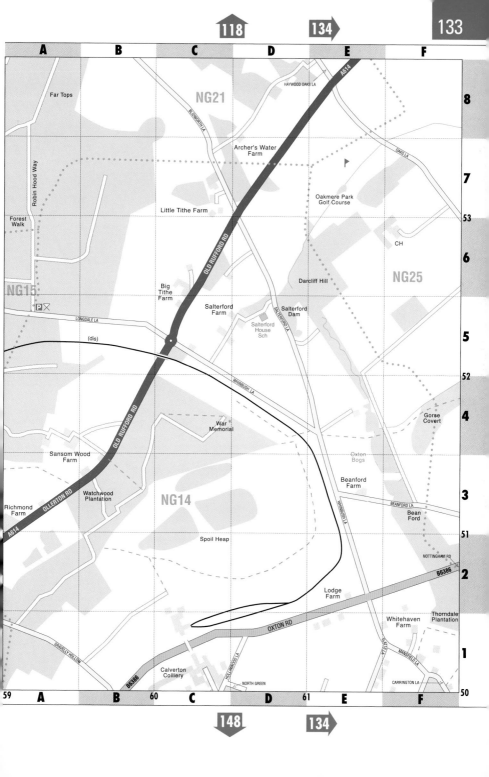

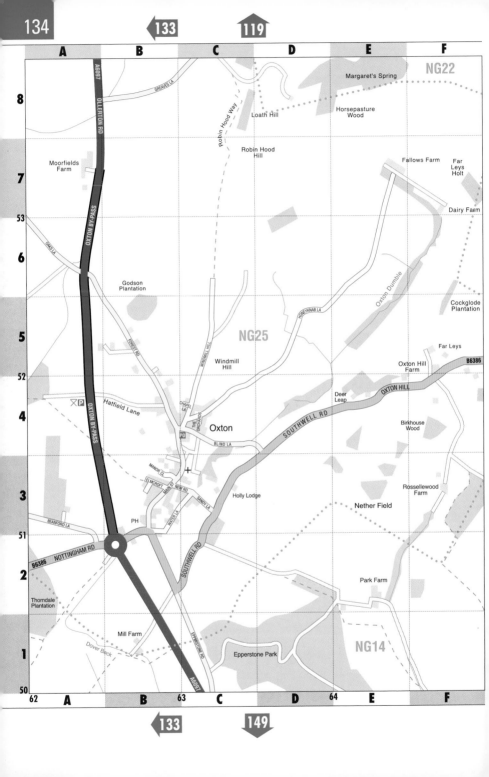

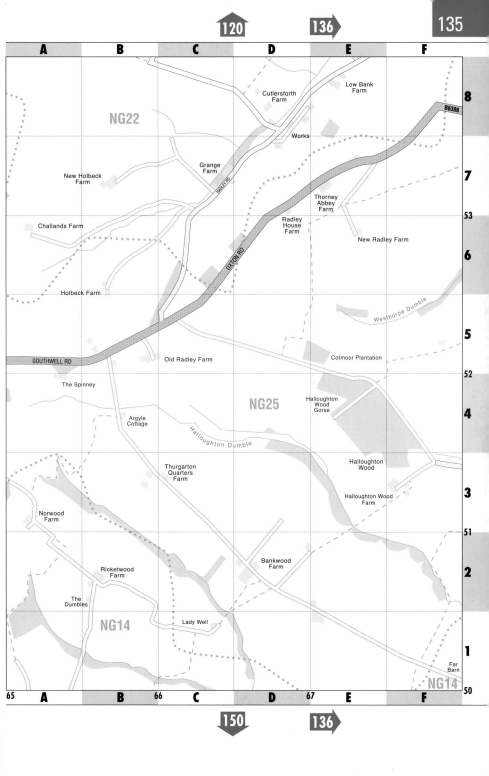

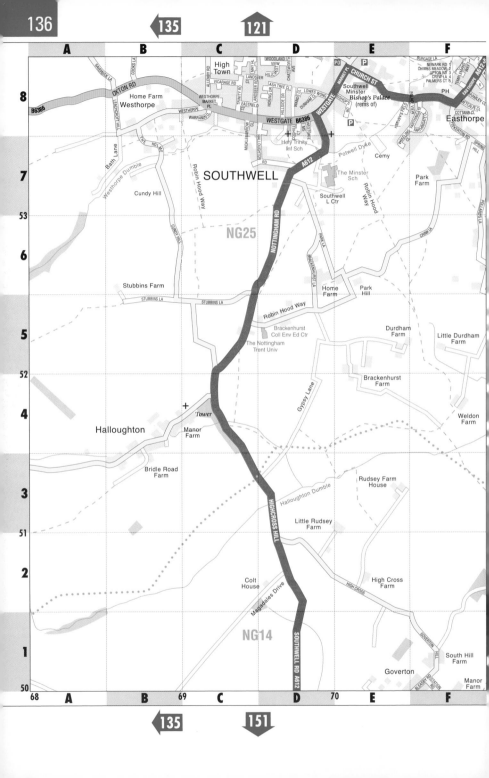

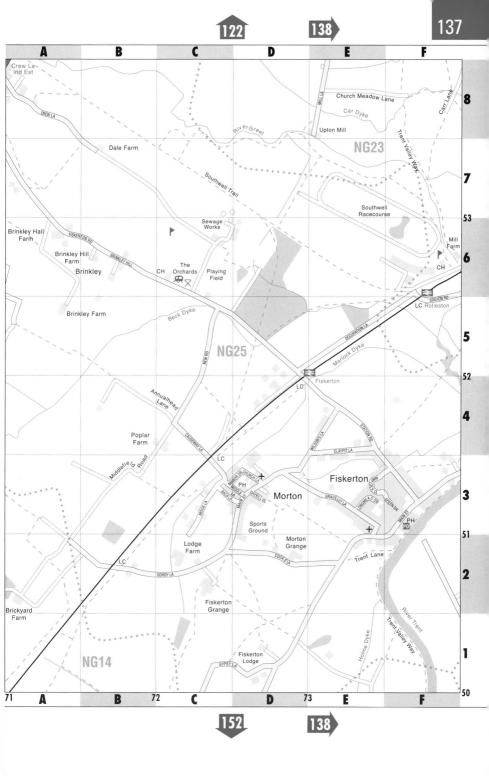

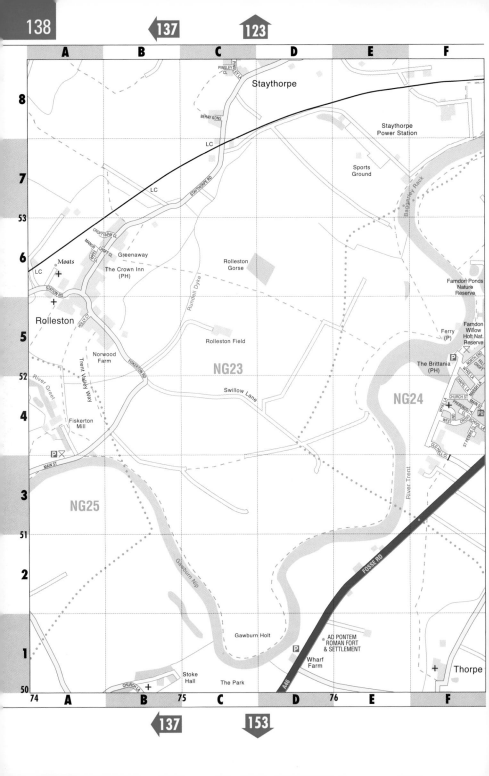

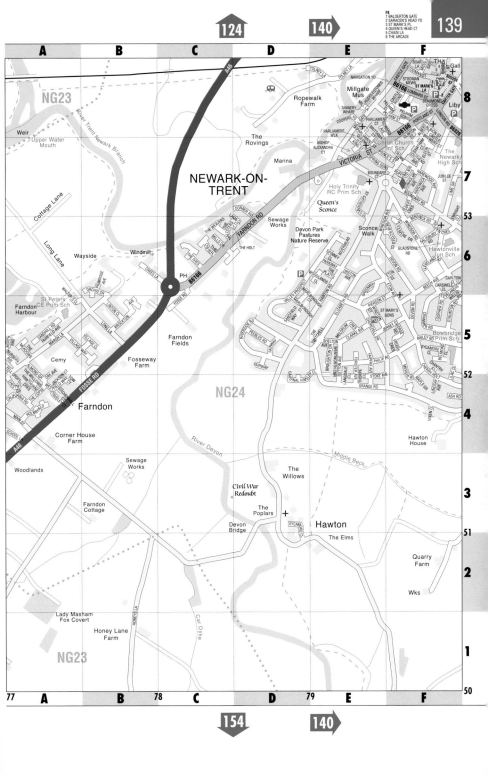

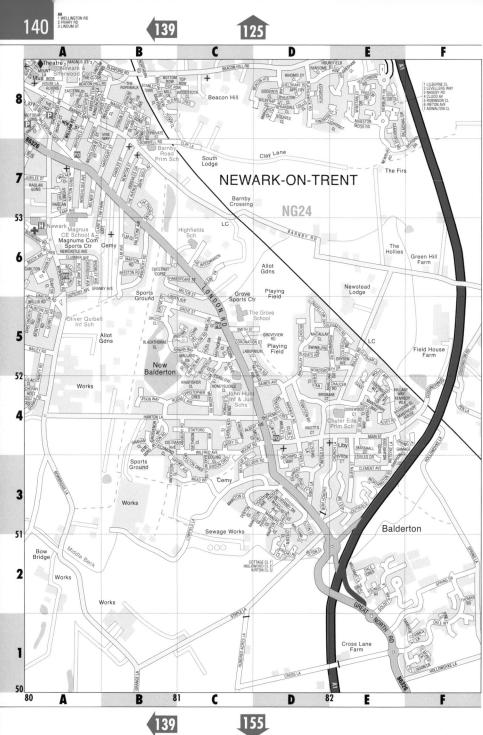

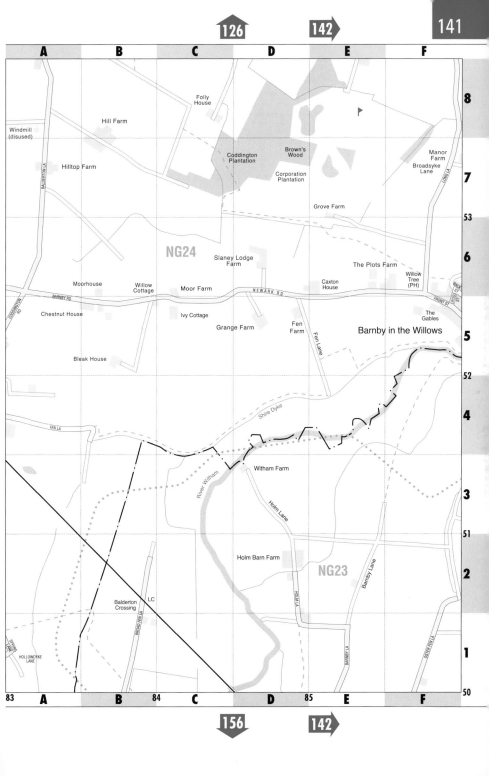

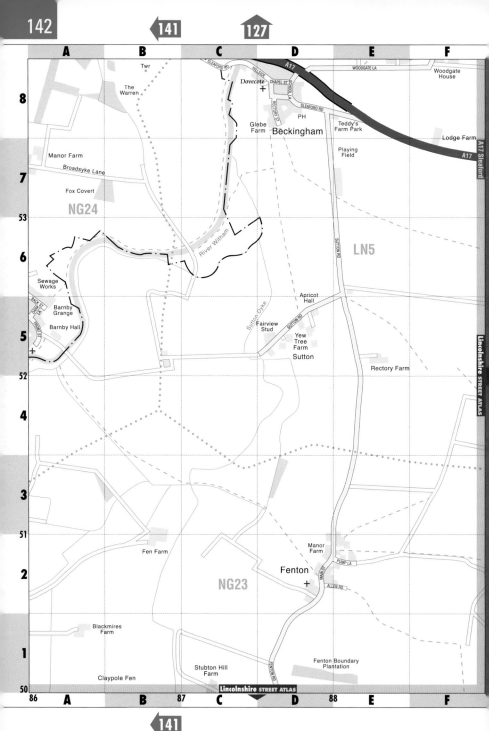

A   B   C   D   E   F

8

WOODGATE LA
Woodgate House

SLEAFORD RD
HILLSIDE
A17
Twr
The Warren
Dovecote
CHAPEL ST
SCHOOL LA
SLEAFORD RD
PH
Glebe Farm
Beckingham
Teddy's Farm Park
Lodge Farm
A17 Sleaford

7
Manor Farm
Broadsyke Lane
Playing Field

Fox Covert

NG24

53

River Witham

6
SUTTON RD
LN5

Sewage Works
BACK ST
FRONT ST
Barnby Grange
Barnby Hall
Sutton Dyke
Apricot Hall
Fairview Stud
Yew Tree Farm
Sutton

5

Rectory Farm

52

4

3

51
Fen Farm
Manor Farm
PUMP LA

2
NG23
Fenton
ALLEN RD
MAIN RD

Blackmires Farm
1
Fenton Boundary Plantation

Stubton Hill Farm
FENTON RD

50
Claypole Fen

86   A   B   87   C   D   88   E   F

Lincolnshire STREET ATLAS

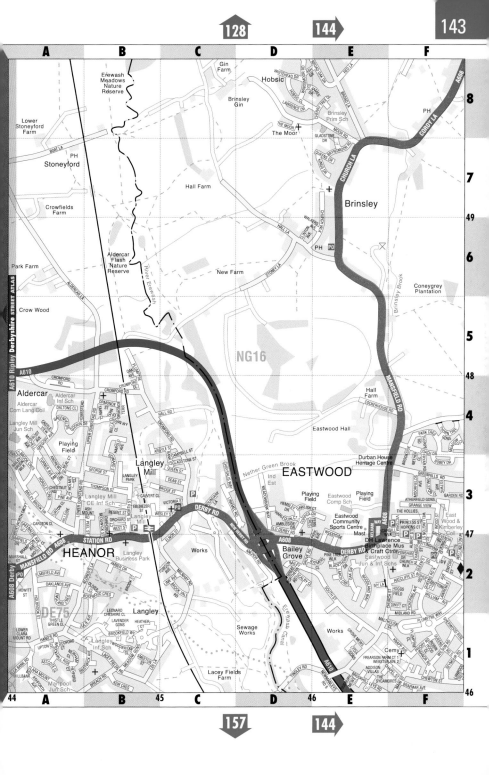

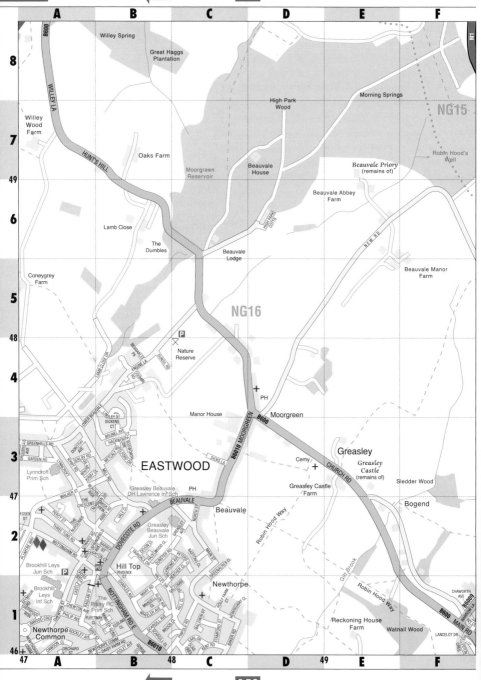

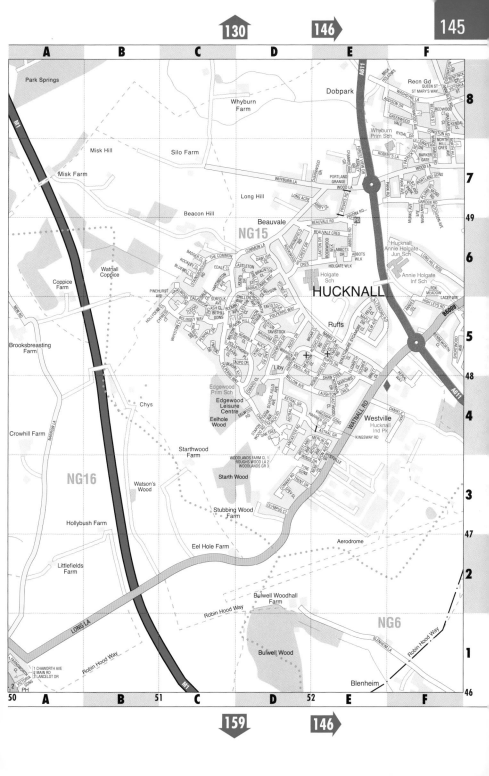

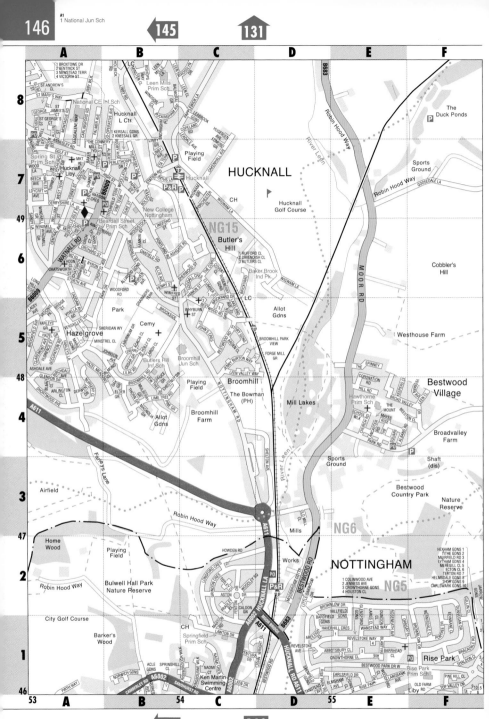

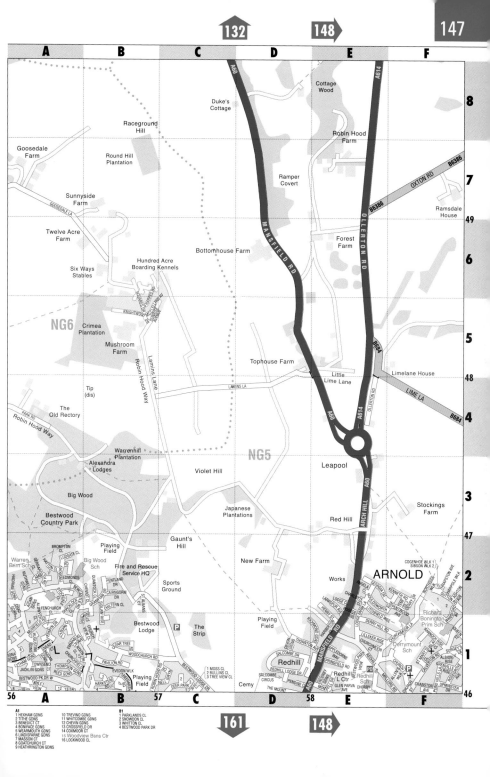

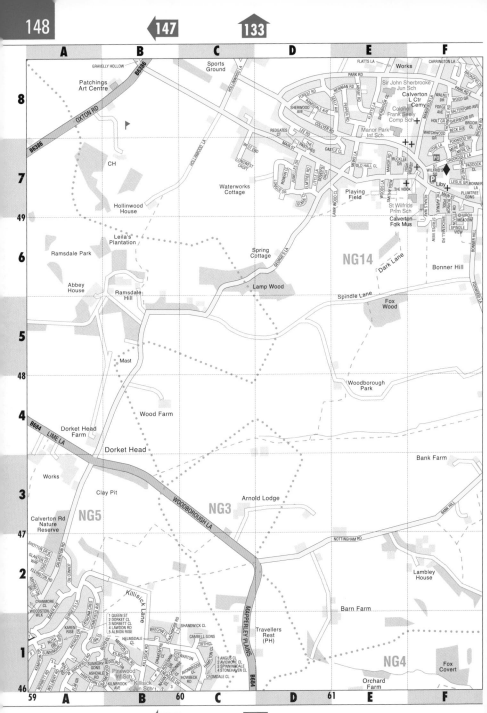

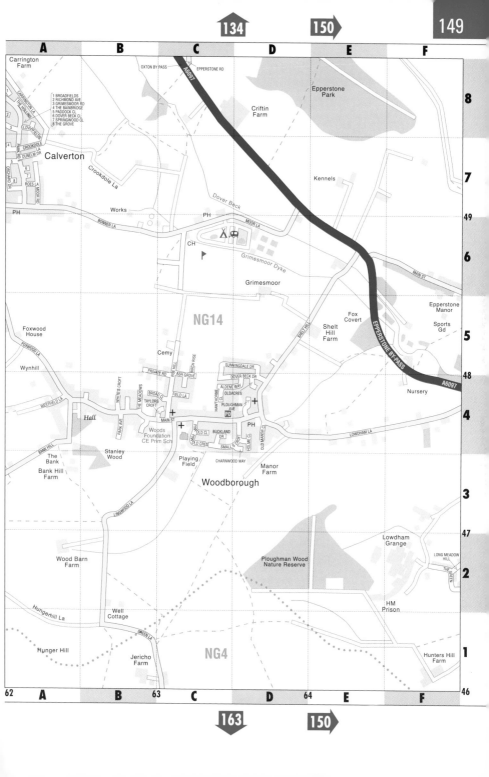

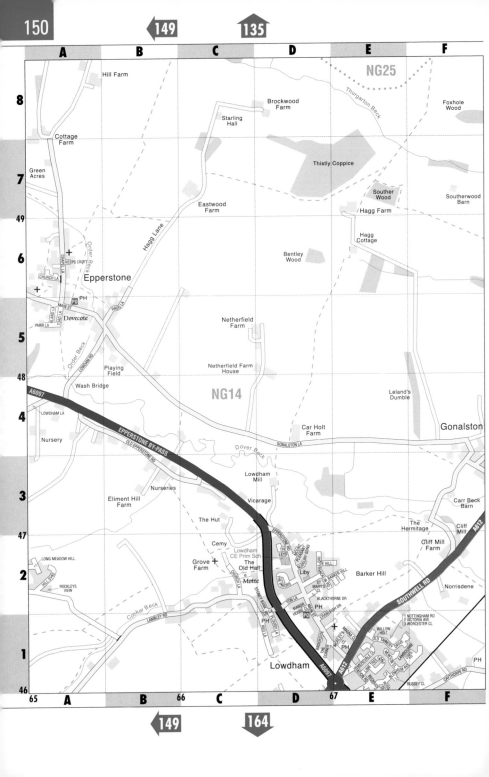

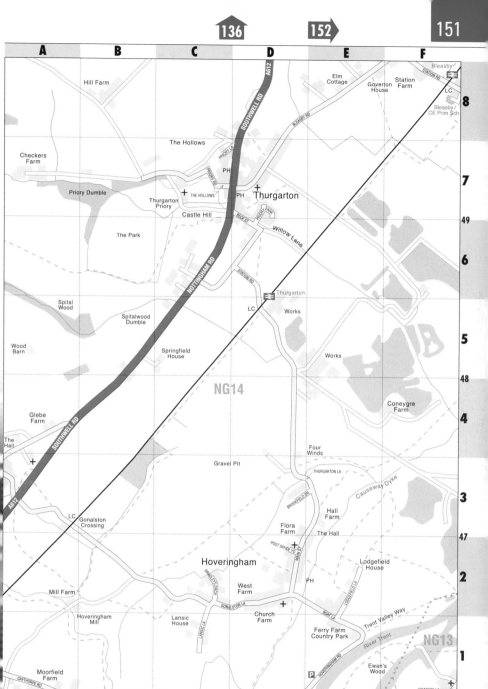

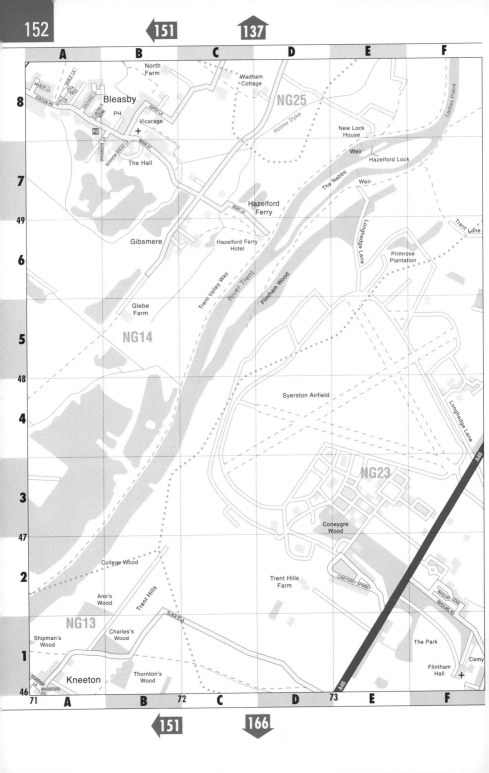

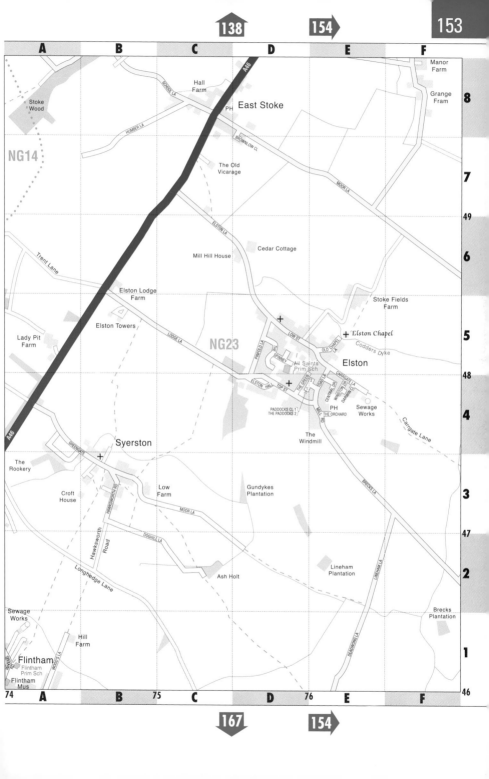

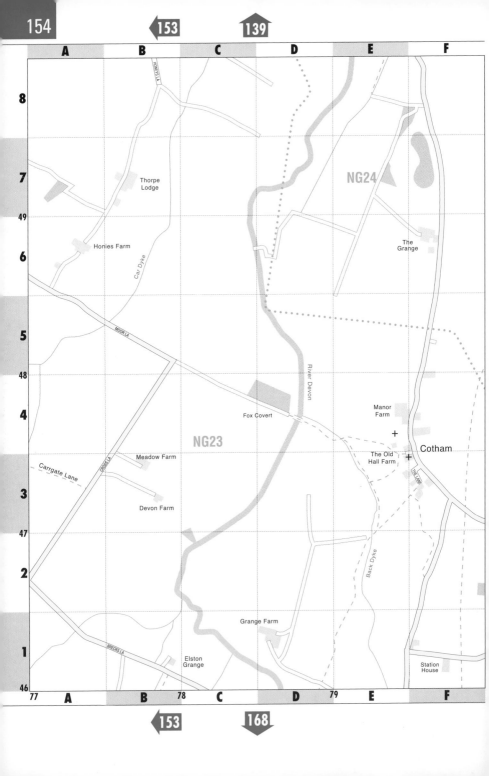

153
139

A B C D E F

8

7

49

6

Thorpe Lodge

Honies Farm

Car Dyke

KINGS LA.

NG24

The Grange

5

48

MOOR LA.

River Devon

4

Fox Covert

NG23

Manor Farm

The Old Hall Farm

Cotham

Carrgate Lane

Meadow Farm

CROSS LA.

3

47

Devon Farm

THE LANE

Back Dyke

2

1

46

Grange Farm

BRECKS LA.

Elston Grange

Station House

77 A B 78 C D 79 E F

153
168

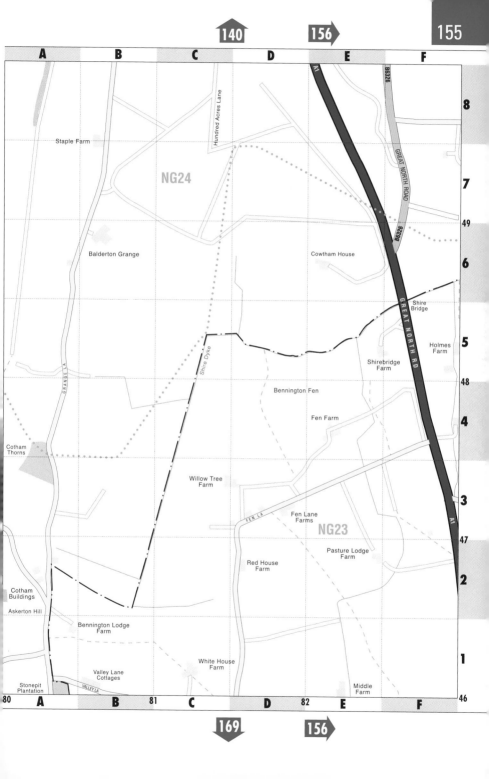

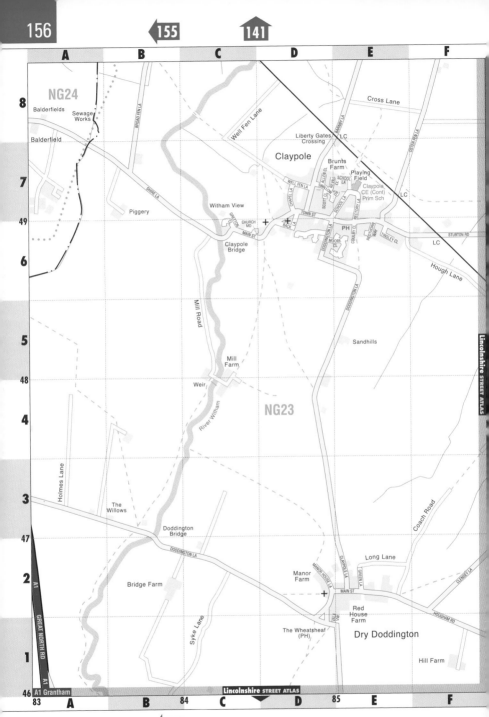

Lincolnshire STREET ATLAS

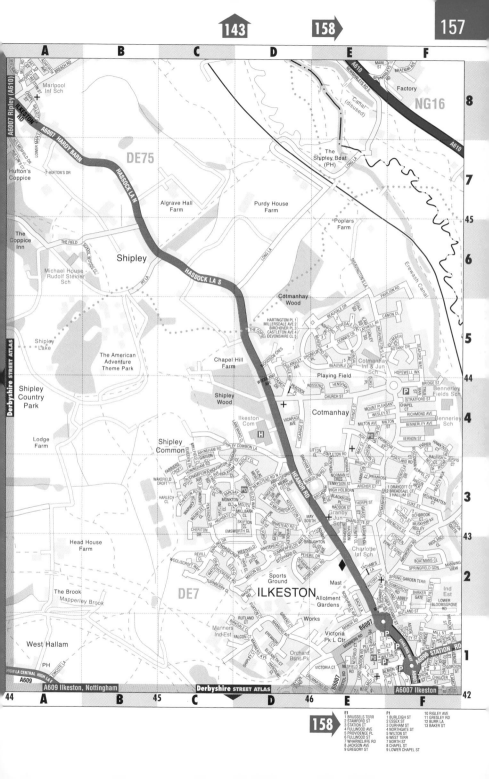

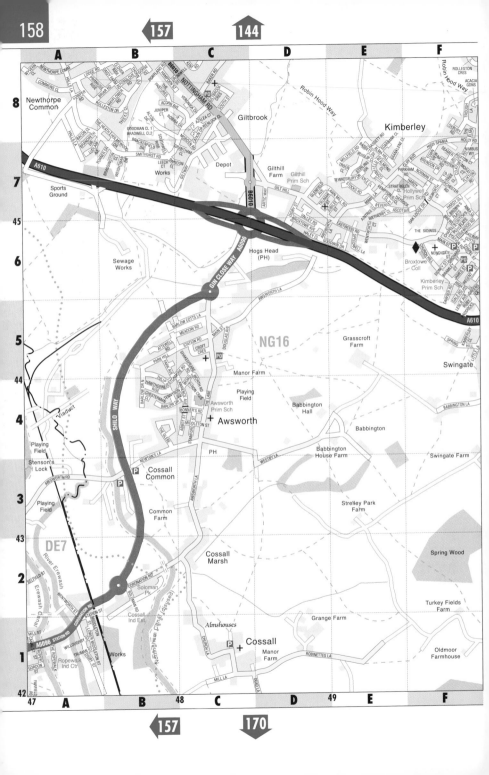

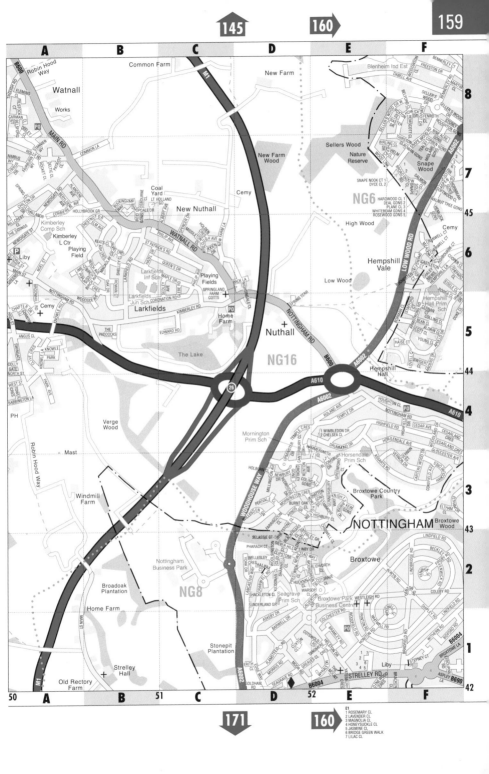

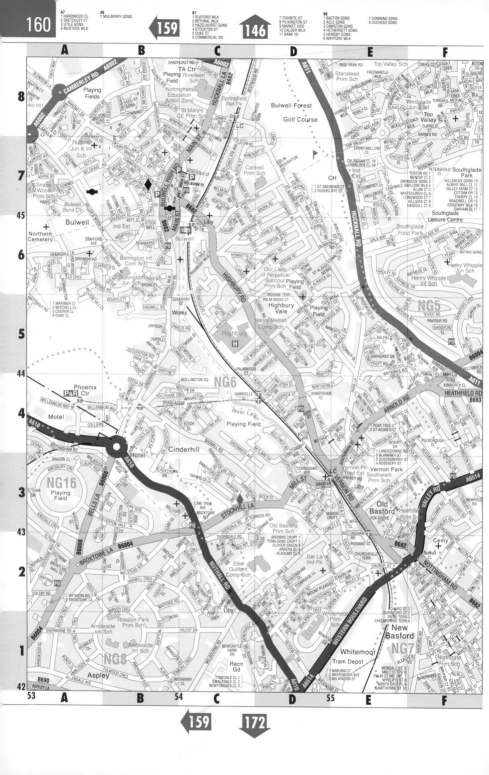

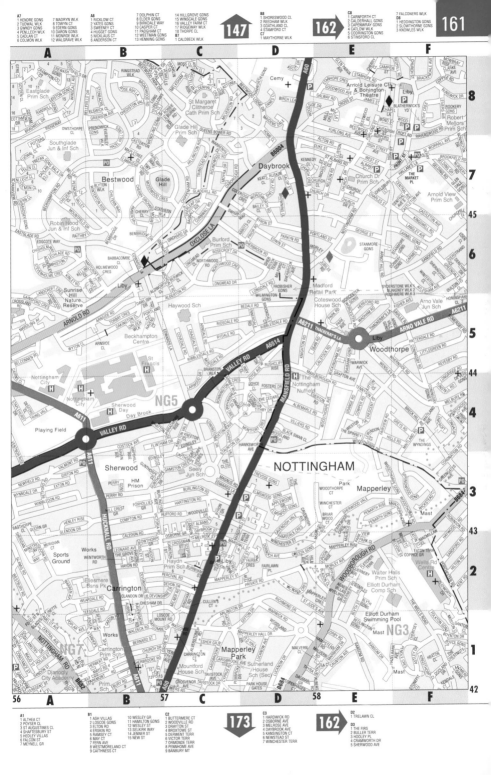

161
148

| | A | B | C | D | E | F |

NG5

ARNOLD

Killisick Jun Sch
Recn Gd
Chestnut Gr
Hawthorne Cres
Spinningdale
Aviemore Cl
Berriedale Cl
Ballantrae Cl

Coppice Farmhouse
Nursery
Coppice Farm Prim Sch
Mapperley Orch

Cottage Farm
Floralands Garden Village
Foxhill Farm
Playworld
Catfoot La

Middlebeck Farm

Christ the King RC Comp Sch
Arnold Hill Sch

Lambley Dumble

Spring Lane Farm

1 HONINGHAM CL
2 BLAKENEY WLK

Ernehale Jun & Inf Sch
The Good Shepherd RC Prim Sch

ARNO VALE RD A6211

GEDLING RD

Crimea Farm

Spring La

Chase Farm

Spoil Heap

PLAINS RD

NG4

The Farmhouse
CH

Mapperley Golf Course

NG3

Mapperley Plains Prim Sch
Westdale Jun & Inf Schs

Scot Grave Farm

Glebe Farm

Recn Gd

1 PERLETHORPE CL
2 PERLETHORPE CRES
3 STOREY AVE
4 HUCKNALL CRES
5 BABBINGTON CRES

Liby
Breck Hill
Hazel Hurst Prep Sch
Whittingham

WOODBOROUGH RD

B684

Westmore
Ward Ave

Carlton Digby Special Sch
Digby Hall Dr
Digby Ave

Stanhope Prim Sch

The Fairway
Turpin Ave

The Gedling Sch
Liby

Gedling
Cemy

1 HEREFORD RD
2 ULLSWATER CL
3 EXETER CL
4 WINDERMERE CL

Porchester

The Mount
Thorpe Cres

Westdale Ct
Grassingdale Cl

Haddon Prim Sch

CARLTON

1 MOUNTBATTEN GR
2 MARGARET CRES
3 ELIZABETH GR
4 PHILIP GR

Church View
Priory

A6211

Trent Valley View
Recn Gd
Carlton Forum Leisure Centre
The Wheldon Sch
Playing Field
Allot Gdns
Huckerbys Field

Porchester Jun Sch
Prospect Rd

Bramble Ct
Tennyson Ave

E1
1 Phoenix Inf Sch

F1
1 Priory Jun Sch
2 All Hallows CE Prim Sch

| A | B | C | D | E | F |

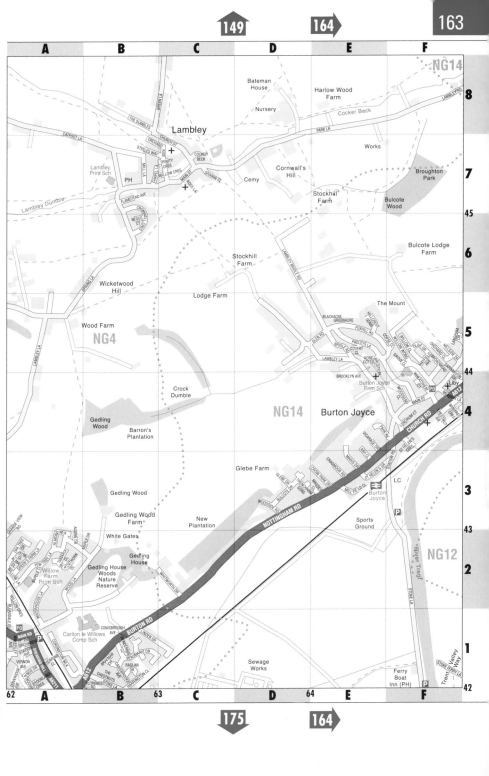

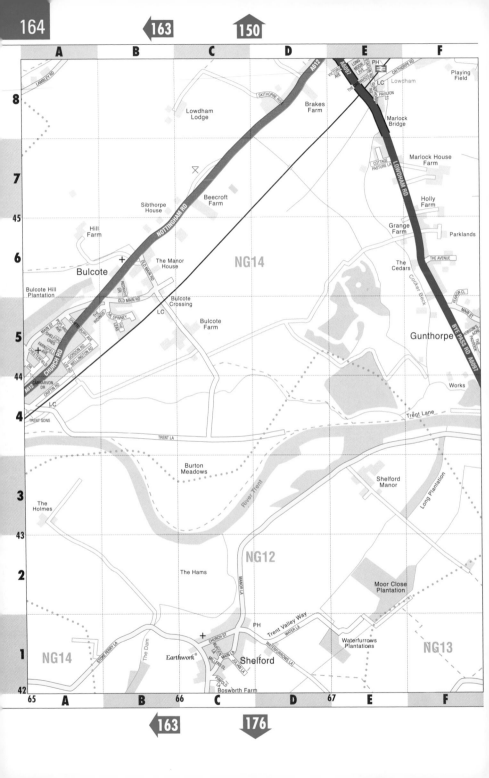

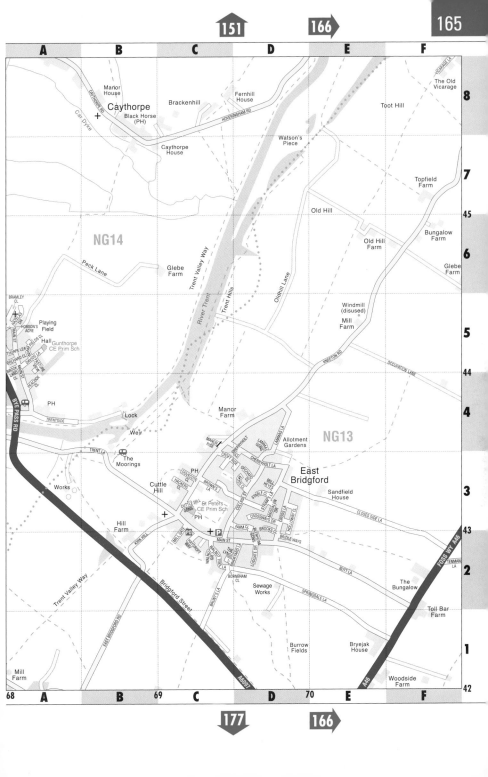

A B C D E F

8

7

NG23

45

6

5

44

4

NG13

3

43

2

1

42

71 A B 72 C D 73 E F

Ti's Wood

Took's Wood

The Park

Jubilee Wood

The Slips

Kennel Wood

Spring Hill

Newfield

The Hollows

Barbara's Wood

RED LODGE LA

BRIDGFORD RD

A46

SPRING LA

PH

Stoneydale Plantation

Barleyholme Wood

Glebe Farm

Fosse Farm

Stony Dale

FOSS WAY

FLINTHAM LA

Shackerdale Wood

LOOSE LA

Fosse Fields Farm

Fosse Poultry Farm

Shackerdale Farm

OCCUPATION LANE

Home Farm

Manor Farm

Royal Oak (PH)

The Shacker

Blagg's Covert

CHURCH LA

Top Farm

White House Farm

Screveton

A46

New Lane

Little Green

KNIGHT PK CL

Rectory

Old Hall

Bedeham Lane

CHURCH LA

Hall Farm

The Hall

Car Hill

Car Hill Barn

TENMAN LA

Car Colston

CAR LA

Moorfield Cottage

Royal Oak Inn (PH)

Gibsons Close

Manor Farm

Manor House

Field House Farm

Car Dyke Bridge

Ebenezer Cottage

MICKLEMOOR LANE

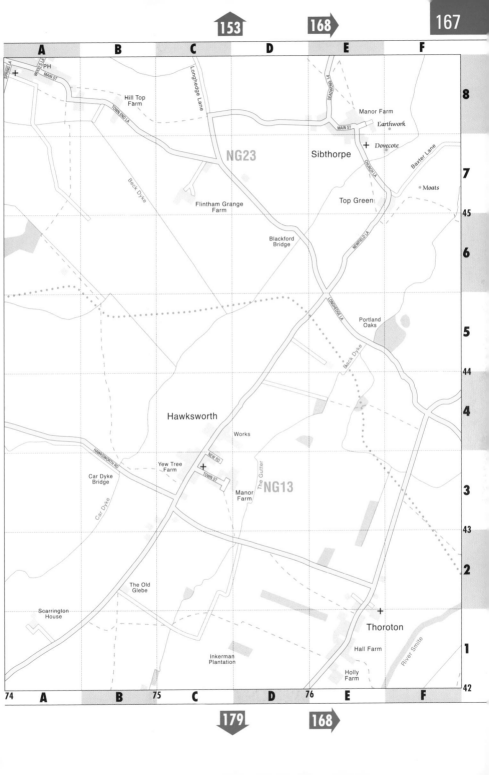

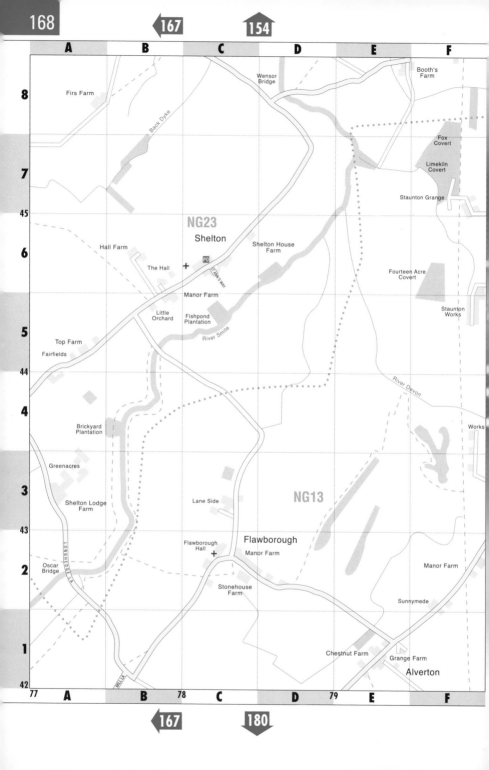

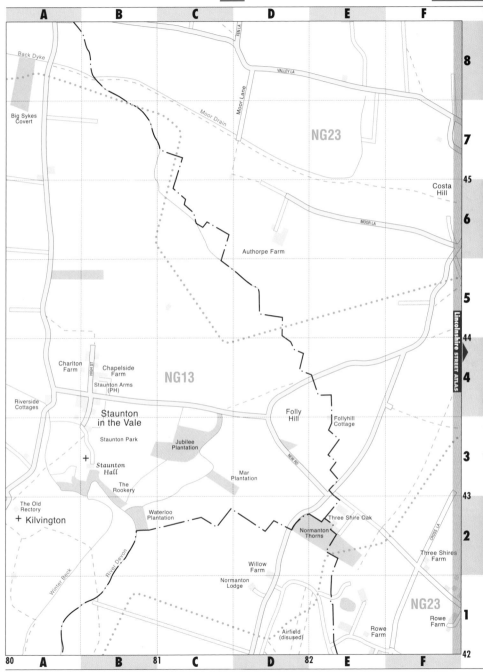

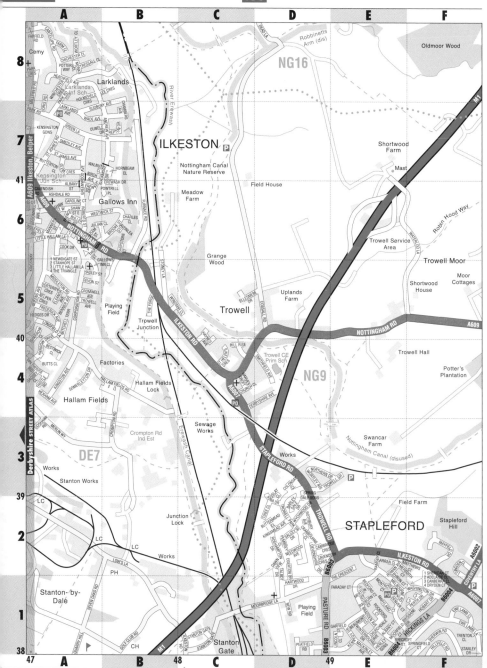

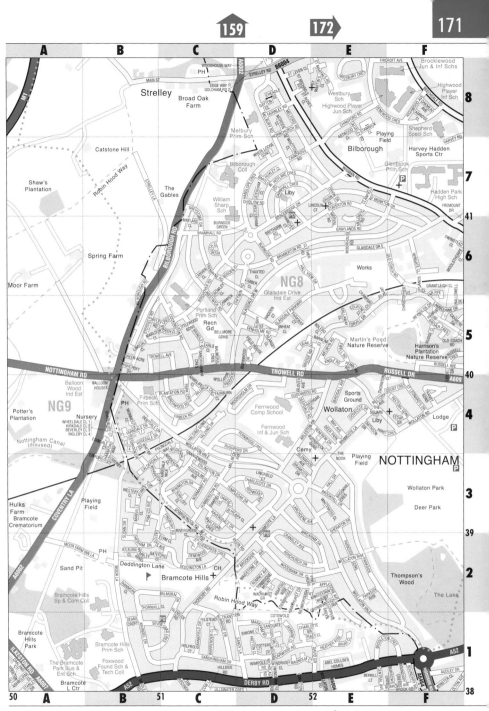

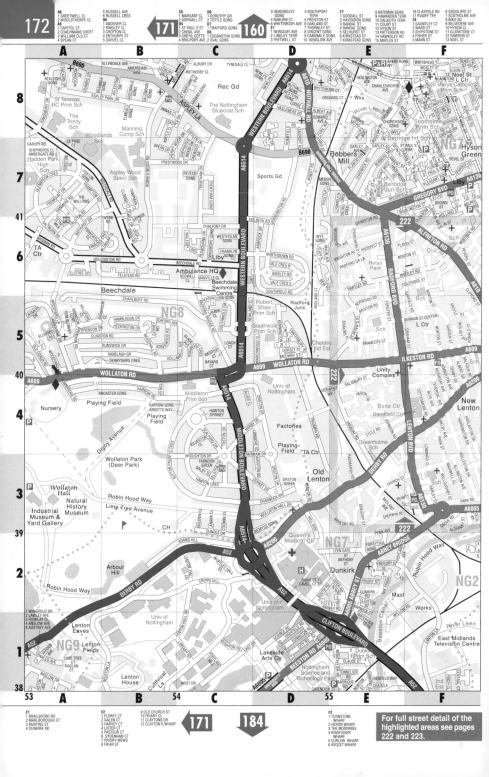

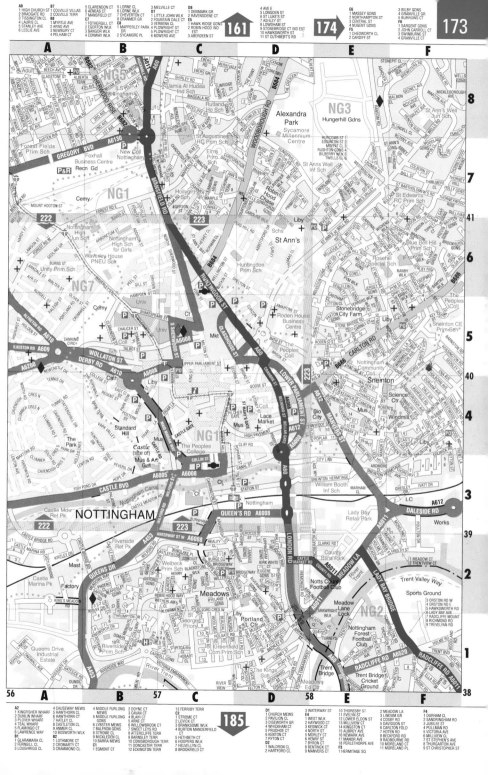

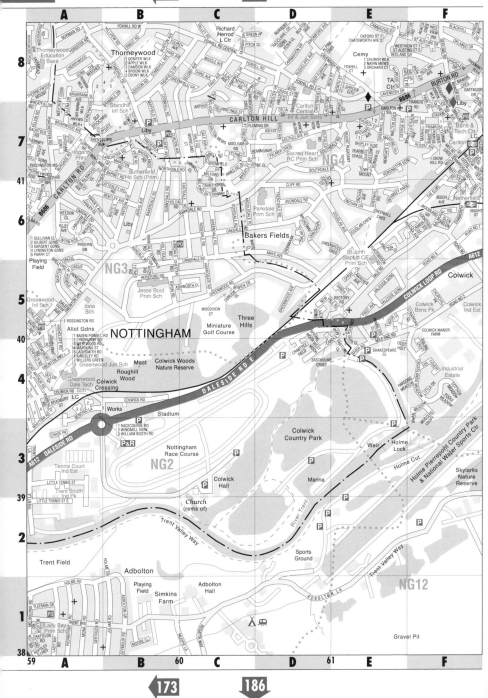

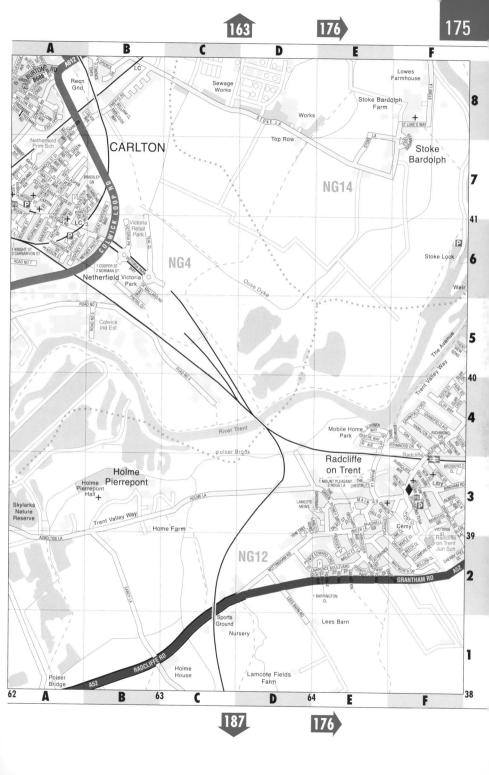

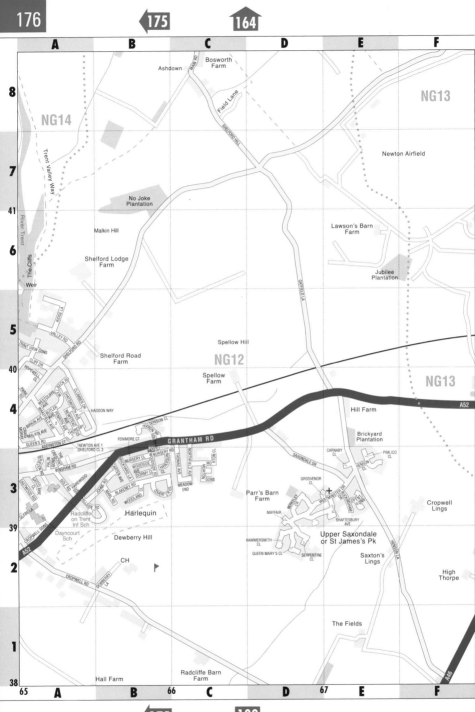

NG13

NG14

Ashdown

Bosworth Farm

Field Lane

MAIN RD

SHELFORD HILL

Newton Airfield

Trent Valley Way

River Trent

No Joke Plantation

Malkin Hill

Lawson's Barn Farm

Shelford Lodge Farm

Jubilee Plantation

The Cliffs

Weir

OXFIELD LA

Spellow Hill

NG12

Spellow Farm

NG13

RIVER LA

VALLEY RD

TRENT VIEW GDNS

CLIFF DR

HOPEWELL CL

SHELFORD RD

PECK LA

CHERRY CL

CHESTNUT CL

WESTCLIFFE AVE

BUTLER DR

MYRTLE CL

THE GREEN

THORESBY DR

BINGHAM AVE

WALLIS AVE

PINFOLD

QUEEN'S RD

ADDINGTON CT

HADDON WAY

DAWSON CL

HUDSON CLOSE

FENIMORE CT

Hill Farm

A52

Brickyard Plantation

GRANTHAM RD

CARNABY CL

PIMLICO CL

BENDIGO CL

SAXONDALE DR

NEWTON AVE 1
SHELFORD CL 2

POST

NURSERY CL

WOODSIDE

DORMY CL

NORTH FIELD AVE

THOMAS AVE

MORTON

NURSERY RD

NOTT CL

MOYGDNS

MEADOW END

PARK AVE

GAMSTON

BINGHAM RD

PAXTON AVE

ACRE END

BLAKENEY RD

WOODLAND

COVERT CL

GROSVENOR CL

Parr's Barn Farm

WESTMINSTER DR

SHREWSBURY CL

BERKELEY CL

GLEBE LA

EASTWO RD

Radcliffe on Trent Inf Sch

Harlequin

MAYFAIR

Dayncourt Sch

A52

CROPWELL RD

DEWBERRY LA

Dewberry Hill

CH

HAMMERSMITH CL

QUEEN MARY'S CL

SERPENTINE CL

Upper Saxondale
or St James's Pk

SHAFTESBURY AVE

Cropwell Lings

Saxton's Lings

High Thorpe

The Fields

A46

Hall Farm

Radcliffe Barn Farm

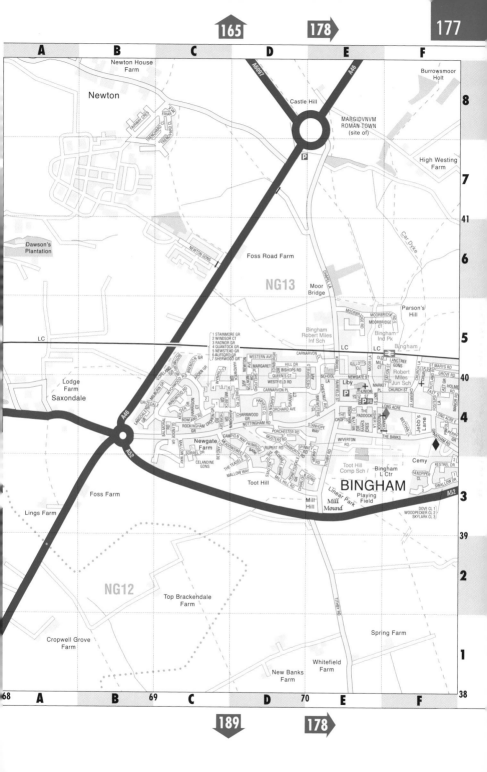

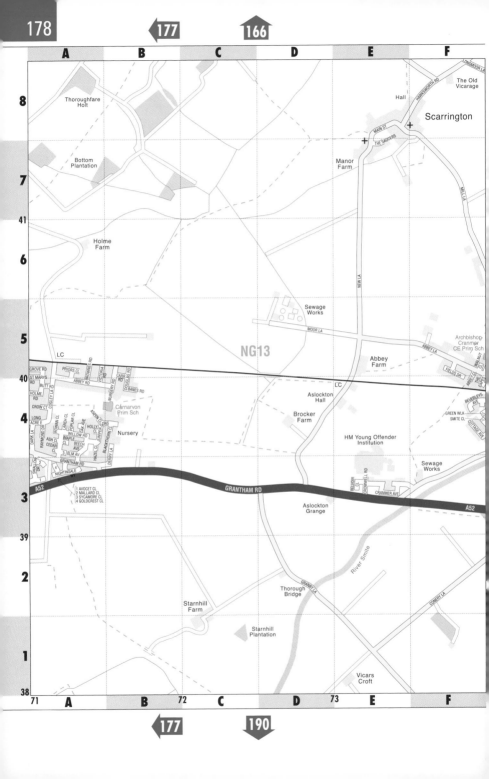

Scarrington

NG13

Thoroughfare
Holt

Bottom
Plantation

Holme
Farm

Hall

The Old
Vicarage

Manor
Farm

Sewage
Works

Archbishop
Cranmer
CE Prim Sch

Abbey
Farm

LC

GROVE RD
ST MARYS
RD
HOLME
RD
CROW CT
LONG
ACRE E
DARK LA
RAYMOND RD

PRIORS CL
BROWNE RD
ABBEY RD
VICTORIA RD
CARR
DOUGLAS RD
OS BANES RD

BUTT RD

NURSERY RD

Carnarvon
Prim Sch

Nursery

Aslockton
Hall

Brocker
Farm

HM Young Offender
Institution

Sewage
Works

LC

BEVERLEYS
AVE
GREEN WLK
SMITE CL
COTTAGE AVE

ROWAN CL
LARCH CL
POPLAR CL
ASPEN CL
ACORN CL
WILLOW RD
HOLLY
JUNIPER
CEDAR
ASH RD
MAPLE
BEECH
AVE
HAZEL CL
ELM AV
BLACKTHORN
DERBY LA

GRANTHAM RD
NIGHTINGALE

1 AVOCET CL
2 MALLARD CL
3 SYCAMORE CL
4 GOLDCREST CL

A52

GRANTHAM RD

Aslockton
Grange

A52

BRIDGR
CROMWELL RD
CRAMMER AVE

River Smite

Starnhill
Farm

Thorough
Bridge

GRANBY LA

Starnhill
Plantation

Vicars
Croft

GOVERT LA

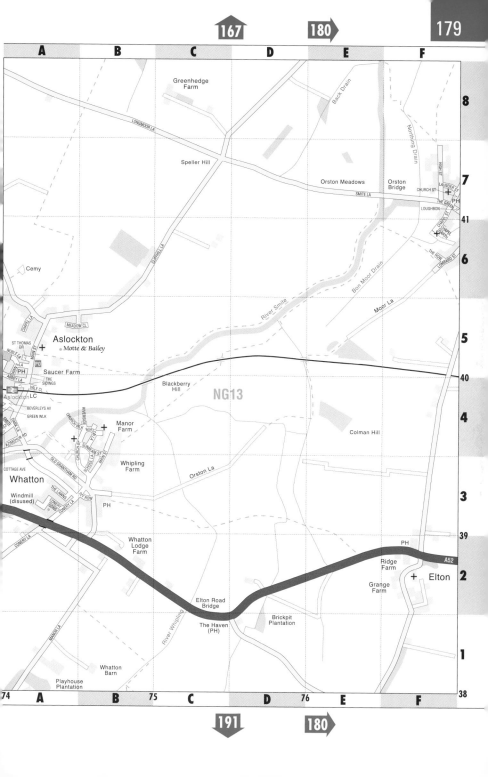

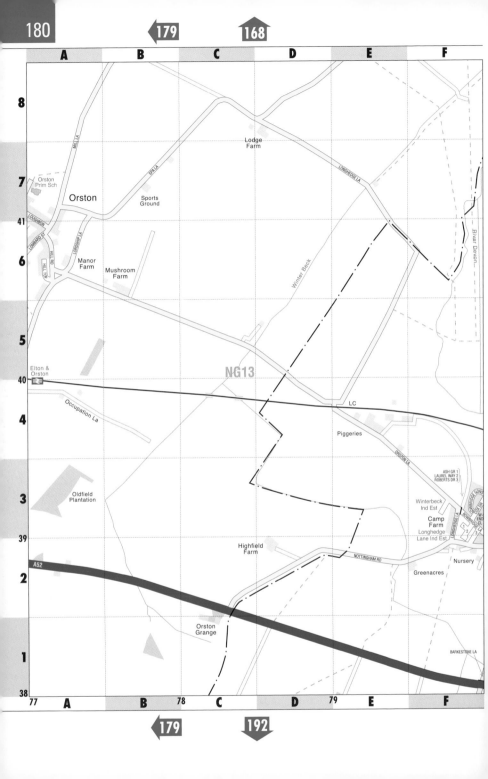

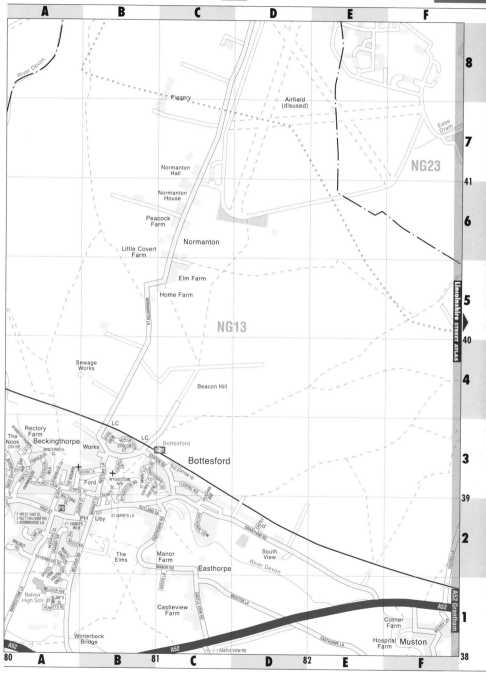

River Devon

Piggery

Airfield
(disused)

Ease
Drain

NG23

Normanton
Hall

Normanton
House

41

Peacock
Farm

Little Covert
Farm

Normanton

Elm Farm

Lincolnshire STREET ATLAS

Home Farm

NORMANTON LA

NG13

5

40

Sewage
Works

Beacon Hill

4

LC

Rectory
Farm

Beckingthorpe

The
Nook
COX RD

WINTERBECK
CL

Works

LC

Bottesford

STROUD
CT

BEACON VIEW

Bottesford

3

STATION RD

OLD STATION YD

FLEMING AVE

DEVON LA

+

Ford

WYGGESTON
RD

RECTORY LA

CHAPEL ST

THE SQUARE

WALFORD
CL

QUEEN ST

MARKET ST

39

C CHURCH VIEW

EASTHORPE VIEW

FARMHOUSE

FISHPOND WALK

BELVOIR RD

CROSS ST

HIGH ST

1 WEST END CL
2 NOTTINGHAM RD
3 BOWBRIDGE LA

PO

PH

Liby

HAND'S
WLK

ST MARY'S LA

RUTLAND LA

GRANTHAM RD

PADDOCKS

GRANBY DR

WALNUT
RD

SILVERWOOD RD

BELVOIR RD

The
Elms

Manor
Farm

MANOR RD

GREEN LA

Easthorpe

South
View

River Devon

2

SOUTH
CL

JAY'S
CL

BELVOIR AVE

CASTLE VIEW RD

Belvoir
High Sch

HOWITTS RD

Castleview
Farm

MUSTON LA

EASTHORPE LA

Cotner
Farm

A52 Grantham

SPERRY LA

1

A52

Hospital
Farm

Muston

A52

Winterbeck
Bridge

A52

CASTLE VIEW RD

38

80   81   82

8

7

6

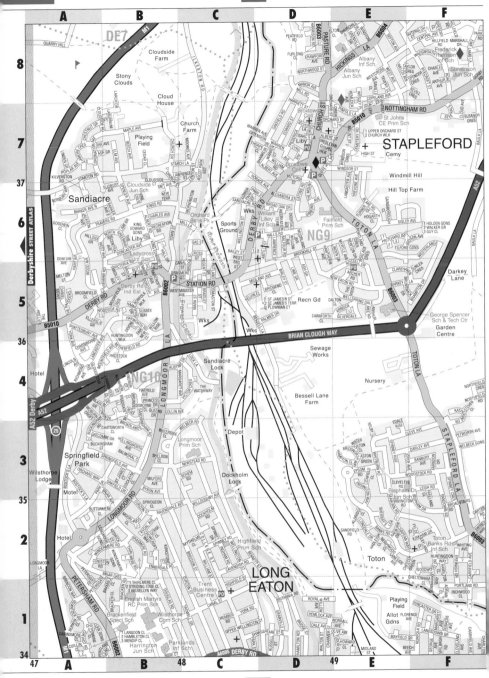

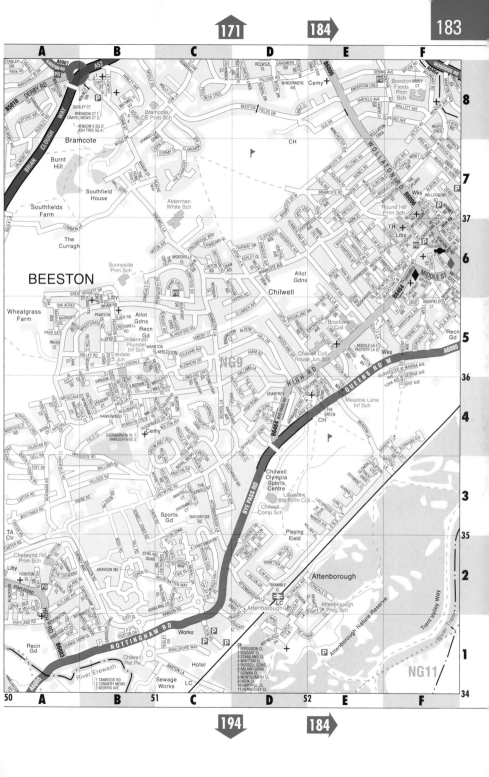

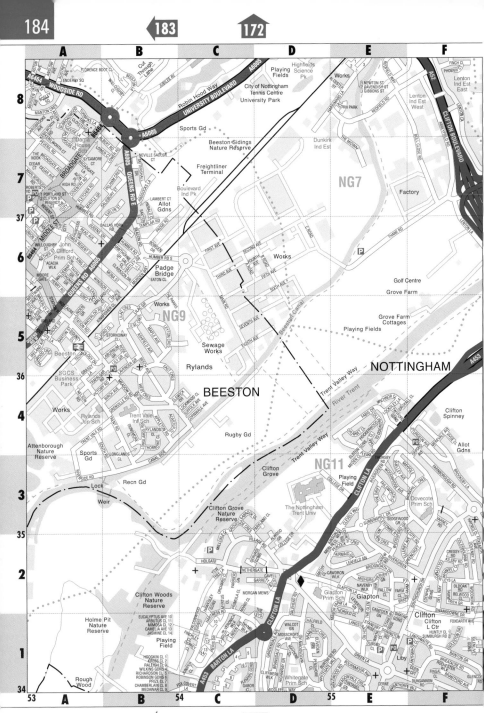

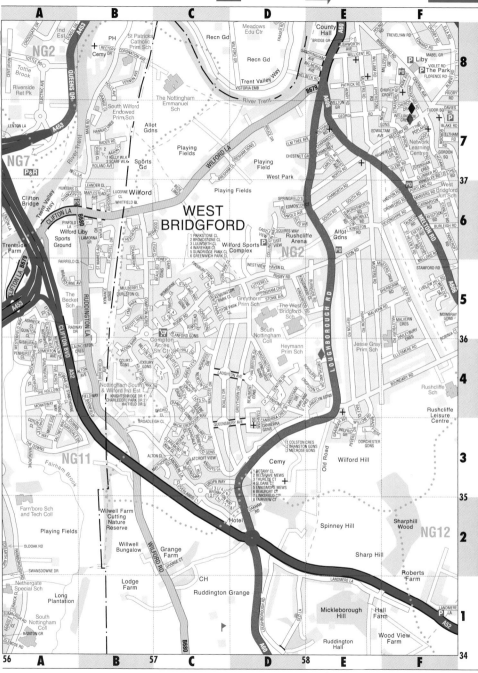

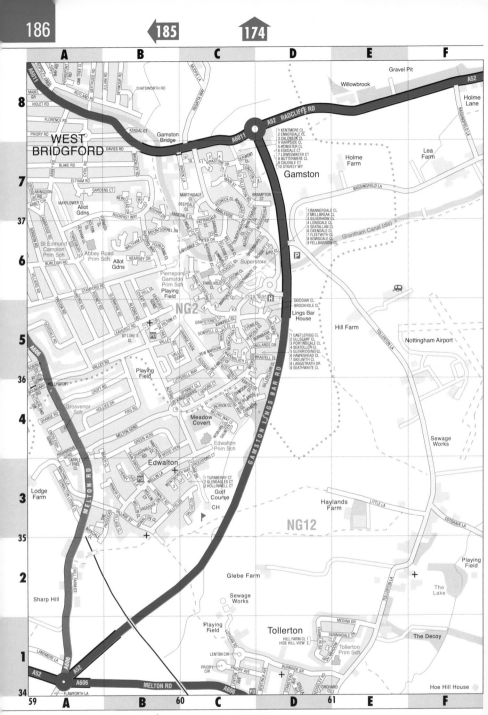

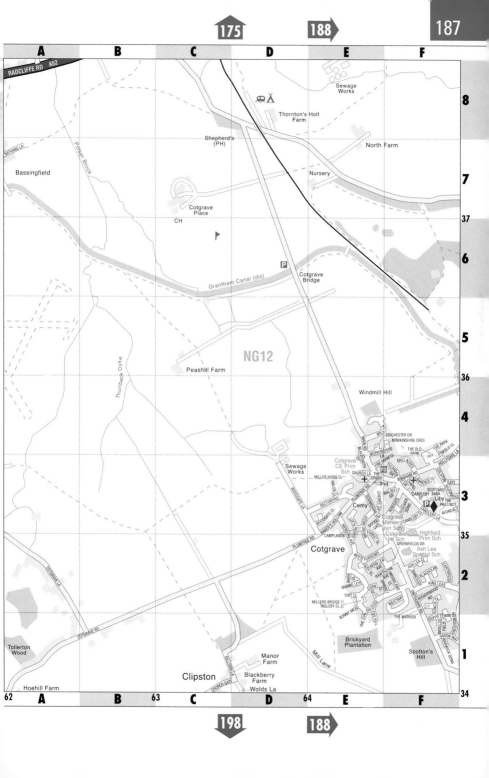

RADCLIFFE RD A52

Bassingfield

NATHANS LA

Polser Brook

Shepherd's
(PH)

Thornton's Holt
Farm

Sewage
Works

North Farm

Nursery

Cotgrave
Place
CH

Grantham Canal (dis)

Cotgrave
Bridge

NG12

Peashill Farm

Thurlbeck Dyke

Windmill Hill

Sewage
Works

Cotgrave
CE Prim
Sch

MILL

CHICHESTER DR
MORKINSHIRE CRES

THE OLD
PARK

EAST ACRE

BLACKSMITH

MORKINSHIRE
LA

LIME FARM CL

LIME PARK

PINFOLD CL

HOLLYGATE LA

MAIN RD

PETWORTH

THE
CROSS

CHURCH LA

BINGHAM RD

SCOTLAND
BANK

MILLER HIVES CL

WALNUT

CANDLEBY
CL

Cmy

Cotgrave
Manvers
(Jun Sch)

RECTORY RD

WOODGATE CL

BAKER'S HOLLOW

HALES CL

PLUMTRE RD

SPOSE
GATE

CHURCH CL

WOODS LA

DIMSDALE

CANDLEBY LA

Lidy
THE
PRECINCT

AVONDALE

Cotgrave
Int Sch

Highfield
Prim Sch

GREENFIELDS DR

Ash Lea
Special Sch

LAMPLANDS

Cotgrave

WHITE FURLONGS

FERN LEA

HAWTHORN
AVE

ASH LEA CL

LAUGHCME

CARTWOOD

RING LEAS

PLUMTREE RD

MANINGLEYS

CORN
CL

MARLWOOD

HAMMERWOOD
RD

MANOR
RD

GRIFFS COMM CL

FALCON

SAXON WAY

CARTWRIGHT GDNS

MILLERS BRIDGE
INGLEBY CL

TOFT CL

BONNY MEAD

JOE LEES

DALSTON RD

THE WARREN

THE HILL

WESTWAY

COTGRAVE LA

COTGRAVE RD

GILLOTTS LA

CHURCH GATE

Tollerton
Wood

Hoehill Farm

Manor
Farm

Blackberry
Farm
Wolds La

Clipston

Mill Lane

Brickyard
Plantation

Scotton's
Hill

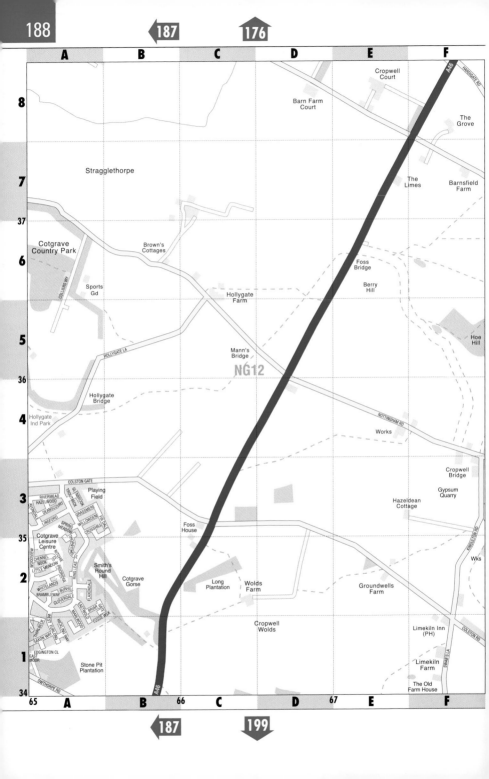

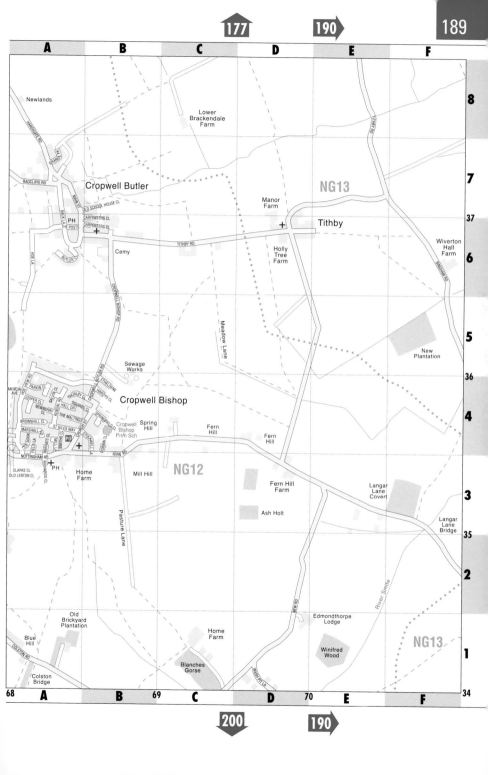

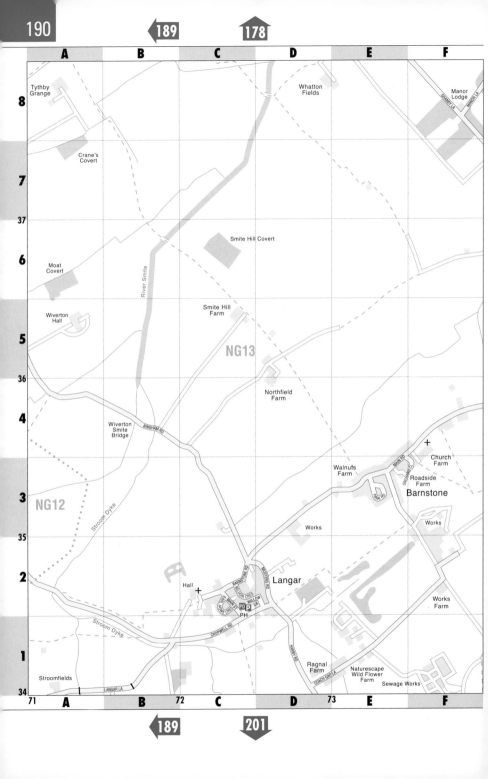

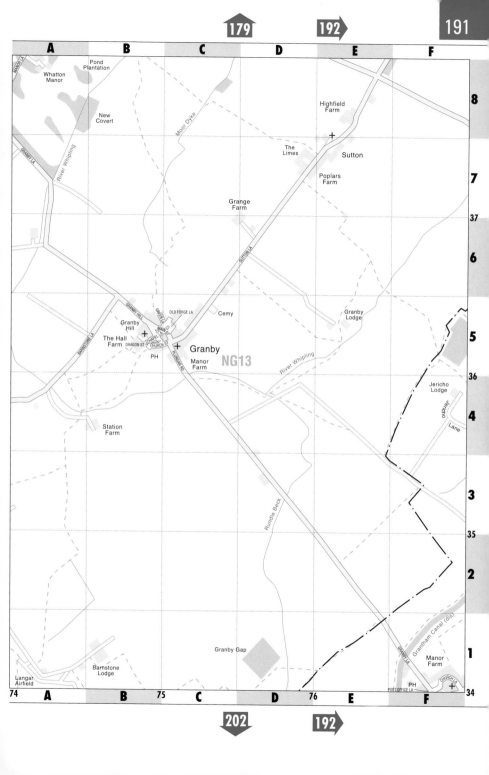

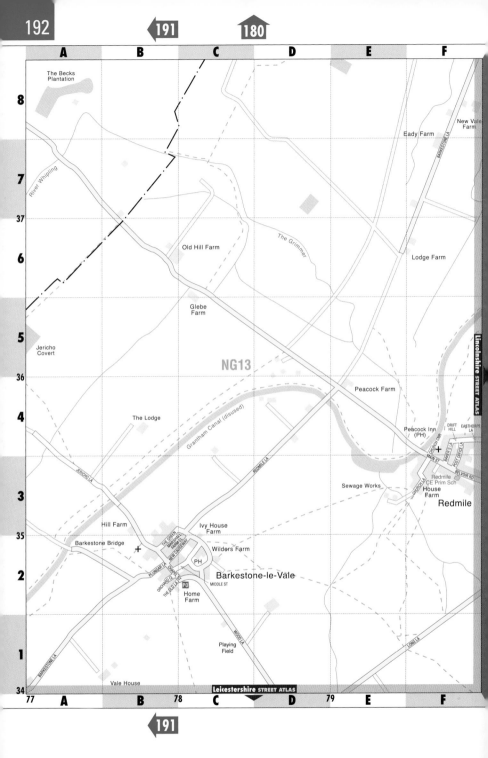

The Becks Plantation

River Whipling

8

7

37

6

Old Hill Farm

The Grimmer

Glebe Farm

Jericho Covert

5

NG13

36

The Lodge

Peacock Farm

Grantham Canal (disused)

4

Peacock Inn (PH)

DRIFT HILL

EASTHORPE LA

Eady Farm

New Vale Farm

Lodge Farm

Lincolnshire STREET ATLAS

MAIN ST

BELVOIR RD

Redmile CE Prim Sch

House Farm

Sewage Works

Redmile

3

Hill Farm

Ivy House Farm

JERICHO LA

35

Barkestone Bridge

THE GREEN

MARSHALL FARM LA

NEW CARSWAY

Wilders Farm

PH

Barkestone-le-Vale

2

PLUNGAR LA

ORCHARD CL

THE OLD LA

PO

MIDDLE ST

Home Farm

BARKESTONE LA

1

MIDDLE LA

LONGS LA

Playing Field

34

Vale House

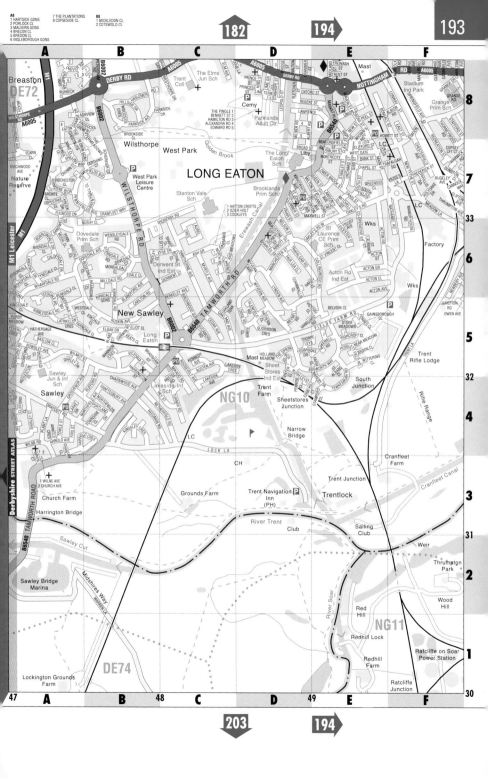

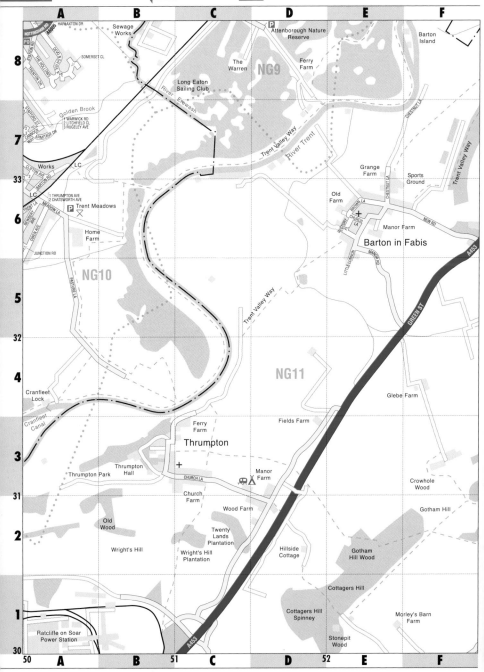

NOTTINGHAM RD A6005

HARLAXTON DR

SOMERSET CL

Sewage Works

Attenborough Nature Reserve

P

Barton Island

8

THE FOLLY

DECOX PADDOX

The Warren

NG9

Ferry Farm

Golden Brook

1 WARWICK RD
2 LITCHFIELD CL
3 RUGELEY AVE

7

CANNOCK WAY

ARMITAGE DR

River Erewash

Long Eaton Sailing Club

Trent Valley Way

River Trent

Trent Valley Way

Grange Farm

Sports Ground

Works

LC

CLIFTON AVE

33

LC

1 THRUMPTON AVE
2 CHATSWORTH AVE

Old Farm

CHESTNUT LA

CHESTNUT LA

NEWPORT RD

TRENT LA

P

Trent Meadows

Home Farm

6

MEADOW LA

OWEN AVE

RESTORED

CHURCH LA

BROWN LA

Manor Farm

NEW RD

Barton in Fabis

JUNCTION RD

LITTLE LUNNON

NG10

PASTURE LA

MANOR RD

A453

5

Trent Valley Way

32

NG11

4

Cranfleet Lock

Glebe Farm

GREEN ST

Cranfleet Canal

Ferry Farm

Fields Farm

3

Thrumpton

Crowhole Wood

Thrumpton Park

Thrumpton Hall

Manor Farm

Gotham Hill

CHURCH LA

31

Church Farm

Wood Farm

Gotham Hill

Old Wood

Twenty Lands Plantation

Hillside Cottage

Gotham Hill Wood

2

Wright's Hill

Wright's Hill Plantation

Cottagers Hill

1

Cottagers Hill Spinney

Morley's Barn Farm

Ratcliffe on Soar Power Station

A453

Stonepit Wood

30

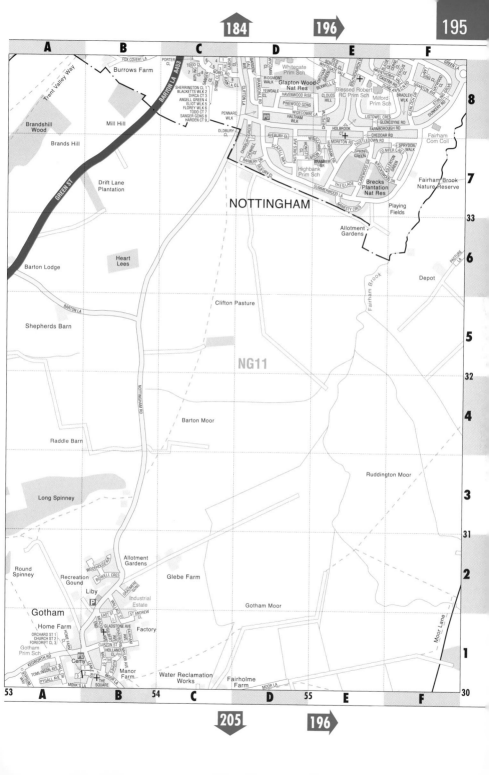

A **B** **C** **D** **E** **F**

Trent Valley Way

FOX COVERT LA
PORTER CL
Burrows Farm
TODD CL
KIRK CL
NOBEL RD
SYKE RD
CLIFTON LA

Brandshill
Wood

Mill Hill

Brands Hill

Whitegate
Prim Sch

Glapton Wood
Nat Res

Blessed Robert
RC Prim Sch

Milford
Prim Sch

Fairham
Com Coll

SHERRINGTON CL 1
BLACKETTS WLK 2
DIRCA CT 3
ANGELL GREEN 4
ELIOT WLK 5
FLOREY WLK 6
TODD CT 7
SANGER GDNS 8
HARDEN CT 9

RIDGMONT
WALK

YEWDALE

HAVENWOOD RISE

PINEWOOD GDNS

WIDECOMBE LA

HALTHAM
WLK

CLOUDS
HILL

LISTOWEL CRES

GLENCOYNE RD

FARNBOROUGH RD

Drift Lane
Plantation

GREEN ST

BARTON LA A453

PENNARD
WLK

OLDBURY
CL

DINSDALE DR
CHISNELL CL

BRAMBER GR

DANEBY WLK

SCARTEL WLK

BANBURY DR
SELBY PL

HOLBROOK

CHEDDAR RD

E SPRYDON
WALK

Fairham
Nature Reserve

PO

AVEBURY GL

Highbank
Prim Sch

MORETON RD

THISTLEDOWN RD

SPRING
GREEN

CO NIFER C/FC

SUMMERWOOD LA

MAJESTY CRES

THE GLADE

Brecks
Plantation
Nat Res

NOTTINGHAM

Barton Lodge

Heart
Lees

Allotment
Gardens

Playing
Fields

Fairham Brook

PASTURE
LA

Depot

BARTON LA

Clifton Pasture

Shepherds Barn

NG11

Barton Moor

Raddle Barn

NOTTINGHAM RD

Ruddington Moor

Long Spinney

Round
Spinney

Allotment
Gardens

Glebe Farm

Recreation
Gound

WIDDOWSON CL
BIDWELL CRES

GRASMERE GDNS

Liby

P

Industrial
Estate

ST ANDREW
CL

Gotham Moor

Moor Lane

Gotham

Home Farm

ORCHARD ST 1
CHURCH ST 2
FOREDRIFT CL 3

Gotham Prim Sch

KEGWORTH RD

HOME FARM

P Cemy

TOMLINSON AVE

PYGALL AVE

MONK'S LA

EAST ST
WALL ST
CURZON ST
GLADSTONE AVE
MOORE LA

THE
SQUARE

Manor
Farm

FERNHAM

ST ANDREW
CL

Factory

Water Reclamation
Works

Fairholme
Farm

MOOR LA

MOOR LA

A **B** **C** **D** **E** **F**

8 7 33 6 5 32 4 3 31 2 1 30

53 54 55

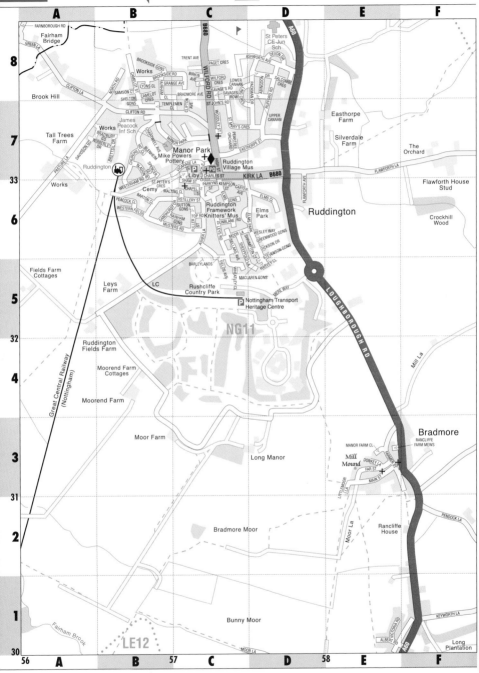

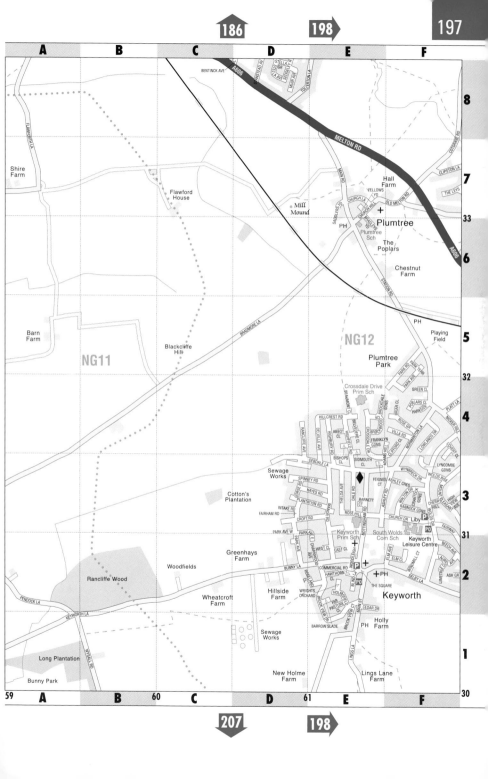

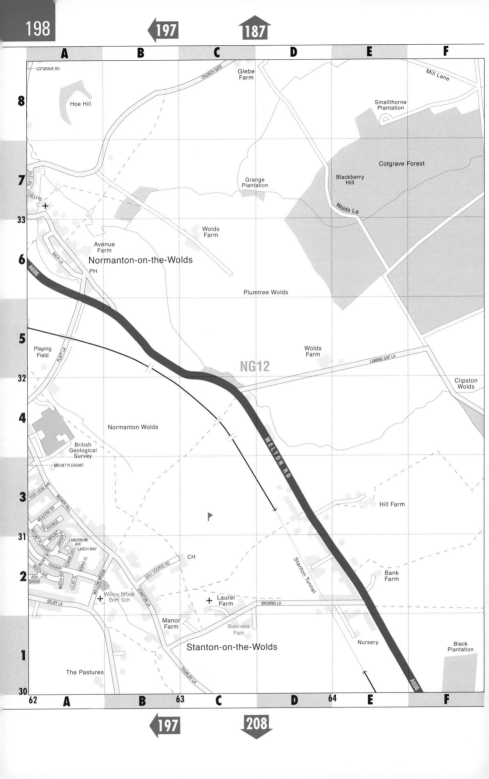

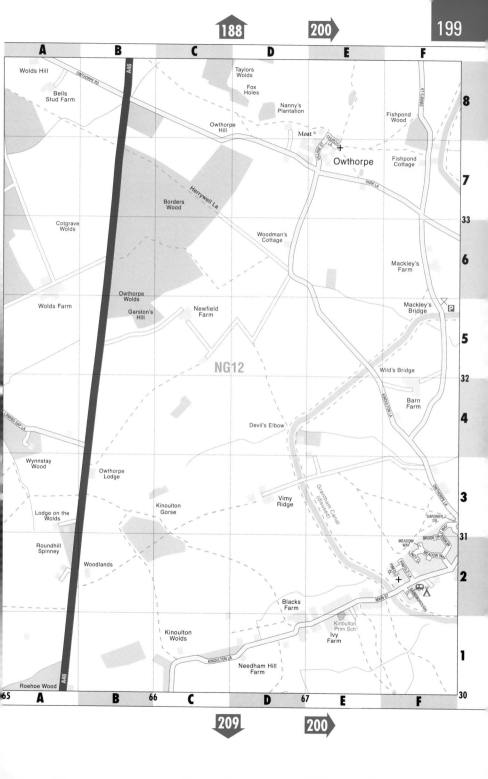

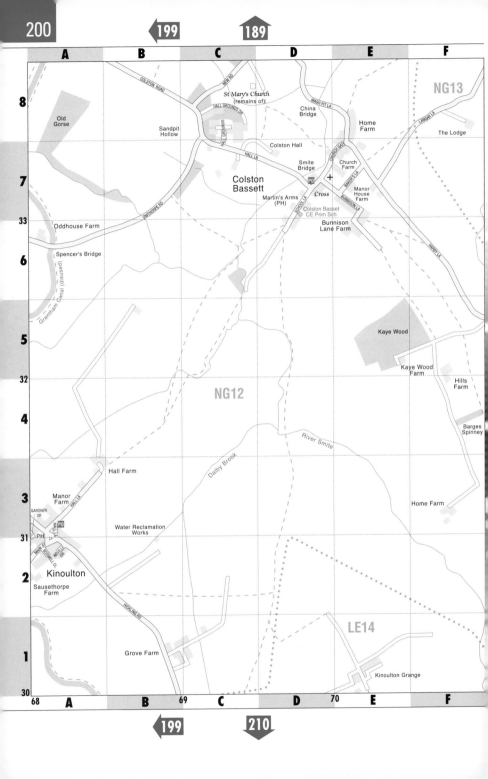

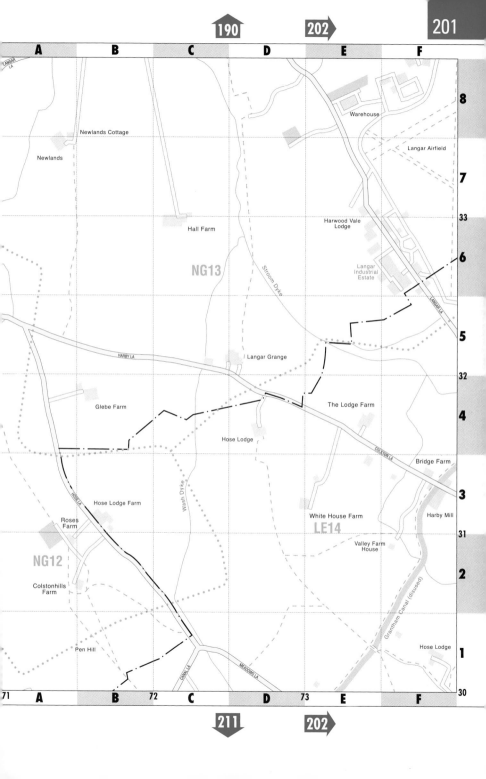

190
202

A   B   C   D   E   F

8

Warehouse

Newlands Cottage

Langar Airfield

Newlands

7

33

Hall Farm

Harwood Vale
Lodge

NG13

Stroom Dyke

6

Langar
Industrial
Estate

LANGAR LA

5

HARBY LA

Langar Grange

32

Glebe Farm

The Lodge Farm

4

Hose Lodge

COLSTON LA

Bridge Farm

HOSE LA

Wash Dyke

Hose Lodge Farm

3

Roses
Farm

White House Farm

Harby Mill

LE14

31

NG12

Valley Farm
House

Grantham Canal (disused)

2

Colstonhills
Farm

Pen Hill

Hose Lodge

CANAL LA

MEADOWS LA

1

71   A   B   72   C   D   73   E   F   30

211
202

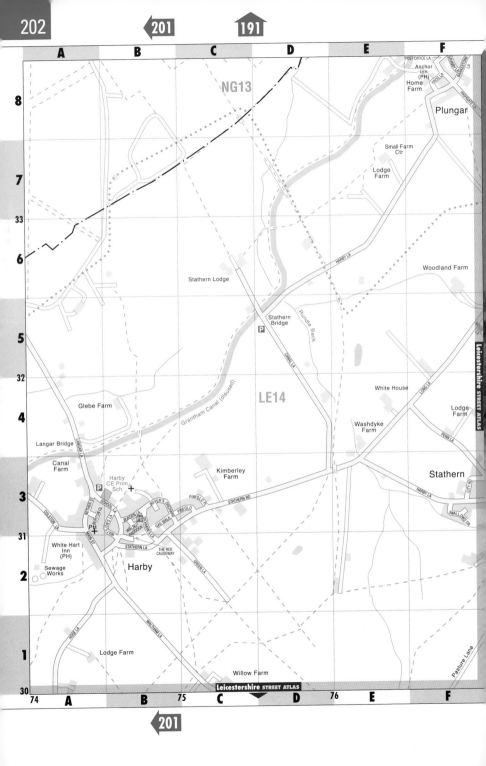

NG13

Plungar

Anchor Inn (PH)
Home Farm
POST OFFICE LA

Small Farm Ctr

Lodge Farm

Woodland Farm

HARBY LA

Stathern Lodge

Stathern Bridge

Rundle Beck

CANAL LA

White House

LONG LA

Lodge Farm

LE14

PENN LA

Washdyke Farm

Stathern

Glebe Farm

Grantham Canal (disused)

Langar Bridge

LANGAR LA

HARBY LA

SWALLOWS DR

CITY RD

Canal Farm

Kimberley Farm

PINFOLD LA

STATHERN RD

Harby CE Prim Sch

ROPER'S CROSSING

PINFOLD

NETHER ST

SCHOOL LA

ST CHAD'S VIEW

BRIDEN LA

ST MARY'S CT

WALNUT

THOMAS'S CL

GAS WALL RD

White Hart Inn (PH)

COLSTON LA

MAIN ST

STATHERN LA

THE RED CAUSEWAY

GREEN LA

Sewage Works

Harby

ROSE LA

WALTHAM LA

Lodge Farm

Willow Farm

Pasture Lane

Leicestershire STREET ATLAS

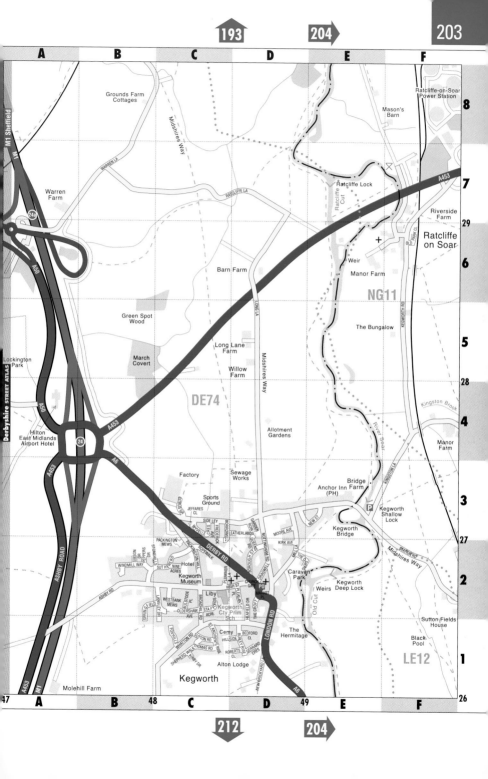

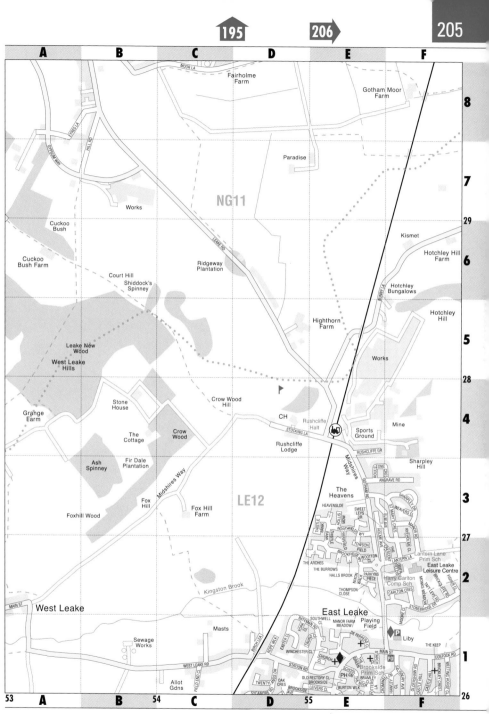

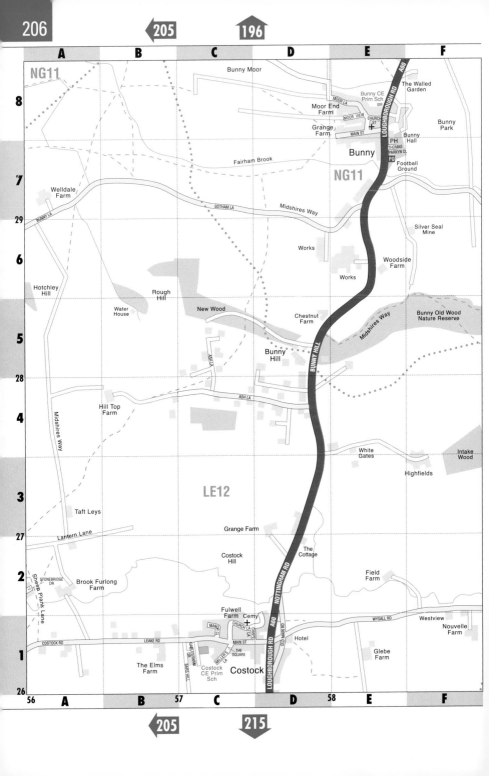

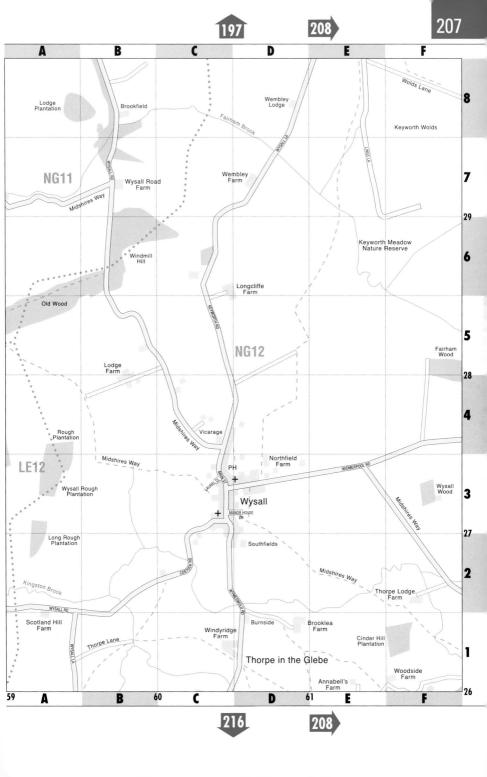

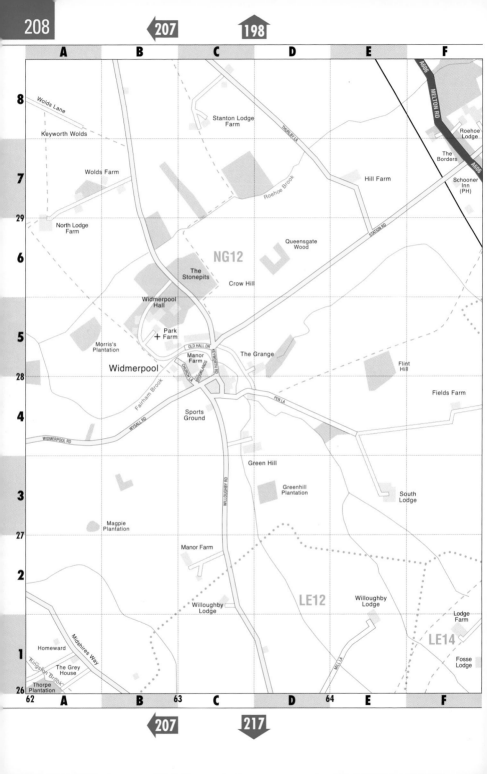

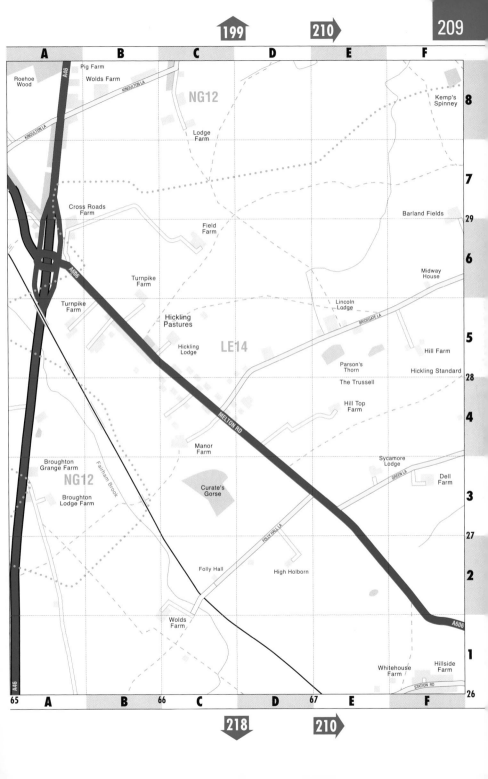

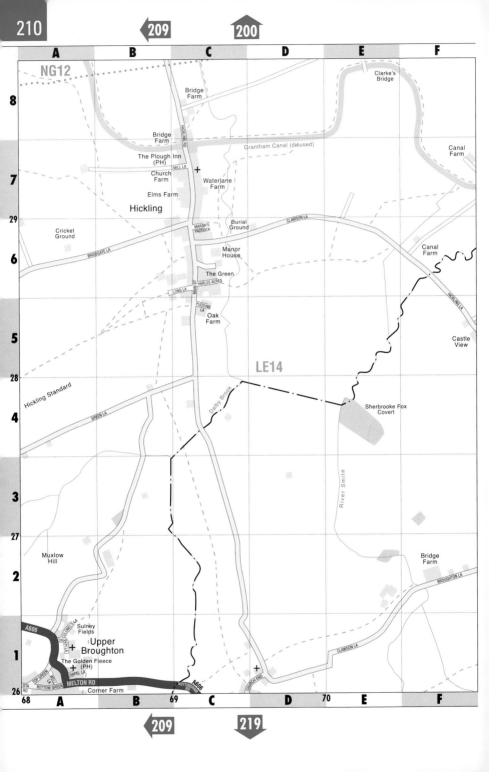

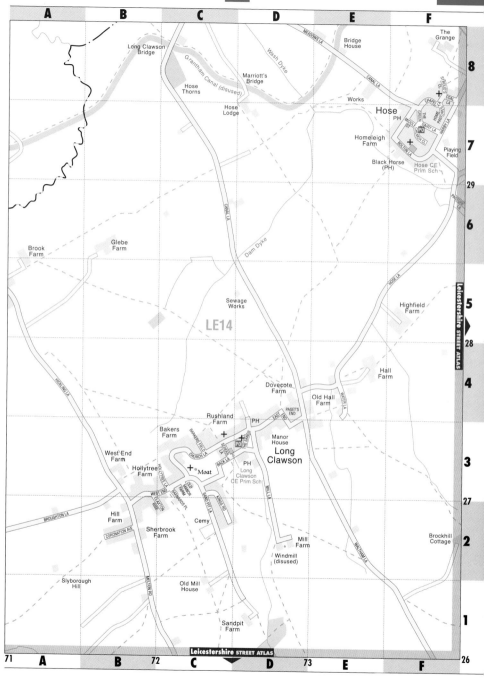

203

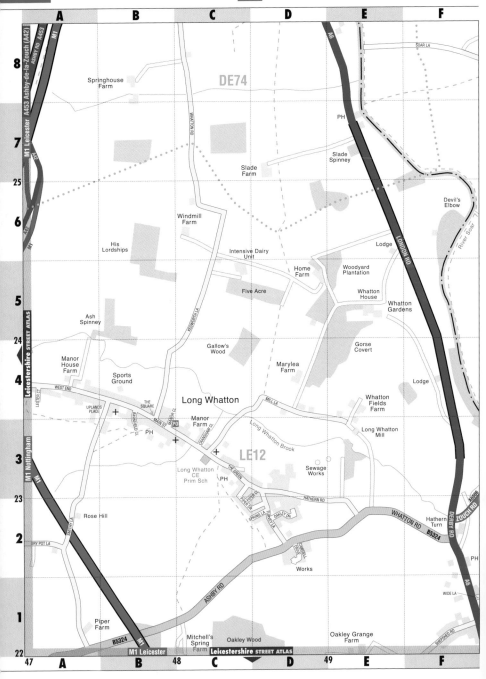

Leicestershire STREET ATLAS

DE74

LE12

Long Whatton

Springhouse Farm

WHATTON RD

Slade Farm

Slade Spinney

PH

Devil's Elbow

River Soar

LONDON RD

Windmill Farm

His Lordships

Intensive Dairy Unit

Home Farm

Lodge

Woodyard Plantation

Whatton House

Whatton Gardens

Five Acre

Ash Spinney

KEGWORTH LA

Gallow's Wood

Marylea Farm

Gorse Covert

Lodge

Manor House Farm

Sports Ground

WEST END

LESTER CT

UPLANDS PLACE

THE SQUARE

BARNS FIELD CL

MAIN ST

MANOR DR

PH

PH

Manor Farm

GRANSHAW CL

MILL LA

Long Whatton Brook

Whatton Fields Farm

Long Whatton Mill

M1 Nottingham

Rose Hill

SUTTON LA

DRY POT LA

Long Whatton CE Prim Sch

THE GREEN

PH

DEER CL

SPRING LA

TINKLE CL

OAKLEY LA

OAKLEY DR

Sewage Works

HATHERN RD

WHATTON RD

Hathern Turn

B5324

DERBY RD

ZOUCH RD

A6

PH

WIDE LA

M1 Leicester

Piper Farm

B5324

M1 Leicester

Mitchell's Spring Farm

ASHBY RD

Oakley Wood

CROMWELL ESTATE

Works

Oakley Grange Farm

SHEPSHED RD

Leicestershire STREET ATLAS

47   48   49

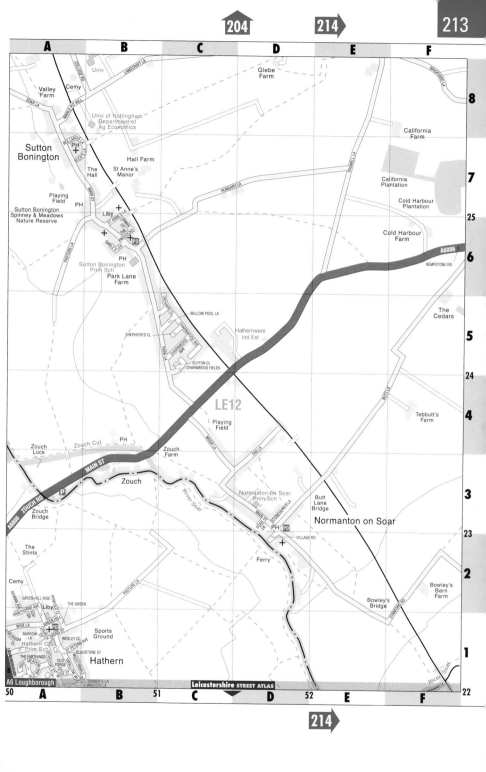

213
205

A **B** **C** **D** **E** **F**

Manor Farm

Calke Hall Farm

Mill Hill

East Leake

Manor Farm Animal Centre & Donkey Sanctuary

8

Sheepwash Brook

Woodgate Farm

WOODGATE RD

OAK CRES

MAPLE CL

MILL CL

PINE CL

SYCAMORE RD

POPLAR AVE

ASH WLK

ORCHARD CL

CEDAR AVE

JOHN LEE RD

BROOKSIDE

BURTON WLK

BROOKSIDE AVE

POTTERS LA

OAKDENE

OLDERSHAW RD

CASTLE HILL

MILL LA

7

Brickyard Plantation

REMPSTONE RD

Riseholme Farm

Sheepwash Farm

LOUGHBOROUGH RD

25

Hills Farm

TRAVELL'S HILL

BRICKYARD LA

6 A6006

Devil's Garden

REMPSTONE RD

Whitehills Farm

Gould's Barn

Home Farm

BUTT LA

Limekiln Plantation

Limekiln Cottages

Stanford Hills Farm

Colonel's Covert

A6006

MELTON RD

North Lodge

5

Trafalgar Wood

LE12

Shaws Park Farm

The Plains

Lings Spinney

24

Normanton Grange Farm

Stanford Hills

Stanford Hall

Dog Kennel Wood

Stanford Park

4

The Evergreens

Firdeal Hill

The Privets

Lewes's Plantation

Underhill Farm

LEAKE LA

3

23

Barn Farm

Black-a-moors Spinney

2

STANFORD RD

King's Brook

Rigget's Spinney

NORMANTON LA

Fox Hill

The Rectory

Five Oaks Farm

Hoton Hills Farm

1

MAIN ST

22

LE11

River Soar

Stanford on Soar

53 **A** **B** **54** **C** **D** **55** **E** **F**

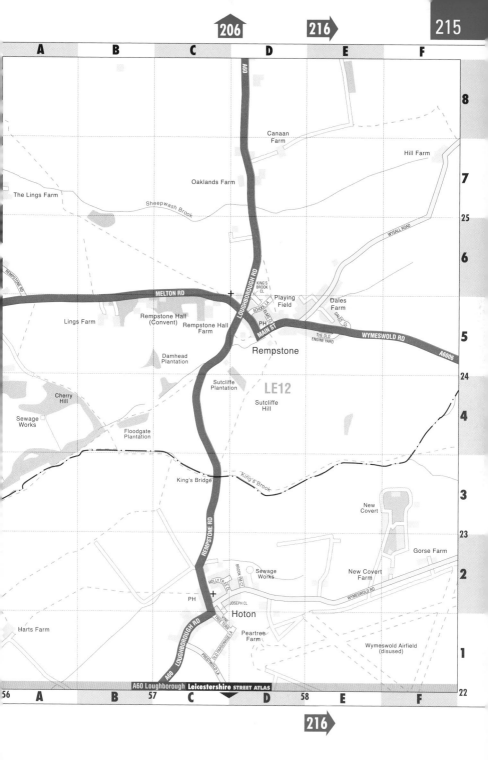

A B C D E F

8

7

25

6

5

24

4

3

23

2

1

22

A60

Canaan Farm

Hill Farm

Oaklands Farm

The Lings Farm

Sheepwash Brook

WYSALL ROAD

MELTON RD

LOUGHBOROUGH RD

Lings Farm

Rempstone Hall (Convent)

Rempstone Hall Farm

KING'S BROOK CL

SCHOOL LA

MAIN ST

PH

Playing Field

Dales Farm

DALES CL

WYMESWOLD RD

A6006

THE OLD ENGINE YARD

Rempstone

LE12

Damhead Plantation

Sutcliffe Plantation

Sutcliffe Hill

Cherry Hill

Sewage Works

Floodgate Plantation

King's Bridge

King's Brook

New Covert

Gorse Farm

New Covert Farm

WYMESWOLD RD

REMPSTONE RD

Sewage Works

BROOK RD

HOLLY TR CT

JOSEPH CL

PH

THE TREE TOPS

Hoton

Peartree Farm

Wymeswold Airfield (disused)

Harts Farm

LOUGHBOROUGH RD

A60

PRESTWOLDS

OLD ASHBY RD

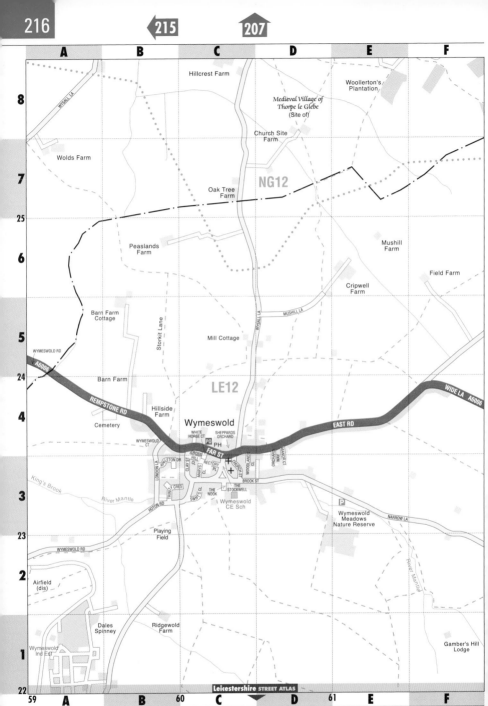

215
207

Hillcrest Farm

Woollerton's Plantation

Medieval Village of
Thorpe le Glebe
(Site of)

Church Site
Farm

Wolds Farm

NG12

Oak Tree
Farm

Mushill
Farm

Peaslands
Farm

Field Farm

Cripwell
Farm

Barn Farm
Cottage

Storkit Lane

Mill Cottage

MUSHILL LA

WYMESWOLD RD

A6006

LE12

Barn Farm

WIDE LA A6006

REMPSTONE RD

Hillside
Farm

Cemetery

Wymeswold

EAST RD

WHITE
HORSE CT

SHEPPARDS
ORCHARD

WYMESWOLD
CT

PO

PH

FAR ST

RECTORY
PL

BROOK ST

BROOK ST

CLAY ST

CROSS
HILL

ST MARY'S
CL

FAR
ST

CONDON LA

STURTON DR

FARM CT CRES

HOTON RD

SWAN
ST

THE
NOOK

Wymeswold
CE Sch

Wymeswold
Meadows
Nature Reserve

NARROW LA

King's Brook

River Mantle

Playing
Field

P

River Mantle

WYMESWOLD RD

Airfield
(dis)

Dales
Spinney

Ridgewold
Farm

Gamber's Hill
Lodge

Wymeswold
Ind Est

215

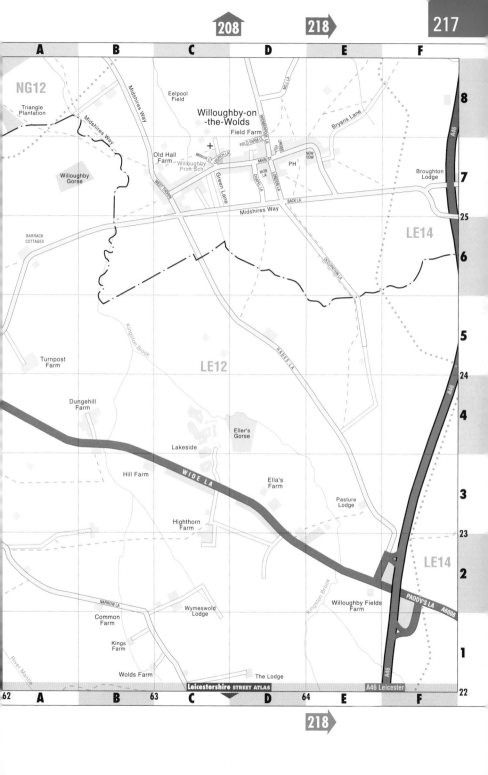

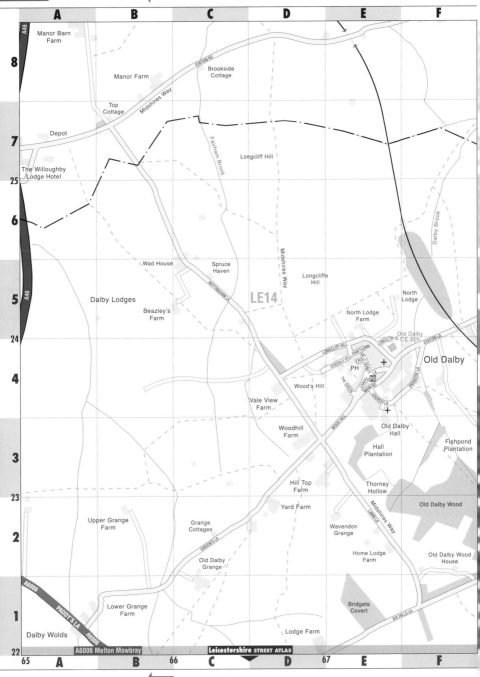

A46
Manor Barn Farm
Manor Farm
Brookside Cottage
STATION RD
Top Cottage
Midshires Way
Depot
Fairham Brook
Longcliff Hill
The Willoughby Lodge Hotel
Dalby Brook
A46
Wad House
Spruce Haven
Midshires Way
Longcliffe Hill
North Lodge
Dalby Lodges
LE14
North Lodge Farm
Beazley's Farm
NOTTINGHAM LA
LONGCLIFF CL
Old Dalby CE Sch
STATION LA
LONGCLIFF HILL
DEBDALE HILL
HAWTHORN
CROFT GDNS
CAPEL LA
Old Dalby
PH
MAIN RD
Wood's Hill
PO
PARADISE LA
Vale View Farm
THE GREEN
WOOD HILL
CHURCH LA
Old Dalby Hall
Woodhill Farm
Hall Plantation
Fishpond Plantation
Thorney Hollow
Hill Top Farm
LAWN LA
Old Dalby Wood
Yard Farm
Midshires Way
Upper Grange Farm
Grange Cottages
Wavendon Grange
Old Dalby Wood House
GIBSON'S LA
Home Lodge Farm
A6006
PADDY'S LA
Old Dalby Grange
Bridgets Covert
SIX HILLS LA
Lower Grange Farm
A6006
Dalby Wolds
Lodge Farm

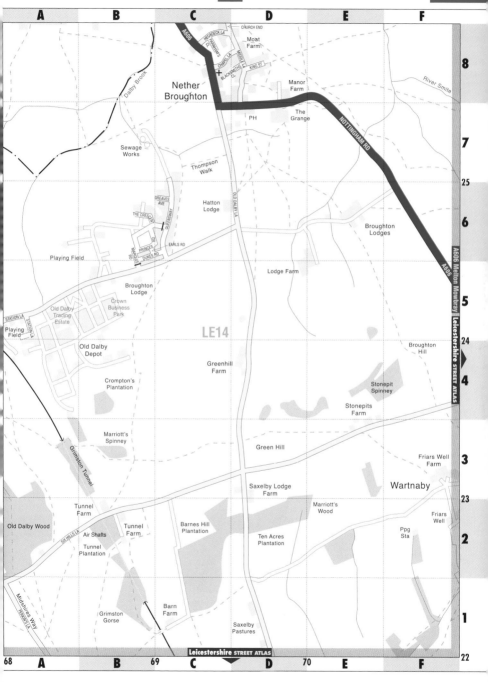

A B C D E F

8

River Smite

A606

Dalby Brook

Nether Broughton

CHURCH END

Moat Farm

MEGADECK LA

CHAPEL LA

ST ANDREWS

MIDDLE LE

KING ST

BLACKSMITHS CL

Manor Farm

PH

The Grange

NOTTINGHAM RD

7

25

Sewage Works

Thompson Walk

Hatton Lodge

OLD DALBY LA

6

GREAVES AVE

THE CRESCENT

QUEENSWAY

Broughton Lodges

EARLS RD

PRINCES RD

INGLES RD

DUKES RD

Playing Field

Lodge Farm

A606 Melton Mowbray

Leicestershire STREET ATLAS

Broughton Lodge

Crown Business Park

Old Dalby Trading Estate

STATION LA

STATION LA

LE14

Playing Field

Old Dalby Depot

Broughton Hill

24

Crompton's Plantation

Greenhill Farm

Stonepit Spinney

4

Marriott's Spinney

Green Hill

Stonepits Farm

Grimston Tunnel

Friars Well Farm

3

Saxelby Lodge Farm

Wartnaby

23

Old Dalby Wood

Tunnel Farm

Air Shafts

SIX HILLS LA

Tunnel Farm

Barnes Hill Plantation

Marriott's Wood

Friars Well

Ppg Sta

2

Tunnel Plantation

Ten Acres Plantation

Midshires Way

PEBBLES LA

Grimston Gorse

Barn Farm

Saxelby Pastures

1

68 A B 69 C

Leicestershire STREET ATLAS

D 70 E F

22

214

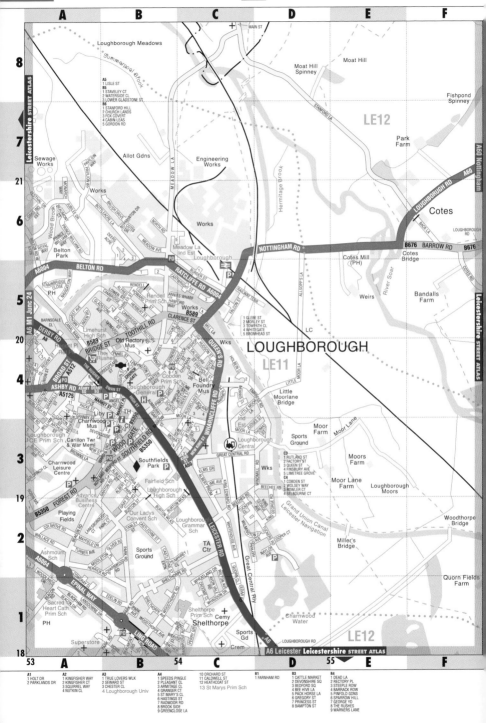

A1
1 HOLT DR
2 PARKLANDS DR

A2
1 KINGFISHER WAY
2 KINGFISHER CT
3 SQUIRREL WAY
4 NUTKIN CL

A3
1 TRUE LOVERS WLK
2 SEWARD ST
3 CHESTER CL
4 Loughborough Univ

A4
1 SPEEDS PINGLE
2 PLEASANT CL
3 ARMITAGE CL
4 GRANGER CT
5 ST MARY'S CL
6 HASTINGS ST
7 RADMOOR RD
8 BROOK SIDE
9 GREENCLOSE LA

10 ORCHARD ST
11 CALDWELL ST
12 HEATHCOAT ST
13 St Marys Prim Sch

B1
1 FARNHAM RD

B3
1 CATTLE MARKET
2 DEVONSHIRE SQ
3 BEDFORD SQ
4 BEE HIVE LA
5 PACK HORSE LA
6 GREGORY ST
7 PRINCESS ST
8 BAMPTON ST

B4
1 DEAD LA
2 RECTORY PL
3 STEEPLE ROW
4 BARRACK ROW
5 PINFOLD GDNS
6 SPARROW HILL
7 GEORGE YD
8 THE RUSHES
9 WARNERS LANE

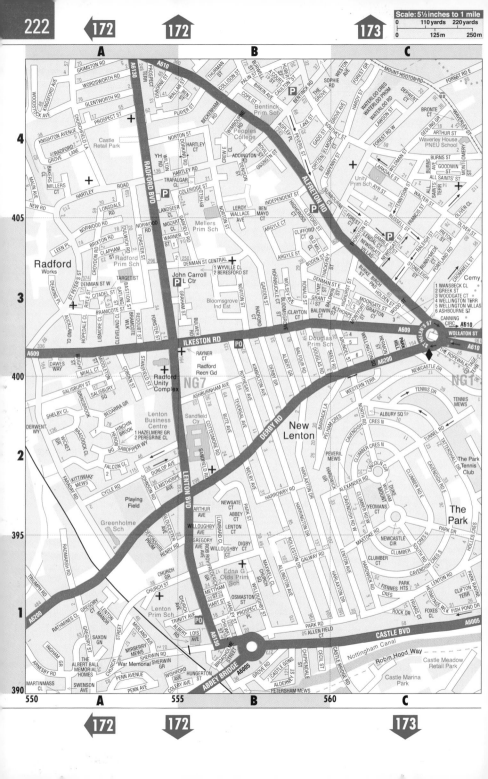

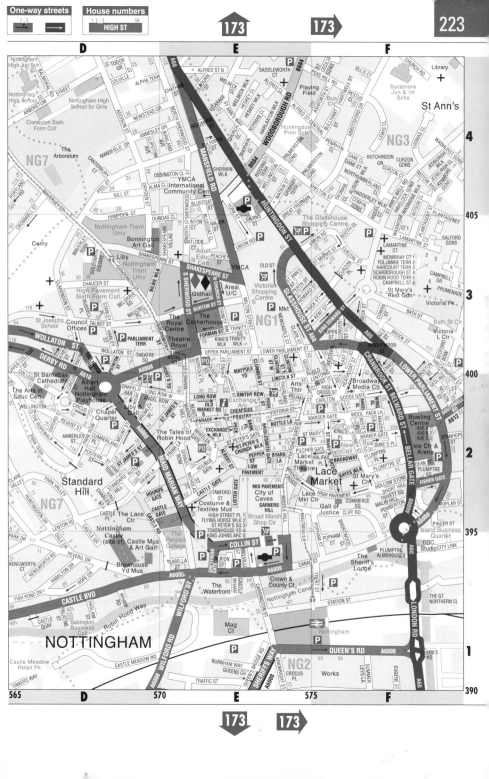

Index

Place name May be abbreviated on the map

Location number Present when a number indicates the place's position in a crowded area of mapping

Locality, town or village Shown when more than one place has the same name

Postcode district District for the indexed place

Page and grid square Page number and grid reference for the standard mapping

Church Rd 6 Beckenham BR2..........**53** C6

Public and commercial buildings are highlighted in magenta   Places of interest are highlighted in blue with a star*

Abbreviations used in the index

Acad	**Academy**	Comm	**Common**	Gd	**Ground**	L	**Leisure**
App	**Approach**	Cott	**Cottage**	Gdn	**Garden**	La	**Lane**
Arc	**Arcade**	Cres	**Crescent**	Gn	**Green**	Liby	**Library**
Ave	**Avenue**	Cswy	**Causeway**	Gr	**Grove**	Mdw	**Meadow**
Bglw	**Bungalow**	Ct	**Court**	H	**Hall**	Meml	**Memorial**
Bldg	**Building**	Ctr	**Centre**	Ho	**House**	Mkt	**Market**
Bsns, Bus	**Business**	Ctry	**Country**	Hospl	**Hospital**	Mus	**Museum**
Bvd	**Boulevard**	Cty	**County**	HQ	**Headquarters**	Orch	**Orchard**
Cath	**Cathedral**	Dr	**Drive**	Hts	**Heights**	Pal	**Palace**
Cir	**Circus**	Dro	**Drove**	Ind	**Industrial**	Par	**Parade**
Cl	**Close**	Ed	**Education**	Inst	**Institute**	Pas	**Passage**
Cnr	**Corner**	Emb	**Embankment**	Int	**International**	Pk	**Park**
Coll	**College**	Est	**Estate**	Intc	**Interchange**	Pl	**Place**
Com	**Community**	Ex	**Exhibition**	Junc	**Junction**	Prec	**Precinct**

Prom	**Promenade**
Rd	**Road**
Recn	**Recreation**
Ret	**Retail**
Sh	**Shopping**
Sq	**Square**
St	**Street**
Sta	**Station**
Terr	**Terrace**
TH	**Town Hall**
Univ	**University**
Wk, Wlk	**Walk**
Wr	**Water**
Yd	**Yard**

Index of localities, towns and villages

A

Adbolton 174 B2
Aldercar 143 A4
Annesley 130 C8
Annesley Woodhouse ...129 E8
Arnold 162 A7
Askham 51 F2
Aslockton 179 A5
Astwith 85 A5
Attenborough 183 E2
Ault Hucknall 85 F7
Austerfield 3 C2
Averham 123 F2
Awsworth 158 C4

B

Babworth 39 A6
Bakers Fields 174 C6
Balderton 140 E3
Barkestone-le-Vale 192 C2
Barnby in the Willows ..141 F5
Barnby Moor 28 C5
Barnstone 190 F3
Barton in Fabis 194 E6
Bathley 110 A3
Bawtry 10 B7
Beckingham
  Lincs 142 D8
  Notts 14 B1
Beechdale 172 B6
Beeston 183 A6
Besthorpe 97 E6
Bestwood 161 B7
Bestwood Village 146 F4
Bilborough 171 E7
Bilsthorpe 105 E6
Bingham 177 E3
Bircotes 9 D4
Bleasby 152 B8
Blidworth 118 B4
Blyth 18 A3
Bobbers Mill 172 C4
Bole 23 E3
Bothamsall 63 E7
Bottesford 181 C3
Boughton 77 F5
Bracebridge 36 A3
Bradmore 196 F3
Bramcote 183 A4
Bramcote Hills 171 C2
Breaston 193 A8
Brinsley 143 E7

C

Calverton 149 A7
Car Colston 166 C2
Carlton 162 D1
Carlton in Lindrick ...25 F5
Carlton-on-Trent 96 E4
Carr Hill 11 A4
Carrington 161 B2
Caunton 109 B4
Caythorpe 165 B8
Chilwell 183 D6
Church Warsop 74 A7
Cinderhill 160 B4
Clarborough 30 E4
Claypole 156 D7
Clayworth 21 D6
Clifton 184 F1
Clipston 187 C1
Clipstone 89 F3
Coates 43 E7
Coddington 126 A2
Collingham 98 A2
Colston Bassett 200 C7
Colwick 174 F5
Cossall 158 C1
Costock 206 C1
Cotes 220 F6
Cotgrave 187 E2
Cotham 154 F4
Cotmanhay 157 E4
Cottam 43 D4
Creswell 58 D8
Cromwell 110 E7
Cropwell Bishop 189 B4
Cropwell Butler 189 B7
Cuckney 60 A4

D

Dalestworth 101 B5
Darlton 67 B7
Daybrook 161 D7
Doddington 71 C1
Drakeholes 11 F1

E

Broadholme 57 B1
Brough 112 B1
Broxholme 57 E8
Budby 75 F8
Bulcote 164 A6
Bulwell 160 A6
Bunny 206 E7
Burton Joyce 163 E4

Dry Doddington 156 E1
Dunham on Trent 54 C2
Dunkirk 172 E2

E

Eagle 84 C3
Eakring 92 F1
East Bridgford 165 D3
East Drayton 53 A3
East Leake 205 E2
East Markham 65 F7
East Stockwith 7 E1
East Stoke 153 D8
Eastwood 143 E3
Eaton 40 A1
Edingley 120 C4
Edwalton 186 B3
Edwinstowe 76 A1
Egmanton 79 E6
Elkesley 50 B3
Elmton 58 A7
Elston 153 E5
Epperstone 150 A6
Everton 11 C3

F

Fardon 139 B4
Farnsfield 119 E6
Fenton
  Balderton 142 D2
  Saxilby 55 D6
Firbeck 16 A6
Fiskerton 137 E3
Flawborough 168 C2
Fledborough 68 C5
Flintham 153 A1
Forest Town 89 B1

G

Gainsborough 24 E5
Gamston
  Retford 51 A5
  West Bridgford 186 D7
Gedling 162 F2
Giltbrook 158 C8
Girton 82 E1
Glapwell 86 C8
Gotham 195 A1
Granby 191 C5
Grassthorpe 81 E4

Greasley 144 E3
Gringley on the Hill ..12 E1
Grove 40 F4
Gunthorpe 164 F5

H

Halam 120 E1
Halloughton 136 B4
Harby
  Leics 202 B2
  Notts 70 E2
Hardstoft 85 A3
Harwell 11 A4
Harworth 8 F5
Hathern 213 B1
Haughton 63 F6
Hawksworth 167 C4
Hawton 139 E3
Hayton 30 D6
Headon 52 B7
Heanor 143 B2
Hemshill Vale 159 E6
Hickling 210 B7
High Marnham 68 B1
Hilcote 99 C1
Hockerton 122 B6
Hodsock 26 E7
Hodthorpe 45 C6
Holbeck 59 C7
Holme 111 A3
Holme Pierrepont 175 B3
Hose 211 F7
Hoton 215 D1
Hoveringham 151 D2
Hucknall 145 E6
Huthwaite 99 E3
Hyson Green 172 F7

I

Ilkeston 170 B7

K

Kegworth 203 C1
Kelham 124 B4
Kersall 94 B1
Kettlethorpe 55 C4
Keyworth 197 F2
Kimberley 158 E8
Kingston on Soar 204 A4
Kinoulton 200 A2

Kirkby in Ashfield 115 C4
Kirkby Woodhouse 114 D1
Kirklington 120 E8
Kirkstead 113 D3
Kirton 78 C5
Kneesall 93 F5
Kneeton 152 A1

L

Lambley 163 C8
Laneham 54 B6
Langar 190 D2
Langford 111 E1
Langley Mill 143 B3
Langold 16 E4
Langwith 72 F8
Laughterton 55 A4
Laxton 79 C3
Lea 24 F2
Letwell 16 A3
Lidgett 91 B8
Linby 131 A3
Little Carlton 34 B8
Long Clawson 211 D3
Long Eaton 193 C7
Long Whatton 212 C4
Loughborough 220 C4
Lound 29 C8
Lowdham 150 D1
Low Marnham 82 A8
Ironville 128 A3

M

Mansfield 102 D3
Mansfield Woodhouse ...88 E3
Manton 36 B1
Mapperley 108 A6
Mapperley Park 161 E3
Market Warsop 74 C4
Marton 44 B8
Mattersey 20 C2
Meadows 173 C2
Meden Vale 74 E8
Misson 4 B2
Misterton 6 F1
Moorhouse 80 C2
Morton
  Lincs 15 C4
  Notts 137 D3
Muston 181 F1

N

Nether Broughton......219 C8
Netherfield......175 B6
Nether Langwith......59 B1
Newark-on-Trent......140 C7
New Balderton......140 B5
New Cross......100 E4
New Houghton......86 F7
Newington......10 E8
New Lenton......172 F4
New Ollerton......77 E5
Newstead......130 E5
Newton......99 B3
Newton on Trent......55 A1
Normanton on Soar......213 E3
Normanton-on-the-
Wolds......198 A6
Normanton on Trent......81 D6
North Clifton......68 E6
North Leverton with
Habblesthorpe......42 D8
North Muskham......110 E1
North Scarle......83 E2
North Wheatley......31 D8
Norwell......110 A7
Nottingham......173 B3
Nuncargate......115 A1
Nuthall......159 D5

O

Old Clipstone......90 C6
Oldcotes......17 A6
Old Dalby......218 F4
Old Lenton......172 D3
Ollerton......77 B3
Ompton......93 B7
Orston......180 A7
Ossington......95 D6

Owthorpe......199 E7
Oxton......134 C4

P

Papplewick......131 D3
Perlethorpe......62 F3
Pinxton......113 C2
Pleasley......87 B6
Pleasleyhill......87 C4
Plumtree......197 E6
Plungar......202 F8
Porchester......162 B2
Pye Bridge......128 A7

R

Radcliffe on Trent......175 E3
Radford......222 A3
Radmanthwaite......87 D3
Ragnall......68 A8
Rainworth......104 A1
Rampton......42 F1
Ranby......38 A6
Ranskill......19 B4
Ratcliffe on Soar......203 F6
Ravenshead......117 B1
Redmile......192 F3
Rempstone......215 D5
Retford......39 E8
Rhodesia......35 A4
Rockley......51 A2
Rolleston......138 A5
Ruddington......196 D6

S

St Ann's......173 D6
Sandiacre......182 A6

Saundby......23 C6
Sawley......193 A4
Saxilby......56 F4
Saxondale......177 A4
Scarrington......178 F8
Screveton......166 E4
Scrooby......10 A2
Selston......128 E7
Shelford......164 C1
Shelton......168 C6
Sherwood......161 B3
Shipley......157 B6
Shirebrook......72 F3
Shireoaks......34 E6
Sibthorpe......167 E7
Skegby......100 E6
Skellingthorpe......71 F3
Sneinton......173 E4
South Clifton......68 E1
South Leverton......42 C6
South Muskham......113 A7
South Normanton......113 A7
South Scarle......98 C5
Southwell......121 C1
South Wheatley......31 E7
Spalford......83 B7
Stainsby......85 B7
Stanford on Soar......214 D1
Stanley......85 D1
Stanton-by-Dale......170 A1
Stanton Hill......100 C5
Stanton-on-the-Wolds......198 C1
Stapleford
  Lincs......127 E8
  Notts......182 E7
Stathern......202 F3
Staunton in the Vale......169 B4
Staythorpe......138 D8
Stoke Bardolph......175 F7
Strelley......171 B8
Sturton le Steeple......32 D5
Styrrup......8 D1

Sutton Bonington......213 A7
Sutton cum Lound......28 F6
Sutton Forest Side......101 B3
Sutton in Ashfield......100 B2
Sutton on Trent......96 E7
Syerston......153 B4

T

Teversal......100 C8
The Park......173 A4
Thoresby......69 F7
Thorneywood......174 B8
Thoroton......167 E2
Thorpe......138 F1
Thorpe Salvin......34 A6
Thrumpton......194 C3
Thurgarton......151 D7
Tibshelf......99 A6
Tickhill......8 B8
Tithby......189 C6
Tollerton......186 D1
Torksey......44 B2
Torworth......19 B2
Toton......182 E2
Treswell......42 C3
Trowell......170 C5
Tuxford......66 B2

U

Upper Broughton......210 B2
Upper Langwith......72 D8
Upton......122 F1

W

Walesby......64 A1
Walkeringham......13 F5

Walkerith......14 D7
Wallingwells......25 C5
Warsop Vale......73 D4
Watnall......159 A8
Wellow......77 E1
West Bridgford......186 A7
West Drayton......51 A2
West Hallam......157 A1
West Leake......205 A1
West Markham......65 B6
Weston......81 B4
West Stockwith......7 D2
Westwood......128 C3
Whaley......59 D4
Whaley Thorns......59 A2
Whatton......179 A3
Whitwell......45 B6
Widmerpool......208 B5
Wilford......185 B6
Willoughby-on-the-
Wolds......217 D8
Winkburn......108 A1
Winthorpe......125 D6
Wollaton......171 E4
Woodbeck......53 A8
Woodborough......149 C3
Woodthorpe......161 E5
Worksop......35 C5
Wymeswold......216 C4
Wysall......207 D3

Z

Zouch......213 B3

Index of streets, hospitals, industrial estates, railway stations, schools, shopping centres, universities and places of interest

1st Ave NG7......173 B8
2nd Ave NG7......173 B8
3rd Ave NG7......173 B8
4th Ave NG7......173 B8

A

Aaron Cl NG11......185 B7
Abba Cl NG16......158 F7
Abbey Bridge NG7......172 E2
Abbey Cir NG2......186 A7
Abbey Cl
  Aslockton NG13......178 F5
  Hucknall NG15......145 E2
Abbey Ct
  Beeston NG9......183 F8
  Mansfield NG18......102 F7
  Nottingham NG7......222 B2
Abbeydale Dr NG18......102 D3
Abbey Dr NG2......183 F7
Abbey Gates Prim Sch
  NG15......117 A1
Abbey Gr NG3......173 F7
Abbey La NG13......178 F5
Abbey Rd
  Beeston NG9......183 F7
  Bingham NG13......178 A4
  Blidworth NG21......118 B5
  Eastwood NG16......144 B2
  Edwinstowe NG21......91 C8
  Kirkby in A NG17......115 D5
  Mansfield NG18......102 E7
  Mattersey DN10......20 C1
  Newstead NG15......130 E6
  West Bridgford NG2......186 A6
Abbey Road Prim Sch
  NG2......186 A6
Abbey St
  Ilkeston DE7......157 F2
  Nottingham NG7......172 E2
  Worksop S80......35 F2
Abbot Cl NG12......197 E4
Abbotsbury Cl NG5......146 E1
Abbots Cl NG5......161 D6
Abbots Dr NG15......115 A4
Abbotsford Dr NG3......223 F4
Abbotsford Mews DE7......157 D3
Abbots Rd NG15......145 E6
Abbot St NG16......158 C4
Abbots Wlk NG15......145 E6
Abbott Lea NG19......101 D8
Abbotts Cres NG22......119 F7
Abbotts Croft NG19......87 E1
Abbott St NG10......193 D6
Abbotts Way NG8......172 A4
Abbott's Way NG8......125 B1
Abel Collin's Homes
  NG8......171 E1
Abercarn Cl NG6......160 B7
Aberconway St NG21......118 A5
Aberdeen St 3 NG3......173 E5
Aberford Ave NG8......172 D8
Abingdon Dr NG11......196 D8
Abingdon Gdns
  Arnold NG5......162 B5
  Beeston NG9......183 D4

Abingdon Rd NG2......186 A7
Abingdon Sq NG8......160 B1
Abingdon View S81......35 C8
Abington Ave NG17......100 F5
Ablard Gdns 6 NG9......183 C2
Acacia Ave
  Annesley Woodhouse
    NG17......130 A8
  Gainsborough DN21......15 D1
Acacia Cl
  Hucknall NG15......146 B5
  Worksop S80......35 C2
Acacia Cres NG4......162 F1
Acacia Ct NG10......182 C5
Acacia Gdns NG16......158 F8
Acacia Rd NG24......140 D5
Acacia Wlk NG9......183 F6
Academy Cl NG6......160 D2
Acaster Cl NG9......184 B4
Acer Cl NG16......113 C3
Ackford Dr S80......35 D3
Acland St DN21......15 C1
Acle Gdns NG6......158 B8
Acorn Ave NG16......158 B8
Acorn Bank NG2......185 B4
Acorn Bsns Pk 11 NG18......102 B6
Acorn Dr NG4......163 A2
Acorn Pk NG7......184 E8
Acorn Ridge NG20......72 D5
Acorn Way NG18......103 B4
Acourt St NG7......222 B4
Acreage La NG20......72 F2
Acre Edge Rd NG22......78 F2
Acre The NG17......115 B3
Acton Ave
  Long Eaton NG10......193 E6
  Nottingham NG6......160 D4
Acton Cl NG10......193 E6
Acton Gr NG10......193 E6
Acton Rd
  Arnold NG5......161 E7
  Long Eaton NG10......193 E6
  Nottingham NG5......160 E4
Acton Rd Ind Est NG10......193 E6
Acton St NG10......193 E5
Adams Ct DE7......157 E3
Adams Hill
  Keyworth NG12......197 F3
  Nottingham NG7......172 C2
Adam St DE7......170 A6
Adamsway NG18......103 A3
Adams Way DN21......44 C8
Adbolton Ave NG4......162 E1
Adbolton Gr NG2......174 B1
Adbolton La NG12......174 D1
Adderley Cl NG5......161 A6
Addington Ct NG12......176 A4
Addington Rd NG7......222 B4
Addison Dr NG15......145 F8
Addison Rd NG4......174 B8
Addison St
  Nottingham NG1......223 D4
  Tibshelf DE55......99 A7
Addison Villas NG16......143 E1
Adelaide Cl
  Gainsborough DN21......24 F6
  Stapleford NG9......170 F1
Adelaide Gr NG5......160 E8

Adel Dr NG4......162 E1
Adenburgh Dr NG9......183 D1
Adrian Cl NG9......182 F1
Adrians Cl NG18......102 E5
Advance Bsns Ctr LE12......220 A2
Adwalton Cl 7 NG24......140 E8
Aegir Cl NG21......24 F6
Aeneas Ct 6 NG5......173 B8
Aerial Way NG15......145 F5
Agnes Villas NG3......161 E2
Aidan Gdns NG5......147 A2
Ainsdale Cres NG8......160 A3
Ainsdale Gn DN22......39 D3
Ainsley Rd NG8......172 D6
Ainsworth Dr NG2......173 B1
Aintree Cl NG16......158 E7
Aira Cl NG2......186 D6
Airdale Ave NG5......161 A1
Airedale 6 NG1......36 A7
Airedale Cl NG10......193 A6
Airedale Ct NG9......183 A4
Airedale Wlk NG8......171 C3
Aisby Wlk DN21......24 F7
Aitchison Ave NG15......145 F7
Ajanta Cl NG9......170 E1
Alandale Ave NG20......72 F5
Alandene Ave NG16......159 A7
Albany Cl
  Arnold NG5......161 E7
  Hucknall NG15......145 C5
  Mansfield Woodhouse NG19......88 C1
Albany Ct NG9......170 E1
Albany Dr NG19......88 C1
Albany Inf Sch NG9......182 E8
Albany Jun Sch NG9......182 E8
Albany Pl NG7......173 A8
Albany St
  Gainsborough DN21......15 C2
  Ilkeston DE7......170 A6
Albemarle Rd NG5......161 D4
Alberta Ave NG16......129 A7
Alberta Terr NG7......173 A8
Albert Ave
  Balderton NG24......140 C4
  Carlton NG4......174 B7
  Nottingham NG8......172 D8
  Nuthall NG16......159 E4
  Stapleford NG9......182 D7
  Westwood NG16......128 B4
Albert Ball Cl NG5......160 F8
Albert Dr NG7......222 B3
Albert Hall NG1......223 D2
Albert Pl LE11......220 B3
Albert Rd
  Beeston NG9......184 B7
  Bunny NG11......196 E1
  Long Eaton NG10......193 D8
  Nottingham, Alexander Park
    NG3......173 D8
  Nottingham NG7......222 A1
  Retford DN22......39 E6
  Sandiacre NG10......182 B6
  West Bridgford NG2......185 F8
Albert St NG12......100 E2
Albert Sq
  Bottesford NG13......181 A3

Albert St continued
  Carlton NG4......162 F1
  Eastwood NG16......143 F3
  Hucknall NG15......146 B7
  Loughborough LE11......220 B3
  Mansfield NG18......102 B6
  Market Warsop NG20......74 A5
  Newark-on-T NG24......139 F8
  Nottingham NG1......223 E2
  Radcliffe on T NG12......175 F3
  South Normanton DE55......113 B6
  Stanton Hill NG17......100 C6
  Stapleford NG9......35 F3
  Worksop S80......35 F3
Albine Rd NG20......72 E6
Albion Cl S80......35 F3
Albion Rd
  Long Eaton NG10......193 F8
  Sutton in A NG17......100 F2
Albion Rise NG5......147 F1
Albion St
  Beeston NG9......183 F7
  Ilkeston DE7......157 F1
  Mansfield NG19......87 F1
  Newark-on-T NG24......139 F8
  Nottingham NG1......223 E1
Albion Terr DN10......7 B1
Albury Dr NG8......160 B1
Albury Sq NG7......222 C2
Alcester St NG7......184 E8
Alcock Ave NG18......102 E7
Aldene Ct NG9......183 D5
Aldene Way NG14......149 C4
Aldercar Com Lang Coll
  NG16......143 A4
Aldercar Flash Nature
  Reserve NG16......143 B6
Aldercar Inf Sch NG16......143 A4
Aldercar La NG16......143 A6
Alder Cl
  Mansfield NG19......88 D1
  New Balderton NG24......140 C5
  Shirebrook NG20......72 E5
  Worksop S80......35 E1
Alder Ct NG19......101 D5
Alder Gdns NG6......160 A7
Alder Gr
  Mansfield Woodhouse
    NG19......88 B5
  New Ollerton NG22......77 D5
Alderman Pounder Inf Sch
  NG9......183 B5
Alderman White Sch
  NG9......183 C7
Aldermens Cl NG2......173 C2
Alderney St NG7......222 B1
Alderson Cl DN11......8 B8
Alderson Dr DN11......8 B8
Alderson Rd S80......35 E1
Aldred's 6 DN21......15 F1
Alderton Rd NG5......161 C6
Alder Way
  Keyworth NG12......198 A2
  Shirebrook NG20......72 D4
  Sutton in A NG17......100 D3
Aldgate Cl NG6......160 A8
Aldred's La DE75......143 D2

Aldridge Cl NG9......182 E2
Aldrin Cl NG6......159 F5
Aldworth Cl NG5......161 C6
Aldwych Cl
  Nottingham NG5......147 A1
  Nuthall NG16......159 D2
Alec Rose Gr DN21......24 F7
Alexander Ave
  Newark-on-T NG24......125 B4
  Selston NG16......128 D7
Alexander Cl NG15......131 B1
Alexander Rd
  Farnsfield NG22......119 F6
  Nottingham NG7......222 C2
Alexander Terr NG16......113 C1
Alexandra Ave
  Mansfield NG18......102 B4
  Mansfield Woodhouse NG19......88 B5
  Sutton in A NG17......100 F4
Alexandra Cres NG9......184 A6
Alexandra Rd
  Bircotes DN11......9 B4
  Long Eaton NG10......193 D8
Alexandra St
  Kirkby in A NG17......115 B6
  Market Warsop NG20......74 A5
  Nottingham NG5......173 B8
  Stapleford NG9......182 D6
Alexandra Terr NG17......100 C6
Alford Cl NG9......184 B5
Alford Rd NG2......186 B5
Alfred Ave NG3......162 A2
Alfred Cl NG3......223 E4
Alfred Ct 4 NG18......102 B7
Alfred St Central NG3......223 E4
Alfred St N NG3......223 E4
Alfred St S NG3......173 E5
Alfred St
  Gainsborough DN21......15 C1
  Kirkby in A NG17......115 A4
  Loughborough LE11......220 B5
  Pinxton NG16......113 C4
  Sutton in A NG17......100 F4
Alfreton Rd
  Huthwaite NG17......113 F1
  Newton DE55......99 A3
  Nottingham NG7......222 B4
  Pinxton NG16......113 C4
  Selston, Selston Green DE55,
    NG16......128 C6
  Selston, Underwood NG16......129 B3
  South Normanton DE55......113 A5
  Sutton in A NG17......100 E3
Allcroft St NG19......88 C4
Allenby Rd NG25......136 C8
Allen Cl NG23......156 D7
Allendale Ave
  Beeston NG9......183 D2
  Nottingham NG8......160 A1
Allendale Rd NG21......118 B8
Allendale Way NG19......88 E1
Allen Dr NG18......102 F5

1st–All

Allen Field Ct NG7..........**222** B1
Allen Rd NG23.............. **142** D2
Allen's Gn Ave NG16 .....**128** F6
Allen St
  Hucknall NG15..........**146** A8
  Worksop S80..............**35** E3
Allen's Wlk NG15...........**147** F1
Allesford La NG22..........**120** B4
All Hallows CE Prim Sch **2**
  NG4........................**162** F1
All Hallows Cl DN22........**39** E4
All Hallows Dr NG4.........**162** F2
All Hallows St DN22........**39** E4
Alliance St NG24............**125** A2
Allington Ave NG7..........**222** B1
Allington Dr NG19...........**101** D7
Allison Ave DN22 ....**40** B3
Allison Gdns NG9...........**183** D4
All Saints CE Inf Sch
  NG17........................**99** F2
All Saints Prim Sch
  NG23......................**153** D5
All Saints RC Comp Sch
  NG19......................**101** F8
All Saints' St NG7..........**222** C4
All Saints' Terr NG7 ....**222** C4
Allsopp Dr S81..............**35** D8
Allsopp's La LE11..........**220** D5
Allwood Dr NG4.............**174** E8
Allwood Gdns NG15........**146** B6
Alma Cl
  Carlton NG4..............**163** A2
  Nottingham NG1.........**223** E4
Alma Hill NG16...............**158** F7
Alma Rd
  Nottingham NG3.........**173** F6
  Retford DN22..............**40** A7
  Selston NG16..............**129** A5
Alma St NG7................**173** A8
Almond Ave NG20...........**72** E5
Almond Cl
  Hucknall NG15..........**146** B5
  Kimberley NG16..........**158** E7
  Saxilby LN1................**57** B4
Almond Gr
  Farndon NG24 ....**139** A5
  6 Kirkby in A NG17 ......**114** F6
  Worksop S80..............**35** E1
Almond Rise NG19..........**88** E1
Almond Wlk NG4............**163** A2
Alnwick Cl NG6..............**160** D6
Alpha Terr NG1..............**223** D4
Alpine Cres NG4.............**174** D8
Alpine Ct S80................**35** C2
Alpine St NG6................**160** E2
Alport Pl NG18...............**103** B7
Althea Ct **1** NG7.............**161** A1
Althorpe St NG7.............**222** C3
Alton Ave NG11..............**185** B4
Alton Cl NG11................**185** C3
Alton Dr NG16................**158** B8
Alum Ct NG5.................**160** F8
Alvenor St DE7...............**157** F1
Alverstone Rd NG3..........**161** C1
Alvey Rd NG24...............**140** E4
Alwood Gr NG11.............**184** D2
Alwyn Rd NG8................**159** F2
Amanda Ave S81.............**25** E6
Amanda Rd DN11............**8** F4
Amber Cl NG21...............**104** C1
Amber Dr NG16..............**143** B2
Ambergate Rd NG8..........**172** A7
Amber Hill NG5..............**161** B7
Amberley St NG1.............**223** D2
Amber St NG18...............**102** C5
Ambleside
  New Ollerton NG22.......**77** C5
  West Bridgford NG2 ......**186** C7
Ambleside Dr NG16 ....**143** D3
Ambleside Grange S81......**35** F8
Ambleside Inf Sch NG8 ...**160** B1
Ambleside Jun Sch NG8 ...**160** A1
Ambleside Rd NG8...........**160** A1
Ambleside Way NG4 ....**175** B8
Amcott Ave DN10...........**14** A8
Amcott Way DN22...........**39** E7
Amen Cnr NG24..............**140** B3
Amen Cnr Karting NG22....**91** E7
American Adventure Theme
  Pk The DE75...............**157** B5
Amersham Rise NG8........**160** B1
Amesbury Circ NG8.........**160** A3
Amethyst Cl NG1............**104** C1
Amhurst Rise S81............**35** D8
Amos La NG23................**98** D4
Ampthill Rise NG5...........**161** B4
Anastasia Cl DN21..........**15** C3
Ancaster Gdns NG8.........**172** A4
Anchor Cl NG8...............**160** D2
Anchor Rd NG16.............**143** D2
Anders Dr NG6...............**159** F5
Anderson Cl NG24...........**140** B3
Anderson Cres NG9.........**183** E8
Anderson Rd DN21..........**24** F7
Andover Cl **1** NG8..........**172** B6
Andover Rd
  Mansfield NG19...........**101** D7
  Nottingham NG5..........**160** C5
Andrew Ave
  Ilkeston DE7...............**170** B7
  Nottingham NG3.........**162** A2
Andrew Dr NG21.............**118** A4
Andrews Dr NG16............**143** A3
Anfield Cl NG3...............**183** A2

Anford Cl NG6..............**160** B5
Angela Ave NG17 ....**115** B1
Angela Cl NG5................**147** E2
Angel Alley NG1..............**223** F2
Angel Gn NG11...............**195** C8
Angel Row NG1...............**223** D2
Angel Row Gall NG1 ....**223** D2
Angel Yd LE11................**220** B4
Anglia Way NG8..............**103** B3
Angrave Cl NG3..............**173** E7
Angus Cl
  Arnold NG5.................**148** B1
  Kimberley NG16..........**159** A5
Anmer Cl **2** NG2............**173** B1
Annan Ct NG8................**172** B8
Anne's Cl NG3................**162** A2
Annesley Cutting NG15....**130** C7
Annesley Gr NG1.............**223** D4
Annesley La NG16............**129** B6
Annesley Prim Sch NG17 **130** B8
Annesley Rd
  Hucknall NG15...........**145** F8
  West Bridgford NG2 ......**185** F7
Annesley Way NG19.........**101** D6
Annesley Woodhouse Quarry
  Nature Reserve NG17.....**129** D2
Annie Holgate Inf Sch
  NG15......................**145** F6
Annies Cl NG15..............**145** F5
Annies Wharf LE11..........**220** B5
Anson Wlk DE7...............**157** F3
Anstee Rd NG10.............**193** C4
Anstey Rise NG3.............**173** F5
Anston Ave S81...............**35** E5
Anthony Bek Prim Sch
  NG19........................**88** F6
Antill St NG9.................**182** D6
Apley Cl DN21................**24** F7
Apollo Dr NG6................**159** F5
Appin Rd NG19...............**101** D5
Appleby Cl NG24.............**140** D8
Appleby Ct S81...............**35** F8
Appleby Rd NG19.............**86** F6
Appledore Ave NG8.........**171** E2
Appledorne Way NG5.......**147** E1
Appleton Dr LE12............**216** B3
Appleton Gate NG24........**125** A1
Appleton Rd
  Beeston NG9..............**184** B4
  Blidworth NG21...........**118** B5
Appleton St NG20............**74** B4
Appletree Cl NG25...........**121** E1
Apple Tree Cl NG12.........**186** A4
Apple Tree La NG4...........**162** F2
Apple Wlk NG4...............**174** A8
Applewood Cl S81............**35** D8
Applewood Gr NG5...........**161** D3
Arboretum St NG1...........**223** D4
Arbrook Dr NG8..............**172** D6
Arbutus Cl NG11............**184** C1
Arcade The NG24............**139** F8
Arcadia Ave NG20............**72** E5
Archbishop Cranmer CE Prim
  Sch NG13..................**178** F5
Archdale Rd NG5.............**161** C6
Archer Cres NG8..............**171** F5
Archer Rd NG9...............**182** E5
Archers Dr NG22.............**106** A5
Archer St DE7................**157** E3
Arches The LE12.............**205** E2
Arch Hill NG5.................**147** E3
Archway Rd NG21............**90** D7
A Rd NG9.....................**184** C6
Arden Cl
  Beeston NG9..............**184** A8
  Hucknall NG15...........**146** C5
Arden Gr NG13...............**177** C5
Ardleigh Cl NG5..............**146** D1
Ardmore Cl NG2..............**173** F3
Ardsley Cl DE75..............**143** A2
Argosy Cl DN11................**9** F8
Argyle Cl NG20...............**73** F4
Argyle Ct NG7................**222** B3
Argyle St
  Langley Mill NG16........**143** C4
  Mansfield NG18...........**102** E6
  Nottingham NG7..........**222** B3
Ariel Cl NG6..................**160** F5
Arkers Cl NG6.................**160** D3
Arklow Cl NG8................**160** B3
Arkwright St
  Gainsborough DN21......**15** C1
  Nottingham NG2.........**173** C1
Arkwright Wlk NG2..........**173** C2
Arleston Dr NG8..............**171** D4
Arlington Ave NG17.........**88** E4
Arlington Cl NG15...........**146** A4
Arlington Dr NG3.............**161** C2
Arlington Way DN22.........**39** F7
Armadale Cl NG5.............**162** C8
Armfield Rd NG5..............**162** C8
Armitage Cl **3** LE11.........**220** A4
Armitage Dr NG10...........**194** A7
Armstrong Rd
  Mansfield NG19...........**101** D7
  Nottingham NG6.........**159** F5
  Retford DN22..............**39** F7
Arncliff Cl NG8................**171** C4
Arndale Rd NG5..............**161** C5
Arne Ct **5** NG2.............**173** C1
Arnesby Rd NG7.............**222** A1
Arno Ave **2** NG7...........**173** B8
Arnold Ave

Arnold Ave *continued*
  Southwell NG25..........**121** E1
Arnold Cres NG10...........**193** A4
Arnold Hill Sch NG5 ....**162** A6
Arnold La NG3................**162** D4
Arnold L Ctr NG5............**161** E8
Arnold Rd NG5...............**161** A5
Arnold View Prim Sch
  NG5........................**161** F7
Arnos Gr NG8................**159** D3
Arnot Hill Rd NG5 ....**161** E6
Arno Vale Gdns NG5.........**161** E5
Arno Vale Jun Sch NG5....**161** F5
Arno Vale Rd NG5............**161** F5
Arnside NG9..................**182** E5
Arnside Cl NG5...............**161** B5
Arnside Rd NG5..............**161** B5
Arran Cl NG9..................**170** E2
Arran Sq NG19................**101** D5
Arthur Ave
  Nottingham NG7.........**222** B2
  Stapleford NG9...........**182** F8
Arthur Cres NG4.............**174** C7
Arthur Gn Ave NG17........**114** E1
Arthur Mee Rd NG9.........**182** E5
Arthur Short Cl S80.........**45** A6
Arthur St
  Carlton NG4...............**175** A6
  Mansfield NG18...........**102** C6
  Nottingham NG7..........**222** C4
  Pinxton NG16.............**113** D3
Artic Way NG16..............**158** D7
Arum Croft DN22............**39** D4
Arun Dale NG19...............**88** D2
Arundel Cl
  Gainsborough DN21......**15** C2
  Sandiacre NG10...........**182** B4
Arundel Dr
  Beeston NG9..............**171** B1
  Carlton in L S81..........**25** F6
  Mansfield NG19...........**101** F8
  Ranskill DN22...............**19** B5
Arundel St NG7...............**222** C3
Arundel Way DN22...........**39** C8
Arundel Wlk DN11............**9** B5
Ascot Ave NG16..............**158** E7
Ascot Cl NG17................**115** C3
Ascot Dr
  Arnold NG5.................**161** D8
  Hucknall NG15...........**145** D5
Ascot Pk Est NG10...........**182** B4
Ascot Rd NG8.................**172** D7
Ascott Gdns NG2.............**185** B4
Ashbourne Cl NG9 ....**171** A1
Ashbourne Ct NG6..........**159** F6
Ashbourne St
  Nottingham NG7.........**222** C3
  Shirebrook NG20..........**72** F4
Ashburnham Ave NG7......**222** B2
Ashby Ave NG19..............**88** D5
Ashby Rd
  Kegworth DE74...........**203** A2
  Kegworth DE74...........**203** B2
  Long Whatton LE12 ......**212** C1
  Loughborough LE11.......**220** A4
Ashby Sq LE11................**220** A4
Ashchurch Dr NG8...........**171** D2
Ash Cl
  Bingham NG13.............**178** A4
  Burton Joyce NG14.......**163** E4
  Pinxton NG16.............**145** C5
  Pinxton NG16.............**113** D2
  Worksop S80...............**35** E1
Ash Cres
  Kirkby in A NG17.........**114** D6
  Nuthall NG16..............**159** B6
Ashcroft DN22................**39** D4
Ashcroft Rd DN21...........**24** D6
Ashdale Ave NG17...........**114** D7
Ashdale Rd
  Arnold NG5................**162** A8
  Ilkeston DE7...............**170** A6
  Nottingham NG3.........**174** B6
Ashdown Cl NG11...........**185** B6
Ashdown Gr NG13...........**177** D3
Ashdown Way DN10..........**6** E1
Ashe Cl NG5..................**162** B7
Asher La NG11...............**196** C6
Ashes Pk Ave S81............**35** D8
Ash Gr
  Brinsley NG16.............**143** D8

Ash Gr *continued*
  Gainsborough DN21 ......**15** D2
  Hathern LE12...............**213** A1
  Keyworth NG12...........**198** A2
  Long Eaton NG10.........**193** C6
  Sandiacre NG10...........**182** A7
  Selston NG16..............**128** F7
  Shirebrook NG20..........**72** D5
  Stapleford NG9...........**182** D5
  Sutton in A NG17.........**100** D7
  Woodborough NG14 ......**149** C4
Ash Holt Dr S81...............**35** F8
Ashington Dr NG5 ....**148** A2
Ash La NG12..................**206** C4
Ashland Rd NG17............**100** C3
Ashland Rd W NG17.........**100** B3
Ashlands Cl NG17............**100** B3
Ashlea DN10....................**6** E2
Ash Lea Cl NG12..............**187** F2
Ash Lea Specl Sch NG12 **187** F2
Ashleigh Way NG19.........**89** D5
Ashley Cl NG9.................**183** D6
Ashley Cres NG12............**197** F3
Ashley Ct S81.................**35** F5
Ashley La NG15...............**145** E7
Ashley La DN22................**41** F2
Ashley Rd
  Keyworth NG12...........**197** E3
  Worksop S81...............**35** F3
Ashley St **7** NG3............**173** E5
Ashley Terr S80................**35** F3
Ashling St NG2...............**173** D2
Ashmore Ave NG17..........**100** C2
Ash Mount Rd NG16.........**143** B3
Ashmount Sch LE11.........**220** A1
Ashness Cl NG2..............**186** C6
Ashover Cl
  Nottingham NG3.........**173** E8
  Ravenshead NG15........**117** B3
Ash Rd NG24.................**139** F4
Ashridge Way NG12.........**186** C4
Ash St DE7....................**157** E4
Ashton Ave NG5..............**147** F2
Ashton Ct NG17...............**101** A5
Ash Tree Ave
  Bawtry DN10..................**9** F7
  Mansfield Woodhouse NG19 **88** C5
Ash Tree Cl NG25............**136** D8
Ash Tree Sq NG9.............**183** B8
Ashvale Rd NG22.............**66** A2
Ash Vale Rd NG22.............**64** A2
Ashview Cl NG10.............**193** A8
Ash Villas **1** NG3............**161** B1
Ashville Cl NG2...............**173** A1
Ashwater Dr NG3............**162** D5
Ashwell Ave NG19...........**88** E5
Ashwell Gdns NG7...........**172** E8
Ashwell St NG4...............**174** F6
Ashwick Cl NG11............**185** A5
Ash Wlk LE12.................**214** D8
Ashwood Ave NG17.........**115** C6
Ashwood Cl NG19............**88** E5
Ashwood Rd S80...............**35** B2
Ashworth Ave NG11.........**196** C8
Ashworth Bsns Ctr NG1 **223** F4
Ashworth Cl
  Newark-on-T NG24 ......**140** D8
  Nottingham NG3.........**174** C5
Ashworth Cres
  North Leverton w H DN22 **32** C1
  Nottingham NG3.........**162** B2
Ashworth Dr NG19..........**88** E4
Askeby Dr NG8...............**159** D1
Askew La NG20...............**74** A3
Askham La NG22.............**52** B5
Askham Rd NG22.............**51** F1
Aslockton Dr NG8............**160** D2
Aslockton Sta NG13.........**179** A4
Aspen Cl
  Bingham NG13.............**178** A4
  Laughterton LN1...........**55** B4
  Tuxford NG22..............**66** A2
  Walesby NG22.............**64** A2
Aspen Ct
  Gainsborough DN21 ......**15** F2
  Mansfield NG19...........**88** E1
  Tuxford NG22..............**66** A2
Aspen Rd NG6.................**159** F7
Aspen St NG4.................**175** A7
Aspinall Ct **2** NG8...........**172** C8
Aspley La NG8................**172** C8
Aspley Pk Dr NG8............**172** B8
Aspley Pl NG17...............**100** D3

Ash Gr
  Brinsley NG16.............**143** D8

Atherton Rise NG8.........**160** B3
Athorpe Gr NG6..............**160** E3
Atkin La NG18................**102** B3
Attenborough La NG9......**183** C3
Attenborough Nature
  Reserve NG9..............**183** E1
Attenborough Prep Sch
  NG9........................**183** E1
Attenborough Sta NG9 ...**183** E1
Attercliffe Terr **8** NG2...**173** C1
Attewell Rd NG16............**158** B5
Attlee Ave NG19................**89** A1
Aubrey Ave **4** NG2.........**173** E4
Aubrey Rd NG5...............**161** B2
Auckland Cl NG7.............**222** A3
Auckland Rd
  Hucknall NG15...........**145** D5
  Retford DN22...............**39** C8
Audley Cl DE7................**157** D3
Audley Dr NG9................**171** F1
Audon Ave NG9...............**183** E5
Audrey Cres NG19............**88** C5
Augustine Gdns NG5.......**147** A1
Ault Hucknall La S44.........**86** A7
Aumberry Gap LE11.........**220** B4
Aurillac Way DN22............**29** D2
Austen Ave
  Long Eaton NG10.........**193** C5
  Nottingham NG7.........**173** A7
Austin Cl NG18...............**102** E8
Austins Dr NG10.............**182** B4
Austin St
  Nottingham NG6.........**160** C7
  Shirebrook NG20..........**73** A4
Austrey Ave NG9.............**184** A8
Autumn Cft Rd NG24.......**125** D1
Avalon Cl NG6................**160** E6
Ave A NG1....................**223** F2
Ave B NG1....................**223** F2
Avebury Cl NG11.............**195** D8
Ave C NG1....................**223** F2
Ave D NG1....................**173** E4
Ave E **4** NG1.................**173** E5
Avenue Cl NG5...............**160** F8
Avenue Rd DN22..............**39** F5
Avenue The
  Calverton NG14...........**148** F7
  Gainsborough DN21 ......**15** E2
  Gunthorpe NG14..........**164** F6
  Mansfield NG18...........**102** E3
  Newark-on-T NG24 ......**140** B7
  Sutton in A NG17.........**100** C1
Averham Cl NG19............**101** D6
Averton Sq NG8..............**172** D3
Aviemore Cl NG5.............**162** B8
Avocet Cl
  Bingham NG13.............**178** A3
  Hucknall NG15...........**131** B1
Avocet Gr S81.................**35** C5
Avocet Wharf **6** NG7....**172** F2
Avon Ave NG15...............**145** E4
Avonbridge Cl NG5 ....**148** C1
Avon Cl NG17................**129** F8
Avondale
  Cotgrave NG12............**188** A3
  Mansfield NG18...........**102** E7
Avondale Cl NG10...........**193** A6
Avondale Rd NG4............**175** B8
Avon Gdns NG2..............**185** F7
Avon Pl NG9..................**184** A7
Avon Rd
  Carlton NG4...............**162** F2
  Nottingham NG3.........**174** B5
Avon Rise DN22..............**40** A7
Avon Vale Rd LE11...........**220** C1
Avon Way
  Mansfield NG18...........**103** A5
  Worksop S81...............**35** E7
Awsworth La NG16..........**158** D4
Awsworth Prim Sch
  NG16......................**158** C4
Awsworth Rd DE7...........**157** F2
Axford Cl NG4................**162** F2
Aylesham Ave NG5..........**161** F4
Aylestone Dr NG8............**172** B8
Ayr St NG7...................**222** C4
Ayscough Ave NG16.........**159** C6
Ayton Cl NG2.................**173** B2
Ayton Gdns NG9.............**183** C2
Azalea Ct NG16...............**158** C8
Azimghur Rd NG13..........**179** A4

B

Babbacombe Cl NG5........**161** B4
Babbacombe Way NG5....**145** D2
Babbington Cres NG4......**162** E2
Babbington La NG16........**158** F4
Babington Ct NG7...........**222** B3
Babworth Cres DN22........**39** C6
Babworth Ct NG18...........**102** D7
Babworth Rd DN22..........**39** B6
Back La
  Claypole NG23............**156** D6
  Cotes LE12.................**220** F6
  Cropwell Butler NG12 ....**189** A6
  Eakring NG22..............**106** E8
  East Markham NG22......**66** A7
  Halam NG22................**120** F2
  Huthwaite NG17...........**99** F3
  Ilkeston DE7...............**157** F2
  Long Clawson LE14 ....**211** C3
  Misson DN10................**4** B2
  Morton NG25...............**137** C3

Back La continued
North Clifton NG23 . . . . .68 E5
Nuthall NG16 . . . . .159 D6
Ollerton NG22 . . . . .77 B3
Ranskill DN22 . . . . .19 A4
Sutton in A NG17 . . . . .100 F6
Thorpe Salvin S80 . . . . .34 A6
Willoughby-on-t-W LE12 . .217 D7

Back St
Barnby in t W NG4 . . . . .142 A5
East Stockwith DN21 . . . . .7 D1
South Clifton NG23 . . . . .68 E1

Back Terr DN22 . . . . .39 F8
Bacon Cl NG16 . . . . .158 A8
Bacon St DN21 . . . . .24 D6
Bacton Ave NG6 . . . . .160 B8
Bacton Gdns 🔟 NG6 . . . . . . .160 B8
Baden Powell Rd NG2 . . . . . .174 A4
Bader NG11 . . . . .185 B7
Bader Rise DN10 . . . . .20 A8
Bader View DN10 . . . . .20 A8
Badger Cl NG15 . . . . .145 C6
Badgers Chase DN22 . . . . .29 F1
Badger Way NG19 . . . . .103 B7
Baggaley Cres NG19 . . . . .88 B1
Bagnall Ave NG5 . . . . .161 C7
Bagnall Rd NG6 . . . . .160 C4
Bagshaw St NG19 . . . . .87 B4
Bagthorpe Cl NG5 . . . . .161 A3
Baildon Cl NG8 . . . . .172 C3
Bailey Brook Cres NG16 . . . .143 A4
Bailey Brook Dr NG16 . . . . . .143 A3
Bailey Brook Wlk NG16 . . . . .143 A3
Bailey Cl NG5 . . . . .161 D7
Bailey Cres NG19 . . . . .101 E7
Bailey Ct NG12 . . . . .175 E2
Bailey Gr Rd NG16 . . . . .143 D2
Bailey La NG12 . . . . .175 E2
Bailey Rd NG4 . . . . .139 F5
Bailey St
Carlton NG4 . . . . .175 A7
Nottingham NG6 . . . . .160 C2
Stapleford NG9 . . . . .182 C6

Bainbridge Rd
Loughborough LE11 . . . . .220 C1
Market Warsop NG20 . . . . .74 B4
Bainbridge Terr NG17 . . . . . .100 D6
Bainbridge The NG14 . . . . . . .149 A7
Baines Ave NG24 . . . . .140 D4
Baines Rd DN21 . . . . .24 F8
Bainton Gr NG7 . . . . .184 F1
Baker Ave NG5 . . . . .148 A2
Baker Brook Ind Pk
NG15 .146 C6
Bakerdale Rd NG3 . . . . .174 B6
Baker La NG12 . . . . .60 A2
Baker Rd
Eastwood NG16 . . . . .144 C1
Mansfield Woodhouse NG19 .88 C6
Bakers Cl NG7 . . . . .222 A4
Baker's Hollow NG14 . . . . . . .187 E3
Baker's La
Colston Bassett NG12 . . . . . . .200 E7
Redmile NG13 . . . . .192 F3
Baker St
Hucknall NG15 . . . . .146 A7
🔟 Ilkeston DE7 . . . . .157 F1
Nottingham NG1 . . . . .173 B7
Bakewell Ave NG4 . . . . .162 E1
Bakewell Cl NG24 . . . . .140 C4
Bakewell Dr NG5 . . . . .160 E7
Bakewell Rd NG10 . . . . .193 E5
Bala Dr NG5 . . . . .161 A7
Balderton Ct NG19 . . . . .101 E7
Balderton Gate NG24 . . . . . .140 A8
Balderton La NG24 . . . . .141 A7
Baldwin Cl NG19 . . . . .89 B2
Baldwin Ct NG7 . . . . .222 B3
Baldwin St
Eastwood NG16 . . . . .144 C1
Nottingham NG7 . . . . .222 C3
Balfour Rd
Nottingham NG7 . . . . .222 B3
Stapleford NG9 . . . . .182 D6
Balfour St
Gainsborough DN21 . . . . .15 C1
Kirkby in A NG17 . . . . .115 C4
Balfron Gdns 🔽 NG2 . . . . . .173 B2
Ballantrae Cl NG5 . . . . .162 B8
Ballater Cl NG19 . . . . .87 E2
Ballerat Cres NG5 . . . . .160 E8
Ballerini Way LN1 . . . . .57 C3
Ball Hill DE55 . . . . .113 C6
Balloon Houses NG9 . . . . . . .171 B4
Balloon Wood Ind Est
NG8 . . . . .171 A4
Balls La NG17 . . . . .115 C2
Ball St NG3 . . . . .173 F7
Balmoral Ave NG2 . . . . .185 E8
Balmoral Cl
Carlton in S81 . . . . .25 F6
Mansfield Woodhouse NG19 .88 D3
Sandiacre NG10 . . . . .182 B3
Balmoral Cres NG8 . . . . .171 C5
Balmoral Ct DN11 . . . . .9 B5
Balmoral Dr
Beeston NG9 . . . . .171 D4
Mansfield NG19 . . . . .87 E2
Newark-on-T NG24 . . . . .140 E8
Radcliffe on T NG15 . . . . .146 B8
Balmoral Rd
Bingham NG13 . . . . .177 C4
Carlton NG4 . . . . .174 F6
Nottingham NG1 . . . . .223 D3
Bamburgh Cl 🔟 NG17 . . . . .114 C7
Bamford Dr NG18 . . . . .103 B6
Bamford St DE55 . . . . .99 A3
Bamkin Cl NG15 . . . . .146 B6

Bampton St 🔠 LE11 . . . . . .220 B3
Banbury Ave NG9 . . . . .182 F3
Banbury Mount 🟦 NG5 . . . .161 C2
Banchory St NG19 . . . . .87 E2
Bancroft La NG18 . . . . .101 F7
Bancroft Rd NG24 . . . . .140 B6
Bancroft St NG6 . . . . .160 C7
Banes Rd NG13 . . . . .178 B4
Bangor Wlk 🔠 NG3 . . . . .173 C7
Bank Ave NG17 . . . . .100 E1
Bank Cl
Creswell S80 . . . . .58 D8
Shirebrook NG20 . . . . .72 F4
Bank End Rd DN10 . . . . .1 C4
Bankfield Dr NG9 . . . . .171 C1
Bank Hill NG14 . . . . .149 A4
Bank Pl NG1 . . . . .223 E2
Banks Ave NG17 . . . . .114 E6
Banks Cres NG5 . . . . .162 B6
Bank Side DN22 . . . . .39 F3
Banks Paddock NG13 . . . . . .177 F4
Banks Rd NG9 . . . . .182 E2
Bank St
Langley Mill NG16 . . . . .143 C3
Long Eaton NG10 . . . . .193 E7
Banks The NG13 . . . . .177 F4
Bankwood Cl NG8 . . . . .160 A1
Bank Yd 🔠 NG6 . . . . .160 B7
Bannerman Rd
Kirkby in A NG17 . . . . .114 F5
Nottingham NG6 . . . . .160 C6
Baptist La NG23 . . . . .111 F8
Barbara Sq NG15 . . . . .130 F1
Barber Cl DE7 . . . . .157 F3
Barber St NG16 . . . . .144 B2
Barbers Wood Cl NG15 . . . .117 A1
Barbrook Cl NG8 . . . . .172 A5
Barbury Dr NG11 . . . . .195 D7
Barclay Ct NG5 . . . . .157 C3
Barden Rd NG3 . . . . .162 A4
Bardfield Gdns NG5 . . . . . . .146 F5
Bardney Dr NG6 . . . . .160 A8
Bardsey Gdns NG5 . . . . .161 A7
Barent Cl NG5 . . . . .160 F6
Barent Wlk NG5 . . . . .160 F6
Bar Gate NG24 . . . . .124 F1
Barker Ave
Sutton in A NG17 . . . . .100 D7
Westwood NG16 . . . . .128 B4
Barker Ave E NG10 . . . . .182 A6
Barker Ave N NG10 . . . . .182 A6
Barker Gate
Hucknall NG15 . . . . .145 F7
Ilkeston DE7 . . . . .157 F2
Nottingham NG1 . . . . .223 F2
Barker Hades Rd S81 . . . . . . .16 B3
Barker Hill NG14 . . . . .150 E2
Barkers Field LE14 . . . . .211 C3
Barker's La NG9 . . . . .183 E4
Barker St NG17 . . . . .99 F4
Barkestone-le-V NG13 . . . . .192 A1
Bottesford NG13 . . . . .181 A1
Barkla Cl NG11 . . . . .195 C8
Barkston Cl NG24 . . . . .140 D3
Bar La NG3 . . . . .160 D2
Bar La Ind Pk NG6 . . . . .160 D2
Barley Croft
South Normanton DE55 . . . . .113 B4
West Bridgford NG2 . . . . .185 C4
Barley Dale Dr NG9 . . . . .170 D2
Barleylands NG11 . . . . .196 C6
Barley Ms NG19 . . . . .88 E6
Barley Wy 🔠 NG24 . . . . .125 B4
Barling Dr DE7 . . . . .157 C2
Barlock Rd NG6 . . . . .160 E4
Barlow Cotts La NG6 . . . . . . .158 B5
Barlow Dr N NG16 . . . . .158 B4
Barlow Dr S NG16 . . . . .158 B4
Barnards Pl LE14 . . . . .211 C3
Barnby Gate NG24 . . . . .140 A8
Barnby La NG23 . . . . .156 C8
Barnby Rd NG24 . . . . .140 A8
Barnby Road Prim Sch
NG24 . . . . .140 B7
Barnby Wlk NG5 . . . . .161 C4
Barn Cl
Cotgrave NG12 . . . . .187 E2
Mansfield NG18 . . . . .102 F5
Worksop S81 . . . . .36 A7
Barn Croft NG9 . . . . .183 B5
Barndale Cl NG2 . . . . .185 C3
Barnes Cres NG17 . . . . .114 E8
Barnes Ct DN22 . . . . .29 C7
Barnes Rd NG5 . . . . .160 E8
Barnet Rd NG3 . . . . .174 B7
Barnett Ct NG12 . . . . .197 E3
Barnfield NG11 . . . . .185 A4
Barnfield Cl LE14 . . . . .212 B4
Barnfield Rd NG23 . . . . .98 B1
Barnsdale Cl LE11 . . . . .220 A5
Barnsley Terr 🟦 NG2 . . . . . .173 C1
Barnstone La NG13 . . . . .191 A5
Barnstone Rd NG13 . . . . . . .190 C2
Barnston Rd NG2 . . . . .174 A5
Barnum Cl NG8 . . . . .171 E5
Barons Cl NG4 . . . . .162 E1
Barons Dr NG22 . . . . .77 F6
Barrack Cotts LE12 . . . . .217 A6
Barrack Rd NG7 . . . . .222 B2
Barrack Row 🔠 LE11 . . . . . .220 B4
Barra Mews 🔟 NG2 . . . . . . .173 B2
Barratt Cl
Beeston NG9 . . . . .183 D1
Cropwell Bishop NG12 . . . . . .189 A4
Barratt Cres NG9 . . . . .183 D2
Barratt La NG9 . . . . .183 D1

Bar Rd DN10 . . . . .23 C7
Bar Rd N DN10 . . . . .23 C8
Bar Rd S DN10 . . . . .23 C8
Barrel Hill Rd NG23 . . . . .96 E7
Barrhead Cl NG5 . . . . .146 E1
Barringer Rd NG18 . . . . .88 D1
Barrington Cl NG12 . . . . .175 E2
Barrique Rd NG7 . . . . .172 E1
Barrowhill Wlk NG18 . . . . . .103 B6
Barrow Rd LE12 . . . . .220 F6
Barrows Gate NG24 . . . . . . .125 B3
Barrows Hill La NG16 . . . . . .128 C5
Barrow Slade NG12 . . . . . . .197 E2
Barrow St LE11 . . . . .220 B3
Barrydale Ave NG9 . . . . .183 F5
Barry St NG6 . . . . .160 B7
Bars Hill LE12 . . . . .206 C1
Bartlow Rd NG8 . . . . .171 D7
Barton Cl
Mansfield Woodhouse
NG19 .89 B1
Ruddington NG11 . . . . .196 B6
Barton La
Barton in F NG11 . . . . .195 A5
Beeston NG9 . . . . .183 C1
Nottingham NG11 . . . . .184 C1
Barton Rd NG10 . . . . .194 A6
Bartons Cl NG16 . . . . .144 C2
Barton St NG9 . . . . .184 A5
Barton Wy NG9 . . . . .183 E5
Barwell Dr NG8 . . . . .159 D1
Basa Cres NG5 . . . . .160 F8
Basford Rd NG6 . . . . .160 D2
Baskin La NG9 . . . . .183 C3
Baslow Ave NG4 . . . . .162 D1
Baslow Cl NG10 . . . . .193 A5
Baslow Dr NG9 . . . . .183 B8
Baslow Way NG18 . . . . .103 B5
Bassetlaw District General
Hospl S81 . . . . .36 A5
Bassetlaw L Ctr S80 . . . . . . .35 F3
Bassetlaw Mus DN22 . . . . . . .39 F7
Bassett Cl NG16 . . . . .144 B1
Bassett Rd NG16 . . . . .144 B1
Bassett Rd NG16 . . . . .158 E7
Bassett The NG20 . . . . .72 E6
Bassingfield La NG12 . . . . . .186 F8
Bastion St NG7 . . . . .222 A3
Bateman Gdns 🔠 NG7 . . . .172 F7
Bateman Rd LE12 . . . . .205 E1
Bateman's Yd NG17 . . . . . . .114 D4
Bath La
Mansfield NG18 . . . . .102 C8
Market Warsop NG19 . . . . . . .73 C2
Bathley La
Little Carlton NG23 . . . . .124 C7
South Muskham NG23 . . . . . .110 B1
Bathley St NG2 . . . . .173 D1
Baths La NG15 . . . . .146 B7
Bath St
Ilkeston DE7 . . . . .157 E1
Nottingham NG1 . . . . .223 F3
Sutton in A NG17 . . . . .100 F4
Bath Street Ctr NG1 . . . . . .225 F5
Bathurst Dr NG8 . . . . .172 A6
Bathurst Terr NG20 . . . . .58 F2
Bathwood Dr
Mansfield NG17, NG18 . . . . .101 E5
Sutton in A NG17, NG18 . . . .101 A2
Batley La NG19 . . . . .86 E4
Baulker La
Blidworth NG21 . . . . .118 E4
Clipstone NG21 . . . . .90 E1
Farnsfield NG22 . . . . .119 A4
Baulk La
Beeston NG9 . . . . .183 A6
Harworth DN11 . . . . .8 F5
Torworth DN22 . . . . .19 A2
Worksop S81 . . . . .35 E5
Baulk The
Clarborough DN22 . . . . .40 E8
Clayworth DN22 . . . . .21 C4
Farnsfield NG22 . . . . .119 A5
Sutton in A NG17, NG19 . . . .101 B6
Baum's La NG18 . . . . .102 C5
Bawtry Cl DN11 . . . . .8 F4
Bawtry Rd
Bawtry DN10 . . . . .10 C8
Bircotes DN10 . . . . .9 C1
Blyth S81 . . . . .18 A6
Everton DN10 . . . . .11 A3
Harworth DN11 . . . . .9 A5
Misson DN10 . . . . .4 A3
Tickhill DN11 . . . . .8 E7
Bawtry Wlk NG3 . . . . .173 F6
Baxter Hill NG19 . . . . .86 F3
Baxter St LE11 . . . . .220 B4
Bayard Ct NG2 . . . . .172 C5
Bayard St DN21 . . . . .15 C1
Bayford Dr NG24 . . . . .140 A8
Bayliss Rd NG4 . . . . .162 D3
Bayswater Rd NG16 . . . . . . .158 F6
Baythorn Rd NG8 . . . . .171 D6
Beacon Dr
Kirkby in A NG17 . . . . .115 C6
Loughborough LE11 . . . . .220 A1
Beacon Hill Conservation
Park NG25 . . . . .121 C1
Beacon Hill Rd
Gringley on t H DN10 . . . . . . .13 A2
Newark-on-T NG24 . . . . .140 C8
Beacon Hill Rise NG3 . . . . . .173 E6
Beacon Hts NG24 . . . . .140 D8
Beacon Rd
Beeston NG9 . . . . .184 B6
Loughborough LE11 . . . . .220 A2

Beaconsfield St continued
Nottingham NG7 . . . . .172 F8
Beacon Vw NG13 . . . . .181 B3
Beacon Vw NG22 . . . . .77 D3
Beacon Way NG24 . . . . .140 D8
Bean Ave S80 . . . . .36 B3
Bean Cl NG6 . . . . .159 F5
Beanford La
Calverton NG14 . . . . .133 F3
Oxton NG25 . . . . .134 A3
Beardall St
🔳 Mansfield NG18 . . . . . . .102 A7
Beardall Street Prim Sch
NG15 .146 B6
Beardsall's Row NG15 . . . . .146 B6
Beardsley Gdns NG2 . . . . . .173 B2
Beardsley Rd NG21 . . . . .76 C1
Beardsmore Gr NG15 . . . . . .130 F1
Beast Mkt Hill
Newark-on-T NG24 . . . . .124 F1
Nottingham NG1 . . . . .223 E2
Beatty Wlk DE7 . . . . .157 F3
Beauclerk Dr NG5 . . . . .160 E8
Beaufit La NG16 . . . . .113 E2
Beaufort Cl NG11 . . . . .185 C3
Beaufort Dr NG9 . . . . .183 C5
Beaufort Gdns NG9 . . . . .9 F7
Beaufort St DN21 . . . . .15 C3
Beaulieu Gdns NG2 . . . . . . .185 C5
Beauly Dr NG19 . . . . .101 D5
Beaumaris Dr
Beeston NG9 . . . . .183 B4
Carlton NG4 . . . . .162 E1
Beaumond Cross NG24 . . . .139 F8
Beaumont Ave NG18 . . . . . .102 F5
Beaumont Cl
Keyworth NG12 . . . . .197 E4
Stapleford NG9 . . . . .170 E1
Beaumont Ct LE11 . . . . .220 A6
Beaumont Gdns NG2 . . . . . .185 D4
Beaumont Rd LE11 . . . . .220 B1
Beaumont Rise S80 . . . . .35 D3
Beaumont St
Gainsborough DN21 . . . . .24 D8
Nottingham NG2 . . . . .173 E4
Beaumont Wlk NG24 . . . . . .125 B2
Beauvale
Annesley Woodhouse
NG17 .129 D8
Hucknall NG15 . . . . .145 E6
Nottingham NG8 . . . . .173 C1
Beauvale Rise NG16 . . . . . . .144 A3
Beaver Pl S80 . . . . .35 F3
Beazley Ave NG18 . . . . .101 F7
Beck Ave NG14 . . . . .148 F8
Beck Cres
Blidworth NG21 . . . . .118 A4
Mansfield NG19 . . . . .101 E7
Beckenham Rd NG7 . . . . . . .222 A4
Becket Sch The NG11 . . . . . .185 A5
Beckett Ave
Carlton in S81 . . . . .25 F7
Gainsborough DN21 . . . . .15 E2
Mansfield NG18 . . . . .101 F7
Beckett Ct NG4 . . . . .162 D3
Beckford Rd NG2 . . . . .173 F3
Beckhampton Ctr NG5 . . . .161 B5
Beckhampton Rd NG5 . . . . .161 A7
Beckingham Ct NG19 . . . . . .101 E7
Beckingham Prim Sch
DN10 .14 B1
Beckingham Rd DN10 . . . . . .14 B3
Beckingthorpe Dr NG13 . . .181 B3
Beck La
Blidworth NG21 . . . . .118 A4
Clayworth DN22 . . . . .21 E4
Farnsfield NG22 . . . . .119 A6
Sutton in A NG17, NG19 . . . .101 A6
Beckland Hill NG22 . . . . .65 F6
Beckley Rd NG8 . . . . .159 F2
Beckon Mdw DN10 . . . . .23 C8
Beckside
Lowdham NG14 . . . . .150 E1
West Bridgford NG2 . . . . .186 C5
Beck St
Carlton NG4 . . . . .174 E6
Nottingham NG1 . . . . .223 F3
Thurgarton NG14 . . . . .151 D7
Bedale S81 . . . . .36 A8
Bedale Ct NG9 . . . . .183 A4
Bedale Rd NG5 . . . . .161 D5
Bedarra Gr NG7 . . . . .222 A2
Bede House La NG24 . . . . . .140 A6
Bede Ling NG2 . . . . .185 C6
Bedford Ave NG16 . . . . .158 C8
Bedford Ct
Beeston NG9 . . . . .183 B5
Bingham NG13 . . . . .178 A4
Carlton NG5 . . . . .162 C4
East Leake LE12 . . . . .214 D8
Gainsborough DN21 . . . . .15 E2
Hucknall NG15 . . . . .146 A4
Huthwaite NG17 . . . . .100 A3

Beech Ave continued
Keyworth NG12 . . . . .198 A2
Kirkby in A NG17 . . . . .114 F5
Long Eaton NG10 . . . . .182 F1
🔳 Mansfield NG18 . . . . . . .102 B6
New Ollerton NG22 . . . . .77 B3
Nottingham, Hyson Green
NG7 . . . . .173 A8
Nottingham, Mapperley
NG3 .162 A4
Nuthall NG16 . . . . .159 B6
Pinxton NG16 . . . . .113 E3
Ravenshead NG15 . . . . .116 F3
Sandiacre NG10 . . . . .182 B7
Tickhill DN11 . . . . .8 B7
Worksop S81 . . . . .35 F6
Beech Cl
Gringley on t H DN10 . . . . .12 F2
Nottingham NG6 . . . . .160 C4
Radcliffe on T NG12 . . . . .175 F2
West Bridgford NG12 . . . . . . .186 A4
Beech Cres
Glapwell S44 . . . . .86 B8
Mansfield Woodhouse
NG19 .88 D2
Beechcroft NG3 . . . . .36 A6
Beech Ct
Nottingham NG3 . . . . .162 A4
Selston NG16 . . . . .129 B3
Beechdale Ave NG17 . . . . . .100 F4
Beechdale Rd
Mansfield Woodhouse
NG19 .89 A2
Nottingham NG8 . . . . .172 B7
Beechdale Swimming Ctr
NG8 .172 C6
Beecher La DN10 . . . . .14 B1
Beeches Rd LE11 . . . . .220 C2
Beeches The
Carlton NG3 . . . . .174 A8
Sutton in A NG17 . . . . .100 D7
Tuxford NG22 . . . . .65 F2
Beech Gr
Blidworth NG21 . . . . .118 C5
Carlton in L S81 . . . . .25 E7
South Normanton DE55 . . . . .113 B5
Beech Hill Ave NG19 . . . . .87 F1
Beech Hill Cres NG19 . . . . . . .87 F1
Beech Hill Dr NG19 . . . . .87 F1
Beech Hill Specl Sch
NG19 .87 F1
Beech Rd
Harworth DN11 . . . . .9 A5
Selston NG16 . . . . .129 B3
Sutton in A NG17 . . . . .100 D7
Beech Tree Ave NG19 . . . . . .88 B5
Beechways DN22 . . . . .39 D4
Beechwood Cl
Mansfield Woodhouse
NG19 .89 A1
Sutton in A NG17 . . . . .101 A5
Beechwood Cres DN22 . . . . .37 F6
Beechwood Dr NG17 . . . . . .101 A5
Beechwood Gr DN22 . . . . . . .38 D6
Beechwood Gr NG17 . . . . . .101 A5
Beechwood Rd
Arnold NG5 . . . . .162 A8
🔳 Kirkby in A NG17 . . . . . .114 F7
Beehive La LN6 . . . . .84 F1
Bee Hive La 🔠 LE11 . . . . . .220 B3
Beehive St NG17 . . . . .100 E1
Beeley Cl NG18 . . . . .103 B6
Beeston Cl NG6 . . . . .146 F4
Beeston Ct NG6 . . . . .160 B8
Beeston Fields Dr NG9 . . . .183 D8
Beeston Fields Prim Sch
NG9 .183 F8
Beeston La NG9 . . . . .184 B8
Beeston Rd
Newark-on-T NG24 . . . . .140 B5
Nottingham NG7 . . . . .172 D1
Beeston Sidings Nature
Reserve NG9 . . . . .184 C2
Beeston Sta NG9 . . . . .184 A5
Beethan Cl NG13 . . . . .177 F4
Beggarlee Pk NG16 . . . . . . .144 B4
Behay Gdns NG23 . . . . .138 C8
Beighton Cl NG12 . . . . .175 F3
Beighton St NG17 . . . . .100 F3
Belconnen Rd NG5 . . . . .161 A5
Belfields Yd DN22 . . . . .120 C4
Belfmoor Cl S80 . . . . .45 A5
Belford Cl NG6 . . . . .159 F8
Belford Ct NG6 . . . . .160 B8
Belfry Cl NG17 . . . . .114 E7
Belfry Way NG2 . . . . .186 C4
Belgrave Ct DN10 . . . . .9 B5
Belgrave Mews NG11 . . . . .185 C3
Belgrave Rd NG6 . . . . .160 A7
Belgrave Sq NG1 . . . . .223 D3
Bella Cl NG23 . . . . .143 B4
Bellamy Rd NG18 . . . . .103 A2
Bellar Gate NG1 . . . . .223 F2
Belle-Isle Rd NG15 . . . . .146 A7
Belleville Dr NG5 . . . . .161 B8
Belle Vue La NG13 . . . . .118 A6
Bell Foundry Mus LE11 . . . .220 C4
Bella La
Collingham NG23 . . . . .111 F8
Nottingham NG1 . . . . .185 A4
Weston NG23 . . . . .81 A5
Bellmore Gdns NG8 . . . . . . .171 D5

Bellsfield Cl S80 45 A5
Bells La NG8 160 A3
Bell St NG4 174 D8
Belmond Cl NG24 139 F5
Belmont Ave NG6 160 C7
Belmont Cl
Beeston NG9 183 B4
Hucknall NG15 146 A4
Mansfield Woodhouse NG19 89 A2
Belmont Rd NG17 115 B1
Belper Ave NG4 162 D1
Belper Cres NG4 162 D1
Belper Rd NG7 172 F7
Belper St NG18 102 D7
Belper Way NG18 102 D7
Belsay Rd NG5 161 A7
Belsford Ct NG16 159 A8
Belton Cl NG10 182 B4
Belton Dr NG2 185 B4
Belton Rd LE11 220 A5
Belton Rd W Extension
LE11 220 A6
Belton St NG7 172 F8
Belt Rd The DN21 15 E3
Belvedere Ave 9 NG7 172 F8
Belvedere St NG18 102 B6
Belvoir Ave NG13 181 A1
Belvoir Cl
Aslockton NG13 178 E3
Long Eaton NG10 193 E5
Belvoir Cres
Langar NG13 190 C2
Newark-on-T NG24 140 A6
Belvoir High Sch NG13 181 A1
Belvoir Hill NG2 173 F4
Belvoir Pl NG24 140 D4
Belvoir Rd
Balderton NG24 140 D3
Bottesford NG13 181 A2
Carlton NG4 175 A7
Redmile NG13 192 F3
West Bridgford NG2 174 A1
Belvoir St
Hucknall NG15 145 F8
Nottingham NG3 161 F2
Belvoir Terr DN21 15 B4
Belward St NG1 223 F2
Belwood Cl NG7 184 F2
Bembridge S81 36 B6
Bembridge Ct NG9 183 A8
Bembridge Dr NG5 161 B6
Bendigo La NG2 174 A4
Benedict Ct 3 NG5 147 A1
Benet Dr NG22 106 A5
Benington Dr NG8 171 C3
Benjamin Adlard Com Sch
DN21 24 E6
Ben Mayo Ct NG7 222 B4
Benner Ave DE7 170 A5
Bennerley Ave DE7 157 F4
Bennerley Ct NG6 159 F8
Bennerley Rd NG6 159 F8
Bennett Ave NG18 102 F6
Bennett Rd NG3 162 A3
Bennett St
Long Eaton NG10 182 C2
Nottingham NG3 161 F2
Sandiacre NG10 182 B5
Benneworth Cl NG15 145 F5
Bennington Wlk NG19 88 E4
Ben St NG7 222 B4
Bentick St NG18 102 D7
Bentinck Ave NG12 186 D1
Bentinck Banks Nature
Reserve NG17 114 E3
Bentinck Cl
Annesley Woodhouse
NG17 114 F1
Boughton NG22 77 E6
Bentinck Ct 8 NG2 173 E4
Bentinck Prim Sch NG7 222 B4
Bentinck Rd
Carlton NG4 162 C2
Newark-on-T NG24 139 F6
Nottingham NG7 222 B4
Bentinck St
Annesley Woodhouse
NG17 129 F8
Hucknall NG15 145 F8
Sutton in A NG17 100 F3
Bentinck Terr NG20 74 B3
Bentley Ave NG3 174 B6
Bentwell Ave NG5 162 A7
Beresford Dr DE7 157 E5
Beresford Rd
Long Eaton NG10 193 A5
Mansfield Woodhouse NG19 88 C6
Beresford St
Mansfield NG18 102 D6
Nottingham NG7 222 A3
Berkeley Ave
Long Eaton NG10 193 C6
Nottingham NG3 173 C8
Berkeley Cres NG12 176 D3
Berkeley Rd NG18 102 C5
Bernard Ave
Hucknall NG15 131 B1
Mansfield Woodhouse NG19 88 B5
Bernard Rd NG19 101 E8
Bernard St NG5 161 B1
Bernisdale Cl NG5 146 F1
Berridge Adult Ctr The
NG7 173 A8
Berridge Inf Sch NG7 172 E7
Berridge Jun Sch NG7 172 E7
Berridge Rd NG7 173 A8
Berridge Rd W NG7 172 E7
Berriedale Cl NG5 162 C8
Berristow Grange NG17 100 D1
Berristow La DE55 113 C7
Berry Ave NG17 114 E6
Berry Hill Cl NG18 102 C4
Berry Hill Gdns NG18 102 F4
Berry Hill Gr NG4 162 E2
Berry Hill La NG18 102 D4
Berry Hill Mews NG18 102 D4
Berry Hill Prim Sch
NG18 102 F4
Berry Hill Rd NG18 102 C4
Berry Pk Lea NG18 102 D3
Berwick Ave NG19 101 D8
Berwick Cl NG5 161 C6
Berwin Cl NG10 182 A1
Beryldene Ave NG16 159 A7
Bescar La NG22 77 A2
Bescoby St DN22 39 F6
Besecar Ave NG4 162 E2
Besecar Cl NG4 162 E2
Bessell La NG9 182 D5
Bessingham Dr NG11 185 C3
Besthorpe Ct NG19 101 E7
Besthorpe Nature Reserve
(North) NG23 97 D6
Besthorpe Nature Reserve
(South) NG23 97 D4
Besthorpe Prim Sch NG23 97 F6
Besthorpe Rd
Collingham NG23 98 A2
North Scarle LN6 83 C1
Bestwick Ave DE75 143 B1
Bestwick Cl DE7 170 A4
Bestwood Ave NG5 161 E8
Bestwood Cl NG5 161 E8
Bestwood Ctry Pk NG6 146 F3
Bestwood Lodge Dr NG5 161 D8
Bestwood Park Drive 4
NG5 147 B1
Bestwood Pk Dr NG5 161 B8
Bestwood Pk Dr W NG5 146 E1
Bestwood Pk View NG5 147 E1
Bestwood Rd
Hucknall NG15 146 C5
Nottingham NG6 146 D2
Pinxton NG16 113 E2
Bestwood Terr NG6 160 C8
Bethel Gdns NG15 145 C5
Bethel Terr S80 34 E7
Bethnal Wlk 2 NG6 160 B7
Betony Cl NG13 177 C4
Betula Cl NG11 184 C1
Beulah Rd NG17 115 B4
Bevan Cl NG21 118 B8
Bevel St NG7 172 F7
Bevercotes Cl NG24 139 F6
Bevercotes Rd NG22 65 D3
Beverley Cl
Nottingham NG8 171 B4
Rainworth NG21 104 B1
Beverley Dr
Kimberley NG16 158 E7
Kirkby in A NG17 115 C3
Mansfield NG18 102 D2
Beverley Gdns NG4 162 F1
Beverley Rd DN11 9 A4
Beverleys Ave NG13 178 F4
Beverley Sq NG3 173 E7
Beverley Wlk S81 25 E7
Bewcastle Rd NG5 147 A2
Bewick Dr NG3 174 C5
Bexhill Ct NG8 171 E1
Bexwell Cl NG11 195 E8
Biant Cl NG8 160 B3
Bidford Rd NG8 159 F1
Bidwell Cres NG11 195 B2
Big Barn La NG18 102 F5
Biggart Cl 2 NG9 183 C2
Biggin St LE11 220 B4
Big La DN22 30 D3
Bigsby Rd DN22 30 A1
Big Wood Sch NG5 147 B2
Biko Sq 8 NG7 172 F8
Bilberry Wlk NG3 173 E7
Bilbie Wlk NG1 223 D3
Bilborough Coll NG8 171 C7
Bilborough Rd NG8 171 C6
Bilby Gdns 3 NG3 173 F5
Billesdon Dr NG5 160 F4
Billingsley Ave NG16 113 D3
Bilsthorpe Rd NG22 92 D1
Bilton Cl NG24 140 D2
Binbrook Ct DN10 9 F6
Bingham Ave NG17 101 A5
Bingham Ind Pk NG13 177 E5
Bingham L Ctr NG13 177 F3
Bingham Rd
Cotgrave NG12 187 F3
Langar NG13 190 B4
Mansfield NG18 103 A3
Nottingham NG5 161 C2
Radcliffe on T NG12 176 A3
Bingham Robert Miles Inf
Sch NG13 177 E5
Bingham Sta NG13 177 F5
Bingley Cl 2 NG8 172 B6
BioCity NG8 173 E4
Birch Ave
Beeston NG9 184 B4
Carlton NG4 174 D7
Farnsfield NG22 119 E7
Ilkeston DE7 170 A7
Nuthall NG16 159 B6
Rainworth NG21 104 C1
Birch Cl
Nuthall NG16 159 B6
Rampton DN22 42 F2
Ravenshead NG15 117 A1
Birch Croft Dr NG19 89 A2
Birch Ct NG22 65 F2
Birchdale Ave NG15 146 A5
Birchenhall Ct NG24 139 A4
Birchen Holme DE55 113 A4
Birches The NG15 117 A3
Birchfield Dr S80 35 B2
Birchfield Rd NG5 148 A1
Birch Gr
Gainsborough DN21 15 D2
Mansfield NG18 103 A4
Shirebrook NG20 72 D5
Birchlands NG19 88 F1
Birch Lea
Arnold NG5 161 D8
East Leake LE12 205 D1
Birchover Pl DE7 157 E5
Birchover Rd NG8 171 C6
Birch Pas NG7 222 C3
Birch Rd
Hodthorpe S80 45 C6
New Balderton NG24 140 C5
New Ollerton NG22 77 D4
Birch Rise NG14 149 C5
Birch St NG20 73 F6
Birch Tree Cl NG19 89 D3
Birch Tree Cres NG17 114 F4
Birchwood Ave
Breaston NG10 193 A7
Long Eaton NG10 193 C5
Birchwood Cl
Ravenshead NG15 117 B1
South Normanton DE55 113 A4
Southwell NG25 121 D1
Sutton in A NG17 100 E6
Birchwood Dr
Ravenshead NG15 117 A1
Sutton in A NG17 100 D7
Birchwood Rd NG8 171 C4
Birchwood View DN21 15 F1
Bircotes & Harworth Com
Sch DN11 9 C5
Bircotes L Ctr DN11 9 C4
Bird Cl NG18 102 C3
Birdcroft La DN10 14 A5
Birding St NG19 88 B1
Birdsall Ave NG8 171 E4
Bird's La NG17 114 E1
Birkdale S81 36 B6
Birkdale Ave NG22 77 D6
Birkdale Cl
Ilkeston DE7 157 D1
West Bridgford NG12 186 A3
Birkdale Dr 3 NG17 114 F6
Birkdale Gr DN22 39 D2
Birkdale Way
Nottingham NG5 160 F8
9 Nottingham NG5 161 A8
Birkin Ave
Beeston NG9 183 A2
Nottingham NG7 172 F7
Radcliffe on T NG12 176 A4
Ruddington NG11 196 C8
Birkland Ave
Mansfield Woodhouse
NG19 88 D3
Market Warsop NG20 74 B4
Nottingham, Mapperley
NG3 162 A4
Nottingham, St Ann's NG1 223 E4
Birkland Dr NG21 76 A2
Birklands Ave
New Ollerton NG22 77 C6
Worksop S80 36 C1
Birklands Cl NG20 74 B5
Birklands Prim Sch NG20 74 B5
Birkland St NG18 102 D7
Birks Cl S80 45 C6
Birks Rd NG19 101 D7
Birley St NG9 182 D5
Birling Cl NG6 159 F7
Birrell Rd NG7 173 A8
Birrel St DN21 15 B2
Bisham Dr NG2 186 B7
Bishop Alexander Prim Sch
NG24 125 A4
Bishop Alexandra Ct
NG24 139 E7
Bishopdale S81 36 A7
Bishopdale Cl NG10 193 A6
Bishopdale Dr NG16 159 B7
Bishopfield La DN22 19 A5
Bishops Cl NG12 197 E4
Bishop's Dr NG25 136 E8
Bishops Hill NG21 103 F1
Bishops Rd NG13 177 D5
Bishop St
Eastwood NG16 143 F2
Loughborough LE11 220 C4
Mansfield NG18 102 B5
Sutton in A NG17 100 E3
Bishops Way NG15 146 B8
Bishop's Wlk NG20 74 A6
Bispham Dr NG9 182 F2
Bispham Dr Jun Sch
NG9 182 E3
Blackacre NG14 163 E5
Blackbird Av 8 S81 35 C7
Blackbrook Rd NG24 125 D1
Blackburn Cl NG23 98 B1
Blackburn Pl DE7 157 E3
Blackcliff Field Cl S80 45 A5
Blacketts Wlk NG11 195 C8
Blackfriars Cl NG8 159 D3
Blackham Rd LE11 220 A1
Blackhill Dr NG4 174 F8
Black La LN6 71 F1
Blackrod Cl NG9 183 A2
Black Scotch La
Mansfield NG18 102 E3
Ravenshead NG18 116 F8
Blacksmith Ct NG12 187 E4
Blacksmith La
Kelham NG23 124 A4
Torworth DN22 19 B2
Blacksmiths Cl LE14 219 D8
Blacksmiths Ct NG15 131 D3
Blacksmiths La LN6 83 D2
Blackstone Wlk NG2 173 C2
Blackstope La DN22 40 A7
Black Swan Cl NG5 161 D4
Blackthorn Cl
Bingham NG13 178 B4
Carlton NG4 163 A2
1 Gainsborough DN21 15 F1
Blackthorn Dr NG6 160 B3
Blackthorne Cl NG24 140 B5
Blackthorne Dr NG14 150 D2
Blackthorn Way NG17 100 C1
Blackwell Rd NG17 99 E3
Bladon Cl NG3 161 E2
Bladon Rd NG11 196 B7
Blair Ct 4 NG2 173 C1
Blair Gr NG10 182 A4
Blaise Cl NG11 195 E8
Blake Cl NG5 162 A7
Blake Cres NG18 102 E7
Blake Ct NG10 193 B5
Blakeney Ct NG19 88 E4
Blakeney Dr NG18 102 C4
Blakeney Rd NG12 176 B3
Blakeney Wlk NG5 161 F5
Blake Rd
Stapleford NG9 182 E6
West Bridgford NG2 186 A7
Blake St
Ilkeston DE7 157 F1
Mansfield Woodhouse NG19 88 B2
Blandford Ave NG10 193 B5
Blandford Dr DN22 39 D4
Blandford Gdns NG2 185 C5
Blandford Rd NG9 183 C5
Bland La NG14 150 A5
Blankney Cl LN1 57 A4
Blankney St NG5 160 E4
Blantyre Ave NG5 146 E1
Blatherwick Rd NG24 140 D8
Blatherwick's Yd NG5 161 F8
Bleaberry Cl NG2 186 C5
Bleachers Yd NG7 160 F1
Bleak Hill Way NG18 101 E4
Bleasby CE Prim Sch
NG14 151 F8
Bleasby Cres NG17 101 B1
Bleasby Rd NG14 151 D8
Bleasby St NG2 173 F4
Bleasby Sta NG14 151 F8
Bleasdale Cl NG4 163 A2
Blencathra Cl NG2 186 C5
Blenheim Ave
Lowdham NG14 150 E1
Nottingham NG3 162 C2
Blenheim Cl
Mansfield NG19 88 D1
Ruddington NG11 196 B7
Blenheim Dr NG9 183 C5
Blenheim Gdns NG13 165 D2
Blenheim Ind Est NG6 159 F8
Blenheim La NG6,NG15 145 E1
Blenheim Pl NG17 99 E3
Blenheim Rise
Bawtry DN10 9 F6
Worksop S81 35 E8
Blenhiem Ct NG10 182 B4
Blessed Robert RC Prim Sch
NG11 195 E8
Bley Ave LE12 214 D8
Blidworth Cl NG8 159 E2
Blidworth Ind Pk NG21 118 B6
Blidworth La
Blidworth NG21 133 C8
Mansfield NG21 103 D1
Rainworth NG21 117 E8
Blidworth Rd
Farnsfield NG22 119 E6
Kirkby in A NG15 115 E4
Blidworth Waye NG15 131 F7
Blind La
Keyworth NG12 197 E2
Oxton NG25 134 C4
Bloomgrove Rd DE7 157 F2
Bloomsbury Dr NG16 159 E3
Bloomsgrove Ind Est
NG7 222 B3
Bloomsgrove St NG7 222 B3
Bluebell Bank NG13 177 D3
Bluebell Cl
Hucknall NG15 145 C6
Selston NG16 128 F2
Shirebrook NG20 72 D3
Stanton Hill NG17 100 B6
Bluebell Gr 2 NG17 114 F7
Blue Bell Hill Prim Sch
NG3 173 F6
Blue Bell Hill Rd NG3 173 E6
Bluebell Pl NG19 88 F4
Bluebells The NG17 101 B1
Bluebell Wood Way
NG17 100 C1
Blue Bell Yd NG22 65 F3
Bluecoat Cl NG1 223 E3
Bluecoat St NG1 223 E4
Blundell Cl NG3 173 F8
Blyth Cl NG19 87 D1
Blyth Gdns NG3 161 E2
Blyth Gr S81 36 A5
Blyth Rd
Blyth, Bilby S81, DN22 27 E5
Blyth, Nornay S81 18 A7
Elkesley S80 48 F4
Harworth DN11 8 F3
New Ollerton NG22 77 A6
Oldcotes S81 16 F6
Ranskill DN22 19 A4
Walesby NG22 63 A3
Worksop, Kilton S81 36 B6
Blyth St NG3 161 E2
Blyton Rd DN21 15 C4
Blyton Wlk NG5 161 B7
BMI The Park Hospl
NG5 132 D2
Boar La NG24 139 F8
Boat La
Aldercar NG16 143 A4
Bleasby NG14 152 C7
Hoveringham NG14 151 E2
Boatmans Cl DE7 157 F2
Bobbers Mill Bridge
NG7 172 D7
Bobbers Mill Rd NG7 172 E7
Boden Dr NG16 159 C6
Boden St NG7 222 B3
Bodmin Ave NG15 145 C5
Bodmin Ct 5 NG18 103 A2
Bodmin Dr NG8 160 C2
Body Rd NG9 183 B2
Bohem Rd NG10 182 C3
Bold Cl NG6 160 B8
Bolero Cl NG8 171 E5
Bolham La DN22 29 F1
Bolingey Way NG15 145 C5
Bollard's La LE12 213 A7
Bolsover St
Hucknall NG15 146 B7
Mansfield NG18 102 D6
Bolton Ave NG9 183 C4
Bolton Cl NG2 186 A7
Bolton La LE14 211 F7
Bolton Terr NG12 175 F3
Bond Cl LE11 220 C1
Bond St
Arnold NG5 161 E8
Nottingham NG2 173 E4
Bonemill La
Clarborough DN22 30 D2
Worksop S81 35 D5
Bonetti Cl NG5 162 C5
Boniface Gdns 4 NG5 147 A1
Bonington Art Gall NG1 223 D3
Bonington Dr NG5 161 F7
Bonington Inf Com Sch
NG6 160 B6
Bonington Jun Sch NG6 160 B6
Bonington Rd
Mansfield NG19 101 E6
Nottingham NG3 162 A3
Bonington Theatre NG5 161 E8
Bonner Hill NG14 148 F6
Bonner La NG14 149 B6
Bonner's Rd NG16 158 C4
Bonnington Cl NG6 160 A6
Bonnington Cres NG5 161 C4
Bonny Mead NG12 187 E2
Bonsal Ct NG18 103 B6
Bonsall St NG10 193 E8
Bonser Cl NG4 174 E7
Bonser Cres NG17 99 E2
Bonser Gdns NG17 100 D2
Booth Ave NG19 87 A5
Booth Cl NG3 223 F3
Booth Cres NG19 87 D2
Booth St NG19 88 B3
Boots Yd NG17 99 F3
Borders Ave NG17 114 E8
Borlace Cres NG9 182 E6
Borman Cl NG6 159 F5
Borough St DE74 203 D2
Borrow Bread La NG14 152 B7
Borrowdale Cl NG2 186 D6
Borrowdale Dr NG10 193 A6
Borrowell DE74 203 C3
Boscombe Rd S81 35 C8
Boscowan Ct DE7 157 F4
Bosden Cl NG8 171 C6
Bosley Sq NG9 184 A8
Bostock's La NG10 182 A3
Boston St NG1 223 F3
Boswell Cl
Kinoulton NG12 200 A2
Mansfield NG18 102 C3
Bosworth Dr NG16 144 B3
Bosworth St NG19 101 D7
Bosworth Way NG10 193 E5
Bosworth Wlk 10 NG2 173 B1
Botany Ave
Mansfield NG18 101 F6
Nottingham NG3 173 F7
Botany Cl NG11 185 C2
Botany Dr DE7 157 F5
Bothe Cl NG10 193 C6
Bottesford Sta NG13 181 C3
Bottleacre La LE11 220 B6
Bottle La NG1 223 E2
Bottom Gn LE14 210 A1
Bottom Row NG24 140 B8
Boughton Cl NG17 100 F5
Boughton Ind Est NG22 78 B5
Boughton Ppg Sta NG22 77 D7
Boughton Rd S80 35 A5
Bould St NG19 87 F1

Boulevard Ind Pk NG7 .. 184 C7
Boundary Cl NG20 .... 72 E6
Boundary Cres
Beeston NG9 .... 171 F1
Blidworth NG21 .... 118 B5
Boundary Ct NG24 ...... 139 F7
Boundary La NG16 ...... 143 C3
Boundary Rd
Beeston NG9 ...... 183 F8
Newark-on-T NG24 .... 139 F7
West Bridgford NG2 .... 185 F4
Boundary Row S80 ..... 35 F2
Boundary Wlk NG20 ..... 58 F1
Bourne Ave
Kirkby in A NG17 ..... 115 B3
Selston NG16 ...... 129 A7
Bourne Cl NG9 ..... 171 D1
Bourne Dr NG15 ..... 117 A2
Bourne Mews NG4 ..... 175 A6
Bourne St NG4 ...... 175 A6
Bournmoor Ave NG7 ..... 184 E1
Bovill St NG7 ..... 222 B4
Bovington Ct DN22 .... 29 E1
Bowbridge Gdns NG13 .. 181 A3
Bowbridge La
Bottesford NG13 ..... 180 F3
New Balderton NG24 .... 140 A3
Bowbridge Prim Sch
NG24 .... 139 F5
Bowbridge Rd NG24 .... 140 A6
Bowden Dr NG9 ..... 184 B6
Bowers Ave 6 NG3 ..... 173 D7
Bowes Well Rd DE7 ..... 157 E2
Bowland Cl NG3 ..... 174 A7
Bowland Rd NG13 ..... 177 C4
Bowler Ct 3 LE11 ..... 220 C4
Bowling Gn Rd DN21 ..... 15 B1
Bowling St NG18 ..... 102 D6
Bowlwell Ave NG5 ..... 160 F8
Bowness Ave NG6 ..... 160 C2
Bowness Cl NG2 ..... 186 C7
Bowne St NG17 ..... 100 F3
Bowscale Cl NG2 ..... 186 C5
Bow St NG19 ..... 88 E4
Box Cres NG17 ..... 114 F6
Boxley Dr NG2 ..... 185 C4
Boyce Gdns NG3 ..... 161 F1
Boycroft Ave NG3 ..... 173 F8
Boyd Cl NG5 ..... 148 A1
Boyer's Orch LE14 ..... 202 B3
Boyer St LE11 ..... 220 C4
Boy La NG21 ..... 76 B1
Boynton Dr NG3 ..... 161 F1
Bracadale Rd NG5 ..... 146 F1
Bracebridge S80 ..... 36 B3
Bracebridge Ave S80 ..... 36 B3
Bracebridge Ct S80 ..... 36 A2
Bracebridge Dr NG8 .... 171 D7
Bracey Rise NG2 ..... 185 E3
Bracken Ave NG22 ..... 77 E6
Bracken Cl
Carlton NG4 ..... 162 D2
Gainsborough DN21 ..... 15 B3
2 Kirkby in A NG17 ..... 114 F6
Long Eaton NG10 ..... 182 B1
Market Warsop NG20 ..... 74 C3
Nottingham NG8 ..... 159 F1
Bracken Ct
Bilsthorpe NG22 ..... 106 A5
Harworth DN11 ..... 8 E4
Brackendale Ave NG5 ..... 161 F8
Brackendale Dr NG22 ..... 64 A2
Brackenfield Ave NG19 ..... 88 E4
Brackenfield Dr NG16 ..... 158 B7
Brackenfield Rise NG15 . 117 A3
Brackenfield Specl Sch
NG10 ..... 182 B1
Bracken Hill NG18 ..... 103 A5
Bracken Hill La
Austerfield DN10 ..... 3 F7
Misson DN10 ..... 4 A5
Bracken Hill Specl Sch
NG17 ..... 115 C5
Brackenhurst Coll Env Ed Ctr
NG25 ..... 136 D5
Brackenhurst La NG25 .. 136 D6
Bracken La DN22 ..... 40 B5
Bracken Lane Prim Sch
DN22 ..... 40 A5
Bracken Rd
Long Eaton NG10 ..... 182 B1
Shirebrook NG20 ..... 72 D3
Bracken Way DN11 ..... 8 E4
Brackenwood Cl NG19 ..... 89 A1
Brackhills Cl NG19 ..... 88 E1
Bracknell Cres NG8 ..... 160 D1
Brackner La NG22 ..... 106 B3
Bracton Dr NG3 ..... 173 F6
Bradbourne Ave NG11 ..... 185 A5
Bradbury Gd NG11 ..... 196 B7
Bradbury St NG2 ..... 174 A4
Bradden Ave NG9 ..... 170 E1
Bradder Way NG18 ..... 102 A5
Braddock Cl NG7 ..... 222 A2
Bradfield Rd NG8 ..... 159 F1
Bradforth Ave NG18 ..... 103 A7
Bradgate Cl NG10 ..... 182 B4
Bradgate Rd 2 NG7 ..... 173 A8
Bradleys Orch NG14 ..... 151 C2
Bradley St NG10 ..... 182 C5
Bradman Gdns NG5 ..... 162 B6
Bradmore Ave NG11 ..... 196 C8
Bradmore Ct NG18 ..... 103 A3
Bradmore La NG12 ..... 197 D5
Bradmore Rise NG5 ..... 161 C4
Bradshaw St NG10 ..... 193 B5
Bradwell Cl NG16 ..... 158 C8
Bradwell Dr NG5 ..... 161 A8
Braefell Cl NG2 ..... 186 D5
Braemar Ave NG16 ..... 143 F1
Braemar Dr NG4 ..... 163 B1
Braemar Rd
Clipstone NG19 ..... 89 E3
Nottingham NG6 ..... 160 C7
Brailsford Ct NG18 ..... 103 B6
Brailsford Rd 1 NG7 ..... 172 E1
Brailsford Way NG9 ..... 183 C1
Brailwood Cl NG22 ..... 106 A6
Brailwood Rd NG22 ..... 106 A6
Brake La NG22 ..... 77 E7
Brake Rd NG22 ..... 63 D1
Brake View NG22 ..... 77 E6
Bramber Gr NG11 ..... 195 E7
Bramble Cl
Beeston NG9 ..... 183 D2
Long Eaton NG10 ..... 182 B1
New Ollerton NG22 ..... 77 D6
North Leverton with
Habblesthorpe DN22 ..... 42 D8
Nottingham NG6 ..... 160 D3
Shirebrook NG20 ..... 72 E6
South Normanton DE55 ..... 113 B6
Bramble Croft NG17 ..... 100 C1
Bramble Ct NG4 ..... 162 F1
Bramble Dr NG3 ..... 174 B8
Bramble Gdns NG8 ..... 172 A8
Bramble La NG18 ..... 103 A5
Bramble Rd DN22 ..... 40 B4
Brambles The NG22 ..... 64 A2
Brambleway NG12 ..... 188 A2
Bramble Way DN11 ..... 8 E4
Brambling Cl NG18 ..... 102 E7
Bramblings The S81 ..... 35 C7
Bramcote Ave NG9 ..... 183 D6
Bramcote CE Prim Sch
NG9 ..... 183 B8
Bramcote Ct NG18 ..... 103 A3
Bramcote Dr
Beeston NG9 ..... 183 E7
Nottingham NG8 ..... 171 D3
Retford DN22 ..... 39 D5
Bramcote Dr W NG9 ..... 183 D7
Bramcote Hills Prim Sch
NG9 ..... 171 B1
Bramcote Hills Sp & Com
Coll NG9 ..... 171 B2
Bramcote La
Beeston NG9 ..... 183 C5
Nottingham NG8 ..... 171 D3
Bramcote L Ctr NG9 ..... 171 A1
Bramcote Lorne Sch
DN22 ..... 51 A5
Bramcote Park Bus & Ent
Sch The NG9 ..... 171 A1
Bramcote Rd NG9 ..... 183 E7
Bramcote St NG7 ..... 222 A3
Bramcote Wlk NG7 ..... 222 A3
Bramerton Rd NG8 ..... 171 D6
Bramhall Rd NG8 ..... 171 C6
Bramley Apple Ex NG25 . 121 D1
Bramley Cl
East Leake LE12 ..... 205 E1
Gunthorpe NG14 ..... 165 A5
Southwell NG25 ..... 136 F8
Bramley Ct
Gainsborough DN21 ..... 15 E1
Kimberley NG16 ..... 158 F6
Sutton in A NG17 ..... 100 F3
Bramley Rd NG8 ..... 159 E1
Bramley Wlk NG19 ..... 101 D7
Brammersack Cl NG23 ..... 124 B7
Brampton Ave DE75 ..... 143 A2
Brampton Ct NG2 ..... 186 C7
Brampton Dr NG9 ..... 182 F5
Brancaster Cl NG6 ..... 160 B4
Brancliffe La S81 ..... 34 F7
Brandish Cres NG11 ..... 184 D1
Brand La NG17 ..... 100 C5
Brandon Cl NG24 ..... 140 E4
Brandreth Ave
Nottingham NG3 ..... 173 F8
Sutton in A NG17 ..... 100 D4
Brandreth Dr NG16 ..... 158 A8
Brand St NG2 ..... 173 F2
Branklene Cl NG16 ..... 158 E7
Branksome Wlk 3 NG2 . 173 C2
Bransdale S81 ..... 36 A8
Bransdale Ave NG19 ..... 88 E1
Bransdale Cl NG10 ..... 193 B6
Bransdale Rd NG11 ..... 184 D1
Branston Ave NG22 ..... 119 F6
Branston Cl NG24 ..... 125 D6
Branston Gdns NG2 ..... 185 D4
Branston Wlk NG5 ..... 161 C4
Brantford Ave NG7 ..... 184 F1
Brantingham Gdns DN10 ... 3 A1
Brassington Cl NG16 ..... 158 B7
Brassington Ct NG19 ..... 88 E4
Braunton Cl NG15 ..... 145 D6
Brayton Cres NG6 ..... 160 D5
B Rd NG9 ..... 184 D6
Breach Rd DE75 ..... 157 A8
Breadsall Ct DE7 ..... 157 F3
Breamer Rd NG23 ..... 112 B8
Brechin S81 ..... 36 B5
Brechin Cl NG5 ..... 148 B1
Brechin Ct NG19 ..... 88 B6
Breckbank NG19 ..... 88 E1
Breck Bank NG22 ..... 77 C5
Breck Bank Cres NG22 ..... 77 C5
Breck Hill Rd NG3 ..... 161 F4
Breck La DN10 ..... 20 A8
Brecknock Dr NG10 ..... 193 A7
Brecks La
Elston NG23 ..... 154 B1
Stapleford LN6 ..... 127 E8
Brecks Plantation Nature
Reserve NG11 ..... 195 D8
Brecks Rd DN22 ..... 39 D3
Breckswood Dr NG11 ..... 195 E7
Brecon Cl
4 Long Eaton NG10 ..... 193 A8
Nottingham NG8 ..... 160 A3
Rainworth NG21 ..... 104 C1
Bredon Cl 5 NG10 ..... 193 A8
Breedon St NG10 ..... 182 C2
Brendon Ct NG9 ..... 183 B8
Brendon Dr
Kimberley NG16 ..... 158 F7
Nottingham NG8 ..... 172 A5
Brendon Gdns NG8 ..... 172 A5
Brendon Gr NG13 ..... 177 C5
Brendon Rd NG8 ..... 172 A5
Brendon Way NG10 ..... 182 A1
Brentcliffe Ave NG3 ..... 174 A7
Brentnall Cl NG10 ..... 193 B7
Bretby Ct NG18 ..... 103 B6
Brett Cl NG15 ..... 145 E5
Bretton Rd NG15 ..... 117 B3
Brettsil Dr NG11 ..... 196 B7
Brewer's Wharf NG24 ..... 124 F1
Brewery La
Everton DN10 ..... 11 C3
Retford DN22 ..... 39 F6
Brewery St NG16 ..... 158 F6
Brewhouse Yd Mus-The Mus
of Nottingham Life
NG7 ..... 223 D1
Brewsters Cl NG13 ..... 177 E4
Brewsters Rd NG3 ..... 173 F8
Brewsters Way DN22 ..... 29 C1
Brewsters Wlk DN10 ..... 10 A8
Brian Clough Way NG9 .. 182 D5
Briar Ave NG10 ..... 182 B3
Briarbank Ave NG3 ..... 174 A8
Briarbank Wlk NG3 ..... 174 A7
Briar Cl
Beeston NG9 ..... 171 E1
Hucknall NG15 ..... 145 E5
Keyworth NG12 ..... 197 F4
Rainworth NG21 ..... 104 B1
Stanton Hill NG17 ..... 100 C6
Worksop S80 ..... 35 C2
Briar Ct
Harworth DN11 ..... 8 E4
New Ollerton NG22 ..... 77 C5
Nottingham NG2 ..... 173 B1
Briar Gate
Cotgrave NG12 ..... 188 A2
Long Eaton NG10 ..... 182 B2
Briar Gn DN11 ..... 8 E4
Briar La NG18 ..... 103 A4
Briar Lea
Retford DN22 ..... 39 D4
Worksop S80 ..... 35 C2
Briar Rd
Eastwood NG16 ..... 158 B8
New Ollerton NG22 ..... 77 C5
Briars The DN10 ..... 4 B3
Briarwood Ave NG3 ..... 174 A7
Briarwood Cl NG19 ..... 89 B1
Briarwood Ct NG3 ..... 161 E3
Briber Hill S81 ..... 18 A1
Briber Rd S81 ..... 18 A2
Brickcliffe Rd LE12 ..... 205 F2
Brickenell Rd NG14 ..... 148 F6
Brickenhole La DN10 ..... 13 F5
Brickings Way DN22 ..... 32 D5
Brick Kiln La NG18 ..... 101 D7
Brickley Cres LE12 ..... 205 F1
Brickyard NG15 ..... 146 C6
Brickyard Dr NG15 ..... 146 C5
Brickyard La
East Bridgford NG13 ..... 165 C2
East Leake LE12 ..... 214 A8
Farnsfield NG22 ..... 120 B6
Misson DN10 ..... 4 D4
Radcliffe on T NG12 ..... 176 B3
South Normanton DE55 ..... 113 A6
Sutton Bonington LE12 ..... 213 F8
Walkeringham DN10 ..... 13 C6
Brick Yd Rd DN22 ..... 50 C6
Bride Church La DN11 ..... 8 A7
Bridegate La LE14 ..... 209 E5
Bridge Ave NG9 ..... 183 E5
Bridge Cl S80 ..... 45 A5
Bridge Ct NG15 ..... 146 A5
Bridge End Ave NG16 ..... 128 F8
Bridge Farm La NG7 ..... 184 E2
Bridgegate DN22 ..... 39 E7
Bridge Gn Wlk 6 NG8 ..... 159 E1
Bridge Gr NG2 ..... 185 E8
Bridgend Cl NG9 ..... 182 D5
Bridge Pl
Saxilby LN1 ..... 57 B3
Worksop S80 ..... 35 E3
Bridge Rd
Gainsborough DN21 ..... 24 D7
Nottingham NG8 ..... 171 D5
Bridge St
Gainsborough DN21 ..... 24 C7
Ilkeston DE7 ..... 157 F4
Langley Mill NG16 ..... 143 C3
Long Eaton NG10 ..... 182 D1
Loughborough LE11 ..... 220 A4
Mansfield NG18 ..... 102 C7
Newark-on-T NG24 ..... 139 F8
Sandiacre NG10 ..... 182 C6
Saxilby LN1 ..... 57 B3
Worksop S80 ..... 35 E2
Bridgeway Ct NG2 ..... 173 D2
Bridgeway Ctr NG2 ..... 173 C2
Bridgford Rd
Kneeton NG13 ..... 166 A8
Bridgford Rd *continued*
West Bridgford NG2 ..... 185 F8
Bridgford St NG18 ..... 102 F5
Bridgnorth Dr NG7 ..... 184 E2
Bridgnorth Way NG9 ..... 182 E3
Bridle Cl NG17 ..... 100 B6
Bridle Rd
Beeston NG9 ..... 183 B8
Burton Joyce NG14 ..... 163 E5
Bridlesmith Gate NG1 ..... 223 E2
Bridle Ways NG13 ..... 165 D2
Bridleway The NG19 ..... 88 F1
Bridlington St NG7 ..... 172 F7
Bridport Ave 4 NG8 ..... 172 D5
Brielen Rd NG12 ..... 176 A3
Brierfield Ave NG11 ..... 185 B4
Brierley Forest Pk NG17. 100 A2
Brierley Gn NG4 ..... 175 A7
Brierly Cotts NG17 ..... 100 E3
Brierly Rd NG17 ..... 100 D4
Brigg Inf Sch DE55 ..... 113 B6
Brightmoor St NG1 ..... 223 F3
Bright Sq NG19 ..... 87 D2
Bright St
Gainsborough DN21 ..... 24 C8
Ilkeston DE7 ..... 157 E3
Nottingham NG7 ..... 222 A3
South Normanton DE55 ... 113 A5
Brimington Ct NG19 ..... 88 E4
Brindley Rd NG8 ..... 171 C5
Brinkhill Cres NG11 ..... 184 F3
Brinkley Hill NG25 ..... 137 B6
Brinsley Cl NG8 ..... 160 A1
Brinsley Hill NG16 ..... 128 C2
Brinsley Prim Sch NG16 .. 143 E8
Brisbane Cl NG19 ..... 88 C6
Brisbane Ct NG24 ..... 140 D4
Brisbane Dr
Nottingham NG5 ..... 160 E8
Stapleford NG9 ..... 170 E1
Bristol Cl NG24 ..... 125 E1
Bristol Rd DE7 ..... 157 E1
Britannia Ave NG6 ..... 160 E5
Britannia Rd NG10 ..... 182 D1
Britannia Terr DN21 ..... 24 D7
British Fields NG22 ..... 65 D3
British Horological Inst
NG23 ..... 122 E2
Brittania Ct NG24 ..... 139 E8
Britten Gdns NG3 ..... 173 F6
Brixham Rd NG15 ..... 145 D5
Brixton Rd NG7 ..... 222 A3
Brixworth Way DN22 ..... 40 B8
Broad Cl NG14 ..... 149 C4
Broad Eadow Rd NG6 ..... 159 F7
Broad Fen La NG23 ..... 156 B8
Broadfields NG14 ..... 148 F8
Broadgate NG9 ..... 184 A7
Broad Gate NG22 ..... 66 E7
Broadgate Ave NG9 ..... 184 A7
Broadgate La
Beeston NG9 ..... 184 A7
Kelham NG23 ..... 123 E6
Broad Gores DN22 ..... 30 D3
Broadhill Rd DE74 ..... 203 C2
Broadholme St NG7 ..... 222 B1
Broadhurst Ave NG6 ..... 160 D2
Broadings La DN22 ..... 54 A6
Broad La
Brinsley NG16 ..... 143 E8
Hodthorpe S80 ..... 45 D6
South Leverton DN22 ..... 43 B6
Broadlands
Sandiacre NG10 ..... 182 B3
South Normanton DE55 ..... 113 A4
Broadleigh Cl NG11 ..... 185 C3
Broadleigh Ct DN22 ..... 39 D4
Broad Marsh Sh Ctr NG1 223 E2
Broadmead NG14 ..... 163 F5
Broad Meer NG12 ..... 187 E3
Broad Oak Cl NG3 ..... 173 E7
Broad Oak Dr
Brinsley NG16 ..... 143 E8
Stapleford NG9 ..... 182 D6
Broadoak Pk NG17 ..... 114 F1
Broad Pl S80 ..... 45 C6
Broad St
Long Eaton NG10 ..... 193 D7
Loughborough LE11 ..... 220 A4
Nottingham NG1 ..... 223 F3
Broadstairs Rd NG9 ..... 182 F2
Broadstone Cl NG2 ..... 185 C5
Broad Valley Dr NG6 ..... 146 E4
Broadway
Carlton NG3 ..... 174 D6
Ilkeston DE7 ..... 157 E3
Nottingham NG1 ..... 223 F2
Broadway E NG4 ..... 174 D6
Broadway Ind Est NG18 . 102 C6
Broadway Media Ctr
NG1 ..... 223 F2
Broadway The NG18 ..... 102 C6
Broad Wlk NG6 ..... 160 C3
Broadwood Ct NG9 ..... 184 A8
Broadwood Rd NG5 ..... 161 B8
Brockdale Gdns NG12 ..... 197 E4
Brockenhurst Rd NG19 .. 101 D6
Brockhall Rise DE75 ..... 143 A1
Brockhole Cl NG2 ..... 186 D5
Brockhurst Gdns NG3 ..... 173 F6
Brocklehurst Dr NG21 ..... 91 C8
Brocklesby Cl DN21 ..... 24 F7
Brocklewood Inf Sch
NG8 ..... 171 F8
Brocklewood Jun Sch
NG8 ..... 171 F8
Brockley Rd NG2 ..... 186 B7
Brockton Ave NG24 ..... 139 B5
Brockwell The DE55 ..... 113 B4
Brockwood Cres NG12 ..... 197 E4
Bromfield Cl NG3 ..... 174 C7
Bromhead St LE11 ..... 220 C5
Bromley Ave NG24 ..... 140 A6
Bromley Cl NG6 ..... 160 B6
Bromley Pl NG1 ..... 223 D2
Bromley Rd NG2 ..... 185 E6
Brompton Cl NG5 ..... 147 A2
Brompton Way NG11 ..... 185 C3
Bronte Cl NG10 ..... 193 A7
Bronte Ct NG7 ..... 222 C4
Brook Ave NG5 ..... 162 B8
Brook Cl
Eastwood NG16 ..... 144 B1
Long Eaton NG10 ..... 193 E5
Nottingham NG6 ..... 160 B6
Brook Cotts DE7 ..... 157 F3
Brook Ct NG16 ..... 143 B2
Brookdale Ct NG5 ..... 161 D5
Brookdale Rd NG17 ..... 101 B3
Brook Dr NG12 ..... 199 F2
Brooke Cl
Balderton NG24 ..... 140 D5
Worksop S81 ..... 36 C4
Brooke St
Ilkeston DE7 ..... 170 B6
Sandiacre NG10 ..... 182 B5
Brookfield Ave
Hucknall NG15 ..... 146 A5
Sutton in A NG17 ..... 100 D4
Brookfield Cl NG12 ..... 175 F3
Brookfield Cres NG20 ..... 72 E5
Brookfield Ct 8 NG2 ..... 173 C2
Brookfield Dr NG14 ..... 151 D3
Brookfield Gdns NG5 ..... 162 A7
Brookfield Rd NG5 ..... 162 A7
Brookfields Way LE12 ..... 205 E2
Brookfield Way DE75 ..... 143 B1
Brook Gdns NG5 ..... 162 A8
Brookhill Ave NG16 ..... 113 D4
Brookhill Cres NG8 ..... 171 E3
Brookhill Dr NG8 ..... 171 E3
Brookhill Ind Est NG16 .. 113 D2
Brookhill La NG16 ..... 113 E5
Brookhill Leys Inf Sch
NG16 ..... 144 A1
Brookhill Leys Jun Sch
NG16 ..... 144 A2
Brookhill Leys Rd NG16 .. 143 E1
Brookhill Rd NG16 ..... 113 D2
Brookhill St NG9 ..... 182 D6
Brook La NG2 ..... 186 C7
Brookland Ave NG18 ..... 101 F7
Brookland Cl NG14 ..... 165 A5
Brookland Dr NG9 ..... 183 D5
Brooklands NG12 ..... 208 C4
Brooklands Cl NG23 ..... 98 A1
Brooklands Cres NG4 ..... 163 A1
Brooklands Dr NG4 ..... 163 A1
Brooklands Prim Sch
NG10 ..... 193 D7
Brooklands Rd NG3 ..... 174 B7
Brooklyn Ave NG14 ..... 163 E5
Brooklyn Cl NG6 ..... 160 D5
Brooklyn Rd NG6 ..... 160 D5
Brook Rd NG9 ..... 183 F8
Brooksby La NG11 ..... 184 F3
Brooks Cl NG13 ..... 165 D3
Brookside
East Leake LE12 ..... 214 E8
Eastwood NG16 ..... 143 F4
Hucknall NG15 ..... 146 B5
Lowdham NG14 ..... 150 D1
Brook Side 8 LE11 ..... 220 A4
Brookside Ave
East Leake LE12 ..... 205 D1
Mansfield Woodhouse NG19 88 C5
Nottingham NG8 ..... 171 D2
Brookside Cl NG10 ..... 193 B8
Brookside Gdns NG11 ..... 196 B8
Brookside Rd NG11 ..... 196 B8
Brookside Way NG17 ..... 99 F1
Brookside Wlk DN11 ..... 9 B4
Brook St
Hucknall NG15 ..... 146 A7
Nottingham NG1 ..... 223 F3
Sutton in A NG17 ..... 100 E2
Tibshelf DE55 ..... 99 A6
Wymeswold LE12 ..... 216 C3
Brook Terr S80 ..... 35 E1
Brookthorpe Way NG11 . 185 A4
Brookvale Cl NG18 ..... 103 A6
Brook Vale Rd NG16 ..... 143 C2
Brook View Ct NG12 ..... 197 E1
Brook View Dr NG12 ..... 197 E2
Brookwood Cres NG4 ..... 174 C7
Broom Cl
Calverton NG14 ..... 148 F8
Carlton in L S81 ..... 25 D1
Tickhill DN11 ..... 8 B7
Broome Acre DE55 ..... 113 C4
Broome Cl NG24 ..... 140 B5
Broomfield Cl NG10 ..... 182 A5
Broomfield La
Farnsfield NG22 ..... 119 F6
Mattersey DN10 ..... 19 E7
Broomhill Ave
Ilkeston DE7 ..... 170 A6
Worksop S81 ..... 35 F8
Broomhill Jun Sch NG15 . 146 B5
Broomhill La NG19 ..... 101 F8
Broomhill Pk View NG15 146 C5
Broomhill Rd
Hucknall NG15 ..... 146 B4

Broomhill Rd *continued*
Kimberley NG16 . . . . **159** A6
Nottingham NG6 . . . . **160** D6
Broom Rd NG14 . . . . **148** F8
Broomston La DN9 . . . . 2 E2
Broom Wlk NG4 . . . . **174** B8
Brora Rd NG6 . . . . **160** D7
Brotts La NG23 . . . . **81** E6
Brotts Rd NG23 . . . . **81** F6
Brougham Ave NG19 . . . . . **87** D2
Brough La
Brough NG23 . . . . **112** B3
Brough NG23 . . . . **112** C2
Elkesley DN22 . . . . **50** B3
Brough Rd LN6 . . . . **127** A8
Broughton Cl
Clipstone NG21 . . . . **89** F4
Ilkeston DE7 . . . . **157** D2
Broughton Dr
Newark-on-T NG24 . . . . . . **139** C5
Nottingham NG8 . . . . **172** C3
Broughton Gdns NG24 . . . **140** E4
Broughton La LE14 . . . . . . **211** A2
Broughton Rd LN6 . . . . . . **127** E7
Broughton St NG9 . . . . . . **183** F7
Broughton Way NG22 . . . . . **78** A4
Brown Ave NG19 . . . . **88** B4
Brown Cres NG17 . . . . **101** A4
Brownes Rd NG13 . . . . **178** A5
Brownhill Cl NG12 . . . . **189** A4
Browning Cl
Arnold NG5 . . . . **161** D7
Worksop S81 . . . . **36** B5
Browning Rd NG24 . . . . . . **140** E5
Browning St NG18 . . . . . . **102** A7
Brown La
Barton in F NG11 . . . . **194** E6
Thorney NG23 . . . . **70** B5
Brownlow Cl NG23 . . . . **153** D7
Brownlow Dr NG5 . . . . **146** F1
Brownlow Rd NG6 . . . . **87** F1
Brownlow's Hill NG24 . . . . **126** A1
Brown Md Rd NG8 . . . . **172** E8
Browns Croft NG6 . . . . **160** D3
Brown's Flats NG16 . . . . . **158** F7
Browns La
Loughborough LE11 . . . . . **220** A3
Stanton-on-t-W NG12 . . . . **198** D2
Brown's La NG13 . . . . **165** C3
Brown's Rd NG10 . . . . **193** E8
Brown St
Mansfield NG19 . . . . **101** F7
Nottingham NG7 . . . . **172** F7
Broxholme La LN1 . . . . **57** C6
Broxton Rise NG8 . . . . **160** B3
Broxtowe Ave
Kimberley NG16 . . . . **158** D6
Nottingham NG8 . . . . **160** C2
Broxtowe Coll
Beeston & Stapleford
NG9 . . . . **183** C5
Kimberley NG16 . . . . **158** F6
Stapleford NG9 . . . . **182** D7
Broxtowe Ctry Pk NG8 . . . **159** E3
Broxtowe Dr
Hucknall NG15 . . . . **131** A1
Mansfield NG18 . . . . **102** C6
Broxtowe Hall Cl NG8 . . . . **160** A2
Broxtowe La NG8 . . . . **160** A2
Broxtowe Pk Bsns Ctr
NG8 . . . . **159** E2
Broxtowe St NG5 . . . . **161** C2
Bruce Cl NG7 . . . . **173** D2
Bruce Dr NG2 . . . . **185** D7
Brunel Ave NG16 . . . . **144** B3
Brunel Cl DN11 . . . . 8 F2
Brunel Dr NG24 . . . . **125** C2
Brunel Gate DN11 . . . . 8 F2
Brunnen The DE55 . . . . . . **113** B4
Brunner Ave NG20 . . . . **72** F3
Brunswick Dr NG9 . . . . . . **182** E5
Brunts NG18 . . . . **102** C8
Brunt's La NG13 . . . . **165** D4
Brunts Sch The NG18 . . . . . **88** D1
Brunts St NG18 . . . . **102** C6
Brush Dr LE11 . . . . **220** B6
Brushfield St NG7 . . . . . . **172** E7
Brussels Terr ☐ DE7 . . . . **157** E1
Brusty Pl NG14 . . . . **163** E5
Bryans Cl La DN10 . . . . 3 F3
Brynsmoor Rd NG16 . . . . . **143** C7
Bryony Way NG11 . . . . **88** F4
Buckfast Way NG2 . . . . . . **186** B7
Buckingham Ave NG15 . . **146** B8
Buckingham Cl
☐ Kirkby in A NG17 . . . . . **114** F6
Mansfield Woodhouse NG19 **88** E5
Buckingham Cl NG10 . . . . **182** A3
Buckingham Dr NG12 . . . **176** E3
Buckingham Rd
Arnold NG5 . . . . **161** E5
Sandiacre NG10 . . . . **182** A3
Buckingham Rise NG8 . . . . **35** E7
Buckingham Way NG16 . . **159** B7
Buckland Dr NG14 . . . . **149** C4
Bucklee Dr NG14 . . . . **148** E8
Bucklow Cl NG8 . . . . **160** D1
Buck's La LE12 . . . . **213** A7
Budby Ave NG18 . . . . **102** C6
Budby Cres NG20 . . . . **74** E8
Budby Rd NG20 . . . . **60** B3
Budby Rise NG15 . . . . **146** B7
Bulcote Dr NG14 . . . . **163** D3
Bulcote Rd NG11 . . . . **184** E3
Bulgrave Mews NG2 . . . . . **185** C3

Bulham La NG23 . . . . **81** F1
Bullace Ct NG19 . . . . **88** E1
Bullace Rd NG3 . . . . **173** E7
Bull Cl Rd NG7 . . . . **184** F7
Buller Cl NG23 . . . . **98** B1
Buller St DE7 . . . . **170** A6
Buller Terr ☐ NG5 . . . . . . **161** D3
Bullfinch Rd NG6 . . . . **160** D4
Bullins Cl NG5 . . . . **147** C1
Bullivant Ave S80 . . . . **58** C8
Bullivant St NG3 . . . . **223** F4
Bullock Cl NG17 . . . . **88** B5
Bullpit Rd NG24 . . . . **140** E5
Bull Yd
Southwell NG25 . . . . **121** E1
Worksop S80 . . . . **35** E2
Bulpit La NG25 . . . . **98** F5
Bulstode Pl DE74 . . . . **203** C2
Bulwell Bsns Ctr NG6 . . . **160** A7
Bulwell Hall Pk Nature
Reserve NG6 . . . . **146** B2
Bulwell High Rd NG6 . . . . **160** B3
Bulwell La NG6 . . . . **160** D4
Bulwell Sta NG6 . . . . **160** C6
Bulwer Rd
Kirkby in A NG17 . . . . **114** F5
Nottingham NG7 . . . . **222** B3
Bunbury St NG2 . . . . **173** D1
Bungalow La NG22 . . . . . . **106** A5
Bunnison La NG12 . . . . **200** E7
Bunny CE Prim Sch
NG11 . . . . **206** E8
Bunny Hill LE12, NG11 . . . **206** D5
Bunny La
East Leake NG11 . . . . **205** E6
Keyworth NG12 . . . . **197** D2
Bunny Wood Nature Reserve
NG11 . . . . **206** F5
Buntings La NG4 . . . . **174** C7
Bunting St ☐ NG7 . . . . . . **172** E1
Bunyan Gn Rd NG16 . . . . **128** D7
Burbage Ct NG18 . . . . **103** B6
Burden Cres DN22 . . . . **53** B8
Burden La
Harby LE14 . . . . **202** B3
Shelford NG12 . . . . **164** C1
Burder St LE11 . . . . **220** A3
Burfield Ave LE11 . . . . **220** A3
Burford Prim Sch NG5 . . . **161** C6
Burford Rd NG7 . . . . **172** F8
Burford St NG5 . . . . **161** E8
Burgage NG25 . . . . **121** E1
Burgage La NG25 . . . . **121** E1
Burgass Rd NG3 . . . . **174** A7
Burge Cl NG2 . . . . **173** C2
Burgh Hall Cl NG9 . . . . . . **183** C2
Burhill NG12 . . . . **188** A2
Burke St NG7 . . . . **222** C3
Burleigh Cl NG4 . . . . **174** E7
Burleigh Rd
Loughborough LE11 . . . . . **220** A4
West Bridgford NG2 . . . . . **186** A6
Burleigh Sq NG9 . . . . **183** C4
Burleigh St ☐ DE7 . . . . . **157** F1
Burley Rise DE74 . . . . **203** D1
Burlington Ave
Nottingham NG5 . . . . **161** B3
Shirebrook NG20 . . . . **72** F6
Burlington Rd
Carlton NG4 . . . . **174** F8
Nottingham NG5 . . . . **161** C3
Burma Rd NG21 . . . . **118** A6
Burmaston Rd NG18 . . . . . **103** B6
Burnaby St NG6 . . . . **160** D4
Burnbank Cl NG2 . . . . **186** D5
Burnbreck Gdns NG8 . . . . **171** E4
Burndale Wlk NG5 . . . . . . **160** F8
Burneham Cl NG13 . . . . . . **165** C2
Burnham Ave NG9 . . . . . . **183** F4
Burnham Cl NG18 . . . . **102** C4
Burnham Way NG5 . . . . . . **161** C2
Burnham Wy NG1 . . . . **173** C3
Burnmoor La NG22 . . . . **80** A7
Burnor Pool NG14 . . . . . . **148** F7
Burns Ave
Mansfield Woodhouse
NG19 . . . . **88** C2
Nottingham NG7 . . . . **222** C4
Stapleford NG9 . . . . **170** E2
Burnside Cl ☐ NG17 . . . . **114** F7
Burnside Dr
Beeston NG9 . . . . **171** C1
Mansfield NG19 . . . . **87** E2
Burnside Gn NG8 . . . . **171** D6
Burnside Gr NG12 . . . . **186** D1
Burnside Rd
Nottingham NG8 . . . . **171** D6
West Bridgford NG2 . . . . . **185** E5
Burns La NG20 . . . . **74** B5
Burns Rd S81 . . . . **36** B4
Burns St
Gainsborough DN21 . . . . . . **15** B1
Mansfield NG18 . . . . **102** A7
Nottingham NG7 . . . . **222** C4
Burnt St NG17 . . . . **101** A3
Burns The NG20 . . . . **74** C5
Burntleys Rd NG22 . . . . **30** D7
Burnt Oak Cl NG16 . . . . . . **159** D3
Burnt Oaks Cl NG19 . . . . . . **88** D3
Burntstump Ctry Pk
NG5 . . . . **132** D1
Burntstump Hill NG5 . . . . **132** D1
Burnwood Ave NG18 . . . . . **103** A7
Burnwood Dr NG8 . . . . **171** C6
Burr La ☐ DE7 . . . . **157** F1
Burrows Ave NG9 . . . . **171** F1

Burrows Cres NG9 . . . . . . **171** F1
Burrows Ct NG3 . . . . **173** F5
Burrows The LE12 . . . . . . **205** E2
Burrow Wlk NG17 . . . . **114** E4
Burtness Rd NG7 . . . . **184** D1
Burton Ave NG4 . . . . **174** A7
Burton Cl
Carlton NG4 . . . . **175** A8
Harby LE14 . . . . **202** A3
Burton Dr NG9 . . . . **183** C4
Burton Joyce Prim Sch
NG14 . . . . **163** F4
Burton Joyce Sta NG14 . . **163** E3
Burton La NG13 . . . . **179** B4
Burton Manderfield Ct ☐
NG2 . . . . **173** C2
Burton Rd
Carlton NG4 . . . . **175** A8
Sutton in A NG17 . . . . **100** C3
Burton Rise
Annesley NG17 . . . . **130** A8
Walesby NG22 . . . . **64** A1
Burton St
Gainsborough DN21 . . . . . . **24** D7
Loughborough LE11 . . . . . **220** B2
Nottingham NG1 . . . . **223** E3
Burton Wlk LE12 . . . . **214** E8
Burton Wlks LE11 . . . . . . **220** B2
Burwell Cl NG19 . . . . **88** E4
Burwell St NG7 . . . . **222** B4
Bush Cl NG5 . . . . **160** F8
Bushmead Mews ☐ S80 . **35** F2
Bushy Cl NG10 . . . . **193** A6
Buskeyfield La NG20 . . . . . **59** F4
Bute Ave NG7 . . . . **222** B2
Butler Ave NG4 . . . . **162** B1
Butler Cl NG12 . . . . **176** A4
Butler Cres NG19 . . . . **87** D2
Butler Dr NG21 . . . . **117** F4
Butlers Cl NG15 . . . . **146** C5
Butlers Hill Inf Sch
NG15 . . . . **146** B5
Butlerwood Cl ☐ NG17 . . **114** E1
Butten Mdw NG10 . . . . 3 C2
Buttercup Cl NG24 . . . . . . **140** C5
Butterhall Cl S80 . . . . **45** A6
Buttermarket Sh Ctr
NG24 . . . . **139** F8
Buttermead Cl NG9 . . . . . **170** D2
Buttermere Cl
Long Eaton NG10 . . . . **182** A2
West Bridgford NG2 . . . . . **186** D7
Buttermere Ct ☐ NG5 . . **161** C2
Buttermere Dr NG9 . . . . . **183** D8
Butterton Cl DE7 . . . . **170** A7
Butterwick Cl NG19 . . . . . . **88** E1
Buttery La NG17 . . . . **100** E7
Butt Hill S80 . . . . **45** A6
Butt La
East Bridgford NG13 . . . . **165** E2
Mansfield Woodhouse NG19 **88** E2
Normanton on S LE12 . . . **213** D4
Butt Rd NG13 . . . . **178** A4
Butts Cl DE7 . . . . **170** A4
Butt St NG10 . . . . **182** B5
Buxton Ave NG4 . . . . **162** D1
Buxton Cl DE7 . . . . **157** D7
Buxton Ct NG18 . . . . **87** D1
Byard La NG1 . . . . **223** E2
Bycroft Rd DN21 . . . . **15** C4
Bye Pass Rd
Beeston NG9 . . . . **183** D3
Gunthorpe NG14 . . . . **164** F5
Bye Path Rd DN22 . . . . **39** F8
Byfield Cl NG7 . . . . **222** B4
Byford Cl NG3 . . . . **161** E2
Byley Rd NG8 . . . . **171** B5
Byrne Ct NG5 . . . . **162** B5
Byron Ave
Kirkby in A NG17 . . . . **115** B7
Long Eaton NG10 . . . . **182** B3
Mansfield Woodhouse NG19 **88** C2
Sutton in A NG17 . . . . **101** B4
Byron Cl
Darlton NG22 . . . . **67** A8
Newark-on-T NG24 . . . . . **140** A6
Byron Cres
Awsworth NG16 . . . . **158** C4
Ravenshead NG15 . . . . . . **116** E3
Byron Ct
Balderton NG24 . . . . **140** E3
☐ Nottingham NG2 . . . . . **173** E4
Byron Gdns NG25 . . . . **121** E1
Byron Gr NG5 . . . . **161** C3
Byron Rd
Annesley NG15 . . . . **130** C8
West Bridgford NG2 . . . . . **185** F7
Byron St
Arnold NG5 . . . . **161** D6
Bilsthorpe NG21 . . . . **118** B5
Hucknall NG15 . . . . **146** A6
Ilkeston DE7 . . . . **157** F1
Mansfield NG18 . . . . **102** A7
Newstead NG15 . . . . **130** D6
Shirebrook NG20 . . . . **72** E4
Byron Way S81 . . . . **36** B4
Bythorn Cl NG17 . . . . **101** B5

C

Cabin Leas ☐ LE11 . . . . . **220** B5
Caddaw Ave NG15 . . . . . . **146** A5
Cad La NG23 . . . . **81** E7
Cadlan Cl NG5 . . . . **161** A7
Cadlan Ct ☐ NG5 . . . . . . **161** A7

Caenby Cl DN21 . . . . **24** F7
Caernarvon Pl NG9 . . . . . . **183** B4
Caincross Rd NG8 . . . . **171** D7
Cairngorm Dr NG5 . . . . . . **147** B2
Cairns Cl NG5 . . . . **161** A5
Cairnsmore Cl NG10 . . . . . **182** A1
Cairo St NG1 . . . . **223** E3
Cairo St NG7 . . . . **160** F1
Caister Rd NG16 . . . . **195** E8
Caithness Ct ☐ NG5 . . . . **161** B1
Calcroft Cl NG8 . . . . **160** C2
Caldbeck Cl NG2 . . . . **186** C7
Caldbeck Ct NG9 . . . . **183** B4
Caldbeck Wlk ☐ NG5 . . . **161** B7
Calderdale NG8 . . . . **171** B3
Calderdale Dr NG10 . . . . . **193** A6
Calderhall Gdns ☐ NG5 . **161** C8
Calder Wlk ☐ NG6 . . . . . **160** B7
Caldon Gn NG6 . . . . **146** C2
Caldwell St ☐ LE11 . . . . . **220** A4
Caledonian Rd DN22 . . . . . **40** A5
Caledon Rd NG5 . . . . **161** B3
Calf Croft S80 . . . . **45** A5
California Rd NG24 . . . . . . **139** A4
Calke Ave NG17 . . . . **99** E2
Calladine Cl NG17 . . . . **100** D1
Calladine Gr NG17 . . . . . . **100** D1
Calladine La NG17 . . . . . . **114** C8
Callaway Cl NG8 . . . . **171** E5
Calstock Rd NG5 . . . . **161** C5
Calveley Rd NG8 . . . . **171** E8
Calver Cl NG8 . . . . **172** C4
Calver St NG19 . . . . **88** E1
Calverton Ave NG4 . . . . . . **162** B1
Calverton Cl NG9 . . . . **183** A2
Calverton Ct ☐ NG18 . . . **103** A3
Calverton Dr NG8 . . . . **159** D2
Calverton Folk Mus
NG14 . . . . **148** E7
Calverton Forum L Ctr
NG14 . . . . **162** C1
Calverton Rd
Arnold NG5 . . . . **148** A2
Blidworth NG21 . . . . **118** A2
Calverton Road Nature
Reserve NG5 . . . . **148** A3
Cambell Gdns NG5 . . . . . . **148** C1
Camberley Rd NG6 . . . . . . **160** A8
Camberley Rd NG6 . . . . . . **160** A8
Camborne Cl DN22 . . . . **29** E1
Camborne Cres DN22 . . . . . **29** E1
Camborne Dr NG8 . . . . **160** C2
Camborne Ms DN22 . . . . . . **29** E1
Cambourne Gdns NG15 . . **116** F2
Cambria Mews NG3 . . . . . **173** C7
Cambria Terr S80 . . . . **35** E4
Cambridge Cl NG23 . . . . . **111** B8
Cambridge Cres NG9 . . . . **170** D2
Cambridge Gdns NG5 . . . **162** B5
Cambridge Ms NG24 . . . . **140** E8
Cambridge Rd
Harworth DN11 . . . . 8 F4
Nottingham NG8 . . . . **172** A4
Rainworth NG21 . . . . **118** A8
West Bridgford NG2 . . . . . **186** A6
Cambridge St
Carlton NG4 . . . . **174** E8
Loughborough LE11 . . . . . **220** B5
Mansfield NG18 . . . . **102** A3
Camb's La DN22 . . . . **31** D8
Camdale Cl NG9 . . . . **183** B6
Camden Cl NG2 . . . . **173** E4
Camelia Ave NG11 . . . . . . **184** C1
Camelot Ave NG5 . . . . **161** A1
Camelot Cres NG11 . . . . . **196** B8
Camelot St NG11 . . . . **196** B8
Cameo Cl NG4 . . . . **174** F6
Cameron La NG24 . . . . **140** E1
Cameron St NG5 . . . . **161** C2
Camerons The NG19 . . . . . **101** D5
Camomile Cl NG5 . . . . **160** E7
Camomile Gdns ☐ NG7 . . **172** E7
Campbell Cl S81 . . . . **35** E8
Campbell Dr NG4 . . . . **174** C8
Campbell Gr NG3 . . . . **223** F3
Campbell St
Gainsborough DN21 . . . . . . **15** B1
Langley Mill NG16 . . . . . . **143** C4
Nottingham NG3 . . . . **223** F3
Campden Gn NG7 . . . . **184** E2
Campion Cl NG20 . . . . **72** D3
Campion St NG5 . . . . **161** E8
Campion Way NG13 . . . . . **177** D4
Camrose Cl NG8 . . . . **171** F8
Canal La
Harby NG13 . . . . **202** D5
Hose LE14 . . . . **211** C6
West Stockwith DN10 . . . . . 7 D2
Canal Side NG9 . . . . **184** B3
Canal St
Ilkeston DE7 . . . . **158** A1
Long Eaton NG10 . . . . **182** C1
Nottingham NG1 . . . . **223** E1
Retford DN22 . . . . **39** F6
Sandiacre NG10 . . . . **182** C5
Canal Terr S80 . . . . **36** A3
Canberra Cl NG9 . . . . **170** F1
Canberra Cres NG24 . . . . **140** E2
Canberra Gdns NG2 . . . . . **185** D3
Candleby Cl NG12 . . . . **187** F3
Candleby Ct NG12 . . . . **187** F3
Candleby La NG12 . . . . **187** F3
Candlemass Ct NG19 . . . . . **88** D2
Candle Mdw NG2 . . . . **174** D5

Canning Circ NG7 . . . . **222** C3
Cannock Way NG10 . . . . . **194** A7
Cannon Cl NG24 . . . . **125** E1
Cannon Sq DN22 . . . . **39** F8
Cannon St NG5 . . . . **161** C3
Canonbie Cl NG5 . . . . **148** B1
Canon Cl DE7 . . . . **157** F5
Canon's Cl NG25 . . . . **121** F1
Cantabury Ave NG7 . . . . . **172** F8
Cantelupe Rd DE7 . . . . . . **170** A4
Canterbury Cl
Mansfield Woodhouse
NG19 . . . . **88** C5
Nuthall NG16 . . . . **159** D3
Worksop S81 . . . . **36** A7
Canterbury Ct ☐ NG1 . . . **223** D4
Canterbury Rd NG8 . . . . . **172** D5
Canterbury Wlk S81 . . . . . . **25** F7
Cantley Ave NG4 . . . . **162** E2
Cantrell Prim Sch NG6 . . **160** C7
Cantrell Rd NG6 . . . . **160** C7
Canver Cl NG8 . . . . **171** C5
Canwick Cl NG8 . . . . **171** C5
Capenwray Gdns ☐ NG5 . **161** C8
Cape St NG18 . . . . **101** F7
Capes The NG13 . . . . **178** F4
Capitol Ct ☐ NG8 . . . . . . **172** A5
Caporn Cl NG6 . . . . **160** C5
Capps Pl NG22 . . . . **66** C3
Capt Ball Meml Homes
NG7 . . . . **222** A1
Carburton Ave NG20 . . . . . **74** D8
Carburton Border S80 . . . . **61** F6
Carburton Way NG17 . . . . **115** D6
Cardale Rd
Nottingham NG3 . . . . **174** A6
Radmanthwaite NG19 . . . . **87** C4
Cardiff St ☐ NG3 . . . . . . **173** F5
Cardinal Cl NG3 . . . . **223** F4
Cardinal Hinsley Cl
NG24 . . . . **139** D4
Carding Cl NG22 . . . . **120** A5
Cardington Cl NG5 . . . . . . **146** E1
Cardle Cl NG19 . . . . **89** A2
Cardwell St NG7 . . . . **172** F8
Carew Rd NG7 . . . . **184** E2
Carey Rd NG6 . . . . **160** C8
Carisbrook Ave NG18 . . . . **103** A2
Carisbrooke Ave
Beeston NG9 . . . . **184** A6
Carlton NG4 . . . . **163** B1
Nottingham NG3 . . . . **161** C1
Carisbrooke Cl NG17 . . . . **115** C5
Carisbrooke Dr NG3 . . . . . **161** C1
Car La NG13 . . . . **166** D2
Carlile Rd NG4 . . . . **174** E8
Carling Ave S80 . . . . **35** D3
Carlingford Rd NG15 . . . . **146** A8
Carlin St NG6 . . . . **160** B7
Carlisle Ave NG6 . . . . **160** C7
Carlisle St DN21 . . . . **15** D1
Carlswark Gdns NG5 . . . . **146** F1
Carlton Ave S81 . . . . **35** C4
Carlton Bsns & Tech Ctr
NG4 . . . . **174** D4
Carlton Central Inf & Jun
Schs NG4 . . . . **174** D8
Carlton Central Jun Sch
NG4 . . . . **174** D8
Carlton Cl
Clipstone NG19 . . . . **89** D3
Heanor DE75 . . . . **143** A3
Newark-on-T NG24 . . . . . **139** F6
Worksop S80 . . . . **35** E7
Carlton Cres LE12 . . . . . . **205** F2
Carlton Digby Specl Sch
NG3 . . . . **162** C3
Carlton Dr DN10 . . . . 9 F6
Carlton Ferry La NG23 . . . . **97** D1
Carlton Fold ☐ NG2 . . . . **173** E4
Carlton Forum L Ctr
NG4 . . . . **162** C1
Carlton Hall La S81 . . . . . . **25** C5
Carlton Hill NG4 . . . . **174** C7
Carlton La
Broxholme LN1 . . . . **57** F7
Sutton on T NG23 . . . . **97** A6
Carlton le Willows Comp Sch
NG4 . . . . **163** A1
Carlton Mews NG4 . . . . . . **174** C7
Carlton Phoenix Ind Est
S80 . . . . **36** A4
Carlton Rd
Long Eaton NG10 . . . . **193** B5
Newark-on-T NG24 . . . . . **140** A5
Nottingham NG3 . . . . **173** F7
Worksop S80, S81 . . . . **35** F5
Carlton Sq NG4 . . . . **174** E7
Carlton St
Mansfield Woodhouse
NG19 . . . . **88** C1
Nottingham NG1 . . . . **223** F2
Carlton Scn Sta NG4 . . . . . **174** E8
Carlton Vale Cl NG4 . . . . . **162** D1
Carlyle Rd NG2 . . . . **185** E7
Carman Cl NG16 . . . . **159** A8
Carmel Gdns NG5 . . . . **161** F6
Carnaby Cl NG12 . . . . **176** E3
Carnarvon Cl NG13 . . . . . **177** E5
Carnarvon Dr NG14 . . . . . **164** A5
Carnarvon Gr
Carlton, Gedling NG4 . . . . **162** F1
Carlton, Thorneywood
NG4 . . . . **174** D8
Sutton in A NG17 . . . . **100** B3
Carnarvon Pl NG13 . . . . . **177** D4
Carnarvon Prim Sch
NG13 . . . . **178** B4

Carnarvon Rd
Huthwaite NG17 . . . . .99 F2
West Bridgford NG2 . . . .185 F6
Carnarvon St
Carlton NG4 . . . . 175 A6
Teversal NG17 . . . . .100 B7
Carnforth Cl NG15 . . . . 182 D5
Carnforth Ct ◨ NG5 . . . 161 C8
Carnoustie S81 . . . . .36 B5
Carnoustie Cl ◷ NG17 . .114 E7
Carnwood Rd NG5 . . . . .161 A5
Carolgate DN22 . . . . .39 F6
Caroline Cl NG15 . . . . . . .117 B3
Caroline Ct DE7 . . . . .170 A6
Caroline Wlk NG3 . . . . . .173 D6
Carpenter Ave NG19 . . . .87 D2
Carpenters Ct NG12 . . . .189 B6
Carradale Cl NG5 . . . . . . .162 C8
Carr Cl DE55 . . . . 113 A7
Carr Farm Rd NG17 . . . . .114 F1
Carrfield Ave NG10 . . . . .182 F1
Carrfield Cl NG17 . . . . . .100 D3
Carrgate La NG23 . . . . . .153 E5
Carr Gr NG17 . . . . .114 E5
Carr Hill Prim Sch NG22 . .29 F1
Carr Hill Way DN22 . . . . . .29 F1
Carrington Ct NG5 . . . . . .161 C1
Carrington La NG14 . . . .149 A8
Carrington Prim Sch
NG5 . . . . .161 B1
Carrington St NG1 . . . . . .223 E1
Carr La
Blyton DN21 . . . . .15 C8
Doddington LN6 . . . . .71 B3
East Stockwith DN21 . . . . .7 E1
Gainsborough DN21 . . . . .24 C6
Market Warsop NG20 . . . .74 A4
Misterton DN10 . . . . .6 E2
South Normanton DE55 . .113 A7
Carrlon Vw ◼ S81 . . . . . . .35 D6
Carroll Gdns NG2 . . . . . .173 C1
Carr Rd
Bingham NG13 . . . . .178 B5
Gringley on t H DN10 . . . .12 C6
Retford DN22 . . . . .39 E6
Carr View DN10 . . . . .11 C3
Carsic La NG17 . . . . .100 E3
Carsic Prim Sch NG17 . .100 D3
Carsic Rd NG17 . . . . .100 D4
Carsington St NG19 . . . . .88 E3
Carson Rd DN21 . . . . .15 C2
Carswell Cl NG24 . . . . . .139 F6
Cartbridge NG17 . . . . . . .187 F2
Carter Ave
Radcliffe on T NG12 . . . .176 B3
Ruddington NG11 . . . . . .196 C6
Carter Gate NG24 . . . . . .139 F8
Carter La
Mansfield NG18 . . . . .102 C6
Shirebrook NG20 . . . . . . .72 E4
Warsop Vale NG19 . . . . . .73 C4
Carter La E DE55 . . . . . .113 C6
Carter La W
Shirebrook NG20 . . . . . . .72 D4
South Normanton DE55 . .113 C5
Carter Rd NG9 . . . . .183 A3
Carters Wood Dr NG16 . .159 F3
Cartwright Cl NG22 . . . . .54 A2
Cartwright St
Loughborough LE11 . . . . .220 C5
Shireoaks S81 . . . . .34 F7
Carver Cl NG21 . . . . .76 B1
Carver's Hollow NG22 . .120 A2
Carver St NG7 . . . . .172 F8
Carwood Rd NG7 . . . . . .171 D1
Caskgate St DN21 . . . . . .24 C8
Caslon Cl DN21 . . . . .161 A8
Castellan Rise NG5 . . . .161 C8
Casterton Rd NG5 . . . . .161 B7
Castle Brewery Ct NG24 .139 F7
Castlebridge NG22 . . . . .173 A2
Castle Bridge Rd NG2 . .173 A2
Castle Bvd NG7 . . . . . . .222 C1
Castle Cl
Bottesford NG13 . . . . . . .181 D2
Calverton NG14 . . . . .148 E7
Castledine St Extension
LE11 . . . . .220 B2
Castledine St LE11 . . . . .220 B2
Castle Farm La S80 . . . . .46 D7
Castlefields NG2 . . . . . . .173 C2
Castle Gate
Newark-on-T NG24 . . . . .139 F8
Nottingham NG1 . . . . . . .223 E2
Tickhill DN11 . . . . .8 A7
Castle Gdns NG7 . . . . . .222 B1
Castle Gr NG2 . . . . .223 D1
Castle Hill LE12 . . . . . . .205 F1
Castle Hill Cl NG17 . . . . .114 E5
Castle Marina Pk NG2 . .173 A2
Castle Marina Rd NG2 . .173 A2
Castle Mdw Rd NG2 . . . .223 D1
Castle Mdw Ret Pk NG2 .222 C1
Castle Mews NG19 . . . . . .88 A8
NG7 . . . . .223 D1
Castle Mus & Art Gall
NG7 . . . . .223 D1
Castle Pk NG2 . . . . .173 B2
Castle Pl NG1 . . . . .223 E2
Castle Quay NG7 . . . . . .223 D1
Castle Rd NG1 . . . . .223 D2
Castlerigg Cl NG2 . . . . .186 C5
Castle Rising NG24 . . . . .139 F8
Castle St
Eastwood NG16 . . . . . . .144 A1
◼ Mansfield NG18 . . . . .102 A7
Mansfield Woodhouse NG19 88 B4
Nottingham NG2 . . . . . . .173 F4
Worksop S80 . . . . .35 E2

Castleton Ave
Arnold NG5 . . . . .161 F6
Carlton NG4 . . . . .162 E1
Ilkeston DE7 . . . . .157 E5
Castleton Cl
Hucknall NG15 . . . . .145 D6
Mansfield Woodhouse NG19 88 C4
◳ Nottingham NG2 . . . . .173 B1
Ravenshead NG15 . . . . . .117 A3
Castleton Ct NG6 . . . . . .159 F6
Castle View
Aldercar NG16 . . . . .143 A4
West Bridgford NG2 . . . .185 D6
Castle View Rd NG13 . . .181 C1
Caterham Cl NG8 . . . . . .171 D7
Catfoot La NG4 . . . . .162 E8
Catherine Ave NG19 . . . . .88 C3
Catherine Cl
◨ Kirkby in A NG17 . . . . .114 F7
Nottingham NG6 . . . . . . .160 A7
Catkin Dr NG16 . . . . .158 C8
Catkin Way NG24 . . . . . .140 B4
Catlow Wlk ◳ NG5 . . . . .161 C8
Caton Cl NG17 . . . . .100 D3
Cator Cl NG4 . . . . .162 D3
Cator La NG9 . . . . .183 D5
Cator La N NG9 . . . . . . .183 D6
Cator Rd NG19 . . . . .87 C3
Catriona Cres NG5 . . . . .148 A1
Catt Cl NG9 . . . . .183 B1
Catterley Hill Rd NG3 . . .174 B6
Cattle Mkt ◼ LE11 . . . . .220 B3
Cattle Mkt Rd NG2 . . . .173 D2
Cattle Rd DN10 . . . . .6 C1
Catton Rd NG5 . . . . .162 A8
Caudale Ct NG2 . . . . . . .186 C7
Caudwell Cl NG25 . . . . .121 E2
Caudwell Dr NG18 . . . . .102 C3
Cauldwell Rd NG17 . . . .101 E2
Caulton St NG7 . . . . . . .222 B4
Caunton Ave NG3 . . . . . .161 E1
Caunton Cl
Mansfield NG18 . . . . .101 F6
Meden Vale NG20 . . . . . .74 D7
Caunton Rd
Bathley NG23 . . . . .109 E4
Hockerton NG25 . . . . . . .122 B6
Caunt's Cres NG17 . . . . .100 D3
Causeway DN21 . . . . .24 E3
Causeway La
Gamston DN22 . . . . .51 B7
Morton NG25 . . . . .137 C4
Causeway Mews ◳ NG3 .173 B1
Cavan Ct ◼ NG2 . . . . . . .173 C1
Cavell Cl
Woodbeck DN22 . . . . .53 B8
Cavell Ct NG7 . . . . .172 D2
Cavendish Ave
Carlton NG4 . . . . .162 D2
Edwinstowe NG21 . . . . . .75 F2
Newark-on-T NG24 . . . . .140 A6
Nottingham NG5 . . . . . . .161 D3
Sutton in A NG17 . . . . . .100 E3
Cavendish Cl
Bawtry DN10 . . . . .9 F6
Hucknall NG15 . . . . .146 C5
Cavendish Cres
Annesley Woodhouse
NG17 . . . . .130 A8
Carlton NG4 . . . . .162 C2
Stapleford NG9 . . . . .170 D2
Cavendish Cres N NG7 .222 C2
Cavendish Cres S NG7 .222 C1
Cavendish Dr
Carlton NG4 . . . . .174 E8
Lea DN21 . . . . .24 F2
Cavendish Pl NG9 . . . . .183 F6
Cavendish Rd
Carlton NG4 . . . . .162 C1
Ilkeston DE7 . . . . .170 A6
Long Eaton NG10 . . . . . .182 C2
Retford DN22 . . . . .40 B4
Worksop S80 . . . . .47 A8
Cavendish Rd E NG7 . . .222 C2
Cavendish Rd W NG7 . .222 C2
Cavendish St
Arnold NG5 . . . . .161 E8
Langwith NG20 . . . . .72 F8
Mansfield NG18 . . . . .102 C5
Nottingham NG7 . . . . . . .184 B8
Sutton in A NG17 . . . . . .101 A4
Cavendish Vale NG5 . . .161 D3
Cave's La DN10 . . . . .13 D6
Cawdell Dr LE12 . . . . . . .212 D2
Cawdron Wlk NG7 . . . . .184 E2
Cawston Gdns ◼ NG6 . .160 B8
Cawthorne Cl NG23 . . . . .98 B1
Cawthorne Way NG18 . .102 F7
Caxmere Dr NG8 . . . . . .171 F5
Caxton Cl NG4 . . . . .174 E7
Caxton Rd NG5 . . . . .161 B1
Caythorpe Cres NG5 . . .161 C3
Caythorpe Rd NG14 . . . .150 F1
Caythorpe Rise NG5 . . . .161 C3
Cecil Cl S80 . . . . .35 A4
Cecil St
Gainsborough DN21 . . . . .15 C1
Nottingham NG7 . . . . . . .222 B1
Cedar Ave
Beeston NG9 . . . . .184 A7
East Leake LE12 . . . . . . .214 D8
Kirkby in A NG17 . . . . . .114 F4
Long Eaton NG10 . . . . . .193 C5
Mansfield Woodhouse NG19 88 C5
Newark-on-T NG24 . . . . .125 B3

Cedar Ave continued
Nuthall NG16 . . . . .159 F4
Cedar Cl
Carlton in L S81 . . . . .25 E7
Gainsborough DN21 . . . . .15 B3
Sandiacre NG10 . . . . . . .182 B7
Sutton in A NG17 . . . . . .100 D7
Cedar Ct NG2 . . . . .184 A7
Cedar Dr
Keyworth NG12 . . . . .197 E2
Selston NG16 . . . . .128 F7
Cedar Gr
Arnold NG5 . . . . .162 B8
Hucknall NG15 . . . . .146 B5
Nottingham NG8 . . . . . . .171 F4
South Normanton DE55 . .113 B4
Cedar La NG22 . . . . .77 C6
Cedarland Cres NG16 . .159 F4
Cedar Rd
Beeston NG9 . . . . .183 E5
Loughborough LE11 . . . .220 C1
Nottingham NG7 . . . . . . .173 A8
Cedar St NG18 . . . . .102 C5
Cedars The NG5 . . . . . . .161 D4
Cedar Tree Rd
Elkesley DN22 . . . . .50 A3
Nottingham NG5 . . . . . . .147 B1
Celandine Cl NG16 . . . . .159 B7
Celandine Gdns NG13 . .177 C4
Celia Dr NG4 . . . . .174 D7
Cemetery Rd
Stapleford NG9 . . . . .182 E7
Worksop S80 . . . . .36 A2
Centenary Cl NG24 . . . .140 C4
Central Ave
Arnold NG5 . . . . .161 F7
Beeston, Chilwell NG9 . . .183 D6
Beeston NG9 . . . . .183 F8
Blidworth NG21 . . . . .118 B5
Creswell S80 . . . . .58 D8
Hucknall NG15 . . . . .146 A6
Kirkby in A NG17 . . . . . .115 B3
Mansfield NG18 . . . . .102 C5
Nottingham, Mapperley
NG3 . . . . .162 A4
Nottingham, New Basford NG7,
NG5 . . . . .161 A1
Sandiacre NG10 . . . . . . .182 B6
South Normanton DE55 . .113 B5
Stapleford NG9 . . . . .182 F8
Walesby NG22 . . . . .64 A1
West Bridgford NG2 . . . .185 F8
Worksop S80 . . . . .35 E3
Central Ave S NG5 . . . . .161 F7
Central Cl NG20 . . . . .72 E2
Central Ct NG7 . . . . .172 F1
Central Dr
Bawtry DN10 . . . . .10 A8
Clipstone NG21 . . . . .89 F2
Elston NG23 . . . . .153 E4
Shirebrook NG20 . . . . . . .72 E5
Central St
◳ Nottingham NG3 . . . . .173 E6
Sutton in A NG17 . . . . . .101 B4
Central Wlk NG15 . . . . . .146 A7
Centre Way NG12 . . . . . .175 E4
Centurion Way NG11 . . .185 A8
Century Ave NG18 . . . . . .101 F5
Century La NG1 . . . . .57 A5
Century Rd DN22 . . . . . . .39 E5
Century St NG24 . . . . . . .140 A8
Cernan Ct NG6 . . . . .159 F5
Cerne Cl NG7 . . . . .184 E1
Chaceley Way NG11 . . . .185 A3
Chadborn Ave NG11 . . . .195 B1
Chadburn Rd NG18 . . . . .102 E8
Chaddesden The NG3 . .173 C7
Chad Gdns NG5 . . . . . . .147 A2
Chadwick Rd NG7 . . . . .172 D7
Chadwick Way DN22 . . . .53 B8
Chaffinch Cl NG18 . . . . .102 F7
Chaffinch Mews DE7 . . .157 C5
Chainbridge Cl LE11 . . .220 A5
Chainbridge La DN22 . . .29 C8
Chainbridge Nature Reserve
DN22 . . . . .29 C8
Chain La
◼ Newark-on-T NG24 . . .139 F8
Nottingham NG7 . . . . . . .172 E1
Chalfield Cl NG11 . . . . . .184 D1
Chalfont Dr NG8 . . . . . . .172 C6
Chalons Cl DE7 . . . . .157 F1
Chamberlain Cl NG8 . . . .184 C1
Chambers Ave DE7 . . . . .170 B7
Champion Ave DE7 . . . . .157 C3
Champion Cres NG1 . . . .101 F8
Chancery Cl NG17 . . . . . .101 A6
Chancery Cl NG1 . . . . . . .185 A6
Chancery La DN22 . . . . . .39 E6
Chancery The NG9 . . . . .183 C7
Chandos Ave NG4 . . . . . .175 A8
Chandos Cl NG22 . . . . . . .65 F3
Chandos St
Carlton NG4 . . . . .174 E7
Nottingham NG3 . . . . . . .173 E7
Chantrey Cl NG9 . . . . . . .183 B1
Chantrey Rd NG2 . . . . . .185 E7
Chantry Cl
Kimberley NG16 . . . . . . .159 A5
Long Eaton NG10 . . . . . .193 A4
Newark-on-T NG24 . . . . .140 A8
Chantry The NG18 . . . . .102 F5
Chantry Wlk NG20 . . . . . .74 B3
Chapel Bar NG1 . . . . . . .223 D2
Chapel Baulk DN9 . . . . . . .2 B1
Chapel Cl
Misterton DN10 . . . . .6 F2

Chapel Cl continued
Walesby NG22 . . . . .64 A2
Chapel Ct DE7 . . . . .157 F4
Chapel Garth NG13 . . . . .179 F6
Chapelgate DN22 . . . . . . .39 F7
Chapel Gate S81 . . . . . . .26 A5
Chapel La
Arnold NG5 . . . . .161 E8
Aslockton NG13 . . . . . . .179 A5
Bathley NG23 . . . . .110 B3
Bingham NG13 . . . . .177 E6
Caunton NG23 . . . . .109 A5
Claypole NG23 . . . . .156 D7
Coddington NG24 . . . . . .126 B1
Costock LE12 . . . . .206 C1
Cotgrave NG12 . . . . .187 F3
Epperstone NG14 . . . . . .150 A6
Everton DN10 . . . . .11 C3
Farndon NG24 . . . . .138 F4
Farnsfield NG22 . . . . . . .119 F5
Granby NG13 . . . . .191 B5
Hose LE14 . . . . .211 F8
Lambley NG4 . . . . .163 B7
Laxton NG22 . . . . .79 C2
Misterton DN10 . . . . .6 F2
Morton DN21 . . . . .15 B4
Nether Broughton LE14 . .219 D8
North Scarle LN6 . . . . . . .83 D3
Old Dalby LE14 . . . . .218 E4
Oxton NG25 . . . . .134 C4
Ravenshead NG15 . . . . . .117 B2
Scrooby DN10 . . . . .10 A2
Upper Broughton LE14 . .210 A1
Walesby NG22 . . . . .64 A2
Willoughby-on-t-W LE12 .217 D7
Worksop S80 . . . . .58 D8
Chapel Mews Ct NG9 . . .183 B8
Chapel Pl NG15 . . . . . . .158 F6
Chapel Quarter Bsns
Development NG1 . . . . .223 D2
Chapel Rd NG16 . . . . . . .128 C6
Chapel St
Annesley Woodhouse
NG17 . . . . .115 A1
Barkestone-le-V NG13 . . .192 B2
Beckingham LN5 . . . . . . .142 D8
Beeston NG9 . . . . .183 B8
Bottesford NG13 . . . . . . .181 A3
Eastwood NG16 . . . . . . .143 F1
Heanor DE7 . . . . .157 A8
Hucknall NG15 . . . . .146 A7
◼ Ilkeston DE7 . . . . .157 F1
Kimberley NG16 . . . . . . .158 F6
Kirkby in A NG17 . . . . . .114 E5
Long Eaton NG10 . . . . . .193 E7
New Houghton NG19 . . . .87 A7
Orston NG13 . . . . .179 F7
Ruddington NG11 . . . . . .196 C6
Selston NG16 . . . . .129 A7
Whaley Thorns NG20 . . . .59 A3
Chapel Staith DN21 . . . . .24 C8
Chapel Wlk S80 . . . . .35 E2
Chapman Ct LE11 . . . . . .220 C4
Chapman St NG18 . . . . .102 B7
Chapter Dr NG16 . . . . . .159 A5
Chard St NG7 . . . . .160 F2
Charlbury Ct NG9 . . . . . .171 B4
Charlbury Rd NG2 . . . . . .172 B5
Charlecote Dr NG8 . . . . .171 D3
Charlecote Pk Dr NG2 . .185 C4
Charles Ave
Beeston, Chilwell NG9 . . .183 C3
Beeston NG9 . . . . .172 A1
Eastwood NG16 . . . . . . .144 B1
Sandiacre NG10 . . . . . . .182 B6
Stapleford NG9 . . . . .182 E8
Charles Baines Com Prim
Sch DN21 . . . . .24 B8
Charles Cl
Carlton NG4 . . . . .162 F2
Ilkeston DE7 . . . . .170 B6
Charles Pk NG6 . . . . . . .160 B5
Charles St
Arnold NG5 . . . . .161 E7
Gainsborough DN21 . . . . .15 D1
Hucknall NG15 . . . . .146 A8
Long Eaton NG10 . . . . . .193 D6
Loughborough LE11 . . . .220 B5
Mansfield NG19 . . . . .88 A1
Mansfield Woodhouse NG19 88 C4
Newark-on-T NG24 . . . . .140 B7
Ruddington NG11 . . . . . .196 C7
Sutton in A NG17 . . . . . .101 A3
Charlesworth Ave NG7 . .172 E8
Charlesworth Ct NG19 . . .88 E3
Charlock Cl NG5 . . . . . . .160 E7
Charlock Gdns NG13 . . .177 D3
Charlotte Cl
Arnold NG5 . . . . .147 E2
Kirton NG22 . . . . .78 B6
Newark-on-T NG24 . . . . .140 A8
Charlotte Gr NG9 . . . . . .171 D1
Charlton Ave NG10 . . . . .182 E4
Charlton Gr NG9 . . . . . . .183 F5
Charnock Ave NG8 . . . . .172 D3
Charnwood Ave
Beeston NG9 . . . . .183 F6
Keyworth NG12 . . . . .197 E2
Long Eaton NG10 . . . . . .193 B4
Sandiacre NG10 . . . . . . .182 B4
Sutton Bonington LE12 . .213 C5
Charnwood Cres DE55 . .113 A6
Charnwood Fields LE12 .213 C5
Charnwood Gr
Bingham NG13 . . . . .177 D4
Hucknall NG15 . . . . .145 D5

Charnwood Gr continued
Mansfield NG18 . . . . .103 A7
Mansfield Woodhouse NG19 88 B5
West Bridgford NG2 . . . .185 E7
Charnwood La NG5 . . . . .162 A6
Charnwood L Ctr LE11 . .220 A3
Charnwood Mus LE11 . . .220 B3
Charnwood Rd LE11 . . . .220 B2
Charnwood St NG17 . . . .100 C1
Charnwood Way NG14 . .149 D4
Charter Pl NG22 . . . . .66 A2
Charters Cl ◻ NG17 . . . . .114 F7
Chartwell Ave NG11 . . . .196 B7
Chartwell Gr NG3 . . . . . .162 C5
Chartwell Rd NG17 . . . . .115 C5
Chase Pk NG2 . . . . .174 A3
Chatham Ct NG24 . . . . . .139 F7
Chatham St
Nottingham NG1 . . . . . . .223 E4
Southwell NG25 . . . . .121 F1
Chatsworth Ave
Beeston NG9 . . . . .183 C2
Carlton NG4 . . . . .162 E1
Long Eaton NG10 . . . . . .194 A6
Nottingham NG7 . . . . . . .160 F2
Radcliffe on T NG12 . . . .176 A4
Selston NG16 . . . . .129 A7
Shirebrook NG20 . . . . . . .72 E6
Southwell NG25 . . . . .121 D1
Chatsworth Cl
Mansfield NG18 . . . . .102 E2
Ravenshead NG15 . . . . . .117 A3
Sandiacre NG10 . . . . . . .182 B4
Sutton in A NG17 . . . . . .100 F5
Chatsworth Ct
Harworth DN11 . . . . .9 B5
Hucknall NG15 . . . . .146 A6
Chatsworth Dr
Hucknall NG15 . . . . .146 A6
Mansfield NG18 . . . . .102 E2
Chatsworth Rd
Creswell S80 . . . . .58 C8
Newark-on-T NG24 . . . . .140 A5
West Bridgford NG2 . . . .186 B8
Worksop S80 . . . . .35 F7
Chatsworth St
Sutton in A NG17 . . . . . .101 A3
Tibshelf DE55 . . . . .99 A6
Chaucer Cres NG17 . . . .101 B4
Chaucer Rd NG24 . . . . . .140 E4
Chaucer St
Ilkeston DE7 . . . . .157 F1
Mansfield NG18 . . . . .102 A7
Nottingham NG1 . . . . . . .223 D3
Chaworth Ave NG16 . . . .145 A1
Chaworth Rd
Bingham NG13 . . . . .177 D4
Carlton NG4 . . . . .174 F6
West Bridgford NG2 . . . .185 E6
Chaworth St N21 . . . . . . .118 B5
Cheadle Cl
Nottingham, Bilborough
NG8 . . . . .171 D8
Nottingham, Portchester
NG3 . . . . .162 B2
Cheapside
Nottingham NG1 . . . . . . .223 E2
Worksop S80 . . . . .36 A2
Cheddar Cl NG21 . . . . . . .104 C1
Cheddar Rd NG11 . . . . . .195 E8
Chedington Ave NG3 . . . .162 D6
Chediston Vale NG5 . . . .161 B8
Chedworth Cl ◻ NG3 . . . .173 F5
Chelmorton Cl NG19 . . . . .88 E3
Chelmsford Rd NG7 . . . .160 F2
Chelmsford Terr NG7 . . .160 F2
Chelsea Cl NG16 . . . . . . .159 E3
Chelsea St NG7 . . . . . . .160 F1
Cheltenham Cl NG9 . . . .182 F1
Cheltenham St NG18 . . .102 F7
Cheltenham St NG5 . . . .160 E4
Chennel Nook NG12 . . . .188 A2
Chepstow Rd NG11 . . . . .195 E8
Chepstow Wlk NG18 . . . .102 F7
Chequers La NG22 . . . . . .54 B2
Cherhill Cl NG11 . . . . . . .195 D7
Cheriton Cl NG19 . . . . . . .87 E1
Cheriton Dr
Ravenshead NG15 . . . . . .117 B2
Shipley DE7 . . . . .157 C3
Chermside Cl NG15 . . . . .117 B1
Chermside NG15 . . . . . . .117 A3
Cherry Ave
Hucknall NG18 . . . . .146 B5
Kirkby in A NG17 . . . . . .114 D7
Cherry Cl
Arnold NG5 . . . . .161 E8
Nottingham NG5 . . . . . . .161 B7
Shirebrook NG20 . . . . . . .72 E6
South Normanton DE55 . .113 B7
Cherry Gr
Mansfield NG18 . . . . .101 E6
Market Warsop NG20 . . . .74 C4
Cherry Hill NG12 . . . . . . .197 F3
Cherry Holt
Newark-on-T NG24 . . . . .139 F5
Retford DN22 . . . . .29 D1
Cherryholt Cl NG13 . . . . .165 D4
Cherryholt La NG13 . . . . .165 D3
Cherry Orch NG12 . . . . . .187 E3
Cherry Orch Mount NG5 .161 B7
Cherry St NG13 . . . . .177 F4
Cherry Tree Ave S81 . . . .34 F7

Cherry Tree Cl
Brinsley NG16 143 E8
Mansfield Woodhouse NG19 88 B4
Radcliffe on T NG12 175 F2
Cherry Tree La NG12 186 B3
Cherry Tree Rd DN21 15 E1
Cherry Tree Wlk DN22 19 C5
Cherry Wood Dr NG8 172 B7
Cherrywood Gdns NG3 174 A8
Chertsey Cl NG3 161 F1
Cherwell Ct NG6 159 F6
Chesham Dr
Beeston NG9 171 B2
Nottingham NG5 161 B1
Cheshire Way NG16 128 C4
Chesil Ave 2 NG8 172 D5
Chesil Cotts 3 NG8 172 D5
Cheslyn Dr NG8 172 C8
Chesnut Cl NG23 81 A4
Chesnut Gdn NG17 100 D1
Chess Burrow NG19 88 D2
Chester Cl 3 LE11 220 A3
Chesterfield Ave
Bingham NG13 177 E5
Carlton NG4 162 D2
Long Eaton NG10 193 F7
Chesterfield Ct NG4 162 D3
Chesterfield Dr
Burton Joyce NG14 164 A5
Retford DN22 40 A7
Chesterfield Rd
Hardstoft DE55 85 A1
Huthwaite NG17 99 E4
New Houghton NG19 86 E7
Pleasley NG19 87 A5
Chesterfield Rd N NG19 87 C4
Chesterfield Rd S NG18 102 B8
Chesterfield St NG4 174 D7
Chester Gn NG9 182 E2
Chesterman Cl NG16 158 B4
Chester Rd NG3 174 B5
Chester St NG19 87 E1
Chesterton Dr S81 36 B5
Chestnut Ave
Beeston NG9 183 F6
Bingham NG13 177 E4
Gainsborough DN21 15 D2
Kirkby in A NG17 114 F4
Newark-on-T NG24 125 B4
Nottingham NG3 162 B2
Ravenshead NG15 117 B1
Retford DN22 39 D4
Chestnut Cl
Bottesford NG13 181 C3
New Ollerton NG22 77 D6
Ravenshead NG18 116 E7
Worksop S80 35 E1
Chestnut Copse NG24 140 B6
Chestnut Dr
Bawtry DN10 9 F7
Mansfield NG18 102 E2
New Ollerton NG22 77 D6
Nuthall NG16 159 B6
Selston NG16 128 F7
Shirebrook NG20 72 D4
South Normanton DE55 113 B4
Chestnut Gdns NG17 100 D1
Chestnut Gr
Arnold NG5 162 A8
Burton Joyce NG14 163 F4
Carlton NG4 162 F1
Farndon NG24 139 A4
Hucknall NG15 146 B4
Kirkby in A NG17 114 F5
Mansfield Woodhouse NG19 88 B5
Nottingham NG3 173 C7
Radcliffe on T NG12 175 F4
Sandiacre NG10 182 A7
West Bridgford NG2 185 D7
Chestnut Hill NG18 102 E2
Chestnut La NG11 194 E6
Chestnut Mews NG18 102 E2
Chestnut Rd
Langley Mill NG16 143 A3
Langold S81 16 F4
Chestnut St LE11 220 A4
Chestnuts The
Carlton NG4 163 B1
Long Eaton NG10 193 A8
Nottingham NG3 161 F1
Radcliffe on T NG12 175 E3
Chestnut Way NG22 66 A2
Chettles Ind Est NG8 172 D5
Chetwin Rd NG8 171 D5
Chetwynd Rd
Beeston, Chilwell NG9 183 C3
Beeston, Toton NG9 183 A2
Chetwynd Road Prim Sch
NG9 183 A2
Cheverton Ct 7 NG3 173 C7
Chevin Gdns 12 NG5 147 A1
Cheviot Cl NG5 147 B2
Cheviot Ct S81 25 E7
Cheviot Dr NG6 159 F8
Cheviot Rd NG10 182 A1
Chewton Ave NG16 144 A1
Chewton Cl NG22 105 E6
Chewton St NG16 144 A1
Cheyne Dr NG22 106 A4
Cheyne Wlk
Bawtry DN10 9 F7
Retford DN22 39 D4
Cheyny Cl NG2 173 C1
Chichester Cl
Ilkeston DE7 170 A8
Chichester Cl *continued*
Mansfield NG19 101 D6
Nottingham NG5 160 E7
Chichester Dr NG12 187 E4
Chichester Wlk S81 25 E7
Chidlow Rd NG8 171 D7
Chigwell Cl NG8 159 E3
Chillon Way NG15 145 D6
Chiltern Cl NG5 147 B2
Chiltern Gdns NG10 182 A1
Chiltern Way
Carlton in L S81 25 E7
Nottingham NG5 161 B7
Chilton Cres NG19 88 C6
Chilton Dr NG16 159 A7
Chilvers Cl NG5 161 A7
Chilwell Coll House Jun Sch
NG9 183 D5
Chilwell Comp Sch NG9 183 D3
Chilwell Ct NG6 160 D7
Chilwell La NG9 183 C6
Chilwell Olympia NG9 183 D3
Chilwell Rd NG9 183 F6
Chilwell Ret Pk NG9 183 A2
Chilwell St NG7 222 B1
Chimes Mdw NG25 136 F8
Chine Gdns NG2 185 C5
Chine The DE55 113 B3
Chingford Rd NG8 171 E8
Chiomere DN22 39 D4
Chippendale St NG7 222 B1
Chippenham Rd NG5 161 C7
Chirnside NG19 101 D5
Chisbury Gn NG11 195 D7
Chisholm Way NG5 161 A6
Chisworth Ct NG19 88 E3
Christ Church Inf Sch
NG24 139 E7
Christchurch Rd NG15 145 D4
Christina Ave NG6 160 C4
Christina Cres NG6 160 C4
Christine Cl NG15 131 C1
Christopher Cl NG8 171 F6
Christopher Cres NG24 140 C4
Christ the King RC Comp Sch
NG5 162 B7
Chrysalis Way NG16 143 C3
Church Ave
Arnold NG5 161 E7
Long Eaton NG10 193 A4
Nottingham NG7 222 B1
Sutton in A NG17 100 D2
Church Cl
Arnold NG5 161 E7
Bingham NG13 177 F5
Church Warsop NG20 74 B6
East Leake LE12 205 E1
Hose LE14 211 F7
North Wheatley DN22 31 E8
Nottingham NG3 223 E4
Radcliffe on T NG12 175 E3
Trowell NG9 170 C4
Church Cnr NG13 192 F4
Church Cres
Arnold NG5 161 D7
Beeston NG9 183 A3
Church Croft NG2 185 F8
Churchdale Ave NG9 170 E1
Church Dr
Arnold NG5 161 E7
Hucknall NG15 146 A7
Ilkeston DE7 157 D4
Keyworth NG12 197 F3
Misterton DN10 6 E2
Nottingham NG5 161 B1
Ravenshead NG15 117 A2
Sandiacre NG10 182 B7
Shirebrook NG20 72 E3
West Bridgford NG2 185 F7
Church Dr E NG5 161 E7
Church Drive Prim Sch
NG5 161 E7
Church End LE14 210 C1
Church Farm Gdns NG22 77 E1
Church Field Cl S81 26 A5
Churchfield Ct NG5 147 A1
Churchfield Dr NG21 103 F2
Churchfield La NG7 222 A4
Churchfield Terr NG7 160 E2
Churchgate DN22 39 F7
Church Gate
Colston Bassett NG12 200 E7
Cotgrave NG12 198 C8
Kegworth DE74 203 D2
Loughborough LE11 220 A4
Loughborough LE11 220 B4
Church Gr NG7 222 A1
Church Hill
Bilsthorpe NG22 106 A5
Keyworth NG12 197 E7
Kimberley NG16 158 F6
Kirkby in A NG17 114 D3
Mansfield Woodhouse NG19 88 C3
Newton DE55 99 A1
North Wheatley DN22 31 E8
Sutton in A NG17 100 E2
Church Hill Ave NG19 88 C3
Church Hill Gdns NG19 88 C3
Churchill Cl NG5 161 F6
Churchill Dr
Newark-on-T NG24 139 E5
Ruddington NG11 196 B7
Stapleford NG9 182 E8
Churchill Pk NG4 174 C3
Churchill Way DN21 24 F3
Church La
Arnold NG5 147 F1
Averham NG23 123 F1
Church La *continued*
Balderton NG24 140 E4
Barton in F NG11 194 E6
Beeston NG9 183 D1
Besthorpe NG23 98 B5
Bingham NG13 177 F5
Bothamsall DN22 63 F7
Bottesford NG13 181 B3
Boughton NG22 77 F5
Brinsley NG16 143 E7
Car Colston NG13 166 C3
Carlton in L S81 25 F4
Carlton-on-Trent NG23 96 F4
Clarborough DN22 30 E3
Clayworth DN22 21 D5
Collingham NG23 98 A1
Cossall NG16 158 C1
Costock LE12 206 C1
Cotgrave NG12 187 E3
Cromwell NG23 110 F7
Eagle LN6 84 D3
Eakring NG22 92 E1
East Drayton DN22 53 A3
East Stoke NG23 138 B1
Epperstone NG14 150 A6
Gamston DN22 50 F4
Halam NG22 120 F1
Harworth DN11 8 E4
Hayton DN22 30 C5
Hucknall NG15 131 B1
Letwell S81 16 A2
Long Clawson LE14 211 C3
Lowdham NG14 150 C2
Mansfield NG18 102 C6
Maplebeck NG22 108 A6
Misterton DN10 6 E2
Morton NG25 137 D3
North Clifton NG23 68 D3
North Scarle LN6 83 D2
Nottingham NG6 160 C7
Old Dalby LE14 218 E4
Owthorpe NG12 199 E8
Pleasley NG19 87 A6
Plumtree NG12 197 E7
Plungar NG13 191 F1
Redmile NG13 192 F3
Retford DN22 39 E4
Saxilby LN1 56 F5
Screveton NG13 166 E4
Scrooby DN10 10 A2
Selston, Selston Green
NG16 128 D7
Selston, Underwood NG16 129 A3
Sibthorpe NG23 167 E7
South Muskham NG23 124 E7
Stapleford NG9 182 D7
Sutton in A NG17 100 E2
Thrumpton NG11 194 C3
Tibshelf DE55 99 A6
Tickhill DN11 8 A7
Torksey LN1 44 B2
Upper Broughton LE14 210 A1
Upton NG23 122 F1
West Drayton DN22 50 F2
Widmerpool NG12 208 C5
Willoughby-on-t-W LE12 217 C7
Church Lands 2 LE11 220 B6
Church Mdw
Calverton NG14 148 F7
Claypole NG23 156 C6
Church Mead NG17 99 F3
Church Mews
1 Nottingham NG2 173 D1
Sutton in A NG17 100 E2
Churchmoor Ct NG5 147 E1
Churchmoor La NG5 147 F1
Church Rd
Bestwood Village NG6 146 E4
Bircotes DN11 9 C4
Burton Joyce NG14 163 F4
Church Warsop NG20 74 B6
Clipstone NG21 89 F3
Greasley NG16 144 E3
Harby NG23 70 D1
Nottingham NG3 223 F4
Saxilby LN1 57 A4
Church St E NG16 113 D4
Church St W NG16 113 D4
Church Side
Farnsfield NG22 119 F6
Huthwaite NG17 99 F3
Mansfield NG18 102 C6
Churchside Gdns NG7 172 E8
Church Sq NG7 222 B1
Church St
Arnold NG5 161 F8
Bawtry DN10 10 A6
Beckingham DN10 14 B1
Beeston, Bramcote NG9 183 B8
Beeston NG9 183 F6
Bilsthorpe NG22 105 F6
Bingham NG13 177 F4
Bottesford NG13 181 B2
Bunny NG11 206 E8
Carlton NG4 174 E7
Collingham NG23 111 F7
Cropwell Bishop NG12 189 A4
East Markham NG22 66 A6
Eastwood NG16 143 F2
Edwinstowe NG21 76 B2
Everton DN10 11 C3
Farndon NG24 138 F4
Gainsborough DN21 15 C1
Gotham NG11 195 B1
Granby NG13 191 B5
Hathern LE12 213 A1
Ilkeston DE7 157 E4
Kirkby in A NG17 114 D4
Church St *continued*
Lambley NG4 163 C7
Langold S81 16 E2
Mansfield NG18 102 B7
Mansfield Woodhouse NG19 88 C3
Market Warsop NG20 74 B5
Misterton DN10 6 E2
Newark-on-T NG24 139 F8
North Wheatley DN22 31 E8
Nottingham NG7 222 A1
Nottingham, Old Basford
NG6 160 E2
Ollerton NG22 77 A3
Orston NG13 179 F7
Pleasleyhill NG19 87 B4
Ruddington NG11 196 C7
Sandiacre NG10 182 B7
Shelford NG12 164 C1
South Leverton DN22 42 C7
South Normanton DE55 113 A6
Southwell NG25 136 E8
Stapleford NG9 182 D7
Sturton le S DN22 32 D4
Sutton in A NG17 100 E2
Sutton on T NG23 97 A8
Whaley Thorns NG20 59 A2
Whatton NG13 179 A3
Wymeswold LE12 216 C3
Church Vale Prim Sch
NG20 74 A7
Church View
Balderton NG24 140 D3
Beckingham DN10 14 B1
Bottesford NG13 181 A3
Carlton NG4 162 F1
Glapwell S44 86 B8
New Houghton NG19 86 F7
Ollerton NG22 77 B3
Scrooby DN10 10 A2
Stanton Hill NG17 100 D6
Church View Cl NG5 147 B1
Church Vw Gd NG17 129 E8
Church Way DN22 29 A6
Church Wlk
Bawtry DN10 10 A7
Brinsley NG16 143 E7
Carlton NG4 174 E7
Eastwood NG16 143 F2
Harworth DN11 8 E4
Stapleford NG9 182 E7
Upton NG23 122 F1
Weston NG23 81 A5
Whatton NG13 179 B4
Worksop S80 35 F3
Churnet Cl NG11 184 E4
Chuter Ede Prim Sch
NG24 140 E4
Cinderhill Gr NG4 162 E2
Cinderhill Rd NG6 160 B5
Cinderhill Wlk NG6 160 B6
Cinder La NG22 77 B2
Circle The NG19 88 B4
Cirrus Dr NG16 159 A7
Citadel St NG7 222 A3
Citrus Gr DE74 203 C3
City Gd (Nottingham Forest
FC) The NG2 173 E1
City Link NG1, NG2 173 F3
City of Caves NG1 223 E2
City of Nottingham Tennis
Ctr NG7 184 C8
City Rd
Beeston NG9 184 A6
Nottingham NG7 172 D1
Stathern LE14 202 F3
City The NG9 184 A6
Clandon Dr NG5 161 B2
Clanfield Rd NG8 171 E7
Clapham St NG7 222 A3
Clapton La NG7 184 E2
Clara Mount Rd DE75 143 A1
Clarborough Dr NG5 162 A6
Clarborough Hill DN22 30 E4
Clarborough Prim Sch
DN22 30 E3
Clarborough Tunnel Nature
Reserve DN22 31 C2
Clare Cl NG6 160 E4
Clarehaven NG9 182 E5
Clare Hill NG21 118 A4
Claremont Ave
Beeston NG9 183 C7
Hucknall NG15 146 A5
Claremont Dr NG11 185 C3
Claremont Prim Sch
NG5 161 B1
Claremont Rd
Gainsborough DN21 24 F6
Nottingham NG5 161 B1
Claremount Cl NG19 88 E4
Clarence Rd
Beeston NG9 183 D3
Long Eaton NG10 193 C6
Worksop S80 35 E4
Clarence St
Loughborough LE11 220 C5
Mansfield NG18 102 A6
Nottingham NG3 173 E5
Pleasleyhill NG19 87 C3
Clarendon Ct 5 NG5 173 B8
Clarendon Dr S81 35 D6
Clarendon Pk NG5 173 B8
Clarendon Rd NG19 101 E8
Clarendon Sixth Form Coll
NG1 223 D4
Clarendon St NG1 223 D3
Clare Rd NG17 114 F8
Clare St NG1 223 E3
Clare Valley NG7 223 D2
Clarewood Gr NG11 195 E7
Clarges St NG6 160 C6
Claricoates Dr NG24 125 E2
Clarke Ave
Arnold NG5 161 F8
Newark-on-T NG24 139 E5
Clarke Cl NG12 189 A4
Clarke Dr NG10 193 A4
Clarke Rd NG2 173 E2
Clarke's La NG9 183 D4
Clark La NG22 65 F2
Clarks La NG24 125 B2
Clarkson Dr NG9 184 B6
Clarkwoods Cl NG22 77 E4
Clater's Cl DN22 40 A8
Claude St NG7 172 E1
Clawson La
Hickling LE14 210 D6
Nether Broughton LE14 210 E1
Claxton Rise LE14 211 C2
Clay Ave NG3 162 A3
Claye St NG10 193 E7
Clayfield Cl NG6 160 A6
Claygate NG3 174 A7
Clay La
Fenton LN1 55 D7
Newark-on-T NG24 140 C7
Claylands Ave S81 35 C6
Claylands Cl S81 35 D5
Claylands La S81 35 D6
Claypit La NG25 137 E3
Claypole CE (Cont) Prim Sch
NG23 156 E7
Claypole La NG23 156 E2
Claypole Rd 16 NG7 172 F7
Clay St LE12 216 C3
Claythorne Dr DN21 24 E8
Clayton Cl NG24 140 A6
Clayton Ct NG7 222 B3
Claytons Dr 11 NG7 172 E2
Clayton's Wharf 12 NG7 172 E2
Clayworth Comm DN22 21 E3
Clayworth Ct 13 NG18 103 A2
Clayworth Rd DN10 12 F1
Clegg Hill Dr NG17 99 E4
Clement Ave NG24 140 E3
Clensey La NG23 156 F2
Clerkson's Alley 6 NG18 102 B7
Clerkson St 4 NG18 102 B6
Clether Rd NG8 171 D6
Cleve Ave NG9 182 E3
Cleveland Ave NG10 182 F1
Cleveland Cl
Carlton in L S81 25 E7
Nottingham NG7 222 A3
Cleveland Sq NG24 139 F6
Cleveland St DN21 24 D7
Cleveleys Rd NG9 182 E3
Clevely Way NG11 184 E3
Cliff Bvd NG16 158 F7
Cliff Cres NG12 175 F4
Cliff Dr NG12 176 A5
Cliffe Hill Ave NG9 182 D7
Cliff Gate NG22 65 C8
Cliffgrove Ave NG9 183 D6
Cliffhill La NG13 179 C6
Cliff La NG16 113 F4
Cliffmere Wlk NG11 184 D1
Cliff Nook DE55 113 B4
Cliff Nook La NG24 125 A1
Clifford Ave NG9 183 F8
Clifford Cl
Keyworth NG12 197 F4
Long Eaton NG10 193 A4
Clifford Ct NG7 222 B3
Clifford St
Long Eaton NG10 193 E7
Mansfield NG18 102 B4
Nottingham NG7 222 B3
Cliff Rd
Carlton NG4 174 D6
Nottingham NG1 223 F2
Radcliffe on T NG12 175 E4
Cliff St NG18 102 C7
Cliff The NG6 160 B4
Cliff Way NG12 175 F4
Clifton Ave
Long Eaton NG10 194 A7
Ruddington NG11 196 C7
Clifton Bvd NG7 184 F8
Clifton Cres
Beeston NG9 183 E3
Newark-on-T NG24 125 B3
Clifton Gr
Carlton NG4 162 E2
Mansfield NG18 102 F4
Clifton Grove Nature Reserve
NG11 184 C3
Clifton La
Nottingham NG11 184 E3
Ruddington NG11 196 A8
Clifton L Ctr NG11 184 F1
Clifton Pl 2 NG18 102 B7
Clifton Rd NG11 196 B7
Clifton St NG9 184 A6
Clifton Terr NG7 222 C1
Clifton Way DN22 39 C8
Clifton Woods Nature
Reserve NG11 184 C3
Clinthill La S80 45 A7
Clinton Ave
Brinsley NG16 143 D6
Nottingham NG5 173 B8
Clinton Ct NG1 223 E3
Clinton Gdn La NG22 65 F2
Clinton St E NG1 223 E3
Clinton St W NG1 223 E3

Clinton St
Arnold NG5 . . . . .161 E7
Beeston NG9 . . . . .183 E7
Newark-on-T NG24 . . . . . .139 F8
Worksop S80 . . . . .36 A1
Clinton Terr DN21 . . . . .24 D7
Clipsham Cl NG24 . . . . .140 E5
Clipstone Ave
Mansfield NG18 . . . . .102 C8
Nottingham, Mapperley
NG3. . . . . .162 A4
Nottingham NG11 . . . . .223 D4
Sutton in A NG17 . . . . .101 A4
Clipstone Cl NG8 . . . . .159 D2
Clipstone Dr NG19 . . . . .89 D3
Clipstone Rd E NG19 . . . . . .89 D3
Clipstone Rd W NG19 . . . . .89 B1
Clipston La NG12 . . . . .197 F7
Clive Cres NG16 . . . . .159 A5
Cliveden Gn NG11 . . . . .184 D1
Cloister St NG7 . . . . .172 E2
Cloisters The NG9. . . . . . . .184 A8
Close Quarters NG6 . . . . . .183 C8
Closes Side La NG13 . . . . . .165 E3
Close The
Averham NG23. . . . . .123 E4
Beeston NG9 . . . . .183 D4
Mansfield NG21. . . . . .103 F2
Newark-on-T NG24 . . . . . .140 A8
Nottingham NG5 . . . . .161 C3
Shirebrook NG20 . . . . .72 F5
Upton NG23 . . . . .122 F1
Cloud Ave NG9 . . . . .182 F7
Clouds Hill NG11 . . . . .195 E8
Cloudside Ct NG10. . . . . . . .182 C7
Cloudside Jun Sch NG10 182 D6
Cloudside Rd NG10 . . . . . . .182 C7
Clough Ct NG8 . . . . .172 B7
Clover Cl S81. . . . . .36 B7
Cloverdale NG12 . . . . .188 A2
Cloverfields NG14. . . . . .149 A8
Clover Gn NG6 . . . . .160 D3
Cloverlands NG11 . . . . .185 C3
Cloverlands Dr NG14. . . . . .159 A7
Clover Rise NG16 . . . . .158 B8
Clover St NG17 . . . . .115 A6
Clover Way NG19 . . . . .88 F4
Club Ct NG24 . . . . .140 D4
Cludd Ave NG24 . . . . .140 E8
Clumber Ave
Beeston NG9 . . . . .183 D5
Brinsley NG16 . . . . .128 C1
Carlton NG4 . . . . .175 A7
Edwinstowe NG21 . . . . .75 F3
Mansfield NG21. . . . . .103 F1
Newark-on-T NG24 . . . . . .140 A6
Nottingham, Hyson Green
NG5. . . . . .173 B8
Nottingham, Mapperley
NG3. . . . . .162 A4
Clumber Cres NG17. . . . . . .100 C6
Clumber Cres N NG7. . . . . .222 C2
Clumber Cres S NG7 . . . . . .222 C1
Clumber Ct
Ilkeston DE7 . . . . .157 F5
Mansfield NG19 . . . . .87 E2
Market Warsop NG20 . . . . .74 B4
Nottingham NG7 . . . . .222 A3
Clumber Dr
Mansfield NG19 . . . . .87 E2
Radcliffe on T NG12. . . . . .176 A4
Clumber Pk Ctry Pk S80 . .48 B3
Clumber Pl S80 . . . . .35 E3
Clumber Rd
West Bridgford NG2 . . . . . .185 F7
Worksop S80 . . . . .47 B5
Clumber Rd E NG7 . . . . . . .222 C2
Clumber Rd W NG7 . . . . . .222 C2
Clumber St
Hucknall NG15. . . . . .146 C6
Kirkby in A NG17 . . . . .115 C5
Long Eaton NG10. . . . . .193 D7
Mansfield NG18 . . . . .102 B7
Market Warsop NG20 . . . . .74 B4
Nottingham NG1 . . . . .223 E3
Retford DN22. . . . . .39 E6
Sutton in A NG17. . . . . .100 D2
Clumber Way NG22 . . . . . .106 A5
Clun Ct NG19 . . . . .88 D2
Clyro Pl DN22 . . . . .28 F6
Coach Dr DN22 . . . . .143 F4
Coach Gap La NG13 . . . . . .190 D1
Coachmans Croft **2**
NG8 . . . . .172 A5
Coach Rd NG20 . . . . .74 C1
Coalfields Cl NG17 . . . . . . .100 C1
Coal La LE14 . . . . .211 F8
Coalpit La DN22 . . . . .49 F4
Coal Yd La NG23 . . . . .82 E8
Coates Ave NG15 . . . . .130 F1
Coates Rd DN22 . . . . .43 D8
Coatsby Rd NG16 . . . . .158 F7
Cobblestone Dr NG18 . . . .102 D5
Cobden Pl NG19 . . . . .88 B6
Cobden Prim Sch LE11. . . .220 B4
Cobden St
Gainsborough DN21 . . . . . .24 C8
Kirkby in A NG17 . . . . .115 A4
Long Eaton NG10. . . . . .193 E7
1 Loughborough LE11. . . .220 C4
Nottingham NG7 . . . . .222 A3
Coburn St NG17 . . . . .100 F1
Cobwell Rd DN22 . . . . .39 E6
Cochrane Terr NG17 . . . . . .100 D8
Cockayne Cl NG10 . . . . .182 B3
Cocker Beck NG14 . . . . . . .150 A5
Cockerhouse Rd NG16 . . . .143 E4
Cockett La NG22 . . . . .119 E7

Cockhill Cl DN10. . . . . .10 A6
Cock Hill La DN10 . . . . .10 A6
Cocking Hill NG22 . . . . .78 C4
Cocking La DN22 . . . . .49 D8
Cockington Rd NG8. . . . . . .171 C5
Cockle Cl NG18 . . . . .102 E5
Cockleys NG10. . . . . .193 C6
Cockshut La NG20 . . . . .59 A4
Coddington CE Prim Sch
NG24. . . . . .126 A1
Coddington La LN6 . . . . . . .127 A6
Coddington Rd NG24. . . . . .140 F5
Codrington Gdns **5**
NG5 . . . . .161 C8
Cogenhoe Wlk NG5 . . . . . .147 F2
Coggin's La NG20. . . . . .74 C6
Coghill Ct NG25 . . . . .136 D8
Cohen Cl
Arnold NG5 . . . . .162 B6
Beeston NG9 . . . . .183 B2
Cokefield Ave NG16. . . . . . .159 F3
Colbeck St S80 . . . . .35 E3
Colborn St NG3 . . . . .173 F7
Colby Cl NG19 . . . . .89 B2
Coleby Ave NG7 . . . . .222 A1
Coleby Rd NG8 . . . . .159 F2
Coledale NG2 . . . . .186 C6
Coleman Ave NG24 . . . . . . .140 B4
Coleridge Cres NG5. . . . . . .161 D7
Coleridge Rd
Balderton NG24 . . . . .140 E5
Worksop S80 . . . . .36 B5
Coleridge St NG7. . . . . .222 B4
Colesbourne Rd NG7. . . . . .184 F2
Colgrove Rd LE11 . . . . .220 A2
Colin Broughton Ct NG6 160 D7
Colindale Gdns NG16 . . . . .159 E3
Colinwood Ave NG5 . . . . . .146 E1
College Dr
Nottingham NG11 . . . . .184 D2
Nottingham NG11 . . . . .184 E3
College La
East Markham NG22 . . . . . .66 A7
Worksop S80 . . . . .36 B1
College Rd
Beeston NG9 . . . . .183 E5
Carlton NG3. . . . . .162 C3
Sutton Bonington LE12 . . .204 A1
College St
East Bridgford NG13 . . . . . .165 D3
Long Eaton NG10. . . . . .182 C2
Nottingham NG1 . . . . .223 D2
Colley La NG23 . . . . .165 A7
Collemoor Leys La NG2 184 F2
Collier Ave NG19 . . . . .88 B5
Colliers Way NG6 . . . . .160 A4
Colliers Wy NG12 . . . . .188 A5
Colliery Cl NG2 . . . . .173 B1
Colliery Rd DN11 . . . . .9 B3
Collin Ave NG10 . . . . .182 B4
Collingham Rd
Collingham LN6 . . . . .98 F1
Mansfield NG19 . . . . .87 D1
Collingham Sta NG23 . . . . .112 B8
Collington St NG9 . . . . .183 E6
Collington Way NG2 . . . . . .185 D6
Collingwood Cl NG11. . . . . .184 E4
Collingwood Rd NG10. . . . .193 E6
Collinridge View NG7. . . . . .64 A2
Collins Ave
South Normanton DE55. . .113 A7
Sutton in A NG17. . . . . .114 E7
Collins Cl NG5 . . . . .159 F5
Collinson La NG24 . . . . .140 F1
Collin St
Beeston NG9 . . . . .183 F6
Nottingham NG1 . . . . .223 E1
Collins Wlk DN22 . . . . .39 F7
Collis Cl NG24 . . . . .140 D8
Collison St NG7. . . . . .222 B4
Collyer Rd NG14 . . . . .148 D8
Colly Gate NG16 . . . . .159 A5
Collygate Rd NG2 . . . . .173 D1
Colmon Cl NG5 . . . . .161 A7
Colmon Wlk **6** NG5 . . . . .161 A7
Clun Ct NG19 . . . . .88 D2
Colne Ct NG19 . . . . .88 D2
Colonel Frank Seely Comp
Sch NG14 . . . . .148 E8
Colonel's La LE14 . . . . .210 A1
Colonsay Cl NG9. . . . . .170 D3
Colsterdale S81 . . . . .36 B8
Colston Basset CE Prim Sch
NG12 .200 D7
Colston Cres NG2 . . . . .185 D4
Colston Gate NG12 . . . . . . .188 A3
Colston La LE14 . . . . .201 E4
Colston Rd
Colston Bassett NG12 . . . .200 B8
Cropwell Bishop NG12. . . .189 A1
Mansfield NG18 . . . . .103 A3
Nottingham NG6 . . . . .160 C7
Colton St DN10. . . . . .6 E2
Columbia Ave
Mansfield NG18 . . . . .102 F5
Sutton in A NG17. . . . . .100 C2
Columbia Cl NG16 . . . . .129 A7
Columbia St NG17 . . . . .100 A2
Columbus St S80 . . . . .35 C2
Colville St NG1 . . . . .173 B7
Colville Terr
Gainsborough DN21 . . . . . .24 D8
2 Nottingham NG1 . . . . . .173 B7
Colville Villas **1** NG1. . . .173 B7
Colwick Bsns Pk NG4. . . . .174 F5
Colwick Cl NG19. . . . . .87 E1

Colwick Ctry Pk NG2 . . . . .174 D3
Colwick Hall NG2. . . . . .174 C3
Colwick Ind Est NG4 . . . . .174 F5
Colwick Loop Rd NG4. . . . .175 B6
Colwick Manor Farm
NG4 . . . . .174 E5
Colwick Pk Cl NG4. . . . . . . .174 E5
Colwick Rd
Nottingham NG2 . . . . .173 C1
West Bridgford NG2 . . . . . .173 E1
Colwick Woods Nature
Reserve NG2. . . . . .174 A3
Combes The NG25 . . . . .121 D2
Comery Ave NG3. . . . . .174 A6
Comfrey Cl NG5 . . . . .160 E7
Commerce Sq NG1 . . . . . . .223 F2
Commercial Ave NG9 . . . . .183 F6
Commercial Gate NG18 . .102 B6
Commercial Rd
Keyworth NG12. . . . . .197 E2
6 Nottingham NG6. . . . . .160 B7
Shirebrook NG20 . . . . .72 D3
Commodore Gdns NG8. . . .160 C2
Common La
Beeston NG9 . . . . .183 A6
Blyth S81. . . . . .18 B4
Hucknall NG15. . . . . .145 D1
Mansfield Woodhouse NG19 88 A4
Ranskill DN22 . . . . .19 C4
Shirebrook NG20 . . . . .72 C2
Sturton le S DN22 . . . . .32 E6
Watnall NG16 . . . . .159 B7
Common Rd
Huthwaite NG17 . . . . .99 F2
Retford DN22. . . . . .39 F7
Thorpe Salvin S80 . . . . .34 A5
Commons Cl NG16 . . . . . . .158 A8
Common Side NG16. . . . . . .128 F8
Common The
Hucknall NG15. . . . . .145 D2
South Normanton DE55. . .113 B6
Compton Acres NG2 . . . . .185 B5
Compton Acres Sh Ctr
NG2 . . . . .185 C5
Compton Rd NG5 . . . . .161 B3
Compton St NG20. . . . . .72 F8
Comyn Gdns NG3 . . . . .223 F4
Conduit Cl NG2 . . . . .173 C2
Coneries The LE11 . . . . . . .220 B4
Conery Gdns NG11 . . . . . . .179 A3
Conery La NG13 . . . . .178 F2
Coneygrey Spinney
NG23. . . . . .152 E2
Conifer Cres NG11. . . . . . . .195 E7
Conifer Wlk NG3. . . . . .174 A8
Coningsby Cl DN21 . . . . . . .24 F8
Coningsby Gdns E NG5. . . .161 F4
Coningsby Rd NG5. . . . . . . .161 F5
Coningswath Rd NG4 . . . . .162 C1
Conisborough Terr **10**
NG2 . . . . .173 C1
Conisbrough Ave NG4 . . . .163 B3
Coniston Ave NG6 . . . . .160 C2
Coniston Cl
Mansfield Woodhouse
NG19. . . . . .88 E4
West Bridgford NG2 . . . . . .186 C7
Coniston Rd
Beeston NG9 . . . . .183 D8
Hucknall NG15. . . . . .145 F8
Kirkby in A NG17 . . . . .115 C6
Long Eaton NG10. . . . . .182 A2
Worksop S81 . . . . .35 E8
Connaught Rd DN21 . . . . . .15 D2
Connelly Cl NG5 . . . . .162 C6
Connery Mews NG5 . . . . . .183 B1
Connery The NG15 . . . . . . .144 E4
Conrad Cl S80 . . . . .36 B3
Constance St NG7 . . . . .161 A1
Convent St NG1 . . . . .223 F3
Conway Ave NG4 . . . . .175 A7
Conway Cl
Mansfield NG19. . . . . .101 D8
Nottingham NG3 . . . . .173 C7
Conway Cres NG4. . . . . .175 A8
Conway Dr NG21. . . . . .25 F6
Conway Gdns
Arnold NG5 . . . . .161 F6
Retford DN22. . . . . .39 B8
Conway Rd
Carlton NG4 . . . . .175 A8
Hucknall NG15. . . . . .145 D3
Conway St NG10 . . . . .163 A1
Conway Wlk **4** NG3 . . . . .173 C7
Cook Dr DE7 . . . . .170 A6
Cooks La
Fiskerton NG25 . . . . .137 D2
Southwell NG25. . . . . .136 B8
Cookson Ave NG4 . . . . .162 D2
Cookson St NG17 . . . . .115 B4
Coombe Cl NG8 . . . . .172 C3
Coombe Rd NG16 . . . . .158 C8
Co-Operative Ave NG15 . .146 B8
Co-Operative St
Long Eaton NG10. . . . . .193 E6
Stanton Hill NG17 . . . . .100 C6
Cooper Cl
Arnold NG5 . . . . .162 C6
Cropwell Bishop NG12. . . .189 A2
Nottingham NG6 . . . . .159 F6
Cooper Ct LE11 . . . . .220 D2
Coopers Gn NG8. . . . . .171 E2
Coopers Rise NG5 . . . . .147 A1
Cooper St NG4 . . . . .175 A4
Coopers Yd NG24 . . . . .139 E8
Copeland Ave
1 Kirkby in A NG17 . . . . . .114 F6
Stapleford NG9 . . . . .182 E8

Copeland Gr NG13 . . . . . . .177 C5
Copeland Rd
Hucknall NG15. . . . . .146 C8
Kirkby in A NG17 . . . . .114 E6
Copenhagen Ct NG3. . . . . .161 D1
Cope St NG7 . . . . .222 B4
Copestake Cl NG10 . . . . . .193 A7
Copper Hill NG23 . . . . .81 E4
Coppice Ave DE7 . . . . .157 D5
Coppice Cl NG15. . . . . .145 E5
Coppice Croft NG17 . . . . . .100 C1
Coppice Dr NG16 . . . . .143 D3
Coppice Form Prim Sch
NG5 . . . . .162 B7
Coppice Gr NG3 . . . . .161 E1
Coppice Rd
Arnold NG5 . . . . .162 B8
Clipstone NG19 . . . . .89 D3
Worksop S81 . . . . .35 F7
Coppice The
Barnby Moor DN22 . . . . . . .28 D5
Shirebrook NG20 . . . . .72 D3
Coppice View DE55 . . . . . . .113 A4
Copplestone Dr NG3 . . . . .162 C6
Coppywood Cl NG17 . . . . . .100 B7
Copse Cl
Burton Joyce NG14 . . . . . .163 F5
Ravenshead NG15 . . . . .116 C3
Copseside Cl **8** NG10. . . .193 A8
Copse The
Beeston NG9 . . . . .183 C6
Farndon NG24. . . . . .139 A4
Hucknall NG15. . . . . .146 C6
Ilkeston DE7 . . . . .157 D5
Mansfield NG18 . . . . .102 C2
Stanton Hill NG17. . . . . . . .100 C5
Copsewood DE55 . . . . .113 A4
Corben Gdns NG6. . . . . .159 F7
Corbiere Ave NG16. . . . . . . .159 F2
Corby Rd NG3 . . . . .161 E1
Cordy La NG16 . . . . .143 F8
Corene Ave NG17 . . . . .100 E1
Coriander Dr NG6 . . . . .160 D3
Corinth St NG7. . . . . .184 E2
Corkhill La NG22 . . . . .121 D5
Cormack La NG24. . . . . .140 F1
Corn Cl NG11 . . . . .184 F1
Corn St
Cotgrave NG12 . . . . .187 E2
South Normanton DE55. . .113 A8
Corncrake Ave NG6 . . . . . . .160 D3
Corncrake Dr NG5 . . . . .162 C7
Cornell Dr NG5 . . . . .162 C8
Cornerhouse The NG1. . . . .223 E3
Corner The NG14 . . . . .150 D1
Cornfield Ave DE55 . . . . . . .113 A4
Cornfield Rd NG16 . . . . .158 B8
Cornhill Rd NG4 . . . . .174 B7
Cornley Rd DN10 . . . . .6 C3
Cornwall Ave
Beeston NG9 . . . . .184 C4
Mansfield NG18 . . . . .102 F6
Cornwall Cl NG16 . . . . .128 C4
Cornwall Dr NG22 . . . . .77 A3
Cornwallis Cl NG10 . . . . . . .193 D6
Cornwall Rd
Arnold NG5 . . . . .161 C7
Retford DN22. . . . . .30 A1
Shireoaks S81 . . . . .34 F7
Coronation Ave
Long Clawson LE14 . . . . . .211 A2
Misson DN10 . . . . .4 B3
New Houghton NG19. . . . . .86 F7
Nottingham NG11 . . . . .185 B8
Sandiacre NG10 . . . . .182 A7
Coronation Dr
Mansfield NG18 . . . . .103 A8
Shirebrook NG20 . . . . .72 F2
South Normanton DE55. . .113 B6
Coronation Rd
Arnold NG3 . . . . .158 A1
Awsworth DE7 . . . . .158 E4
Bestwood Village NG6. . . .146 E4
Cossall NG16. . . . . .158 B2
Hucknall NG15. . . . . .145 F8
Nuthall NG16. . . . . .159 C5
Coronation St
Mansfield NG18 . . . . .102 B6
New Balderton NG24. . . . . .140 C5
Retford DN22. . . . . .39 E6
Sutton in A NG17. . . . . .100 E8
Whitwell S80 . . . . .45 A6
Coronation Wlk NG4 . . . . .163 A1
Corporation Oaks NG3 . . .173 C7
Corporation Rd DE7 . . . . . .170 A5
Corporation St **8** NG18 . .102 A7
Corringham Rd DN21 . . . . .15 C8
Corsham Gdns NG3 . . . . . . .174 A7
Cosby Rd **4** NG2 . . . . .173 F3
Cosgrove Ave NG17 . . . . . .101 B5
Cossall Ind Est NG16. . . . .158 B2
Cossall Rd NG9 . . . . .170 D3
Costhorpe Ind Est S81 . . . .16 E1
Costhorpe Villas S81 . . . . . .16 E1
Costock Ave NG5 . . . . .161 B4
Costock Rd
East Leake LE12 . . . . .206 A1
Wysall NG12 . . . . .207 D2
Costume & Textile Mus
NG1 . . . . .223 E2
Cotes Dr LE11 . . . . .220 B6
Cotes Rd LE12 . . . . .220 F5
Coteswood House Sch
NG5 . . . . .161 C5
Cotgrave Ave NG4 . . . . .162 D2
Cotgrave CE Prim Sch
NG12 .187 F2
Cotgrave Cl NG8. . . . . .159 E2

Cotgrave Ctry Pk NG12. . .188 A6
Cotgrave Inf Sch NG12. . . .187 F3
Cotgrave La NG12. . . . . .187 F3
Cotgrave La NG12 . . . . .187 F3
Cotgrave Rd NG12. . . . . . . .188 A3
Cotgrave Manvers Jun Sch
NG12 .187 F3
Cotgrave Rd
Cotgrave NG12 . . . . .187 A1
Mansfield NG19. . . . . .87 F2
Cotmanhay Rd DE7 . . . . . . .157 E3
Coton Cl
Mansfield Woodhouse
NG19. . . . . .88 C4
Nottingham NG11 . . . . .185 A3
Cotswold Cl **2** NG10. . . . .193 B8
Cotswold Ct
Beeston NG9 . . . . .171 D1
Carlton in L S81. . . . . .25 C7
Cotswold Gr NG18 . . . . . . .103 B6
Cotswold Rd NG8 . . . . .159 E1
Cottage Ave NG13 . . . . . . .178 F4
Cottage Cl
Balderton NG24 . . . . .140 D2
Blidworth NG21 . . . . .117 F4
Ilkeston DE7 . . . . .157 D3
Cottage La
Collingham NG23 . . . . .111 F6
Market Warsop NG20 . . . . .74 C2
North Clifton NG23 . . . . . . .69 B4
Cottage Mdw NG4 . . . . . . .174 F4
Cottage Pasture La
NG14. . . . . .164 E7
Cottage Terr NG1 . . . . .222 C3
Cottam Dr NG5 . . . . .161 A8
Cottam Gdns NG5. . . . . . . .161 A8
Cottam Gr NG19 . . . . .101 D6
Cottam Rd
Cottam DN22 . . . . .43 C4
South Leverton DN22 . . . . .42 E7
Cottans Cl NG25 . . . . .136 F8
Cottesmore Rd NG7. . . . . .222 B2
Cotton Mill La NG22 . . . . .120 A5
Coulby Cl NG23 . . . . .156 E6
Coulton's Ave NG17 . . . . . .100 C3
Coulton's Cl NG17. . . . . . . .100 C3
County Bsns Pk NG2. . . . . .173 E2
County Cl NG9 . . . . .184 A5
County Rd
Carlton NG4 . . . . .162 C3
Nottingham NG2 . . . . .173 E2
Coupland Cl **6** DN21 . . . . .15 F1
Courtenay Gdns NG3 . . . . .173 D7
Court-Field Rd NG17. . . . . .101 A6
Courtlett Way NG6 . . . . . . .159 B8
Courtney Cl NG8 . . . . .171 E5
Court St **11** NG7 . . . . .172 F7
Covedale Rd NG5 . . . . .161 C5
Covent Gdns NG12. . . . . . . .176 E3
Coventry Cl NG6 . . . . .160 C5
Coventry Dr S81 . . . . .36 A6
Coventry La NG9. . . . . .171 A3
Coventry Rd
Beeston NG9 . . . . .184 A7
Nottingham NG6 . . . . .160 B6
Cove Rd DN9 . . . . .2 E6
Coverdale S81 . . . . .36 B7
Covert Cl
Burton Joyce NG14 . . . . . .163 E5
Hucknall NG15. . . . . .146 C6
Keyworth NG12 . . . . .197 F4
Covert Rd NG2 . . . . .186 B6
Cowan St NG1 . . . . .223 F3
Cowdray Cl LE11. . . . . .220 A1
Cowdrey Gdns NG5 . . . . . . .162 B6
Cow La
Beeston NG9 . . . . .183 C8
Newark-on-T NG24 . . . . . .124 F1
Cowlairs NG5. . . . . .160 E7
Cowley St NG6 . . . . .160 D3
Cowpasture La NG17 . . . . .100 E1
Cow Pasture La NG17 . . . . .114 C5
Cowper Cl S81 . . . . .36 B5
Cowper Rd
Arnold NG5 . . . . .161 E4
Eastwood NG16 . . . . .158 A4
Cowpes Cl NG17 . . . . .100 E6
Cox Dr NG13. . . . . .180 F3
Coxmoor Cl NG2 . . . . .186 C4
Coxmoor Ct **14** NG5 . . . . .147 A1
Coxmoor Prim Sch
NG17 .115 C5
Coxmoor Rd NG17, NG15. .115 C7
Cox's Hill DN21 . . . . .15 D1
Cox's La NG19 . . . . .101 A6
Crab La NG23. . . . . .110 F1
Crab Nook La NG22 . . . . . .119 F6
Crabtree Field NG12 . . . . .174 D4
Crabtree La
Beckingham DN10 . . . . .23 A8
High Marnham NG23. . . . . .67 D2
Crabtree Rd NG6 . . . . .160 A6
Craddock St LE11. . . . . .220 B4
Crafts Way NG25 . . . . .121 E1
Cragdale Rd NG5 . . . . .161 C5
Cragg La DE55 . . . . .99 A2
Cragmoor Rd NG14 . . . . . .163 E3
Crags Rd S80. . . . . .45 A1
Craig Moray NG12 . . . . . . .176 A4
Craigs Gn NG19 . . . . .101 E5
Craig St NG10 . . . . .193 E7
Craigston Rd S81 . . . . .25 E6
Crammond Cl **3** NG2 . . . .173 B2

Crampton Cl NG17......100 B3
Crampton Ct NG5......161 A8
Crampton Rd NG18......102 E8
Cramworth Dr 4 NG5...161 D3
Cranberry Cl NG2......185 B5
Cranborne Cl NG19....101 D7
Cranbourne Cl NG9....170 D2
Cranbourne Gr NG15....145 E7
Cranbrook St NG1......88 C6
Cranbrook St NG1......223 F3
Cranfleet Way NG10....193 B7
Cranford Gdns NG12....165 C4
Cranleigh Dr NG14....150 D1
Cranmer Ave NG13....178 E3
Cranmer Gr
  8 Nottingham NG3...173 C7
  Radmanthwaite NG19....87 D3
Cranmer Rd NG24....139 F5
Cranmer St
  Ilkeston DE7......157 F1
  Long Eaton NG10....182 D1
  Nottingham NG3....173 C7
Cranmore Cl NG5....148 A2
Cranshaw Cl LE12....212 C3
Cransley Ave NG5....171 D2
Cranston Ave NG5....147 F1
Cranston Rd NG9....171 C1
Cranswick Cl NG19....89 A2
Cranthorne Dr NG3....174 C6
Crantock Gdns NG12...197 F3
Cranwell Cl NG21....125 D1
Cranwell Ct NG6....159 F6
Cranwell Rd NG6....159 D2
Craster Dr
  Arnold NG5....148 A2
  Nottingham NG6....159 F8
Craster St NG17....100 E1
Crathie Rd S81....25 E6
Craven Rd NG7....172 E7
Crawford Ave NG9....182 D8
Crawford Ct NG8....171 E5
Crawford Rise NG5....162 E7
C Rd NG9....184 D6
Crees La NG24....139 B6
Crescent Ave NG4....162 E1
Crescent Prim Sch NG19...87 D2
Crescent Rd NG16....128 D3
Crescent The
  Arnold NG5....161 E4
  Beckingham DN10....14 B1
  Beeston, Chilwell NG9....183 C3
  Beeston, Toton NG9....183 A2
  Bilsthorpe NG22....105 E6
  Bircotes DN11....9 C4
  Blidworth NG21....118 B5
  East Leake LE12....205 F2
  Eastwood NG16....144 A2
  Lea DN21....24 F2
  Mansfield NG18....102 C3
  Newark-on-T NG24....140 A6
  Nottingham NG3....173 D8
  Old Dalby LE14....219 B6
  Radcliffe on T NG12....176 A3
  Retford DN22....39 D6
  Shirebrook NG20....72 E6
  Stapleford NG9....170 E2
  Sutton in A NG17....100 D7
Cresswell Rd
  Beeston NG9....183 B5
  Worksop S80....35 E4
Cresswell St S80....35 E3
Cressy Rd NG7....184 F2
Cresta Gdns NG3....161 D2
Creswell Crags Mus & Ed Ctr
  S80....45 B1
Creswell Ct NG19....88 E4
Creswell Rd NG20....60 A3
Crewe Cl
  Blidworth NG21....118 A6
  Nottingham NG7....222 B4
Crewe Rd DN11....9 B4
Crew La NG25....137 A8
Crew La Ind Est NG25....137 A8
Crew Rd NG23....98 B1
Cribb Cl NG11....185 B7
Crich View
  Newton DE55....99 A4
  Nottingham NG2....173 D2
Cricket Cl NG17....129 F8
Cricketers Ct NG2....173 F1
Cricket Field La DN22....39 E8
Criftin Rd NG14....164 A4
Crink La NG25....136 F6
Cripps Hill NG7....172 C2
Critchley St DE7....157 F1
Critch's Flats NG16....158 F6
Crocus St
  Kirkby in A NG17....115 B4
  Nottingham NG2....173 D2
Croft Ave
  Hucknall NG15....146 A6
  Mansfield NG18....102 C2
Croft Cl
  Pinxton NG16....113 C3
  Rolleston NG23....138 A6
Croft Cres NG16....158 C5
Croft Ct NG17....99 F4
Croft Dr DN11....8 A8
Croft Farm Cl
  Everton DN10....11 C3
  Rolleston NG23....138 B6
Croft Gdns LE14....218 E4
Crofton Cl
  Beeston NG9....183 D3
  3 Nottingham NG8....172 B6

Crofton Rd NG9......183 D2
Croft Prim Sch NG17....100 F2
Croft Rd
  Arnold NG5....161 F8
  Finningley DN10....1 A1
  Keyworth NG12....197 D3
  West Bridgford NG12....186 A4
Croft Rise NG13....165 C3
Crofts The NG13....177 E4
Croft The
  Beckingham DN10....23 C8
  Kegworth DE74....203 D2
  Newark-on-T NG24....140 A8
  Retford DN22....39 F8
  South Normanton DE55....113 A6
  Stanton Hill NG17....100 C5
Croft Way DN10....11 C3
Croft Wlk S80....45 A6
Cromarty Cl NG19....101 D5
Cromarty Ct 2 NG2....173 B2
Cromdale Cl NG5....148 C1
Cromer Cl NG18....102 C4
Cromer Rd NG3....173 E7
Cromford Ave
  Carlton NG4....174 D8
  Mansfield NG18....102 A4
Cromford Cl
  Aldercar NG16....143 B4
  Long Eaton NG10....193 A5
Cromford Ct
  Annesley Woodhouse
    NG17....115 A1
  Langley Mill NG16....143 B4
  West Bridgford NG2....185 F6
Cromford Rd DN21....15 C1
Crompton Cl
  Bilsthorpe NG22....105 F3
  Ilkeston DE7....170 B3
  Radmanthwaite NG19....87 D3
Crompton St
  New Houghton NG19....86 F8
  Teversal NG17....100 B7
Crompton View Prim Sch
  NG22....105 F6
Cromwell Ave DE7....170 A5
Cromwell Cres NG4....163 B7
Cromwell Dr LE12....205 E1
Cromwell Rd
  Aslockton NG13....178 E3
  Beeston NG9....183 E6
  Newark-on-T NG24....140 B7
Cromwell St
  Carlton NG4....174 E7
  Eastwood NG16....158 C8
  Gainsborough DN21....24 C8
  Mansfield NG18....102 C6
  Nottingham NG7....222 C3
Cromwell Way DN21....24 F3
Crookdole La NG14....148 F7
Crooked Billet St DN21....15 B4
Crookes Ave NG19....87 A5
Crook's Ave NG19....88 C3
Croome Cl LE11....220 C1
Cropston Cl NG2....185 E4
Cropton Cres NG8....172 B6
Cropton Gr NG13....177 C4
Cropwell Bishop Prim Sch
  NG12....189 B4
Cropwell Bishop Rd
  NG12....189 B4
Cropwell Butler Rd
  NG12....189 A8
Cropwell Gdns NG18....102 D7
Cropwell Gdns NG12....176 A2
Cropwell Gn NG3....173 F6
Cropwell Rd
  Langar NG13....190 C1
  Radcliffe on T NG12....176 A2
Crosby Cl NG17....89 A1
Crosby Rd NG2....185 F3
Cross Comm La DN22....33 A5
Crossdale Dr NG12....197 E4
Crossdale Drive Prim Sch
  NG12....197 E4
Crossdale Wlk NG5....160 E8
Cross Dr
  Kirkby in A NG17....115 B7
  Rainworth NG21....104 B1
Crossfield Dr
  13 Nottingham NG5....147 A1
  Nottingham NG5....161 A8
Crosshill LE12....205 A1
Crosshill NG12....188 A3
Cross Hill DN10....12 F2
Cross Hill Cl LE12....216 C3
Cross La
  Austerfield DN10....3 C5
  Balderton NG24....140 E1
  Blidworth NG21....117 D6
  Collingham NG23....112 C8
  East Bridgford NG13....165 D3
  Eikesley DN22....49 F4
  Elston NG23....154 A3
  Farndon NG24....138 F4
  Gringley on t H DN10....5 A1
  Harby NG23....70 D2
  Huthwaite NG17....100 A3
  Stanton Hill NG17....100 C4
  Staunton in the Vale NG23...169 F2
Crossland Rd NG5....161 A5
Crosslands Mdw NG4....174 F4
Crossley Ave NG17....100 A3
Crossley Hill La S81....26 C4
Crossley St NG5....161 B2
Crossman St NG5....161 C2
Cross St
  Arnold NG5....161 E8
  Barnby in t W NG24....141 F5

Cross St continued
  Beeston NG9....183 F7
  Bilsthorpe NG22....105 F5
  Carlton, Netherfield NG4...175 A7
  Carlton, Thorneywood
    NG4....174 D8
  Eastwood NG16....144 A2
  Gainsborough DN21....24 D8
  Hathern LE12....213 A1
  Langold S81....16 E3
  Long Eaton NG10....193 E8
  Loughborough LE11....220 C5
  Mansfield Woodhouse NG19 88 B2
  Morton DN21....15 B4
  Newark-on-T NG24....140 B8
  Retford DN22....40 A6
  Sandiacre NG10....182 C6
  Sturton le S DN22....32 D5
Cross The
  Carlton in L S81....26 A6
  Cotgrave NG12....187 E3
Crossways
  East Markham NG22....66 A7
  Retford DN22....39 F8
Crossways Dr NG13....165 D3
Crowborough Ave NG8....171 E2
Crowcroft Way NG10....182 B2
Crow Ct NG13....178 A4
Crow Hill NG18....87 B5
Crow Hill Ct NG18....102 B8
Crow Hill Dr NG18....102 B8
Crow Hill Rd NG4....88 B2
Crow Hill Rd NG4....174 F7
Crow Hi Rd NG18....102 B8
Crow La NG23, NG24....124 D7
Crowley Cl NG18....171 C6
Crown Ave NG19....103 A8
Crown Cl
  Collingham NG23....98 A1
  Long Eaton NG10....193 A7
  Rainworth NG21....118 C8
Crown Ct DN22....32 D5
Crown Farm Way NG10....103 B8
Crown St
  Mansfield NG18....102 F6
  Newark-on-T NG24....139 F7
  Worksop S80....35 E4
Crow Pk Ave NG23....81 E1
Crow Pk Dr NG14....163 E3
Crowthorne Cl NG5....146 E1
Crowthorne Gdns NG5....146 E1
Croxall Cl NG11....184 E4
Croxley Gdns NG16....159 D3
Croxton Ct NG19....88 E3
Croydon Rd NG7....222 A3
Crummock Cl NG9....183 C8
Cuckney CE Prim Sch
  NG20....60 A2
Cuckney Hill NG20....74 B7
Cuckoo Holt S81....35 C7
Cuckstool The NG23....96 F8
Cudworth Dr NG3....161 F2
Culdewood Cl NG5....146 E1
Cul-de-sac NG22....105 F6
Cullen Cl NG24....124 E1
Cullen's Ct NG5....161 C2
Cullin Cl NG5....146 F2
Cumberland Ave
  Beeston NG9....183 B3
  Market Warsop NG20....74 A5
Cumberland Cl
  Bircotes DN11....9 C4
  Carlton in L S81....25 F7
  Westwood NG16....128 C4
Cumberland Dr NG7....101 D7
Cumberland Pl NG1....223 D2
Cumbria Rd S81....36 A6
Cunily Hill NG25....136 B6
Cunningham Cl DN10....19 F8
Cupar Cl NG20....72 D2
Curie Ct NG7....172 D2
Curlew Cl NG3....174 C5
Curlew Wharf 5 NG7....172 F2
Currie Rd NG24....125 A2
Cursley Way NG9....183 C2
Curtis Cl NG23....98 A1
Curtis St NG15....146 A6
Curzon Ave NG4....174 B7
Curzon Cl NG21....118 A8
Curzon Ct NG3....223 F4
Curzon Dr S81....35 F7
Curzon Gdns NG3....223 F4
Curzon Pl NG3....223 F3
Curzon St
  Carlton NG4....175 A7
  Gainsborough DN21....15 C2
  Gotham NG11....195 B1
  Long Eaton NG10....182 B2
  Loughborough LE11....220 A3
  Nottingham NG3....223 F3

D

Dabek Rise NG17....115 A1
Dabell Ave NG6....159 F8
Dadley Rd S81....25 F7
Dadsley Rd DN11....8 A8
Dagfa House Sch NG9....184 A7
Dagmar Gr
  Beeston NG9....184 A6
  Nottingham NG3....161 D1
Dahlia Ave DE55....113 B7
Dairy La LE14....211 F7
Daisy Cl NG12....187 E2
Daisy Farm Rd NG16....158 B8
Daisy Rd NG3....162 A1
Dakeyne St NG3....173 E5
Dalbeattie Cl NG5....162 B8
Dalby Sq NG8....172 C3
Dale Ave
  Carlton NG4....174 C7
  Long Eaton NG10....182 D1
  Newton DE55....99 A3
  Nottingham NG3....162 A2
Dalebrook Cres NG15....145 C5
Dale Cl
  Hucknall NG15....145 C5
  Langwith NG20....72 E8
  Retford DN22....39 E3
  Sutton in A NG17....101 A5
Dale Cres NG24....140 E2
Dale Farm Ave NG3....174 A5
Dale Gr NG2....173 F4
Dalehead Rd NG11....184 D2
Dale La
  Ault Hucknall S44....86 D7
  Beeston NG9....183 E5
  Blidworth NG21....118 B5
Dalemoor Gdns NG8....172 B8
Dale Rd
  Carlton NG4....174 C7
  Keyworth NG12....197 E3
  Kimberley NG16....158 F5
  Market Warsop NG20....74 C5
Dales Ave NG17....100 F5
Dales Cl LE12....215 E5
Daleside NG12....187 E2
Daleside Rd NG3....174 A3
Daleside Rd E NG2, NG3....174 C4
Dales La DN10....4 F4
Dale St
  Mansfield NG19....88 B1
  Nottingham NG2....173 E4
Dalestorth Ave NG17....87 D1
Dalestorth Cl NG17....101 A5
Dalestorth Gdns NG17....101 A5
Dalestorth Prim Sch
  NG17....101 A4
Dalestorth Rd NG17....101 A5
Dalestorth St NG17....100 F5
Dale View NG11....36 B7
Dale View Rd NG3....174 B7
Dalewood Cl NG15....145 A5
Dale Wy NG24....140 F1
Dalkeith Terr 10 NG7....172 F7
Dallas St NG18....102 A6
Dallas York Rd NG9....184 B6
Dalley Cl NG9....182 F7
Dalton Cl NG9....182 E5
Daltons Cl NG16....143 A4
Dame Flogan St NG18....102 B6
Dame La DN10....4 B2
Dam Rd DN11....8 A6
Damson Wlk NG8....174 B8
Dane Cl NG3....223 F4
Dane Ct NG3....223 F4
Danes Cl NG5....161 D8
Danesfield Rd S80....35 F1
Daneshill Gravel Pits Nature
  Reserve NG22....19 D1
Dane Cl NG20....20 A1
Danes Rd DN11....15 F1
Daneswood Jun Sch
  NG17....100 D7
Danethorpe La NG24....126 B8
Danethorpe Vale NG5....161 C4
Daniel Cres NG17....101 F7
Daniel Mews NG10....182 A5
Daniels Way NG15....145 E4
Danners Hill NG15....131 E5
Danvers Dr NG17....101 E7
Darfield Ct DN11....8 A7
Darfield Dr DE75....143 A2
Darkey La NG9....182 E5
Dark La
  Aslockton NG13....179 A4
  Barnby in t W NG24....142 A5
  Bradmore NG11....197 B3
  Calverton NG14....133 B6
  West Leake LE12....204 F2
Darley Ave
  Beeston NG9....182 F3
  Carlton NG4....162 E1
  Kirkby in A NG17....115 C5
  Nottingham NG7....172 E7
Darleydale Cl NG18....102 D3
Darley Dr NG10....193 A5
Darley Rd NG7....172 E7
Darley Sq DE7....157 E5
Darley St NG7....162 B7
Darlton Dr NG5....161 B8
Darlton Rd
  East Drayton DN22....53 A1
  Tuxford NG22....66 C4
Darlton St NG19....101 D6
Darnal Cl NG5....160 E7
Darnhall Cres NG8....171 D7
Daron Gdns 18 NG5....161 A7

Darrel Rd DN22....39 E5
Darricott Cl NG21....118 B8
Darvel Cl 6 NG8....172 B6
Darwin Cl
  Elston NG23....153 E4
  Mansfield NG18....102 C3
  Nottingham NG5....160 E8
Darwin Dr DN22....42 B1
Darwin Rd NG10....193 B5
Darwin St DN21....24 D4
Daubeney Ave LN1....57 B3
Davey Rd NG18....102 A8
David Gr NG9....171 E1
David La NG6....160 D3
Davids La NG14....165 A5
Davidson Cl NG5....162 C7
Davidson Gd NG11....196 A4
Davidson St 5 NG2....173 F3
David St NG17....115 B7
Davies Ave NG17....100 E3
Davies Cl NG17....100 E3
Davies Rd NG2....186 A7
Davis Cl NG21....90 B4
Davis Rd NG9....183 B3
Davy Cl NG15....131 B2
Dawber St S81....35 C7
Dawes Way NG7....222 A3
Dawgates La NG19....86 F1
Dawlish Cl NG15....145 D6
Dawlish Ct NG16....143 D3
Dawlish Dr NG5....161 B5
Dawn Cl NG15....131 C1
Dawn House Sch NG21....103 E3
Dawn's La NG13....179 A5
Dawn View NG9....170 D2
Dawson Cl NG16....144 A1
Dawver Rd NG16....158 F6
Daybill Cl NG13....181 B3
Daybill Ct NG25....137 D3
Daybrook Ave 4 NG5....161 C3
Daybrook St NG5....161 C3
Dayncourt Sch NG12....176 A3
D'Ayncourt Wlk NG22....120 A6
Deabill St NG4....175 A6
Dead La
  Cossall NG16....158 D1
  1 Loughborough LE11....220 B4
Deadwong La NG23....153 E1
Deakins Pl NG7....222 A3
Deal Gdns NG6....159 F7
Dean Ave NG3....162 A3
Dean Cl
  Mansfield NG18....102 C4
  Nottingham NG8....171 D5
Dean Hole CE Prim Sch
  NG23....109 A5
Dean Rd NG5....161 E5
Deans Cl DN10....6 E2
Dean's Cl NG23....109 B5
Deanscourt NG12....188 A3
Deans Croft NG9....171 B1
Deansgate NG19....87 A5
Dean St
  Langley Mill NG16....143 C3
  Nottingham NG1....223 F2
Death La DN22....21 D6
Debdale Gate NG19....88 A2
Debdale La
  Keyworth NG12....197 D2
  Mansfield NG19....88 A2
Debdhill Rd DN10....6 E2
Deben Down NG19....88 E2
Deddington La NG9....171 C2
Deeley Cl NG16....159 A7
Deepdale Ave NG9....182 D6
Deepdale Cl NG2....186 A7
Deepdale Gdns NG17....100 F4
Deepdale Rd NG17....100 F4
Deepdene Cl NG8....160 A2
Deepdene Way NG8....160 A2
Deep Furrow Ave NG4....174 D8
Deeps La S45....85 B3
Deeps La DN10....4 B7
Deerdale La
  Bilsthorpe NG22....105 A8
  Edwinstowe NG21....91 C1
Deerleap Dr NG5....161 C7
Deer Pk NG8....171 E4
Deer Pk Dr
  Arnold NG5....147 C1
  Nottingham NG8....161 B8
Deers Acres LE14....220 B6
Deetleton Cl NG16....129 A7
De Lacy Ct NG22....77 B4
Delamere Cl NG18....102 C4
Delamere Dr NG18....102 C4
Delia Ave NG15....131 C1
Dell Lea NG18....102 C6
Dell The NG17....129 F8
Dell Way NG7....184 E5
Dellwood Cl NG4....162 C2
Delta St NG7....160 F1
Deltic Cl NG16....159 A7
Delville Ave NG12....197 E4
De Morgan Cl NG16....129 A2
Denacre Ave NG10....182 F1
Denbigh Cl NG21....93 A1
Denbigh Ct NG16....129 A7
Denbury Rd NG15....117 A2

Denby Dr NG18 . . . . 102 D2
Dendy Dr DN22 . . . . 53 B8
Dene Cl DN10 . . . . 20 B7
Denehurst Ave NG8 . . . . 160 C1
Dene The S80 . . . . 35 C2
Denewood Ave NG9 . . . . 171 C2
Denewood Cres NG8 . . . 171 E8
Denholme Rd NG8 . . . . . 171 D5
Denison Ave DN22 . . . . . . 40 A4
Denison St
  Beeston NG9 . . . . 183 E7
  Nottingham NG7 . . . . . 222 B4
Denman Cl DN22 . . . . 39 D8
Denman St Central NG7 . 222 B3
Denman St E NG7 . . . . . 222 B3
Denman St W NG7 . . . . . 222 A3
Denmark Gr ❶ NG3 . . . . 173 D8
Dennett Cl NG3 . . . . 173 E6
Dennis Ave NG9 . . . . 183 E8
Dennis St
  Carlton NG4 . . . . 175 A7
  Worksop S80 . . . . 35 F2
Dennor Dr NG19 . . . . 88 E5
Denstone Rd NG3 . . . . . 173 E5
Dentdale Dr NG8 . . . . . . 171 B4
Denton Ave NG10 . . . . . 182 A6
Denton Cl
  Balderton NG24 . . . . . . 140 C3
  Mansfield NG19 . . . . 88 E1
Denton Dr NG2 . . . . 185 D4
Denton Gn NG8 . . . . 159 F2
Denver Ct NG9 . . . . 170 E1
Deptford Cres NG6 . . . . 160 C5
Derby Gr NG7 . . . . 222 B3
Derby Rd
  Annesley Woodhouse NG15,
    NG17 . . . . 130 B7
  Beeston NG9 . . . . 171 E1
  Eastwood NG16 . . . . . . 143 E2
  Hathern LE12 . . . . 212 F2
  Kegworth DE74 . . . . . . 203 C2
  Kirkby in A NG17 . . . . . 115 D4
  Langley Mill NG16 . . . . 143 C3
  Long Eaton NG10 . . . . . 193 B8
  Loughborough LE11 . . . 220 A5
  Mansfield NG17, NG18 . 116 B8
  Nottingham NG7 . . . . . 222 B2
  Sandiacre NG10 . . . . . . 182 D4
Derbyshire Ave NG9 . . . 170 D4
Derbyshire Cres NG8 . . 172 A5
Derbyshire Dr NG1 . . . . 146 A7
Derbyshire La NG15 . . . . 146 A7
Derby Sq LE11 . . . . 220 A4
Derby St
  Arnold NG5 . . . . 161 F7
  Beeston NG9 . . . . 183 F7
  Mansfield NG18 . . . . . . 102 C6
  Nottingham NG1 . . . . . 223 D3
Dereham Dr NG5 . . . . . . 162 A6
Derry Dr NG5 . . . . 147 F2
Derry Hill Rd NG5 . . . . . 147 E1
Derry La NG13 . . . . 178 B3
Derrymount Sch NG5 . . 147 F1
Derwent Ave
  Ilkeston DE7 . . . . 157 D2
  Mansfield NG18 . . . . . . 103 A5
Derwent Cl
  Beeston NG9 . . . . 183 E3
  Mansfield NG18 . . . . . . 103 A5
  Market Warsop NG20 . . . 74 C5
  Rainworth NG21 . . . . . . 118 B8
  West Bridgford NG2 . . . 186 C7
  Worksop S81 . . . . 35 F6
Derwent Cres NG5 . . . . 162 A6
Derwent Ct
  Balderton NG24 . . . . . . 140 D3
  Nottingham NG7 . . . . . 222 C4
Derwent Dr
  Annesley Woodhouse
    NG17 . . . . 130 A8
  Hucknall NG15 . . . . . . 146 A4
  Selston NG16 . . . . 129 A7
Derwent St Ind Est
  NG10 . . . . 193 D6
Derwent St NG10 . . . . . 193 C6
Derwent Terr ❶ NG5 . . 161 C2
Derwent Way
  Newark-on-T NG24 . . . . 125 B2
  Nottingham NG7 . . . . . 172 D4
  Nottingham NG7 . . . . . 222 A2
Desborough Rd NG16 . . 128 D7
Desford Cl NG5 . . . . 161 A4
De Vere Gdns NG5 . . . . 162 A4
Devitt Dr NG15 . . . . 131 C1
Devon Cir NG5 . . . . 147 D1
Devon Cl
  Eastwood NG16 . . . . . . 144 B2
  Sandiacre NG10 . . . . . . 182 B5
Devon Dr
  Mansfield NG18 . . . . . . 101 F8
  Nottingham NG5 . . . . . 161 C2
  Ruddington NG11 . . . . . 196 D8
  Nottingham NG5 . . . . . 181 B3
**Devon Pk Pastures Nature
  Reserve** NG24 . . . . . 139 D6
Devon Rd NG24 . . . . . . 139 D6
Devonshire Ave
  Beeston NG9 . . . . 183 F6
  Long Eaton NG10 . . . . . 194 A8
Devonshire Cl
  Ilkeston DE7 . . . . 157 E5
  ❶ Sutton in Ashfield
    NG17 . . . . 100 A2
Devonshire Cres NG5 . . 161 B2
Devonshire Dr
  Eastwood NG16 . . . . . . 143 F2
  Langwith NG20 . . . . 72 F8
  Ollerton NG22 . . . . 77 A3

Devonshire Dr continued
  Stapleford NG9 . . . . . . 170 D2
Devonshire La LE11 . . . . 220 B3
Devonshire Prom NG7 . . 222 A1
Devonshire Rd
  Harworth DN11 . . . . 8 F4
  Nottingham NG5 . . . . . 161 B2
  Retford DN22 . . . . 39 D6
  West Bridgford NG2 . . . 185 F6
Devonshire Sq ❷ LE11 . 220 B3
Devonshire St
  New Houghton NG19 . . . 87 A7
  Worksop S80 . . . . 35 C2
Devon St
  Ilkeston DE7 . . . . 170 A5
  Nottingham NG3 . . . . . 173 F5
Dewberry La NG12 . . . . 186 A4
DH Lawrence Birthplace Mus
  NG16 . . . . 143 F3
Dial The NG12 . . . . 187 E1
Diamond Ave
  Kirkby in A NG17 . . . . . 115 C4
  Rainworth NG21 . . . . . . 104 C1
Dickens Ct NG16 . . . . . . 144 B3
Dickenson Terr DN21 . . . 24 D7
Dickenson Way NG23 . . 110 F3
Dickens Rd S81 . . . . 36 B3
Dickman's La LE14 . . . . 202 B3
Dicks La NG16 . . . . 144 C3
Dickson Dr NG11 . . . . . . 196 D6
Didcot Dr NG8 . . . . 160 D1
Digby Ave NG3 . . . . 162 C3
Digby Ct NG7 . . . . 222 B1
Digby Hall Dr NG4 . . . . . 162 C3
Digby St
  Cossall DE7 . . . . 158 A1
  Kimberley NG16 . . . . . . 158 D7
Dingley Cl NG19 . . . . 88 E5
Dirca Cl NG11 . . . . 195 C8
Diseworth Gr ❸ NG2 . . 173 D1
Distillery St NG11 . . . . . 196 C6
Division Rd NG20 . . . . . . 72 E4
Dixie St NG16 . . . . 128 B4
Djanogly City Acad NG7 161 A1
Dobbin Cl NG12 . . . . . . 189 B4
Dockholm Rd NG10 . . . . 182 C2
Dock Rd S80 . . . . 35 E3
Doddington Hall LN6 . . . . 71 B1
Doddington La
  Claypole NG23 . . . . 156 B2
  Dry Doddington NG23 . . 156 E5
Dodford Ct DE75 . . . . . . 143 A1
Dodsley Way NG21 . . . . . 90 A4
Dog & Duck La DN21 . . . . 15 B4
Doghill La NG23 . . . . . . 153 B2
Dog La DN10 . . . . 10 A2
Dogwood Ave NG6 . . . . 160 A7
Doles La
  Kirkby in A NG17 . . . . . 114 C6
  Whitwell S80 . . . . 45 B7
Dolphin Ct ❼ NG5 . . . . 161 A8
Dominie Cross Rd DN22 . . 39 F4
Donbas Cl NG6 . . . . 160 B4
Doncaster Ave NG10 . . . 182 B6
Doncaster Gr NG10 . . . . 182 F1
Doncaster Rd
  Bawtry DN10 . . . . 10 A8
  Carlton L S81 . . . . 25 F7
  Langold S81 . . . . 16 F3
  Tickhill DN11 . . . . 8 A8
  Westwoodside DN9 . . . . . 2 B1
Doncaster Terr ❶❶ NG2 . 173 C1
Donington Rd NG7 . . . . 184 E1
Donkey La NG11 . . . . . . 196 E3
Donner Cres DE7 . . . . . 157 E5
Dooland Dr NG3 . . . . . . 161 F1
Dorchester Cl NG18 . . . 102 D2
Dorchester Dr NG18 . . . 102 D2
Dorchester Gdns NG2 . . 185 E3
Dorchester Rd
  Annesley Woodhouse
    NG17 . . . . 115 B1
  Harworth DN11 . . . . 9 B5
  Kimberley NG16 . . . . . . 158 F7
Doreen Dr NG17 . . . . . . 100 D2
Dorewood Ct NG24 . . . . 140 E4
Doris Rd DE7 . . . . 170 A7
Dorket Cl NG5 . . . . 148 A1
Dorket Dr NG8 . . . . 172 D3
Dorking Rd NG7 . . . . . . 222 B4
Dormy Cl
  Beeston NG9 . . . . 183 C7
  Mansfield Woodhouse NG19 88 E5
  Radcliffe on T NG12 . . . 176 B3
Dormy Ct NG6 . . . . 160 A8
Dormer Ave NG24 . . . . . 139 D7
Dornoch Ave
  Nottingham NG5 . . . . . 161 D2
  Southwell NG25 . . . . . . 121 F1
Dorothy Ave
  Eastwood NG16 . . . . . . 144 A3
  Hucknall NG15 . . . . . . 131 B1
  Mansfield Woodhouse NG19 88 C1
  Sandiacre NG10 . . . . . . 182 B5
Dorothy Dr NG19 . . . . . . 88 F1
Dorothy Gr ❶ NG8 . . . . 172 D6
Dorset Dr
  Nottingham NG11 . . . . . . 8 F4
Dorset Gdns NG2 . . . . . 185 C5
Dorset St NG8 . . . . 172 D5
Dorset Way NG18 . . . . . 103 A4
Dorterry Cres DE7 . . . . 170 A5
Dorton Ave DN21 . . . . . . 24 F8
Douglas Ave
  Awsworth NG16 . . . . . . 158 C5
  Carlton NG4 . . . . 174 E6
Douglas Cl NG12 . . . . . . 175 E2
Douglas Cres NG4 . . . . 174 E6
Douglas Dr NG9 . . . . . . 183 A2

Douglas Prim Sch NG7 . 222 B3
Douglas Rd
  Bingham NG13 . . . . 178 B4
  Long Eaton NG10 . . . . . 182 B1
  Mansfield Woodhouse NG19 89 B2
  Nottingham NG7 . . . . . 222 B3
  Sutton in A NG17 . . . . . 100 D2
Douro Dr NG5 . . . . 148 B1
Dove Cl
  Bingham NG13 . . . . 177 F3
  Ollerton NG22 . . . . 77 B4
  Worksop S81 . . . . 35 E7
Dovecote St LE12 . . . . . 213 A1
Dovecote Cl NG13 . . . . . 165 C3
Dovecote Dr NG8 . . . . . 171 E4
Dovecote La NG9 . . . . . 184 A5
Dovecote Prim Sch
  NG11 . . . . 184 F3
Dovecote Rd NG16 . . . . 144 B2
Dove Croft NG22 . . . . . . 77 B4
Dovedale Ave
  Long Eaton NG10 . . . . . 193 A6
  Sutton in A NG17 . . . . . 100 D1
Dovedale Cir DE7 . . . . . 157 E5
Dovedale Cl
  Edwinstowe NG21 . . . . . 76 A2
  Mansfield NG18 . . . . . . 102 D3
  Nottingham NG10 . . . . 193 B6
Dovedale Prim Sch
  NG10 . . . . 193 A6
Dovedale Rd
  Nottingham NG3 . . . . . 174 C6
  West Bridgford NG2 . . . 186 A5
Dove Dr NG16 . . . . 129 A7
Dove La NG10 . . . . 193 C8
Dovenby Rd NG7 . . . . . . 184 F2
Dover Beck Cl
  Calverton NG14 . . . . . . 149 A7
  Ravenshead NG15 . . . . 116 F2
Dover Beck Dr NG14 . . . 149 D4
Dover Bottom DN22 . . . . 50 D3
Doveridge Ave NG4 . . . . 175 A8
Doveridge Rd NG4 . . . . 175 A8
Dover St NG25 . . . . 121 E1
Dove St NG6 . . . . 160 B7
Dovey's Orch NG14 . . . . 148 D7
Downes Cl NG6 . . . . 160 A7
Downham Cl NG5 . . . . . 162 A6
Downham Gdns NG15 . . 117 B2
Downing Cl NG6 . . . . . . 160 B8
Downing Gdns ❼ NG6 . 160 B8
Downing St
  Nottingham NG6 . . . . . 160 B8
  South Normanton DE55 . 113 A6
  Sutton in A NG17 . . . . . 100 F3
Downs The NG11 . . . . . . 185 A3
Dowson Cl NG12 . . . . . . 176 B4
Dowson St NG3 . . . . 173 F6
Doyne Ct NG2 . . . . 173 C1
Dragon St NG13 . . . . . . 191 B5
Dragwell DE74 . . . . 203 D2
Drakemyre Cl NG5 . . . . 148 B1
Drake Rd NG4 . . . . 175 B6
Drake St DN21 . . . . 24 C6
Draycott Ct DE7 . . . . . . 157 F3
Draycott Rd NG10 . . . . . 193 A4
Draymans Ct NG7 . . . . . 172 F7
Drayton Ave NG19 . . . . . 87 D1
Drayton St ❽ NG5 . . . . 161 C2
Drift Hill NG13 . . . . 192 F4
Drift The
  Hucknall NG15 . . . . . . 131 B1
  Nottingham NG11 . . . . . 184 E3
Drinking Pit La S80 . . . . . 46 B3
Drinsey Nook La NG23 . . 70 C7
Drive The
  Beeston NG9 . . . . 183 E3
  Clipstone NG21 . . . . 90 A3
  Gainsborough DN21 . . . . 24 F7
  Winthorpe NG24 . . . . . 125 C6
Drive The Pk La DN22 . . . 30 A1
Drmonde Terr ❼ NG3 . . 161 C2
Dronfield Pl DE7 . . . . . . 157 D5
Dronley Dr NG20 . . . . . . 74 C7
Drove La NG21 . . . . 117 A3
Drovers Ct DN21 . . . . . . 24 E5
Droversdale Rd DN11 . . . . 9 C4
Drummond Ave NG4 . . . 175 B7
Drummond Dr NG16 . . . 159 E4
Drummond Rd DE7 . . . . 157 E1
Drury La DN11 . . . . 8 A7
Dryden Ave NG24 . . . . . 140 E5
Dryden Cl NG9 . . . . 170 F1
Dryden Dale S81 . . . . 36 B3
Dryden St NG1 . . . . 223 D4
Dry Pot La LE12 . . . . . . 212 A2
Drysdale Cl NG6 . . . . . . 160 B5
Duchess Gdns ❽ NG6 . 160 B5
Duchess St
  Nottingham NG6 . . . . . 160 B8
  Whitwell S80 . . . . 45 A6
Ducie La DN22 . . . . 43 D8
Dudley Ct NG9 . . . . 183 A8
Dudley Doy Rd NG25 . . 121 C1
Duesbury The DE55 . . . . 113 B4
Duffield Cl NG10 . . . . . . 193 A5
Duffield Ct NG5 . . . . . . 160 F8
Duke Cl NG6 . . . . 160 A5
Duke Cres NG16 . . . . . . 144 C1
Duke Pl S80 . . . . 35 E3
Dukeries Cl S81 . . . . 35 C6
Dukeries Com Coll NG22 77 D5
Dukeries Complex The
  NG22 . . . . 77 D5
Dukeries Cres
  Edwinstowe NG21 . . . . . 76 B1
  Worksop S80 . . . . 36 C1

Dukeries Ind Est The S81 35 C6
Dukeries L Ctr NG22 . . . . 77 D6
Dukeries Way S81 . . . . . 35 C6
Dukes Cl NG17 . . . . 101 C2
Duke's Dr S44 . . . . 86 A7
Dukes Pl DE7 . . . . 157 E4
Duke's Pl NG1 . . . . 223 F2
Dukes Rd LE14 . . . . 219 B6
Duke St
  Arnold NG5 . . . . 161 E7
  Hucknall NG15 . . . . . . 146 B7
  Huthwaite NG17 . . . . . 100 A3
  Ilkeston DE7 . . . . 157 F3
  Loughborough LE11 . . . 220 B5
  ❺ Nottingham NG7 . . . 160 B7
  Retford DN22 . . . . 39 E6
  South Normanton DE55 . 113 B6
  Whitwell S80 . . . . 45 A6
Duke's Terr DN10 . . . . . . 10 A7
Duke's Wood Nature Reserve
  NG22 . . . . 107 A5
Duke William Mount
  NG7 . . . . 222 C2
Dulverton Vale NG8 . . . . 160 B3
Dulwich Rd NG7 . . . . . . 222 A3
Dumb Hall La S80 . . . . . . 34 B4
Dumbles The
  Lambley NG4 . . . . 163 B8
  Sutton in A NG17 . . . . . 100 C1
Dunham Cl
  Newton on T LN1 . . . . . . 55 A1
  Southwell NG25 . . . . . . 136 D8
**Dunham on Trent CE Prim
  Sch** NG22 . . . . 54 A1
Dunham Rd
  Laneham DN22 . . . . 54 A5
  Newton on T DN22, LN1 . 54 E1
Dunholme Ave NG24 . . . 139 F7
Dunholme Cl
  Gainsborough DN21 . . . . 24 E8
  Nottingham NG6 . . . . . 160 B8
Dunholme Rd NG11 . . . . 195 F8
Dunkery Rd NG11 . . . . . 195 B8
Dunkirk Ind Est NG7 . . . 184 D7
Dunkirk Prim Sch NG7 . 172 E1
Dunkirk Rd ❹ NG7 . . . . 172 C1
Dunlin Wharf ❷ NG2 . . 173 A2
Dunlop Ave NG7 . . . . . . 222 A2
Dunn Brigg NG19 . . . . . . 88 E5
Dunnett Rd NG19 . . . . . 101 E5
Dunoon Cl NG5 . . . . 146 E1
Dunoon Rd NG19 . . . . . 101 E5
Dunsby Cl NG7 . . . . 184 E1
Dunsford Dr NG3 . . . . . 162 C6
Dunsil Cl NG11 . . . . 185 A8
Dunsil Rd
  Eastwood NG16 . . . . . . 144 B4
  Pinxton NG16 . . . . 113 D2
Dunsmore Cl NG9 . . . . . 184 B4
Dunstall Wlk DN21 . . . . . 24 F7
Dunstan Cres S80 . . . . . . 35 F1
Dunstan St NG4 . . . . . . 175 A7
Dunster Rd
  Eastwood NG16 . . . . . . 144 B1
  Gainsborough DN21 . . . . 15 F1
  West Bridgford NG2 . . . 186 A6
Dunston Cl NG10 . . . . . . 193 F7
Dunvegan Dr NG5 . . . . . 146 E1
Dunwoody Cl NG18 . . . . 102 F7
Durban House Heritage Ctr
  NG16 . . . . 143 F3
Durham Ave NG2 . . . . . 173 F4
Durham Cl
  Mansfield Woodhouse
    NG19 . . . . 88 C4
  ❶ Nottingham NG2 . . . 173 F4
  Worksop S81 . . . . 35 F2
Durham Cres NG6 . . . . . 160 C6
Durham Gr DN22 . . . . . . 30 A1
Durham St ❹ DE7 . . . . 157 F1
Durlston Cl NG2 . . . . . . 185 B5
Durnford St NG7 . . . . . . 160 F7
Dursley Cl NG6 . . . . 160 B5
Dyce Cl NG6 . . . . 159 F7
Dykes End NG23 . . . . . . 112 A8
Dylan Thomas Rd NG5 . 160 F8
Dyscarr Cl S81 . . . . 16 F3
**Dyscarr Wood Nature
  Reserve** S81 . . . . 16 E3

E

Eagle Cl
  Arnold NG5 . . . . 162 A7
  Beeston NG9 . . . . 183 D8
Eagle Ct NG6 . . . . 160 A7
Eagle Moor LN6 . . . . 84 F4
Eagle Rd DN21 . . . . 24 F6
Eagle Rd
  Eagle LN6 . . . . 84 B4
  North Scarle LN6, NG23 . 83 E3
Eakring Cl NG18 . . . . . . 102 F7
**Eakring Meadow Nature
  Reserve** NG22 . . . . . . 93 E1

Eakring Rd
  Kneesall NG22 . . . . 93 E5
  Mansfield NG18, NG21,
    NG22 . . . . 103 D7
  Wellow NG22 . . . . 92 D8
Ealing Ave NG6 . . . . 160 D4
Eardley Rd NG5 . . . . . . 160 E6
Earl Cres NG4 . . . . 162 F3
Earl Dr NG16 . . . . 144 C1
Earles Ct DN22 . . . . 29 C1
Earl Howe Cres NG13 . . 190 C2
Earls Cl NG8 . . . . 171 C5
Earlsfield Dr NG5 . . . . . 146 E1
Earls Rd LE14 . . . . 219 B6
Earlswood Dr NG12 . . . . 186 B4
Earp Ave NG24 . . . . 140 A2
Easedale Cl NG2 . . . . . . 186 C7
Easegill Ct NG5 . . . . . . 160 F8
East Acres NG12 . . . . . . 187 F3
Eastbourne Professional Ctr
  NG17 . . . . 101 A2
East Bridgford Rd NG13 . 165 B1
East Cir St NG1 . . . . 223 D2
East Cl LE12 . . . . 197 E2
Eastcliffe Ave NG4 . . . . 162 D3
Eastcote Ave NG9 . . . . . 171 B2
East Cres NG9 . . . . 184 B5
Eastcroft LN1 . . . . 57 A5
Eastcroft La NG22 . . . . . 52 A2
Eastdale Rd NG3 . . . . . . 174 C6
East Dr NG7 . . . . 172 C1
East End LE14 . . . . 211 D4
Eastern Ave DN21 . . . . . . 15 F1
Eastern Ct NG24 . . . . . . 140 A8
Eastern Terr La NG24 . . 140 A8
Eastfield
  North Muskham NG23 . . 110 F2
  North Wheatley DN22 . . . 31 E8
Eastfield Cl NG21 . . . . . . 89 F2
Eastfield Ct NG25 . . . . . 136 C8
Eastfield Dr DE55 . . . . . 113 A5
Eastfield Side NG17 . . . 101 A4
Eastgate
  Normanton on T NG23 . . 81 E7
  Worksop S80 . . . . 35 F3
Eastglade Prim Sch S61 161 A8
Eastglade Rd NG5 . . . . . 161 A6
East Gr
  Bingham NG13 . . . . 177 F4
  Nottingham NG7 . . . . . 173 A8
Eastham Cl NG3 . . . . . . 173 E6
Eastham Rd NG5 . . . . . . 162 C6
Eastholme Croft NG2 . . 174 D5
Easthorpe NG25 . . . . . . 136 F8
Easthorpe La NG13 . . . . 192 F4
Easthorpe Rd NG13 . . . . 181 C2
Easthorpe St NG11 . . . . 196 C7
Eastlands La NG20 . . . . . 74 B6
Eastland Terr NG20 . . . . 74 C8
East Leake L Ctr LE12 . . 205 F2
Eastleigh Dr NG19 . . . . . 88 B6
East Markham Prim Sch
  NG22 . . . . 65 F8
East Moor NG12 . . . . . . 188 A1
Eastmoor Dr NG4 . . . . . 174 F8
East Rd LE12 . . . . 216 C4
East St
  Bingham NG13 . . . . 177 F4
  Bole DN22 . . . . 23 E3
  Gotham NG11 . . . . 195 B1
  Harworth DN11 . . . . 9 A5
  Heanor DE75 . . . . 157 A8
  Long Eaton NG10 . . . . . 193 F8
  Nottingham NG1 . . . . . 223 F2
  Retford DN22 . . . . 39 F6
  Sutton in A NG17 . . . . . 101 A3
East View
  Bawtry DN10 . . . . 10 A8
  East Markham NG22 . . . . 65 F6
  Shirebrook NG20 . . . . . . 72 F6
  West Bridgford NG2 . . . 185 D6
Eastwell St NG15 . . . . . 146 A8
East Wlk DN22 . . . . 39 C8
Eastwold NG12 . . . . 188 A2
Eastwood Ave NG20 . . . . 74 B5
Eastwood Cl NG15 . . . . 145 E4
Eastwood Comp Sch
  NG16 . . . . 143 E3
Eastwood Com Sports Ctr
  NG16 . . . . 143 E3
Eastwood Ct S81 . . . . . . 35 F8
Eastwood Inf Sch NG16 143 E2
Eastwood Jun Sch NG16 143 E2
Eastwood & Kimberley Coll
  NG16 . . . . 143 F2
Eastwood La DN10 . . . . . . 4 D3
Eastwood Rd
  Kimberley NG16 . . . . . . 158 E6
  Radcliffe on T NG12 . . . 176 A3
Eastwood St NG6 . . . . . 160 C5
Easy Par S80 . . . . 45 A5
Eather Ave NG19 . . . . . . 88 C4
Eaton Cl
  Beeston NG9 . . . . 184 B6
  Farnsfield NG22 . . . . . . 119 F6
  Rainworth NG21 . . . . . 118 B5
Eaton Ct ❹ NG18 . . . . . 103 A3
Eaton Grange Dr NG10 . 193 A8
Eatons Rd NG9 . . . . 182 D6
Eaton St NG3 . . . . 161 E1
Eaton Terr NG3 . . . . 161 F2

Eaton Wood Nature Reserve
DN22 . . . . .51 D8
Ebenezer St
Ilkeston DE7 . . . . .157 F3
Langley Mill NG16 . . . . . . .143 B3
Ebers Gr NG3 . . . . .173 C8
Ebers Rd NG3 . . . . .173 C8
Ebony Wlk NG3 . . . . .174 B8
Ebury Rd NG5 . . . . .161 B1
Eckington Terr **12** NG2 . . .173 C1
Eckington Wlk NG3 . . . . . .103 B6
Eclipse Yd **3** NG18 . . . . . .102 B7
Ecton Cl NG5 . . . . .146 F1
Edale Cl
Hucknall NG15 . . . . .145 C6
Long Eaton NG10 . . . . .193 B6
Mansfield NG18 . . . . .103 A3
Edale Cl NG17 . . . . .100 E4
Edale Rd
Mansfield NG18 . . . . .103 B6
Nottingham NG2 . . . . .174 A5
Edale Rise NG3 . . . . .182 E3
Edale Sq DE7 . . . . .157 E5
Eddery View NG18 . . . . . . .102 F7
Eddison Cl S81 . . . . .36 A7
Eddison Pk Ave S81. . . . . . . .35 E8
Edison Rd S81 . . . . .35 C8
Eddleston Dr NG7 . . . . . . .184 F1
Edelin Rd LE11 . . . . .220 B1
Edenbridge Ct NG8 . . . . . .171 D2
Eden Cl NG5 . . . . .162 A6
Eden Ct DN22 . . . . .39 E3
Edenhall Gdns NG7 . . . . . .184 F2
Eden Low NG19 . . . . .88 E3
Eden Cl NG5 . . . . .161 A7
Edern Gdns NG5 . . . . .161 A7
Edgar Ave NG18 . . . . .102 C8
Edgbaston Gdns **1** NG8. .172 D8
Edgcote Way NG5 . . . . .161 A6
Edge Cl NG23 . . . . .110 F4
Edge Hill Ct NG10 . . . . . . .193 D4
Edgehill Dr NG24 . . . . .140 A8
Edgehill Gr NG19 . . . . .88 C2
Edge Way NG8 . . . . .159 E1
Edgewood Dr NG15 . . . . . .145 D5
Edgewood L Ctr NG15. . . .145 D4
Edgewood Prim Sch
NG15 . . . . .145 C4
Edgewood Rd NG16 . . . . . .158 F6
Edgington Ct NG12 . . . . . .188 A1
Edginton St NG3 . . . . .173 F7
Edgware Rd NG6 . . . . .160 D7
Edinbane Cl NG5 . . . . .146 F1
Edinburgh Dr NG13 . . . . . .177 D5
Edinburgh Rd S80 . . . . .47 B8
Edinburgh Wlk S80 . . . . . . .47 A8
Edingale Ct NG9 . . . . .171 B4
Edingley Ave
Mansfield NG19 . . . . .101 D7
Nottingham NG5 . . . . .161 C4
Edingley Hill NG22 . . . . . . .120 D4
Edingley Sq NG5 . . . . .161 B3
Edison St NG17 . . . . .114 F1
Edison Way NG5 . . . . .162 C7
Edlington Dr NG8 . . . . .171 C3
Edmond Gr NG15 . . . . .146 C7
Edmonds Cl NG5 . . . . .147 A2
Edmonton Ct NG2 . . . . . . .185 D6
Edmonton Rd NG21 . . . . . . .89 E2
Edna G Olds Prim Sch
NG7 . . . . .222 B1
Ednaston Rd NG7 . . . . .172 D1
Edwald Rd NG12 . . . . .186 B3
Edwaltam Ave NG2 . . . . . .185 E7
Edwalton Cl NG12 . . . . . . .186 B3
Edwalton Ct
4 Mansfield NG18 . . . . . .103 A3
Nottingham NG6 . . . . .160 E6
Edwalton Lodge Cl
NG12 . . . . .186 A3
Edwalton Prim Sch
NG12 . . . . .186 C4
Edward Ave
Newark-on-T NG24 . . . . . .139 E8
Nottingham NG8 . . . . .172 D8
Sutton in A NG17 . . . . .100 A4
Westwood NG16 . . . . .128 B4
Edward Cl NG15 . . . . .145 D4
Edward Rd
Eastwood NG16 . . . . .144 A2
Gainsborough DN21 . . . . . . .15 D1
Long Eaton NG10 . . . . .193 D8
Nuthall NG16 . . . . .159 C5
West Bridgford NG2 . . . . . .185 F8
Edwards Ct S80 . . . . .35 D3
Edwards La NG5 . . . . .161 C5
Edward St
Aldercar NG16 . . . . .143 B3
Kirkby in A NG17 . . . . .115 B6
Market Warsop NG20 . . . . . .74 A5
Stapleford NG9 . . . . .182 D7
Worksop S80 . . . . .35 F4
Edwin St
Arnold NG5 . . . . .161 D6
Sutton in A NG17 . . . . .100 E3
Edwinstowe Dr
Nottingham NG5 . . . . .161 C4
Selston NG16 . . . . .129 B7
Eel La NG22 . . . . .79 C2
Eel Pool Rd DN10 . . . . .11 E1
Eelwood Rd NG15 . . . . . . .145 D4
Egerton Cl NG18 . . . . .103 A7
Egerton Dr NG9 . . . . .170 D2
Egerton Rd NG5 . . . . .161 C2
Egerton St NG3 . . . . .173 C7

Egerton Wlk **2** NG3 . . . . .173 C7
Egham Cl NG21 . . . . .104 C1
Egling Croft NG4 . . . . .174 F4
Egmanton Rd
Laxton NG22 . . . . .79 C3
Mansfield NG18 . . . . .103 A3
Meden Vale NG20 . . . . .74 D7
Tuxford NG22 . . . . .65 C1
Egmont Ct **1** NG2 . . . . . .173 C1
Egypt Rd NG7 . . . . .160 F1
Eider Cl NG20 . . . . .72 D3
Eighth Ave
Beeston NG9 . . . . .184 C5
Mansfield NG19 . . . . .103 A8
Eisele Cl NG6 . . . . .159 F6
Ekowe St NG7 . . . . .160 F2
Eland Rd NG20 . . . . .72 F5
Eland St NG7 . . . . .160 F1
Elder Cl NG5 . . . . .148 A1
Elder Gdns **8** NG5. . . . . .161 A8
Elder St NG15 . . . . .146 B4
Elder St
Kirkby in A NG17 . . . . .114 C6
Sutton in A NG17 . . . . .100 E7
Eldon Gn NG22 . . . . .65 F3
Eldon Rd NG9 . . . . .183 C1
Eldon St
Newark-on-T NG24 . . . . . .139 F7
Tuxford NG22 . . . . .65 F3
Eleanor Ave DE7 . . . . .170 A5
Eleanor Cres NG9 . . . . .182 F7
Electric Ave NG11 . . . . . . .185 A8
Eley Cl DE7 . . . . .157 C2
Elford Rise NG3 . . . . .173 F5
Elgar Dr NG10 . . . . .193 B5
Elgar Gdns NG3 . . . . .173 F7
Eliot Cl NG10 . . . . .193 B5
Eliot Wlk NG11 . . . . .195 C8
Elizabethan High Sch The
DN22 . . . . .39 D8
Elizabeth Cl
Gainsborough DN21 . . . . . . .15 C3
Hucknall NG15 . . . . .145 E5
Elizabeth Ct DE7 . . . . .157 D1
Elizabeth Gr NG4 . . . . .162 E2
Elizabeth Rd NG24 . . . . . . .139 E5
Elkesley Prim Sch DN22. . . .50 A3
Elkesley Rd NG20 . . . . .74 E8
Ella Bank Rd DE75 . . . . . . .143 A1
Ella Rd NG2 . . . . .173 F1
Ellastone Ave NG5 . . . . . . .161 C8
Ellerby Ave NG7 . . . . .184 E2
Ellerslie Cl NG24 . . . . .125 A1
Ellerslie Gr NG10 . . . . .182 A5
Ellesmere Bsns Pk NG5. . .161 B2
Ellesmere Ct NG5 . . . . .162 B7
Ellesmere Dr NG9. . . . . . . .170 C5
Ellesmere Rd
Mansfield NG18 . . . . .102 F8
West Bridgford NG2 . . . . . .185 F4
Ellington Rd NG5 . . . . .148 A2
Elliott Durham Comp Sch
NG3 . . . . .161 F5
Elliott Durham Swimming
Pool NG3 . . . . .161 E1
Elliott St NG7 . . . . .222 C3
Ellis Ave NG15 . . . . .146 B6
Ellis Cl NG10 . . . . .193 C6
Ellis Ct NG3 . . . . .223 F4
Ellis Gr NG9 . . . . .183 F5
Ellis Guilford Comp Sch
NG6 . . . . .160 C2
Ellis St NG17 . . . . .115 B5
Ellsworth Rise NG5 . . . . . .160 F6
Ellwood Cres NG8 . . . . . . .172 A5
Elma La NG20 . . . . .59 D6
Elm Ave
Beeston, Attenborough
NG9. . . . . .183 D2
Beeston, Chilwell NG9. . . . .183 E6
Binghan NG13 . . . . .178 A4
Carlton NG4 . . . . .174 F7
East Leake LE12 . . . . .205 F3
Hucknall NG15 . . . . .145 E5
Keyworth NG12 . . . . .197 F2
Long Eaton NG10 . . . . .193 C8
Newark-on-T NG24 . . . . . .140 B6
Nottingham NG3 . . . . .173 C7
Nuthall NG16 . . . . .159 D8
Sandiacre NG10 . . . . .182 B7
Elm Bank NG3 . . . . .173 C8
Elm Bank Dr NG3 . . . . .173 C8
Elmbridge NG5 . . . . .161 B7
Elm Cl
Keyworth NG12 . . . . .197 F2
Newark-on-T NG24 . . . . . .140 B6
Nottingham NG3 . . . . .173 C7
Pinxton NG16 . . . . .113 D2
Saxilby LN1 . . . . .57 B4
Elmcroft NG25 . . . . .134 B3
Elmdale Gdns NG8 . . . . . . .172 B8
Elm Dr NG4 . . . . .174 F7
Elm Gr
Arnold NG5 . . . . .148 A1
Church Warsop NG20 . . . . . .74 A6
Elmhurst Ave
Nottingham NG3 . . . . .162 C2
South Normanton DE55 . . .113 A4
Elmhurst Cl DE55 . . . . .113 A4
Elmhurst Dr NG17 . . . . . . .100 A3
Elmhurst Rd NG19 . . . . .88 F1
Elmore Ct NG7 . . . . .222 B4
Elmore's Mdw NG14 . . . . .152 A8
Elms Cl
Rempstone LE12 . . . . .215 D5
Ruddington NG11 . . . . .196 D6
Elmsfield Ave DE75 . . . . . .143 A2
Elms Gdns NG11 . . . . .196 C6

Elms Gr LE11 . . . . .220 C3
Elmsham Ave NG5 . . . . . . .146 E1
Elms Jun Sch The NG10. . .193 C8
Elmsmere Dr S81 . . . . .17 A4
Elms Pk NG11 . . . . .196 D6
Elms Rd S80 . . . . .35 F4
Elms The
Carlton NG4 . . . . .174 F6
Watnall NG16 . . . . .158 F8
Elmsthorpe Ave NG7 . . . . .222 A2
Elmswood Gdns NG5. . . . .161 D3
Elmton Cl S80 . . . . .58 D8
Elmton Rd S80 . . . . .58 D8
Elmtree Ave NG16 . . . . . . .128 F7
Elm Tree Ave
Mansfield Woodhouse
NG19. . . . . .88 A4
Shirebrook NG20 . . . . .72 D4
West Bridgford NG2 . . . . . .185 D7
Elmtree Cl S81 . . . . .34 F7
Elm Tree Cl S80 . . . . .9 E2
Elm Tree Dr DN10 . . . . .9 F7
Elm Tree Pl DN22 . . . . .50 B4
Elmtree Rd NG14 . . . . .148 D7
Elm Tree Rd NG17 . . . . . . .114 F6
Elm Tree Rise NG22 . . . . . . .93 E5
Elm Tree St NG18 . . . . .102 C7
Elm Wlk DN22 . . . . .40 A5
Elmwood Cl DN22 . . . . .30 A1
Elnor St NG16 . . . . .143 C3
Elsham Wlk DN21 . . . . .24 F8
Elson St NG7 . . . . .172 F8
Elston Cl NG19 . . . . .87 D1
Elston Gdns NG11 . . . . . . .184 C4
Elston Hall NG23 . . . . .153 D4
Elston La NG23 . . . . .153 C6
Elswick Cl NG5 . . . . .161 B8
Elswick Dr NG9 . . . . .184 C4
Elterwater Dr NG2 . . . . . . .186 C6
Eltham Cl NG8 . . . . .159 F3
Eltham Dr NG8 . . . . .160 A2
Eltham Rd NG2 . . . . .186 A7
Elton Cl
Balderton NG24 . . . . .140 D3
Mansfield NG18 . . . . .103 B6
Stapleford NG9 . . . . .182 D8
Elton & Orston Sta NG13 180 A5
Elton Rd
Mansfield NG18 . . . . .102 F6
3 Nottingham NG5. . . . . .161 B1
Elton Rd N NG5 . . . . .161 A1
Elton Terr NG7 . . . . .172 F7
Elvaston Ct NG18 . . . . .103 B6
Elvaston Dr NG10 . . . . .193 A4
Elvaston Rd NG8 . . . . .172 B5
Elveden Dr DE7 . . . . .157 C3
Ely Cl
Mansfield Woodhouse
NG19. . . . . .88 D4
Worksop S80 . . . . .36 A2
Emerald Cl NG19 . . . . .87 F1
Emerald Gr NG17 . . . . .115 C4
Emerys Rd NG4 . . . . .175 B8
Emma Bates Way NG21 . .118 B6
Emmanuel Ave
Nottingham, Portchester
NG3. . . . . .162 A1
Nottingham, Rise Park
NG5. . . . . .147 A1
Emmendingen Av NG24 . .125 B3
Emmerson Dr NG21 . . . . . . .90 A5
Emneth Cl NG3 . . . . .173 F8
Empingham Cl NG9 . . . . . .183 B2
Empire St NG18 . . . . .102 D6
Empress Rd LE11 . . . . .220 D4
Emsworth Ave DN22 . . . . . .29 E1
Emsworth Cl DE7 . . . . .157 D3
Ena Ave NG3 . . . . .173 F5
Enderby Cres
Gainsborough DN21 . . . . . . .24 E7
Mansfield NG18 . . . . .102 F6
Enderby Gdns NG5. . . . . . .147 E1
Enderby Sq NG9 . . . . .183 F8
Endsleigh Gdns
Beeston NG9 . . . . .183 F7
West Bridgford NG12 . . . . .186 A4
Enfield St NG9 . . . . .183 E7
Engine La NG16 . . . . .144 B4
England Cres DE7 . . . . .143 A2
English Martyrs RC Prim Sch
NG10 . . . . .182 B1
Ennerdale Cl NG2 . . . . .186 C7
Ennerdale Rd
Long Eaton NG10 . . . . .182 B2
Nottingham NG5 . . . . .161 D5
Ennismore Mews NG11. . .185 C2
Enright Cl NG24 . . . . .139 F6
Enterprise Bsns Ctr SK1. .119 C7
Enterprise Rd NG11 . . . . . .185 A7
Enterprise Wy NG21 . . . . .118 A6
Enthorpe St **4** NG8. . . . . .172 B6
Epinal Way LE11 . . . . .220 A1
Epperstone By-pass
NG14 . . . . .150 B4
Epperstone Ct **4** NG18 . .103 A2
Epperstone Rd
Lowdham NG14 . . . . .150 D2
Oxton NG25 . . . . .134 C1
West Bridgford NG2 . . . . . .185 E8
Epping Way NG19 . . . . . . .103 B8
Epsom Rd NG9 . . . . .182 E3
Epsom St NG18 . . . . .102 F6
Erdington Way NG9 . . . . . .182 E3
Erewash Ct DE7 . . . . .157 F3
Erewash Dr DE7 . . . . .170 B6
Erewash Gdns NG5 . . . . . .161 A8
Erewash Gr NG9 . . . . .182 F2

Erewash Meadows Nature
Reserve
Aldercar NG16. . . . . .143 B8
Jacksdale NG16. . . . . .128 B1
Erewash Rd NG16 . . . . .113 E2
Erewash Sq DE7 . . . . .170 A6
Erewash St
Kirkby in A NG17 . . . . .115 A5
Long Eaton NG10 . . . . .193 E8
Pye Bridge DE55 . . . . .128 A6
Erica Dr DE55 . . . . .113 B7
Eric Ave NG15 . . . . .130 F1
Erith Cl NG8 . . . . .159 D1
Ermehale Jun & Inf Sch
NG5 . . . . .162 A6
Ernest Rd NG4 . . . . .162 B1
Erskine Rd **4** NG5. . . . . . .161 B1
Esher Gr NG3 . . . . .161 C1
Eshton Rise DN10 . . . . .3 A1
Eskdale Cl NG10 . . . . .193 B5
Eskdale Ct NG2 . . . . .186 C7
Eskdale Dr
Beeston NG9 . . . . .183 B5
Nottingham NG8 . . . . .172 B8
Worksop S81 . . . . .35 E8
Eskdale Jun Sch NG9 . . . .183 B5
Eskhouse Cl NG2 . . . . .186 C4
Essex Dr DN11. . . . . .9 D4
Essex Rd DN11. . . . . .9 D4
Essex St **2** DE7 . . . . .157 F1
Estfeld Cl DN11. . . . . .8 A8
Estwic Ave NG16 . . . . .143 F3
Ethel Ave
Hucknall NG15 . . . . .131 C1
Nottingham NG3 . . . . .162 A1
Ethelbert Ave NG17 . . . . . .115 C1
Etheldene NG12 . . . . .189 B4
Ethel Rd NG2 . . . . .185 F7
Ethel Wainright Prim Sch
NG19 . . . . .101 F8
Etherington St DN21 . . . . . .24 D8
Eton Cl NG24 . . . . .139 F6
Eton Gr NG8 . . . . .172 B4
Eton Rd NG2 . . . . .185 E6
Eucalyptus Ave NG11. . . . .184 C1
Eugene Gdns NG2 . . . . . . .173 D2
Eugene St NG2 . . . . .223 F1
Europa Way NG2 . . . . .185 C3
Evans Ave NG17 . . . . .100 C3
Evans Rd NG6 . . . . .160 D3
Evedon Wlk NG5 . . . . .147 B1
Evelyn St
Beeston NG9 . . . . .184 B7
11 Nottingham NG2. . . . .173 E4
Eversley Wlk NG5 . . . . .161 B8
Everton Prim Sch DN10. . . .11 B3
Everton Sluice La DN10 . . . .11 C4
Everton St NG19 . . . . .87 E1
Evesham Ct NG9 . . . . .183 A1
Evesham Mews **7** S80. . . .35 F2
Ewart Rd NG7 . . . . .173 A8
Ewe Lamb Cl NG9 . . . . . . .170 F1
Ewe Lamb La NG9 . . . . . . .170 F1
Ewell Rd NG8 . . . . .171 E5
Exbourne Rd NG8 . . . . .159 F1
Exbury Gdns NG2 . . . . . . .185 B4
Exchange Arc NG1. . . . . . .223 E2
Exchange Rd NG2 . . . . . . .185 F7
Exchange Row **13** NG18 . .102 B7
Exchange St DN22 . . . . .39 E7
Exchange Wlk NG1 . . . . . . .223 E2
Exe Fold NG19 . . . . .88 D2
Exeter Cl
Carlton NG4 . . . . .162 F2
East Leake LE12 . . . . .205 D1
Exeter Rd
Nottingham NG7 . . . . .173 A8
West Bridgford NG2 . . . . . .185 F6
Export Dr NG17 . . . . .113 F8
Exton Rd NG5 . . . . .161 A3
Eyam Cl
Beeston NG9 . . . . .171 C2
Mansfield NG18 . . . . .103 B6
Eyam Cl
Beeston NG9 . . . . .183 E5
Ilkeston DE7 . . . . .157 E2
Factory Rd NG17. . . . . .115 A5
Factory Rd **2 LE11**. 220 C3
Factory Yd NG17 . . . . .101 A4
Failsworth Cl NG11 . . . . . .184 E3
Fairbank Cres NG5 . . . . . . .161 D2
Fairburn Cl NG8 . . . . .171 C4
Fairburn Way NG16 . . . . . .159 A7
Faircroft Ave NG10 . . . . . .182 B5
Fairdale Dr NG16 . . . . .144 B2
Fairfax Cl
Gainsborough DN21 . . . . . . .24 F6
Nottingham NG7 . . . . .160 F2
Fairfield DN22 . . . . .39 E3
Fairfield Ave
Nether Langwith NG20 . . . .59 A2
Nottingham NG11 . . . . . . .185 B5
Fairfield Cres NG10 . . . . . .193 A4

Fairfield Dr
Mansfield NG18. . . . . .103 A7
Ravenshead NG15 . . . . . . .116 C3
Fairfield Prim Sch NG9 . .182 D6
Fairfield Rd NG17. . . . . . . .101 B3
Fairfield St NG13 . . . . .177 E4
Fairham Ave NG11. . . . . . . .195 B1
Fairham Ct NG11 . . . . .196 B8
Fairham Dr NG8 . . . . .172 D4
Fairham Rd NG12 . . . . .197 D3
Fairhaven NG17 . . . . .113 B3
Fairholme Cl NG21. . . . . . . .89 F2
Fairholme Dr NG19 . . . . . . .87 E1
Fairisle Cl NG11 . . . . .185 A1
Fairland Cres NG2 . . . . . . .185 D4
Fairlawn Pl NG5 . . . . .161 D2
Fairlawns NG18 . . . . .103 B7
Fair Lea Cl NG10. . . . . .193 D6
Fairlie Ave NG18 . . . . .103 B6
Fairlight Way NG5 . . . . . . .161 B7
Fairmaid Gr NG7. . . . . .184 E2
Fairmead Cl NG3 . . . . .174 A8
Fairnley Rd NG8 . . . . .171 D8
Fair Vale NG23 . . . . .110 A8
Fair View NG19 . . . . .89 A2
Fairview Ave NG16. . . . . . .128 F2
Fairview Ct NG11 . . . . .185 D2
Fairview Rd NG5 . . . . .161 E4
Fairway
Keyworth NG12 . . . . .198 A2
Newark-on-T NG24 . . . . . .139 D5
Retford DN22 . . . . .39 D4
Fairway Cres NG13 . . . . . . .177 B8
Fairway Dr
Beeston NG9 . . . . .183 D6
Nottingham NG4 . . . . .174 C8
Nottingham NG6 . . . . .160 D7
Fairways Dr NG17. . . . . . . .114 F7
Fairways The NG19 . . . . . . .88 D6
Fairway The NG4 . . . . .162 E3
Fairweather Cl NG22 . . . . . .77 F5
Falcon Cl
Eagle LN6 . . . . .84 D3
Nottingham NG7 . . . . .222 A2
Falcon Ct DE7 . . . . .157 D1
Falconers Wlk **7** NG5 . . .161 C8
Falcon Gr NG7 . . . . .161 A1
Falcon St
Loughborough LE11 . . . . . .220 C5
6 Nottingham NG7. . . . . .161 A1
Falconwood Gdns NG11. . .184 C1
Fallow Cl
Nottingham NG7 . . . . .184 E2
Retford DN22 . . . . .29 E1
Fallow Ct S81 . . . . .36 B7
Fal Paddock NG19 . . . . .88 D2
Falstone Ave NG24 . . . . . . .140 B6
Falston Rd NG8 . . . . .172 A7
Faraday Ave NG22 . . . . .66 A3
Faraday Ct NG9 . . . . .170 C1
Faraday Rd
Mansfield NG18 . . . . .102 E5
Nottingham NG7 . . . . .222 A2
Far Back La NG22 . . . . .119 F6
Far Croft Ave NG17 . . . . . .100 C3
Farfield Ave NG9 . . . . .183 B8
Farfield Gr NG9 . . . . .183 B8
Farfield Rd DE7. . . . . .170 A8
Far Holme La NG23 . . . . . . .97 A8
Far La LE12 . . . . .213 D3
Farleys Gr NG15 . . . . .146 A5
Farleys La NG15 . . . . .146 A5
Farley St NG6 . . . . .160 B7
Farm Ave NG15 . . . . .145 D4
Farm Cl
East Bridgford NG13 . . . . .165 D3
Ilkeston DE7 . . . . .170 A8
Long Eaton NG10. . . . . . . .193 E5
Nottingham NG11 . . . . . . .195 F8
Farm Croft Rd NG19 . . . . . .88 C6
Farmers Branch S81. . . . . . .36 A7
Farmer St NG11 . . . . .196 E3
Farm Gr S81 . . . . .36 B7
Farmhouse Cl NG13. . . . . .181 A3
Farmilo Cres NG18 . . . . .87 F1
Farmilo Prim Sch NG19 . . .87 C4
Farm La NG22 . . . . .65 F7
Farm Rd
Arnold NG5 . . . . .162 B7
Beeston NG9 . . . . .183 D5
Farm View DN22 . . . . .39 E3
Farm View Rd NG17 . . . . . .115 C5
Farnborough Rd NG11 . . . .185 A2
Farnborough Sch S81 . . . . . .36 B7
Farndale Cl
Long Eaton NG10. . . . . . . .193 A5
Sutton in A NG17 . . . . .100 F5
Farndale Dr NG8. . . . . .171 B4
Farndale Rd NG17 . . . . . . .100 F5
Farndon Dr NG9 . . . . .182 F3
Farndon Gn NG8. . . . . .172 C3
Farndon Rd NG24 . . . . .125 A2
Farndon St S81 . . . . .35 D7
Farndon Ponds Nature
Reserve NG24 . . . . .138 F6
Farndon Rd
Newark-on-T NG24,
NG23. . . . . .139 D5
Sutton in A NG17 . . . . .101 D1
Farndon Way NG19 . . . . . .101 E7
Farndon Willow Holt Nature
Reserve NG24 . . . . .138 F5
Farnets Ct S81 . . . . .36 B5
Far New Cl NG10 . . . . .182 B5

F

Farnham Rd **1** LE11 . . . . . .220 B1
Farnsfield Ave NG14 . . . . . .164 A5
Farnsfield Ct **15** NG18 . . .103 A2
Farnsfield Rd
Bilsthorpe NG22 . . . . .105 F3
Blisthorpe NG22 . . . . .106 A4
Farnsfield St Michael Prim
Sch NG22 . . . . .119 F7
Farnsworth Ave NG21 . . . . .103 E2
Farnsworth Ct NG16 . . . . . .145 A1
Farnsworth Gr NG17 . . . . . . .99 F3
Far Pasture Cl NG12 . . . . . .197 E2
Farrar Cl NG24 . . . . .125 C2
Far Rd NG22 . . . . .67 D4
Farrendale Cl NG19 . . . . .88 D1
Farriers Croft DE7 . . . . .157 C3
Farriers Gn NG11 . . . . .184 C2
Farrington Cl NG8 . . . . .159 D3
Farr Way NG21 . . . . .118 A4
Far Rye NG8 . . . . .171 F6
Far St
Bradmore NG11 . . . . .196 E3
Wymeswold LE12 . . . . .216 C4
Farthingate NG25 . . . . .136 F8
Farthingate Cl NG25 . . . . . .136 F8
Farthing Ct NG10 . . . . .193 B7
Farthings The LE12 . . . . . . .213 A1
Farwells Cl NG6 . . . . .160 C3
Faulconbridge Cl NG6 . . . . .160 B6
Fawcett St DN21 . . . . .15 C1
Fearn Chase NG4 . . . . .174 E2
Fearn Cl DE72 . . . . .193 A7
Fearnleigh Dr NG6 . . . . .160 D2
Fearon Cl NG14 . . . . .164 F5
Featherbed La NG25 . . . . . .127 D7
Featherston Ave NG80 . . . . . .36 B2
Featherstone Cl
Carlton NG4 . . . . .162 C6
Mansfield NG18 . . . . .101 D4
Feignes Ct NG12 . . . . .197 E3
Feilding Way DN21 . . . . .15 E1
Felen Cl NG5 . . . . .161 A7
Fellbarrow Cl NG2 . . . . .186 C5
Fell Croft NG24 . . . . .139 A5
Felley Ave NG17 . . . . .114 E7
Felley Mill La N NG16 . . . . .129 C2
Felley Mill La S NG16 . . . . .129 B1
Felley Priory Gdn NG16 . . . .129 C3
Fellows Rd NG9 . . . . .183 E7
Fellows Yd NG12 . . . . .197 E7
Fell Side NG5 . . . . .162 A5
Fellside Cl NG2 . . . . .186 C6
Fell Wilson St NG20 . . . . .74 C4
Felly Cl NG15 . . . . .145 E5
Felly Mill La S NG16 . . . . . .129 B1
Felstead Ct NG9 . . . . .171 C1
Felton Ave NG19 . . . . .88 C6
Felton Cl NG9 . . . . .183 B5
Felton Rd NG2 . . . . .173 D1
Fenchurch Cl NG5 . . . . .147 A1
Fenchurch Ct NG12 . . . . . . .176 B3
Fen La
Balderton NG23 . . . . .155 D3
Balderton NG24 . . . . .141 A4
Fennel St LE11 . . . . .220 B4
Fenroth Cl NG6 . . . . .159 F8
Fenton Cl NG24 . . . . .125 B2
Fenton Dr NG6 . . . . .146 C2
Fenton Rd
Fenton NG23 . . . . .142 D1
Nottingham NG5 . . . . .160 F4
Fenwick Cl NG8 . . . . .159 F2
Fenwick Rd NG8 . . . . .159 F2
Fenwick St NG20 . . . . .74 C4
Ferguson Ave NG19 . . . . .88 A4
Ferguson Cl **1** NG9 . . . . .183 C2
Fern Ave NG5 . . . . .161 B1
Fern Cl
Beeston NG9 . . . . .183 C7
Bilsthorpe NG22 . . . . .106 A5
Ravenshead NG15 . . . . .117 B1
Shirebrook NG20 . . . . .72 E6
Southwell NG25 . . . . .121 D1
Fern Cres NG16 . . . . .143 D3
Ferndale Cl
Beeston NG9 . . . . .183 B4
New Ollerton NG22 . . . . .77 E6
Ferndale Gr NG3 . . . . .174 B6
Ferndale Rd NG3 . . . . .174 B6
Ferndene Dr NG10 . . . . .193 A7
Ferngill Cl **2** NG2 . . . . . .173 B1
Fern Lea Ave NG12 . . . . . . .187 E2
Fernleigh Ave NG3 . . . . .162 B2
Fernleigh Rise NG19 . . . . . . .88 D1
Fern Rd NG12 . . . . .189 B3
Fern St NG17 . . . . .100 E4
Fernwood Cl NG19 . . . . .89 A1
Fernwood Comp Sch
NG8 . . . . .171 D4
Fernwood Cres NG8 . . . . . . .171 D4
Fernwood Dr NG12 . . . . . . .175 F4
Fernwood Inf & Jun Sch
NG8 . . . . .171 D4
Ferny Hollow Cl NG5 . . . . . .160 E8
Ferous Cl NG11 . . . . .195 F8
Ferrers Wlk NG3 . . . . .173 E5
Ferriby Terr **13** NG2 . . . .173 C1
Ferry La Cotry Pk
NG14 . . . . .151 E1
Ferry La
Carlton-on-Trent NG23 . . . . . .96 F5
Everton DN10 . . . . .11 C3
North Muskham NG23 . . . . . .110 F2
Festival Ave DN11 . . . . .9 A4
Festival Dr LE11 . . . . .220 A6
Festival Hall L Ctr NG17 . . .115 A4
Festus Cl NG3 . . . . .223 F4

Festus St
Carlton NG4 . . . . .175 A7
Kirkby in a NG17 . . . . .115 A4
Field Ave NG17 . . . . .145 D4
Field Cl
Beeston NG9 . . . . .183 B4
Carlton NG4 . . . . .162 F2
Mansfield Woodhouse
NG19 . . . . .88 D5
Worksop S81 . . . . .36 A7
Field Dr NG20 . . . . .72 E2
Fielden Ave NG19 . . . . .87 D2
Field End Cl LE12 . . . . .205 C1
Fieldfare Dr S81 . . . . .35 C7
Field House NG8 . . . . .171 D5
Fieldings The NG17 . . . . . . .100 B2
Field La
Ault Hucknall NG19, S44 . . . .86 C6
Beeston NG9 . . . . .183 B4
Blidworth NG21 . . . . .117 F3
Cropwell Bishop NG12 . . . . .189 A4
Morton DN21 . . . . .15 A4
Woodborough NG14 . . . . . . .149 C4
Field Maple Dr NG7 . . . . . . .172 E8
Field Mill (Mansfield Town
FC) NG18 . . . . .102 B5
Field PI NG17 . . . . .114 D8
Fields Ave NG11 . . . . .196 C5
Fields Dr NG13 . . . . .178 F5
Fields Farm Rd NG10 . . . . . .193 E5
Field The DE75 . . . . .157 A6
Field View
South Normanton DE55 . . . . .113 A7
Sutton in A NG17 . . . . .100 C1
Fieldway NG11 . . . . .185 B4
Fiennes Cres NG7 . . . . .222 C1
Fifth Ave
Beeston NG9 . . . . .184 D6
Clipstone NG21 . . . . .89 F3
Edwinstowe NG21 . . . . .75 F2
Mansfield NG19 . . . . .103 A8
Fifteyeights Rd DN10 . . . . . . .1 D3
Filey St NG6 . . . . .160 C8
Finch Cl NG7 . . . . .184 F8
Finchley Cl NG11 . . . . .184 C1
Findern Cl NG18 . . . . .103 B6
Findern Gn NG3 . . . . .174 A6
Fingal Cl NG7 . . . . .184 E2
Fingle St DN22 . . . . .32 D1
Fingleton S81 . . . . .36 B6
Finkell St DN10 . . . . .12 F3
Finley Way DE55 . . . . .113 B4
Finningley Rd NG18 . . . . . . .103 A3
Finsbury Ave
5 Loughborough LE11 . . .220 C3
Nottingham NG2 . . . . .173 F4
Finsbury Pk Cl NG2 . . . . . . .185 C5
Finsbury Rd
Beeston NG9 . . . . .171 C3
Nottingham NG5 . . . . .147 A2
Firbank Ct NG9 . . . . .183 B4
Firbeck Ave NG18 . . . . .102 F5
Firbeck Cres NG18 . . . . .16 F3
Firbeck Prim Sch NG8 . . . . .171 B4
Firbeck Rd
Arnold NG5 . . . . .162 A8
Nottingham NG8 . . . . .171 C4
Fir Cl
Nottingham NG6 . . . . .159 F7
Shirebrook NG20 . . . . .72 E6
Fircroft Ave NG8 . . . . .171 F8
Fircroft Dr NG15 . . . . .145 C5
Fir Dale NG12 . . . . .188 A3
Firecrest Way NG6 . . . . .160 D3
Firemen's Row NG17 . . . . . .100 E2
Firs Ave NG9 . . . . .183 F7
Firsby Rd NG8 . . . . .159 F2
Firs Rd NG12 . . . . .186 B4
Firs St NG10 . . . . .193 A4
First Ave
Beeston NG9 . . . . .184 C6
Carlton, Colwick NG4 . . . . . .174 E5
Carlton, Gedling NG4 . . . . . .162 F1
Carlton, Thorneywood
NG4 . . . . .174 C8
Clipstone NG21 . . . . .90 A3
Edwinstowe NG21 . . . . .76 A2
Mansfield NG21 . . . . .103 F2
Mansfield Woodhouse NG19 . .89 A1
Nottingham NG6 . . . . .160 B7
Firs The **1** NG5 . . . . .161 D3
Firth Cl NG5 . . . . .148 C1
Firth Dr NG9 . . . . .183 C2
Firth Rd DN22 . . . . .39 C8
Firth Way NG6 . . . . .146 A1
Fir Tree Cl NG19 . . . . .89 D2
Fir View NG22 . . . . .77 D5
Fisher Ave NG5 . . . . .161 F5
Fisher Cl
Collingham NG23 . . . . .98 B1
East Leake LE12 . . . . .205 F2
Sutton in Ashfield NG17 . . . .100 C5
Fisher La
Bingham NG13 . . . . .177 E4
Mansfield NG18 . . . . .102 C5
Worksop S80 . . . . .36 C5
Fishers St NG17 . . . . .115 A1
Fisher St **4** NG7 . . . . . . .172 F8
Fish Pond Dr NG7 . . . . .223 D1
Fishpool Rd NG21 . . . . .117 D3
Fiskerton Ct **8** NG18 . . . .103 A3
Fiskerton Rd
Rolleston NG23 . . . . .138 B5
Southwell NG25 . . . . .137 A6
Fiskerton Sta NG25 . . . . . . .137 E4
Fitzherbert St NG20 . . . . .74 C4

Five Acres NG11 . . . . .185 A4
Five Fields Cl DN22 . . . . .40 A4
Five Fields La DN22 . . . . .40 A4
Flagholme NG12 . . . . .187 F2
Flamingo Ct **5** NG2 . . . . .173 C1
Flamstead Ave NG4 . . . . . . .163 B7
Flamstead Rd DE7 . . . . .157 F1
Flamsteed Rd NG8 . . . . .159 D1
Flash La NG22 . . . . .93 B7
Flat La S81 . . . . .16 A6
Flatts La
Calverton NG14 . . . . .133 E1
Westwood NG16 . . . . .128 D3
Flatts The NG9 . . . . .183 B5
Flawforth Ave NG11 . . . . . . .196 D6
Flawforth La NG11 . . . . .196 E7
Flaxendale NG12 . . . . .188 A2
Flaxton Way NG5 . . . . .160 F7
Fleam Rd NG11 . . . . .184 E4
Fleeman Gr NG2 . . . . .174 A1
Fleet Cl NG7 . . . . .172 D6
Fleetway S81 . . . . .35 E2
Fleetway NG16 . . . . .144 B1
Fleetwith Cl NG2 . . . . .186 C5
Fleming Ave
Bottesford NG13 . . . . .181 C3
Tuxford NG22 . . . . .66 A3
Fleming Cl NG16 . . . . .159 A8
Fleming Dr
Carlton NG4 . . . . .174 C7
Newark-on-T NG24 . . . . .125 B4
Woodbeck DN22 . . . . .53 B8
Fleming Gdns NG11 . . . . . . .184 C1
Fletcher Ct NG22 . . . . .119 E2
Fletcher Gate NG1 . . . . .223 E2
Fletcher Rd NG9 . . . . .184 A7
Fletcher St NG10 . . . . .193 D8
Fletcher Terr NG3 . . . . .161 E3
Fletcher Way NG19 . . . . . . .103 B8
Flewitt Gdns NG3 . . . . .173 E6
Flint Ave NG19 . . . . .88 F1
Flintham Dr NG5 . . . . .161 C4
Flintham La NG13 . . . . .166 E5
Flintham Mus NG23 . . . . . . .153 A1
Flintham Prim Sch NG23 . . .153 A1
Flixton Rd NG16 . . . . .158 F7
Flood Rd The DN21 . . . . .24 F7
Floralands Gdn Village
NG4 . . . . .162 E8
Floral Villas NG5 . . . . .96 F7
Florence Boot Cl NG9 . . . . .184 B7
Florence Cres NG4 . . . . .175 B8
Florence Ct DE7 . . . . .157 F1
Florence Gr NG3 . . . . .174 A7
Florence Rd
Carlton NG4 . . . . .175 B8
West Bridgford NG2 . . . . . . .186 A8
Florence St NG15 . . . . .146 A5
Florence Terr 24 D7
Florey Ct NG7 . . . . .172 E2
Florey Wlk NG11 . . . . .195 A8
Florin Gdns NG10 . . . . .193 A7
Floss La DN22 . . . . .43 D4
Flowers Cl NG5 . . . . .162 B6
Flying Horse Wlk NG1 . . . . .223 E2
Foljambe Terr NG3 . . . . .223 F3
Folkton Gdns NG3 . . . . .161 F1
Folly Hall La LE12 . . . . .209 D3
Folly La
Besthorpe NG23 . . . . .98 B8
Stapleford LN6 . . . . .112 F5
Folly Nook La DN22 . . . . .19 A4
Fonton Hall Dr NG17 . . . . . .114 B8
Forbes Cl NG10 . . . . .193 E5
Fordbridge La DE55 . . . . . . .113 A7
Fordham Gn NG11 . . . . .195 E8
Ford La NG23 . . . . .109 A5
Ford St N NG7 . . . . .161 A1
Ford St NG7 . . . . .161 A1
Foredrift Cl NG13 . . . . .195 A1
Forest Ave NG18 . . . . .102 C5
Forest Cl
Annesley Woodhouse
NG17 . . . . .130 A8
Cotgrave NG12 . . . . .187 E3
Rainworth NG21 . . . . .104 C1
Selston NG16 . . . . .129 B7
Forest Ct
Mansfield NG18 . . . . .103 B7
Nottingham NG7 . . . . .222 C1
Forester Cl NG9 . . . . .183 C4
Forester Gr NG4 . . . . .174 D8
Forester Rd NG3 . . . . .174 A8
Forester St NG4 . . . . .175 A7
Forest Fields Prim Sch
NG7 . . . . .173 A8
Forest Glade Prim Sch
NG17 . . . . .101 A4
Forest Gr NG7 . . . . .222 C4
Forest Hill NG18 . . . . .102 C2
Forest Hill Rd S81 . . . . .36 A7
Forest La
Papplewick NG15 . . . . .131 E3
Walesby NG22 . . . . .63 D3
Worksop S80 . . . . .36 C5
Forest Link NG22 . . . . .105 F5
Forest Rd
Annesley Woodhouse
NG17 . . . . .130 A8
Bingham NG13 . . . . .177 D4
Blidworth NG21 . . . . .118 B5
Calverton NG14 . . . . .148 D8
Clipstone NG21 . . . . .89 F3
Loughborough LE11 . . . . . . .220 A3

Forest Rd continued
Market Warsop NG20 . . . . . . .74 D1
New Ollerton NG22 . . . . .77 C4
Oxton NG25 . . . . .134 B5
Sutton in A NG17 . . . . .101 A5
Forest Rd E NG1 . . . . .173 B7
Forest Rd W NG7 . . . . .222 C4
Forest Rise NG20 . . . . .74 C2
Forest St
Annesley Woodhouse
NG17 . . . . .130 A8
Kirkby in a NG17 . . . . .115 A4
Sutton in A NG17 . . . . .100 F2
Forest Town Prim Sch
NG19 . . . . .89 A1
Forest View
New Ollerton NG22 . . . . .77 B4
Retford DN22 . . . . .39 D3
Forest View Dr NG15 . . . . . .145 E2
Forest View Jun Sch
NG22 . . . . .77 D5
Forewood La NG22 . . . . .42 A4
Forge Ave NG14 . . . . .148 F8
Forge Cl
South Muskham NG23 . . . . .124 C7
Sutton on T NG23 . . . . .96 F8
Forge Hill NG9 . . . . .183 D4
Forge Mill Gr NG15 . . . . . . .146 C5
Forge The NG9 . . . . .170 B5
Forman St NG1 . . . . .223 E3
Forrests Yd S80 . . . . .35 E2
Forster Ave NG24 . . . . .139 E5
Forster St
Gainsborough DN21 . . . . .15 C1
Kirkby in a NG17 . . . . .114 F5
Nottingham NG7 . . . . .172 D7
Forsythia Gdns NG7 . . . . . . .172 E2
Forum Rd NG5 . . . . .160 E6
Fosbrooke Dr NG10 . . . . . . .193 D5
Fosdyke Gdns LN1 . . . . .57 B3
Fosse Cl LN1 . . . . .57 B3
Fosse Rd NG23 . . . . .139 A4
Fossett's Ave NG16 . . . . . . .128 F7
Fosseway **3** DN21 . . . . . . .15 F1
Fosse Wlk NG12 . . . . .188 A1
Fosse Way NG13 . . . . .166 B5
Foster Ave NG9 . . . . .183 F6
Foster Dr NG5 . . . . .161 C4
Fosters Dr NG5 . . . . .161 D4
Fosters La NG13 . . . . .177 F4
Foster St NG18 . . . . .102 C6
Foston Cl NG18 . . . . .103 B6
Fothergill Ct **1** NG3 . . . .173 C7
Foundry Cl NG24 . . . . .124 F2
Fountain Dale Ct **2**
NG3 . . . . .173 D7
Fountaindale Specl Sch
NG18 . . . . .116 D6
Fountain Hill DN10 . . . . .13 D7
Fountain Hill Rd DN10 . . . . .13 D7
Fountains Cl
Kirkby in a NG17 . . . . .115 C5
West Bridgford NG2 . . . . . . .186 B6
Four Seasons Sh Ctr
NG18 . . . . .102 B7
Fourth Ave
Beeston NG9 . . . . .184 D6
Carlton NG4 . . . . .174 B8
Clipstone NG21 . . . . .89 F3
Edwinstowe NG21 . . . . .76 A2
Mansfield NG21 . . . . .103 A8
Rainworth NG21 . . . . .103 F2
Fowler St NG3 . . . . .173 D8
Foxby Hill DN21 . . . . .24 E6
Foxby La DN21 . . . . .24 F6
Fox Cl NG10 . . . . .193 D5
Fox Covert
Carlton NG4 . . . . .174 F4
1 Loughborough LE11 . . .220 B6
Fox Covert Cl NG17 . . . . . . .100 C1
Fox Covert La
Misterton DN10 . . . . .14 A8
Nottingham NG11 . . . . .184 C1
Foxcovert Plantation Nature
Reserve NG14 . . . . .132 C2
Fox Covert Way NG10 . . . . .103 B7
Foxearth Ave NG11 . . . . . . .185 A2
Foxes Cl NG7 . . . . .222 C1
Foxglove Cl
New Balderton NG24 . . . . . .140 C5
Worksop S80 . . . . .36 B2
Foxglove Rd NG16 . . . . .158 B8
Foxgloves The NG13 . . . . . .177 D3
Fox Gr NG5 . . . . .160 D3
Fox Gr Ct NG6 . . . . .160 E3
Foxhall Rd NG7 . . . . .173 A8
Foxhill Rd NG12 . . . . .187 E2
Foxhill Ct NG4 . . . . .174 E8
Foxhill
Burton Joyce NG14 . . . . . . .163 E5
Carlton NG4 . . . . .174 C8
Foxhill Rd Central NG4 . . . .174 D8
Foxhill Rd E NG4 . . . . .174 E8
Foxhill Rd W NG4 . . . . .174 B8
Foxhills DE74 . . . . .203 C1
Foxhollies Gr NG5 . . . . .161 B3
Fox Mdw NG15 . . . . .145 C6
Fox Rd
Nottingham NG2 . . . . .173 E1
Clipstone NG21 . . . . .89 F3
Fox St
Annesley Woodhouse
NG17 . . . . .130 A8

Fox St continued
Sutton in A NG17 . . . . .100 F3
Foxton Cl NG6 . . . . .159 F8
Foxwood Cl S81 . . . . .25 D1
Foxwood Found Sch & Tech
Coll NG9 . . . . .171 B1
Foxwood Gr NG14 . . . . .148 F7
Foxwood La NG14 . . . . .149 A5
Fradley Cl NG6 . . . . .146 C2
Frampton Rd NG8 . . . . .172 A7
Frances Gr NG15 . . . . .131 B1
Frances St NG16 . . . . .128 D5
Francis Chichester Wlk
DN21 . . . . .24 C7
Francis Gr NG6 . . . . .160 E3
Francis Rd NG4 . . . . .174 F8
Francis St
Mansfield NG18 . . . . .102 C7
Nottingham NG7 . . . . .222 C4
Franklin Rd NG21 . . . . .150 D2
Franklin Ct NG14 . . . . .114 E5
Frank Ave NG18 . . . . .101 F5
Franklin Cl NG5 . . . . .161 C8
Franklin Dr NG12 . . . . .186 D1
Franklin Rd NG16 . . . . .128 A4
Franklyn Gdns
Keyworth NG12 . . . . .197 E4
Nottingham NG8 . . . . .172 C6
Fraser Cres NG4 . . . . .162 B1
Fraser Rd
Carlton NG4 . . . . .162 B1
Nottingham NG2 . . . . .173 D1
Fraser Sq NG4 . . . . .162 B1
Fraser St NG15 . . . . .130 D6
Frearson Farm Ct NG16 . . . .143 F1
Freckingham St NG1 . . . . . .223 F2
Freda Ave NG4 . . . . .162 D2
Freda Cl NG4 . . . . .162 D3
Frederick Ave
Carlton NG4 . . . . .174 B7
Ilkeston DE7 . . . . .170 A5
Kegworth DE74 . . . . .203 C3
Kirkby in a NG17 . . . . .114 D6
Frederick Gent Sch
DE55 . . . . .113 B5
Frederick Harrison Inf Sch
NG9 . . . . .182 F8
Frederick Rd NG9 . . . . .182 D7
Frederick St
Long Eaton NG10 . . . . .193 F7
Loughborough LE11 . . . . . . .220 A3
Mansfield NG18 . . . . .102 A7
Retford DN22 . . . . .39 F6
Sutton in A NG17 . . . . .100 C1
Worksop S80 . . . . .35 E3
Freeby Ave NG19 . . . . .88 D5
Freehold St LE11 . . . . .220 C4
Freeland Cl NG9 . . . . .182 F3
Freeman's La DN22 . . . . .32 C5
Freemans Rd NG4 . . . . .175 A8
Freemans Terr NG4 . . . . . . .175 A8
Freemantle Wlk NG5 . . . . . .160 E8
Freeston Dr NG6 . . . . .159 F8
Freeth St NG2 . . . . .173 F2
Freiston St **5** NG7 . . . . . .172 E7
Fremount Dr NG8 . . . . .171 D5
French St DE7 . . . . .170 A6
French Terr NG20 . . . . .59 A2
Fretwell St **3** NG7 . . . . . .172 E7
Friar La
Market Warsop NG20 . . . . . . .74 C2
Nottingham NG1 . . . . .223 D2
Friars Cl NG16 . . . . .129 B7
Friars Cres NG24 . . . . .139 F5
Friars Ct NG7 . . . . .222 C1
Friar St
Long Eaton NG10 . . . . .193 D7
Nottingham NG7 . . . . .222 C1
Friar Wlk NG13 . . . . .177 C8
Friary Cl NG7 . . . . .172 E2
Friary **10** NG7 . . . . .172 E2
Friary Gdns NG24 . . . . .125 A1
Friary Rd **2** NG24 . . . . . .140 A8
Friary The NG7 . . . . .172 E2
Friday La NG4 . . . . .162 F1
Friend La NG21 . . . . .76 B1
Frinton Rd NG8 . . . . .159 E1
Frisby Ave NG10 . . . . .193 E6
Fritchley Ct NG18 . . . . .103 B6
Frith Gr NG19 . . . . .101 E7
Frithwood La DE55 . . . . .58 D7
Frobisher Gdns NG5 . . . . . . .161 D6
Frog La NG13 . . . . .202 F8
Frogmore St NG1 . . . . .223 E4
Front St
Arnold NG5 . . . . .161 F7
Barnby in t W NG24 . . . . . . .141 F5
East Stockwith DN21 . . . . . . .7 D2
Morton DN21 . . . . .15 B3
South Clifton NG23 . . . . .68 E1
Frost Ave NG16 . . . . .143 A4
Fryar Rd NG16 . . . . .143 F3
Fulford Ave DN22 . . . . .39 C8
Fulforth St NG1 . . . . .223 E4
Fuller Cl NG18 . . . . .102 B4
Fuller St NG11 . . . . .196 C6
Fullwood Ave **4** DE7 . . . .157 E1
Fullwood Cl NG9 . . . . .183 C4
Fullwood St DE7 . . . . .157 E1
Fulmar Way S81 . . . . .35 C7
Fulwood Cres NG8 . . . . .160 B1
Fulwood Dr NG10 . . . . .193 A7
Fulwood Rd N
Huthwaite NG17 . . . . .99 F1
Sutton in A NG17 . . . . .114 A8

Fulwood Rd S NG17.... 114 A8
Fulwood Rise NG17 .... 114 A8
Furlong Ave NG5 ...... 161 E8
Furlong Cl NG9......... 182 D8
Furlong St NG5......... 161 E8
Furnace Rd DE7........ 170 B6
Furness Cl NG2......... 186 A7
Furness Rd NG6 .... 160 C3
Furnival St S80......... 36 A1
Furrobrook Rd NG4.... 174 E6
Furze Gdns NG3 .... 173 D7
Furze The NG22......... 78 C6
Fylde Cl NG9........... 182 F2
Fylingdale Way NG8 ... 171 C4

G

Gables Farm Dr LE12 .... 206 C1
Gable's Lea LE12....... 213 B6
Gables The NG22....... 106 A5
Gabor Cl NG11......... 195 C8
Gabrielle Cl NG6....... 160 D4
Gaddick View NG22 ..... 79 F6
Gadd St NG7 .... 222 B4
Gadsby Cl DE7......... 170 A4
Gainas Ave DN21 .... 15 C2
Gainsborough Central Sta
DN21................. 24 D8
Gainsborough Cl
Kinoulton NG12........ 199 F2
Long Eaton NG10....... 193 E5
Stapleford NG9 .... 182 E6
Gainsborough Dr NG24...125 B3
Gainsborough Lea Rd Sta
DN21................. 24 D5
Gainsborough Rd
Bawtry DN10........... 10 A6
Everton DN10 .... 11 D2
Girton NG23............ 82 F3
Gringley on t H DN10 ... 12 B1
Lea DN21.............. 24 F2
North Wheatley DN22 ... 23 C5
Saundby DN22.......... 23 C5
Saxilby LN1 .... 56 E2
Sturton le S DN22 ...... 32 C6
Winthorpe NG24........ 125 C6
Gainsborough Waterfront
Enterprise Ctr DN21....24 C6
Gainsborough W Lindsey L
Ctr DN21.............. 15 D2
Gainsford Cl NG5....... 160 F5
Gainsford Cres NG5..... 160 F5
Gaitskell Cres NG11 ..... 76 C1
Gaitskell Way NG24..... 140 E4
Gala Way
Nottingham NG5........ 160 E6
Retford DN22.......... 39 F5
Gale Cl NG9 .... 184 B6
Galena Dr NG3 .... 174 A7
Galen Ave DN22........ 42 A1
Galen Ct **3** NG7 ...... 172 E2
Galleries of Justice NG1 .223 F2
Galley Hill Rd NG25..... 122 B1
Gallows Inn Cl DE7 .... 170 A5
Galway Ave DN11....... 9 D5
Galway Cres DN22 ...... 39 C8
Galway Dr DN11 .... 9 D5
Galway Rd
Arnold NG5 .... 161 E8
Bircotes DN11.......... 9 D5
Nottingham NG7........ 222 B1
Gamage Cl NG24....... 140 F4
Gamble St NG7 .... 222 C3
Gamston CE Prim Sch
DN22................. 50 F5
Gamston Cres NG5..... 161 C3
Gamston Lings Bar Rd
NG12................. 186 C3
Gamston Rd NG18 ..... 103 B3
Gamston Wood Nature
Reserve DN22......... 51 D6
Gant Ct DN11.......... 8 A8
Ganton Cl NG3 .... 161 F1
Garden Ave
Carlton NG4........... 174 D8
New Houghton NG19..... 86 F7
Rainworth NG21 .... 104 A1
Shirebrook NG20....... 72 E4
Garden City NG4....... 174 E8
Gardendale Ave NG11... 184 D1
Gardenia Cres NG3 .... 162 B2
Gardenia Gr NG3 ...... 162 B2
Garden La NG17 .... 101 A3
Garden Rd
Bingham NG13.......... 177 D4
Eastwood NG16........ 144 A3
Hucknall NG15......... 145 F7
3 Mansfield NG18...... 102 B6
Garden Row DE74...... 203 D3
Gardens Ct NG2 .... 186 A7
Garden St NG7 .... 222 B3
Gardiner Terr NG17 .... 100 D6
Gardinia Cl NG9....... 183 A2
Gardner Dr NG12...... 199 F3
Garfield Cl NG9........ 170 E1
Garfield Rd NG7....... 222 B3
Garfield St DN21....... 15 C1
Garforth Cl NG8....... 172 E8
Garibaldi Rd NG19...... 89 D2
Garibaldi Sch NG19..... 89 E2
Garners Hill NG1....... 223 F2
Garnet Cl NG18........ 102 C5
Garnet St NG3......... 173 E5
Garnet St NG4......... 174 F7

Garnon St NG18 .... 101 E6
Garratt Ave NG18 ..... 102 C7
Garrett Gr NG11 ...... 184 D2
Garsdale Cl NG2 ...... 186 C6
Garsdale Dr NG11..... 185 A3
Garside Ave NG17..... 100 D1
Garside St S80 .... 36 A3
Garth Ave NG17....... 114 E8
Garth Rd NG18 .... 102 A4
Garton Cl
Beeston NG9 .... 183 B5
Nottingham NG6 .... 160 B5
Garton Rd LE11........ 220 A3
Garwick Cl NG19....... 89 B2
Gas St NG10........... 182 C6
Gas Wlk LE14.......... 202 B3
Gatcombe Cl NG12..... 176 A3
Gatcombe Gr NG10 .... 182 A3
Gateford Cl
Beeston NG9 .... 171 C2
Worksop S81 .... 35 D7
Gateford Dr S81 ...... 35 D6
Gateford Gdns S81..... 35 D6
Gateford Glade S81..... 35 D6
Gateford Park Prim Sch
S81................. 35 D7
Gateford Rd S81, S80... 35 D7
Gateford Rise S81...... 35 D7
Gateside Rd NG2...... 173 A1
Gatling St NG7 .... 222 A3
Gattlys La NG22......... 77 B4
Gaul St NG6 .... 160 B7
Gauntley Ct **1** NG7.... 172 F8
Gauntley St NG7....... 172 E8
Gautries Cl NG5....... 161 A8
Gawthorne St NG7..... 161 A1
Gayhurst Gn NG6...... 160 C5
Gayhurst Rd NG6...... 160 C5
Gaynor Ct NG8 .... 172 B6
Gayrigg Ct NG9....... 183 B4
Gayton Cl NG8........ 171 D8
Gayton Rd DE7 .... 157 D1
Gaywood Cl NG11..... 195 F8
Gedling Gr NG7........ 222 C4
Gedling Rd
Arnold NG5 .... 162 B5
Carlton NG4........... 162 E3
Gedling Sch The NG4 ... 162 E3
Gedling St
Mansfield NG18........ 102 B5
Nottingham NG1 ...... 223 F2
Gedney Ave NG3....... 173 F8
Gelding Gr NG5........ 161 F7
Gelding House Woods
Nature Reserve NG4...163 B2
Gell Rd NG9 .... 183 A3
George Ave
Beeston NG9 .... 183 F5
Long Eaton NG10....... 182 F1
George Dere Cl NG22 ... 77 D6
George Rd
Carlton NG4........... 174 E7
West Bridgford NG2 .... 185 E7
George's La NG14...... 148 D6
George Spencer Sch & Tech
Ctr NG9............. 182 E5
George St
Arnold NG5 .... 161 E6
Gainsborough DN21 .... 15 B2
Hucknall NG15......... 146 A8
Langley Mill NG16 ..... 143 B3
Mansfield NG18........ 101 F8
Mansfield Woodhouse, Forest
Town NG19.......... 89 A1
Mansfield Woodhouse
NG19.............. 88 D3
Market Warsop NG20 ... 74 B4
Newark-on-T NG24 .... 125 A1
Nottingham NG1 ...... 223 E3
Pinxton NG16.......... 113 C4
Retford DN22.......... 39 F5
Sutton in A NG17....... 100 B3
Whaley Thorns NG20.... 59 A2
Worksop S80 .... 35 F3
George Yd **7** LE11...... 220 B4
Georgia Dr NG5....... 147 E2
Georgia Rd NG9....... 183 F5
Gerrard Cl NG5........ 147 A2
Gerrard Cres DE74..... 203 D1
Gertrude Rd NG2 ...... 174 A1
Gervase Gdns NG11.... 184 D2
Ghest Villas S81....... 16 F1
Ghost House La NG9....183 B4
Gibbet Hill La DN10..... 9 F4
Gibbons Ave NG9...... 182 D6
Gibbons Rd NG18...... 101 F5
Gibbons St NG7....... 172 E1
Gibb St NG10.......... 193 E7
Gibdyke DN10 .... 4 C3
Gibson Cres NG24..... 140 C3
Gibson Rd NG7........ 173 A8
Gibson's La LE14...... 218 C2
Gifford Gdns NG2......173 B2
Gilbert Ave
Gotham NG11.......... 195 B1
Tuxford NG22.......... 66 A3
Gilbert Bvd NG5....... 162 C2
Gilbert Gdns NG3..... 174 A6
Gilbert St NG15....... 130 D8
Gilbert Wy NG21...... 118 B6
Gilcroft St

Gillercomb Cl NG2..... 186 D5
Gill Gn Wlk DN22...... 30 D4
Gillies The NG19....... 101 E5
Gilliver La NG12....... 187 C1
Gillot St DE75 .... 157 A8
Gillotts Cl NG13....... 177 E5
Gill St
Nottingham NG1 ...... 223 D4
Selston NG16.......... 129 A6
Sutton in A NG17....... 100 C2
Gilmores La NG24...... 140 F1
Gilpet Ave NG3 .... 173 F8
Gilstrap Cl NG24....... 140 D8
Gilstrap Ctr NG24..... 124 E1
Giltbrook Cres NG16 ... 158 C8
Gilt Hill NG16......... 158 D7
Gilthill Prim Sch NG16... 158 D7
Gilt Way NG16........ 158 C8
Gimson Cl DE7........ 157 C3
Gin Cl Way NG16...... 158 C6
Gipsy La NG14......... 152 B8
Girton Ct NG18........ 103 B2
Girton La LN6......... 83 B1
Girton Rd NG5........ 161 A3
Gisburn Cl NG11...... 185 A4
Gisburn Gr NG19...... 103 B8
Glade Ave NG8........ 172 C5
Glade Hill Prim Sch NG5 161 C8
Gladehill Rd NG5...... 161 C7
Glade The NG11....... 195 E7
Gladstone Ave
Gotham NG11.......... 195 B1
Loughborough LE11..... 220 B5
Gladstone Dr NG16 .... 143 E7
Gladstone Rd NG24.... 139 F6
Gladstone St
Beeston NG9 .... 183 F6
Carlton NG4........... 174 D7
Gainsborough DN21 .... 15 C1
Hathern LE12.......... 213 A1
Kirkby in A NG17....... 115 B5
Langley Mill NG16 ..... 143 C4
Long Eaton NG10....... 193 D6
Loughborough LE11..... 220 B5
Mansfield NG18........ 102 D7
Mansfield Woodhouse NG19 88 C2
Nottingham NG7 ...... 173 A8
South Normanton DE55... 113 B6
Worksop S80 .... 35 E1
Gladstone Terr
1 Kirkby in A NG17...... 114 F5
Mansfield Woodhouse NG19 88 C2
Gladys St NG7......... 161 A1
Glaisdale S81.......... 36 B7
Glaisdale Dr E NG8 .... 171 E6
Glaisdale Drive Ind Est
NG8................. 171 D6
Glaisdale Dr W NG8.... 171 D5
Glaisdale Parkway NG8 . 171 D5
Glamis Rd
Carlton in L S81........ 25 E6
Nottingham NG5 ...... 161 A2
Glannis Sq NG20...... 74 C6
Glanton Way NG5..... 148 A2
Glapton Prim Sch NG11 . 184 D2
Glapton Rd NG2....... 173 C1
Glapton Wood Nature
Reserve NG11........ 195 C8
Glaramara Cl **1** NG2 .. 173 B1
Glasby Cl NG2......... 77 B4
Glasshouse St NG1 .... 223 E3
Glastonbury Cl NG19.... 88 D4
Glaven Cl NG3........ 88 D2
Glebe Ave
Market Warsop NG20 ... 74 C4
Pinxton NG16.......... 113 D3
Glebe Cl
North Wheatley DN22 ... 31 E8
South Normanton DE55... 113 A5
Worksop S80 .... 35 D3
Glebe Cres DE7........ 170 A7
Glebe Dr NG14........ 163 D3
Glebe Farm Cl NG2 .... 185 C4
Glebe Farm View NG6... 162 F3
Glebe Jun Sch DE55 .... 113 A5
Glebe Pk NG24 .... 140 C6
Glebe Rd
Carlton NG4........... 162 C2
Retford DN22.......... 159 C4
West Bridgford NG2 .... 185 F7
Glebe St
Annesley Woodhouse
NG17.............. 129 F8
Beeston NG9 .... 183 E6
Hucknall NG15......... 146 A8
Loughborough LE11..... 220 C5
Glebe View
Awsworth NG16........ 158 B4
Retford DN22.......... 39 D8
Glen Ave NG16........ 144 B1
Glenbrook Cl NG8..... 188 A3
Glenbrook Cres NG8 ... 172 A7
Glenbrook Prim Sch
NG8................. 171 F7
Glencairn Dr NG8...... 172 A8
Glen Cl DN55 .... 99 A3
Glencoe Rd NG11...... 185 A1
Glencoyne Rd NG11.... 195 E8
Glendale Cl NG4....... 162 D2
Glendale Ct NG9....... 183 B3
Glendale Gdns NG5.... 161 F7
Glendoe Gr NG13...... 177 C4
Glendon Dr
Hucknall NG15......... 146 A5
Nottingham NG5 .... 161 B5
Gleneagles Ct NG12.... 186 C3

Gleneagles Dr
Arnold NG5 .... 148 B1
Kirkby in A NG17....... 114 E7
Glen Eagles Way DN22.... 39 D3
Glenfield Ave NG16 .... 158 D7
Glenfield Rd NG10..... 193 D5
Glen Helen NG4....... 174 F6
Glenlivet Gdns NG7.... 184 F1
Glenloch Dr NG11 ..... 195 F8
Glen Mooar Cl NG19.... 89 A2
Glenmore Rd NG2..... 186 B6
Glenorchy Cres NG5.... 160 E8
Glen Parva Ave NG5.... 147 E1
Glen Rd NG14......... 163 E5
Glenridding Cl NG2.... 186 D5
Glensford Gdns NG5 ... 146 E2
Glenside
Arnold NG5 .... 162 B5
Kirkby in A NG17....... 115 C5
Glenside Rd NG9 ..... 171 C1
Glen St NG17......... 100 E4
Glenstone Ct **1** NG7...172 F8
Glen Thorn NG17...... 184 F2
Glenthorn Cl S81....... 34 F7
Glentworth Rd NG7.... 222 A4
Glenwood Ave NG8 ... 171 D3
Glinis Rd NG5......... 160 F8
Glossop Ave NG18 .... 103 B6
Gloucester Ave
Beeston NG9 .... 183 F5
Nottingham NG7 ...... 222 A2
Nuthall NG16.......... 159 F4
Sandiacre NG10........ 182 A4
Gloucester Rd S81...... 36 A7
Glover Ave NG8....... 171 D4
Glover Cl DN22 .... 42 C6
Glovers Cl NG20....... 60 A3
Glovers La NG24...... 140 D4
Glovers Rd NG24...... 140 D3
Go Ape! NG21......... 90 D4
Goatchurch Ct **8** NG5... 147 A1
Goathland Cl **3** NG5... 161 B8
Godber Rd NG15...... 145 E5
Godfrey's Ct S80....... 35 E3
Godfrey St NG4 ...... 175 A6
Godkin Dr NG16...... 143 A4
Goldcrest Cl NG13..... 178 A3
Goldcrest Rd NG6..... 160 B4
Goldcrest Rise S81...... 35 C7
Goldenholme La DN22 ... 43 A1
Goldfinch Cl
Loughborough LE11..... 220 A3
Mansfield NG18........ 102 E7
Goldham Rd NG8...... 171 D8
Goldsmith Rd
Balderton NG24........ 140 D5
Worksop S81 .... 36 B5
Goldsmith Sq NG1 .... 223 D3
Goldsmith St
Mansfield NG18........ 102 A7
Nottingham NG1 ...... 223 D3
Goldstraw La NG24.... 140 E2
Goldswong Terr NG3 ... 173 C7
Goldthorpe Ave NG18... 88 F6
Goldthorpe Cl S81...... 16 F3
Golf Club Rd DE7...... 170 B1
Golf Course Rd NG12 ... 198 B2
Golf Rd NG12......... 176 A3
Gomersall Cl DN22..... 40 A6
Gonalston La
Epperstone NG14 ...... 150 D4
Hoveringham NG14 .... 151 D2
Goodacre St NG18..... 102 C7
Goodall Cres NG15..... 146 C5
Goodall St **1** NG7..... 172 F7
Goodhand Cres NG18... 101 E6
Goodliffe St **6** NG7.... 172 F8
Goodman Cl NG16 .... 158 B4
Good Shepherd RC Prim Sch
The NG5............. 162 A5
Goodwin Cl
Newark-on-T NG24 .... 140 D8
Sandiacre NG10........ 182 A6
Goodwin Dr NG16..... 158 E6
Goodwin St NG7 ...... 222 C4
Goodwood Ave NG5.... 161 E8
Goodwood Dr NG9..... 182 F2
Goodwood Rd NG8.... 171 D4
Goodwood Way NG18 ... 102 F7
Goosedale La NG6..... 147 A7
Goose Gate
Cotgrave NG12........ 187 E3
Nottingham NG1 ...... 223 F2
Goosemoor La DN22.... 39 F4
Gopher Rd NG24...... 139 F5
Gordon Ave NG18..... 102 E6
Gorebridge Rd NG11 ... 102 C3
Gordon Cl
Beeston NG9 .... 183 D2
Farnsfield NG22........ 119 F5
Worksop S80 .... 36 B3
Gordon Cres DE55..... 113 A4
Gordondale Rd NG18.... 88 B1
Gordon Rd
Burton Joyce NG14 .... 164 A5
Loughborough LE11..... 220 B6
Nottingham NG3 ...... 173 F6
West Bridgford NG2 .... 185 F7
Gordon Rise NG3 ..... 161 E2
Gordon Sq NG2........ 185 F7
Gordon St
Gainsborough DN21 .... 24 D5
Ilkeston DE7 .... 158 A1
Nottingham NG6 .... 160 D4
Gorman Ct NG5........ 162 B7
Gorse Ave NG18 ...... 103 A5
Gorse Cl
Calverton NG14........ 148 D7

Gorse Cl continued
Eastwood NG16........ 158 B8
Long Eaton NG10....... 182 B2
Gorse Ct NG6.......... 160 E5
Gorse Hill NG15 ...... 114 D5
Gorselands Ave S80..... 36 C1
Gorse Rd
Keyworth NG12........ 197 D3
Newark-on-T NG24 .... 139 F5
Gorseway NG21........ 90 A3
Gorsey Rd NG3........ 173 D8
Gorsey Rd NG13...... 173 C2
Gorsy La NG25........ 137 C2
Gosforth Ct NG2...... 173 D1
Goshawk Rd DE7...... 170 A3
Gotham La NG11...... 206 C7
Gotham Prim Sch NG11. 195 A1
Gotham Rd
East Leake LE12 ...... 205 F3
Kingston-on-S NG11 ... 204 C5
Gothic Cl NG6......... 160 E4
Goverton Hill NG14 ... 136 F1
Goverton Sq NG6...... 160 D5
Gowan Cl **7** NG9..... 183 C2
Goyden Cl NG5........ 161 A8
Grace Ave NG9....... 184 B6
Grace Dr NG8 .... 172 D8
Gracefield La NG23 .... 81 F7
Grafton Ave NG5...... 161 D5
Grafton Cl NG17...... 101 B5
Grafton Ct NG7....... 222 C3
Grafton St S80 .... 35 C4
Graham Cl NG24...... 140 B4
Graham St NG7....... 222 B3
Grainger Ave
Annesley Woodhouse
NG17.............. 115 B1
West Bridgford NG2 .... 185 E3
Grainger St NG2...... 173 E2
Graingers Terr NG15 ... 146 B6
Grampian Dr NG5..... 147 B2
Grampian Way NG10 ... 193 A8
Granary Cl DN21...... 15 B1
Granary Ct S81........ 26 A6
Granby Ave
Mansfield NG18........ 102 B8
Newark-on-T NG24 .... 125 A1
Granby Ct NG13....... 177 D4
Granby Dr
Balderton NG24........ 140 D3
Bottesford NG13....... 181 A2
Granby Hill NG13..... 191 B5
Granby La
Plungar NG13 .... 191 F1
Whatton NG13......... 178 D2
Granby St
Ilkeston DE7 .... 157 E2
Loughborough LE11..... 220 A4
Grandfield Ave NG12.... 175 F4
Grandfield Cres NG12... 175 F4
Grange Ave
Bawtry DN10........... 9 A5
Beeston NG9 .... 183 F6
Mansfield NG18........ 101 F5
Misterton DN10........ 14 A4
Newark-on-T NG24 .... 139 E4
Ollerton NG22.......... 77 B3
Ruddington NG11....... 196 C8
Grange Cl
Carlton in L S81........ 26 A6
Lambley NG4.......... 163 C7
Misterton DN10........ 14 A8
Nottingham NG11...... 185 B8
Grange Cres NG4 ..... 162 F3
Grange Ct
Kirkby in A NG17....... 115 D5
West Bridgford NG2 .... 185 C2
Grange Dr
Harworth DN11......... 9 A5
Long Eaton NG10....... 193 F8
Misterton DN10........ 14 A8
Grange Farm Cl NG9.... 183 A1
Grange La NG24....... 155 A4
Grangelea Gdns NG9.... 183 B8
Grange Pk
Cropwell Butler NG12 ... 189 C7
Gainsborough DN21 .... 15 B5
West Bridgford NG2 .... 186 C5
Grange Prim Sch NG10 . 193 F8
Granger Ct **1** LE11...... 220 A4
Grange Rd
Arnold NG5 .... 161 E4
Blidworth NG21........ 118 B5
Long Eaton NG10....... 193 F8
Nottingham NG6 .... 160 D3
Retford DN22.......... 39 D8
West Bridgford NG2 .... 186 A4
Grange The
North Muskham NG23 ... 110 F3
Retford DN22.......... 39 D8
South Normanton DE55... 113 A6
Grange View
Eastwood NG16........ 143 F3
Harworth DN11......... 9 A5
Grange View Rd NG4.... 163 A2
Grange Wlk DN10........ 7 A1
Grangewood Ct NG8.... 171 D3
Grangewood Rd
3 Kirkby in A NG17...... 114 F7
Nottingham NG8 ...... 172 B3
Grannis Dr NG8....... 172 A8
Grantham Cl NG16..... 144 A1
Grantham Rd
Bingham NG13......... 178 C3
Bottesford NG13....... 181 D2
Radcliffe on T NG4..... 175 F7
Grantleigh Cl NG8..... 171 D6
Granton Ave NG11.... 195 F8
Granton Rise NG19 .... 101 D5

Grant St NG7 . . . . .222 B3
Granville Ave NG10 . . . .182 D1
Granville Cres NG15 . . . .175 E2
Granville Ct 4 NG3 . . . .173 F6
Granville Gr 3 NG3 . . . .173 F5
Granville St LE11 . . . . . .220 A4
Grasmere Cl
　Gainsborough DN21 . . . . . .15 E2
　Hucknall NG15 . . . . .145 F8
Grasmere Rd
　Beeston NG9 . . . . .183 D8
　Long Eaton NG10 . . . . . .182 B2
　Worksop S81 . . . . .35 F7
Grasmere St NG10 . . . . .182 B2
Grassdale Cl NG4 . . . . . .162 D2
Grassington Rd NG8 . . . .172 D7
Grassmere NG12 . . . . . . .188 A3
Grass St DE7 . . . . .157 F8
Grassthorpe Rd NG23 . . . .81 E2
Grassy La NG9 . . . . .184 A5
Gratton Ct 1 NG1 . . . . .114 F7
Gravelholes La DN10 . . . . . .6 E1
Gravel La NG22 . . . . .79 D7
Gravelly Hollow NG14 . . .133 A1
Gravelly La NG15 . . . . . .137 E3
Gravel Pit La DN22 . . . . . .50 F1
Gravency Gdns NG5 . . . .162 C6
Graves Moor La S81 . . . . .18 E2
Gray Fallow DE55 . . . . . .113 B4
Gray La NG22 . . . . .120 E1
Graylands Rd NG8 . . . . .171 E6
Grays Dr NG15 . . . . .132 B6
Grayson Ms NG9 . . . . . .183 B2
Gray St LE11 . . . . .220 B2
Graystones Cl NG2 . . . . .186 C5
Grazingfield NG11 . . . . . .185 A4
Greasley Ave NG16 . . . . .144 C2
Greasley Beauvale DH
　Lawrence Inf Sch
　NG16 . . . . .144 B3
Greasley Beauvale Jun Sch
　NG16 . . . . .144 B2
Greasley Ct NG18 . . . . . .103 B3
Greasley St NG6 . . . . . . .160 B7
Great Central Rd
　Loughborough LE11 . . . . .220 C3
　Mansfield NG18 . . . . . . .102 C3
Great Central Rly LE11 . . .220 C2
Great Central Sta LE11 . . .220 C3
Great Freeman St NG3 . . .223 E4
Great Hoggett Dr NG9 . . .183 B6
Great La NG22 . . . . .65 F7
Great Northern Cl The
　NG2 . . . . .223 F1
Great Northern Rd NG16 143 D2
Great Northern Way
　NG4 . . . . .175 B6
Great N Rd
　Balderton NG23, NG24 . . .155 C5
　Barnby Moor DN22 . . . . . .28 C5
　Bircotes DN10 . . . . .9 F6
　Carlton-on-T NG23 . . . . . .96 F6
　Claypole NG24 . . . . .155 F7
　Eaton DN22 . . . . .40 A2
　Gamston DN22 . . . . .51 A4
　North Muskham NG23 . . . .110 F5
　Ranskill DN22 . . . . .19 B3
　Scrooby DN10 . . . . .10 A2
　South Muskham NG23,
　　NG24 . . . . .124 D5
　West Markham NG22 . . . . .65 C6
　Weston NG23 . . . . .81 C3
Greaves Ave LE14 . . . . . .219 C6
Greaves Cl
　Arnold NG5 . . . . .162 B5
　Newark-on-T NG24 . . . . .140 D8
　Nottingham NG8 . . . . . . .159 D1
Greaves La NG22 . . . . . .120 B3
Grebe Cl NG24 . . . . .140 C5
Greek St NG7 . . . . .222 C3
Greenacre
　Burton Joyce NG14 . . . . .163 E5
　Mansfield NG18 . . . . . . .102 F5
　Stanton Hill NG17 . . . . . .100 C5
Green Acre
　Nottingham NG8 . . . . . . .171 B5
　West Bridgford NG2 . . . . .186 B4
Greenacre Ave DE75 . . . .143 A3
Greenacre Rd S81 . . . . . . .36 A6
Greenacres NG17 . . . . . .115 B2
Greenacres Cl NG16 . . . .144 C2
Greenacres Dr DE55 . . . .113 B6
Green Ap NG4 . . . . .174 C8
Green Ave NG4 . . . . .175 A7
Greenbank NG4 . . . . . . .174 D6
Green Bank NG21 . . . . . .118 C8
Greenbank Dr NG17 . . . .100 E2
Greenburn Cl NG2 . . . . .186 D6
Green Cl
　Blidworth NG21 . . . . . . .118 A4
　Hucknall NG15 . . . . .146 C5
　Keyworth NG12 . . . . . . .197 F4
　Newton DE55 . . . . .99 A3
Greenclose La 3 LE11 . . .220 A4
Green Cres NG16 . . . . . .128 F6
Greencroft NG11 . . . . . . .184 E4
Greendale Ave DE75 . . . . .76 A3
Greendale Cl
　Market Warsop NG20 . . . . .74 A4
　Stanton Hill NG17 . . . . . .100 C6
Greendale Cres NG9 . . . . .90 B4
Greendale Gdns NG8 . . . .172 B8
Greendale Rd
　Arnold NG5 . . . . .161 F6
　Nottingham NG3 . . . . . . .174 C6
Green Farm Rd NG16 . . . .128 D6
Greenfield Ave S80 . . . . . .45 C6

Greenfield Cl
　Edwinstowe NG21 . . . . . . .91 B8
　Mansfield Woodhouse NG19 89 B1
Greenfield Com Prim Sch
　NG2 . . . . .173 D1
Greenfield Gr NG4 . . . . . .174 C8
Greenfields NG16 . . . . . .143 A4
Greenfields Cres NG22 . . . .77 C4
Greenfields Dr NG12 . . . .187 F2
Greenfield St NG7 . . . . . .172 D1
Greenfield Way 2 S81 . . . .25 F7
Greenfinch Dale S81 . . . . .35 C7
Greenford Cl NG16 . . . . .159 E3
Greengate NG23 . . . . . . .153 A4
Greengate Rd DN22 . . . . .53 B4
Greengates Ave NG3 . . . .161 F3
Green Hill LE12 . . . . .213 A1
Greenhill Cres NG4 . . . . .174 E6
Greenhill La NG17 . . . . . .129 F8
Greenhill Rd NG4 . . . . . .174 E6
Greenhill Rise NG4 . . . . .174 E7
Greenhills Ave NG16 . . . .144 A3
Greenhills Rd NG16 . . . . .143 F5
Greenholme NG17 . . . . . .115 A4
Greenholme Pk NG19 . . . . .88 E6
Green In Inf Sch The DE55 .113 A7
Green La
　Babworth DN22 . . . . .38 E5
　Bathley NG23 . . . . .110 B2
　Bottesford NG13 . . . . . . .181 C1
　Collingham NG23 . . . . . .112 B7
　Darlton NG22 . . . . .67 C4
　Dry Doddington NG23 . . .156 E2
　Elton LE14 . . . . .84 F4
　Granby NG13 . . . . .191 B5
　Harby LE14 . . . . .202 C2
　Hodthorpe S80 . . . . .45 C5
　Ilkeston DE7 . . . . .170 A4
　Lambley NG4 . . . . .149 B1
　Laxton NG22 . . . . .79 D1
　Lea DN21 . . . . .24 F3
　Mansfield, Moorhaigh NG19 .87 A2
　Mansfield NG18 . . . . . . .101 E5
　Pleasley S44 . . . . .86 B8
　Ranskill DN10 . . . . .18 F8
　South Leverton DN22 . . . . .42 D6
　Upper Broughton LE14 . . .210 A4
　Walesby NG22 . . . . .64 A2
Greenland Cres NG9 . . . .183 C4
Greenland Rd NG17 . . . . .100 E7
Green Leys NG2 . . . . . . .186 A6
Green Mile La DN22 . . . . .38 E8
Green Platt NG12 . . . . . . .187 E3
Green Rd DN10 . . . . .13 A2
Greens Ct DE7 . . . . .157 D1
Green's Farm La NG4 . . . .163 A2
Greensfields NG17 . . . . . .101 A5
Greenside Ave NG21 . . . . .42 F2
Greenside Cl NG10 . . . . .193 E7
Greensquare Rd NG16 . . .113 A6
Green St
　Barton in F NG11 . . . . . .195 A7
　Nottingham NG2 . . . . . . .173 D1
Green The
　Barkestone-le-V NG13 . . .192 B2
　Beeston NG9 . . . . .183 E4
　Bilsthorpe NG22 . . . . . . .105 F7
　Carlton in L S81 . . . . .26 A6
　Coddington NG24 . . . . . .126 B2
　Collingham NG23 . . . . . .111 F7
　East Leake LE12 . . . . . . .205 E1
　Elston NG23 . . . . .153 D4
　Gainsborough DN21 . . . . .24 F7
　Glapwell S44 . . . . .86 B8
　Hadstock S45 . . . . .85 A1
　Harworth DN11 . . . . .8 E4
　Hathern LE12 . . . . .213 A1
　Hose LE14 . . . . .211 F7
　Huthwaite NG17 . . . . .99 F1
　Kingston-on-S LE12 . . . . .204 A4
　Kirklington NG22 . . . . . . .120 F8
　Long Whatton LE12 . . . . .212 C3
　Lowdham NG14 . . . . .149 F2
　Mansfield Woodhouse NG19 88 B4
　Orston NG13 . . . . .179 F7
　Radcliffe on T NG12 . . . . .175 E3
Greentrees Ct NG17 . . . . .100 D1
Greenvale NG24 . . . . . . .120 A6
Greenview Cl NG19 . . . . . .89 B1
Greenway
　Carlton in L S81 . . . . .26 A6
　Clipstone NG19 . . . . .89 D3
　Newark-on-T NG24 . . . . .139 E6
　Retford DN22 . . . . .39 D3
Greenway Cl NG12 . . . . .175 E3
Greenway The NG10 . . . .182 B6
Greenwich Ave NG6 . . . .160 C4
Greenwich Pk Cl NG2 . . .185 C5
Green Wlk NG15 . . . . . . .178 F4
Greenwood Ave
　Edwinstowe NG21 . . . . . . .76 B2
　Harworth DN11 . . . . .8 F5
　Hucknall NG15 . . . . .145 F8
　Huthwaite NG17 . . . . .99 F2
　Ilkeston DE7 . . . . .170 A4
　Mansfield Woodhouse NG19 88 B4
　Nottingham NG3 . . . . . . .174 D5
Greenwood Cl
　Carlton in L S81 . . . . .25 D1
　Farnsfield NG22 . . . . . . .120 A6
　Worksop S81 . . . . .35 D8
Greenwood Cotts S81 . . .102 F8
Greenwood Craft Ctr
　NG18 . . . . .116 E6

Greenwood Cres
　Boughton NG22 . . . . .77 E5
　Carlton NG4 . . . . .174 E6
Greenwood Dale Tech Sch
　NG3 . . . . .174 A4
Greenwood Dr NG17 . . . .114 F5
Greenwood Gdns NG11 . .196 D6
Greenwood Inf Sch NG2 . .174 A5
Greenwood Jun Sch
　NG2 . . . . .174 A4
Greenwood Prim Sch
　NG17 . . . . .114 E6
Greenwood Rd NG3 . . . . .174 C5
Greenwood Vale NG15 . . .145 F8
Greer La S44 . . . . .86 D8
Greet Park Cl NG25 . . . . .121 F1
Greetwell Cl 1 NG8 . . . .172 A6
Gregory Ave
　Aldercar NG16 . . . . .143 A4
　NG7 . . . . .222 B1
　Nottingham, Porchester
　　NG3 . . . . .162 A2
　Nottingham, West Bridgford
Gregory Bvd NG7 . . . . . .173 A7
Gregory Cl NG9 . . . . .182 F8
Gregory Cres DN11 . . . . . .8 E4
Gregory Ct
　Beeston NG9 . . . . .183 B4
　Nottingham NG7 . . . . . . .222 A1
Gregory Gdns NG22 . . . . .119 F5
Gregory St
　9 Ilkeston DE7 . . . . .157 E1
　6 Loughborough LE11 . . .220 B3
　Nottingham NG7 . . . . . . .172 E2
Gregson Gdns NG9 . . . . .183 B1
Gregson Rd NG9 . . . . . . .183 B1
Gregson Way NG17 . . . . .101 B5
Grenville Dr
　Ilkeston DE7 . . . . .157 F3
　Stapleford NG9 . . . . .182 E8
Grenville Rd NG4 . . . . . . .184 B4
Grenville Rise NG5 . . . . . .147 F1
Gresham Cl
　Newark-on-T NG24 . . . . .140 E8
　West Bridgford NG2 . . . . .185 C7
Gresham Gdns
　Arnold NG5 . . . . .162 A5
　West Bridgford NG2 . . . . .185 D7
Gresley Ave DN10 . . . . . . .10 A8
Gresley Dr NG2 . . . . .173 F3
Gresley Rd
　11 Ilkeston DE7 . . . . . . .157 F1
　Retford DN22 . . . . .39 D5
Greta N Rd NG23 . . . . . . .96 F3
Gretton Cl NG23 . . . . . . .156 C6
Gretton Rd NG3 . . . . .162 A4
Greyfriar Gate NG1 . . . . .223 E1
Greyhound St NG1 . . . . . .223 E2
Greys Rd NG5 . . . . .161 F4
Grey St
　Eastwood NG16 . . . . .144 A1
　Gainsborough DN21 . . . . .15 B2
　Kirkby in A NG17 . . . . . . .114 D5
Greystoke Dr NG8 . . . . . .171 C7
Greystones Rd DN21 . . . . .15 B3
Greythorn Dr NG2 . . . . . .185 D4
Greythorn Prim Sch
　NG2 . . . . .185 D5
Griceson Cl NG22 . . . . . . .77 B2
Grierson Ave NG5 . . . . . .147 A1
Griffs Hollow NG4 . . . . . .174 E7
Grimesmoor Rd NG14 . . .149 A8
Grimsby Terr NG3 . . . . . .223 E4
Grimston Rd NG7 . . . . . .222 A4
Grindon Cres NG6 . . . . . .146 C2
Gringley Rd
　Clayworth DN22 . . . . .21 E6
　Misterton DN10 . . . . .6 E1
　Walkeringham DN10 . . . . .13 E4
Grinsbrook NG7 . . . . .222 A2
Gripps Comm NG12 . . . . .187 F1
Grisedale Ct NG9 . . . . . . .183 A4
Gritley Mews NG2 . . . . . .173 B2
Grives La NG17 . . . . .115 B2
Grizedale Cl NG19 . . . . . .103 A8
Grizedale Gr NG13 . . . . . .177 B4
Grizedale Ri NG19 . . . . . .103 A8
Grosvenor Ave
　Long Eaton NG10 . . . . . .193 A4
　Nottingham NG3 . . . . . . .161 C1
　Sutton in A NG17 . . . . . . .100 D2
Grosvenor Cl NG12 . . . . .176 D3
Grosvenor Rd
　Bircotes DN11 . . . . .9 B4
　Eastwood NG16 . . . . .143 F2
　New Balderton NG24 . . . . .140 B4
　Skegby Sutton NG12 . . . . .186 A4
Grouville Dr NG5 . . . . . . .162 A5
Grove Ave
　Beeston NG9 . . . . .183 F6
　Nottingham NG7 . . . . . . .222 C4
　Sutton in A NG17 . . . . . . .100 F3
Grove Coach Rd DN22 . . . .40 B4
Grove La DN22 . . . . .40 B6
Grove Mews NG16 . . . . . .143 E1
Grove Pk DN10 . . . . .6 E1
Grover Ave NG3 . . . . .162 A3
Grove Rd
　Church Warsop NG20 . . . . .74 A6
　Grove DN22 . . . . .41 C6
　Nottingham NG7 . . . . . . .222 B1
　Retford DN22 . . . . .40 C3
Grove Sch The NG24 . . . .140 C5
Groveside Cres NG11 . . . .184 C1
Grove Sports Ctr NG24 . . .140 C5
Grove St
　Beeston NG9 . . . . .184 A5

Grove St continued
　6 Mansfield NG18 . . . . . .102 B6
　Mansfield Woodhouse NG19 88 B3
　New Balderton NG24 . . . . .140 B5
　Retford DN22 . . . . .39 F7
Grove The
　Beckingham DN10 . . . . . . .14 B1
　Calverton NG14 . . . . .149 A7
　Newton on T N1 . . . . .55 A1
　Nottingham, Carrington
　　NG5 . . . . .161 B2
　Nottingham NG7 . . . . . . .222 B4
Grove Wood Rd DN10 . . . . .6 F1
Grundy Ave NG16 . . . . . .128 D7
Grundy Nook S80 . . . . . . .45 A5
Grundy St NG7 . . . . .172 E7
Guildford Ave NG18 . . . . .88 C6
Guildhall St NG24 . . . . . .140 A8
Guinea Cl NG10 . . . . .193 A7
Gunn Cl NG6 . . . . .160 A7
Gunnersbury Way NG16 . .159 E3
Gunthorpe CE Prim Sch
　NG14 . . . . .165 A5
Gunthorpe Cl NG5 . . . . . .161 B3
Gunthorpe Ct NG18 . . . . .103 B3
Gunthorpe Dr NG5 . . . . . .161 B3
Gunthorpe Rd
　Carlton NG4 . . . . .162 D3
　Lowdham NG14 . . . . .164 E8
　West Stockwith DN9 . . . . . .7 E8
Gutersloh Ct NG9 . . . . . .182 F8
Guy Cl NG9 . . . . .182 E6
Guylers Hill Dr NG21 . . . . .89 F2
Gwenbrook Ave NG9 . . . .183 E5
Gwenbrook Rd NG9 . . . . .183 D5
Gwndy Gdns 3 NG5 . . . .161 A7
Gypsum Way NG11 . . . . .205 A7

H

Habblesthorpe Cl DN22 . . . .32 E1
Habblesthorpe Rd DN22 . . .32 E1
Hackers Cl NG13 . . . . . . .165 C3
Hackworth Cl NG16 . . . . .144 B3
Hadbury Rd NG5 . . . . . . .160 F3
Hadden Ct NG8 . . . . .171 C5
Hadden Pk High Sch
　NG8 . . . . .172 A7
Hadderley Wlk NG3 . . . . .223 F4
Haddon Cl
　Carlton NG4 . . . . .162 D2
　Hucknall NG15 . . . . .146 A6
　Selston NG16 . . . . .129 B7
Haddon Cres NG9 . . . . . .183 C2
Haddon Dr NG12 . . . . . . .198 A6
Haddon Nurseries DE7 . . .157 E3
Haddon Pl NG20 . . . . .72 D7
Haddon Prim Sch NG4 . . .162 D1
Haddon Rd
　Mansfield NG18 . . . . . . .102 B8
　Ravenshead NG15 . . . . . .117 A3
　Retford DN22 . . . . .40 B4
　West Bridgford NG2 . . . . .185 F6
Haddon St
　Ilkeston DE7 . . . . .157 E3
　Nottingham NG5 . . . . . . .161 B2
　Sutton in A NG17 . . . . . . .100 E2
Haddon Way NG12 . . . . . .176 A4
Hades La LE12 . . . . .217 D5
Hadfield Wlk NG18 . . . . . .103 B6
Hadleigh Cl NG9 . . . . . . .182 E2
Hadley St DE7 . . . . .170 A5
Hadrian Gdns NG5 . . . . . .147 A2
Hadstock Cl NG10 . . . . . .182 B4
Hagg La
　Bawtry DN10 . . . . .10 E8
　Egmanton NG22 . . . . .80 A5
　Epperstone NG14 . . . . . . .150 B5
Haggonfields Prim Sch
　S80 . . . . .35 A4
Hagley Cl NG3 . . . . .174 A6
Haileybury Cres NG2 . . . .185 F5
Haileybury Rd NG2 . . . . . .185 F5
Hainton Cl DN21 . . . . .24 E7
Haise Ct NG6 . . . . .159 F5
Halam CE Prim Sch
　NG22 . . . . .120 F2
Halam Cl NG19 . . . . .101 D7
Halam Hill NG22 . . . . . . .121 A1
Halberton Dr NG2 . . . . . .185 D3
Haldane Ct DN21 . . . . . . .15 B1
Hales Cl NG12 . . . . .187 E3
Haley Cl NG16 . . . . .158 D6
Halfmoon Dr NG17 . . . . . .115 B3
Halifax Cl NG8 . . . . .160 A4
Halifax Dr S81 . . . . .35 E8
Halifax Pl NG1 . . . . .223 E2
Hallam Fields Rd DE7 . . . .170 B4
Hallam Rd
　Beeston NG9 . . . . .183 F6
　Nottingham NG3 . . . . . . .162 A2
Hallams La NG9 . . . . .183 E5
Hallam's La NG5 . . . . . . .161 F7
Hallamway NG18 . . . . . . .88 C1
Hall Barn La NG19 . . . . . .101 D3
Hall Cl
　Radcliffe on T NG12 . . . . .175 E3
　Rainworth NG21 . . . . . . .104 B1
Hall Cl The NG22 . . . . . . .106 B5
Hall Croft NG9 . . . . .183 F5
Hallcroft Ave DN22 . . . . . .29 C1
Hallcroft Ind Est DN22 . . . .29 D2
Hallcroft Inf Sch DN22 . . . .29 C1

Hallcroft Rd DN22 . . . . . . .29 D2
Hall Dr
　Beeston NG9 . . . . .183 D5
　Clayworth DN22 . . . . .21 D5
　Cropwell Bishop NG12 . . .189 A4
　Gotham NG11 . . . . .195 A1
　Nottingham NG8 . . . . . . .171 E3
　Sandiacre NG10 . . . . . . .182 B6
　Worksop S80 . . . . .35 D2
Hallfield Rd DE55 . . . . . . .99 A3
Hallfields NG12 . . . . .186 B3
Hall Gdns
　Beeston NG9 . . . . .183 B7
　East Leake LE12 . . . . . . .214 F8
Hall Grounds NG12 . . . . .200 C7
Hall Grounds Dr NG12 . . .200 C8
Halliday Cl S80 . . . . .35 D3
Hallifax Ave NG20 . . . . . . .74 B7
Halliwell Cl NG24 . . . . . .125 B4
Hall La
　Brinsley NG16 . . . . .143 D6
　Colston Bassett NG12 . . . .200 C7
　East Markham NG22 . . . . .66 A7
　Kinoulton NG12 . . . . .200 A3
　Newton DE55 . . . . .99 A3
Halloughton Rd NG25 . . . .136 D7
Hallowell Dr NG8 . . . . . . .171 F5
Hall Rd NG16 . . . . .143 C4
Halls Brook LE12 . . . . . . .205 E2
Halls La NG16 . . . . .158 A8
Halls Rd NG16 . . . . .182 D6
Hall's Rd DN10 . . . . .13 A3
Hall St
　Mansfield NG18 . . . . . . .102 E6
　Nottingham NG5 . . . . . . .161 D3
　Sutton in A NG17 . . . . . .100 E6
Hallum Ct DE7 . . . . .157 F3
Hall View
　Mattersey DN10 . . . . .20 B7
　Worksop S80 . . . . .35 D2
Hall View Dr NG8 . . . . . . .171 D6
Halstead Cl
　Beeston NG9 . . . . .183 C4
　Mansfield Woodhouse NG19 88 F2
　Nottingham NG8 . . . . . . .160 B3
Haltham Gn 2 DN21 . . . . .24 F8
Haltham Wlk NG11 . . . . . .195 D8
Hamble Cl NG8 . . . . .88 D3
Hambledon Dr NG8 . . . . .172 B5
Hambleton Cl NG10 . . . . .182 A1
Hambleton Ct S81 . . . . . . .25 E7
Hambling Cl NG6 . . . . . . .160 A7
Hamilton Cl
　Arnold NG5 . . . . .148 C1
　Beeston NG9 . . . . .182 F2
Hamilton Dr
　Market Warsop NG20 . . . . .74 A2
　Nottingham NG7 . . . . . . .223 D1
　Radcliffe on T NG12 . . . . .175 F4
Hamilton Gdns 1 NG5 . . .161 B1
Hamilton Rd
　Long Eaton NG10 . . . . . .182 D1
　Nottingham NG5 . . . . . . .173 B8
　Sutton in A NG17 . . . . . . .101 C2
Hamilton St
　Mansfield NG18 . . . . . . .102 E6
　Worksop S81 . . . . .35 E6
Hamlet La DE55 . . . . .113 A5
Hamlet The DE55 . . . . . . .113 A5
Hammersmith Cl
　Nuthall NG16 . . . . .159 E4
　Radcliffe on T NG12 . . . . .176 D2
Hammerwater Dr NG20 . . . .74 A3
Hammond Gr NG17 . . . . .115 B2
Hampden Gr NG9 . . . . . .183 E6
Hampdens Cl NG14 . . . . .125 E2
Hampden St
　Eastwood NG16 . . . . .158 B8
　Kirkby in A NG17 . . . . . . .114 F5
　Nottingham NG1 . . . . . . .223 D3
Hampshire Cl NG16 . . . . .128 B4
Hampshire Dr NG10 . . . . .182 B5
Hampstead Rd NG3 . . . . .161 E1
Hampton Cl NG9 . . . . . . .182 E3
Hampton Rd NG2 . . . . . .185 E6
Hanbury Ct NG18 . . . . . .103 B6
Handel House Sch DN21 . . .24 C8
Handel St NG3 . . . . .173 E5
Handley Arc 5 NG18 . . . .102 B7
Hand's Rd DE75 . . . . .143 A1
Hand's Wlk NG13 . . . . . . .181 A2
Hanford Way LE11 . . . . . .220 B5
Hankin St NG15 . . . . .146 C6
Hanley Ave NG9 . . . . .183 B8
Hanley St NG1 . . . . .223 D3
Hannah's Yd DN22 . . . . . . .39 C7
Hanover Ct NG8 . . . . .171 D6
Hanslope Cres NG8 . . . . .171 D7
Hanson Cres NG15 . . . . . .146 F6
Hanstubbin Rd NG16 . . . .128 F6
Hanworth Gdns NG5 . . . .161 D8
Harberton Cl NG5 . . . . . .147 E1
Harby Ave
　Mansfield Woodhouse
　　NG19 . . . . .88 D5
　Sutton in A NG17 . . . . . . .101 C1
Harby Cl NG24 . . . . .140 D3
Harby Dr NG8 . . . . .172 C4
Harby La
　Colston Bassett NG12 . . . .200 F5
　Hose LE14 . . . . .211 F7

Harby La continued
Plungar LE14 . . . . **202** F3
Harby Rd NG13 . . . . **190** D1
Harcourt Cl DE7 . . . . **157** D1
Harcourt Cres NG16 . . . . **159** F7
Harcourt Pl DN22 . . . . **40** A4
Harcourt Rd NG7 . . . . **173** A8
Harcourt St
Beeston NG9 . . . . **183** E6
Kirkby in A NG17 . . . . . . **115** A5
Mansfield NG18 . . . . **102** A6
Newark-on-T NG24 . . . . . **140** B7
Harcourt Terr NG3 . . . . . **223** F3
Harden Cl NG11 . . . . **195** C8
Hardie Ave DE55 . . . . **113** A6
Hardigate Rd NG12 . . . . . **189** A8
Hardstaff Cl
Annesley Woodhouse
NG17 . . . . **114** E1
Retford DN22 . . . . **29** C1
Hardstaff Rd NG2 . . . . . . **174** A4
Hardwick Ave
Mansfield NG21 . . . . **103** F1
Newark-on-T NG24 . . . . . **139** F7
Shirebrook NG20 . . . . **72** E4
Sutton in A NG17 . . . . . . **101** A6
Hardwick Cl
Saxilby LN1 . . . . **56** F4
Sutton in A NG17 . . . . . . **101** A6
Hardwick Cres S80 . . . . . **36** B2
Hardwick Ct DN11 . . . . **9** B5
Hardwick Dr
Ollerton NG22 . . . . **77** A3
Selston NG16 . . . . **129** B7
Hardwicke Rd NG6 . . . . . **183** C3
Hardwick Gr
Mansfield NG7 . . . . **222** B2
West Bridgford NG2 . . . . **173** F1
Hardwick Hall S44 . . . . **85** E4
Hardwick Hall Ctry Pk
S44 . . . . **85** F5
Hardwick La NG17 . . . . . **100** F2
Hardwick Old Hall S44 . . . **85** E4
Hardwick Pk Nature Wlk
S44 . . . . **85** C4
Hardwick Rd
☑ Nottingham, Carrington
NG5 . . . . **161** C3
Nottingham, The Park NG7 **222** C1
Hardwick Rd E S80 . . . . . **36** B2
Hardwick Rd W S80 . . . . . **36** B2
Hardwick St
Langwith NG20 . . . . **72** F8
Mansfield NG18 . . . . **102** D7
Shirebrook NG20 . . . . **73** A4
Sutton in A NG17 . . . . . . **100** F2
Tibshelf DE55 . . . . **99** A7
Hardwick View NG17 . . . . **101** A6
Hardwood Cl
☑ Nottingham NG6 . . . . **159** F7
Nottingham NG6 . . . . . . **159** F7
Hardy Barn DE75 . . . . . . **157** A7
Hardy Cl
Kimberley NG16 . . . . **158** F7
Long Eaton NG10 . . . . . . **193** D6
Hardy Pl NG18 . . . . **101** F6
Hardys Cl NG12 . . . . **189** B4
Hardy's Dr NG4 . . . . **162** F1
Hardy St
Kimberley NG16 . . . . **158** F7
Mansfield NG7 . . . . **222** C4
Worksop S80 . . . . **35** E3
Harefield LE12 . . . . **205** E3
Hareholme St NG18 . . . . . **102** A8
Harewood Ave
Newark-on-T NG24 . . . . . **139** F7
Nottingham NG6 . . . . . . **160** D5
Retford DN22 . . . . **39** C5
Harewood Cl
Radcliffe on T NG12 . . . . **176** A3
Sandiacre NG10 . . . . **182** B4
Harewood Ct DN11 . . . . . . **9** B5
Harewood Dr DN10 . . . . . **10** A8
Harewood Rd S81 . . . . **35** F7
Hargon La NG24 . . . . **125** B6
Harkstead Rd NG5 . . . . . **147** B1
Harlaxton Dr
Long Eaton NG10 . . . . . . **194** A8
Nottingham NG7 . . . . **222** B2
Harlaxton Wlk NG3 . . . . . **223** E4
Harlech Cl DE7 . . . . **157** C3
Harlech Rise NG9 . . . . . . **183** B4
Harlequin Cl NG12 . . . . . **176** B3
Harlequin Ct NG16 . . . . . **143** D3
Harles Acres LE14 . . . . . **210** C6
Harley Cl S80 . . . . **46** E8
Harley Gall The S80 . . . . . **45** E1
Harley St NG2 . . . . **222** B1
Harlow Ave NG18 . . . . . . **102** C3
Harlow Cl
Mansfield Woodhouse
NG19 . . . . **88** C6
Sutton in A NG17 . . . . . . **100** F6
Harlow Gr NG4 . . . . **162** E2
Harlow St NG21 . . . . **118** C8
Harmston Rise NG5 . . . . **160** F4
Harold Ave NG16 . . . . . . **143** B4
Harold St NG2 . . . . **173** E4
Harpenden Sq NG8 . . . . . **160** B3
Harpham Rd DN21 . . . . . . **44** B8
Harpole Wlk NG5 . . . . . . **147** F2
Harrier Gr NG17 . . . . **145** E4
Harriers Gr NG17 . . . . . . **101** B4
Harriett St NG9 . . . . **182** D7
Harrimans La NG7 . . . . . **184** E8

Harrington Cl NG4 . . . . . **163** B1
Harrington Dr NG7 . . . . . **222** B2
Harrington Jun Sch
NG10 . . . . **182** B1
Harrington St
Long Eaton NG10 . . . . . . **193** B5
Mansfield NG18 . . . . **102** A6
Worksop S80 . . . . **35** D2
Harris Cl NG8 . . . . **171** F5
Harrison Cl NG13 . . . . . . **177** C4
Harrison Dr S81 . . . . **16** E3
Harrison Rd
Mansfield NG18 . . . . **101** E6
Stapleford NG9 . . . . **182** D8
Harrison's Plantation Nature
Reserve NG8 . . . . **171** F5
Harris Rd NG9 . . . . **183** D6
Harrogate Rd NG3 . . . . . **174** C5
Harrogate St NG4 . . . . . . **174** F7
Harrop White Rd NG19 . . **101** F8
Harrowby Rd NG7 . . . . . . **222** B2
Harrow Ct
Gainsborough DN21 . . . . . **15** F2
Rainworth NG21 . . . . **118** A8
Harrow Dr DE7 . . . . **170** A4
Harrow Gdns NG8 . . . . . **172** C4
Harrow La NG22 . . . . **77** F5
Harrow Rd
Hucknall NG15 . . . . **145** D5
Nottingham NG8 . . . . . . **172** B4
West Bridgford NG2 . . . . **185** C5
Harstoft Ave S81 . . . . **35** F5
Hart Ave NG10 . . . . **182** A5
Hartcroft Rd NG5 . . . . . . **161** B6
Hartford Cl ☑ NG2 . . . . . **173** D2
Harthill Cl ☑ NG9 . . . . . **183** C2
Hartill Dr NG19 . . . . **101** D5
Hartington Ave
Carlton NG4 . . . . **162** D1
Hucknall NG15 . . . . **145** C6
Hartington Ct NG18 . . . . **103** B6
Hartington Dr
Selston NG16 . . . . **129** A7
Sutton in A NG17 . . . . . . **101** B4
Hartington Pl DE7 . . . . . **157** E5
Hartington Rd NG5 . . . . . **161** C3
Hartland Rd NG20 . . . . . . **72** F8
Hartley Cl NG7 . . . . **222** B4
Hartley Dr NG9 . . . . **184** B6
Hartley Rd
Kirkby in A NG17 . . . . . . **114** F5
Nottingham NG7 . . . . . . **222** B4
Hartness Rd NG11 . . . . . **184** C1
Hartside Cl NG4 . . . . **186** C7
Hartside Gdns ☑ NG10 . . **193** A8
Hart St NG7 . . . . **222** B1
Hartwell St NG3 . . . . **223** F4
Hartwood Dr NG9 . . . . . . **170** D1
Harvest Cl
Bingham NG13 . . . . **177** D4
Carlton in L S81 . . . . **25** F7
Nottingham NG5 . . . . . . **160** F8
Worksop S81 . . . . **36** B7
Harvest Dr NG24 . . . . . . **125** C4
Harvey Cl NG11 . . . . **196** D5
Harvey Croft NG9 . . . . . **170** C4
Harvey Ct ☑ NG7 . . . . . **172** E2
Harvey Hadden Sports Ctr
NG8 . . . . **171** F7
Harvey Rd
Mansfield NG18 . . . . **102** C3
Nottingham, Bilborough
NG8 . . . . **171** F7
Nottingham, Dunkirk NG7 **172** E2
Harvey's Field NG25 . . . . **136** E8
Harwall Sluice La DN10 . . **11** D3
Harwich Cl NG6 . . . . **160** A8
Harwill Cres NG8 . . . . . . **160** B2
Harwood Cl
Arnold NG5 . . . . **162** B8
Sutton in A NG17 . . . . . . **101** A4
Harwood Pl NG17 . . . . . . **101** A4
Harworth Ave S81 . . . . . . **18** A6
Harworth CE Prim Sch
DN11 . . . . **9** A4
Harworth Cl NG19 . . . . . **101** D6
Haslam St NG7 . . . . **223** D1
Haslehurst Gdns S80 . . . . **35** E2
Haslemere Gdns NG15 . . **116** F2
Haslemere Rd
Long Eaton NG10 . . . . . . **193** B8
Nottingham NG8 . . . . . . **172** D8
Hassock La N DE75 . . . . . **157** B7
Hassock La S DE75 . . . . . **157** C6
Hassocks La NG9 . . . . . . **184** B7
Hassop Wlk NG18 . . . . . . **103** B6
Hastings St
Carlton NG4 . . . . **174** C7
☑ Loughborough LE11 . . **220** A4
Haswell Rd NG6 . . . . **160** B5
Hatchet's La NG24 . . . . . **125** A5
Hatfield Ave
Meden Vale NG20 . . . . . . **74** F8
Sandiacre NG10 . . . . **182** B4
Hatfield Cl NG21 . . . . . . **104** B1
Hatfield Dr NG2 . . . . **185** C4
Hatfield Rd NG3 . . . . **161** C1
Hatfield St DN22 . . . . **40** A6
Hather Cl DN22 . . . . **51** A5
Hatherleigh Cl NG3 . . . . . **162** C6
Hathern Cl NG10 . . . . . . **193** D5
Hathern Gn NG9 . . . . **184** A8
Hathern Rd LE12 . . . . . . **212** D2
Hathern Turn LE12 . . . . . **212** B2
Hathernware Ind Est
LE12 . . . . **213** D5
Hathersage Ave NG10 . . **193** A5

Hathersage Rise NG15 . . **117** A3
Hathersage Wlk NG4 . . . . **100** E4
Hathersage Wlk NG18 . . . **103** B6
Hatley Cl ☑ NG2 . . . . . . **173** B1
Hatton Cl NG5 . . . . **147** A2
Hatton Crofts NG10 . . . . . **193** C6
Hatton Ct NG18 . . . . **103** B6
Hatton Gdns
Newark-on-T NG24 . . . . . **140** B8
Nuthall NG8 . . . . **159** E3
Haughgate Hill DN22 . . . . **22** B1
Havelock Gdns NG3 . . . . **223** F4
Haven Cl
Clipstone NG21 . . . . **89** F3
Sutton in A NG17 . . . . . . **100** D3
West Bridgford NG2 . . . . **185** D5
Havenden Gdns ☑ NG7 . . **172** F7
Haven Hill S81 . . . . **16** D6
Havenwood Rise NG11 . . **195** D8
Haverhill Cres NG5 . . . . . **146** D1
Haversham Cl NG6 . . . . . **160** D2
Hawarden Terr ☑ NG7 . . **172** F7
Hawbush Rd NG22 . . . . . . **81** A6
Hawkesworth Ave NG19 . . **89** B1
Hawkhill Cl NG22 . . . . . . **77** A3
Hawkhurst Dr NG8 . . . . . **171** D2
Hawking La S44 . . . . **85** A7
Hawkins Ct DE7 . . . . **157** F4
Hawk Ridge Gdns ☑
NG5 . . . . **173** E5
Hawkshead Cl NG2 . . . . . **186** D5
Hawksley Gdns NG11 . . . **184** C2
Hawksley Rd ☑ NG7 . . . . **172** F7
Hawksworth Ave NG5 . . . **161** D4
Hawksworth Rd
Hawksworth NG13 . . . . . **167** B3
Scarrington NG13 . . . . . . **178** F8
Syerston NG23 . . . . **153** B3
West Bridgford NG2 . . . . **173** F1
Hawksworth St
Gainsborough DN21 . . . . . **24** D8
☑ Nottingham NG3 . . . . **173** E5
Hawley Cl LE12 . . . . **205** F1
Hawson Way S81 . . . . **35** C7
Hawthorn Ave
Gainsborough DN21 . . . . . **15** D1
Glapwell S44 . . . . **86** B8
Hucknall NG15 . . . . **145** F7
Hawthorn Cl
Beckingham DN10 . . . . . . **23** B8
Keyworth NG12 . . . . **197** E2
New Ollerton NG22 . . . . . **77** D5
☑ Nottingham NG3 . . . . **173** B1
Old Dalby LE14 . . . . **218** E4
West Bridgford NG12 . . . **186** B4
Hawthorn Cres
Arnold NG5 . . . . **148** A1
☑ Kirkby in A NG17 . . . **114** F6
Kirkby in A NG17 . . . . . . **115** A6
Hawthorn Ct ☑ NG6 . . . . **173** B1
Nottingham NG2 . . . . **77** D5
Hawthorne Ave
Hathern LE12 . . . . **213** A1
Long Eaton NG10 . . . . . . **193** C6
Shirebrook NG20 . . . . **72** D4
Tibshelf DE55 . . . . **99** B8
Hawthorne Cl
North Leverton with
Habblesthorpe DN22 . . **42** D8
Stanton Hill NG17 . . . . . **100** B6
Woodborough NG14 . . . . **149** C4
Hawthorne Cres NG24 . . . **139** A4
Hawthorne Gr NG9 . . . . . **184** B6
Hawthorne Prim Sch
NG6 . . . . **146** E4
Hawthorne Rd NG16 . . . . **113** D3
Hawthorne Rise NG16 . . . **158** B4
Hawthorne Way NG21 . . . . **91** B8
Hawthorn Gr NG21 . . . . . . **91** B8
Hawthorn Way S81 . . . . . . **25** E7
Hawthorns The
Kirkby in Ashfield NG17 . . **114** F6
Market Warsop NG20 . . . . **74** A4
Walesby NG22 . . . . **64** A2
Hawthorn Way S81 . . . . . . **25** E7
Hawton Cl
Gainsborough DN21 . . . . . **15** E2
Mansfield NG19 . . . . **87** F1
Hawton Cres NG8 . . . . . . **172** C3
Hawton La NG24 . . . . **140** B4
Hawton Rd NG24 . . . . . . **139** E5
Hawton Spinney NG8 . . . **172** C4

Haxey Gate Rd DN10 . . . . . **6** F5
Haxey Rd DN10 . . . . **6** F2
Haycroft Cl NG19 . . . . . . **88** E5
Haycroft Way NG13 . . . . **165** C2
Hayden La NG15 . . . . **131** B1
Haydn Ave NG5 . . . . **161** B2
Haydn Prim Sch NG5 . . . . **161** C2
Haydn Rd NG5 . . . . **161** B2
Haydock Cl NG16 . . . . . . **158** E7
Hayes Cl NG16 . . . . **143** E2
Hayes La NG23 . . . . **197** E3
Hayles Cl NG5 . . . . **161** B8
Hayling Cl DE7 . . . . **157** C3
Hayling Dr NG8 . . . . **160** D1
Haynes Ave NG9 . . . . . . **170** C5
Haynes Cl
Nottingham NG11 . . . . . **184** F3
Tuxford NG22 . . . . **66** A3
Hays Cl DE7 . . . . **157** D2
Hayside Ave NG4 . . . . . . **174** C8
Hayward Ave LE11 . . . . . **220** C2
Haywood Ave NG21 . . . . **118** A5
Haywood Rd ☑ NG2 . . . . **173** E4

Haywood Oaks La NG21 . . **118** C3
Haywood Rd NG3 . . . . . . **162** A3
Haywood St NG5 . . . . . . **161** C4
Haywood St NG2 . . . . . . **173** E4
Hazelas Dr NG14 . . . . . . **165** A5
Hazel Bank NG18 . . . . . . **102** E8
Hazelbank Ave NG3 . . . . **161** F1
Hazelby Rd S80 . . . . **58** E8
Hazel Cl NG13 . . . . **178** A4
Hazel Cres NG20 . . . . **72** D4
Hazel Dr NG16 . . . . **144** C6
Hazelford Way NG15 . . . . **130** D7
Hazel Gr
Edwinstowe NG21 . . . . . . **76** B1
Hucknall NG15 . . . . **146** A5
Kirkby in A NG17 . . . . . . **115** C5
Mansfield Woodhouse NG19 **88** B5
New Balderton NG24 . . . . **140** C5
Nottingham NG3 . . . . . . **162** A4
South Normanton DE55 . . **113** B5
Hazel Hill Cres NG5 . . . . **161** B8
Hazelhurst Gdns ☑ NG6 **160** B7
Hazel Hurst Prep Sch
NG3 . . . . **159** F5
Hazelmere Gr NG7 . . . . . **222** A2
Hazel Rd NG22 . . . . **77** D5
Hazel St
Nottingham NG6 . . . . . . **160** B8
Sutton in A NG17 . . . . . . **100** D7
Hazel Way NG15 . . . . **131** B2
Hazelwood NG12 . . . . . . **188** A3
Hazelwood Cl
Eastwood NG16 . . . . **144** B2
Mansfield Woodhouse NG19 **89** B2
Hazelwood Dr NG15 . . . . **145** C6
Hazelwood Gr S80 . . . . . . **35** C2
Hazelwood La NG22 . . . . . **41** E1
Hazelwood Rd NG7 . . . . . **172** E7
Headingley Gdns ☑
NG8 . . . . **172** D8
Headland Ave DN22 . . . . . **50** A3
Headstead Bank DN22 . . . **43** D6
Head Stocks The NG17 . . **100** A1
Heafield Dr DE74 . . . . . . **203** D2
Healdswood Inf Sch
NG17 . . . . **100** D6
Healdswood St NG17 . . . **100** D7
Healey Cl
Collingham NG23 . . . . . . **112** A8
Nottingham NG2 . . . . . . **173** C2
Heanor Rd DE7 . . . . **157** D3
Heanor Wlk NG18 . . . . . . **103** B6
Heapham Cres DN21 . . . . **24** F8
Heapham Rd ☑ DN21 . . . . **24** F8
Heard Cres NG9 . . . . **183** F8
Heath Ave NG16 . . . . . . **103** B7
Heath Ave NG3 . . . . **161** F1
Heathcoat St
☑ Loughborough LE11 . . **220** A4
Nottingham NG1 . . . . . . **223** F3
Heathcote Pl NG17 . . . . . **101** A1
Heather Cl
Eastwood NG16 . . . . **144** C2
☑ Kirkby in A NG17 . . . **114** F7
Mansfield NG18 . . . . **102** A6
Nottingham NG3 . . . . . . **173** D7
South Normanton DE55 . . **113** A3
Tickhill DN11 . . . . **8** B4
Heather Croft NG2 . . . . . **185** C4
Heather Ct DE75 . . . . . . **143** B1
Heather La NG15 . . . . . . **132** B8
Heatherley Dr
Mansfield NG18 . . . . **88** A1
Nottingham NG6 . . . . . . **160** F4
Heatherley Prim Sch
NG18 . . . . **88** E1
Heather Rd NG4 . . . . **162** D1
Heather Rise NG9 . . . . . **171** E1
Heathers The NG22 . . . . . **77** F5
Heathervale NG2 . . . . . . **185** B6
Heather Way NG18 . . . . . **103** B6
Heathfield Ave NG15 . . . . **117** A1
Heathfield Ct ☑ NG17 . . **114** F7
Heathfield Gdns
Retford DN22 . . . . **39** E8
Tibshelf DE55 . . . . **99** A7
Heathfield Gr NG9 . . . . . **183** C3
Heathfield Prim Sch
NG5 . . . . **160** F3
Heathfield Rd NG5 . . . . . **160** F4
Heathfield Way NG18 . . . **102** D5
Heath Gdns DE72 . . . . . . **193** A8
Heathland Cl NG18 . . . . . **103** A6
Heathlands Prim Sch
NG21 . . . . **118** C5
Heathrington Gdns ☑
NG5 . . . . **147** A1
Heath The NG16 . . . . **158** B8
Heaton Cl
Newark-on-T NG24 . . . . . **140** D8
Nottingham NG3 . . . . . . **161** F1
Heaton St DN21 . . . . **24** D8
Heavenside LE12 . . . . . . **205** E3
Heavytrees Ave NG15 . . . **117** A1
Hecadeck La LE14 . . . . . **219** C8
Heckdyke La DN10 . . . . . . **7** E5
Heckington Dr NG8 . . . . . **172** B5
Heddington Gdns ☑
NG5 . . . . **161** D8
Heddon Bar NG19 . . . . . . **88** E3
Hedgerow Cl NG17 . . . . . **100** C1
Hedges Dr DE7 . . . . **170** A5
Hedley St NG7 . . . . **172** F8
Hedley Villas ☑ NG7 . . . . **161** A1
Helen Cl NG9 . . . . **183** D6
Helenship La DN22 . . . . . . **54** B7
Hellebore Cl NG5 . . . . . . **160** E7
Helm Cl NG6 . . . . **159** F7

Helmsdale Cl
Arnold NG5 . . . . **148** B1
Mansfield NG19 . . . . **101** E5
Helmsdale Gdns NG5 . . . **146** F1
Helmsley Rd NG21 . . . . . **103** E3
Helston Dr NG8 . . . . **159** E1
Helvellyn Cl ☑ NG2 . . . . **173** C2
Helvellyn Way NG10 . . . . **182** B2
Hemingway Cl
Carlton NG4 . . . . **174** C7
Eastwood NG16 . . . . **144** C1
Hemlock Ave
Long Eaton NG10 . . . . . . **182** D3
Stapleford NG9 . . . . **182** E8
Hemlock Gdns NG6 . . . . **159** F6
Hemmingfield Cl S81 . . . . **35** F8
Hemmingfield Cres S81 . . **35** F7
Hemmingfield Rd S81 . . . . **36** A7
Hemmingfield Way S81 . . . **36** A8
Hemplands La NG23 . . . . . **96** E8
Hemplands The NG23 . . . . **98** A1
Hempshill Hall Prim Sch
NG6 . . . . **159** F5
Hempshill La NG6 . . . . . . **160** A6
Hemsby Gdns ☑ NG6 . . . **160** B8
Hemscott Cl NG6 . . . . . . **159** F8
Hemsley Dr NG16 . . . . . . **143** D3
Hemswell Cl NG3 . . . . . . **174** A3
Hendon Rise NG3 . . . . . . **173** F8
Hendre Gdns ☑ NG5 . . . **161** A7
Henley Cl NG4 . . . . **175** A6
Henley Ct DN21 . . . . **15** C2
Henley Gdns NG9 . . . . . **170** E1
Henley Rise NG5 . . . . . . **161** A3
Hennessey Cl ☑ NG9 . . . **183** C2
Henning Gdns ☑ NG5 . . . **161** A8
Henning La NG17 . . . . . . **100** B1
Hennymoor Cl S80 . . . . . . **45** C8
Hennymoor La S80 . . . . . . **45** C2
Henrietta St NG6 . . . . . . **160** C6
Henry Ave NG19 . . . . **88** B5
Henry Ct NG2 . . . . **173** C2
Henry Mellish Comp Sch
NG6 . . . . **160** D5
Henry Rd
Beeston NG9 . . . . **184** A6
Nottingham NG7 . . . . . . **222** A1
West Bridgford NG2 . . . . **185** E8
Henry St
Arnold NG5 . . . . **147** E2
Hucknall NG15 . . . . **146** A6
☑ Nottingham NG2 . . . . **173** C4
Sutton in A NG17 . . . . . . **100** F1
Henry Whipple Inf Sch
NG5 . . . . **160** F6
Henry Whipple Jun Sch
NG5 . . . . **160** F6
Henshaw Pl DE7 . . . . **157** E4
Henson Cl NG12 . . . . . . **176** E3
Henson La NG12 . . . . . . **176** E2
Henson's Sq NG9 . . . . . . **183** B8
Henton Cl NG24 . . . . **125** B1
Hepburn Rd NG16 . . . . . . **76** C1
Hepple Dr NG6 . . . . **159** F7
Herald Cl NG9 . . . . **183** B8
Herbert Rd
Annesley Woodhouse
NG17 . . . . **115** B1
Nottingham NG5 . . . . . . **161** B1
Herbert St
Loughborough LE11 . . . . **220** B5
Mansfield NG18 . . . . **102** A6
Hercules Dr NG24 . . . . . . **140** D7
Hereford Ave
Mansfield Woodhouse
NG19 . . . . **88** C6
Ollerton NG22 . . . . **77** B4
Hereford Cl S81 . . . . **36** A6
Hereford Rd
Carlton NG4 . . . . **162** F2
Nottingham NG3 . . . . . . **174** B5
Ravenshead NG15 . . . . . . **117** A3
Herewood Cl NG20 . . . . . . **72** F6
Hermes Cl DN10 . . . . **9** F8
Hermitage Ave NG18 . . . . **101** F5
Hermitage La NG18 . . . . . **101** E4
Hermitage Sq ☑ NG2 . . . **173** F3
Hermitage Wlk NG7 . . . . **222** C1
Hermon St NG7 . . . . **222** A2
Herne St NG17 . . . . **101** A4
Heron Dr NG7 . . . . **222** A2
Heron Glade S81 . . . . **35** C7
Herons Ct NG2 . . . . **186** C4
Heron Way
Mansfield NG19 . . . . **87** C1
New Balderton NG24 . . . . **140** C5
Heron Wharf ☑ NG7 . . . . **172** F2
Herrick Rd LE11 . . . . . . **220** A2
Herriot Gr DN11 . . . . **9** A4
Herrods View NG17 . . . . **100** C6
Hervey Gn NG7 . . . . **184** E2
Heskey Cl NG3 . . . . **223** F4
Heslington Ave NG8 . . . . **172** E8
Heslop Cl S80 . . . . **35** D3
Hethbeth Ct ☑ NG2 . . . . **173** C2
Hethersett Gdns ☑ NG6 . . **160** B8
Hetley Rd NG9 . . . . **184** B5
Hett's La NG20 . . . . **74** B5
Hetts Lane Inf Sch NG20 . . **74** B5
Hewett St NG20 . . . . **74** B3
Hewson's La NG23 . . . . . **112** A5
Hexham Ave DE7 . . . . . . **170** A4
Hexham Cl
Mansfield NG18 . . . . **102** C3

Hexham Cl *continued*
West Bridgford NG2 . . . . . . 186 A6
Hexham Gdns 🔟 NG5 . . . . . 147 A1
Heyes The NG15 . . . . 117 A1
Heyford Ct DE75 . . . . 143 A1
Heymann Prim Sch NG2 . . 185 D4
Hey St NG10 . . . . 193 C4
Heyward St NG18 . . . . 102 D7
Heywood Cl NG25 . . . . 121 F1
Heywood St NG18 . . . . 102 D7
Hibbert Cres NG17 . . . . . . 101 A3
Hibbert Rd NG18 . . . . 102 D7
Hickings La NG9 . . . . 182 E8
Hickling Ct NG18 . . . . 102 D7
Hickling La LE14 . . . . 211 A4
Hickling Rd
Kinoulton NG12 . . . . 200 B2
Nottingham NG3 . . . . 162 A2
Hickling Way NG12 . . . . . . 188 A1
Hickman Cres DN21 . . . . . . 15 C4
Hickman Ct DN21 . . . . 24 E8
Hickman St DN21 . . . . 24 D8
Hickory Cl 🔟 NG17 . . . . . . 114 F7
Hickton Dr NG3 . . . . 183 B1
Hide Hill View NG12 . . . . . 186 D1
Highbank Dr NG11 . . . . . . 195 E7
Highbank Prim Sch
NG11 . . . . 195 D7
Highbury Ave NG6 . . . . . . 160 D5
Highbury Cl NG8 . . . . 159 E3
Highbury Hospl NG6 . . . . . 160 C5
Highbury Rd
Keyworth NG12 . . . . 197 E4
Nottingham NG6 . . . . 160 C6
Highbury Wlk NG6 . . . . . . 160 C6
High Church St NG7 . . . . . 161 A1
High Church Street 🔟
NG7 . . . . 173 A8
High Cl NG12 . . . . 115 B1
Highclere Dr NG4 . . . . 174 F8
Highcliffe Ave NG20 . . . . . 72 D4
Highcliffe Rd NG3 . . . . . . 174 A5
High Common La
Austerfield DN10 . . . . 3 A6
Tickhill DN11 . . . . 9 A8
High Cres NG17 . . . . 115 B1
Highcroft NG3 . . . . 161 F4
Highcroft Cl NG10 . . . . . . 193 E5
Highcroft Dr NG8 . . . . 171 B5
Highcross Ct NG6 . . . . . . 136 E2
Highcross Ct NG7 . . . . . . 222 B4
Highcross Hill NG25,
NG14 . . . . 136 D3
High Cross St NG1 . . . . . . 223 F3
Highfield DN21 . . . . 29 C1
Highfield Ave
Kirkby in A NG17 . . . . 114 C6
Mansfield NG19 . . . . 88 B1
Shirebrook NG20 . . . . 72 D6
Highfield Cl
Gainsborough DN21 . . . . . . 15 E1
Mansfield NG19 . . . . 88 B1
Ravenshead NG15 . . . . . . 117 A2
Highfield Ct NG9 . . . . 183 F6
Highfield Dr
Bilsthorpe NG22 . . . . 105 F4
Carlton NG4 . . . . 174 B8
Nuttall NG16 . . . . 159 F4
South Normanton DE55 . . . 113 B5
Stapleford LN6 . . . . 127 A4
Highfield Gr
Carlton in L S81 . . . . 26 B5
West Bridgford NG2 . . . . . 185 F7
Highfield La S80 . . . . 36 C1
High Field La DN10 . . . . . . 3 B3
Highfield Prim Sch
Cotgrave NG12 . . . . 187 F3
Long Eaton NG10 . . . . 182 C2
Highfield Rd
Bawtry DN10 . . . . 10 B8
Beeston NG9 . . . . 183 A3
Clipstone NG21 . . . . 90 A4
Keyworth NG12 . . . . 197 E4
Nottingham NG7 . . . . 172 D1
Nuttall NG16 . . . . 159 E4
Saxilby LN1 . . . . 57 A4
Sutton in A NG17 . . . . 100 C3
West Bridgford NG2 . . . . . 185 F7
Highfields Ct NG15 . . . . . . 146 A6
Highfields Dr NG22 . . . . . . 106 A4
Highfields Sch NG24 . . . . 140 C6
Highfield St NG10 . . . . . . 182 C1
Highfield Terr 🔟 NG18 . . . 102 B6
Highfield Villas S81 . . . . . 25 F8
Highfield Way NG18 . . . . . 102 A6
Highgate Cl NG4 . . . . 162 C2
Highgate Dr DE7 . . . . 157 C3
Highgate La NG13 . . . . . . 202 F8
High Gr NG19 . . . . 88 E1
High Grounds Rd S80 . . . . 35 C4
High Grounds Way S80 . . 35 B4
Highgrove Ave NG9 . . . . . 183 D6
Highgrove Gdns NG12 . . . 186 A3
High Hazles Cl NG4 . . . . . 162 E3
High Hazles Dr NG17 . . . . 100 A2
High Hoe Ct S80 . . . . 36 A3
High Hoe Dr S80 . . . . 36 A3
High Hoe Rd S80 . . . . 36 B3
High Holborn DE7 . . . . . . 157 E3
High Hurst NG14 . . . . 148 E7
High La Central DE7 . . . . . 157 A1
High La E DE7 . . . . 157 A1
Highland Cl NG19 . . . . 88 D3
Highland Rd S81 . . . . 36 A5
Highland Rd NG18 . . . . . . 102 E2
High Leys Dr NG15 . . . . . 116 C3
High Leys Rd NG15 . . . . . 145 F5

High Mdw
Bawtry DN10 . . . . 9 F7
Hathern LE12 . . . . 213 A1
Tollerton NG12 . . . . 186 D1
High Oakham Dr NG18 . . . 102 B3
High Oakham Hill NG18 . . 102 A4
High Oakham Prim Sch
NG18 . . . . 102 B3
High Oakham Rd NG18 . . . 102 B4
High Pavement
Nottingham NG1 . . . . 223 F2
Sutton in A NG17 . . . . 100 E2
High Pavement Sixth Form
Coll NG1 . . . . 223 F2
High Pk Cotts NG16 . . . . . 144 D6
High Rd
Beeston, Chilwell NG9 . . . . 183 D4
Beeston NG9 . . . . 184 A7
Beeston, Toton NG9 . . . . . 183 A1
Carlton in L S81 . . . . 26 A5
High Ridge NG19 . . . . 88 F2
High St Ave NG5 . . . . 161 E7
High St Pl NG1 . . . . 223 E2
High Spania NG16 . . . . . . 158 F7
High St
Arnold NG5 . . . . 161 E7
Bawtry DN10 . . . . 10 A7
Beckingham DN10 . . . . 23 B8
Blyth S81 . . . . 18 B2
Bottesford NG13 . . . . 181 A2
Brinsley NG16 . . . . 128 E1
Collingham NG23 . . . . 112 A8
Eagle LN6 . . . . 84 D3
East Markham NG22 . . . . . . 65 F7
Edwinstowe NG21 . . . . 76 B1
Elkesley DN22 . . . . 50 B4
Everton DN10 . . . . 11 C3
Gainsborough DN21 . . . . . . 24 D7
Girton NG23 . . . . 82 F1
Gringley on t H DN10 . . . . . 12 F2
Harby NG23 . . . . 70 E2
Hucknall NG15 . . . . 146 B7
Huthwaite NG17 . . . . 100 A3
Kegworth DE74 . . . . 203 C2
Kimberley NG16 . . . . 158 F6
Laxton NG22 . . . . 79 B3
Long Eaton NG10 . . . . 193 E8
Loughborough LE11 . . . . . 220 B4
Mansfield Woodhouse NG19 88 C3
Market Warsop NG20 . . . . . 74 A4
Marton DN21 . . . . 44 C7
Misson DN10 . . . . 4 B2
Misterton DN10 . . . . 6 E5
Newton on T LN1 . . . . 55 A1
North Scarle LN6 . . . . 83 D2
Nottingham NG1 . . . . 223 E2
Orston NG13 . . . . 179 F7
Pleasleyhill NG19 . . . . 87 B5
Retford DN22 . . . . 39 E3
Ruddington NG11 . . . . 196 C7
South Leverton DN22 . . . . . 42 C6
South Normanton DE55 . . . 113 A6
Stanton Hill NG17 . . . . . . 100 C6
Stapleford NG9 . . . . 182 E7
Staunton in t V NG13 . . . . 169 B4
Sutton in A NG17 . . . . 100 E2
Sutton on T NG23 . . . . 96 F8
Tibshelf DE55 . . . . 99 A7
Walkeringham DN10 . . . . . 13 F6
High Tor NG17 . . . . 100 E7
Highurst St NG7 . . . . 222 C3
High View Ave NG12 . . . . 198 A3
High View Rd DE55 . . . . . 113 C7
High View Rd Ind Units
DE55 . . . . 113 C7
Highwood Ave NG8 . . . . . 171 F8
Highwood Player Inf Sch
NG8 . . . . 171 E8
Highwood Player Jun Sch
NG8 . . . . 171 E8
Highwray Gr NG11 . . . . . . 184 D1
Hilary Cl NG8 . . . . 171 D3
Hilcot Dr NG8 . . . . 160 C1
Hilcote La DE55 . . . . 99 A1
Hilcote St DE55 . . . . 113 A6
Hillary Way NG24 . . . . . . 140 E4
Hillbeck Cres NG8 . . . . . . 171 C4
Hill Cl
Eastwood NG16 . . . . 144 C1
West Bridgford NG2 . . . . . 186 B6
Hill Cres
Gainsborough DN21 . . . . . . 15 F1
Sutton in A NG17 . . . . 101 B4
Hillcrest NG25 . . . . 136 D8
Hill Crest NG20 . . . . 72 D3
Hillcrest Ave DE55 . . . . . 113 A4
Hillcrest Cl NG15 . . . . 159 A6
Hillcrest Dr NG15 . . . . . . 145 D6
Hillcrest Gdns NG14 . . . . 163 E5
Hill Crest Gr NG5 . . . . 161 B3
Hillcrest Mews DN22 . . . . 40 A7
Hillcrest Rd NG12 . . . . . . 197 E4
Hillcrest View NG4 . . . . . 162 E3
Hill Dr NG13 . . . . 177 D5
Hill Farm Cl NG12 . . . . . . 186 D1
Hill Farm Ct NG12 . . . . . . 186 A2
Hillfield Gdns NG5 . . . . . . 146 E1
Hillfield Rd NG9 . . . . 170 F1
Hill Fields DE55 . . . . 113 A3
Hillgrove Gdns 🔟 NG5 . . . 161 A8
Hilliers Ct NG5 . . . . 146 E1
Hillington Rise NG5 . . . . . 161 D8
Hillmoor St NG19 . . . . . . 87 C3
Hillocks Prim Sch NG17 . 101 B3
Hill Rd
Beeston NG9 . . . . 183 B2
Bestwood Village NG6 . . . . 146 E4

Hill Rd *continued*
Gotham NG11 . . . . 205 B7
Harworth DN11 . . . . 8 F3
Orston NG13 . . . . 180 A6
Hill Rise NG9 . . . . 170 D4
Hillsborough Ave NG17 . . 114 D8
Hillsborough Way NG17 . . 114 D8
Hillsford Cl NG8 . . . . 172 A5
Hillside
Beckingham LN5 . . . . 142 C8
Kegworth DE74 . . . . 203 D1
Langley Mill NG16 . . . . . . 143 A3
Marton DN21 . . . . 44 C8
Tuxford NG22 . . . . 66 B3
Hill Side NG7 . . . . 172 D3
Hillside Ave
Misterton DN10 . . . . 7 A2
Nottingham NG3 . . . . 162 A4
Hillside Cres
Beeston NG9 . . . . 183 E8
Worksop S81 . . . . 35 F5
Hillside Dr
Burton Joyce NG14 . . . . . 163 F5
Long Eaton NG10 . . . . 193 B8
Southwell NG25 . . . . 136 D8
Hillside Gr NG10 . . . . 182 A6
Hillside Rd
Beeston, Bramcote NG9 . . 183 D8
Beeston, Chilwell NG9 . . . . 183 B3
Blidworth NG21 . . . . 118 A4
Radcliffe on T NG12 . . . . . 176 A3
Hillside Wlk NG21 . . . . . . 118 A4
Hills Rd NG5 . . . . 161 F4
Hill St
Pleasleyhill NG19 . . . . 87 B5
Retford DN22 . . . . 39 E2
Worksop S80 . . . . 35 F3
Hillsway NG20 . . . . 72 D3
Hillsway Cres NG18 . . . . . 102 A4
Hill Syke NG14 . . . . 150 A2
Hill The NG17 . . . . 114 A8
Hill Top NG15 . . . . 180 A6
Hill Top Ave NG20 . . . . . . 72 E4
Hilltop Cl LN6 . . . . 84 D3
Hill Top Rd NG16 . . . . . . 113 C3
Hill Top View NG11 . . . . . 100 C1
Hillview Ave NG3 . . . . . . 161 D2
Hillview Cres DN22 . . . . . 30 E4
Hillview Ct NG19 . . . . 88 D4
Hillview Rd
Carlton NG4 . . . . 162 A1
Retford DN22 . . . . 39 E3
Hill View Rd
Beeston NG9 . . . . 183 A2
Kirkby in A NG17 . . . . 115 C5
Hill Vue Ave NG24 . . . . . . 140 B8
Hill Vue Gdns NG24 . . . . . 140 B8
Hillwood Cl S80 . . . . 45 A8
Hilton Cres NG2 . . . . 186 B5
Hilton Ct NG2 . . . . 186 B5
Hilton Rd NG3 . . . . 162 A4
Hinchin Brook NG7 . . . . . 222 A2
Hindlow Ct NG18 . . . . . . 103 B6
Hind St DN22 . . . . 40 A6
Hine Ave NG24 . . . . 125 A2
Hinsley Cl NG5 . . . . 162 B8
Hirst Cres NG8 . . . . 171 E4
Hirst Rd DN22 . . . . 40 A8
Hives La LN6 . . . . 83 D3
Hobart Cl NG2 . . . . 173 C1
Hobart Dr NG9 . . . . 170 F1
Hobhouse Rd NG19 . . . . . 87 D2
Hobsic Cl NG16 . . . . 143 D8
Hobsic La NG16 . . . . 128 E8
Hobson's Acre NG14 . . . . 165 A5
Hockerton Hts NG23 . . . . 122 B6
Hockerton Rd NG25,
NG23 . . . . 122 F2
Hockerwood NG11 . . . . . 184 E4
Hockerwood La NG23 . . . 122 C2
Hockley NG1 . . . . 223 F2
Hockley Pl NG17 . . . . 114 E4
Hodgkin Cl NG11 . . . . . . 184 C1
Hodgkinson Rd NG17 . . . 115 B4
Hodgkinson St NG4 . . . . 175 A6
Hodmire La S44 . . . . 85 E7
Hodsock La S81 . . . . 26 B7
Hodsock Priory Gdns S81 26 B7
Hodthorpe Prim Sch S80 . 45 C5
Hoe La
Halam NG22 . . . . 120 F3
Langford NG23 . . . . 111 E3
Normanton on T NG23 . . . . 82 B4
Radcliffe on T NG12 . . . . . 175 C3
Rockley DN22 . . . . 51 C2
Winthorpe NG24 . . . . 125 D7

Holdale Rd NG3 . . . . 174 B6
Holdenby Cl DN22 . . . . . . 40 A8
Holden Cres
Newark-on-T NG24 . . . . . . 139 F6
Nuttall NG16 . . . . 159 C6
Holden Gdns NG9 . . . . . . 182 E6
Holden Rd NG9 . . . . 183 E7
Holden St
Mansfield NG18 . . . . 102 A6
Nottingham NG7 . . . . 222 C3
Holderness Cl DN11 . . . . . . 9 A4
Holding S81 . . . . 36 A1
Holds La DN22 . . . . 19 B2
Holgate NG11 . . . . 184 C2
Holgate Rd NG2 . . . . 173 C1
Holgate Sch NG15 . . . . . . 145 E6
Holkham Ave NG9 . . . . . . 183 C5
Holkham Cl
Arnold NG5 . . . . 162 A6
Shipley DE7 . . . . 157 C3
Holland Cl NG11 . . . . 195 B1
Holland Cres NG16 . . . . . 129 B7
Holland Mdw NG10 . . . . . 193 D5
Holland St NG7 . . . . 172 F7
Holles Ave NG24 . . . . 77 E5
Holles Cres NG7 . . . . 222 C1
Holles St S80 . . . . 35 F2
Holles Ave NG24 . . . . 125 A4
Hollies Cl NG12 . . . . 186 A4
Hollies The
Eastwood NG16 . . . . 143 F2
Rainworth NG21 . . . . 104 B1
Ravenshead NG15 . . . . . . 116 F1
Sandiacre NG10 . . . . 182 A5
Hollington Rd NG8 . . . . . 172 B6
Hollington Way NG18 . . . 103 B7
Hollingwell Dr 🔟 NG18 . . 103 B7
Hollingworth Ave NG10 . . 182 B3
Hollins The NG14 . . . . . . 149 A8
Hollinwell Ave NG8 . . . . 172 C5
Hollinwell Cl NG17 . . . . . 114 E7
Hollinwell Ct 🔟 NG12 . . . 186 B3
Hollinwood Lane NG14 . . 148 C8
Hollis St NG7 . . . . 161 A1
Holloway Cl NG13 . . . . . . 165 D3
Hollowdyke La NG24 . . . . 140 F3
Hollowgate La NG23 . . . . 68 B1
Hollows The
Long Eaton NG10 . . . . 194 A8
Maplebeck NG22 . . . . 108 A7
Nottingham NG11 . . . . . . 185 A4
Thurgarton NG14 . . . . . . 151 C7
Hollow Stone NG1 . . . . . . 223 F2
Holly Ave
Carlton NG4 . . . . 174 D8
Nottingham, Wilford NG11 . 185 B8
Hollyberry Croft NG17 . . 100 D1
Hollybrook Gr NG16 . . . . 159 B7
Holly Bush Cl DN22 . . . . . 50 B4
Holly Cl
Bingham NG13 . . . . 178 A4
Hucknall NG15 . . . . 146 B5
Hollycroft NG2 . . . . 186 A4
Holly Ct
Beeston NG9 . . . . 183 C8
Harworth DN11 . . . . 8 E4
Mansfield NG19 . . . . 88 E1
Retford DN22 . . . . 39 F6
Rolleston NG23 . . . . 138 A5
Hollydale Rd NG3 . . . . . . 174 B6
Hollydene Cl NG15 . . . . . 145 C5
Hollydene Cres NG6 . . . . 160 B4
Holly Farm Ct NG16 . . . . 144 C1
Holly Gdns NG3 . . . . 173 F7
Hollygate La NG12 . . . . . 188 B5
Hollygate Sch NG3 . . . . . 173 F7
Holly Gr NG17 . . . . 114 F6
Holly Hill Prim Sch
NG16 . . . . 129 A7
Holly Hill Rd NG16 . . . . . 129 A6
Hollyhouse Dr DE55 . . . . 113 B6
Holly La NG9 . . . . 183 E5
Holly Prim Sch NG15 . . . . 146 B5
Holly Rd
Mansfield Woodhouse
NG19 . . . . 89 A2
Watnall NG16 . . . . 159 A7
Holly Rise NG24 . . . . 77 D5
Hollythorpe Pl NG15 . . . 145 C5
Hollytree Cl LE14 . . . . . . 215 C2
Hollytree La LE14 . . . . . . 211 C3
Hollywell Prim Sch
NG16 . . . . 158 F7
Holme Ave LE12 . . . . 205 E3
Holme Cl
Ilkeston DE7 . . . . 157 D2
Woodborough NG14 . . . . . 149 D4
Holme Croft NG17 . . . . . 100 F5
Holmefield NG24 . . . . . . 140 E8
Holmefield Cres DE7 . . . 170 A8
Holmefield Rd S80 . . . . . . 45 A6
Holmefield Wlk NG18 . . . 103 B6
Holme Gr NG24 . . . . 174 B2
Holme La
Egmanton NG22 . . . . 79 C6
Halam NG22 . . . . 120 F3
Langford NG23 . . . . 111 E3
Normanton on T NG23 . . . . 82 B4
Radcliffe on T NG12 . . . . . 175 C3
Rockley DN22 . . . . 51 C2
Winthorpe NG24 . . . . 125 D7

Holme Pierrepont Ctry Pk
NG12 . . . . 174 F3
Holme Pierrepont Hall
NG12 . . . . 175 B3
Holme Pit Nature Reserve
NG11 . . . . 184 C3
Holme Rd
Bingham NG13 . . . . 178 A4
West Bridgford NG2 . . . . . 174 A1
Holmes Cl NG16 . . . . 143 A3
Holmesfield Dr DE75 . . . . 157 A7
Holmes Rd DN22 . . . . 39 F7
Holme St NG2 . . . . 173 E2
Holme The NG25 . . . . 136 B7
Holme Way S81 . . . . 25 D1
Holme Wlk DN21 . . . . 15 F1
Holmewood Cres NG5 . . 161 B6
Holmewood Dr NG16 . . . 158 B8
Holmfield Cl S81 . . . . 36 A5
Holmfield Rd NG9 . . . . . . 183 C3
Holmhurst Cl S81 . . . . 35 C5
Holmsfield NG12 . . . . 197 E2
Holmwood Rd NG21 . . . . 104 C1
Holocaust Ctr The NG22 . . 78 E3
Holroyd Ave NG2 . . . . . . 173 F4
Holt Dr 🔟 LE11 . . . . 220 A1
Holt Gr NG14 . . . . 148 F7
Holt The
Gainsborough DN21 . . . . . . 15 F1
Newark-on-T NG24 . . . . . . 139 D6
Holwood Ct NG6 . . . . 160 A6
Holy Cross RC Prim Sch
NG15 . . . . 131 B1
Holy Family RC Prim Sch
NG5 . . . . 47 A8
Holyoake Rd NG3 . . . . . . 162 C3
Holyrood Ct NG9 . . . . . . 171 C1
Holy Trinity Inf Sch
NG25 . . . . 136 D7
Holy Trinity RC Prim Sch
NG24 . . . . 139 E7
Holywell Rd DE7 . . . . 157 C3
Home Cl NG5 . . . . 161 D8
Homecroft Dr NG16 . . . . 128 E7
Home Croft The NG9 . . . . 183 B7
Home Farm Cl
Gotham NG11 . . . . 195 A1
Laughterton LN1 . . . . 55 B4
Homefarm La NG23 . . . . . 70 A6
Homefield Ave NG5 . . . . 148 A1
Homefield Croft DN10 . . . 10 A2
Homefield Rd NG8 . . . . . 172 D7
Home Fm Ct NG16 . . . . . 128 D6
Homelands The NG17 . . . 100 F1
Home Mdws DN11 . . . . . . 8 A6
Home Pastures LE14 . . . . 211 F4
Homestead NG16 . . . . . . 143 A4
Homesteads The NG20 . . . 74 B4
Honeycourt Cl DE55 . . . . 113 B4
Honeyknab La NG25 . . . . 134 D5
Honeys La NG23 . . . . 139 B1
Honeysuckle Cl
New Balderton NG24 . . . . . 140 C4
🔟 Nottingham NG5 . . . . . 159 C1
Honeysuckle Gr
Bingham NG13 . . . . 177 D3
Nottingham NG3 . . . . 162 C3
Honeywood Dr NG3 . . . . 174 A7
Honeywood Wlk NG3 . . . 174 A7
Honing Dr NG25 . . . . 136 D7
Honingham Cl NG5 . . . . . 162 A6
Honingham Rd DE7 . . . . . 157 C3
Honister Cl
Mansfield NG18 . . . . 102 C4
Nottingham NG11 . . . . . . 195 D7
West Bridgford NG2 . . . . . 186 C7
Honister Ct NG18 . . . . . . 102 C4
Honiton Cl NG9 . . . . 183 A2
Honiton Rd NG8 . . . . 159 E1
Hood St NG5 . . . . 161 D2
Hook Cl 🔟 NG5 . . . . 183 C2
Hooley Cl NG10 . . . . 193 B6
Hooley Pl 🔟 NG5 . . . . . . 161 D3
Hooley St NG16 . . . . 128 F6
Hoopers Cl NG13 . . . . . . 181 A2
Hoopers Wlk 🔟 NG2 . . . 173 C2
Hooton Rd NG4 . . . . 174 C7
Hooton St NG3 . . . . 173 F5
Hope Cl NG2 . . . . 173 B2
Hopedale Cl NG7 . . . . . . 222 A3
Hope Dr NG7 . . . . 223 D1
Hope St
Beeston NG9 . . . . 183 E7
Mansfield NG18 . . . . 102 D6
Hopewell Cl NG12 . . . . . . 175 F3
Hopewell Wlk DE7 . . . . . 157 F5
Hopkin La NG25 . . . . 121 C1
Hopkins Ct NG16 . . . . . . 143 F3
Hopyard La
Egmanton NG22 . . . . 79 A8
Ridgeway NG22 . . . . 82 A6
Horace Ave NG9 . . . . 182 E6
Hornbeam Cl DE7 . . . . . . 170 B7
Hornbeam Gdns NG6 . . . 159 F7
Hornbuckle Ct NG7 . . . . 222 B3
Hornchurch Rd NG8 . . . . 171 D8
Hornsby Wlk NG5 . . . . . . 160 E8
Horridge St DE7 . . . . 157 F4
Horsecroft Cl DE7 . . . . . . 157 C2
Horsendale Ave NG16 . . . 159 C7
Horsendale Prim Sch
NG16 . . . . 159 E3
Horsewells St DN10 . . . . . 12 F2

Horsham Dr NG5..........160 F8
Horsley Cres NG16.........143 A3
Hose CE Prim Sch LE14 ..211 F7
Hose La
　Colston Bassett LE14......201 A3
　Harby LE14...............202 A1
　Hose LE14................211 F5
Hoselett Field Rd NG10..193 E5
Hosiery St NG17...........115 A5
Hospital Rd DN22..........39 E7
Hotchkin Ave LN1..........57 C3
Hoten Rd 7 NG2...........173 F3
Hoton Rd LE12............216 B3
Hotspur Cl NG6...........160 E5
Hotspur Rd DN21..........15 C2
Houfton Rd NG18..........102 E8
Hougham Rd NG23.........156 F1
Houghton Ave DE7..........5 F2
Houghton Cl NG16.........159 E4
Houldsworth Rise NG5....147 E2
Hound Rd NG2............185 E8
Hounds Gate NG1.........223 D2
Hounsfield Cl NG24.......140 E8
Hounsfield Way NG23......96 F8
Houseman Gdns NG2......173 C2
Houston Cl NG5...........146 E1
Hove Rd NG5.............160 E5
Hoveringham Rd NG14.....161 D6
Howard Cl NG10...........182 E1
Howard Rd
　Bircotes DN11..............9 C4
　Mansfield NG19...........101 F8
Howard's Gdns NG4........140 C4
Howard St
　Loughborough LE11.......220 B5
　Nottingham NG1..........223 E3
　Sutton in A NG17.........100 F4
　Worksop S80...............36 B2
Howbeck La DN22..........30 E4
Howbeck Rd NG5.........162 B8
Howden Rd NG6...........146 C1
Howell-Jones Rd NG9....183 B3
Howells Cl NG5...........161 C8
Howe Rd LE11............220 A3
Howes Ct NG24..........140 A8
Howick Dr NG6...........159 F8
Howitts Rd NG13..........181 A1
Howitt St
　Heanor DE75...............143 A2
　Long Eaton NG10.........193 E7
Hoylake Cl NG19...........88 E6
Hoylake Cres NG8.........172 E2
Hubert St NG7............222 B4
Huckerby Rd DE7..........157 C2
Huckerbys Field NG4......162 C1
Hucklow Ct NG18..........103 B6
**Hucknall Annie Holgate Jun
　Sch** NG15................145 F6
Hucknall Cl NG8...........159 D2
Hucknall Cres NG4.........162 E2
Hucknall Ind Pk NG15.....145 E4
Hucknall La NG6...........146 D2
Hucknall L Ctr NG15......146 B8
Hucknall Rd
　Newstead NG15...........130 D5
　Nottingham NG6..........160 E6
　Hucknall Sta NG15........146 C7
Huddlestones Wharf
　NG24....................139 E8
Hudson St
　Loughborough LE11.......220 C4
　Nottingham NG3..........173 F6
Hudson Wy NG12.........176 B4
Hufton's Ct DE75..........157 A7
Hufton's Dr DE75..........157 A7
Hugessen Ave NG15.......146 C8
Hugget Gdns 4 NG5......161 A8
Humber Cl NG2...........173 C2
Humber La NG23..........153 B8
Humber Rd
　Beeston NG9.............184 A7
　Long Eaton NG10.........182 C1
Humber Rd S NG9.........184 B6
Humber St
　Retford DN22.............40 A6
　Worksop S80...............35 E4
Humberston Rd NG8.......171 C3
Hume St LE11............220 B2
Humphrey Cl LE11........220 B2
Humphries Gdns S80.......35 E1
Hundred Acre La S81......26 C3
Hundred Acres La NG24..140 D1
Hundreds La DN10..........5 B2
Hungary La LE12..........213 C7
Hungerhill Rd NG3.........173 D7
Hungerton St NG7.........222 B1
Hunston Cl NG8...........172 A7
Hunt Cl NG12.............175 F3
Hunter Rd NG5............162 C6
Hunters Chase NG19.......88 B2
Hunters Cl NG11..........185 A6
Hunters Ct NG17..........114 E5
Hunter's Dr DN10.........12 E2
Huntingdon Dr NG7........223 D2
Huntingdon Prim Sch
　NG3....................223 E4
Huntingdon St NG1.......223 E3
Huntingdon Way NG2.....182 F2
Huntingdon Wlk NG10....182 B5
Huntly Cl
　Mansfield NG19..........101 D5
　Nottingham NG7..........184 F1
Hunt's Hill NG16.........144 A7
Huntsman Pl DN22.........19 B2

Hurcomb St NG3..........173 F7
Hurst Cl NG21...........103 F1
Hurts Croft NG9..........183 D4
Hurt's Yd NG1............223 E2
Huss's La NG10...........193 F7
Hutchinson Gn NG3.......223 F4
Hutchinson Rd NG24......140 E8
Huthwaite La DE55........99 C2
Huthwaite L Ctr NG17.....99 F3
Huthwaite Rd NG17.......100 C2
Hutton Cl NG9............171 D1
Hutton St NG2...........173 F3
Huxley Cl NG8............171 D7
Hyde Cl NG11............184 F4
Hyde Pk Cl NG2..........185 C5
Hyson Cl 10 NG7.........172 F8
Hyson St 12 NG7.........172 F7

I

Ian Gr NG4..............174 F8
**IBTE Mus of
　Telecommunications**
　S81.....................35 F2
Idle Bank DN9.............2 D5
Idle Ct DN10..............10 A7
Idle View DN22...........29 F1
Idlewells Sh Ctr NG17....100 E2
Ilam Sq DE7.............157 E5
Ilford Cl DE7............157 D3
Ilion St NG19.............87 F2
Ilkeston Com Hospl DE7 .157 D4
Ilkeston Rd
　Sandiacre NG10..........182 C8
　Stapleford NG9...........170 F2
　Trowell NG9..............170 C5
ILS Nottingham NG5......173 B8
Imperial Ave
　Beeston NG9.............183 E6
　Carlton NG4.............162 E1
Imperial Rd
　Beeston NG9.............183 E6
　Nottingham NG6..........160 D6
Inchwood Cl NG9.........182 F2
Incinerator Rd NG2.......173 E2
Independent St NG7.......172 D3
Industrial Mus & Yd Gall
　NG8....................172 A3
Infield La
　Cuckney NG20.............60 B5
　North Leverton w H DN22..32 E1
　Weston NG23.............81 B3
Ingamells Dr LN1..........57 C3
Ingham Gr NG7...........222 A1
Ingham Rd
　Bawtry DN10..............9 F8
　Long Eaton NG10.........182 C2
Ingleborough Gdns 6
　NG10...................193 A8
Ingleby Cl
　Cotgrave NG12...........187 E2
　Nottingham NG8..........171 B4
Ingleby Medieval Village of
　LN1.....................57 A8
Inglefield Rd DE7.........170 A6
Inglemere Cl S81..........36 A5
Inglewood Ct NG24.......140 D2
Inglewood Rd NG7........184 E1
Ingram Rd NG6...........160 D6
Ingrams La NG23..........82 A3
Ingram Terr NG6..........160 C6
Ings Rd DN10.............12 E6
Inham Cl NG9............183 C6
Inham Cl NG9............183 A5
Inham Fields NG14........165 A5
Inham Rd NG9............183 B6
Inholms Gdns NG23.......152 F2
Inholms Rd NG23..........152 F2
Inkerman Rd NG16........128 F5
Inkerman St NG16.........128 F5
Innes Rd NG4.............174 C7
Institute St NG17.........100 C6
Instow Rise NG3..........223 F4
Intake Ave NG18..........101 F5
Intake Farm Prim Sch
　NG19...................101 E7
Intake Rd
　Clipstone NG21............90 A3
　Keyworth NG12...........197 D3
Iona Cl DN21.............15 E2
Iona Dr NG9..............170 D2
Iona Gdns NG5...........147 A1
Iona Sq NG3..............174 A5
Ipswich Cir NG3..........174 A5
Ireland Ave NG9..........184 A5
Ireland Cl NG9...........184 A5
Iremonger Rd NG2.........173 D2
Irene Terr NG7............160 F2
Ireton Ave 8 NG24......140 E8
Ireton Gr NG9............183 D2
Ireton St
　Beeston NG9.............183 E6
　Nottingham NG7..........222 C3
Irving Cl NG22...........120 A5
Irwin Dr NG6.............160 A6
Isaac's La NG9...........182 D7
Isabella St NG7..........223 D1
Island Bsns Quarter NG1 .223 F1
Islay Cl
　Arnold NG5..............147 F1
　Stapleford NG9...........170 D3
Ivatt Cl DN10............10 A8
Ivatt Dr NG2.............173 F3
Iveagh Cl NG20...........74 C5
Ives Cl NG2.............185 C4
Ivies The NG24...........139 C6
Ivy Cl NG16.............144 F1

Ivy Gr
　Carlton NG4.............174 D7
　Kirkby in A NG17.........114 F6
　Nottingham NG7..........173 A8
Ivy La NG16.............143 E2
Ivy Lodge La S81..........16 B3
Ivy Row NG13............179 B3

J

Jacklin Gdns NG5.........147 A1
Jacksdale Nature Reserve
　NG16...................128 B3
Jacksdale Prim Sch
　NG16...................128 B3
Jackson Ave
　8 Ilkeston DE7...........157 E1
　Sandiacre NG10..........182 A6
Jackson Terr NG20........74 E8
James Murray Mews
　NG18...................102 C7
James Peacock Inf Sch
　NG11...................196 B7
James St
　Annesley Woodhouse
　　NG17.................115 A1
　Arnold NG5..............161 E8
　Nottingham NG16.........158 F6
　Worksop S80..............35 E5
James William Turner Ave
　NG17...................100 E1
Jamia Al Hudaa Ind Sch
　NG3....................163 A2
Jamia Al-Karam DN22......40 A1
Japan Rd DN21...........15 B1
Japonica Dr NG6..........160 B4
Jardine S81..............36 B6
Jardines The NG9.........171 C1
Jarrow Gdns NG5.........146 F2
Jarvis Ave NG3...........174 B6
Jasmin Cl NG20...........72 C6
Jasmine Cl
　5 Nottingham, Broxtowe
　　NG8...................171 D1
　Nottingham, Glapton NG11 184 C1
Jasmine Dr DE55...........99 B7
Jasmine Rd NG5..........160 E3
Jasper Cl NG12...........175 E2
Jayne Cl
　Carlton NG4.............163 A2
　Nottingham NG8..........171 E5
Jay's Cl NG13............181 A1
Jedburgh Cl NG3..........223 F4
Jedburgh Wlk NG3........223 F4
Jeffares Cl DE74..........203 C3
Jeffries Prim Sch NG7....114 F5
Jellicoe St NG20..........59 A2
Jenford St NG18..........101 E6
Jenkins Ave NG6..........101 D7
Jenned Rd NG5...........148 A2
Jenner St 14 NG5........161 B1
Jenness Ave NG5.........146 E1
Jennison St
　Mansfield NG18...........88 A1
　Nottingham NG6..........160 C7
Jenny Beckett's La NG18 .102 F4
Jenny Burton Way NG15 .146 C5
Jensen Way NG5..........161 B1
Jephson Rd NG17.........114 F8
Jericho La NG13..........192 A3
Jericho Rd NG24..........140 D2
Jermyn Dr NG5...........147 A1
Jersey Gdns NG3..........173 E6
Jersey St NG24...........139 F5
Jerusalem LN6............71 F2
Jerusalem Rd LN6.........71 F3
Jervis Ct DE7............157 F3
Jesmond Rd NG6..........160 D6
Jesse Gray Prim Sch
　NG2....................174 B5
Jessop Cl NG24...........125 C1
Jessop's La NG4..........162 F2
Jessop Way NG24.........125 C1
Job La DN10..............20 B7
Jockey La NG18...........84 F2
Jockey La DN22...........50 A5
John Barrow Cl NG21.....118 C8
John Blow Prim Sch
　NG23...................142 E1
John Carroll Ct 2 NG3 .173 F6
John Carroll L Ctr NG7...222 B3
John Clifford Prim Sch
　NG9....................184 A6
John Coupland Hospl
　DN21....................15 B3
John Davies Prim Sch
　NG17....................99 F4
John Gold Av NG24......140 A7
John Hunt Inf Sch NG24 .140 C4
John Hunt Jun Sch
　NG24...................140 C4
John King Workshop Mus
　NG16...................113 D3
John Pope Way NG24.....125 B4
Johnson Ave NG15.......146 B5
Johnson Dr NG18.........102 C3
Johnson Rd NG7..........222 A2
Johns Rd NG12...........176 B3
John St
　Ilkeston DE7.............157 F1
　Kirkby in A NG17.........160 F1
　Sutton in A NG17.........100 F4
　Worksop S80..............35 E3
John T Rice Inf Sch NG19 .89 E3

John Wright Cl NG5.......146 D1
Joseph Whitaker Sch
　NG21...................117 F8
Joyce Ave
　Beeston NG9.............182 E3
　Nottingham NG5..........161 D5
Joyce Cl NG5.............161 D4
Jubilee Ave NG18.........184 B8
Jubilee Cl DN10............4 B3
Jubilee Dr LE11...........220 A6
Jubilee Rd
　Arnold NG5..............161 E6
　Retford DN22.............39 D5
　Sutton in A NG17.........100 D3
Jubilee St
　Kimberley NG16..........158 E7
　Newark-on-T NG24........140 A7
　3 Nottingham NG2.......173 F4
Jubilee Way N NG18......103 C6
Jubilee Way S NG18......103 B4
Judges St LE11...........220 C3
Judson Ave NG9..........182 F6
Julian Cl DE7............170 A6
Julian La NG12...........164 C1
Julian Rd NG2............174 B1
Julius Wy NG17...........115 B8
Julie Ave DE75...........143 A1
Jumelles Dr NG14.........148 D2
Junction Rd
　Long Eaton NG10.........194 A6
　Sutton in A NG17.........101 B2
Juniper Cl
　Bilsthorpe NG22..........106 A5
　Nottingham NG11.........184 C1
Juniper Ct NG16..........158 C8
Juniper Gdns NG13........178 A4

K

Kansington Ct 5 NG5...161 C3
Kappler Cl NG4...........175 A7
Karen Rise NG5...........148 A1
Katherine Dr NG9.........182 F4
Kaye Rd NG19............101 D7
Kayes Wlk NG1...........223 F2
Keats Ave NG17..........100 B3
Keats Cl
　Arnold NG5..............161 D7
　Long Eaton NG10.........193 B5
　Nuthall NG16............159 B6
Keats Cres S81............36 A4
Keats Dr NG15............145 D6
Keats Rd NG24...........140 D5
Kedleston Cl
　Beeston NG9.............183 C5
　Long Eaton NG10.........193 A5
Kedleston Dr DE7.........157 D3
Kedleston Rd S81..........35 F6
Keel Dr NG13............181 A2
Keeling Cl NG16..........129 A7
Keepers Cl NG6..........146 E4
Keep The LE12...........205 F1
Kegworth La DE74.........212 C5
Kegworth Mus DE74......203 C2
Kegworth Rd
　Gotham NG11.............195 A1
　Kingston-on-S NG11......204 D8
　Ratcliffe on S NG11......203 F5
Keighton Hill NG7........172 C2
Keilder Dr NG13..........177 C4
Kelfield Cl NG6...........160 E5
Kelham Gn NG3...........173 F6
Kelham La NG24..........124 D3
Kelham Rd
　Mansfield NG19..........101 C7
　Newark-on-T NG24........124 E1
Kelham Way NG16........143 E3
Keller Ct DN22............53 B8
Kelling Cl NG5............161 A6
Kelly Wlk NG2............185 B7
Kelsey Cl NG9............183 C3
Kelso Gdns NG2..........173 B2
Kelstedge Dr NG18.......103 B6
Kelstern Cl
　Mansfield NG18...........103 A7
　Nottingham NG8..........160 C3
Kelvedon Gdns NG3.......173 E6
Kelvin Cl NG9............182 C5
Kelvin Rd
　Clipstone NG19...........89 D3
　Nottingham NG3..........174 A7
Kemmel Rd NG6..........160 D5
Kempsey Cl NG5..........160 E8
Kempson St NG11........196 C6
Kempton Cl NG16.........158 E7
Kempton Dr NG5.........148 A1
Kempton Rd NG18.........102 F7
Kendal Cl
　Annesley Woodhouse
　　NG17.................130 A8
　Hucknall NG15............145 F8
　Worksop S81..............35 E8
Kendal Cres NG4..........162 E3
Kendal Dr NG9............183 D8
Kendale Ct NG3...........161 F1
Kendal Rd NG18..........189 A4
Kenia Cl NG24............174 D8
Kenilworth Ave NG17.....101 B4
Kenilworth Cl
　Saxilby LN1...............57 A4
　Worksop S80..............36 A1
Kenilworth Ct
　Beeston NG9.............184 A7
　Nottingham NG7..........223 D1
Kenilworth Dr S81.........25 F6

Kenilworth Rd
　Beeston NG9.............184 A8
　Nottingham NG7..........223 D1
Kenley Cl S81.............35 D8
Kenmare Cres DN21.......24 F6
Ken Martin Swimming Ctr
　NG6....................146 C1
Kenmore Cl NG19.........101 C5
Kenmore Gdns NG3.......223 F4
Kennack Cl DE55.........113 C6
Kennedy Ave
　Long Eaton NG10.........193 C5
　Mansfield Woodhouse
　　NG19..................88 D4
Kennedy Cl NG5...........161 E7
Kennedy Ct
　Walesby NG22.............64 A2
　Worksop S81..............36 A4
Kennedy Dr NG9..........170 E2
Kennedy Rise NG22........64 A2
Kennedy Wlk NG24.......140 E4
Kennel Dr DN22...........28 C5
Kennel La LN6............71 C3
Kenneth Rd NG5..........147 F2
Kennet Paddock NG19....128 A5
Kennington Rd NG8.......172 D5
Kenrick Rd NG3...........162 A2
Kenrick St NG4...........175 A4
Kensington Cl
　Beeston NG9.............183 A8
　Mansfield Woodhouse NG19 88 E5
　Sutton in A NG17.........100 E3
Kensington Gdns
　Carlton NG4.............174 E2
　Ilkeston DE7.............170 A7
Kensington Pk Cl NG2....185 C5
Kensington Rd NG10......182 A4
Kenslow Ave 10 NG7....172 E2
Kent Ave
　Beeston NG9.............183 F4
　Westwood NG16..........128 A4
Kent Cl S81..............36 A6
Kentmere Cl NG2.........186 C2
Kenton Ave NG16.........159 D3
Kenton Ct 6 NG2.........173 D3
Kent Rd
　Eastwood NG16...........158 C5
　Nottingham NG3..........162 A1
Kent St NG1.............223 F3
Kentwood Rd NG2.........173 F4
Kenyon Rd NG7...........172 D3
Keppel Ct DE7............157 F5
Kersall Cres NG5..........160 D5
Kersall Dr NG6...........160 D5
Kersall Gdns NG15........146 B2
Kestral Dr NG13...........177 F5
Kestral Rd NG18..........162 B3
Kestrel Cl NG4...........162 B3
Kestrel Dr NG21..........118 B8
Kestrel Mews NG19.......35 C2
Kestrel Rise LN6..........84 D2
Keswick Cl
　Beeston NG9.............183 D8
　West Bridgford NG2......186 C2
Keswick Ct
　Long Eaton NG10.........182 B2
　3 Nottingham NG2.......173 E4
Keswick Rd S81............35 E8
Keswick St NG2..........173 E4
Kettlebury Cl NG15.......145 C2
Kettlethorpe Rd LN1......55 D7
Ket St NG6..............160 B8
Keverne Cl NG8...........160 C2
Kevin Rd NG8............171 D2
Kew Cl NG11.............185 C5
Kew Cres DE75...........143 E3
Kew Gdns
　New Balderton NG24......140 B4
　Nuthall NG16............159 E7
Kexby Wlk DN21...........24 F
Keyes Ct DN10............19 F
Keyes Ct DN10............19 F
Keyes Rise DN10..........19 F
Keys Cl NG6..............160 A
Key St NG3..............173 F
Keyworth Cl NG19.........101 E
Keyworth Dr NG19.........89 C
Keyworth L Ctr NG12.....197 F
**Keyworth Mdw Nature
　Reserve** NG12...........207 E
Keyworth Prim Sch
　NG12...................197 E
Keyworth Rd
　Carlton NG4.............162 A
　Widmerpool NG12........208 C
　Wysall NG12.............207 C
Keyworth Cl NG16.........160 F
Kiddier Ave NG5..........162 B
Kid La S81...............16 A
Kighill La NG15...........132 B
Kilbourn St NG3..........223 E
Kilburn Cl NG9...........171 C
Kilburn Dr DE7...........170 A
Kilby Ave NG3............174 A
Kildare Rd NG3...........174 A
Kildonan Cl NG8..........159 D
Killarton Cl NG8..........195 E
Killerton Pk Dr NG11.....195 E
Killisick Jun Sch NG5.....162 B
Killisick Rd NG5..........148 A
Kilnbrook Ave NG5........148 A
Kilnwood Cl NG3..........174 A
Kilsby Rd NG7............184 E
Kilton Ave NG18..........103 B
Kilton Cl S81.............36 B
Kilton Cres S81...........36 B
Kilton Glade S81..........36 A
Kilton Hill S81............36 A

Kilton Rd S80 . . . . 36 A3
Kilton Terr S80 . . . . 36 A3
Kilverston Rd NG10 . . . 182 A6
Kilverton Cl NG8 . . . . . 172 C4
Kilvington Rd NG5 . . . . 162 B7
Kimber Cl NG8 . . . . 171 D6
Kimberley Cl NG16 . . . . 158 F5
Kimberley Comp Sch
  NG16 . . . . 159 A6
Kimberley L Ctr NG16 . . 159 A6
Kimberley Prim Sch
  NG16 . . . . 158 F6
Kimberley Rd
  Nottingham NG2 . . . . 174 A4
  Nuthall NG16 . . . . 159 C5
Kimbolton Ave NG7 . . . 222 B2
Kindlewood Dr NG9 . . . 183 B1
King Charles St NG1 . . . 223 D2
King Edward Ave NG18 . 102 B4
King Edward Gdns NG10 182 B6
King Edward Prim Sch
  NG18 . . . . 102 C6
King Edward Rd LE11 . . 220 C3
King Edward St
  Hucknall NG15 . . . . . . 146 A6
  Nottingham NG1 . . . . . 223 F3
  Sandiacre NG10 . . . . . 182 B6
  Shirebrook NG20 . . . . . 72 F4
King Edward's Terr DN22 . 39 F6
King Edwin Prim Sch
  NG21 . . . . 75 F1
Kingerby Cl DN21 . . . . . 24 E7
Kingfield Cl NG21 . . . . 118 B8
Kingfisher Cl
  New Balderton NG24 . . 140 C5
  Nottingham NG6 . . . . . 160 D4
Kingfisher Ct
  Beeston NG9 . . . . 184 B5
  2 Long Eaton LE11 . 220 A2
Kingfishers Ct NG2 . . . 174 A6
Kingfisher Way **1** LE11 . 220 A2
Kingfisher Wharf
  4 Nottingham NG7 . . 172 F2
  1 Nottingham NG7 . . 173 A2
Kingfisher Wlk S81 . . . . 35 C7
King George Ave LE11 . . 220 D2
King George Rd LE11 . . 220 D2
King George V Ave NG18 . 102 E5
King Johns Arc NG1 . . . 223 E2
King John's Rd NG21 . . . 90 A4
Kinglake Pl NG2 . . . . . . 173 C2
King Rd NG20 . . . . 74 A4
Kingrove Ave NG9 . . . . 183 D6
King St E DN21 . . . . 24 D7
Kings Ave NG4 . . . . 162 E2
Kingsbridge Ave NG3 . . 162 C6
Kingsbridge Way NG9 . . 183 C6
Kingsbury Dr NG8 . . . . 172 A8
Kings Ct NG25 . . . . 121 E1
Kingsdale Cl 36 B8
Kingsdale Cl NG10 . . . . 193 A5
Kingsdown Mount NG8 . 171 E2
Kings Dr NG16 . . . . 143 E7
Kingsford Ave NG7 . . . . 222 A4
Kingshaugh Camp (Ancient
  Mon) NG22 . . . . 66 F8
Kingsley Ave NG19 . . . . 88 C3
Kingsley Cres NG19 . . . . 88 D4
Kingsley Cres NG19 . . . 193 B4
Kingsley Cl NG19 . . . . . 88 C5
Kingsley Dr NG4 . . . . . 175 A7
Kingsley Rd NG2 . . . . . 174 A3
Kingsley St NG17 . . . . . 115 B4
Kings Lodge Dr NG18 . . 101 E4
King's Marina NG18 . . . 124 F2
King's Mdw Rd NG2 . . . 173 A2
Kingsmead DN22 . . . . . 39 D3
Kingsmeadow NG9 . . . . 170 D2
Kingsmeadow NG17 . . . 118 C8
King's Mill Ctr Hospl
  NG17 . . . . 101 C5
Kings Mill La NG17 . . . 101 D4
Kings Mill Rd E NG17,
  NG18 . . . . 114 E8
Kings Mill Way NG18 . . 101 E4
Kings Moor NG5 . . . . . . 160 F7
Kingsnorth NG24 . . . . . 140 A8
King's Pl NG1 . . . . 223 F2
Kings St
  Long Clawson LE14 . . . 211 C2
  Sandiacre NG10 . . . . . 182 B6
King's Rd NG24 . . . . . . 124 F1
Kings Sch The NG2 . . . . 173 D1
Kings Stand NG18 . . . . 102 E4
King St
  Beeston NG9 . . . . 184 A6
  Eastwood NG16 . . . . . 143 F2
  Gainsborough DN21 . . . 24 D7
  Hodthorpe S80 . . . . . . 45 C6
  Huthwaite NG17 . . . . . 100 B3
  Ilkeston DE7 . . . . 157 F1
  Kirkby in a NG17 . . . . 115 A4
  Long Eaton NG10 . . . . 193 D8
  Loughborough LE11 . . 220 C3
  Mansfield NG18 . . . . . 102 D7
  Mansfield Woodhouse
    NG19 . . . . 88 B2
  Nether Broughton LE14 . 219 D8
  Newark-on-T NG24 . . . 139 E7
  Nottingham NG1 . . . . . 223 E3
  Pinxton NG16 . . . . 113 D4
  South Normanton DE55 . 113 A5
  Southwell NG25 . . . . . 121 E1
  Sutin in A NG17 . . . . . 100 E2
  Tibshelf DE55 . . . . 99 A7
  Warsop Vale NG20 . . . . 73 D5

King St continued
  Worksop S80 . . . . 35 E2
Kingsthorpe Cl
  Mansfield NG19 . . . . . . 88 E1
  Nottingham NG3 . . . . . 161 F1
Kingston Ave DE7 . . . . 170 A4
Kingston Cl S80 . . . . . . 47 C8
Kingston Ct
  Kingston-on-S NG11 . . 204 D5
  14 Nottingham NG2 . 173 E4
Kingston Dr
  Cotgrave NG12 . . . . . . 187 F1
  Ollerton NG22 . . . . 77 A3
Kingston La DE74 . . . . . 203 F3
Kingston Pk Prim Sch
  S81 . . . . 25 F6
Kingston Rd
  Carlton in L S81 . . . . . . 25 D6
  Mansfield NG18 . . . . . 102 D7
  West Bridgford NG2 . . 185 E6
  Worksop S80 . . . . 47 B8
Kingsway
  Ilkeston DE7 . . . . 170 A6
  Kirkby in A NG17 . . . . 115 B3
  Mansfield Woodhouse NG19 89 A1
  New Balderton NG24 . . 140 C3
  Radcliffe on T NG12 . . 175 E2
  Worksop S81 . . . . 36 A4
Kingsway Ave NG22 . . . 77 D6
Kingsway Gdns NG15 . . 145 E4
Kingsway Prim Sch
  NG17 . . . . 115 B3
Kingswell Rd NG16 . . . 161 F6
Kings Wlk NG1 . . . . 223 E3
Kingswood Cl S81 . . . . . 16 E5
Kings Wood Cl NG10 . . . 10 A8
Kingswood Dr NG17 . . . 114 F6
Kingswood Rd
  Nottingham NG8 . . . . . 172 B5
  West Bridgford NG2 . . 185 D5
Kinlet Rd NG5 . . . . 161 A6
Kinoulton La
  Kinoulton NG12 . . . . . 209 B8
  Kinoulton, Owthorpe NG12 .199 F4
Kinoulton Prim Sch
  NG12 . . . . 199 E1
Kinoulton Rd NG12 . . . 188 F2
Kinsdale Wlk NG11 . . . 184 E3
Kipling Cl
  Nottingham NG5 . . . . . 195 C8
  Worksop S81 . . . . 36 B5
Kipling St **5** NG18 . . . 102 A7
Kipps St NG1 . . . . 223 F3
Kirby Cl
  Blidworth NG21 . . . . . 118 A4
  Eastwood NG16 . . . . . 144 A3
Kirby Dr DE74 . . . . 203 C1
Kirby Rd NG16 . . . . . . 144 A3
Kirk Ave DE74 . . . . 203 D2
Kirkbride Ct NG9 . . . . . 183 B4
Kirkby Cl NG15 . . . . . . 121 E2
Kirkby Folly Rd NG17 . . 101 B1
Kirkby Gdns NG2 . . . . . 173 D2
Kirkby House Dr NG17 . 114 F2
Kirkby-in-Ashfield Sta
  NG17 . . . . 115 A5
Kirkby La NG16 . . . . . . 114 B4
Kirkby Mill View NG17 . 114 C5
Kirkby Rd
  Ravenshead NG15 . . . . 116 C3
  Sutton in A NG17 . . . . 100 E1
Kirkby Woodhouse Prim Sch
  NG17 . . . . 114 E1
Kirk Cl NG9 . . . . 183 D4
Kirkdale Cl NG8 . . . . . . 171 B4
Kirkdale Gdns NG10 . . . 193 B6
Kirkdale Rd
  Long Eaton NG10 . . . . 193 B6
  Nottingham NG3 . . . . . 174 B6
Kirk Dr NG18 . . . . 77 E6
Kirke Cl NG20 . . . . 66 B7
Kirke St DN22 . . . . 39 F7
Kirkewhite Ave NG10 . . 193 D7
Kirkfell Cl NG12 . . . . . 186 C5
Kirk Gate NG24 . . . . . . 124 F1
Kirkham Dr NG9 . . . . . 182 F2
Kirkhill NG13 . . . . 177 C5
Kirk Hill NG13 . . . . 165 B2
Kirk La NG11 . . . . 196 C1
Kirkland Ave NG18 . . . 101 F6
Kirkland Cl NG17 . . . . . 115 B8
Kirkland Dr NG9 . . . . . 183 C2
Kirkley Gdns NG5 . . . . 162 A8
Kirk Ley Rd LE12 . . . . . 214 D8
Kirklington Prim Sch
  NG22 . . . . 120 E7
Kirklington Rd
  Bilsthorpe NG22 . . . . . 105 D2
  Eakring NG22 . . . . 106 E8
  Rainworth NG21, NG22 . 104 C1
  Southwell NG25 . . . . . 121 D1
Kirkpatrick Dr S81 . . . . 35 C7
Kirk Rd NG3 . . . . 162 A2
Kirk's Bldgs NG4 . . . . . 174 D7
Kirkstall Cl NG16 . . . . . 113 D3
Kirkstead Gdns **7** NG7 .172 F7
Kirkstead Jun Sch NG16 .113 D3
Kirkstead Rd NG16 . . . . 113 D3
Kirkstead St **6** NG7 . . 172 F7
Kirkstone Ct NG10 . . . . 182 B2
Kirkstone Dr NG2 . . . . . 186 C7
Kirk White Ct NG2 . . . . 173 C1
Kirtle Cl NG8 . . . . 172 B8
Kirtley Dr NG2 . . . . 173 A2
Kirton Ave NG10 . . . . . 193 D7

Kirton Cl
  Balderton NG24 . . . . . 140 D2
  Mansfield NG19 . . . . . 101 D7
  Meden Vale NG20 . . . . 74 E8
Kirton Ct NG22 . . . . 78 C6
Kirton Pk NG22 . . . . 78 C6
Kirton Rd NG22 . . . . 78 C6
Kirton Wood Nature Reserve
  NG22 . . . . 78 F5
Kitchener Dr NG18 . . . . 102 C6
Kitchener Gdns S81 . . . . 35 E8
Kitchener Terr NG20 . . . 59 A2
Kitson Ave NG16 . . . . . 128 C4
Kittiwake Mews NG7 . . 222 A2
Kiwi Cl NG15 . . . . 145 D5
Knapp Ave NG16 . . . . . 143 F1
Knaton Rd S81 . . . . 25 E7
Kneesall Cl NG20 . . . . . 74 D7
Kneesall Gr NG15 . . . . . 146 B7
Kneeton Cl
  Carlton NG4 . . . . 162 D4
  Nottingham NG5 . . . . . 161 C4
Kneeton Rd NG13 . . . . . 165 E5
Kneeton Vale NG5 . . . . 161 C4
Knighton Av NG7 . . . . . 172 E6
Knighton Rd NG5 . . . . . 161 D5
Knightsbridge Dr
  Nuthall NG8 . . . . 159 E3
  West Bridgford NG2 . . 185 C4
Knightsbridge Gdns
  NG15 . . . . 130 F1
Knights Cl
  Nottingham NG5 . . . . . 160 F8
  West Bridgford NG2 . . 185 C3
Knight's Cl NG13 . . . . . 166 E4
Knight's Ct NG24 . . . . . 140 A8
Knight St NG4 . . . . 175 A6
Knipton Cl NG24 . . . . . 140 D3
Knole Rd NG8 . . . . 171 E5
Knoll Ave NG15 . . . . . . 145 D5
Knoll The
  Mansfield NG18 . . . . . 101 E6
  Shirebrook NG20 . . . . . 72 D3
Knott End S81 . . . . 16 E3
Knott's Ct NG24 . . . . . . 140 A8
Knowle Hill NG16 . . . . . 159 A5
Knowle La NG16 . . . . . 159 A5
Knowle Pk NG16 . . . . . 159 A5
Knowles Wlk **3** NG5 . . 161 A8
Krebs Cl NG11 . . . . 184 C1
Kyle View NG5 . . . . 147 A1
Kyme St NG7 . . . . 222 B3
Kynance Cl DE55 . . . . . 113 C6
Kynance Gdns NG11 . . . 185 B5

L

Labray Rd NG14 . . . . . . 148 E8
Laburnum Cl NG24 . . . . 140 C5
Laburnum Ave
  Gainsborough NG12 . . . 15 D2
  Keyworth NG12 . . . . . 198 A2
  Kirkby in A NG17 . . . . 114 D3
  Shirebrook NG20 . . . . . 72 E5
Laburnum Cl
  Hathern LE12 . . . . 213 A1
  Sandiacre NG10 . . . . . 182 A5
  South Normanton DE55 . 113 B4
  Worksop S80 . . . . 35 D1
Laburnum Gr
  Beeston NG9 . . . . 184 B5
  Hucknall NG15 . . . . . . 146 B5
  Mansfield Woodhouse NG19 88 A4
Laburnum Rd S81 . . . . . 16 F4
Laburnum St NG3 . . . . . 173 D7
Laceby Ct NG19 . . . . . . 88 E4
Lace Ctr The NG1 . . . . . 223 E2
Lace Market Theatre The
  NG1 . . . . 223 E2
Lace Mkt Ctr The NG1 . 223 E2
Lace Rd NG9 . . . . 183 F7
Lace St NG7 . . . . 172 D1
Lace Wy NG1 . . . . 173 E3
Lacey Ave NG15 . . . . . . 146 A5
Lacey Cl DE7 . . . . 157 C3
Lacey Fields Rd DE75 . . 143 B1
Ladbrooke Cres NG6 . . . 160 C3
Ladybank Rise NG5 . . . 162 C8
Lady Bay Ave NG2 . . . . 173 F1
Lady Bay Bridge NG2 . . 173 E2
Lady Bay Prim Sch NG2 . 174 A1
Lady Bay Rd NG2 . . . . . 174 A1
Lady Bay Ret Pk NG2 . . 173 E3
Ladybridge Cl NG9 . . . . 183 A3
Ladybrook La NG18 . . . 101 F7
Ladybrook Pl NG19 . . . . 101 E7
Ladybrook Primary Sch
  NG19 . . . . 101 D8
Ladybrook Prim Sch
  NG19 . . . . 101 D8
Ladycroft Ave NG15 . . . 146 A8
Ladycross Inf Sch NG10 . 182 A6
Ladydale Cl NG18 . . . . . 101 E6
Ladylea Rd NG10 . . . . . 193 A4
Lady Lee Quarry Nature
  Reserve S80 . . . . 35 A4
Ladysmith St NG2 . . . . . 174 A4
Ladysmock Gdns NG2 . . 173 E4
Lady Well La DN22 . . . . 52 B8
Lady Wlk S81 . . . . 35 E7
Ladywood La NG23 . . . . 80 E5
Lake Farm Rd NG21 . . . 103 F1
Lakeland Ave NG15 . . . 146 C5
Lakeside Arts Ctr NG7 . . 172 D6

Lakeside Ave NG10 . . . . 193 C4
Lakeside Cl NG10 . . . . . 193 C5
Lakeside Inf Sch NG10 . .193 B4
Lakeside View NG21 . . . 101 B4
Lake Vw NG7 . . . . 222 B4
Lake View Dr NG17 . . . . 129 F6
Lakeview Prim Sch
  NG21 . . . . 103 F1
Lakeview Sixth Form Coll
  NG9 . . . . 183 D3
Lamartine Cl NG3 . . . . . 223 F3
Lamartine St NG3 . . . . . 223 F3
Lamb Cl NG24 . . . . 139 C7
Lamb Cl Dr NG16 . . . . . 144 B4
Lambcroft Rd NG16 . . . 113 D4
Lambert Cl NG9 . . . . . . 184 B7
Lambert Gdns NG8 . . . . 172 C2
Lambert St NG7 . . . . . . 172 E7
Lambeth Rd NG5 . . . . . 147 A2
Lambie Cl NG8 . . . . 172 C5
Lamb La S81 . . . . 16 C5
Lambley Ave
  Mansfield NG18 . . . . . 102 F5
  Nottingham NG3 . . . . . 162 B3
Lambley Bridle Rd NG14 163 D6
Lambley La
  Burton Joyce NG14 . . . 163 E5
  Carlton NG4 . . . . 162 F3
Lambley Prim Sch NG4 . 163 B7
Lambourne Cres NG14 . 150 F1
Lambourne Dr NG8 . . . . 172 A5
Lambourne Gdns NG5 . . 162 A5
Lambton Cl DE7 . . . . . . 157 E3
Lamcote Gdns NG4 . . . . 175 A4
Lamcote Gr NG2 . . . . . . 173 D1
Lamcote Mews NG4 . . . 175 A4
Lamcote St NG2 . . . . . . 173 D1
Laming Gap La NG12 . . 198 E5
Lammas La NG5 . . . . . . 147 D4
Lammas Gdns
  East Bridgford NG13 . . 165 D4
  Nottingham NG2 . . . . . 173 D2
Lammas La NG5 . . . . . . 165 D4
Lammas Rd NG17 . . . . . 100 C3
Lammas Sch NG17 . . . . 100 C3
Lamond Cl NG19 . . . . . 101 E5
Lamorna Gr NG11 . . . . . 185 B6
Lamplands NG12 . . . . . 187 E3
Lamp Wood Cl NG14 . . . 148 E7
Lanark Cl NG8 . . . . 172 C3
Lancaster Ave
  Sandiacre NG10 . . . . . 182 A4
  Stapleford NG9 . . . . . . 182 E7
Lancaster Cl NG11 . . . . . 8 B7
Lancaster Dr DN10 . . . . . 9 F8
Lancaster Rd
  Bestwood Village NG6 . . 146 E4
  Gringley on t H DN10 . . 22 A8
  Hucknall NG15 . . . . . . 145 D4
  Newark-on-T NG24 . . . 125 C2
  Nottingham NG3 . . . . . 174 B7
Lancaster Way NG8 . . . 159 D2
Lancaster Wlk S81 . . . . . 36 A6
Lancastrian Way S81 . . . 36 A6
Lancelot Dr NG16 . . . . . 145 A1
Lancelyn Gdns NG2 . . . 185 E4
Lancster Cres DN11 . . . . 8 B7
Landa Gr NG22 . . . . 66 A3
Landcroft Cres NG5 . . . 161 C4
Landcroft La LE12 . . . . . 204 D1
Landmere Cl DE7 . . . . . 157 C3
Landmere Gdns NG3 . . . 161 F1
Landmere La
  West Bridgford NG11 . . 185 C3
  West Bridgford NG11,
    NG12 . . . . 185 D1
Landsdowne Ct DN22 . . 39 D4
Landsdowne Rd NG5 . . 160 E4
Landsdown Gr NG10 . . . 182 F1
Landseer Cl
  Nottingham NG7 . . . . . 222 A4
  Southwell NG25 . . . . . 136 C8
Landseer Rd NG25 . . . . 136 C8
Lane The NG25 . . . . 136 C8
Lane End NG17 . . . . 115 A5
Laneham Ave NG5 . . . . 162 A7
Laneham Rd
  Dunham on T NG22 . . . 54 A2
  Rampton DN22 . . . . . . 53 D6
Lanercost Mews **3** S80 . 35 F2
Lanesborough Ct **1** NG2 220 E2
Laneside Ave NG9 . . . . 182 E2
Lane The
  Awsworth NG16 . . . . . 158 C4
  Cotham NG23 . . . . 154 F3
Laneward Cl DE7 . . . . . 157 D4
Langar Cl NG5 . . . . 161 C8
Langar Ind Est NG13 . . . 201 E6
Langar La
  Colston Bassett NG12 . . 200 D8
  Harby LE14 . . . . 202 A4
Langar Pl NG19 . . . . . . 103 B8
Langar Rd NG13 . . . . . . 177 E4
Langdale Cl NG24 . . . . . 139 E4
Langdale Dr
  Long Eaton NG10 . . . . 193 A6
  Tickhill DN11 . . . . 8 B8
Langdale Gr NG13 . . . . 177 B4
Langdale Rd
  Nottingham NG3 . . . . . 174 C5
  Worksop S81 . . . . 35 F7
Langdon Cl NG10 . . . . . 182 A1
Langdown Cl NG6 . . . . . 160 A8
Langford La NG23 . . . . . 111 A3

Langford Rd
  Arnold NG5 . . . . 162 B7
  Mansfield NG19 . . . . . 101 D6
Langford St NG17 . . . . . 100 E3
Langham Ave NG3 . . . . 174 A3
Langham Dr NG14 . . . . 163 F5
Langham Pl NG18 . . . . . 101 F7
Langley Ave
  Arnold NG5 . . . . 161 F6
  Ilkeston DE7 . . . . 157 F5
Langley Cl NG19 . . . . . . 87 E1
Langley Dr DE74 . . . . . 203 C2
Langley Mill Business Park
  NG16 . . . . 143 E3
Langley Mill CE Inf Sch
  NG16 . . . . 143 B3
Langley Mill Jun Sch
  NG16 . . . . 143 A4
Langley Mill Sta NG16 . .143 B2
Langley Pk NG16 . . . . . 143 B3
Langley St **1** S80 . . . . . 35 F2
Langold Dyscarr Com Sch
  S81 . . . . 16 D3
Langstrath Dr NG2 . . . . 186 C4
Langstrath Rd NG7 . . . . 184 E1
Langton Ave NG17 . . . . 114 D6
Langton Cl NG4 . . . . . . 174 D7
Langton Hollow NG16 . . 128 D6
Langton Rd NG17 . . . . . 100 E2
Langtree Gdns NG13 . . . 177 F5
Langtry Gr NG7 . . . . . . 161 A1
Langwell Dr NG19 . . . . . 89 C2
Langwith Bassett Prim Sch
  NG20 . . . . 72 E7
Langwith Dr NG20 . . . . . 58 F1
Langwith Maltings NG20 .72 F8
Langwith Rd
  Cuckney NG20 . . . . 60 A2
  Shirebrook NG20 . . . . . 72 F5
Langwith-Whaley Thorns Sta
  NG20 . . . . 58 F2
Lansbury Ave NG22 . . . . 77 C6
Lansbury Dr
  Bilsthorpe NG22 . . . . . 105 F7
  South Normanton DE55 . 113 A6
Lansbury Gdns NG18 . . 102 E8
Lansbury Rd
  Bilsthorpe NG22 . . . . . 105 F7
  Edwinstowe NG21 . . . . 76 B2
  New Balderton NG24 . . 140 C4
  Sutton in A NG17 . . . . 100 F1
Lansdall Gr DN21 . . . . . 24 C3
Lansdown Cl NG9 . . . . . 183 B4
Lansdowne Ave NG18 . . 102 D2
Lansdowne Dr
  Loughborough LE11 . . 220 A1
  West Bridgford NG2 . . 185 D4
Lansic La NG14 . . . . . . 151 C1
Lansing Cl NG11 . . . . . 195 F8
Lantern La LE12 . . . . . . 205 F2
Lanthwaite Cl NG7 . . . . 184 F1
Lanthwaite Rd NG7 . . . 184 F1
Lapford Cl NG3 . . . . . . 162 D6
Larch Ave
  Mansfield Woodhouse
    NG19 . . . . 88 B5
  Shirebrook NG20 . . . . . 72 D4
Larch Cl
  Bingham NG13 . . . . . . 178 A4
  Hucknall NG15 . . . . . . 146 B5
  Nottingham NG5 . . . . . 161 C8
Larch Cres
  Beeston NG9 . . . . 183 D7
  Eastwood NG16 . . . . . 143 E2
Larch Ct DN21 . . . . 15 C2
Larchdale Cl DE55 . . . . 113 A4
Larch Dr NG10 . . . . 182 B4
Larch Gdns NG6 . . . . . 160 A7
Larch Rd NG22 . . . . 77 D5
Larch Way NG22 . . . . . 198 A2
Largs Cl NG5 . . . . 146 E1
Lark Cl NG9 . . . . 183 A5
Larkdale St NG7 . . . . . . 222 C4
Larkfield Ave NG17 . . . 114 C1
Larkfield Rd NG16 . . . . 159 B6
Larkfields Jun Sch NG16 159 B5
Larkhall Pl NG19 . . . . . 101 E5
Larklands Ave DE7 . . . . 170 A7
Lark Spinney NG17 . . . . 35 C6
Larkspur Ave NG15 . . . 147 E2
Larkspur Cl
  Mansfield NG19 . . . . . . 88 D2
  South Normanton DE55 . 113 A4
Larpit Gn S80 . . . . 45 A5
Larwood S81 . . . . 36 B5
Larwood Cres NG17 . . . 114 F1
Larwood Gr NG5 . . . . . 161 C4
Lascelles Ave NG4 . . . . 162 D2
Latham St NG6 . . . . 160 B7
Lathkill Ave DE7 . . . . . . 157 F5
Lathkill Cl NG6 . . . . 160 A8
Lathkilldale Cres NG10 . 193 A5
Latimer Cl NG6 . . . . . . 160 C6
Latimer Dr NG9 . . . . . . 171 B3
Latimer Way NG22 . . . . 77 C4
Laughton Ave NG2 . . . . 185 C4
Laughton Cres NG15 . . 145 A4
Laughton Rd NG11 . . . . 185 A4
Launceston Cres NG11 . 185 A4
Launder St
  Nottingham NG2 . . . . . 173 C2

Launder St *continued*
Orston NG13 . . . . .179 F7
Launds Ave NG16 . . . . .128 D7
Laurel Ave
Church Warsop NG20 . . . . . .74 A7
Keyworth NG12 . . . . .197 F2
Mansfield NG18 . . . . .102 C5
Mansfield Woodhouse NG19 .89 A1
Misterton DN10 . . . . .6 E3
Laurel Cl
Gainsborough DN21 . . . . . . .15 E2
Shirebrook NG20 . . . . .72 D6
Wysall NG12 . . . . .207 C3
Laurel Cres
Long Eaton NG10 . . . . .193 C6
Nuthall NG16 . . . . .159 B6
Laurel Gr
Kirkby in A NG17 . . . . .115 C5
South Normanton DE55 . . . .113 A4
Laurel Rd NG4 . . . . .174 C8
Laurie Ave NG7 . . . . .173 A8
Laurie Cl ■ NG7 . . . . .173 A8
Lauriston Dr NG6 . . . . .160 D4
Lavender Cl
■ Nottingham NG8 . . . . . .159 E1
Tibshelf DE55 . . . . .99 B7
Lavender Cres NG4 . . . . . . .162 D1
Lavender Gdns DE75 . . . . . .143 B1
Lavender Gr NG9 . . . . .184 B5
Lavender Wlk NG13 . . . . . .173 D7
Lavenham Mews ■ S80 . . . .35 F2
Laver Cl NG5 . . . . .162 B7
Laverick Rd NG16 . . . . .128 A4
Lawdon Rd NG5 . . . . .148 A1
Lawley Ave NG9 . . . . .172 A1
Lawn Ave NG17 . . . . .100 F2
Lawn La
Old Dalby LE14 . . . . .218 E2
Sutton in A NG17 . . . . .100 F2
Lawn Mill Rd NG16 . . . . . .158 E7
Lawn Rd
Carlton in L S81 . . . . .25 E8
Sutton in A NG17 . . . . .101 B3
Lawns Rd NG17 . . . . .129 F8
Lawns The
Collingham NG23 . . . . .98 B1
Whatton NG13 . . . . .179 A3
Lawnwood Ave DN22 . . . . . .50 A3
Lawnwood La DN22 . . . . . . .50 A3
Lawrence Ave
Awsworth NG16 . . . . .158 C4
Carlton NG4 . . . . .174 E5
Eastwood NG16 . . . . .143 F2
Kirkby in A NG17 . . . . .114 E5
Mansfield Woodhouse NG19 .88 B4
Lawrence Cl NG12 . . . . . . .187 F3
Lawrence Cres NG17 . . . . . .101 B4
Lawrence Dr NG16 . . . . . . .143 D8
Lawrence Pk NG16 . . . . . . .129 B3
Lawrence Pl NG24 . . . . . . .125 A1
Lawrence St
Long Eaton NG10 . . . . .193 D8
Newark-on-T NG24 . . . . . . .125 A1
Sandiacre NG10 . . . . .182 B7
Stapleford NG9 . . . . .182 D6
Lawrence Way ■ NG2 . . . . .173 A2
Lawson Ave NG10 . . . . .193 E7
Lawson Cl DN22 . . . . .50 F2
Lawson Sq S81 . . . . .18 B2
Lawson St NG7 . . . . .222 C4
Lawton Dr NG6 . . . . .146 C1
Laxton Ave
Nottingham NG6 . . . . .160 D5
Sutton in A NG17 . . . . .101 C1
Laxton Dr
Hucknall NG15 . . . . .145 E6
Meden Vale NG20 . . . . .74 D8
Laxton Heritage Mus
NG22 . . . . .79 B3
Laxton Rd NG22 . . . . .79 D4
Laxton Visitors Ctr NG22 . . .79 C2
Laycock Ave DN10 . . . . .12 E2
Layton Ave NG18 . . . . .102 A7
Layton Burroughs ■
NG18 . . . . .102 A7
Leabrook Cl NG11 . . . . .184 C3
Leabrook Gdns NG15 . . . . .146 C8
Leabrooks Ave
Mansfield Woodhouse
NG19 . . . . .88 D5
Sutton in A NG17 . . . . .101 C1
Leach Cl NG22 . . . . .54 C1
Leachcroft Hill NG25 . . . . .136 B8
Leach Wy NG21 . . . . .118 B6
Lea Cl NG15 . . . . .117 B2
Leacroft Rd NG18 . . . . .172 D8
Lea Ct S80 . . . . .35 C2
Leadale Ave NG15 . . . . .146 C8
Leadale Cres NG19 . . . . .88 E5
Lead Hill S80 . . . . .35 E2
Leaf Cl NG15 . . . . .131 B1
Leafe Cl NG9 . . . . .183 C2
Leafield DN22 . . . . .39 D8
Leafield Gn NG11 . . . . .184 E2
Leahurst Gdns NG2 . . . . . . .186 B6
Leahurst Rd NG2 . . . . .186 B5
Leake La LE12 . . . . .214 D3
Leake Rd
Costock LE12 . . . . .206 B1
Gotham NG11 . . . . .205 C6
Lea La NG16 . . . . .128 F6
Leam Glen NG19 . . . . .88 D2
Leamington Dr
Beeston NG9 . . . . .183 C4
South Normanton DE55 . . . .113 B5

Leamington Dr *continued*
Sutton in A NG17 . . . . .114 E8
Leamington Hall NG17 . . . .100 E1
Leamington Prim Sch
NG17 . . . . .114 F8
Leander Cl NG11 . . . . .185 B6
Lea Rd
Gainsborough DN21 . . . . . . .24 E5
Market Warsop NG20 . . . . . .74 C3
Ravenshead NG15 . . . . .117 B2
Lea Rd W DN21 . . . . .24 D5
Leas Ave NG19 . . . . .87 A5
Leas Park Jun Sch NG19 . . . .88 C4
Leas Rd NG19 . . . . .88 D4
Leas The NG14 . . . . .164 B5
Leatherlands DE74 . . . . . . .203 D3
Lea Vale DE55 . . . . .113 A4
Leaway The NG20 . . . . .72 D3
Le Brun Sq S81 . . . . .25 E7
Lechlade Rd NG5 . . . . .161 A6
Ledbury Vale NG8 . . . . .172 B8
Leech Ct NG16 . . . . .158 B7
Lee Cres DE7 . . . . .170 A8
Leeds Rd S81 . . . . .34 F7
Leeks Rd NG25 . . . . .121 E1
Lee La DE75 . . . . .143 B1
Leeming Cl NG20 . . . . .74 C5
Leeming La NG19, NG20 . . . .88 C7
Leeming La N NG19 . . . . . . .88 B5
Leeming La S NG19 . . . . . . .88 C2
Leeming Pk NG19 . . . . .88 C3
Leeming St NG18 . . . . .102 B7
Lee Rd
Bestwood Village NG6 . . . . .146 F4
Hucknall NG15 . . . . .146 F4
Leen Ct NG22 . . . . .78 A4
Leen Dr
Hucknall NG15 . . . . .131 B1
Nottingham NG6 . . . . .146 C1
Leen Gate NG7 . . . . .172 E2
Leen Mills La NG15 . . . . . .131 A1
Leen Mills Prim Sch
NG15 . . . . .146 B8
Leen Pl NG7 . . . . .222 A3
Leen Valley Dr NG20 . . . . . .72 E3
Leen Valley Way NG15 . . . .146 C6
Lee Rd
Burton Joyce NG14 . . . . . . .164 A5
Calverton NG14 . . . . .148 D8
Lees Ave NG19 . . . . .101 D7
Lees Barn Rd NG12 . . . . . . .175 D2
Lees Hill St NG2 . . . . .173 E4
Lees La DE55 . . . . .113 A6
Lees Rd NG3 . . . . .162 A2
Leeway Cl NG21 . . . . .103 E2
Leeway Rd
Mansfield NG21 . . . . .103 E2
Southwell NG25 . . . . .121 D1
Legion Dr NG17 . . . . .100 D6
Leicester Cres S81 . . . . .35 E7
Leicester Rd LE11 . . . . .220 C2
Leicester St NG10 . . . . .193 E6
Leigh Cl NG2 . . . . .185 C6
Leigh Rd NG9 . . . . .182 F3
Leighton St NG3 . . . . .173 F6
Leiston Gdns NG5 . . . . .161 A8
Leivers Ave NG5 . . . . .161 F8
Leivers Cl LE12 . . . . .205 E1
Lema Cl NG6 . . . . .160 D7
Lemont Rd NG19 . . . . .89 A2
Lemynton St LE11 . . . . .220 B4
Lendrum Ct NG14 . . . . .163 F4
Lennox St NG1 . . . . .223 F3
Lenton Ave
Nottingham NG7 . . . . .222 C1
Tollerton NG12 . . . . .186 C1
Lenton Bvd NG7 . . . . .222 B2
Lenton Cir NG12 . . . . .186 C1
Lenton Ct NG7 . . . . .222 B2
Lenton Hall Dr NG7 . . . . . .172 C1
Lenton Ind Est E NG7 . . . . .184 F8
Lenton Ind Est W NG7 . . . .184 F8
Lenton Inf Sch NG7 . . . . . .222 A2
Lenton La NG7 . . . . .184 F8
Lenton Manor NG7 . . . . . . .222 A1
Lenton Prim Sch NG7 . . . . .222 B1
Lenton Rd NG7 . . . . .223 D2
Lenton St NG10 . . . . .182 C7
Leonard Ave NG5 . . . . .161 B2
Leonard Cheshire Cl
DE75 . . . . .143 B1
Leonard St NG6 . . . . .160 B5
Leopold St
Long Eaton NG10 . . . . .193 D8
Loughborough LE11 . . . . . . .220 A5
Sutton in A NG17 . . . . .100 E1
Le Page Ct NG8 . . . . .172 A7
Leroy Wallace Ave NG7 . . .222 A4
Lerwick Cl NG11 . . . . .185 A1
Leslie Ave
Beeston NG9 . . . . .183 F5
Kimberley NG16 . . . . .158 F5
■ Nottingham NG7 . . . . . .173 A8
Leslie Gr NG14 . . . . .148 F7
Leslie Rd NG7 . . . . .173 A8
Letchworth Cres NG9 . . . . .183 C4
Letcombe Rd NG11 . . . . . . .184 E3
Letwell Ave S81 . . . . .16 A7
Levellers Way NG24 . . . . . .140 E8
Levels La
Blaxton DN9 . . . . .1 A8
Misson DN10 . . . . .4 B6
Levens Cl NG2 . . . . .186 C5
Leverton Gn NG7 . . . . .184 E2
Leverton Rd
Mansfield NG19 . . . . .101 E7
Retford DN22 . . . . .40 C7
Sturton le S DN22 . . . . .32 D4
Leverton Wlk NG5 . . . . . . .162 A8

Levick Ct ■ NG2 . . . . .173 C2
Lewcote La DE7 . . . . .157 A1
Lewindon Ct NG5 . . . . .161 E4
Lewis Cl NG3 . . . . .223 F4
Lewis St NG3 . . . . .24 D8
Lexington Ct NG22 . . . . .65 F2
Lexington Gdns
Nottingham NG5 . . . . .161 D4
Tuxford NG22 . . . . .65 F2
Leybourne Dr NG5 . . . . . . .160 E6
Ley Croft NG19 . . . . .88 D5
Ley La
East Drayton DN22 . . . . .53 D3
Mansfield Woodhouse
NG19 . . . . .88 D4
Leyland Cl NG9 . . . . .182 F2
Leys La DN10 . . . . .12 E2
Leys Rd NG11 . . . . .196 C6
Ley St NG4 . . . . .175 A7
Leys The
Lowdham NG14 . . . . .150 D2
Normanton-on-t-W NG12 . . .197 F7
Nottingham NG11 . . . . .184 D1
Leyton Ave NG17 . . . . .101 A5
Leyton Cres NG9 . . . . .184 B5
Liber Cl NG18 . . . . .102 F8
Library Rd NG7 . . . . .172 C1
Lichfield Ave NG18 . . . . . . .102 C2
Lichfield Cl
Beeston NG9 . . . . .182 E3
Mansfield NG18 . . . . .102 C2
Worksop S81 . . . . .36 A7
Lichfield La NG18 . . . . .102 D3
Lichfield Rd NG2 . . . . .174 A4
Lichfield Wlk S81 . . . . .25 E7
Liddell Gr NG8 . . . . .171 F4
Liddington St NG7 . . . . . . .160 F1
Lidget La DN22 . . . . .40 A8
Lifton Ave DN22 . . . . .29 E1
Lightfoot Cl NG24 . . . . .140 E8
Lilac Ave NG4 . . . . .174 C8
Lilac Cl
Keyworth NG12 . . . . .198 A2
Newark-on-T NG24 . . . . . . .139 F4
■ Nottingham NG8 . . . . . .159 E1
Lilac Cres NG9 . . . . .184 B5
Lilac Gr
Bawtry DN10 . . . . .9 F7
Beeston NG9 . . . . .184 B5
Carlton in L S81 . . . . .25 E7
Clipstone NG19 . . . . .89 D2
Glapwell S44 . . . . .86 B8
Market Warsop NG20 . . . . . .73 F7
Shirebrook NG20 . . . . .72 E5
South Normanton DE55 . . . .113 A4
Lilac Mews DE7 . . . . .157 D3
Lilac Rd NG15 . . . . .146 B5
Lilburne Cl NG24 . . . . .140 E8
Lillee Ct S81 . . . . .36 B5
Lilleker Rise NG5 . . . . .147 E1
Lilley Cl NG16 . . . . .128 E6
Lillington Rd NG6 . . . . .160 B7
Lily Ave NG4 . . . . .175 A7
Lily Gr NG9 . . . . .184 B5
Limb Cres NG17 . . . . .100 F1
Lime Ave
Firbeck S81 . . . . .16 A6
Huthwaite NG17 . . . . .100 A3
Langley Mill NG16 . . . . . . .143 C2
Loughborough LE11 . . . . . . .220 C3
Sutton in A NG17 . . . . .100 F4
Lime Cl
Nuthall NG16 . . . . .159 A6
Pinxton NG16 . . . . .113 D3
Radcliffe on T NG12 . . . . . .175 F3
Lime Cres NG20 . . . . .73 F7
Lime Gr
Bottesford NG13 . . . . .181 A2
Long Eaton NG10 . . . . .193 D8
Mansfield Woodhouse NG19 .89 C1
Newark-on-T NG24 . . . . . . .139 F7
Retford DN22 . . . . .39 D7
Sandiacre NG10 . . . . .182 B6
South Normanton DE55 . . . .113 A5
Stapleford NG9 . . . . .182 D5
Lime Gr Ave NG9 . . . . .183 E5
Limehurst Ave LE11 . . . . . .220 A5
Limehurst High Sch
LE11 . . . . .220 A5
Limekiln Ct NG6 . . . . .160 A8
Lime Kiln Pl NG18 . . . . . . .102 B6
Lime La NG5 . . . . .147 F4
Limes Ave NG20 . . . . .59 A2
Limes Cres NG20 . . . . .72 D5
Limes Ct NG17 . . . . .101 C1
Lime St
Kirkby in A NG17 . . . . .115 A6
Nottingham NG6 . . . . .160 B7
Sutton in A NG17 . . . . .101 A3
Lime Tree Ave
Carlton in L S81 . . . . .25 E7
Gainsborough DN21 . . . . . . .15 D1
Glapwell S44 . . . . .86 B8
Kirkby in A NG17 . . . . .114 F5
Mansfield Woodhouse NG19 .88 A4
Nottingham NG8 . . . . .160 C3
Retford DN22 . . . . .39 D7
Sutton in A NG17 . . . . .100 D8
Limetree Cl NG12 . . . . .197 F2
Lime Tree Cl
Collingham NG23 . . . . .112 A8
New Ollerton NG22 . . . . . . .77 D5

Lime Tree Cres DN10 . . . . . . .9 F7
Lime Tree Gr NG9 . . . . .172 A1
Lime Tree Dr NG18 . . . . . . .116 E7
Lime Tree Gdns NG14 . . . . .150 E1
Limetree Gr ■ LE11 . . . . . .220 C3
Lime Tree Pl
Mansfield NG18 . . . . .102 C6
Rainworth NG21 . . . . .104 C1
Lime Tree Rd
Elkesley DN22 . . . . .50 B3
Hucknall NG15 . . . . .146 B4
New Ollerton NG22 . . . . . . .77 C5
Limmen Gdns NG3 . . . . . . .173 E6
Limpenny St NG7 . . . . .222 C4
Linby Ave
Hucknall NG15 . . . . .146 B7
Mansfield NG19 . . . . .101 D6
Linby Cl
Carlton NG4 . . . . .162 E2
Nottingham NG5 . . . . .161 D5
Linby Cum Papplewick CE
Prim Sch NG15 . . . . .131 B3
Linby Dr NG8 . . . . .159 D2
Linby Gr NG15 . . . . .146 B7
Linby La NG15 . . . . .131 C3
Linby Rd NG15 . . . . .146 B8
Linby Wlk NG15 . . . . .146 A8
Lincoln Ave NG10 . . . . .182 A4
Lincoln Cir NG7 . . . . .222 C2
Lincoln Cl
Stapleford NG9 . . . . .170 E1
Tibshelf DE55 . . . . .99 A6
Lincoln Coll NG18 . . . . .15 C1
Lincoln Ct
Newark-on-T NG24 . . . . . . .125 B2
Nottingham NG8 . . . . .171 E7
Lincoln Dr NG19 . . . . .88 D4
Lincoln Gr NG12 . . . . .175 F3
Lincoln Rd
East Markham NG22 . . . . . . .66 A7
Fenton LN1 . . . . .55 D6
Newark-on-T NG24 . . . . . . .125 B3
Saxilby LN1 . . . . .57 D3
Tuxford NG22 . . . . .66 A3
Lincoln Rd Bridge NG24 . . .125 A2
Lincoln St
Gainsborough DN21 . . . . . . .15 C1
Newark-on-T NG24 . . . . . . .125 A2
Nottingham NG1 . . . . .223 E2
Nottingham, Old Basford
NG6 . . . . .160 E3
Tibshelf DE55 . . . . .99 A6
Worksop S80 . . . . .36 A1
Lincoln View S80 . . . . .36 A2
Lindale Cl NG2 . . . . .186 C6
Lindbergh Cl S80 . . . . .35 C2
Lindbridge Rd NG8 . . . . . . .159 F2
Lind Cl NG21 . . . . .103 F1
Linden Ave
New Balderton NG24 . . . . . .140 B5
Nottingham NG11 . . . . .184 C1
Tuxford NG22 . . . . .66 A2
Linden Gr
Beeston NG9 . . . . .184 A5
Carlton NG4 . . . . .163 B1
Kirkby in A NG17 . . . . .114 D6
Sandiacre NG10 . . . . .182 A7
Shirebrook NG20 . . . . .72 F4
Stapleford NG9 . . . . .182 E6
Linden Pl NG5 . . . . .162 C6
Linden Rd
Loughborough LE11 . . . . . . .220 A5
Mansfield NG18 . . . . .102 F8
Linden St
Mansfield NG19 . . . . .88 A1
Nottingham NG3 . . . . .173 D7
Shirebrook NG20 . . . . .72 F4
Linden Terr DN21 . . . . .24 D7
Lindfield Cl NG8 . . . . .160 A2
Lindfield Rd NG8 . . . . .159 F2
Lindholme Way NG17 . . . . .100 F5
Lindhurst La NG18 . . . . . . .102 F4
Lindisfarne Gdns ■
NG5 . . . . .147 A1
Lindley's La NG17 . . . . .115 A3
Lindley St
Eastwood NG16 . . . . .144 B4
Mansfield NG18 . . . . .102 A7
Selston NG16 . . . . .128 D6
Lindley Terr ■ NG7 . . . . . .172 E7
Lindrick ■ DN11 . . . . .8 A6
Lindrick Cl
Carlton in L S81 . . . . .25 F7
Mansfield Woodhouse
NG19 . . . . .88 D6
West Bridgford NG2 . . . . . .186 C4
Worksop S81 . . . . .35 F5
Lindrick Ct DN22 . . . . .39 D2
Lindrick La DN11 . . . . .8 A6
Lindrick Rd NG17 . . . . .114 F7
Lindsay Ave
Annesley Woodhouse
NG17 . . . . .115 B1
Newark-on-T NG24 . . . . . . .139 F4
Lindsay Cl NG18 . . . . .102 A6
Lindsay Dr NG18 . . . . .103 A3
Lindsey Rd DN11 . . . . .9 A5
Lindum Gr ■ NG2 . . . . . . .173 F3
Lindum Mews NG24 . . . . . .140 A8
Lindum Rd NG6 . . . . .160 D3
Lindum St ■ NG24 . . . . . . .140 A8
Lindwall Ct S81 . . . . .36 B5
Lindy Cl NG12 . . . . .199 F2
Linecroft La DN10 . . . . .14 C7
Linette Cl NG5 . . . . .161 A2
Linford NG9 . . . . .171 B3
Ling Beeches DN22 . . . . . . .39 D4
Ling Cres NG11 . . . . .196 C8

Lingdale Cl LE11 . . . . .220 B1
Lingfield Cl NG18 . . . . .102 F5
Lingfield Ct NG8 . . . . .171 D3
Lingford NG12 . . . . .188 A3
Lingford St NG15 . . . . .146 B6
Lingforest Cl NG18 . . . . . . .103 A5
Lingforest Ct ■ NG18 . . . . .103 A5
Lingforest Rd NG18 . . . . . .103 A5
Ling Rd NG15 . . . . .146 B6
Lings Bar Hospl NG2 . . . . .186 D6
Lings La NG12 . . . . .207 E2
Lings View NG20 . . . . .74 C3
Lingwood Gr NG18 . . . . . . .103 A7
Lingwood La NG14 . . . . . . .149 B3
Linkin Rd NG9 . . . . .183 C6
Linkmel Cl NG2 . . . . .173 A1
Linkmell Cl NG2 . . . . .186 C6
Linkmel Rd NG16 . . . . .143 C3
Linksfield Ct NG11 . . . . . . .185 C2
Links The NG18 . . . . .103 B6
Linley St NG23 . . . . .113 A8
Linnell St NG3 . . . . .173 F6
Linnets Dr NG18 . . . . .102 F6
Linnets The S81 . . . . .35 D7
Linsdale Cl NG8 . . . . .171 B5
Linsdale Gdns NG4 . . . . . . .162 D4
Lintin Ave NG21 . . . . .75 F2
Linton Cl
Farndon NG24 . . . . .139 B5
Mansfield NG18 . . . . .103 B6
Linton Dr NG22 . . . . .77 F5
Linton Rise NG3 . . . . .174 A6
Linwood Cl DN21 . . . . .24 F7
Linwood Cres
Eastwood NG16 . . . . .144 A1
Ravenshead NG15 . . . . .116 F3
Linwood Ct NG19 . . . . .88 E4
Lion Cl NG8 . . . . .160 C2
Liquorice La NG14 . . . . .26 B4
Lisle St ■ LE11 . . . . .220 A5
Lismore Cl NG7 . . . . .222 A3
Lismore Ct NG19 . . . . .101 D5
Lissington Rd DN21 . . . . . . .24 E7
Lister Ct ■ NG7 . . . . .172 E2
Lister Gate NG1 . . . . .223 E2
Lister Rd NG7 . . . . .172 E2
Listowel Cres NG11 . . . . . . .195 E8
Litchen Cl DE7 . . . . .157 F2
Litchfield Cl NG10 . . . . . . .194 A7
Litchfield Rise NG5 . . . . . . .147 E2
Little Acre NG18 . . . . .88 E5
Little Barn Ct NG18 . . . . . .102 F6
Little Barn Gdns NG18 . . . .102 F6
Little Barn La NG18 . . . . . .102 F6
Little Belt The DN11 . . . . . .33 B3
Little Birch Ave NG18 . . . . .33 B3
Little Breck DE55 . . . . .113 A4
Little Carter La NG18 . . . . .102 E7
Little Debdale La NG19 . . . .87 F1
Little Hallam La DE7 . . . . . .170 A6
Little Hayes NG2 . . . . .185 C4
Little Holland Gd NG16 . . .159 B7
Little Hollies NG5 . . . . .89 A2
Little John Ave NG20 . . . . . .74 C2
Little John Cl NG22 . . . . . . .77 D6
Little John Dr NG21 . . . . . .104 A1
Little John Wlk ■ NG3 . . . .173 D7
Little La
Blyth S81 . . . . .18 B3
Calverton NG14 . . . . .148 D7
Collingham NG23 . . . . .111 F7
Edingley NG22 . . . . .120 D3
Gringley on t H DN10 . . . . . .12 F2
Huthwaite NG17 . . . . .99 E2
Kimberley NG16 . . . . .158 F5
Pleasleyhill NG19 . . . . .87 B5
Shirebrook NG20 . . . . .72 D3
Thorpe Salvin S80 . . . . .34 B6
Tollerton NG12 . . . . .186 E3
Little Lunnon NG11 . . . . . . .194 E6
Little Mdw NG12 . . . . .188 A2
Littlemoor La NG11 . . . . . . .196 E3
Little Moor La LE11 . . . . . .220 C4
Little Oak Ave NG17 . . . . . .130 A7
Little Oak Dr NG17 . . . . . . .115 B1
Little Oakwood Dr NG5 . . .146 D2
Littleover Ave NG18 . . . . . .103 B6
Little Ox NG4 . . . . .174 F4
Little Ricket La NG15 . . . . .116 D3
Little Tennis St S NG2 . . . . .174 A2
Little Tennis St NG2 . . . . . .174 A3
Little Top La DN10 . . . . .20 C1
Little Wlk DN21 . . . . .7 D1
Littlewood Gdns NG8 . . . . .171 C5
Littlewood La NG19 . . . . . . .88 A6
Littleworth NG18 . . . . .102 D7
Litton Ave NG17 . . . . .101 A5
Litton Cl
Arnold NG5 . . . . .161 E4
Ilkeston DE7 . . . . .157 E4
Ravenshead NG15 . . . . .116 F4
Littondale S81 . . . . .36 A1
Litton Rd NG19 . . . . .88 E3
Liverpool St NG3 . . . . .173 E5
Livingstone St NG15 . . . . . .130 E6
Llanberis Gr NG8 . . . . .160 C2
Lloyd St NG5 . . . . .161 C2
Loach Ct NG8 . . . . .172 A5
Lobelia Cl NG3 . . . . .173 D7
Lockerbie St NG4 . . . . .174 F6
Lock La
Long Eaton NG10 . . . . .193 C4
Sandiacre NG10 . . . . .182 C4
Locksley La NG11 . . . . .184 E4
Lockwood Cl
Beeston NG9 . . . . .184 C4
■ Nottingham NG5 . . . . . .147 A1

Lockwood Rd DN22 . . . . . . .39 D3
Lodge Cl
  Arnold NG5 . . . . .147 E2
  Nottingham NG8 . . . . .172 D8
Lodge Farm La NG25 . . . . .147 E1
Lodgefield La NG14 . . . . . .151 E2
Lodge La
  Elston NG23 . . . . .153 C5
  Kirkby in A NG17 . . . . .115 D4
  Screveton NG13 . . . . .166 D5
  Tuxford NG22 . . . . .66 A1
Lodge Rd
  Eastwood NG16 . . . . .158 A8
  Long Eaton NG10 . . . . .193 D5
Lodgewood Cl NG6 . . . . . .160 A6
Lodore Cl NG2 . . . . .186 C6
Lodore Rd S81 . . . . .35 F7
Logan St NG6 . . . . .160 D6
Lois Ave NG7 . . . . .222 B1
Lombard Cl NG7 . . . . .222 B2
Lombard St
  Newark-on-T NG24 . . . . . . .139 E7
  Orston NG13 . . . . .180 A6
Lonan Cl NG19 . . . . .89 A2
London La
  Willoughby-on-t-W LE12 . . .217 D7
  Wymeswold LE12 . . . . .216 B3
London Rd
  Kegworth DE74 . . . . .203 D1
  Newark-on-T NG24 . . . . . . .140 C5
  Nottingham NG2 . . . . .173 D2
  Retford DN22 . . . . .40 A3
Longacre NG5 . . . . .161 F4
Long Acre NG15 . . . . .145 D7
Longbeck Ave NG11 . . . . . .185 A4
Long Brecks La S81 . . . . . . .18 C1
Long Clawson CE Prim Sch
  LE14 . . . . .211 D3
Longcliff Cl LE14 . . . . .218 E4
Longcliff Hill LE14 . . . . . . .218 E4
Longcroft View S80 . . . . . . .45 A6
Longdale NG19 . . . . .88 E1
Longdale Ave NG15 . . . . . .117 A1
Longdale Craft Ctr & Mus
  NG15 . . . . .132 D6
Longdale La
  Calverton NG21 . . . . .133 B5
  Ravenshead NG15 . . . . . . .132 C6
Longdale Rd NG5 . . . . .161 D6
Longden Cl NG9 . . . . .170 F2
Longden St **5** NG3 . . . . .173 E5
Longden Terr
  Market Warsop NG20 . . . . . .74 B4
  Stanton Hill NG17 . . . . . . .100 D6
Long Eaton Sch The
  NG10 . . . . .193 D7
Long Eaton Sta NG10 . . . . .193 C5
Longfellow Dr
  Balderton NG24 . . . . .140 E4
  Worksop S81 . . . . .36 B4
Longfellows Cl NG5 . . . . . .161 B8
Longfield La DE7 . . . . .170 A5
Longford Cres NG6 . . . . . .146 C2
Longford Wlk NG18 . . . . . .103 B6
Longhedge La
  Bottesford NG13 . . . . .180 F3
  Flawborough NG13, NG23 . .168 A2
  Orston NG13 . . . . .180 E7
  Pleasley NG19 . . . . .86 F8
  Sibthorpe NG13 . . . . .167 E5
Longhill Rise NG17 . . . . . . .114 F1
Long Hill Rise NG15 . . . . . .145 F6
Longholme Rd DN22 . . . . . .40 B8
Longhurst S81 . . . . .36 B5
Longhurst View NG25 . . . . .45 A5
Long La
  Barkestone-le-V NG13 . . . . .192 F1
  Barnby in t W NG24 . . . . . .141 F7
  Beeston NG9 . . . . .183 E3
  Carlton in L S81 . . . . .25 F6
  East Drayton DN22 . . . . . . .53 C3
  Farndon NG24 . . . . .139 B5
  Hickling LE14 . . . . .210 C6
  Kegworth DE74 . . . . .203 D5
  Shipley DE75 . . . . .157 D6
  Stathern LE14 . . . . .202 F4
  Watnall NG16 . . . . .145 A1
Longland La NG24 . . . . . . .119 D4
Longlands Cl NG9 . . . . . . .184 B4
Longlands Dr NG2 . . . . . . .186 D5
Longlands Rd NG9 . . . . . . .184 B4
Longleat Cres NG9 . . . . . . .183 C5
Long Mdw
  Farnsfield NG22 . . . . .120 A6
  Mansfield Woodhouse
    NG19 . . . . .88 D3
Long Mdw Hill NG14 . . . . . .150 A2
Long Mdws DN10 . . . . .11 B3
Longmead Cl NG5 . . . . . . .161 C6
Longmead Dr
  Fiskerton NG25 . . . . .137 E3
  Nottingham NG5 . . . . .161 C6
Longmoor Ave NG14 . . . . . .164 E8
Longmoor Gdns NG10 . . . . .182 B2
Longmoor La
  Long Eaton NG10 . . . . .182 A2
  Scarrington NG13 . . . . .179 B8
Longmoor Prim Sch
  NG10 . . . . .182 C3
Longmoor Rd NG10 . . . . . .182 B2
Longmor Wlk NG18 . . . . . .103 B6
Longore Sq NG8 . . . . .172 D4
Longridge Rd NG5 . . . . . . .161 F4
Long Row
  Kingston-on-S LE12 . . . . . .204 A4
  Newark-on-T NG24 . . . . . . .140 B8
  Nottingham NG1 . . . . .223 E2

Long Row W NG1 . . . . .223 E2
Longshaw Rd NG18 . . . . . .103 B6
Longster La NG20 . . . . .73 C3
Longstone Way NG19 . . . . .101 D6
Long Stoop Way NG19 . . . . .103 B7
Longue Dr NG14 . . . . .148 D7
Longwall Ave NG2 . . . . . . .173 A1
Longwest Croft NG14 . . . . .148 C7
Long Whatton CE Prim Sch
  LE12 . . . . .212 C3
Longwood Com Inf Sch
  NG6 . . . . .113 C1
Longwood Ct NG5 . . . . . . .160 F8
Longwood Dr NG17 . . . . . .100 E1
Longwood Rd NG16 . . . . . .113 E2
Lonscale Cl NG2 . . . . .186 C5
Lonsdale Dr NG9 . . . . .182 E1
Lonsdale Rd NG7 . . . . .222 A4
Lord Hadon Rd DE7 . . . . . .157 E1
Lord Nelson St NG2 . . . . . .173 F4
Lordship La NG13 . . . . .180 A6
Lord St
  Gainsborough DN21 . . . . . .24 C8
  Mansfield NG18 . . . . .102 B5
  Nottingham NG2 . . . . .173 E4
Lorimer Ave NG4 . . . . .162 F2
Lorne Cl **8** NG3 . . . . . . .173 E6
Lorne Ct NG12 . . . . .175 F3
Lorne Wlk **6** NG3 . . . . . .173 C7
Lortas Rd NG5 . . . . .160 F2
Loscoe Gdns **2** NG5 . . . .161 B1
Loscoe Mount Rd NG5 . . . .161 C2
Loscoe Rd NG5 . . . . .161 C1
Lothian Rd NG12 . . . . .186 C1
Lotmore Ct **1** NG2 . . . . . .173 B2
Lotus Cl NG3 . . . . .173 E7
Loughan Cl NG5 . . . . .180 A7
Loughborough Ave NG2 . . .173 F4
Loughborough Carillon Twr
  & War Meml LE11 . . . . . . .220 B3
Loughborough CE Prim Sch
  LE11 . . . . .220 A3
Loughborough Gram Sch
  LE11 . . . . .220 B2
Loughborough General Hospl
  LE11 . . . . .220 B4
Loughborough High Sch
  LE11 . . . . .220 B3
Loughborough Rd
  Bradmore NG11 . . . . .196 E5
  Bunny NG11 . . . . .206 E8
  East Leake LE12 . . . . .214 F7
  Hathern LE12 . . . . .213 A1
  Hoton LE12 . . . . .215 C1
  Loughborough LE11 . . . . . .220 D1
  Rempstone LE12 . . . . .215 D5
  West Bridgford NG12 . . . . .185 E5
Loughborough Sta LE11 . . .220 C5
Loughborough Uni **4**
  LE11 . . . . .220 A3
Loughborough Rd
  Bradmore NG11 . . . . .196 E5
Loughrigg Cl **3** NG2 . . . .173 B1
Louis Ave NG9 . . . . .183 E7
Louise Ave NG4 . . . . .175 A8
Lound House Ct NG17 . . . . .100 F5
Lound House Rd NG17 . . . .100 F5
Lound Low Rd DN22 . . . . . .29 D7
Louwil Ave NG19 . . . . .88 E5
Loveden Cl NG24 . . . . .140 D3
Love La DN21 . . . . .15 C2
Lovell Cl NG6 . . . . .159 F5
Lover's La NG24 . . . . .125 A1
Lowater St NG4 . . . . .174 B7
Low Comm DN11 . . . . .8 A4
Lowcroft NG5 . . . . .161 F4
Lowdam Rd NG14 . . . . .150 A5
Lowdham CE Prim Sch
  NG14 . . . . .150 D2
Lowdham La NG14 . . . . . . .149 E4
Lowdham Rd
  Carlton NG4 . . . . .162 C3
  Gunthorpe NG14 . . . . .164 E7
Lowdham St **8** NG3 . . . . .173 E5
Lowdham Sta NG14 . . . . . .164 E8
Lower Bagthorpe NG16 . . . .128 F3
Lower Beauvale NG16 . . . . .144 A1
Lower Bloomsgrove Rd
  DE7 . . . . .157 F2
Lower Brook St NG10 . . . . .193 E7
Lower Cambridge St
  LE11 . . . . .220 B5
Lower Canaan NG11 . . . . . .196 D8
Lower Chapel St **9** DE7 . .157 F1
Lower Clara Mount Rd
  DE75 . . . . .143 A1
Lower Dunstead Rd
  NG16 . . . . .143 A3
Lower Eldon St **12** NG2 . .173 E4
Lower Gladstone St **3**
  LE11 . . . . .220 B5
Lower Granby St **7** DE7 . .157 F2
Lower Kirklington Rd
  NG25 . . . . .121 D2
Lower Maples DE75 . . . . . .157 A7
Lower Middleton St NG7 . . .158 A1
Lower Oakham Way
  NG18 . . . . .101 F3
Lower Orch St NG9 . . . . . . .182 D7
Lower Parliament St
  NG1 . . . . .223 F2
Lower Pasture La DN22 . . . .31 E8
Lower Pk St NG9 . . . . .182 C5
Lower Regent St NG9 . . . . .184 B7
Loweswater Ct NG2 . . . . . .186 C7

Lowes Wong NG25 . . . . . . .136 D8
Lowes Wong Inf & Jun Sch
  NG25 . . . . .121 D1
Lowfield NG22 . . . . .29 D1
Lowfield Cl DN10 . . . . .3 C1
Lowfield La NG24 . . . . .140 C2
Low Field La DN10 . . . . .3 C1
Low Holland La DN22 . . . . .32 E4
Lowlands Dr NG12 . . . . . . .175 E3
Low Moor Rd NG17 . . . . . . .115 B6
Lowmoor Rd Ind Est
  NG17 . . . . .115 A6
Low Pavement NG1 . . . . . . .223 E2
Low Rd
  Besthorpe NG23 . . . . .97 F6
  Scrooby DN10 . . . . .10 A2
  Sutton in A NG17 . . . . .100 F7
Low's La DE7 . . . . .170 B2
Low St
  Beckingham DN10 . . . . .14 C1
  Carlton in L S81 . . . . .26 A5
  Collingham NG23 . . . . .111 F8
  East Drayton DN22 . . . . . . .53 B3
  East Markham NG22 . . . . . .66 A6
  Elston NG23 . . . . .153 D5
  Gringley on t H DN10 . . . . .12 F2
  Harby NG23 . . . . .70 D2
  Sutton in A NG17 . . . . .100 E2
  Torworth DN22 . . . . .19 B2
Lowther Sq S81 . . . . .25 E7
Lowther Way LE11 . . . . . . .220 A5
Lowtown Cl S80 . . . . .36 A2
Lowtown St S80 . . . . .36 A2
Lowtown View S80 . . . . .36 A2
Low Wood La LN6 . . . . .98 F7
Low Wood Rd NG6 . . . . . . .159 F6
Loxley Dr NG18 . . . . .103 A3
Lucerne Cl NG11 . . . . .185 B6
Lucknow Ave NG3 . . . . . . .161 D1
Lucknow Cl NG3 . . . . .173 D8
Lucknow Dr
  Mansfield NG17, NG18 . . . .101 E5
  Nottingham NG3 . . . . .161 D1
  Sutton in A NG17, NG18 . . .101 B3
Lucknow Rd NG3 . . . . .173 D8
Ludborough Wlk NG19 . . . . .88 E4
Ludford Cres DN21 . . . . . . .24 E7
Ludford Rd NG6 . . . . .160 C7
Ludgate Cl NG5 . . . . .147 A2
Ludgate Dr NG13 . . . . .165 D2
Ludham Ave NG6 . . . . .160 B8
Ludlam Ave NG16 . . . . .158 A7
Ludlow Cl NG9 . . . . .171 D1
Ludlow Hill Rd NG2 . . . . . .185 E5
Lulworth Cl NG2 . . . . .185 C5
Lulworth Ct NG16 . . . . .158 F7
Lumley Dr DN11 . . . . .8 B7
Lune Cl NG9 . . . . .183 E3
Lune Mdw NG19 . . . . .88 E3
Lunn La NG23 . . . . .111 F7
Lupin Cl NG3 . . . . .173 D7
Luther Ave NG17 . . . . .100 E2
Luther Cl NG3 . . . . .173 E7
Luton Cl NG8 . . . . .160 D1
Lutterell Cl NG2 . . . . .185 D5
Lutterell Way NG2 . . . . . . .186 C5
Lydia Gdns NG16 . . . . .143 E1
Lydney Pk NG2 . . . . .185 C5
Lyle Cl NG16 . . . . .158 B8
Lyme Pk NG2 . . . . .185 B5
Lymington Gdns NG3 . . . . .174 B6
Lymington Rd NG19 . . . . . .101 D6
Lymn Ave NG4 . . . . .162 F2
Lyncombe Ct DN22 . . . . . . .39 D4
Lyncombe Gdns NG12 . . . .197 F3
Lyndale Rd NG9 . . . . .183 A8
Lyndhurst Ave NG21 . . . . . .76 A1
Lynden Ave NG10 . . . . .193 E5
Lyndhurst Ave NG18 . . . . . .118 B5
Lyndhurst Gdns NG2 . . . . .185 D6
Lyndhurst Rd NG2 . . . . . . .173 F4
Lynds Cl NG21 . . . . .76 B2
Lynmouth Cres NG7 . . . . . .172 E7
Lynmouth Dr DE7 . . . . .157 D3
Lynncroft NG16 . . . . .144 A3
Lynncroft Prim Sch
  NG16 . . . . .144 A3
Lynnes Cl NG21 . . . . .118 A4
Lynstead Dr NG15 . . . . . . .145 C5
Lynton Gdns NG5 . . . . .162 A8
Lynton Rd NG9 . . . . .183 C6
Lyons Cl NG11 . . . . .196 B8
Lytham Dr NG12 . . . . .186 B3
Lytham Gdns NG5 . . . . . . .147 A1
Lytham Rd NG17 . . . . .114 E7
Lythe Cl NG11 . . . . .185 A5
Lytton Cl NG3 . . . . .173 E5

M

Mabel Ave NG17 . . . . .101 A1
Mabel Gr NG2 . . . . .186 A8
Mabel St NG2 . . . . .173 D2
Mable St S80 . . . . .35 A4
McArthur Glen Designer
  Outlet NG16 . . . . .113 E6
MacAulay Cl
  Balderton NG24 . . . . .140 D5
  Worksop S81 . . . . .36 B4
MacAulay Dr NG24 . . . . . . .140 D5
MacAulay Gr NG16 . . . . . . .159 B6
McClelland Av NG6 . . . . . .147 B5
Machin St S81 . . . . .35 C7
Machins La NG12 . . . . .186 A3

McIntosh Rd NG4 . . . . .162 D3
Mackinley Ave NG9 . . . . . .170 E1
Mackleys La NG23 . . . . . . .110 F2
Mackworth Ct NG18 . . . . . .103 B5
MacLaren Gdns NG11 . . . . .196 D5
Maclean Rd NG4 . . . . .174 C7
Macmillan Cl NG3 . . . . . . .161 F2
McPhail Cres NG8 . . . . . . .171 E8
Madison Dr DN10 . . . . .9 F6
Madryn Wlk **6** NG5 . . . . .161 A7
Mafeking St NG2 . . . . .174 A4
Magdala Rd NG3 . . . . .173 C8
Magdalen Dr NG13 . . . . . . .165 D3
Magdalene View NG4 . . . . .140 B8
Magdalene Way NG15 . . . . .146 A7
Mag La NG20 . . . . .58 D5
Magna Cl NG14 . . . . .150 E1
Magnolia Cl **3** NG8 . . . . .159 E1
Magnolia Ct NG9 . . . . .171 E4
Magnolia Gr NG15 . . . . . . .146 B4
Magnums Com Sports Ctr
  NG24 . . . . .140 A6
Magnus CE Sch NG24 . . . . .140 A6
Magnus Rd NG5 . . . . .161 C3
Magnus St NG24 . . . . .140 A8
Magpie Cl S81 . . . . .35 C7
Magpie La DN22 . . . . .42 B2
Magson St NG3 . . . . .173 E5
Maida La NG22 . . . . .77 B4
Maiden La NG1 . . . . .223 F2
Maidens Dale NG5 . . . . . . .146 F8
Maid Marian Ave NG16 . . . .129 B6
Maid Marian Way NG1 . . . . .223 E2
Maid Marion Rd NG22 . . . .106 A4
Maid Marrion Dr NG21 . . . . .76 C2
Maidstone Dr NG8 . . . . . . .171 D2
Main Ave NG19 . . . . .103 A8
Main La NG12 . . . . .164 C1
Main Rd
  Annesley Woodhouse
    NG17 . . . . .114 C1
  Barnstone NG13 . . . . .190 E3
  Beeston NG9 . . . . .184 C5
  Boughton NG22 . . . . .77 E3
  Carlton NG4 . . . . .163 A1
  Cotgrave NG12 . . . . .187 E4
  Kelham NG23 . . . . .124 A4
  Nether Langwith NG20 . . . . .59 A1
  Nottingham NG11 . . . . .185 B7
  Old Dalby LE14 . . . . .218 E4
  Plumtree NG12 . . . . .197 E2
  Pye Bridge DE55 . . . . .128 A6
  Radcliffe on T NG12 . . . . . .175 E3
  Radcliffe on T, Shelford
    NG12 . . . . .176 C8
  Ravenshead NG15 . . . . . . .117 B3
  Selston NG16 . . . . .128 F2
  Upton NG23 . . . . .122 C2
  Watnall NG16 . . . . .159 A7
  Westwood NG16 . . . . .128 B3
Mainside Cres NG16 . . . . . .129 A1
Main St
  Annesley Woodhouse
    NG17 . . . . .129 F8
  Aslockton NG13 . . . . .179 A5
  Awsworth NG16 . . . . .158 C5
  Balderton NG24 . . . . .140 E4
  Bathley NG23 . . . . .110 B3
  Bleasby NG14 . . . . .152 B7
  Blidworth NG21 . . . . .117 F4
  Bothamsall DN22 . . . . .63 E7
  Bradmore NG11 . . . . .196 E5
  Brinsley NG16 . . . . .128 D1
  Bunny NG11 . . . . .206 E8
  Burton Joyce NG14 . . . . . .163 F4
  Calverton NG14 . . . . .148 F7
  Carlton-on-Trent NG23 . . . .96 F4
  Clarborough DN22 . . . . . . .30 F8
  Claypole NG23 . . . . .156 C6
  Coddington NG24 . . . . . . .126 B2
  Costock LE12 . . . . .206 C1
  Cromwell NG23 . . . . .110 F8
  Cropwell Butler NG12 . . . .189 A7
  Doddington LN6 . . . . .71 C1
  Dry Doddington NG23 . . . .156 F2
  Eakring NG22 . . . . .92 E1
  East Bridgford NG13 . . . . .165 C2
  East Leake LE12 . . . . .205 E1
  Eastwood, Beauvale NG16 . .144 C2
  Eastwood NG16 . . . . .143 F1
  Edingley NG22 . . . . .120 C4
  Egmanton NG22 . . . . .79 F6
  Farndon NG24 . . . . .139 A4
  Farnsfield NG22 . . . . .119 F6
  Fenton NG23 . . . . .142 D2
  Fiskerton NG25 . . . . .137 F3
  Flintham NG23 . . . . .167 A8
  Granby NG13 . . . . .191 B5
  Gunthorpe NG14 . . . . .165 A5
  Harby LE14 . . . . .202 A3
  Harworth DN11 . . . . .8 F4
  Hickling LE14 . . . . .210 C6
  Hoveringham NG14 . . . . . .151 D2
  Huthwaite NG17 . . . . .99 F3
  Keyworth NG12 . . . . .197 E2
  Kimberley NG16 . . . . .158 F6
  Kinoulton NG12 . . . . .199 D2
  Kirton NG22 . . . . .78 B6
  Lambley NG4 . . . . .163 C7
  Laneham DN22 . . . . .54 A5
  Langar NG13 . . . . .190 C2
  Laxton NG22 . . . . .79 C3
  Linby NG15 . . . . .131 B3
  Long Eaton NG10 . . . . . . .193 E7
  Long Whatton LE12 . . . . . .212 B3

Main St continued
  Lowdham NG14 . . . . .150 D2
  Mattersey DN10 . . . . .20 B7
  Morton NG25 . . . . .137 D3
  Newton DE55 . . . . .99 A4
  Normanton on S LE12 . . . . .213 D3
  North Leverton w H DN22 . . .32 D1
  North Muskham NG23 . . . .110 F2
  Nottingham NG6 . . . . .160 C7
  Ollerton NG22 . . . . .77 A3
  Ossington NG23 . . . . .95 D6
  Oxton NG25 . . . . .134 B3
  Papplewick NG15 . . . . .131 C5
  Redmile NG13 . . . . .192 F3
  Scarrington NG13 . . . . . . .178 A8
  Shirebrook NG20 . . . . .72 E3
  Sibthorpe NG23 . . . . .167 E8
  South Muskham NG23 . . . .124 D7
  South Normanton DE55 . . . .113 B6
  Stanford on S LE12 . . . . . .214 C1
  Strelley NG16 . . . . .159 A1
  Sutton Bonington LE12 . . . .213 B4
  Sutton on T NG23 . . . . . . .96 F7
  Torksey LN1 . . . . .44 B2
  Upper Broughton LE14 . . . .210 A1
  Welby NG22 . . . . .64 A2
  West Bridgford NG12 . . . . .186 C2
  West Leake LE12 . . . . .204 F1
  Weston NG23 . . . . .81 A4
  West Stockwith DN10 . . . . . .7 E2
  Whaley Thorns S44 . . . . . . .59 A2
  Whatton NG13 . . . . .179 B3
  Willoughby-on-t-W LE12 . . .217 D7
  Woodborough NG14 . . . . . .149 C4
  Worksop S80 . . . . .35 E2
  Zouch LE12 . . . . .213 B3
Maitland Ave NG5 . . . . . . .161 F4
Maitland Rd NG5 . . . . .161 F4
Majestic Theatre DN22 . . . . .39 E7
Major St NG1 . . . . .223 E3
Making It! NG18 . . . . .102 C6
Malbon Cl NG3 . . . . .173 F8
Malcolm Cl NG3 . . . . .173 C7
Maldon Cl NG9 . . . . .183 B4
Malham Cl DN10 . . . . .9 F8
Malin Cl NG5 . . . . .162 B8
Malin Hill NG1 . . . . .223 F2
Malkin Ave NG12 . . . . .176 A4
Mallam Rd NG22 . . . . .77 D6
Mallard Cl
  Bingham NG13 . . . . .178 A3
  Nottingham NG6 . . . . .160 F4
  Shirebrook NG20 . . . . .72 D3
Mallard Ct NG9 . . . . .184 A5
Mallard Gn NG24 . . . . .140 C5
Mallard Rd NG4 . . . . .175 B6
Mallards The S81 . . . . .35 C7
Mallatratt Pl NG19 . . . . . . .88 B4
Mallow Way NG13 . . . . . . .177 C4
Malmesbury Rd NG3 . . . . .162 A4
Malpas Ave DN21 . . . . .15 C1
Maltby Cl NG8 . . . . .160 B2
Maltby Rd
  Mansfield NG18 . . . . .102 C6
  Nottingham NG3 . . . . .162 A4
  Oldcotes S81 . . . . .16 E6
Malt Cotts NG7 . . . . .160 F1
Malthouse Cl NG16 . . . . . .143 F1
Malthouse Rd
  Ilkeston DE7 . . . . .170 A4
  Whitwell S80 . . . . .45 A6
Malting Cl NG11 . . . . .196 C6
Maltings The
  Blyth S81 . . . . .18 B3
  Cropwell Bishop NG12 . . . .189 A4
Maltkiln Cl NG22 . . . . .77 C2
Maltkiln La NG24 . . . . .125 A2
Maltkiln Rd LN1 . . . . .56 D6
Maltkins The DN22 . . . . . . .42 C8
Maltmill La NG1 . . . . .223 E2
Malton Rd NG5 . . . . .160 F2
Malt St NG11 . . . . .195 B1
Maltsters The NG14 . . . . . .139 C6
Malvern Cl NG3 . . . . .161 E1
Malvern Cres NG2 . . . . . . .185 F5
Malvern Rd
  Nottingham NG3 . . . . .161 E1
  West Bridgford NG2 . . . . . .185 E5
Manby St DN20 . . . . .74 D8
Mandalay St NG6 . . . . .160 D4
Mandeen Gr NG18 . . . . . . .103 A4
Manesty Cres NG11 . . . . . .195 C7
Mangham La DN11 . . . . .9 D4
Manham Hill NG23 . . . . . . .111 F8
Manifold Dr NG16 . . . . . . .129 A7
Manifold Gdns DE7 . . . . . .157 E3
Manitoba Way NG16 . . . . . .128 F7
Manly Cl NG5 . . . . .160 F8
Manners Ave DE7 . . . . .157 D1
Manners Ind Est DE7 . . . . .157 F2
Manners Rd
  Balderton NG24 . . . . .140 D3
  Ilkeston DE7 . . . . .157 E1
  Newark-on-T NG24 . . . . . . .124 E1
  Nottingham NG5 . . . . .147 A6
Manners Sutton Prim Sch
  NG23 . . . . .123 F2
Manning Comp Sch NG8 . . .172 B8
Manning St **5** NG3 . . . . .173 D7
Manning View DE7 . . . . . . .157 E1
Mannion Cres NG10 . . . . . .193 B5
Manns Leys NG12 . . . . . . .187 E2
Mann St **5** NG7 . . . . . . .172 F8

Manor Ave
Beeston NG9 . . . .**183** F5
17 Nottingham NG2. . . . .**173** E4
Stapleford NG9 . . . .**182** D8
Manor Cl
Bleasby NG14 . . . .**152** A8
Boughton NG22 . . . .**77** F6
Costock LE12 . . . .**206** C1
Eagle LN6 . . . .**84** D3
Gamston DN22 . . . .**50** F5
Long Whatton LE12 . . . .**212** B3
Misson DN10 . . . .**4** C3
Newton DE55. . . . .**99** A3
Oxton NG25 . . . .**134** B3
Southwell NG25 . . . .**121** E1
Walesby NG22 . . . .**64** A2
West Bridgford NG12 . . . . . .**186** B3
Worksop S80 . . . .**35** C2
Manor Cres
Carlton NG4 . . . .**174** E8
Kirkby in A NG17 . . . .**115** B3
Manor Croft NG6 . . . .**160** E3
Manor Ct
Beeston NG9 . . . .**183** B7
Carlton NG4 . . . .**174** F7
Church Warsop NG20 . . . .**74** C6
Wymeswold LE12 . . . .**216** D4
Manor Dr NG25 . . . .**137** D3
Manor Farm Animal Ctr &
Donkey Sanctuary
LE12 . . . .**214** F8
Manor Farm Cl
Bradmore NG11. . . . .**196** E3
Rolleston NG23 . . . .**138** A6
Manor Farm La NG7 . . . . . .**184** E2
Manor Farm Mdw LE12 . . .**205** E1
Manor Farm Rise DN22 . . . .**32** C1
Manor Gn Wlk NG4 . . . .**174** F8
Manor Gr S80 . . . .**35** C2
Manor House Cl NG14 . . . . .**150** D2
Manor House Ct NG17 . . . . .**114** C4
Manor House Dr
North Muskham NG23. . . . . .**110** F3
Wysall NG12 . . . .**207** C3
Manor House La NG23 . . . . .**156** D2
Manor House Rd NG10. . . . .**193** F6
Manor La
Broadholme LN6 . . . .**71** A8
Shelford NG12 . . . .**164** C2
Whatton NG13 . . . .**179** A1
Manor Pk NG11. . . . .**196** C7
Manor Rd
Barton in F NG11. . . . .**194** E6
Bingham NG13 . . . .**177** F4
Bottesford NG13 . . . .**181** C2
Calverton NG14 . . . .**148** E7
Carlton NG4 . . . .**174** F8
Caunton NG23 . . . .**109** A4
Church Warsop NG20 . . . .**74** C6
Collingham NG23. . . . .**112** A8
East Leake LE12 . . . .**205** F3
Eastwood NG16 . . . .**143** F1
Ilkeston DE7 . . . .**157** E1
Keyworth NG12 . . . .**197** E3
Mansfield Woodhouse NG19 . **88** A4
Morton DN21 . . . .**15** B4
Saxilby LN1 . . . .**57** A4
Scrooby DN10 . . . .**10** A2
Sutton in A NG17 . . . .**100** E7
Manor Rise NG13 . . . .**165** C4
Manor Sch The NG19. . . . . . .**88** C5
Manor St
Nottingham NG2 . . . .**173** E4
Sutton in A NG17 . . . .**100** E2
Manorwood Rd NG12 . . . . .**187** F2
Manse Ave S80 . . . .**58** D8
Manse Cl S80 . . . .**58** D8
Mansell Cl NG16 . . . .**144** B1
Mansey Common Nature
Reserve NG22 . . . .**107** A6
Mansfield Bsns Ctr NG18 . . .**88** B1
Mansfield Com Hospl
NG18 . . . .**102** A6
Mansfield Ct **7** NG5 . . . . . .**173** B8
Mansfield Gr NG1 . . . .**223** D4
Mansfield La
Calverton NG14 . . . .**148** F7
Sutton in A NG17 . . . .**101** A7
Mansfield L Ctr NG18 . . . . . .**102** A8
Mansfield L Pk NG18 . . . . . .**102** B5
Mansfield Mus NG18 . . . .**102** C7
Mansfield Prep Sch The
NG19 . . . .**88** C3
Mansfield Rd
Annesley NG17 . . . .**130** A6
Arnold NG5, NG15 . . . .**147** D6
Babworth DN22 . . . .**38** D3
Blidworth NG21 . . . .**118** A5
Brinsley NG16 . . . .**143** F4
Clipstone NG21 . . . .**90** B5
Cuckney NG20 . . . .**60** B3
Dalesworth NG17 . . . .**101** D4
Edingley NG22 . . . .**120** C5
Edwinstowe NG21 . . . .**75** E2
Farnsfield NG22 . . . .**119** C7
Glapwell S44 . . . .**86** D8
Heanor DE75 . . . .**143** A2
Mansfield Woodhouse NG18 . **88** C2
Market Warsop NG20 . . . .**73** F1
Nottingham NG5 . . . .**161** D4
Ollerton NG22 . . . .**76** F3
Ravenshead NG15 . . . .**116** F1
Selston, Friezeland NG16 . . .**129** C4
Selston NG16 . . . .**128** F7

Mansfield Rd *continued*
South Normanton DE55 . . . . .**113** D6
Sutton in A, Skegby NG17 . . .**100** C6
Sutton in A, Sutton Forest Side
NG17. . . . .**101** B4
Tibshelf DE55 . . . .**99** B7
Worksop S80 . . . .**46** A8
Mansfield St NG5 . . . .**161** C2
Mansfield Town Sta
NG18 . . . .**102** B6
Mansfield Woodhouse Sta
NG19 . . . .**88** B3
Manston Way S81 . . . .**35** C8
Manthorpe Cres NG5. . . . . .**161** F3
Manthorpe House NG24 . . .**140** E4
Manthorpe Way NG24 . . . . .**140** E4
Manton CI NG21 . . . .**118** B8
Manton Cres
Beeston NG9 . . . .**184** A8
Worksop S80 . . . .**36** B1
Manton Dale S80 . . . .**36** B1
Manton Villas S80. . . . .**36** C1
Manton Wood Enterprise
Zone S81 . . . .**36** F1
Manvers Cres NG21 . . . .**75** F2
Manvers Ct
Market Warsop NG20 . . . .**74** A4
9 Nottingham NG2. . . . .**173** E4
Manvers Gr NG12 . . . .**175** F3
Manvers Rd
Retford DN22 . . . .**39** D5
West Bridgford NG2 . . . .**185** F6
Manvers St
Carlton NG4 . . . .**175** A6
Mansfield NG18 . . . .**102** A7
Mansfield Woodhouse NG19 . **88** A3
Market Warsop NG20 . . . .**74** B3
Nottingham NG2 . . . .**173** E4
Shirebrook NG20 . . . .**73** A4
Worksop S80 . . . .**35** E3
Manvers View NG22 . . . .**77** E6
Manville Ct
Beeston NG9 . . . .**171** B3
Nottingham NG8 . . . .**172** C6
Maori Ave NG15 . . . .**145** D5
Maple Ave
Beeston NG9 . . . .**184** B5
Sandiacre NG10 . . . .**182** B7
Maplebeck Ave NG20 . . . .**74** D8
Maplebeck Rd
Arnold NG5 . . . .**162** A7
Caunton NG23 . . . .**108** E6
Maple Cl
East Leake LE12 . . . .**214** D8
Gainsborough DN21 . . . .**15** B3
Keyworth NG12 . . . .**198** A2
Mansfield NG18 . . . .**88** E1
Radcliffe on T NG12 . . . .**175** F2
Tuxford NG22 . . . .**66** A2
Maple Cres NG17 . . . .**114** F6
Maple Ct **4** DE75 . . . .**143** F1
Mapledene Cres NG8 . . . . .**171** C3
Maple Dr
Carlton NG4 . . . .**163** B2
Elkesley DN22 . . . .**50** B3
Hucknall NG15 . . . .**145** E5
Nuthall NG16 . . . .**159** C6
Ravenshead NG18 . . . .**116** D7
South Normanton DE55 . . . . .**113** B6
Worksop S81 . . . .**36** A7
Maple Gr
Bawtry DN10 . . . .**9** F7
Gainsborough DN21 . . . .**86** B8
Newark-on-T NG24 . . . .**139** F4
Maples St **18** NG7 . . . .**172** F6
Maplestead Ave NG11. . . . .**185** B6
Mapletoft Ave NG19. . . . .**88** A5
Mapleton Way NG17 . . . . . .**101** A4
Mapletree Cl NG5. . . . .**161** B7
Maple Wy NG16. . . . .**128** F7
Mapperley Cres NG3 . . . . . .**161** E2
Mapperley Hall Dr NG3 . . .**161** D2
Mapperley Orch NG5. . . . . .**162** C7
Mapperley Pk Dr **1** NG3 .**173** C8
Mapperley Plains NG3 . . . .**162** C6
Mapperley Plains Prim Sch
NG3 . . . .**162** B3
Mapperley Rd NG3. . . . .**173** C7
Mapperley Rise NG3 . . . . . .**161** E2
Mapperley St NG5 . . . .**161** C2
Mappleton Dr NG18 . . . .**103** B5
Mapplewells Cres NG17 . . .**100** B1
Mapplewells Prim Sch
NG17. . . . .**100** B1
Mapplewells Rd NG17. . . . . .**100** C1
March Cl NG5 . . . .**160** F2
Marches Cl NG15 . . . .**145** E4
Marchwood Cl NG8 . . . .**172** D5
Mardale Cl NG2 . . . .**186** C6
Mardling Av NG5 . . . .**161** A5
Margaret Ave
Long Eaton NG10 . . . .**182** F1
Sandiacre NG10. . . . .**182** B4
Margaret Cres NG4 . . . .**162** E2
Margaret Pl NG13 . . . .**177** D5
Margaret's Ct NG9 . . . .**183** A8
Marham Ct NG2 . . . .**173** E3
Marhill Rd NG4 . . . .**174** F7
Marie Gdns NG15 . . . .**146** A5
Marina Ave NG9 . . . .**183** F5
Mariner Ct NG6 . . . .**160** A6
Marion Ave
Hucknall NG15 . . . .**131** C1
Kirkby in A NG17 . . . .**115** B3
Marion Murdoch Ct NG4 .**162** E2
Maris Cl NG11 . . . .**184** C2
Maris Dr NG14. . . . .**163** E3
Marjorie St S80. . . . .**35** A4

Market Cl
Shirebrook NG20. . . . .**72** F3
South Normanton DE55 . . . . .**113** A6
Market House Pl **12**
NG18 . . . .**102** B7
Market Pl
Bingham NG13 . . . .**177** E4
Gainsborough DN21 . . . .**24** C8
Hucknall NG15 . . . .**146** A7
Kegworth DE74 . . . .**203** D2
Long Eaton NG10 . . . .**193** E8
Loughborough LE11 . . . .**220** B4
9 Mansfield NG18 . . . .**102** B7
Mansfield Woodhouse NG19 . **88** C3
Nottingham NG6 . . . .**160** B7
Ollerton NG22 . . . .**77** A3
Retford DN22 . . . .**39** F7
South Normanton DE55 . . . . .**113** A6
Southwell NG25 . . . .**136** E8
Stanton Hill NG17 . . . .**100** E2
Tickhill DN11 . . . .**8** A7
Tuxford NG22 . . . .**65** F3
Worksop S80 . . . .**35** F2
Market Pl The NG5. . . . .**161** F7
Market Side **9** NG6. . . . . . .**160** B7
Market St
Bingham NG13 . . . .**177** E4
Bottesford NG13 . . . .**181** B2
Gainsborough DN21 . . . .**24** D8
Huthwaite NG17 . . . .**99** F3
Loughborough LE11 . . . .**220** A4
15 Mansfield NG18 . . . .**102** B7
Nottingham NG1 . . . .**223** E2
Shirebrook NG20 . . . .**72** F4
South Normanton DE55 . . . . .**113** A5
Sutton in A NG17 . . . .**35** F3
Worksop S80 . . . .**35** E3
Markham Ave NG24 . . . .**125** B3
Markham Cl NG22 . . . .**77** B4
Markham Cres NG5 . . . .**161** C4
Markham Pl NG19 . . . .**101** D7
Markham Rd
Beeston NG9 . . . .**171** D1
Langold S81 . . . .**16** E3
Tuxford NG22 . . . .**65** F3
Markham St NG15 . . . .**130** D6
Markhams The NG22 . . . .**77** B4
Mark La NG20 . . . .**58** A8
Marklew Cl NG21 . . . .**118** A5
Mark St NG10 . . . .**182** C5
Markwick Cl NG24 . . . .**140** D8
Marlborough Cl
Newark-on-T NG24 . . . .**139** D5
Worksop S81 . . . .**35** D8
Marlborough Ct NG24. . . . .**139** D6
Marlborough Rd
Arnold NG5 . . . .**161** E4
Beeston NG9 . . . .**183** F7
Kirkby in A NG17 . . . .**115** B5
Long Eaton NG10 . . . .**182** F1
Mansfield NG19 . . . .**87** F1
Marlborough St
Gainsborough DN21 . . . .**24** D7
2 Nottingham NG7. . . . .**172** E1
Marldon Cl NG8 . . . .**171** C5
Marle Pit Hill LE12 . . . .**213** A8
Marlock Cl NG25. . . . .**137** E3
Marlow Ave NG6 . . . .**160** E2
Marlowe Dr NG24 . . . .**140** D4
Marlowe Gdns S81. . . . .**36** B4
Marlow Rd DN21. . . . .**15** E2
Marl Rd NG12 . . . .**176** B3
Marmion Rd NG3 . . . .**174** A6
Marnham Dr NG3 . . . .**161** E1
Marnham Rd NG22 . . . .**66** D2
Marples Ave NG19 . . . .**88** E5
Marple Sq NG3 . . . .**173** C7
Marquis Ave NG24 . . . .**140** D3
Marquis Gdns DN22. . . . .**40** A4
Marquis Rd LE14 . . . .**219** B6
Marriots La NG21 . . . .**117** F4
Marriott Ave
Beeston NG9 . . . .**183** A5
Mansfield NG18 . . . .**101** F7
Marriott Cl NG18 . . . .**101** F7
Marrison Way NG25 . . . .**121** F1
Marsant Cl **1** NG8 . . . .**172** C5
Marshall Ave NG17 . . . .**115** C4
Marshall Ct NG24 . . . .**140** E4
Marshall Dr NG9. . . . .**183** A8
Marshall Farm Cl NG13 . . .**192** B2
Marshall Hill Dr NG3. . . . . .**162** B2
Marshall Rd
Cropwell Bishop NG12 . . . . . .**189** A4
Nottingham NG3 . . . .**162** A1
Marshall St
Heanor DE75 . . . .**143** A2
Nottingham NG5 . . . .**161** C2
Marshall Terr NG17 . . . .**100** D6
Marsh La
Farndon NG24 . . . .**139** A5
Laughterton LN1 . . . .**55** A4
Misterton DN10 . . . .**7** B1
North Leverton w H DN22 . . . .**33** D1
North Muskham NG23 . . . . . .**110** F2
Saundby DN22. . . . .**23** D5
Marsh Rd DN22 . . . .**32** D4
Marston Ave NG20 . . . .**74** D8
Marston Cl NG24 . . . .**140** E4
Marston Moor Rd NG24 . . .**140** E8
Marston Rd NG3 . . . .**174** B7
Martin Cl NG6 . . . .**160** A8
Martin Ct NG6 . . . .**160** A8

Martindale Cl NG2 . . . .**186** C7
Martin La DN10. . . . .**9** F8
Martinmass Cl NG7 . . . .**222** A1
Martins Hill NG4. . . . .**174** E7
Martin's Pond Nature
Reserve NG8. . . . .**171** E5
Martlet Way S80 . . . .**47** A8
Marton Rd
Beeston NG9 . . . .**183** C3
Newark-on-T NG24 . . . .**140** C1
Nottingham NG6 . . . .**146** C1
Martyn Ave NG17 . . . .**100** F1
Marvin Rd NG9 . . . .**183** F6
Marwood Cres NG4 . . . .**162** C2
Marwood Rd NG4 . . . .**162** C2
Maryfield Cl DN22 . . . .**29** E1
Maryland Ct NG9 . . . .**170** E1
Mary Rd NG16 . . . .**144** B1
Marys Cl LE12 . . . .**216** C3
Mary St
Kirkby in A NG17 . . . .**115** B6
Rhodesia S80. . . . .**35** B4
Whaley Thorns NG20 . . . .**59** A2
Masefield Cres NG24 . . . . . .**140** D4
Masefield Pl S81 . . . .**36** B4
Masonic Pl NG1 . . . .**223** D3
Mason Rd DE7 . . . .**157** D2
Mason St NG17 . . . .**101** B4
Massey Cl NG14 . . . .**163** E3
Massey Gdns **1** NG3. . . . . .**173** E6
Massey St NG24 . . . .**140** B8
Masson Ct **7** NG5 . . . .**147** A1
Mather Rd NG24 . . . .**124** F1
Matlock Ave NG18 . . . .**102** A5
Matlock Ct NG1. . . . .**223** C3
Matlock St NG4 . . . .**174** F7
Mattersey Ct NG19. . . . .**88** B1
Mattersey Prim Sch DN10 . .**20** A7
Mattersey Rd
Everton DN10 . . . .**11** C1
Lound DN22 . . . .**20** B2
Ranskill DN22 . . . .**19** D6
Matthew Holland Sch The
NG16 . . . .**128** F7
Mattingley Rd NG5 . . . .**170** F2
Mattingly Rd NG6. . . . .**160** A5
Mattley Ave NG17 . . . .**115** A1
Maud St NG7 . . . .**161** A1
Maun Ave
Kirkby in A NG17 . . . .**115** B7
Nottingham NG7 . . . .**172** D6
Maun Cl
Mansfield NG18 . . . .**101** F4
Retford DN22. . . . .**39** F5
Maun Cres NG22 . . . .**77** C5
Maundale Ave NG17 . . . .**101** B4
Maun Gn NG24 . . . .**125** B2
Maun Inf Sch NG22 . . . .**77** B5
Maunleigh NG19 . . . .**88** E1
Maunside NG18 . . . .**101** F4
Maunside Ave NG17 . . . .**101** B1
Maun Valley Ind Pk
NG17. . . . .**101** C2
Maun Way
Mansfield NG18 . . . .**101** F4
Wellow NG22 . . . .**78** A4
Maurice Dr NG3 . . . .**161** E2
Mavis Ave NG15 . . . .**117** A2
Mawkin La NG16. . . . .**113** F5
Maws La NG16 . . . .**158** C7
Maxtoke Rd NG2 . . . .**222** C1
Maxwell Cl NG7 . . . .**222** B1
May Ave NG8 . . . .**171** E4
Maycroft Gdns NG3 . . . .**174** A7
May Ct **6** NG5. . . . .**161** B1
Maydene Cl NG11 . . . .**184** D1
Mayes Rise NG6 . . . .**146** E4
Mayfair NG12 . . . .**176** D3
Mayfair Ave NG18. . . . .**102** D5
Mayfair Cl DN11 . . . .**8** F4
Mayfair Ct NG7 . . . .**172** E8
Mayfair Gdns NG5 . . . .**160** F5
May Fair Pl NG22 . . . .**66** A2
Mayfield Ave
Burton Joyce NG14 . . . .**163** F5
Gainsborough DN21 . . . .**15** B3
Mayfield Cl NG18 . . . .**103** B5
Mayfield Ct NG2 . . . .**173** C2
Mayfield Dr
Loughborough LE11 . . . .**220** A2
Stapleford NG9 . . . .**170** F2
Mayfield Gr NG10 . . . .**182** E1
Mayfield Rd NG17 . . . .**100** D2
Mayfield Rd NG4 . . . .**174** B7
Mayfield St NG17 . . . .**114** D3
Mayfield Terr NG20 . . . .**74** B3
Mayflower Ave DN10 . . . .**10** A2
Mayflower Cl
Bawtry DN10 . . . .**10** A8
Gainsborough DN21 . . . .**24** E4
West Bridgford NG2 . . . .**186** A7
Mayflower Ct NG20 . . . .**72** E4
Mayflower Jun & Inf Sch
DN10 . . . .**10** B8
Mayflower Rd NG16. . . . . . .**158** B8
Mayhall Ave NG19 . . . .**88** A4
May Hill NG25 . . . .**136** C8
Mayland Cl NG8 . . . .**171** C6
May Lodge Dr NG22. . . . .**91** E6
Mayo Rd NG5. . . . .**161** B1
Maypole NG11 . . . .**184** E3
Maypole Rd NG2 . . . .**92** E8
Maypole Rd NG4 . . . .**162** F4
Maypole Yd NG1 . . . .**223** E3
Mays Cl NG4 . . . .**174** D6
Mays La LN1. . . . .**57** C3

May St DE7. . . . .**157** E4
Maythorn Cl NG11 . . . .**185** C3
Maythorne Cl NG14. . . . .**150** F8
Maythorne Wlk **1** NG5 . . .**161** C7
Maythorn Gr NG21 . . . .**76** B3
Meade Dr S81 . . . .**36** A7
Meadow Ave
Loughborough LE11. . . . .**220** B6
Mansfield NG18 . . . .**102** C5
Meadow Bank
Mansfield Woodhouse
NG19. . . . .**88** E6
South Normanton DE55 . . . . .**113** A7
Meadowbank Day Hospl
NG2 . . . .**173** B1
Meadowbank Way NG16. . .**128** F7
Meadow Cl
Aslockton NG13 . . . .**179** A5
Eastwood NG16. . . . .**143** F4
Farnsfield NG22 . . . .**120** A6
Hucknall NG15 . . . .**145** D5
2 Kirkby in A NG17 . . . .**114** E6
North Muskham NG23 . . . . . .**110** F1
Nottingham NG2 . . . .**173** E1
Retford DN22. . . . .**29** E1
Tibshelf DE55 . . . .**99** B7
Meadow Cotts
Carlton NG4 . . . .**174** F7
Mansfield Woodhouse NG19 . **88** C3
Meadow Ct
Nottingham NG2 . . . .**173** F2
South Normanton DE55 . . . . .**113** A4
Meadow Dr
Keyworth NG12 . . . .**198** A3
Misterton DN10 . . . .**6** F2
Sutton in A NG17 . . . .**100** C3
Tickhill DN11 . . . .**8** A7
Worksop S80 . . . .**35** C2
Meadow End
Gotham NG11 . . . .**195** B1
Radcliffe on T NG12. . . . .**176** C3
Meadow Farm View
NG17 . . . .**114** E5
Meadow Gdns
Beeston NG9 . . . .**183** A5
Heanor DE75 . . . .**143** B1
Meadow Gr
Bilsthorpe NG22 . . . .**106** A4
Newton NG13 . . . .**99** A3
Nottingham NG2 . . . .**173** E2
Meadow La
Beeston NG9 . . . .**183** E4
Bothamsall DN22 . . . .**63** E7
Burton Joyce NG14 . . . .**163** F4
Girton NG23. . . . .**82** F4
Long Eaton NG10 . . . .**193** F7
Loughborough LE11. . . . .**220** B7
North Scarle LN6 . . . .**83** F2
2 Nottingham NG2. . . . .**173** F3
Shirebrook NG20 . . . .**72** D2
South Normanton DE55 . . . . .**113** A3
Weston NG23 . . . .**81** B4
Meadow La Ind Est LE11. . . .**220** B6
Meadow Lane Inf Sch
NG9 . . . .**183** E4
Meadow La (Notts Cty FC)
NG2 . . . .**173** E2
Meadow Pl NG20 . . . .**74** A4
Meadow Rd
Awsworth NG16. . . . .**158** C5
Beeston NG9 . . . .**184** B4
Blidworth NG21 . . . .**118** A5
Carlton NG4. . . . .**174** F7
New Balderton NG24 . . . .**140** C4
Worksop S80 . . . .**35** C2
Meadow Rise
Nottingham NG6 . . . .**159** F6
Saxilby LN1 . . . .**57** B4
Meadows Ed Ctr NG2 . . . . .**173** D1
Meadows La LE14 . . . .**201** D1
Meadow St DE7 . . . .**157** F1
Meadows The
Beckingham DN10 . . . .**23** B8
Farndon NG24 . . . .**139** A4
South Wheatley DN22 . . . .**31** E8
Woodborough NG14 . . . .**149** B4
Meadowsweet Hill NG13 . . .**177** D4
Meadow The DN22 . . . .**39** F8
Meadowvale Cres NG7 . . . .**184** E1
Meadow View NG25 . . . .**121** F1
Meadow Way
Harworth DN11. . . . .**8** F5
Kinoulton NG12 . . . .**199** F2
Mead Way NG24 . . . .**140** C3
Medavar Cl NG11. . . . .**184** C1
Meden Ave
Market Warsop NG20 . . . .**74** C5
New Houghton NG19. . . . .**86** F7
Meden Bank
Bothamsall DN22 . . . .**63** F7
Pleasleyhill NG19 . . . .**87** B5
Stanton Hill NG17 . . . .**100** C6
Meden Cl
Nottingham NG11 . . . .**184** E3
Pleasleyhill NG19 . . . .**87** B5
Meden Cres NG17. . . . .**100** C6
Meden Gdns NG7 . . . .**172** D7
Meden Glen NG20 . . . .**74** C6
Meden Rd
Mansfield Woodhouse
NG19. . . . .**88** D3
Meden Sch & Tech Coll The
NG20 . . . .**74** A4
Meden Sports Ctr NG20. . . . .**74** B5
Meden Sq NG19 . . . .**87** B5
Meden Way DN22 . . . .**39** F5

Medina Dr NG12 . . . . 186 E1
Medway DN22 . . . . 29 D1
Medway Cl NG9 . . . . 183 C5
Meeks Rd NG5 . . . . 162 B8
Meering Ave NG24 . . . . . 125 B4
Meering Cl NG23 . . . . 98 A1
Meerings The NG23 . . . . . . 81 E1
Meer Rd NG9 . . . . 183 A5
Meeting House Cl LE12 . . 205 F1
Meetinghouse La DN22 . . . 42 B6
Melbourne Ct
  Mansfield NG18 . . . . . . 103 B6
  Nottingham NG8 . . . . . 160 C1
Melbourne Gr DN11 . . . . . . 8 F4
Melbourne Rd
  Nottingham NG8 . . . . . 160 C1
  Stapleford NG9 . . . . . . 170 E1
  West Bridgford NG2 . . . 174 A1
Melbourne St
  Mansfield Woodhouse
  NG19 . . . . 88 C6
  Selston NG16 . . . . 129 B6
Melbury Prim Sch NG8 . . 171 D8
Melbury Rd
  Nottingham, Bilborough
  NG8 . . . . 171 D8
  Nottingham, Woodthorpe
  NG3 . . . . 162 A4
Meldreth Rd NG8 . . . . . . 171 E6
Meldrum Cres NG14 . . . . 139 E5
Meldrum Dr DN21 . . . . . . 24 E5
Melford Hall Dr NG2 . . . . 185 C4
Melford Rd NG8 . . . . 171 D8
Melksham Rd NG5 . . . . . 161 C8
Mellbreak Cl NG7 . . . . . . 182 B3
Mellers Prim Sch NG7 . . 222 B3
Mellish Rd S81 . . . . 16 E2
Mellors Rd
  Arnold NG5 . . . . 147 F1
  Mansfield NG19 . . . . . 101 D8
  West Bridgford NG2 . . . 185 F6
Melrose Ave
  Beeston NG9 . . . . 184 A5
  Mansfield NG18 . . . . . 102 D5
  ③ Nottingham NG5 . . . 161 C3
Melrose Gdns NG2 . . . . . 185 C4
Melrose Rd DN11 . . . . . . 15 C2
Melrose St NG5 . . . . 161 C2
Melton Cl NG10 . . . . 182 A5
Melton Gdns NG12 . . . . . 186 B4
Melton Gr NG2 . . . . 185 E7
Melton La LE12 . . . . 204 C2
Melton Rd
  East Leake LE12 . . . . . 214 E5
  Long Clawson LE14 . . . 211 B1
  Plumtree NG12 . . . . . . 197 E8
  Rempstone LE12 . . . . . 215 C6
  Stanton-on-t-W NG12 . . 198 D4
  Upper Broughton LE14 . . 210 A1
  West Bridgford NG12 . . 186 A3
  Widmerpool NG12, LE12 . 209 C4
Melton Way NG18 . . . . . . 110 E1
Melville Ct ③ NG3 . . . . 173 C8
Melville Gdns NG3 . . . . . 173 E6
Melville St NG1 . . . . 223 E1
Melvyn Dr NG13 . . . . 177 E4
Memorial Ave S80 . . . . . . 35 F2
Mendip Cl
  Long Eaton NG10 . . . . 182 A1
  Mansfield NG18 . . . . . 102 E4
Mendip Ct
  Carlton in S, S81 . . . . . 25 E7
  Nottingham NG5 . . . . . 160 F8
Mensing Ave NG12 . . . . . 187 E3
Mercer Rd DN21 . . . . 15 B2
Merchant St
  Nottingham NG6 . . . . . 160 B8
  Shirebrook NG20 . . . . . 73 A4
Mercia Ave NG12 . . . . . . 189 A4
Mercia Cl S81 . . . . 36 A7
Mercia Rd NG24 . . . . . . 139 F5
Mercury Cl NG6 . . . . 160 C5
Mere Ave NG14 . . . . 148 F7
Mere Cl NG14 . . . . 148 F7
Meredith Cl NG21 . . . . . . 173 B1
Meredith Ct NG9 . . . . . . 170 E2
Meregill Cl NG5 . . . . 146 F1
Merevale Ave NG11 . . . . 184 C4
Merevale Cl NG14 . . . . . 150 E1
Mere Way NG11 . . . . 196 D5
Meriac Cl NG5 . . . . 160 F8
Meriden Ave NG1 . . . . . . 184 A8
Meridian Cl DE7 . . . . 157 E4
Meridian Ct NG5 . . . . . . 161 A2
Merlin Cl NG7 . . . . 184 E2
Merlin Dr NG15 . . . . 145 E4
Merlin Way DE7 . . . . 157 E3
Merrick Dr S81 . . . . 36 C3
Merrivale Cl NG14 . . . . . 173 C8
Merryvale Dr NG19 . . . . . 101 D6
Merryweather Cl
  Edwinstowe NG21 . . . . 91 C8
  Southwell NG25 . . . . . 121 E2
Mersey St NG6 . . . . 160 B7
Merton Ave DN22 . . . . . . 29 E1
Merton Cl NG5 . . . . 148 B1
Merton Ct NG5 . . . . 170 E1
Metcalf Cl NG25 . . . . 136 F8
Metcalfe Rd NG16 . . . . . 144 B3
Methuen St NG18 . . . . . . 102 E6
Metro Ave DE55 . . . . 99 A3
Mettham St NG7 . . . . 222 B1
Meunt La NG14 . . . . 148 E8
Mews The S81 . . . . 18 A3
Meynell Gr ⑦ NG7 . . . . 161 A1
Meynell Rd NG10 . . . . . . 193 D5

Meyrick Rd NG24 . . . . . . 125 A1
Miall Ct NG7 . . . . 222 A3
Michaels Vw St NG16 . . . 129 A5
Micklebarrow Cl NG25 . . 136 C8
Mickleborough Ave NG3 . 174 A8
Mickleborough Way
  NG2 . . . . 185 C3
Mickledale Cl NG22 . . . . 105 E4
Mickledale La NG22 . . . . 105 E6
Mickleden Cl ⑨ NG2 . . . 173 B2
Mickledon Cl ① NG10 . . 193 B8
Middle Ave NG4 . . . . 174 C8
Middlebeck Ave NG5 . . . 162 C8
Middlebeck Dr NG5 . . . . 162 C8
Middlebridge Rd DN10 . . 12 E4
Middlebrook Rd NG16 . . 129 B4
Middledale Rd NG4 . . . . 174 C6
Middlefell Way NG11 . . . 184 D1
Middlefield La DN21 . . . . 24 E7
Middlefield Rd ① NG10 . 193 B8
Middle Furlong Gdns ⑤
  NG2 . . . . 173 B2
Middle Furlong Mews ④
  NG2 . . . . 173 B2
Middle Gate NG24 . . . . . 125 A1
Middlegate Field Dr S80 . . 45 A5
Middle Hill NG1 . . . . 223 E2
Middle Holme La NG23 . . 97 A8
Middle La
  Beeston NG9 . . . . 183 E5
  Morton NG25 . . . . 137 D3
  Nether Broughton LE14 . 219 D8
Middle Pavement NG1 . . 223 E2
Middle St
  Barkestone-le-V NG13 . 192 C2
  Beeston NG9 . . . . 184 A6
  Hose LE14 . . . . 211 F7
  Misson DN10 . . . . 4 C2
Middleton Bvd NG8 . . . . 172 C3
Middleton Cl NG16 . . . . 159 C6
Middleton Cres NG9 . . . 171 E1
Middleton Ct
  Mansfield NG18 . . . . . 103 B6
  New Ollerton NG22 . . . . 77 C5
Middleton Prim Sch
  NG8 . . . . 172 C4
Middleton Rd
  Clipstone NG21 . . . . . . 89 F4
  Ilkeston DE7 . . . . 170 A5
  Mansfield Woodhouse NG19 88 C5
  Newark-on-T NG24 . . . 125 C3
Middleton St
  Awsworth NG16 . . . . . 158 C4
  Beeston NG9 . . . . 183 F7
  Cossall DE7 . . . . 158 A1
  Nottingham NG7 . . . . . 222 A3
Middle Wood La DN10 . . . 4 C6
Midfield Rd NG17 . . . . . . 115 B1
Midhurst Cl NG19 . . . . . 183 C4
Midhurst Way NG7 . . . . . 184 E2
Midlame Gdns NG6 . . . . 159 F7
Midland Ave
  Carlton NG4 . . . . 175 A7
  Nottingham NG7 . . . . . 222 A1
  Stapleford NG9 . . . . . . 182 C5
Midland Cres NG4 . . . . . 174 F7
Midland Ct NG7 . . . . 172 D5
Midland Gr NG4 . . . . 175 A8
Midland Rd
  Carlton NG4 . . . . 174 F7
  Eastwood NG16 . . . . . 143 F2
  Sutton in A NG17 . . . . 101 B2
Midland St NG10 . . . . . . 193 E8
Midland Way NG18 . . . . 102 B5
Midway The NG7 . . . . . . 184 E7
Mikado Rd NG10 . . . . . . 193 C5
Mike Powers Pottery
  NG11 . . . . 196 C7
Milburn Gr NG13 . . . . . . 177 C4
Mildenhall Cres NG5 . . . 161 C8
Mile End Rd NG4 . . . . . . 174 E5
Miles Yd LE11 . . . . 220 B3
Milford Ave NG10 . . . . . 182 B3
Milford Cl NG6 . . . . 160 A8
Milford Cres NG19 . . . . . 101 D7
Milford Ct NG5 . . . . 161 D6
Milford Dr
  Ilkeston DE7 . . . . 157 D3
  Nottingham NG3 . . . . . 174 C7
Millash La S80 . . . . 45 A4
Millbank DE75 . . . . 157 A8
Millbank Cl DE7 . . . . 157 D3
Millbaulk La NG22 . . . . . . 93 E7
Mill Baulk Rd DN10 . . . . 114 A6
Millbeck Ave NG8 . . . . . 171 C3
Millbeck Cl NG2 . . . . 186 C6
Millbrook Dr NG4 . . . . . 162 C1

Millers Bridge NG12 . . . 187 E2
Millers Cl NG12 . . . . 164 C1
Millers Ct
  Clarborough DN22 . . . . 30 E4
  Nottingham NG7 . . . . . 222 A4
Millersdale Ave
  Ilkeston DE7 . . . . 157 E5
  Mansfield NG18 . . . . . 101 E4
Millers Gn ⑦ NG2 . . . . 174 A4
Miller's La LE12 . . . . 206 C1
Millers Way
  Kirkby in Ashfield NG17 . 115 A5
  Retford DN22 . . . . 39 C8
Millers Wy NG17 . . . . . . 101 D5
Millfield Ave LN1 . . . . . . 57 B4
Millfield Cl
  Ilkeston DE7 . . . . 157 C3
  Retford DN22 . . . . 39 E3
Mill Field Cl
  Burton Joyce NG14 . . . 163 E3
  Harby NG23 . . . . 70 D2
Millfield Rd
  Ilkeston DE7 . . . . 170 A8
  Kimberley NG16 . . . . . 158 E7
  South Leverton DN22 . . 42 A6
Millfield View S80 . . . . . . 35 C2
Mill Gate
  East Bridgford NG13 . . 165 C3
  Newark-on-T NG24 . . . 139 E8
Mill Gdns S80 . . . . 35 D2
Mill Gn NG24 . . . . 140 E8
Mill Heyes NG13 . . . . . . 165 D3
Mill Hill NG10 . . . . 12 D2
Mill Hill Rd NG13 . . . . . 177 D3
Mill Holme DE55 . . . . . . 113 B4
Millicent Gr NG2 . . . . . . 185 F8
Millicent Rd NG2 . . . . . . 185 E8
Millidge Cl NG5 . . . . 160 F5
Millingdon Ave NG16 . . . 159 D3
Mill La
  Annesley Woodhouse
  NG17 . . . . 114 C2
  Arnold NG5 . . . . 161 E8
  Caunton NG23 . . . . . . 109 A5
  Cossall NG16 . . . . 158 C1
  Cotgrave NG12 . . . . . . 187 E4
  Eagle LN6 . . . . 84 E4
  East Leake LE12 . . . . . 214 F8
  Edwinstowe NG21 . . . . 76 A1
  Hickling LE14 . . . . 210 C2
  Huthwaite NG17 . . . . . 100 A2
  Kegworth DE74 . . . . . . 203 D2
  Lambley NG4 . . . . 163 B7
  Long Clawson LE14 . . . 211 D3
  Long Whatton LE12 . . . 212 D4
  Loughborough LE11 . . . 220 A5
  Morton DN21 . . . . 15 C5
  Newark-on-T NG24 . . . 139 E8
  Normanton on T NG23 . . 81 D7
  North Clifton DN22 . . . . 68 F5
  North Leverton w H DN22 42 B8
  North Muskham NG23 . . 110 F1
  Orston NG13 . . . . 180 A7
  Pinxton NG16 . . . . 113 D2
  Rockley DN22 . . . . 39 C4
  Sandiacre NG10 . . . . . 182 C6
  Saxilby LN1 . . . . 57 B4
  Scarrington NG13 . . . . 178 F7
  Scrooby DN10 . . . . 10 A3
  South Leverton DN22 . . 42 C7
  Stainsby S44 . . . . 86 C6
  Upton NG23 . . . . 137 E8
  Walesby NG22 . . . . 63 F2
  Walkeringham DN10 . . . 13 F4
  Whitwell S80 . . . . 45 A6
  Willoughby-on-t-W LE12 . 217 D8
Mill Lakes NG6 . . . . 146 B2
Millman Way NG22 . . . . . 29 C1
Mill Mdw View S81 . . . . . 18 B3
Mill Pk NG25 . . . . 121 F1
Mill Rd
  Eastwood NG16 . . . . . 144 B3
  Elston NG23 . . . . 153 E4
  Heanor DE75 . . . . 157 A8
  Stapleford NG9 . . . . . . 182 D8
Mills Dr NG24 . . . . 139 C6
Mill St
  Ilkeston DE7 . . . . 157 D3
  Mansfield NG18 . . . . . 102 D4
  Nottingham NG6 . . . . . 160 B7
  Retford DN22 . . . . 39 E6
  Sutton in A NG17 . . . . 100 F3
  Worksop S80 . . . . 35 E4
Millstone Cl NG18 . . . . . 102 E4
Millview Cl ⑥ NG2 . . . . 173 F4
Millview Ct ⑬ NG2 . . . . 173 F4
Millway NG19 . . . . 88 D1
Mill Wlk S80 . . . . 35 C3
Mill Yd
  Beeston NG9 . . . . 183 F6
  Hucknall NG15 . . . . . . 146 A7
Milne Ave DN11 . . . . 9 C4
Milne Dr DN11 . . . . 9 C4
Milne Gr DN11 . . . . 9 C4
Milner Ave NG14 . . . . . . 148 F7
Milner Rd
  Long Eaton NG10 . . . . 193 D8
  Nottingham NG5 . . . . . 161 C2
Milner St
  Newark-on-T NG24 . . . 140 A7
  Nottingham NG2 . . . . . 173 D1
Milnhay Rd NG16 . . . . . 143 B5
Milton Ave DE7 . . . . 157 E4
Milton Cl NG17 . . . . 101 B4

Milton Cres
  Beeston NG9 . . . . 183 C2
  Ravenshead NG15 . . . . 117 A2
Milton Ct NG5 . . . . 162 B7
Milton Dr
  Ravenshead NG15 . . . . 117 A2
  Worksop S81 . . . . 36 B4
Milton Rd
  Gainsborough DN21 . . . 15 E2
  Ilkeston DE7 . . . . 157 F4
  West Markham NG22 . . . 65 B6
Milton Rise NG15 . . . . . 145 C5
Milton St
  Ilkeston DE7 . . . . 157 F4
  Kirkby in A NG17 . . . . 115 B5
  Long Eaton NG10 . . . . 193 D7
  Mansfield NG18 . . . . . 102 A7
  New Balderton NG24 . . 140 C6
  Nottingham NG1 . . . . . 223 E3
Milton Wlk S81 . . . . 36 B4
Milverton Rd NG5 . . . . . 161 C8
Mimosa Cl NG11 . . . . . . 184 C1
Minas Ave NG4 . . . . 160 B8
Minster Cl
  Hucknall NG15 . . . . . . 146 B8
  Kirkby in A NG17 . . . . 114 F6
Minster Gdns NG16 . . . . 144 B1
Minster Rd DN10 . . . . . . 6 E2
Minster Sch The NG25 . . 136 E7
Minstrel Ave NG5 . . . . . 161 A2
Minstrel Cl NG15 . . . . . . 146 A5
Mint Cl NG10 . . . . 193 A4
Minton Pastures ③ NG19 . 89 A1
Minver Cres NG8 . . . . . . 160 B2
Mirberry Mews NG7 . . . . 222 A1
Mire La DN22 . . . . 28 F6
Misk Hollows NG15 . . . . 145 E8
Misk View NG16 . . . . . . 144 B2
Misson Carr Nature Reserve
  DN9 . . . . 5 A7
Misson Bank DN10 . . . . . 1 F4
Misson Prim Sch DN10 . . 4 B3
Misterton Cres NG15 . . . 116 F1
Misterton Ct NG19 . . . . . 88 B1
Mitchell Ave NG16 . . . . 143 A4
Mitchell Cl
  Nottingham NG6 . . . . . 160 A6
  Worksop S81 . . . . 35 B8
Mitchell St NG10 . . . . . . 193 E7
Mitchell Terr DE7 . . . . . 170 A5
M Lark Cl NG17 . . . . 100 D1
Mob La LE12 . . . . 217 D7
Model Village NG20 . . . . 58 E3
Model Village Prim Sch
  NG20 . . . . 72 E8
Moffat Cl NG3 . . . . 173 F7
Moira St LE11 . . . . 220 B3
Mollington Sq NG6 . . . . 160 B3
Monarch Way LE11 . . . . 220 A6
Mona Rd NG2 . . . . 174 A1
Mona St NG9 . . . . 184 B6
Monckton Dr NG25 . . . . 121 C1
Monckton St
  Bircotes DN11 . . . . 9 C3
  Retford DN22 . . . . 39 C4
Monks Cl DE7 . . . . 170 A8
Monk's La NG11 . . . . . . 195 A1
Monks Mdw LE12 . . . . . 205 F2
Monksway NG11 . . . . . . 185 A4
Monks Way S81 . . . . 34 F7
Monkton Cl DE7 . . . . . . 170 A8
Monkton Dr NG8 . . . . . . 171 E7
Monkwood Cl NG23 . . . . 98 B1
Monmouth Cl NG8 . . . . 171 B4
Monmouth Rd S81 . . . . . 36 A6
Monroe Wlk ⑪ NG5 . . . 161 A7
Monsaldale Cl NG10 . . . 193 B6
Monsall Ave DE7 . . . . . . 157 E5
Monsall St NG7 . . . . 160 F1
Monsell Dr NG5 . . . . 147 E1
Montague Rd NG15 . . . . 146 A8
Montague St
  Beeston NG9 . . . . 183 E7
  Mansfield NG18 . . . . . 102 E6
  Nottingham NG6 . . . . . 160 B7
Montfort Cres NG5 . . . . 161 D4
Montfort St NG7 . . . . . . 222 C3
Montgomery Rd NG24 . . 140 A5
Montgomery St NG7 . . . 172 D7
Montgomery St NG7 . . . 222 C4
Montpelier Rd NG7 . . . . 172 E1
Montrose S81 . . . . 36 B6
Montrose Cl NG9 . . . . . . 170 E1
Montrose Sq NG19 . . . . . 88 B6
Montys Mdw S81 . . . . . . 35 D8
Monyash Cl DE7 . . . . . . 157 D3
Moor Bridge NG6 . . . . . 146 C2
Moorbridge Cotts NG6 . . 146 D2
Moorbridge La NG9 . . . . 170 D1
Moorbridge Rd NG16 . . . 170 D1
Moorbridge Rd E NG13 . 177 C5
Moore Ave DE74 . . . . . . 203 D3
Moore Cl
  Claypole NG23 . . . . . . 156 D6
  East Leake LE12 . . . . . 205 F2
  West Bridgford NG2 . . . 174 B1
Moore Gate NG9 . . . . . . 184 A6
Moore Rd NG15 . . . . . . 162 A2
Moores Ave NG10 . . . . . 182 C5
Moore St NG6 . . . . 160 C5
Moor Farm Inn La NG9 . . 171 A5
Moorfield Cres NG10 . . . 182 B5
Moorfield Ct NG9 . . . . . 170 E1
Moorfield La NG22 . . . . . 78 B6
Moorfield Pl NG20 . . . . . 74 C5
Moorfields Ave NG16 . . . 143 F3

Moorgate Ave NG19 . . . . 86 F7
Moorgate Pk DN22 . . . . . 39 F8
Moorgate St NG7 . . . . . 222 C3
Moorgreen NG16 . . . . . 144 C3
Moorgreen Dr NG8 . . . . 159 D2
Moorhaigh La NG19 . . . . 87 A3
Moorhouse Rd
  Egmanton NG22 . . . . . 80 C4
  Nottingham NG8 . . . . . 171 E6
Moorings The ③ NG2 . . 172 F2
Moor La
  Aslockton NG13 . . . . . 178 D5
  Beeston NG9 . . . . 171 B2
  Besthorpe NG23 . . . . . 98 C6
  Bingham NG13 . . . . . . 177 E5
  Blyth S81 . . . . 18 D2
  Bunny NG11 . . . . 206 E8
  Calverton NG14 . . . . . 146 D6
  Dry Doddington NG23 . . 169 E6
  Elston NG23 . . . . 154 B5
  Gotham NG11 . . . . 205 C8
  Loughborough LE11 . . . 220 C3
  Mansfield NG18 . . . . . 101 F6
  Morton NG25 . . . . 137 C3
  Norton on S LE12 . . . . 213 C4
  North Clifton NG23 . . . 69 D3
  South Clifton NG23 . . . 69 D3
  Stathern NG13 . . . . . . 202 F5
  Syerston NG23 . . . . . . 153 C3
  Upper Langwith S44 . . . 72 A8
Moorland Ave
  Stapleford NG9 . . . . . . 182 D6
  Walkeringham DN10 . . . 13 F6
Moorland Cl
  Sutton in A NG17 . . . . 101 A6
  Walkeringham DN10 . . . 13 F6
Moorlands Cl NG10 . . . . 182 B2
Moorland Way NG18 . . . 103 A6
Moorland Wlk DN10 . . . . 13 F6
Moor Rd
  Bestwood Village NG6 . . 146 E6
  Brinsley NG16 . . . . . . 143 E8
  Calverton NG14 . . . . . 149 A7
  Collingham NG23 . . . . . 98 B1
  Nottingham NG8 . . . . . 159 D1
Moorsholm Dr NG8 . . . . 171 D4
Moor St
  Carlton NG4 . . . . 175 A7
  Mansfield NG18 . . . . . 102 A6
Moor The NG16 . . . . . . 143 D8
Moor Top Rd NG17 . . . . . 8 F5
Moor View NG17 . . . . . . 206 E8
Moray Ct NG16 . . . . 158 F7
Moray Sq NG19 . . . . . . 101 D5
Morden Cl NG8 . . . . 171 D8
Morden Rd NG16 . . . . . 158 C8
Moreland Ct
  Carlton NG4 . . . . 174 C7
  ⑩ Nottingham NG2 . . . 173 F3
Moreland Pl ⑪ NG2 . . . 173 F3
Moreland St NG2 . . . . . 173 F3
Morello Ave NG4 . . . . . . 174 F7
Moreton Rd NG11 . . . . . 195 E7
Morgan Mews NG7 . . . . 184 D2
Morgans Cl NG24 . . . . . 126 B2
Morkinshire Cres LE12 . . 187 F4
Morkinshire La LE12 . . . 187 E4
Morley Ave
  Nottingham NG3 . . . . . 161 E2
  Retford DN22 . . . . 29 C1
Morley Cl NG18 . . . . . . 103 B5
Morley Dr DE7 . . . . 157 D3
Morley Rd NG3 . . . . 162 A1
Morley St ⑤ NG2 . . . . 173 E4
Morley St
  Arnold NG5 . . . . 161 D6
  Gainsborough DN21 . . . 24 C8
  Kirkby in A NG17 . . . . 115 B4
  Loughborough LE11 . . . 220 C5
  Stanton Hill NG17 . . . . 100 C6
  Sutton in A NG17 . . . . 100 F3
Mornington Cl NG10 . . . 182 C6
Mornington Cres NG8 . . 159 D3
Mornington Prim Sch
  NG16 . . . . 159 D4
Morrell Bank NG5 . . . . . 160 F6
Morris Ave NG9 . . . . . . 183 B1
Morris Cl LE11 . . . . 220 C4
Morris Rd NG8 . . . . 159 D1
Morris St NG4 . . . . 175 A7
Morton Cl
  Mansfield NG18 . . . . . 103 B6
  Morton DN21 . . . . 15 B4
  Radcliffe on T NG12 . . . 176 C3
Morton Gdns NG12 . . . . 176 C3
Morton Hall Gdns DN22 . 38 A5
Morton Terr DN21 . . . . . 15 C3
Morton Trentside Prim Sch
  DN21 . . . . 15 A4
Morval Rd NG8 . . . . 171 C6
Morven Ave
  Hucknall NG15 . . . . . . 146 B6
  Mansfield Woodhouse NG19 88 B2
  Sutton in A NG17 . . . . 100 E2
Morven Park Prim Sch
  NG17 . . . . 115 B5
Morven St S80 . . . . 58 F8
Morven Terr DN21 . . . . . 15 B4
Mosborough Rd NG17 . . 100 A1

Moseley Rd NG15 . . . . 130 C8
Moses View S81 . . . . 34 F7
Mosgrove Cl S81 . . . . 35 C7
Mosley St
  Hucknall NG15 . . . . 146 A6
  Nottingham NG7 . . . . 172 F8
Moss Cl
  Arnold NG5 . . . . 147 C1
  East Bridgford NG13 . . . . 165 D3
Mosscroft Ave NG11 . . . . 184 D1
Mossdale S81 . . . . 36 A8
Mossdale Rd
  Mansfield NG18 . . . . 102 E8
  Nottingham NG5 . . . . 161 C5
Moss Dr NG9 . . . . 183 B7
Moss Rd NG15 . . . . 145 F7
Moss Rise NG3 . . . . 162 B2
Moss Side NG11 . . . . 185 A3
Mosswood Cres NG5 . . . . 161 B7
Mottram Rd NG9 . . . . 183 C6
Moulton Cres NG24 . . . . . 140 C3
Mount Ave S81 . . . . 35 E5
Mountbatten Ct DE7 . . . . 157 F3
Mountbatten Dr NG4 . . . . 162 E2
Mountbatten Way NG9 . . 183 C2
Mount CE Prim Sch
  NG24 . . . . 125 A1
Mount Cl DN11 . . . . 8 F5
Mount Cres
  Market Warsop NG20 . . . . 74 C3
  South Normanton DE55 . . 113 A3
Mount Ct NG24 . . . . 140 D4
Mountfield Ave NG18 . . . . 182 B4
Mountfield Dr NG5 . . . . . . 161 A7
Mountford House Sch
  NG5 . . . . 161 C1
Mount Hooton Rd NG7 . . 222 C4
Mount Hooton St NG7 . . . 173 A7
Mount La NG24 . . . . 140 A8
Mount Milner NG18 . . . . . 102 D6
Mount Pleasant
  Carlton NG4 . . . . 174 E7
  Ilkeston DE7 . . . . 157 E4
  Keyworth NG12 . . . . 198 A2
  Lowdham NG14 . . . . 150 D2
  2 Mansfield NG18 . . . . 102 A7
  Nottingham NG6 . . . . 160 E2
  Radcliffe on T NG12 . . . . 175 E3
  Retford DN22 . . . . 39 F7
  Sutton in A NG17 . . . . . . 100 F4
Mount Sorrel Dr NG2 . . . 186 B6
Mount St
  Nottingham, New Basford
    NG7 . . . . 160 F1
  Nottingham NG1 . . . . 223 D2
  Stapleford NG9 . . . . 182 E7
Mount The
  Arnold NG5 . . . . 147 D1
  Bestwood Village NG6 . . . 146 E4
  Clipstone NG19 . . . . 89 D3
  Nottingham, Broxtowe
    NG8 . . . . 159 E1
  Nottingham, Portchester
    NG3 . . . . 162 C2
  Stapleford NG9 . . . . 182 D6
Mount Vernon Pk DN22 . . . 40 A4
Mount View Cl NG18 . . . . 102 D6
Mowbray Cl NG3 . . . . 223 F3
Mowbray Gdns NG5 . . . . . 185 F5
Mowbray Rise NG5 . . . . . 161 F8
Mowbray Str DN21 . . . . . 15 C2
Mowlands Cl NG17 . . . . . 101 B2
Moyra Dr NG5 . . . . 161 C7
Mozart Cl NG7 . . . . 222 A3
Mr Straw's House S80 . . . 36 A5
Muir Ave NG12 . . . . 197 D8
Muir Cl S81 . . . . 36 B6
Muirfield Cl **6** NG17 . . 114 E7
Muirfield Rd NG5 . . . . 147 A1
Muirfield Way NG19 . . . . . 88 E6
Mulberry Cl NG5 . . . . 185 B5
Mulberry Cres S81 . . . . . . 25 F7
Mulberry Gdns **1** NG6 160 A8
Mulberry Gr NG15 . . . . . . 146 B4
Mumby Cl NG24 . . . . 125 A1
Mundella Rd NG2 . . . . 173 D1
Mundy St DE7 . . . . 157 E2
Munford Circ NG6 . . . . . . 160 B3
Munks Ave NG15 . . . . 145 F7
Murby Cres NG6 . . . . 160 B8
Murden Way NG9 . . . . 184 B6
Muriel Rd NG9 . . . . 183 F7
Muriel St NG6 . . . . 160 B7
Murray Cl NG5 . . . . 160 F5
Murray St NG18 . . . . 102 B5
Muschamp Terr NG20 . . . . 74 B3
Mushill La LE12 . . . . 216 D5
Muskham Ave DE7 . . . . . . 157 F3
Muskham Ct NG19 . . . . . . 88 B1
Muskham La NG23 . . . . . . 110 C2
Muskham Prim Sch
  NG23 . . . . 110 F2
Muskham St NG2 . . . . 173 D1
Musters Cres NG2 . . . . . . 185 F5
Musters Croft NG4 . . . . . . 174 F4
Musters Rd
  Bingham NG13 . . . . 177 D4
  Langar NG13 . . . . 190 D2
  Newstead NG15 . . . . 130 D6
  Ruddington NG11 . . . . . . 196 C6
  West Bridgford NG2 . . . . 185 E5
Musters St NG20 . . . . 73 A4
Musters Wlk **4** NG6 . . 160 A7
Muston Cl NG3 . . . . 161 F1

Muston La NG13 . . . . 181 D1
Mutton La DN10 . . . . 23 A8
Muttonshire Hill DN22 . . . 50 F5
Mynd The NG18 . . . . 88 E5
Myrtle Ave
  Long Eaton NG10 . . . . . . 193 C6
  1 Nottingham NG7 . . . 173 B8
  Stapleford NG9 . . . . 182 E6
Myrtle Cl NG20 . . . . 72 D6
Myrtle Gr NG9 . . . . 184 A7
Myrtle Rd NG4 . . . . 174 C8
Myrtle St DN22 . . . . 39 D6
Myrtus Cl NG11 . . . . 184 C2
Mytholme Cl NG10 . . . . . 182 C2

N

Nabbs La NG15 . . . . 145 E5
Naburn Ct **4** NG8 . . . . 172 D8
Nairn Cl
  Arnold NG5 . . . . 148 B1
  Farnsfield NG22 . . . . 119 F5
Nairn Mews NG4 . . . . 174 E7
Nan Sampson Bank DN9 . . 1 D8
Nansen St NG6 . . . . 160 C6
Naomi Cres NG6 . . . . 146 C1
Naomi Ct NG6 . . . . 146 C1
Narrow La
  Bawtry DN10 . . . . 10 B8
  Greasley NG16 . . . . 145 A4
  Hathern LE12 . . . . 213 A1
  Wymeswold LE12 . . . . . . 217 B2
Naseby Cl NG5 . . . . 160 F4
Naseby Dr NG10 . . . . 193 E4
Naseby Rd NG16 . . . . 128 E8
Nash Cl S81 . . . . 36 C4
Nathaniel Rd NG10 . . . . . 193 F7
Nathans La NG12 . . . . 187 A7
National CE Inf Sch
  NG15 . . . . 146 A8
National Jun Sch **1**
  NG15 . . . . 146 A8
National Sch The NG15 . . 130 F1
National Water Sports Ctr
  NG12 . . . . 174 F3
Naturescape Wild Flower
  Farm NG13 . . . . 190 E1
Navenby Wlk NG7 . . . . . . 184 E2
Navigation Way LE11 . . . . 220 A5
Navigation Yd NG18 . . . . 139 F8
Naworth Cl NG6 . . . . 160 E5
Naylor Ave
  Gotham NG11 . . . . 195 B1
  Loughborough LE11 . . . . . 220 D2
Neal Ct NG16 . . . . 143 A3
Neale St NG10 . . . . 193 E7
Near Mdw NG10 . . . . 193 E5
Nearsby Dr NG2 . . . . 186 B6
Needham Rd NG5 . . . . . . 162 A8
Needham St NG13 . . . . . . 177 E4
Needwood Ave NG9 . . . . . 170 D2
Neeps Croft NG14 . . . . . . 150 A6
Negus St NG4 . . . . 163 B6
Neighwood Cl NG9 . . . . . 182 E2
Nell Gwyn Cres NG5 . . . . 147 C1
Nelper Cres DE7 . . . . 170 A5
Nelson La NG23 . . . . 110 F2
Nelson Rd
  Arnold NG5 . . . . 161 E7
  Beeston NG9 . . . . 184 A4
  New Balderton NG24 . . . . 140 B4
  Nottingham NG6 . . . . 160 C7
Nelson St
  Gainsborough DN21 . . . . . 15 C2
  Ilkeston DE7 . . . . 157 F3
  Long Eaton NG10 . . . . . . 193 D6
  Nottingham NG1 . . . . 223 F2
  Retford DN22 . . . . 39 F6
Nene Cl NG15 . . . . 145 E3
Nene Wlk S81 . . . . 35 E7
Nesbitt St NG7 . . . . 100 F1
Nesfield Ct DE7 . . . . 157 E1
Nesfield Rd DE7 . . . . 157 E1
Neston Dr NG6 . . . . 160 C4
Nether Cl
  Eastwood NG16 . . . . 143 F4
  Nottingham NG3 . . . . 161 F2
Nether Cl NG22 . . . . 120 A6
Nethercross Dr NG20 . . . . 74 C5
Netherfield Inf Sch NG20 . 74 D8
Netherfield La
  Church Warsop NG20 . . . . 74 D7
  Market Warsop NG20 . . . . 61 C1
Netherfield Prim Sch
  NG4 . . . . 175 A7
Netherfield Rd
  Long Eaton NG10 . . . . . . 193 C4
  Sandiacre NG10 . . . . 182 B4
Netherfield Sta NG4 . . . . . 174 F6
Nethergate NG11 . . . . 184 C2
Nethergate Specl Sch
  NG11 . . . . 185 A1
Nether Pasture NG4 . . . . . 175 B6
Nether St
  Beeston NG9 . . . . 184 A4
  Harby LE14 . . . . 202 A3
Netherton Pl S80 . . . . 36 A1
Netherton Rd S80 . . . . . . 47 A7
Nettlecliff Wlk NG5 . . . . . 160 E8
Nettle Croft DN11 . . . . 8 C7
Nettleworth Inf Sch NG19 88 C4
Neville Dr NG12 . . . . 200 A2
Neville Rd NG14 . . . . 148 F6
Neville Sadler Ct NG9 . . . 184 B7
Newall Dr
  Beeston NG9 . . . . 183 C2

Newall Dr continued
  Everton DN10 . . . . 11 A1
Newark Air Mus NG24 . . . 126 A5
Newark Ave **18** NG2 . . 173 E4
Newark Castle NG24 . . . . 139 F8
Newark Castle Sta NG24 . 124 F1
Newark Cl NG18 . . . . 102 F2
Newark Cres NG2 . . . . . . 173 E4
Newark Ct NG5 . . . . 160 F5
Newark Dr NG18 . . . . 102 F2
Newark High Sch The
  NG24 . . . . 139 F7
Newark Hospl NG24 . . . . . 140 A6
Newark Mus & Tudor Hall
  NG24 . . . . 140 A8
Newark North Gate Sta
  NG24 . . . . 125 D1
Newark Rd
  Barnby in t W NG24 . . . . 141 D6
  Caunton NG23 . . . . 109 B4
  Coddington NG24 . . . . . . 125 F1
  Collingham LN6 . . . . 112 F3
  Eakring NG22 . . . . 92 F1
  Kirklington NG22 . . . . . . 120 F8
  Laughterton LN1 . . . . 55 B7
  Ollerton NG22 . . . . 77 A3
  Southwell NG25 . . . . 121 F1
  Stapleford LN6 . . . . 127 C8
  Sutton in A NG17 . . . . . . 101 C1
  Tuxford NG22 . . . . 65 F2
  Wellow NG22 . . . . 77 D2
Newark & Sherwood Coll
  Blidworth NG21 . . . . 118 A6
  Edwinstowe NG21 . . . . . . 76 B2
  Newark-on-Trent NG24 . . 140 A8
  Rainworth NG21 . . . . 104 B2
Newark St NG2 . . . . 173 E4
Newark Way NG18 . . . . . . 103 A2
Newbarn Cl NG20 . . . . . . 72 D2
Newberry Cl NG12 . . . . . . 189 A4
Newbery Ave NG10 . . . . . 193 F6
Newbery Cl NG21 . . . . 76 A3
Newbold Way NG12 . . . . . 199 F2
Newbound La NG17 . . . . . 86 C2
Newboundmill La NG19 . . 87 A2
New Brickyard La DE74 . . 203 D1
Newbury Cl NG3 . . . . 162 A4
Newbury Ct **3** NG5 . . . 173 B8
Newbury Dr NG16 . . . . . . 159 D3
Newbury Mews **5** S80 . . 35 F2
Newbury Rd
  Balderton NG24 . . . . 140 E8
  Newark-on-T NG24 . . . . . 125 E1
Newcastle Ave
  Beeston NG9 . . . . 183 F6
  Carlton NG4 . . . . 162 E1
  Newark-on-T NG24 . . . . . 140 A6
  Worksop S80 . . . . 35 E1
Newcastle Cir NG7 . . . . . . 222 C2
Newcastle Dr NG7 . . . . . . 222 C3
Newcastle Farm Dr NG8 . 160 C1
Newcastle St
  Huthwaite NG17 . . . . 100 A3
  4 Mansfield NG18 . . . . 102 A7
  Mansfield Woodhouse NG19 88 B3
  Market Warsop NG20 . . . . 74 B4
  Nottingham, Bulwell NG6 . 160 C8
  Nottingham NG1 . . . . 223 E3
  Tuxford NG22 . . . . 65 F2
  Worksop S80 . . . . 35 E1
New Cl
  Blidworth NG21 . . . . 118 A5
  Kirkby in A NG17 . . . . . . 115 A5
New Coll Nottingham
  Hucknall NG15 . . . . 146 B7
  Nottingham NG1 . . . . 223 E4
  Nottingham NG5 . . . . 173 B8
Newcombe Dr NG5 . . . . . 162 C7
New Cotts NG22 . . . . 106 A2
New Cross St NG17 . . . . . 100 F4
New Cswy NG13 . . . . 192 C2
New Derby Rd NG16 . . . . 143 C3
Newdigate Rd NG16 . . . . 159 A7
Newdigate St
  Ilkeston DE7 . . . . 170 A6
  Kimberley NG16 . . . . 159 A6
  Nottingham NG7 . . . . 222 C3
New Eaton Rd NG9 . . . . . 182 E5
New England Way NG19 . . 87 F2
New Fall St NG17 . . . . 99 F3
New Farm La NG16 . . . . . 159 A6
Newfield La NG23 . . . . . . 167 A6
Newfield Rd NG5 . . . . 161 A3
Newgate Cl NG4 . . . . 174 E7
Newgate Ct NG7 . . . . 222 B2
Newgate La NG18 . . . . . . 102 C7
Newgate Lane Prim Sch
  NG18 . . . . 102 C7
Newgate St
  Bingham NG13 . . . . 177 E5
  Worksop S80 . . . . 35 F2
Newhall Gr NG2 . . . . 173 F1
Newhall La NG22 . . . . 120 C2
Newham Cl DE75 . . . . 143 A1
Newhaven Ave NG19 . . . . 88 B3
New Hill
  Farnsfield NG22 . . . . 119 F6
  Walesby NG22 . . . . 64 A2
New Holles Ct S80 . . . . . . 35 F2
Newholm Dr NG11 . . . . . . 185 A4
New Hucknall Way **2**
  NG17 . . . . 100 A1
Newings La DN22 . . . . 42 F8
Newington Rd NG10 . . . . . 10 C8
New Inn Wlk DN22 . . . . . . 39 F5
New King St LE11 . . . . . . 220 C3

Newton Dr continued
  West Bridgford NG2 . . . . 185 C4
Newton Gdns NG13 . . . . . 177 C6
Newton Prim Sch DE55 . . 99 A3
Newton Rd
  Carlton NG4 . . . . 162 E3
  Newton DE55 . . . . 99 A4
Newton's La NG16 . . . . . . 158 B4
Newton St
  Beeston NG9 . . . . 183 E6
  Mansfield NG18 . . . . 102 C6
  Newark-on-T NG24 . . . . . 140 A7
  Nottingham NG7 . . . . 172 E1
  Retford DN22 . . . . 39 F4
Newtonwood La DE55 . . . 99 C5
New Tythe St NG10 . . . . . 193 F7
New Vale Rd NG4 . . . . . . 174 E6
Nicholas Pl NG22 . . . . 66 A3
Nicholas Rd NG9 . . . . 171 D1
Nicholson's Row NG20 . . . 72 F3
Nicholson St NG24 . . . . . . 140 A7
Nicker Hill NG12 . . . . 198 A3
Nicklaus Ct **5** NG5 . . . 161 A8
Nidderdale NG8 . . . . 171 C4
Nidderdale Cl NG8 . . . . . . 171 C4
Nightingale Ave
  Balderton NG24 . . . . 140 E4
  Nuthall NG16 . . . . 159 D6
Nightingale Cres NG16 . . 129 B6
Nightingale Dr NG19 . . . . 87 E1
Nightingale Gr S81 . . . . . 35 D7
Nightingale Way
  Bingham NG13 . . . . 178 A3
  Woodbeck DN22 . . . . 53 B8
Nile St NG1 . . . . 223 F3
Nilsson Rd NG9 . . . . 183 B3
Nimbus Wy NG16 . . . . . . 159 A7
Nine Acre Gdns NG6 . . . . 159 F8
Nine Acres DE74 . . . . 203 C2
Nine Scores La DN9 . . . . . . 1 A2
Ninth Ave NG19 . . . . 103 A8
Nixon Rise NG15 . . . . 145 D5
Nixon Walk LE12 . . . . 205 E2
Noble La NG13 . . . . 179 A5
Noburn Cres NG6 . . . . . . 160 F3
Noel St
  Gainsborough DN21 . . . . . 15 C2
  Kimberley NG16 . . . . 159 A6
  Mansfield NG18 . . . . 102 A7
  Nottingham NG7 . . . . 172 F8
Nook The
  Beeston, Chilwell NG9 . . . 183 B6
  Beeston NG9 . . . . 184 A7
  Calverton NG14 . . . . 148 F7
  East Leake LE12 . . . . 205 E1
  Nottingham NG8 . . . . 171 E4
  Shirebrook NG20 . . . . . . 72 D3
Norbett Cl NG9 . . . . 183 C3
Norbett Ct NG5 . . . . 148 A1
Norbett Rd NG5 . . . . 148 A1
Norbreck Cl NG8 . . . . 160 B3
Norbury Dr NG18 . . . . 102 E4
Norbury Way NG10 . . . . . 182 A6
Nordean Rd NG5 . . . . 162 A5
Norfolk Ave
  Beeston NG9 . . . . 183 A1
  Bircotes DN11 . . . . 9 D4
Norfolk Cl
  Hucknall NG15 . . . . 145 D5
  Market Warsop NG20 . . . . 74 F4
Norfolk Ct NG19 . . . . 88 C5
Norfolk Dr
  Arnold NG5 . . . . 162 B5
  Nottingham NG1 . . . . 223 B3
Norfolk Pl
  Bircotes DN11 . . . . 9 C4
  Long Eaton NG10 . . . . . . 182 F1
Norfolk St S80 . . . . 35 E2
Norfolk Wlk NG10 . . . . . . 182 B5
Norland Cl NG3 . . . . 173 E7
Norman Ave
  Newark-on-T NG24 . . . . . 125 B4
  Sutton in A NG17 . . . . . . 101 A1
Normanby Rd NG8 . . . . . . 171 C3
Norman Cl
  Beeston NG9 . . . . 183 A3
  Nottingham NG3 . . . . 173 C6
  Nottingham NG3 . . . . 223 E4
Norman Dr
  Eastwood NG16 . . . . 144 B2
  Hucknall NG15 . . . . 145 E4
Norman Rd NG3 . . . . 174 A8
Norman St
  Carlton NG4 . . . . 175 A4
  Ilkeston DE7 . . . . 157 F3
  Kimberley NG16 . . . . 158 F7
Normanton Dr
  Loughborough LE11 . . . . . 220 B6
  Mansfield NG18 . . . . 102 E7
Normanton La
  Bottesford NG13 . . . . 181 B5
  Keyworth NG12 . . . . 197 F4
  Stanford on S LE12 . . . . . 214 B1
Normanton on Soar Prim Sch
  LE12 . . . . 213 D3
Norman Way
  Newark-on-T NG24 . . . . . 125 D1
  Southwell NG25 . . . . 121 F2

Nornay Cl S81 .... 18 A4
Northall Ave NG6 .... 160 B6
Northampton St 2 NG3 .. 173 E6
North Ave
Bawtry DN10 .... 10 A8
Rainworth NG21 .... 104 A1
Sandiacre NG10 .... 182 B6
North Carr Rd DN10 .... 7 C3
North Church St NG1 .... 223 E3
North Cir St NG1 .... 223 D2
Northcliffe Ave NG3 .... 162 B2
North Clifton Prim Sch NG23 .... 68 E3
Northcote St NG10 .... 193 E7
Northcote Way NG6 .... 160 C5
North County Prim Sch DN21 .... 15 B2
North Cres
Bottesford NG13 .... 181 A2
Clipstone NG21 .... 90 A3
Northcroft LN1 .... 57 A5
Northdale Rd NG3 .... 174 B7
Northdown Dr NG9 .... 183 C4
Northdown Rd NG8 .... 172 D6
North Dr
Beeston NG9 .... 183 E6
Bilsthorpe NG22 .... 105 F7
North End NG24 .... 138 F5
Northern Ct NG6 .... 160 D4
Northern Dr NG9 .... 170 D3
Northern Rd NG24 .... 125 B1
Northern Rd Ind Est NG24 .... 125 B1
Northern View NG17 .... 100 F3
Northfield Ave
Ilkeston DE7 .... 157 E2
Long Eaton NG10 .... 193 A4
Mansfield Woodhouse NG19 88 A4
Radcliffe on T NG12 .... 176 C3
Northfield Cres NG9 .... 183 A4
Northfield Dr NG18 .... 102 E6
Northfield La
Mansfield Woodhouse NG19 .... 88 A5
Treswell DN22 .... 42 B4
Northfield Pk NG19 .... 88 B5
Northfield Prim Sch NG19 88 B5
Northfield Rd
Beeston NG9 .... 183 A4
North Leverton w H DN22 ... 33 B1
Northfields NG10 .... 193 B4
Northfields Cl NG17 .... 100 E3
Northfields Way LE12 .... 205 E3
Northfield Way DN22 .... 39 D8
North Gate
Newark-on-T NG24 .... 125 A2
Nottingham NG7 .... 160 F1
Tickhill DN11 .... 8 A8
Northgate Bsns Ctr NG24 .... 124 F1
North Gate Pl NG7 .... 160 F1
Northgate Prim Sch NG7 160 F1
Northgate Ret Pk NG24 . 125 A2
Northgate St 4 DE7 .... 157 F1
North Gn
Calverton NG14 .... 133 D1
East Drayton DN22 .... 53 B3
North Hill Ave NG15 .... 145 F7
North Hill Cres NG15 .... 145 F7
North Leverton CE Prim Sch DN22 .... 32 D1
North Leverton Windmill DN22 .... 32 B1
North Leys Rd DN22 .... 43 C8
North Marsh Rd DN21 .... 15 C2
North Moor Dr DN10 .... 13 F6
North Moor Rd DN10 .... 13 F6
North Nottinghamshire Coll
1 East Retford DN22 .... 39 F6
Worksop S81 .... 35 F5
Northolme DN21 .... 15 D1
Northolme Ave NG6 .... 160 C7
Northolt Dr NG8 .... 159 D3
North Par DN21 .... 24 F7
North Pk NG18 .... 102 E3
North Rd
Long Eaton NG10 .... 193 C6
Loughborough LE11 .... 220 B6
Nottingham NG7 .... 222 C2
Retford DN22 .... 29 B2
Ruddington NG11 .... 196 B8
West Bridgford NG2 .... 185 E7
Northrowe NG17 .... 129 E8
North Scaffold La NG23 .. 112 B2
North Scarle Rd NG23 .... 98 E7
North Sherwood St NG1 . 223 E4
Northside La DN22 .... 32 F1
Northside Wlk NG5 .... 147 F2
North St
Beeston NG9 .... 183 E6
Eastwood NG16 .... 144 C2
Gainsborough DN21 .... 15 C1
Huthwaite NG17 .... 100 A3
7 Ilkeston DE7 .... 157 F1
Kimberley NG16 .... 159 A5
Kirkby in A NG17 .... 115 B2
Langley Mill NG16 .... 143 B3
Morton DN21 .... 15 B4
4 Nottingham NG2 .... 173 E4
Pinxton NG16 .... 113 D3
South Normanton DE55 .... 113 A5
Sturton le S DN22 .... 32 D6
Sutton in A NG17 .... 100 F3
Warsop Vale NG20 .... 73 D4
Whaley Thorns NG20 .... 59 A2
Northumberland Ave S81 . 25 E8
Northumberland Cl NG3 . 223 F4
Northumbria Cl S81 .... 36 B6
Northumbria Dr DN22 .... 39 D5
North Warren Rd DN21 .... 15 B2
North Way S81 .... 25 F7
North Wheatley CE Prim Sch DN22 .... 31 E8
North Wlk DN22 .... 39 C8
Northwold Ave NG2 .... 185 D6
Northwood S81 .... 36 A6
Northwood Ave NG17 .... 100 D4
Northwood Cres NG5 .... 161 C6
Northwood Rd NG5 .... 161 C6
Northwood St NG9 .... 182 D8
Norton La NG20 .... 60 B3
Norton Rd LN6 .... 127 E8
Norton St NG7 .... 222 B3
Norwell CE Prim Sch NG23 .... 110 A8
Norwell Ct NG19 .... 88 B1
Norwell La
Brough NG23 .... 112 C1
Cromwell NG23 .... 110 D8
Norwell Rd NG23 .... 109 C5
Norwich Cl NG19 .... 88 D5
Norwich Gdns NG6 .... 146 B1
Norwood Cl NG17 .... 100 B3
Norwood Gdns NG25 .... 121 E2
Norwood Rd NG7 .... 222 A3
Nostell Mews 6 S80 .... 35 F2
Notintone St NG2 .... 173 E4
Nottingham Airport NG12 .... 186 F5
Nottingham Arts Theatre NG1 .... 223 F2
Nottingham Bluecoat Sch The NG8 .... 172 C8
Nottingham Canal Nature Reserve NG9 .... 170 C7
Nottingham Castle (site of) NG7 .... 223 D2
Nottingham Cath NG1 .... 223 D2
Nottingham City Hospl NG5 .... 161 A4
Nottingham Com Coll NG3 .... 173 E5
Nottingham Emmanuel Sch The NG11 .... 185 C8
Nottingham High Jun Sch NG7 .... 223 D4
Nottingham High Sch NG7 .... 223 D4
Nottingham High Sch for Girls NG1 .... 223 D4
Nottingham Ice Ctr & Arena NG1 .... 223 F2
Nottingham La LE14 .... 218 C5
Nottingham Nuffield Hospl The NG5 .... 161 D4
Nottingham Playhouse NG1 .... 223 D2
Nottingham Racecourse NG2 .... 174 B3
Nottingham Rd
Arnold NG5 .... 161 E6
Beeston NG9 .... 183 B1
Bingham NG13 .... 177 D4
Bottesford NG13 .... 180 E2
Burton Joyce NG14 .... 163 D3
Costock LE12 .... 206 D2
Cropwell Bishop NG12 .... 188 E4
Eastwood, Giltbrook NG16 158 C8
Eastwood NG16 .... 144 A2
Gotham NG11 .... 195 B4
Gunthorpe NG14 .... 164 B6
Hucknall NG15 .... 146 C4
Ilkeston DE7 .... 170 A6
Kegworth DE74 .... 203 D2
Keyworth NG12 .... 197 E3
Kimberley NG16 .... 159 A5
Kirkby in A NG17 .... 115 B2
Long Eaton NG10 .... 193 E8
Loughborough LE11 .... 220 D6
Mansfield NG18 .... 102 C3
Nether Broughton LE14 .... 219 E7
Nottingham, New Basford NG7 .... 160 F1
Nuthall NG16 .... 159 F4
Oxton NG25 .... 134 A2
Radcliffe on T NG12 .... 175 D2
Ravenshead NG15 .... 116 E3
Selston NG16 .... 129 A6
Southwell NG25 .... 136 D6
Stapleford NG9 .... 182 E7
Thurgarton NG14 .... 151 C6
Trowell NG9 .... 170 E5
Woodborough NG14 .... 148 E2
Nottingham Rd E NG16 .... 144 B1
Nottingham Science & Tech Pk NG2 .... 172 D1
Nottingham Sta NG2 .... 223 F1
Nottingham S & Wilford Ind Est NG2 .... 185 B4
Nottingham Transport Her Ctr NG11 .... 196 C5
Nottingham Trent Univ The
Clifton NG11 .... 184 D3
Nottingham NG1 .... 223 D3
Southwell NG25 .... 136 D5
Nuart Rd NG9 .... 183 F7
Nugent Gdn NG3 .... 173 E6
Nugent Gdns 4 NG3 .... 173 E6
Nuncar Ct NG17 .... 115 A1
Nuncargate Rd NG17 .... 115 A1
Nunn Brook Rd NG17 .... 99 E1
Nunn Brook Rise NG17 .... 99 E2
Nunn Cl NG17 .... 99 E1
Nurseries The NG16 .... 144 A2
Nursery Ave
Beeston NG9 .... 183 C5
Nursery Ave *continued*
Farndon NG24 .... 139 A5
Sutton in A NG17 .... 100 C2
Nursery Cl
Hucknall NG15 .... 146 A4
Radcliffe on T NG12 .... 176 B3
Saxilby LN1 .... 57 B4
Nursery Ct
Mansfield NG18 .... 102 C8
Newark-on-T NG24 .... 125 A1
Nursery Dr NG4 .... 174 D8
Nursery End NG25 .... 121 D1
Nursery Gdns DE55 .... 113 C4
Nursery La
Morton DN21 .... 15 A5
Nottingham NG6 .... 160 E4
Sutton on T NG23 .... 96 F8
Nursery Rd
Arnold NG5 .... 162 A7
Bingham NG13 .... 178 B4
Radcliffe on T NG12 .... 176 B3
Nursery St NG18 .... 102 C8
Nursery Vale DN21 .... 15 B5
Nursury Gdns NG14 .... 150 D2
Nuthall Gdns NG8 .... 172 D8
Nuthall Rd NG8 .... 160 C2
Nuthatch Cres S81 .... 25 D1
Nutkin Cl 4 LE11 .... 220 A2

O

Oak Acres NG9 .... 183 A5
Oak Ave
Aldercar NG16 .... 143 B5
Bingham NG13 .... 178 A4
Blidworth NG21 .... 118 B4
Farndon NG24 .... 139 A4
Mansfield NG18 .... 102 C8
New Ollerton NG22 .... 77 D4
Radcliffe on T NG12 .... 175 E4
Rainworth NG21 .... 104 C1
Sandiacre NG10 .... 182 A7
Shirebrook NG20 .... 72 D4
Oak Bank Cl NG18 .... 102 B8
Oak Cl
Pinxton NG16 .... 113 C3
Worksop S80 .... 35 E1
Oak Cres LE12 .... 214 D8
Oakdale Dr NG9 .... 183 C4
Oakdale Rd
Arnold NG5 .... 162 B8
Carlton NG3 .... 174 C6
Mansfield NG18 .... 101 F7
Retford DN22 .... 39 E8
South Normanton DE55 .... 113 A4
Oak Dr
Eastwood NG16 .... 143 E2
Mansfield Woodhouse NG19 88 E2
New Balderton NG24 .... 140 C4
Nuthall NG16 .... 159 B6
Oakenhall Ave NG15 .... 146 C7
Oakfield LN1 .... 57 A3
Oakfield Ave
Market Warsop NG20 .... 74 B3
Sutton in A NG17 .... 114 E8
Oakfield Cl
Mansfield NG18 .... 102 F2
Nottingham NG8 .... 171 C3
Oakfield Dr NG10 .... 182 B3
Oakfield La NG20 .... 74 B2
Oakfield Rd
Hucknall NG15 .... 146 B6
Nottingham NG8 .... 171 C3
Stapleford NG9 .... 182 D7
Oakfields Rd NG2 .... 174 A1
Oak Flatt NG9 .... 183 A5
Oakford Cl NG8 .... 160 A2
Oak Gr NG15 .... 146 A4
Oakham Bsns Pk NG18 .... 101 F3
Oakham Cl
Mansfield NG18 .... 102 B4
Nottingham NG5 .... 160 F7
Oakhampton Cres NG3 .. 162 C6
Oakham Rd NG11 .... 185 D2
Oakham Way DE7 .... 157 D3
Oakholme Ave S81 .... 35 F5
Oakholme Rise S81 .... 35 F6
Oakington Cl NG5 .... 161 B5
Oakland Ave
Huthwaite NG17 .... 99 F2
Long Eaton NG10 .... 193 C5
Oakland Ct NG9 .... 171 A1
Oakland Gr NG14 .... 148 F7
Oakland Rd NG18 .... 102 F8
Oaklands NG23 .... 112 A8
Oaklands Ave DE75 .... 143 A2
Oaklands Dr DN11 .... 8 D2
Oaklands La DN22 .... 40 A5
Oakland St 6 NG7 .... 172 E7
Oaklands The DE55 .... 113 A4
Oakland Terr NG10 .... 193 C5
Oakleaf Cres NG17 .... 100 C1
Oakleigh Ave
Mansfield Woodhouse NG19 .... 88 E4
Nottingham NG3 .... 162 C2
Oakleigh St NG6 .... 160 D4
Oakley Dr LE12 .... 212 D2
Oakley Mews NG6 .... 159 F6
Oakley's Rd NG10 .... 193 E7
Oakley's Rd W NG10 .... 193 D6
Oak Lodge Dr NG16 .... 158 F7
Oakmead Ave NG8 .... 171 F8
Oakmere Cl NG2 .... 186 C4
Oakridge Cl NG19 .... 88 F1
Oak Rise NG22 .... 105 E7
Oaks Ave S80 .... 58 C8
Oaks Cl DN22 .... 19 B5
Oaks Ind Est LE11 .... 220 A6
Oaks La
Oxton NG25 .... 133 F7
Walkeringham DN10 .... 13 E3
Oak St
Kirkby in A NG17 .... 115 B5
Nottingham NG5 .... 161 B1
Sutton in A NG17 .... 100 D7
Oaks The
Mansfield NG18 .... 102 C3
Newark-on-T NG24 .... 140 E4
Oak Tree NG14 .... 152 A8
Oaktree Ave DN21 .... 15 F2
Oak Tree Ave
Edwinstowe NG21 .... 76 A2
Glapwell S44 .... 86 B8
Radcliffe on T NG12 .... 175 F4
Oak Tree Bsns Pk NG18 .. 103 B4
Oak Tree Cl
Hucknall NG15 .... 145 D4
Mansfield NG18 .... 103 B7
West Bridgford NG2 .... 186 A8
Oak Tree Cres NG19 .... 88 B4
Oaktree Dr NG22 .... 106 A4
Oak Tree Dr NG4 .... 163 A2
Oak Tree La NG18 .... 103 A6
Oak Tree La L Ctr NG18 .. 103 B5
Oak Tree Prim Sch NG18 .... 103 C6
Oaktree Rd DE55 .... 99 C1
Oak Tree Rd
Bawtry DN10 .... 9 F7
Sutton in A NG17 .... 101 A4
Oak Tree Rise S81 .... 25 E7
Oak View Rise NG18 .... 116 D7
Oakwood Dr
Nottingham NG8 .... 172 C7
Ravenshead NG15 .... 117 A1
Oakwood Gr NG21 .... 91 B8
Oakwood Mews S80 .... 35 C3
Oakwood Rd NG18 .... 103 B4
Oatfield La NG12 .... 176 D6
Oban Rd NG9 .... 183 C6
Observatory Way NG17 .. 115 B8
Occupation La
Edwinstowe NG21 .... 76 B1
Kirkby in A NG17 .... 114 F6
Rolleston NG25 .... 137 E5
Willoughby-on-t-W LE12 .. 217 E6
Occupation Rd
Hucknall NG15 .... 146 A5
New Houghton NG19 .... 86 F7
Nottingham NG6 .... 160 B5
Ochbrook Ct DE7 .... 157 F3
Ockerby St NG6 .... 160 C6
Oddicroft La NG17 .... 101 A1
Odesa Dr NG6 .... 160 B4
Ogdon Ct NG3 .... 173 F6
Ogle Dr
Nottingham NG1 .... 173 B3
Nottingham NG7 .... 223 D1
Ogle St NG15 .... 146 A7
Oldacres NG14 .... 149 D4
Old Basford Prim Sch NG6 .... 160 D3
Old Bell La NG23 .... 96 F4
Old Blyth Rd DN22 .... 38 A6
Old Bowling Gn The S81 .. 35 B4
Old Brickyard NG3 .... 174 A7
Oldbury Cl NG11 .... 195 D7
Old Chapel Cl NG17 .... 114 E5
Old Chapel La
Elston NG23 .... 153 E5
Selston NG16 .... 129 A3
Old Church St 9 NG7 .... 172 E2
Old Coach Rd
Nottingham NG8 .... 171 F5
Nottingham NG8 .... 171 F6
Worksop S80 .... 47 E7
Old Ctyd The DN21 .... 44 C8
Old Dalby CE Sch LE14 .. 218 E5
Old Dalby La LE14 .... 219 D6
Old Derby Rd NG16 .... 143 D3
Old Dr NG9 .... 183 E8
Old Engine Yd The LE12 .. 215 E5
Old Epperstone Rd NG14 150 B4
Oldershaw Ave DE74 .... 203 C2
Oldershaw Rd LE12 .... 205 F1
Old Farm Rd NG5 .... 160 F8
Old Forge Cl LE12 .... 213 A1
Old Forge La NG13 .... 191 C5
Old Forge Rd DN10 .... 6 E2
Old Gateford Rd S81 .... 35 C8
Old Grantham Rd NG13 .. 179 A3
Old Great N Rd NG23 .... 96 E8
Old Hall Cl
Calverton NG14 .... 148 E7
Farndon NG24 .... 138 F4
Market Warsop NG20 .... 74 C5
Old Hall Dr
Nottingham NG3 .... 161 D2
Widmerpool NG12 .... 208 C5
Old Hall Gdns NG24 .... 125 F2
Old Hall La
East Markham NG22 .... 65 F7
Norwell NG23 .... 110 B8
Old Hall The DN21 .... 15 C1
Oldknow St NG7 .... 172 F7
Old La NG12 .... 185 D1
Old La The NG13 .... 192 B2
Old Lenton Cl NG12 .... 189 A4
Old Lenton St NG1 .... 223 F2
Old Liby Arts Ctr The NG18 .... 102 B7
Old London Rd
Babworth DN22 .... 49 F8
Barnby Moor DN22 .... 28 C3
Old London Rd *continued*
West Drayton DN22 .... 50 F2
Old Main Rd
Bulcote NG14 .... 164 B5
Costock LE12 .... 206 D1
Old Manor Cl NG14 .... 149 D4
Old Manor Rd NG19 .... 88 B3
Old Melton Rd NG12 .... 197 F7
Old Mill Cl
Beeston NG9 .... 183 A2
Bestwood Village NG6 .... 146 D3
Nottingham NG7 .... 222 B3
Old Mill Cres NG24 .... 140 B8
Old Mill Ct NG13 .... 177 F5
Old Mill La
Cuckney NG20 .... 60 B3
Mansfield NG19 .... 88 E1
Old Mkt Pl
Mansfield NG18 .... 102 B7
South Normanton DE55 .... 113 A6
Old Mkt Sq NG1 .... 223 E2
Old Newark Rd NG18 .... 102 E2
Oldoak Rd NG11 .... 185 A2
Old Parsonage La LE12 .. 215 C1
Old Pk Cl NG11 .... 203 F6
Old Pk The NG12 .... 187 F4
Old Post Office St DN10 .. 11 C3
Old Rd NG17 .... 100 F7
Old Rectory Cl LE12 .... 205 E1
Old Rectory Mus & Wildlife Gdn LE11 .... 220 B4
Old Rufford Rd
Bilsthorpe NG22 .... 105 C4
Calverton NG14 .... 133 C6
Edwinstowe NG22 .... 91 D4
Farnsfield NG22 .... 119 B5
Ollerton NG22 .... 77 A3
Old Sch Cl NG11 .... 195 E8
Old Sch House Cl NG12 .. 189 B7
Old Sch La NG19 .... 87 A5
Old Showfields DN21 .... 15 D2
Old Sookholme La NG20 .. 74 A4
Old St NG1 .... 223 E3
Old Sta Yd NG13 .... 181 C3
Old Storth La DE55 .... 113 B4
Old Tannery Dr NG14 .... 150 E1
Old Terr NG19 .... 86 F4
Old Tollerton Rd NG2 .... 186 C7
Old Trent Rd DN10 .... 14 F1
Old Way LE12 .... 213 A1
Olga Ct NG3 .... 173 F6
Olga Rd NG3 .... 173 F6
Olive Ave
Long Eaton NG10 .... 182 E1
Shirebrook NG20 .... 72 D6
Olive Ct NG17 .... 100 F4
Olive Gr
Burton Joyce NG14 .... 163 F5
Mansfield NG19 .... 103 A8
Oliver Cl
Heanor DE75 .... 143 B2
Nottingham NG7 .... 222 C4
Oliver Ct NG24 .... 140 B8
Oliver Quibell Inf Sch NG24 .... 140 A5
Oliver Rd LE11 .... 220 B2
Oliver St NG7 .... 222 C3
Ollerton Prim Sch NG22 .. 77 D5
Ollerton Rd
Arnold NG5 .... 147 E6
Calverton NG14 .... 132 F2
Edwinstowe NG21 .... 76 D3
Farnsfield NG22 .... 119 A1
Gamston DN22 .... 50 E5
Kelham NG23 .... 124 A5
Kirton NG22 .... 78 F8
Ollerton NG22 .... 77 A4
Retford DN22 .... 39 E4
South Muskham NG23 .... 124 B7
Tuxford NG22 .... 65 C2
Worksop S80 .... 47 B4
Ollerton Water Mill NG22 . 77 A3
Olton Ave NG9 .... 171 F1
Olympus Ct NG15 .... 145 D3
Omberley Ave NG17 .... 101 B6
Onchan Ave NG4 .... 174 E6
Ontario Dr NG16 .... 129 A7
Opal Cl
Mansfield NG18 .... 102 E4
Rainworth NG21 .... 104 C1
Orange Cl NG20 .... 72 E6
Orange Croft DN11 .... 8 B8
Orange Gdns NG2 .... 173 D2
Orby Cl NG3 .... 173 F6
Orby Wlk NG3 .... 173 F6
Orchard Ave
Bingham NG13 .... 177 D4
Carlton NG4 .... 174 E7
North Leverton w H DN22 .. 42 D8
Orchard Bsns Pk
Ilkeston DE7 .... 157 D1
Sandiacre NG10 .... 182 C6
Orchard Cl
Barkestone-le-Vale NG13 .... 192 B2
Barnstone NG13 .... 190 F3
Bleasby NG14 .... 152 A8
Burton Joyce NG14 .... 163 F5
East Bridgford NG13 .... 165 D3
East Leake LE12 .... 214 D8
Gunthorpe NG14 .... 165 A5
Mansfield NG18 .... 102 C2
Morton DN21 .... 15 B5
North Leverton w H DN22 .. 42 D8
Radcliffe on T NG12 .... 175 E3

Orchard Cl continued
Shirebrook NG20 . . . . **72** E5
South Muskham NG23 . . . . **124** E7
Southwell NG25 . . . . **121** D2
Sutton Bonington LE12 . . . **213** C5
Tollerton NG12 . . . . **186** D1
Orchard Cres
Beeston NG9 . . . . **183** C5
Glapwell S44 . . . . **86** B8
Tuxford NG22 . . . . **65** F2
Orchard Ct
Carlton NG4 . . . . **174** E7
Gelding NG4 . . . . **162** D2
Hucknall NG15 . . . . **146** A6
Langley Mill NG16 . . . . **143** B3
Nottingham NG8 . . . . **172** E8
Orchard Dr NG14 . . . . **149** A7
Orchard Gr
Arnold NG5 . . . . **161** C6
Misterton DN10 . . . . **14** A8
Orchard La LN1 . . . . **57** A4
Orchard Leigh DN22 . . . . . . **39** D4
Orchard Pk **125** F2
Orchard Prim Sch NG17 . . **114** C5
Orchard Rd NG17 . . . . **114** C5
Orchard Rise NG4 . . . . **163** C7
Orchard Sch DN22 . . . . **42** C7
Orchard Specl Sch NG24 **125** A1
Orchard St
Eastwood NG16 . . . . **144** A1
Gotham NG11 . . . . **195** B1
Hucknall NG15 . . . . **146** A6
Kimberley NG16 . . . . **158** F6
Langley Mill NG16 . . . . **143** B3
Long Eaton NG10 . . . . **193** E7
10 Loughborough LE11 . . . **220** A4
Mansfield NG19 . . . . **88** B1
Stapleford NG9 . . . . **182** D7
Orchards The
Carlton NG4 . . . . **163** A1
Lowdham NG14 . . . . **164** E8
Oxton NG25 . . . . **134** C4
Westwood NG16 . . . . **128** B4
Orchard The
Elston NG23 . . . . **153** E4
Sutton in A NG17 . . . . **101** B1
Orchard View NG19 . . . . . . **88** B3
Orchard Way
Balderton NG24 . . . . **140** D3
Sandiacre NG10 . . . . **182** A3
Sutton in A NG17 . . . . **114** C8
Wymeswold LE12 . . . . **216** D3
Orchard Wlk NG17 . . . . . . **114** C5
Orchid Cl
4 Kirkby in A NG17 . . . . . **114** F7
New Balderton NG24 . . . . **140** B5
West Bridgford NG11 . . . . **185** C4
Orchid Dr
Farndon NG24 . . . . **139** B6
Sutton in A NG17 . . . . **101** B1
Orchid Way NG20 . . . . **72** D3
Ordsall Pk Cl DN22 . . . . **39** D6
Ordsall Pk Dr DN22 . . . . . . **39** D6
Ordsall Rd DN22 . . . . **39** D6
Ordsall Prim Sch DN22 . . . **39** D4
Ordsall Rd DN22 . . . . **39** C5
Orford Ave
Nottingham NG11 . . . . **184** F4
Radcliffe on T NG12 . . . . . **175** F2
Orion Cl NG8 . . . . **171** E7
Orion Dr NG8 . . . . **171** E7
Orlando Dr NG4 . . . . **174** F8
Orlock Wlk NG5 . . . . **161** B5
Ormonde St NG16 . . . . **143** B4
Ormonde Terr
Aldercar NG16 . . . . **143** B4
Nottingham NG5 . . . . **161** C2
Ornsay Cl NG5 . . . . **146** E1
Orpean Way NG9 . . . . **182** E2
Orston Ave
Arnold NG5 . . . . **162** A7
Newark-on-T NG24 . . . . . . **139** E6
Orston Dr NG8 . . . . **172** D4
Orston Gn NG8 . . . . **172** D3
Orston La NG13 . . . . **180** F3
Orston Prim Sch NG13 . . **180** A7
Orston Rd E NG2 . . . . **173** F1
Orston Rd W NG2 . . . . **173** F1
Orton Ave NG9 . . . . **183** C6
Ortzen St NG7 . . . . **222** B4
Orville Rd NG5 . . . . **160** E5
Osberne Wy NG19 . . . . **89** F2
Osberton Rd DN22 . . . . **39** F6
Osberton View S81 . . . . . . **36** B5
Osborne Ave 2 NG5 . . . . . **161** C3
Osborne Cl NG10 . . . . **182** B4
Osborne Gr NG5 . . . . **161** C3
Osborne St NG7 . . . . **222** A4
Osbourne Cl NG16 . . . . . . **159** B7
Osbourne St NG17 . . . . . . **129** F8
Osgood Rd NG5 . . . . **162** C5
Osier Dr NG15 . . . . **130** A6
Osier Fields LE12 . . . . **205** F2
Osier Rd NG2 . . . . **173** C2
Osiers The
Kegworth DE74 . . . . **203** D2
Newark-on-T NG24 . . . . . . **139** C6
Osman Cl NG2 . . . . **173** B1
Osmanthorpe Nature Reserve
NG22 . . . . **120** F6
Osmaston St
Nottingham NG7 . . . . **222** B1
Sandiacre NG10 . . . . **182** C5
Osprey Cl NG11 . . . . **184** C1

Ossington Cl
Meden Vale NG20 . . . . **74** D8
Nottingham NG1 . . . . **223** E4
Ossington Rd NG22 . . . . **93** E5
Ossington St NG7 . . . . **222** B4
Ossington Way NG24 . . . . . **124** F1
Oster Fen La NG23 . . . . . . **156** F7
Osterley Gr NG8 . . . . **159** D2
Otter Ave LN1 . . . . **57** A4
Otter Way NG19 . . . . **87** D1
Oulton Cl NG5 . . . . **161** F6
Oundle Dr
Ilkeston DE7 . . . . **170** A7
Mansfield NG19 . . . . **87** D1
Nottingham NG8 . . . . **172** C3
Our Lady of Perpetual
Succour Prim Sch NG6 **160** D8
Our Ladys Convent Sch
LE11 . . . . **220** B2
Oursham St NG17 . . . . **100** F3
Ousebridge Cres NG4 . . . **175** A8
Ouse Bridge Dr NG4 . . . . **175** A8
Outgang La
Mansfield Woodhouse
NG19 . . . . **88** D4
Pleasley NG19 . . . . **87** C6
Treswell DN22 . . . . **42** F4
Outram St NG17 . . . . **100** F3
Oval Gdns 2 NG8 . . . . **172** D8
Oval The
Retford DN22 . . . . **39** D4
Sutton in A NG17 . . . . **100** D4
Tickhill DN11 . . . . **8** B8
Overdale Ave NG17 . . . . . . **100** E7
Overdale Cl NG10 . . . . **193** A6
Overdale Rd NG6 . . . . **160** C3
Overend Rd S80 . . . . **35** F4
Overmoor View DE55 . . . . . **99** B7
Overstone Cl NG17 . . . . . . **100** F5
Overstrand Cl NG5 . . . . . . **161** F6
Oveday La S81 . . . . **25** D3
Owen Ave NG10 . . . . **194** A6
Owlston Cl NG6 . . . . **143** F3
Owsthorpe Cl NG5 . . . . . . **161** A8
Owston Ferry Rd DN9 . . . . . . **7** D7
Owston Rd DN10 . . . . **7** C4
Owthorpe Gr NG5 . . . . **161** B2
Owthorpe La NG12 . . . . . . **199** F3
Owthorpe Rd
Colston Bassett NG12 . . . . **200** B7
Cotgrave NG12 . . . . **187** F2
Oxborough Rd NG5 . . . . . . **161** C7
Oxbow Cl NG2 . . . . **173** C1
Oxbury Rd NG16 . . . . **158** F8
Oxclose La
Mansfield Woodhouse
NG19 . . . . **88** A3
Nottingham NG5 . . . . **161** C6
Radmanthwaite NG19 . . . . . **87** D3
Oxcroft La NG20 . . . . **58** A8
Oxendale Cl NG2 . . . . **186** C6
Oxengate NG5 . . . . **161** C6
Oxford Cl NG21 . . . . **118** A8
Oxford Dr DN11 . . . . **8** F5
Oxford Rd
Carlton NG4 . . . . **174** E8
Eastwood NG16 . . . . **143** F2
Kirkby in A NG17 . . . . **115** D4
Long Eaton NG10 . . . . **193** D8
Loughborough LE11 . . . . . **220** A4
Mansfield Woodhouse NG19 **88** C1
Nottingham NG1 . . . . **223** D2
Sutton in A NG17 . . . . **100** C5
Oxpasture La NG20 . . . . **58** B6
Oxton Ave NG5 . . . . **161** C4
Oxton By-Pass NG25 . . . . **134** A4
Oxton Cl
Mansfield NG19 . . . . **101** E7
Retford DN22 . . . . **39** E3
Oxton Hill NG25 . . . . **134** E4
Oxton Rd
Calverton NG14 . . . . **133** D1
Southwell NG25 . . . . **135** C6
Ozier Holt
Carlton NG4 . . . . **174** E4
Long Eaton NG10 . . . . **193** C6

P

Packe St LE11 . . . . **220** A4
Pack Horse La 5 LE11 . . . **220** B3
Packington Hill DE74 . . . . **203** C2
Packman Dr NG11 . . . . **196** D8
Paddington Ms NG3 . . . . . . **174** A7
Paddock Cl
Calverton NG14 . . . . **148** F7
Edwinstowe NG21 . . . . **76** A3
Nottingham NG6 . . . . **160** B5
Radcliffe on T NG12 . . . . . **175** E5
Paddocks Cl
Elston NG23 . . . . **153** D4
Pinxton NG16 . . . . **113** C4
Paddocks The
Beckingham DN10 . . . . **14** B1
Bottesford NG13 . . . . **181** A2
Elston NG23 . . . . **153** E4
Hockerton NG25 . . . . **122** B6
Lound DN22 . . . . **20** C2
Mansfield Woodhouse NG19 **88** E5
Marton DN21 . . . . **44** C8
Newark-on-T NG24 . . . . . . **140** B7
Newton on T LN1 . . . . **55** A1
Sandiacre NG10 . . . . **182** A5
Stapleford LN6 . . . . **127** E8

Paddocks The continued
Sutton Bonington LE12 . . . **213** B6
West Bridgford NG12 . . . . **186** B3
Worksop S81 . . . . **36** B7
Paddocks View NG10 . . . . **193** A8
Paddock The
Beeston NG9 . . . . **183** D2
Bingham NG13 . . . . **177** E4
Collingham NG23 . . . . **112** A7
Gunthorpe NG13, NG14 . . **164** F5
Kirkby in A NG17 . . . . **114** F4
Retford DN22 . . . . **40** A4
Stanton Hill NG17 . . . . **100** C5
Tickhill DN11 . . . . **8** B8
Paddy's La LE14 . . . . **218** A1
Padge Rd NG9 . . . . **184** B6
Padgham Ct 11 NG5 . . . . . **161** A8
Padley Hill NG18 . . . . **102** A6
Padleys La NG14 . . . . **163** C5
Padstow Cl NG18 . . . . **103** B2
Padstow Rd NG5 . . . . **161** A7
Pagdin Dr DN11 . . . . **8** E1
Paget Cres NG11 . . . . **196** C8
Paget St 5 LE11 . . . . **220** A5
Paignton Cl NG8 . . . . **160** B2
Paisley Gr NG9 . . . . **183** C1
Palace Theatre NG24 . . . . **140** A8
Palace View NG25 . . . . **136** F8
Palatine St
Nottingham NG1 . . . . **173** B3
Nottingham NG7 . . . . **223** D1
Paling Cres NG17 . . . . **100** E3
Palin Gdns NG12 . . . . **176** A3
Palin St NG7 . . . . **222** B4
Palm Ct Ind Ctr NG7 . . . . **160** F1
Palmer Ave NG15 . . . . **146** A8
Palmer Cres NG4 . . . . **174** D7
Palmer Dr NG9 . . . . **182** D5
Palmer Rd
Retford DN22 . . . . **30** A1
Sutton on T NG23 . . . . **96** F8
Palmers Ct 5 NG25 . . . . . **136** F8
Palmerston Gdns NG3 . . **223** E4
Palmerston St
Selston NG16 . . . . **128** F2
Westwood NG16 . . . . **128** C4
Palm St NG7 . . . . **160** F1
Palmwood Ct NG6 . . . . **160** C5
Palm Wood Ct NG6 . . . . . . **160** C5
Paper Mill La NG11 . . . . **8** C8
Papplewick Grange
NG15 . . . . **131** D3
Papplewick Hall & Gdns
NG15 . . . . **131** D4
Papplewick La NG15 . . . . **146** C8
Papplewick Ppg Sta
NG15 . . . . **132** C5
Paradise La LE14 . . . . **218** F4
Parfitt Dr NG12 . . . . **120** A5
Park Ave
Annesley Woodhouse
NG17 . . . . **130** B8
Arnold NG5 . . . . **161** E5
Awsworth NG16 . . . . **158** B5
Bildworth NG21 . . . . **118** B5
Burton Joyce NG14 . . . . . **163** E4
Carlton NG4 . . . . **174** F8
Eastwood NG16 . . . . **143** E3
Hucknall NG15 . . . . **145** F7
Keyworth NG12 . . . . **197** F4
Kimberley NG16 . . . . **159** A4
Loughborough LE11 . . . . . **220** B1
Mansfield NG18 . . . . **102** C8
Misterton DN10 . . . . **6** E3
Nottingham NG3 . . . . **173** C7
Shirebrook NG20 . . . . **72** E4
West Bridgford NG2 . . . . . **185** F8
Woodborough NG14 . . . . . **149** B4
Park Ave E NG12 . . . . **197** D3
Park Ave W NG12 . . . . **197** D3
Park Chase NG6 . . . . **160** B5
Park Cl
Lea DN21 . . . . **24** F1
Nottingham NG3 . . . . **161** E2
Pinxton NG16 . . . . **113** C2
Park Cres
Eastwood NG16 . . . . **143** F4
Ilkeston DE7 . . . . **170** A4
Newark-on-T NG24 . . . . . . **125** B4
Nottingham NG8 . . . . **171** C3
Retford DN22 . . . . **40** A8
Parkcroft Rd NG12 . . . . . . **185** F6
Park Ct
Loughborough LE11 . . . . . **220** B2
Mansfield NG18 . . . . **102** C8
Parkdale Prim Sch NG4 . **174** D6
Parkdale Rd NG3 . . . . **174** C6
Park Dr
Blyth S81 . . . . **18** A3
Hucknall NG15 . . . . **146** B6
Nottingham NG7 . . . . **222** C2
Sandiacre NG10 . . . . **182** A3
Parker Cl NG5 . . . . **162** C8
Parker's La NG19 . . . . **88** C3
Parker St
Hucknall NG15 . . . . **146** A7
Newark-on-T NG24 . . . . . . **140** A8
Parkes Cl NG24 . . . . **126** B2
Park Farm Cotts LN1 . . . . . **55** F1
Park Gate NG15 . . . . **131** B1
Park Gdn NG17 . . . . **100** A3
Park Hall Gdns NG15 . . . . . **88** C5
Park Hall Rd NG19 . . . . **88** C5
Parkham Rd NG16 . . . . **158** F7
Park Hill NG16 . . . . **158** B5
Park Hill Dr S81 . . . . **35** A5
Park House Gates NG3 . . **161** D1

Park Hts NG7 . . . . **222** C1
Parkin Cl NG12 . . . . **189** A4
Park La
Elkesley DN22 . . . . **50** C3
Holbeck NG20 . . . . **59** C6
Kirkby in A NG17 . . . . **114** C2
Lambley NG4 . . . . **163** E8
Mansfield NG18 . . . . **102** B5
Nottingham NG6 . . . . **160** E4
Owthorpe NG12 . . . . **199** E7
Pinxton NG16 . . . . **113** C2
Retford DN22 . . . . **40** A8
Southwell NG25 . . . . **136** D6
Sutton Bonington LE12 . . . **213** C5
Parkland Cl
Mansfield NG18 . . . . **102** E2
Nottingham NG11 . . . . **184** D3
Parklands Adult Ctr
NG10 . . . . **193** D8
Parklands Cl
Coddington NG24 . . . . **125** F2
4 Nottingham NG5 . . . . . **147** B1
Parklands Dr 2 LE11 . . . . **220** A1
Parklands Inf Sch NG10 . .**182** B1
Park Mews
Mansfield Woodhouse
NG19 . . . . **88** C4
Nottingham NG3 . . . . **173** C8
Retford DN22 . . . . **40** A8
Park Ravine NG7 . . . . **222** C1
Park Rd
Arnold NG5 . . . . **161** E5
Barnstone NG13 . . . . **190** E3
Bawtry DN10 . . . . **9** F7
Beeston, Bramcote NG9 . . **183** A8
Beeston, Chilwell NG9 . . . **183** E6
Bestwood Village NG6 . . . **146** E4
Calverton NG14 . . . . **148** E7
Carlton NG4 . . . . **174** F7
Hucknall NG15 . . . . **145** F7
Ilkeston DE7 . . . . **170** A7
Keyworth NG12 . . . . **197** F5
Loughborough LE11 . . . . . **220** B2
Radcliffe on T NG12 . . . . . **175** F4
Shirebrook NG20 . . . . **72** E5
Park Rd E NG14 . . . . **149** A7
Park Rd N NG9 . . . . **183** E6
Park Row NG1 . . . . **223** D2
Parkside
Huthwaite NG17 . . . . **100** A3
Keyworth NG12 . . . . **197** F4
Nottingham NG8 . . . . **171** E2
Parkside Ave NG10 . . . . . . **193** B8
Parkside Dr NG10 . . . . **193** B8
Parkside Gdns NG8 . . . . . **171** E2
Parkside Rd NG21 . . . . **75** E2
Parkside Rise NG8 . . . . . . **171** E2
Park Springs Rd DN21 . . . **24** F6
Park St
Beeston NG9 . . . . **183** E6
Kirkby in A NG17 . . . . **114** F5
Long Eaton NG10 . . . . **182** C1
Loughborough LE11 . . . . . **220** B3
Mansfield Woodhouse NG19 **88** B3
Newark-on-T NG24 . . . . . . **140** A7
Stapleford NG9 . . . . **182** C5
Sutton in A NG17 . . . . **100** F3
Parkstone Ave NG21 . . . . **103** F2
Parkstone Cl NG2 . . . . **185** C5
Park Terr
Keyworth NG12 . . . . **197** F5
Nottingham NG1 . . . . **223** D2
Park The
Cotgrave NG12 . . . . **187** F4
Mansfield NG18 . . . . **102** C8
Newark-on-T NG24 . . . . . . **140** A7
North Muskham NG23 . . . . **110** F3
Park Valley NG7 . . . . **223** D2
Park View
Beeston NG9 . . . . **183** D6
Mansfield NG18 . . . . **161** E2
Pleasley NG19 . . . . **87** A5
Parkview Rd NG5 . . . . **161** A7
Park View Way NG18 . . . . **102** C5
Parkway
Clipstone NG19 . . . . **89** D3
Newark-on-T NG24 . . . . . . **139** E6
Nottingham NG11 . . . . **100** B3
Whitwell S80 . . . . **45** A6
Parkway Ct NG8 . . . . **171** D5
Parliament Cl NG24 . . . . . **139** E8
Parliament Rd NG18 . . . . . **101** E8
Parliament St
Newark-on-T NG24 . . . . . . **139** E7
Sutton in A NG17 . . . . **100** F2
Parliament Terr NG1 . . . . **223** D3
Parliament Wlk NG24 . . . **139** E8
Parnell St DN21 . . . . **24** C8
Parnham's Cl LE14 . . . . . . **219** C8
Parr Gate NG9 . . . . **183** A4
Parr La NG14 . . . . **150** A5
Parrs The NG9 . . . . **184** B6
Parry Ct 5 NG3 . . . . **174** A6
Parry Way NG5 . . . . **162** B8
Parsons Mdw NG4 . . . . . . **174** F4
Parthenon Cl NG19 . . . . . . **86** F5
Partridge Cl NG21 . . . . . . **118** B8
Paschall Rd NG17 . . . . **115** B1
Pasteur Ct 5 NG7 . . . . . . **172** E2

Pasture Rd
Carlton in L S81 . . . . **26** A7
Carlton NG2 . . . . **174** E4
Nottingham NG12 . . . . **100** C5
Worksop S80 . . . . **35** C2
Pasture Farm & Victorian
Carriages Mus NG22 . . . . . **78** B7
Pasture La
Hathern LE12 . . . . **213** B2
Hilcote DE55 . . . . **99** C1
Hose LE14 . . . . **211** F6
Long Eaton NG10 . . . . **194** A5
Nottingham NG11 . . . . **196** A7
Sutton Bonington LE12 . . . **213** A6
Pasture Rd
Gainsborough DN21 . . . . . . **24** F8
Stapleford NG9 . . . . **170** D1
Pastures Ave NG11 . . . . . **195** D7
Pastures The
Bawtry DN10 . . . . **10** A5
Calverton NG14 . . . . **148** D7
Eastwood NG16 . . . . **158** B8
Mansfield Woodhouse NG19 **88** E5
Rampton DN22 . . . . **43** A1
Tuxford NG22 . . . . **65** E2
Pasture View NG14 . . . . . . **165** A5
Patchills The NG18 . . . . . . **102** E6
Patchings Art Ctr NG14 . . **148** A8
Pateley Rd NG3 . . . . **162** A4
Paton Rd NG5 . . . . **160** E5
Patricia Dr NG5 . . . . **148** A1
Patrick Rd NG2 . . . . **185** E8
Patriot Cl NG16 . . . . **159** A7
Patterdale Cl NG2 . . . . **186** C6
Patterdale Rd NG5 . . . . . . **161** F5
Patterson Pl NG18 . . . . . . **102** D7
Patterson Rd 13 NG7 . . . . **172** F7
Paul Ave NG18 . . . . **103** A6
Paulson's Dr NG18 . . . . . . **102** B7
Pavilion Cl
Market Warsop NG20 . . . . . **74** B4
2 Nottingham NG2 . . . . . **173** D1
Pavilion Ct NG14 . . . . **164** E8
Pavilion Gdns
New Houghton NG19 . . . . . . **86** F8
Sutton in A NG17 . . . . **101** A6
Pavilion Rd
Ilkeston DE7 . . . . **157** F6
Kirkby in Ashfield NG17 . . **115** B6
Nottingham NG5 . . . . **147** B1
West Bridgford NG2 . . . . . **173** E1
Pavillion Way LE11 . . . . . . **220** A7
Paviour Rd NG5 . . . . **160** F5
Paxton Gdns NG3 . . . . **173** E5
Paxtons Ct NG24 . . . . **124** F1
Payne Rd NG9 . . . . **183** B3
Peach Ave
Selston NG16 . . . . **128** F6
South Normanton DE55 . . **113** B7
Peache Way NG9 . . . . **183** C2
Peachey St NG1 . . . . **223** E3
Peacock Cl
Gunthorpe NG14 . . . . **165** A4
Ruddington NG11 . . . . **196** B6
Peacock Cres NG7 . . . . . . **184** C2
Peacock Dr NG21 . . . . **118** C8
Peacock Pl DE7 . . . . **157** D4
Peacock St 2 NG18 . . . . . **102** B6
Peafield La NG19 . . . . **88** E4
Peafield Lane Prim Sch
NG19 . . . . **88** F4
Peakdale Cl NG10 . . . . **193** A6
Peaks's Croft DN10 . . . . . . **10** A7
Peak Hill Cl S81 . . . . **25** D1
Peak The NG20 . . . . **72** E3
Pearce Dr NG8 . . . . **172** B7
Pearl Ave NG17 . . . . **115** B3
Pearl Cl NG21 . . . . **104** C3
Pearmain Dr NG3 . . . . **173** F7
Pearson Ave NG9 . . . . **183** B5
Pearson St
Carlton NG4 . . . . **175** A6
Nottingham NG7 . . . . **160** F2
Pear Tree Cl DN22 . . . . **30** D4
Pear Tree Ct NG6 . . . . **160** E4
Pear Tree Dr NG20 . . . . . . **72** E6
Peartree La NG17 . . . . **86** B2
Peartree Orch NG11 . . . . . **196** C7
Pear Tree St NG5 . . . . **160** F6
Peas Hill Rd NG3 . . . . **223** F4
Peatfield Rd NG9 . . . . **170** D1
Peck La NG1 . . . . **223** E2
Pecks Hill NG18 . . . . **102** E7
Pedmore Valley NG5 . . . . **161** A7
Peebles Rd NG24 . . . . **139** D5
Peel Ave
Retford DN22 . . . . **40** B3
Tuxford NG22 . . . . **65** E4
Peel Cres NG19 . . . . **87** D2
Peel Dr LE11 . . . . **220** C4
Peel Rd NG19 . . . . **101** E8
Peel St
Langley Mill NG16 . . . . . . **143** B3
Long Eaton NG10 . . . . **193** E8
Nottingham NG1 . . . . **223** D4
South Normanton DE55 . . **113** B6
Peets Dr NG23 . . . . **110** F2
Pelham Ave
Ilkeston DE7 . . . . **157** C1
Nottingham NG5 . . . . **173** B8
Pelham Cl NG24 . . . . **139** F8
Pelham Cres
Beeston NG9 . . . . **184** B7
Nottingham NG7 . . . . **222** B2
Pelham Ct 4 NG5 . . . . **173** B8
Pelham Gdns NG24 . . . . . **139** F8

Pelham Rd
Kirkby in A NG17 . . . . 115 A6
Nottingham NG5 . . . . 173 B8
Retford DN22 . . . . 39 D6
Pelham St
Mansfield NG18 . . . . 102 C7
Newark-on-T NG24 . . . . . . 139 F8
Nottingham NG1 . . . . 223 E2
Sutton in A NG17 . . . . 100 D2
Worksop S80 . . . . 36 A1
Pelham Way NG19 . . . . 89 D3
Pemberley Ch NG17 . . . . . 100 D1
Pemberton St NG1 . . . . . . 223 F2
Pemberton The DE55 . . . 113 B4
Pembleton Dr NG19 . . . . . . 87 D1
Pembrey Cl NG19 . . . . 170 D2
Pembridge Cl NG6 . . . . . . 160 D2
Pembroke Cres NG24 . . . . 125 C3
Pembroke Dr
Carlton in L S81 . . . . 25 E6
Nottingham NG3 . . . . 161 C1
Pembroke Rd S81 . . . . 34 F7
Pembury Rd NG8 . . . . 171 E5
Penarth Gdns NG5 . . . . . . 161 E3
Penarth Rise NG5 . . . . . . 161 E3
Pen Cl DE55 . . . . 99 A3
Pendennis Cl DN21 . . . . . . 15 E2
Pendennis Cl NG3 . . . . . . 163 B1
Pendine Cl
Arnold NG5 . . . . 147 D1
South Normanton DE55 . . . 113 C6
Pendle Cres NG3 . . . . 161 F1
Pendock La NG12 . . . . 197 A2
Penfold Cl LE12 . . . . 213 A1
Penhale Dr NG15 . . . . 145 C5
Penhurst Cl NG11 . . . . 185 A4
Pen La NG12 . . . . 208 D4
Penllech Cl NG5 . . . . 161 A7
Penllech Wlk 4 NG5 . . . . 161 A7
Pennant Rd NG6 . . . . 160 D2
Pennard Wlk NG11 . . . . . . 195 D8
Penn Ave NG7 . . . . 222 A1
Pennhome Ave 8 NG5 . . 161 C2
Penniment La NG19 . . . . . . 87 B2
Pennine Cl
Huthwaite NG17 . . . . 99 E4
Long Eaton, Breaston
NG10 . . . . 182 A1
Long Eaton, New Sawley
NG10 . . . . 193 D4
Mansfield Woodhouse NG19 88 C4
Newton DE55 . . . . 99 A3
Pennine Dr NG5 . . . . 147 B1
Pennine Dr
Kirkby in A NG17 . . . . 114 D4
Selston NG16 . . . . 128 F7
Pennington Wlk DN22 . . . . 40 A6
Penn La LE14 . . . . 202 F4
Penn Moor Cl NG10 . . . . . 193 A6
Penn St NG17 . . . . 100 F3
Pennyfields Bvd NG10 . . . 193 A7
Pennyfoot St NG1 . . . . 173 E4
Penny Gn S80 . . . . 45 A5
Penrhyn Cl NG3 . . . . 223 F4
Penrhyn Cres NG9 . . . . . . 183 B4
Penrith Ave NG12 . . . . 176 A4
Penrith Cres NG8 . . . . 160 C2
Penrith Pl NG19 . . . . 101 D8
Penshore Cl NG11 . . . . . . 184 D1
Penswick Gr NG24 . . . . . . 125 F2
Pentland Ct NG19 . . . . 101 D5
Pentland Dr
Carlton in L S81 . . . . 25 E7
Nottingham NG5 . . . . 147 B2
Pentland Gdns NG10 . . . . 182 A1
Pentrich Wlk NG18 . . . . . . 103 B5
Pentwood Ave NG5 . . . . . . 147 F2
Penzance Pl NG18 . . . . . . 103 B7
Peoples Coll The Nottingham
NG1 . . . . 223 E2
Peppercorn Gdns NG8 . . . 172 C5
Pepper Rd NG14 . . . . 148 E8
Peppers Dr DE74 . . . . 203 B2
Pepper St
Nottingham NG1 . . . . 223 E2
Sutton in A NG17 . . . . 101 B2
Percival Cl NG17 . . . . 100 E3
Percival Cres NG17 . . . . . 100 E3
Percival Rd NG5 . . . . 161 C2
Percival St S35 . . . . 35 E5
Percy St
Eastwood NG16 . . . . 144 A2
Nottingham NG6 . . . . 160 D3
Sutton in A NG17 . . . . 100 C7
Peregrine Cl NG7 . . . . 222 A2
Peregrine Ct S81 . . . . 35 C7
Perivale Cl NG16 . . . . 159 D3
Perkin's La LE14 . . . . 219 A1
Perlethorpe Ave
Carlton NG4 . . . . 162 E2
Mansfield NG19 . . . . 88 A1
18 Nottingham NG2 . . . . . 173 E4
Perlethorpe Cl
Carlton NG4 . . . . 162 E2
Edwinstowe NG21 . . . . 75 F3
Perlethorpe Cres NG4 . . . 162 E2
Perlethorpe Dr
Carlton NG4 . . . . 162 E2
Hucknall NG15 . . . . 145 E5
Perlthorpe Ave NG20 . . . . . 74 D8
Perry Gr
Bingham NG13 . . . . 177 F4
Loughborough LE11 . . . . . . 220 C1
Perry Rd NG5 . . . . 161 B3
Perth Cl NG19 . . . . 88 C5
Perth Dr NG9 . . . . 170 F1
Perth St NG1 . . . . 223 E3

Peterborough Rd NG23 . . . 98 B1
Peter Donnelly Ctr The
NG18 . . . . 102 E4
Peters Cl
Arnold NG5 . . . . 162 C6
Eastwood NG16 . . . . 144 C2
Petersfield Cl
Mansfield NG19 . . . . 101 C8
Nottingham NG5 . . . . 160 F7
Petersgate NG10 . . . . 182 A1
Petersgate Cl NG10 . . . . . 182 A1
Petersham Mews NG7 . . . 222 B1
Petersham Rd NG10 . . . . . 182 A1
Petersmiths Cl NG22 . . . . . 77 C6
Petersmiths Cres NG22 . . . 77 C6
Petersmiths Dr NG22 . . . . . 77 C6
Petworth Ave NG9 . . . . . . 182 F3
Petworth Dr NG5 . . . . 160 F4
Peveril Cres NG10 . . . . . . 193 A5
Peveril Dr
Ilkeston DE7 . . . . 157 D2
Nottingham NG7 . . . . 223 D1
Sutton in A NG17 . . . . 100 C2
West Bridgford NG2 . . . . . . 185 D3
Peveril Mews NG7 . . . . . . 222 C2
Peveril Rd NG9 . . . . 184 A7
Peveril St
Hucknall NG15 . . . . 146 A8
Nottingham NG7 . . . . 222 B4
Pharaoh Ct NG8 . . . . 159 D2
Pheasant Hill NG19 . . . . . . 88 A1
Philip Ave
Eastwood NG16 . . . . 144 A1
Kirkby in A NG17 . . . . 115 B2
Nuthall NG16 . . . . 159 C6
Philip Cl NG11 . . . . 118 C8
Philip Gr NG4 . . . . 162 E2
Philip Rd NG24 . . . . 139 E5
Phoenix Ave NG4 . . . . 162 E2
Phoenix Ct
Eastwood NG16 . . . . 144 A1
Nottingham NG7 . . . . 184 F8
Phoenix Ctr NG6 . . . . 160 A4
Phoenix Inf Sch 11 NG4 . . . 162 F1
Phoenix St NG17 . . . . 101 B4
Phyllis Cl NG15 . . . . 130 F1
Phyllis Gr NG10 . . . . 193 F7
Piccadilly NG6 . . . . 160 D6
Pickard St NG18 . . . . 102 E7
Pickering Ave NG16 . . . . . 143 F2
Pieris Dr NG11 . . . . 184 C1
Pierpoint Pl NG17 . . . . . . 114 F6
Pierrepont Ave NG4 . . . . . 162 E2
Pierrepont Gamston Prim
Sch NG2 . . . . 186 B6
Pierrepont Rd NG2 . . . . . . 174 A1
Pierson St NG4 . . . . 139 E5
Pilcher Gate NG1 . . . . 223 E2
Pilgrim Cl
Ranby DN22 . . . . 38 E6
Ravenshead NG15 . . . . 116 F2
Pilgrim Ct S81 . . . . 34 F7
Pilgrim Rise DN10 . . . . 3 C1
Pilgrim Way S80 . . . . 35 F2
Pilkington Rd NG3 . . . . . . 162 A1
Pilkington St 8 NG6 . . . . 160 B7
Pillared House La DN21 . . 24 D7
Pimlico Ave NG9 . . . . 171 B3
Pimlico Cl NG12 . . . . 176 E3
Pinder St NG1 . . . . 223 F2
Pine Ave
Langley Mill NG16 . . . . 143 A3
New Ollerton NG22 . . . . 77 D4
Pine Cl
East Leake LE12 . . . . 214 D8
Everton DN10 . . . . 11 C3
Kirkby in A NG17 . . . . 114 F6
Mansfield NG18 . . . . 103 F1
Mansfield Woodhouse NG19 88 C5
Newark-on-T NG24 . . . . . . 125 B4
Newark-on-T NG24 . . . . . . 140 F1
Shirebrook NG20 . . . . 72 E6
Pine Hill Cl NG5 . . . . 146 F1
Pinehurst Ave NG15 . . . . . 145 C5
Pines The
Gainsborough DN21 . . . . . . 24 F6
Worksop S80 . . . . 35 F2
Pines Way NG18 . . . . 116 D7
Pine Tree Cl S80 . . . . 35 E1
Pine Tree Wlk NG16 . . . . . 143 E2
Pineview Cl NG18 . . . . 102 F2
Pinewood Ave
Arnold NG5 . . . . 148 B1
Edwinstowe NG21 . . . . 91 C8
Pinewood Cl
Kirkby in A NG17 . . . . 115 C6
Southwell NG25 . . . . 121 D1
Pinewood Dr NG18 . . . . . . 102 F2
Pinewood Gdns NG11 . . . 195 D8
Pinewood Inf Sch NG5 . . . 148 B1
Pinfold NG13 . . . . 177 F4
Pinfold Cl
Bottesford NG13 . . . . 181 A3
Cotgrave NG12 . . . . 98 A1
Cotgrave NG12 . . . . 187 F4
Kinoulton NG12 . . . . 199 F2
Lound DN22 . . . . 20 C1
Woodborough NG14 . . . . . . 149 C4
Pinfold Cres NG14 . . . . . . 149 C4
Pinfold Dr S81 . . . . 25 F7
Pinfold Gate LE11 . . . . . . 220 B4
Pinfold Jetty 5 LE11 . . . . 220 C4
Pinfold La
Averham NG23 . . . . 123 C2
Balderton NG24 . . . . 140 D3
Bottesford NG13 . . . . 181 A3

Pinfold La continued
Clarborough DN22 . . . . 40 E8
Elston NG23 . . . . 153 D5
Harby LE14 . . . . 202 C3
Kinoulton NG12 . . . . 199 F2
Misterton DN10 . . . . 6 E2
Nottingham NG11 . . . . 185 B6
Shelford NG12 . . . . 164 C1
Stapleford NG9 . . . . 182 E7
Styrrup DN11 . . . . 8 D2
Pinfold Cl LE14 . . . . 202 C3
Pinfold Rd NG16 . . . . 144 C1
Pinfold The DN10 . . . . 4 B2
Pingle Cl DN21 . . . . 24 E8
Pingle Cres NG5 . . . . 160 F8
Pingle The NG10 . . . . 193 D8
Pingley NG23 . . . . 138 C8
Pingley La NG23 . . . . 138 C8
Pintail Cl NG4 . . . . 175 B5
Pinxton Ct NG18 . . . . 103 B7
Pinxton Gn NG16 . . . . 113 F3
Pinxton La
Kirkby in A, Fulwood
NG17 . . . . 114 A7
Kirkby in A, Tichfield Park
NG17 . . . . 114 C4
South Normanton DE55 . . . 113 C5
Pinxton Rd NG17 . . . . 114 D3
Piper Cl
Hucknall NG15 . . . . 131 B1
Long Whatton LE12 . . . . . . 212 C2
Piper Dr LE12 . . . . 212 C2
Piper La S80 . . . . 61 D7
Pippin Cl
Newark-on-T NG24 . . . . . . 125 B2
Nottingham NG3 . . . . 173 F7
Pitcairn Cl NG2 . . . . 173 C1
Pitch Cl NG4 . . . . 174 C8
Pithouse La LE12 . . . . 204 E1
Pit La DE75 . . . . 157 B6
Pitt Hill NG20 . . . . 58 F2
Pitt La DN10 . . . . 12 F3
Plains Farm Cl NG3 . . . . . 162 C5
Plains Gr NG3 . . . . 162 A4
Plainspot Rd NG16 . . . . . 128 E2
Plains Rd NG3 . . . . 162 B4
Plane Cl NG6 . . . . 159 F7
Plantagenet Ct NG3 . . . . . 223 F3
Plantagenet St NG3 . . . . . 223 F3
Plantation Ave NG22 . . . . . 66 A7
Plantation Cl NG5 . . . . . . 147 A1
Plantation Dr DN10 . . . . . . 11 A1
Plantation Hill S81 . . . . . . 36 B4
Plantation La S81 . . . . 27 B8
Plantation Rd
East Markham NG22 . . . . . . 66 A6
Keyworth NG12 . . . . 197 D3
Nottingham NG8 . . . . 171 C4
Plantation Side NG7 . . . . . 172 E7
Plantations The 7 NG10 . 193 A8
Plant La NG10 . . . . 193 A4
Plants Yd S80 . . . . 35 F2
Platt La NG12 . . . . 198 A5
Platt St NG16 . . . . 113 D2
Platts The NG24 . . . . 139 E5
Player St NG7 . . . . 222 B4
Playworld NG4 . . . . 162 F8
Plaza Gdns NG6 . . . . 160 E4
Pleasant Cl 2 LE11 . . . . . 220 A4
Pleasant Pl DE74 . . . . 203 D2
Pleasant Row NG7 . . . . . . 172 F7
Pleasley Rd NG17 . . . . . . 101 A6
Pleasley Vale Nature Reserve
NG19 . . . . 87 D7
Plot La NG23 . . . . 98 E4
Plough Dr S81 . . . . 25 F7
Plough La
Lowdham NG14 . . . . 150 D1
Nottingham NG2 . . . . 173 E4
Ploughman Ave NG14 . . . 149 D4
Ploughman Wood Nature
Reserve NG14 . . . . 149 D2
Plover Dene S81 . . . . 35 C7
Plover Wharf 3 NG2 . . . . 173 A2
Plowman Ct NG9 . . . . 182 D6
Plowright Ct 6 NG3 . . . . . 173 D7
Plowright St 4 NG3 . . . . . 173 D7
Plumb Rd NG15 . . . . 146 C7
Plummer La DE74 . . . . . . 203 C2
Plumptre NG16 . . . . 143 B5
Plumptre Almshouses
NG1 . . . . 223 F1
Plumptre Cl NG16 . . . . . . 143 F1
Plumptre Pl NG1 . . . . 223 F2
Plumptre Sq NG1 . . . . 223 F2
Plumptre Sch NG12 . . . . . 197 E6
Plumtre Way NG16 . . . . . . 143 F1
Plum Tree Ave NG19 . . . . . 89 B1
Plumtree Gdns NG14 . . . . 148 F7
Plumtree Rd
Bircotes DN11 . . . . 9 C6
Cotgrave NG12 . . . . 187 E3
Plumtree Sch NG12 . . . . . 197 E6
Plungar Cl NG8 . . . . 172 B6
Plungar La NG13 . . . . 192 B2
Plungar La NG13 . . . . 191 C5
Plymouth Ave NG16 . . . . . 113 E2
Poacher's La DN22 . . . . . . 31 D8
Pocklington Cres NG24 . . 125 D6
Pocklington Rd NG23 . . . . . 98 B1
Podder La NG3 . . . . 162 C6
Point The NG3 . . . . 173 D8
Pollard Cl NG13 . . . . 165 D3
Pollard's La NG25 . . . . . . 136 F7
Polly Taylor's Rd NG23 . . . 67 C1
Polperro Way NG15 . . . . . 145 D5
Pond Hills La NG5 . . . . . . 147 F1
Pond St NG17 . . . . 115 B5

Pool Cl NG16 . . . . 113 D2
Poole Mdw NG12 . . . . 174 F4
Popham Ct NG1 . . . . 223 F1
Popham St NG1 . . . . 223 F1
Poplar Ave
East Leake LE12 . . . . 214 D8
Kirkby in A NG17 . . . . 115 C5
Nottingham NG5 . . . . 161 A1
Sandiacre NG10 . . . . 182 A7
Poplar Cl
Bingham NG13 . . . . 178 A4
Carlton NG3 . . . . 174 D6
Sutton on T NG23 . . . . 96 F8
Worksop S80 . . . . 35 D1
Poplar Cres NG16 . . . . . . 159 B6
Poplar Dr
Church Warsop NG20 . . . . . 74 A6
Mansfield Woodhouse NG19 89 C1
Poplar Rd DE55 . . . . 113 B7
Poplars Ave NG14 . . . . . . 164 A5
Poplars Cl NG12 . . . . 197 F4
Poplar St
Mansfield Woodhouse
NG19 . . . . 88 C3
New Ollerton NG22 . . . . 77 D4
Nottingham NG2 . . . . 173 E4
Retford DN22 . . . . 39 F6
Poplars The
Beeston NG9 . . . . 183 F7
Nottingham NG7 . . . . 172 E8
Sutton in A NG17 . . . . 101 A3
West Bridgford NG2 . . . . . . 185 F7
Poppy Cl NG20 . . . . 72 D3
Poppy Gdn DE55 . . . . 99 B7
Porchester Cl NG15 . . . . . 146 C7
Porchester Jun Sch NG4 . 162 A1
Porchester Rd
Bingham NG13 . . . . 177 D4
Nottingham NG3 . . . . 162 A3
Porlock Cl 2 NG10 . . . . . . 193 A8
Portage Cl NG12 . . . . 175 E2
Port Arthur Rd NG2 . . . . . 174 A4
Porter Cl NG11 . . . . 195 C8
Porters Wlk NG3 . . . . 174 A7
Portinscale Cl NG2 . . . . . 186 C5
Portland Cres
Mansfield Woodhouse
NG19 . . . . 88 D3
Stapleford NG9 . . . . 182 E6
Portland Ct NG5 . . . . 161 B5
Portland Ct Mews NG19 . . 88 C4
Portland Gdns NG15 . . . . 145 F7
Portland Grange NG15 . . . 145 F7
Portland Hill NG7 . . . . 172 C1
Portland Inf & Jun Sch
NG17 . . . . 101 A5
Portland L Ctr NG3 . . . . . . 173 D1
Portland Mdws DN22 . . . . . 29 A6
Portland Pk Cl NG15 . . . . 145 F7
Portland Pk Nature Reserve
NG17 . . . . 114 F3
Portland Pl
Sutton DN22 . . . . 29 A6
Worksop S80 . . . . 35 F4
Portland Prim Sch 8 NG1 . 173 D1
Portland Rd
Beeston NG9 . . . . 182 F1
Carlton NG4 . . . . 162 C2
Eastwood NG16 . . . . 158 B8
Hucknall NG15 . . . . 146 A6
Ilkeston DE7 . . . . 157 F3
Long Eaton NG10 . . . . 193 B4
Nottingham NG7 . . . . 222 C3
Retford DN22 . . . . 39 F5
Selston NG16 . . . . 129 A7
Shirebrook NG20 . . . . 72 F4
West Bridgford NG2 . . . . . . 185 F6
Whaley Thorns NG20 . . . . . 59 A2
Portland Ret Pk NG18 . . . 102 A5
Portland Row NG17 . . . . . . 91 C8
Portland Sch S80 . . . . 46 F8
Portland Sq NG17 . . . . . . 100 F2
Portland St
Arnold NG5 . . . . 161 E6
Beeston NG9 . . . . 184 A7
Kirkby in A NG17 . . . . 115 B4
Mansfield NG18 . . . . 102 B6
Market Warsop NG20 . . . . . 74 B4
Newark-on-T NG24 . . . . . . 139 F8
New Houghton NG19 . . . . . . 87 A7
Sutton in A NG17 . . . . 100 F2
Worksop S80 . . . . 35 E3
Portland Terr
Gainsborough DN21 . . . . . . 24 D7
Meden Vale NG20 . . . . 60 E1
Whaley Thorns NG20 . . . . . 59 A2
Portman Ct DN10 . . . . 9 F7
Porto Rd NG5 . . . . 146 F1
Postern St NG1 . . . . 223 D2
Post Office La
Plungar NG13 . . . . 202 F8
Redmile NG13 . . . . 192 F3
Post Office Rd NG17 . . . . 115 B2
Post Office Yd NG14 . . . . 151 D2
Posts The NG12 . . . . 189 A6
Potter La NG22 . . . . 92 D8
Potters Cl NG5 . . . . 161 A7
Potters Ct NG9 . . . . 171 D1
Potters La LE12 . . . . 216 C3
Potters Nook S81 . . . . 34 F7
Potter St
Sutton in A NG17 . . . . 101 A4

Potter St continued
Worksop S80 . . . . 35 F2
Potters Way DE7 . . . . 170 A8
Pot Yd The NG22 . . . . 119 F6
Poulter Cl NG7 . . . . 172 D7
Poulter St NG20 . . . . 58 F1
Poulter View DN22 . . . . 39 F5
Poulton Dr NG2 . . . . 173 D2
Poultry NG1 . . . . 223 E2
Powell Ct NG2 . . . . 119 F5
Powell Gdns S81 . . . . 35 D7
Powtrell Pl DE7 . . . . 170 B6
Poynton St NG1 . . . . 223 D3
Poyser Cl 2 NG7 . . . . 161 A1
Pratt Cl NG19 . . . . 87 D1
Prebends Cl NG24 . . . . . . 138 F4
Precinct Rd NG17 . . . . . . 115 B5
Precinct The NG12 . . . . . . 187 F3
Premier Rd NG7 . . . . 173 A8
Prendwick Gdns NG5 . . . . 161 B8
Prest Ave NG20 . . . . 74 E8
Preston Rd
Balderton NG24 . . . . 140 E8
Rainworth NG21 . . . . 118 A8
Prestwich Cl NG8 . . . . . . 159 D2
Prestwold Ave
Mansfield NG18 . . . . 103 B8
Mansfield Woodhouse NG19 89 B1
Prestwold La LE12 . . . . . . 215 C1
Prestwood Dr NG8 . . . . . . 172 B7
Previn Gdns NG3 . . . . 173 F6
Priestgate NG22 . . . . 65 E6
Priestsic Prim Sch NG17 . 100 F3
Priestsic Rd NG17 . . . . . . 100 E3
Primrose Ave
Farndon NG24 . . . . 139 B6
Newark-on-T NG24 . . . . . . 125 B4
Selston NG16 . . . . 128 F2
Primrose Bank NG13 . . . . 177 D4
Primrose Cl
7 Kirkby in A NG17 . . . . . 114 F7
Nottingham NG3 . . . . 173 D7
South Normanton DE55 . . . 113 B7
Primrose Cres NG4 . . . . . 174 F7
Primrose Ct NG17 . . . . . . 101 B1
Primrose La NG22 . . . . 78 C5
Primrose Rise NG16 . . . . 158 A8
Primrose St
Carlton NG4 . . . . 174 F7
Gainsborough DN21 . . . . . . 24 D7
Primrose Way
Sutton in A NG17 . . . . 100 C1
Worksop S81 . . . . 36 A6
Primula Cl NG11 . . . . 184 C2
Prince Charles Rd S81 . . . . 35 D6
Prince Edward Cres
NG12 . . . . 175 E2
Prince of Wales St DN22 . . 39 E6
Princes Rd LE14 . . . . 211 C3
Princess Anne Rd S81 . . . . 35 E6
Princess Ave
Beeston NG9 . . . . 184 A6
Mansfield NG19 . . . . 103 A8
Market Warsop NG20 . . . . . 74 C4
South Normanton DE55 . . . 113 A5
Princess Cl NG4 . . . . 162 F2
Princess Diana Ct DN21 . . 15 C3
Princess Dr NG10 . . . . . . 182 B4
Princess St
Eastwood NG16 . . . . 143 F3
Kirkby in A NG17 . . . . 114 D3
Long Eaton NG10 . . . . 193 B4
7 Loughborough LE11 . . 220 B3
Princes St NG18 . . . . 102 A5
Prince's St NG24 . . . . 139 F7
Princes Wlk DN21 . . . . 15 F1
Prince St
Ilkeston DE7 . . . . 157 E4
Long Eaton NG10 . . . . 193 D8
Prince William Rd LE11 . . 220 A4
Prince William Way
LE11 . . . . 220 A6
Prior Cl NG17 . . . . 101 B4
Prioridge NG12 . . . . 188 A2
Prior Rd NG5 . . . . 161 D6
Priors The NG13 . . . . 178 A5
Priorswell Rd S80 . . . . 35 F2
Priory Ave
Annesley Woodhouse
NG17 . . . . 130 B8
Ravenshead NG15 . . . . 117 B1
Priory Cl NG12 . . . . 186 C1
Priory Cir NG12 . . . . 186 C1
Priory Cres NG4 . . . . 162 F1
Priory Ctr NG12 . . . . 162 F1
Priory Ctr The S80 . . . . 45 E4
Priory Jun Sch 1 NG4 . . . 162 F1
Priory La NG14 . . . . 151 C7
Priory Mews 7 NG7 . . . . . 172 E2
Priory Pk NG14 . . . . 151 C7
Priory RC Prim Sch The
NG4 . . . . 144 B1
Priory Rd
Blidworth NG21 . . . . 118 A5
Carlton NG4 . . . . 162 F1
Eastwood NG16 . . . . 143 F4
Hucknall NG15 . . . . 145 E7

Priory Rd continued
Mansfield Woodhouse NG19 . . **88** B3
West Bridgford NG2 . . . . **186** A8
Priory Sq NG19 . . . . **88** B3
Priory St NG7 . . . . **172** E2
Pritchard Dr NG9 . . . . **182** E6
Private Rd
Hucknall NG15 . . . . **145** E7
Nottingham NG5, NG3 . . . . . **161** D2
Southwell NG25 . . . . **121** E1
Woodborough NG14 . . . . **149** B5
Private St NG24 . . . . **140** B8
Privet Ave NG17 . . . . **115** A6
Prize Cl NG11 . . . . **184** C1
Procters Dr NG23 . . . . **82** E1
Promenade NG3 . . . . **223** F4
Promenade The NG17 . . . . **115** D6
Prospect Cl NG17 . . . . **115** B7
Prospect Ct NG17 . . . . **99** C1
Prospect Dr
Shirebrook NG20 . . . . **72** E3
Worksop S81 . . . . **35** F6
Prospect Hill Inf Sch S81 . . **36** A6
Prospect Hill Jun Sch
S81 . . . . **36** A7
Prospect Pl
Nottingham NG7 . . . . **222** B1
Sutton in A NG17 . . . . **100** E1
Prospect Prec S81 . . . . **36** A6
Prospect Rd
Carlton NG4 . . . . **162** B1
Heanor DE75 . . . . **157** A8
Prospect St
Mansfield NG18 . . . . **102** D6
Nottingham NG7 . . . . **222** A4
Prospect Terr
Gainsborough DN21 . . . . **24** D7
Nottingham NG7 . . . . **222** A4
Providence Pl DE7 . . . . . . **157** E1
Providence Rd NG16 . . . . . **128** A4
Prudhoe Ct NG2 . . . . **173** D1
Pudding La LE14 . . . . **210** C5
Pulborough Cl NG5 . . . . . . **160** F4
Pullman Rd NG2 . . . . **173** F4
Pump Hollow La NG18 . . . **103** A7
Pump Hollow Rd NG19 . . . **103** A8
Pump La
Fenton NG23 . . . . **142** E2
Walesby NG22 . . . . **64** A2
Purbeck Cl
Long Eaton NG10 . . . . **193** A8
Mansfield Woodhouse NG19 . **88** C6
Purbeck Dr NG2 . . . . **185** C5
Purdy Mdw NG10 . . . . **193** A5
**Pureland Japanese Gdn and
Meditation Ctr** NG23 . . . . **68** E5
Pyatt St NG2 . . . . **173** D1
Pye Ave NG19 . . . . **101** D7
Pye Hill Rd NG16 . . . . **128** A4
Pygall Ave NG11 . . . . **195** A1
Pym St NG3 . . . . **173** F6
Pym Wlk NG3 . . . . **173** F6
Python Hill Rd NG21 . . . . . **104** B1

Q

Quadrangle The
Blidworth NG21 . . . . **118** A5
Newstead NG15 . . . . **130** D6
Quakefield Rd NG22 . . . . **66** B6
Quaker La
Farnsfield NG22 . . . . **119** F5
11 Mansfield NG18 . . . . **102** B7
Quaker Way NG18 . . . . **102** B7
Quantock Cl NG5 . . . . **147** B2
Quantock Gr NG13 . . . . **177** C4
Quantock Rd NG10 . . . . **182** A1
Quarries Way NG17 . . . . . . **114** E4
Quarry Ave NG6 . . . . **160** B6
Quarry Cl NG15 . . . . **132** B8
Quarrydale Ave NG17 . . . . **100** F5
Quarrydale Dr NG17 . . . . . **100** E5
Quarrydale Rd NG17 . . . . . **100** F4
Quarrydale Sch NG17 . . . . **100** E5
Quarry Dr Vw NG18 . . . . . **102** E5
Quarry Dr NG17 . . . . **115** B3
Quarry Gr S81 . . . . **35** C7
Quarry Hill NG18 . . . . **182** A8
Quarry La
Linby NG15 . . . . **131** B4
Mansfield NG18 . . . . **102** A5
Quarry Rd NG15 . . . . **132** B8
Quarry Yd NG17 . . . . **100** E2
Quartz Ave NG18 . . . . **102** E4
Quayside Cl NG2 . . . . **173** E1
Queen Eleanor Prim Sch
NG23 . . . . **70** E3
Queen Elizabeth Cres
S80 . . . . **35** A4
Queen Elizabeth Rd NG9 . **183** A3
Queen Elizabeth Sch The
NG19 . . . . **88** A1
Queen Elizabeths High Sch
DN21 . . . . **15** C3
Queen Mary's Cl NG12 . . . **176** D2
Queens Ave DE7 . . . . **170** A5
Queen's Ave NG4 . . . . **162** E2
Queensberry St NG6 . . . . . **160** E4
Queens Bower Rd NG5 . . . **161** C8
Queen's Bridge Rd NG2 . . **223** E1
Queensbury Ave NG2 . . . . **185** C3
Queens Cl S80 . . . . **45** C5
Queen's Cres DN10 . . . . **10** A7

Queen's Ct
Bingham NG13 . . . . **177** D5
Clipstone NG19 . . . . **89** D3
Newark-on-T NG24 . . . . **125** A1
Queens Dr
Beeston NG9 . . . . **184** A6
Brinsley NG16 . . . . **143** E7
Nottingham NG11 . . . . **185** A8
Sandiacre NG10 . . . . **182** B4
Queen's Dr NG16 . . . . **159** C6
Queens Dr Ind Est NG2 . . **173** A1
Queensfield DN21 . . . . **15** B3
Queens Gr NG2 . . . . **223** E1
Queen's Head Ct NG24 . . . **139** F7
**Queen's Medical Ctr (Univ
Hospl)** NG7 . . . . **172** D2
Queens Rd
Beeston NG9 . . . . **184** A6
Carlton in L S81 . . . . **25** F7
Hodthorpe S80 . . . . **45** C6
Kegworth DE74 . . . . **203** D2
Queen's Rd
Loughborough LE11 . . . . **220** C4
Newark-on-T NG24 . . . . **125** A1
Nottingham NG2 . . . . **223** F1
Radcliffe on T NG12 . . . . . . **176** A4
Queens Rd E NG9 . . . . **184** B7
Queens Rd N NG16 . . . . . . **143** F3
Queens Rd S NG16 . . . . . . **143** F1
Queens Rd W NG9 . . . . . . **183** E4
Queen's Sq NG16 . . . . **143** F2
Queen St
Arnold NG5 . . . . **148** A1
Balderton NG24 . . . . **140** E3
Bottesford NG13 . . . . **181** A2
Collingham NG23 . . . . **98** A1
Gainsborough DN21 . . . . **24** D7
Hucknall NG15 . . . . **145** F8
Kirkby in A NG17 . . . . **115** A4
Langley Mill NG16 . . . . **143** C3
Long Eaton NG10 . . . . **193** E7
3 Loughborough LE11 . . . . **220** B3
10 Mansfield NG18 . . . . **102** B7
Market Warsop NG20 . . . . . . **74** A5
Newark-on-T NG24 . . . . **139** F7
Nottingham NG1 . . . . **223** E3
Pinxton NG16 . . . . **113** C3
Retford DN22 . . . . **39** D6
South Normanton DE55 . . . **113** A5
Southwell NG25 . . . . **121** D1
Sutton in A NG17 . . . . **100** F4
Worksop S80 . . . . **35** F2
Queensway
Gainsborough DN21 . . . . **24** F8
Kirkby in A NG17 . . . . **115** B2
Mansfield Woodhouse NG19 **89** A1
Nether Broughton LE14 . . . **219** C6
Saxilby LN1 . . . . **57** B3
Skellingthorpe LN6 . . . . **71** F3
Worksop S80 . . . . **35** F1
Queens Wlk **14** NG16 . . . . **143** F2
Queen's Wlk
Nether Langwith NG20 . . . . . **59** A1
Nottingham NG2 . . . . **173** B1
Querneby Ave NG3 . . . . . . **161** E2
Querneby Rd NG3 . . . . **161** E2
Quibell Rd NG24 . . . . **140** A5
Quibell's La NG24 . . . . **125** A3
Quines Hill Rd NG19 . . . . . . **89** A2
Quinton Cl NG11 . . . . **185** A5
Quorn Cl
Beeston NG9 . . . . **183** E3
Loughborough LE11 . . . . **220** C2
Quorndon Cres NG10 . . . . **193** D5
Quorn Gr NG5 . . . . **161** A3
Quorn Rd NG5 . . . . **161** A2

R

Rabbithill La NG23 . . . . **83** B6
Racecourse Rd
Mansfield NG18 . . . . **102** E5
Nottingham NG2 . . . . **174** A4
Rachel Cl DN21 . . . . **15** C3
Radbourne Rd **9** NG2 . . . **173** F3
Radbourne St NG19 . . . . **88** E4
Radburn Ct NG9 . . . . **170** E1
Radcliffe Gdns NG4 . . . . . . **174** D8
Radcliffe Mount NG2 . . . . **174** A4
Radcliffe on Trent Inf Sch
NG12 . . . . **176** A3
Radcliffe on Trent Jun Sch
NG12 . . . . **175** F3
Radcliffe Rd
Carlton NG12 . . . . **175** B3
Cropwell Butler NG12 . . . . . **189** A7
West Bridgford NG2 . . . . . . **186** D8
Radcliffe St NG2 . . . . **173** D1
Radcliffe Sta NG12 . . . . . . **175** F3
Radford Bridge Rd NG8 . . **172** C5
Radford Bvd NG7 . . . . **222** A4
Radford Cres NG4 . . . . **162** E2
Radford Ct NG7 . . . . **222** B3
Radford Gr La NG7 . . . . . . **222** A4
Radford Prim Sch NG7 . . . **222** A3
Radford Rd NG7 . . . . **172** F7
Radford St
1 Mansfield NG18 . . . . . . **102** B6
Worksop S80 . . . . **36** A1
Radley Rd NG24 . . . . **125** C2
Radley Sq NG6 . . . . **160** D5
Radmanthwaite Rd NG19 . . **87** D3
Radmarsh Rd NG7 . . . . **222** A1
Rad Mdws NG10 . . . . **193** C6
Radnoor Rd **8** LE11 . . . . . **220** A4
Radnor Gr NG13 . . . . **177** C4
Radnor Pl NG19 . . . . **87** C4

Radstock Rd NG3 . . . . **174** A7
Radway Dr NG7 . . . . **185** A5
Raeburn Dr NG9 . . . . **182** E2
Ragdale Rd NG6 . . . . **160** B8
Ragdale Cl NG3 . . . . **173** D7
Raglan Ct
Beeston NG9 . . . . **172** A1
Newark-on-T NG24 . . . . **140** A7
Raglan Rd NG3 . . . . **163** B1
Raglan Rd DN22 . . . . **39** E5
Raglan Gdns NG24 . . . . **140** A7
Raglan St NG16 . . . . **144** A1
Raibank Gdns NG5 . . . . . . **161** E5
Railway Ave S80 . . . . **58** D8
Railway Cotts NG16 . . . . . . **158** F6
Railway Ct LN1 . . . . **57** A3
Railway Terr LE11 . . . . **220** C5
Raines Ave S81 . . . . **35** E6
Raines Pk Rd S81 . . . . **35** E7
Rainham Gdns NG11 . . . . . **196** C6
**Rainworth Heath Nature
Reserve** NG21 . . . . **104** A3
Rainworth L Ctr NG21 . . . . **117** B8
Rainworth Wr Rd NG21 . . . **103** F1
Raithby Cl NG5 . . . . **161** A6
Raleigh Cl
Ilkeston DE7 . . . . **157** F3
Nottingham NG11 . . . . **184** C1
Raleigh Rd NG19 . . . . **101** E8
Raleigh St NG7 . . . . **222** C3
Ralf Cl NG2 . . . . **185** E4
Ramblers Cl NG4 . . . . **174** E5
Ramper La LN1 . . . . **55** C7
Ramper Rd
Letwell S81 . . . . **16** A3
Saundby DN22 . . . . **23** D7
Rampton Gn Rd DN22 . . . . . **42** F1
Rampton Hospl DN22 . . . . . . **53** B8
Rampton La DN22 . . . . **42** D5
Rampton Prim Sch DN22 . . **42** D1
Rampton Rd
Laneham DN22 . . . . **54** A6
Retford DN22 . . . . **42** E3
Ramsdale Ave NG14 . . . . . **148** D8
Ramsdale Cres NG5 . . . . . **161** D2
Ramsdale Rd NG4 . . . . **162** E1
Ramsden Ave NG21 . . . . . . **116** F2
Ramsden Cres S81 . . . . **25** F7
Ramsden Croft NG21 . . . . **104** A1
Ramsden Prim Sch S81 . . . **26** A5
Ramsey Cl
Mansfield Woodhouse
NG19 . . . . **89** A2
Ramsey Ct **8** NG5 . . . . . . **161** B1
Ramsey Dr NG5 . . . . **162** C6
Ranby CE Prim Sch DN22 . . **38** A7
Ranby House Sch DN22 . . . **38** B7
Rancliffe Ave NG12 . . . . . . **197** D3
Rancliffe Farm Mews
NG11 . . . . **196** E3
Randal Gdns **4** NG7 . . . . **172** F7
Randall Cl NG24 . . . . **140** D8
Randall Way DN22 . . . . **29** C1
Randal St **3** NG7 . . . . **172** F7
Randol Cl NG24 . . . . **101** D4
Ranelagh Gr NG8 . . . . **172** B5
Ranmere Rd NG8 . . . . **172** A7
Ranmoor Rd NG4 . . . . **162** F1
Rannerdale Cl NG12 . . . . . **186** C6
Rannoch Dr NG19 . . . . **101** E5
Rannoch Rise NG5 . . . . . . **147** F1
Rannoch Way NG12 . . . . . . **197** F3
Ranskill Gdns NG5 . . . . . . **161** A8
Ranskill Prim Sch DN22 . . . **19** B5
Ranskill Rd DN22 . . . . **19** E6
Ransom Dr NG3 . . . . **161** E1
Ransome Ct NG4 . . . . **140** D8
Ransom Rd
Mansfield NG21 . . . . **103** D3
Nottingham NG3 . . . . **173** D8
Ransom Wood Bsns Pk
NG21 . . . . **103** D3
Ranson Rd NG9 . . . . **183** C2
Ratcher Way NG19 . . . . . . **103** B8
Ratcliffe Gate NG18 . . . . . **102** C6
Ratcliffe La DE74 . . . . **203** C2
Ratcliffe St NG16 . . . . **143** F2
Rathgar Cl NG8 . . . . **171** D4
Rathmines Cl NG7 . . . . **222** A1
Rathvale Cl NG9 . . . . **183** A4
Raven Ave NG5 . . . . **161** B4
Ravencroft La DN10 . . . . **14** B1
Ravendale Rd DN21 . . . . **24** E7
Ravenhill Cl NG9 . . . . **183** B4
Ravenscourt S81 . . . . **36** A6
Ravens Ct NG5 . . . . **161** B6
Ravensdale Ave
Long Eaton NG10 . . . . **182** B2
Mansfield NG18 . . . . **102** D8
Ravensdale Dr NG8 . . . . . . **171** C3
Ravensdale Rd NG18 . . . . **102** E8
Ravensfield Rd NG12 . . . . **173** D8
Ravensfleet Rd DN21 . . . . . . **7** F3
Ravenshead CE Prim Sch
NG15 . . . . **117** A2
Ravenshill Cl DN22 . . . . **19** B4
Ravensmore Rd NG5 . . . . . **161** B2
Ravenswood Rd NG5 . . . . **162** A8
Ravensworth Rd NG6 . . . . **160** B8
Rawson St
Nottingham NG7 . . . . **160** F1
Selston NG16 . . . . **129** A6
Raylawn St NG18 . . . . **103** A6
Raymede Dr NG5 . . . . **160** F6

Raymede Dr NG5 . . . . **160** E6
Raymond Cl NG17 . . . . **114** E7
Raymond Dr NG13 . . . . **178** A4
Raymoth La S81 . . . . **35** E7
Rayneham Rd DE7 . . . . **157** C4
Rayner Ct NG7 . . . . **222** B3
Raynford Ave NG9 . . . . **183** C4
Raysmith Cl NG25 . . . . **121** E2
Rayton Ct DN11 . . . . **9** A4
Rayton La S81 . . . . **36** C3
Rayton Spur S81 . . . . **36** B3
Read Ave NG9 . . . . **184** A6
Readman Rd NG9 . . . . **183** A3
Rearsby Cl NG8 . . . . **171** D5
Recreation Dr NG20 . . . . **72** F2
Recreation Rd
Annesley NG15 . . . . **130** C8
New Houghton NG19 . . . . . . **86** F7
Sandiacre NG10 . . . . **182** B6
Shirebrook NG20 . . . . **72** E6
Recreation St
Long Eaton NG10 . . . . **193** F8
Mansfield NG18 . . . . **102** C7
Selston NG16 . . . . **129** B6
Sutton in A NG17 . . . . **100** D2
Recreation Terr NG9 . . . . . **182** D6
Recreation View NG20 . . . . **72** E6
Rectors Gate DN22 . . . . **39** E8
Rectory Ave
Gainsborough DN21 . . . . **15** D1
Nottingham NG8 . . . . **171** E4
Rectory Dr NG11 . . . . **185** B8
Rectory Dr The NG4 . . . . . **162** F2
Rectory Gdns
Beckingham DN10 . . . . **14** B1
Kirton NG22 . . . . **78** B6
Nottingham NG8 . . . . **171** F4
Rectory La
Bottesford NG13 . . . . **181** B3
Claypole NG23 . . . . **156** E7
Gamston DN22 . . . . **50** F5
Lea DN21 . . . . **24** F2
Rectory Pl
Barton in F NG11 . . . . **194** E6
2 Loughborough LE11 . . . . **220** B4
Wymeswold LE12 . . . . **216** C3
Rectory Rd
Carlton NG4 . . . . **174** E5
Church Warsop NG20 . . . . . . **74** C7
Cotgrave NG12 . . . . **187** E3
Loughborough LE11 . . . . **220** B5
Retford DN22 . . . . **39** E7
Treswell DN22 . . . . **42** B3
West Bridgford NG2 . . . . . . **185** F7
Rectory St LN5 . . . . **142** D8
Red Barn Cl DN55 . . . . **99** B3
Redbarn La DE55 . . . . **99** B3
Redbarn Way NG17 . . . . . . **100** C1
Redbourne Dr NG8 . . . . . . **172** C6
Redbridge Dr NG16 . . . . . . **159** D3
Redcar Cl
Carlton NG4 . . . . **162** E2
Mansfield NG18 . . . . **102** E5
Redcliffe Gdns NG3 . . . . . **173** C8
Redcliffe Rd
Mansfield NG18 . . . . **102** B6
Nottingham NG3 . . . . **173** C8
Redcroft Cl NG21 . . . . **75** F2
Redfield Rd NG7 . . . . **184** E8
Redfield Way NG7 . . . . **184** E8
Redforde Ave DN22 . . . . **29** C1
Redforde Pk Ave DN22 . . . . **29** C1
Redforde Pk Dr DN22 . . . . . **29** C1
Redforde Pk Rd DN22 . . . . . **29** C1
Redgate Cl NG19 . . . . **101** E8
Redgates Ct NG14 . . . . **148** D7
Redgate Specl Sch NG19 . . **101** E7
Redgate St
Pinxton NG16 . . . . **113** D2
Redhill La DN22 . . . . **63** E8
Red Hill La NG22 . . . . **92** E4
Redhill L Ctr NG5 . . . . **147** E1
Redhill Lodge Dr NG5 . . . . **147** D1
Redhill Rd NG5 . . . . **147** E1
Redhill Sch NG5 . . . . **147** E1
Red Kite Cl **6** S81 . . . . **35** C7
Red La
Brinsley NG16 . . . . **128** C1
Carlton in L S81 . . . . **26** A2
Lowdham NG14 . . . . **150** D1
Redland Ave NG4 . . . . **174** F8
Redland Cl
Beeston NG9 . . . . **183** C4
Ilkeston DE7 . . . . **157** F2
Redland Dr NG9 . . . . **183** C4
Redland Gr NG4 . . . . **174** E8
Redland Rd NG18 . . . . **101** E8
Redlands Prim Sch S80 . . . . **35** D4
Red Lodge La NG13 . . . . . . **166** B7
Redman Cl DN21 . . . . **15** C2
Redmays Dr NG14 . . . . **164** B6
Redmile CE Prim Sch
NG13 . . . . **192** F3
Redmile La NG13 . . . . **192** F3
Redmile Rd NG8 . . . . **160** C2
Redoubt St NG7 . . . . **222** A3
Redruth Cl NG8 . . . . **171** C6
Redruth Dr NG18 . . . . **103** B2
Redthorn Way NG23 . . . . . **156** E6
Redwing Cl S81 . . . . **35** C6
Redwood NG2 . . . . **185** C6
Redwood Ave NG8 . . . . **171** D3
Redwood Cres NG9 . . . . . . **184** A4
Redwood Inf Sch NG15 . . . **145** F8
Redwood Wlk **2** NG5 . . . . **161** B8
Reedman Rd NG10 . . . . **193** B4
Rees Gdns NG5 . . . . **147** A1

Rees Row DN22 . . . . **42** B1
Reform St
Annesley Woodhouse
NG17 . . . . **129** E8
Sutton in A NG17 . . . . **100** F2
Regal Arts Ctr S80 . . . . **35** F4
Regatta Way NG2 . . . . **186** C8
Regency Ct NG9 . . . . **184** A7
Regents Cl NG23 . . . . **112** B8
Regents Pk Cl NG2 . . . . . . **185** C5
Regent St
Beeston NG9 . . . . **184** A7
Kimberley NG16 . . . . **158** F6
Kirkby in A NG17 . . . . **114** F4
Langley Mill NG16 . . . . **143** B3
Long Eaton NG10 . . . . **193** D8
Loughborough LE11 . . . . **220** A4
Mansfield NG18 . . . . **102** B7
Nottingham, New Basford
NG7 . . . . **161** A1
Nottingham, Standard Hill
NG1 . . . . **223** D2
Stapleford NG10 . . . . **182** C5
Sutton in A NG17 . . . . **100** D2
Regina Cl NG12 . . . . **175** E2
Regina Cres NG15 . . . . **116** F1
**Reg Taylor's Swan &
Waterfowl Sanctuary**
NG25 . . . . **121** F2
Reid Gdns NG16 . . . . **159** B7
Reigate Cl NG9 . . . . **183** C2
Reigate Dr NG9 . . . . **183** C2
Reigate Rd NG7 . . . . **160** F2
Reindeer St NG18 . . . . **102** E6
Rempstone Dr NG6 . . . . . . **160** D5
Rempstone Rd
East Leake LE12 . . . . **214** E7
East Leake, Stanford Hills
LE12 . . . . **214** A6
Hoton LE12 . . . . **215** C2
Wymeswold LE12 . . . . **216** A4
Renals Way NG14 . . . . **148** F7
Rendell Prim Sch LE11 . . . **220** B5
Renfrew Ct NG19 . . . . **101** E5
Renfrew Dr NG8 . . . . **171** E4
Repton Ct NG19 . . . . **88** E4
Repton Dr DE7 . . . . **170** B7
Repton Rd
Nottingham NG6 . . . . **160** D6
West Bridgford NG2 . . . . . . **185** E5
Retford Coll The DN22 . . . . **39** F7
Retford Gate DN22 . . . . **41** E2
Retford Hospl DN22 . . . . . . **39** D8
Retford L Ctr DN22 . . . . **39** C6
Retford Little Theatre
DN22 . . . . **39** E6
Retford Oaks High Sch
DN22 . . . . **39** C5
Retford Rd
Askham DN22 . . . . **52** E3
Blyth S81 . . . . **18** B2
Boughton NG22 . . . . **77** D4
Mattersey DN10 . . . . **20** C6
North Leverton w H DN22 . . **41** F8
North Wheatley DN22 . . . . . . **31** C7
Nottingham NG5 . . . . **161** A3
Rampton DN22 . . . . **42** D1
Ranby S81 . . . . **37** C4
South Leverton DN22 . . . . . . **42** A8
Worksop S80 . . . . **36** C2
Retford Sta DN22 . . . . **39** E5
Revelstoke Ave NG5 . . . . . **146** D1
Revelstoke Way NG5 . . . . . **146** E1
Revesby Gdns NG8 . . . . . . **172** C2
Revesby Rd NG5 . . . . **161** F5
Revill Cl
Claypole NG23 . . . . **156** D7
Ilkeston DE7 . . . . **157** C2
Revill Ct **15** NG17 . . . . . . **114** E7
Reydon Dr NG8 . . . . **160** D1
Reynolds Dr NG8 . . . . **171** F5
Rhodes Wlk NG18 . . . . **101** C6
Rhyl Cres NG4 . . . . **162** E2
Ribblesdale S81 . . . . **36** A4
Ribblesdale Ct NG9 . . . . . . **183** A4
Ribblesdale Rd
Long Eaton NG10 . . . . **193** A5
Nottingham NG5 . . . . **161** C5
Riber Cl
Annesley Woodhouse
NG17 . . . . **115** A1
Long Eaton NG10 . . . . **193** D5
Riber Cres NG5 . . . . **160** F5
Richard Bonington Prim Sch
NG5 . . . . **147** F1
Richard Herrod Ctr NG4 . . **174** D8
Richards Cl NG12 . . . . **176** A3
Richardson Cl NG11 . . . . . **184** C1
Richard St DN22 . . . . **40** A5
Richborough Pl NG8 . . . . . **171** D2
Richey Cl NG5 . . . . **148** A1
Richmond Ave
Breaston DE72 . . . . **193** A8
Calverton NG14 . . . . **149** A8
Eastwood NG16 . . . . **144** B2
Ilkeston DE7 . . . . **157** F4
Nottingham NG3 . . . . **173** F7
Sandiacre NG10 . . . . **182** A4
Richmond Cl NG24 . . . . **140** B4
Richmond Dr
Beeston NG9 . . . . **183** C4
Mansfield Woodhouse
NG19 . . . . **88** D2
Nottingham NG3 . . . . **161** D2
Radcliffe on T NG12 . . . . . . **175** E4
Richmond Gdns NG5 . . . . . **147** E1
Richmond La DN10 . . . . **9** F6

Richmond Rd
Carlton in L S81 25 E6
Gainsborough DN21 24 F8
Kirkby in A NG17 115 D5
Retford DN22 30 A1
West Bridgford NG2 173 F1
Worksop S80 36 A1
Richmond St NG18 102 F5
Richmond Terr NG12 175 F3
Ricket La
Blidworth NG21 117 C5
Ravenshead NG15 116 F4
Ricklow Ct 1 NG5 161 A8
Rick St NG1 223 F3
Riddell Ave S81 16 E3
Ridding La DN10 3 A4
Ridding Terr NG3 223 E4
Ridge Cl NG17 100 D3
Ridge Hill NG14 150 D2
Ridge La NG12 176 A5
Ridgeway
Nottingham NG5 161 A8
Shirebrook NG20 72 F5
Southwell NG25 121 D2
Worksop S81 36 B6
Ridgeway Cl NG22 119 F6
Ridgeway La NG20 74 B3
Ridgeway St NG3 173 E6
Ridgeway Terr NG20 74 B4
Ridgeway The NG22 120 A6
Ridgeway Wlk 17 NG5 161 A8
Ridgewood Dr NG9 183 C4
Ridgewood Gr NG15 117 A2
Ridgmont Wlk NG11 195 D8
Ridgway Cl NG2 186 C5
Riding La DN10 3 A4
Ridings The
Bulcote NG14 164 B5
Keyworth NG12 198 A3
Mansfield Woodhouse NG19 88 F1
Ridsdale Rd NG5 161 C5
Rifle St NG7 222 A3
Rigg La
Blidworth NG21 132 E7
Hucknall NG15 132 E5
Rigley Ave 10 DE7 157 F1
Rigley Dr NG5 160 E7
Riley Ave NG17 100 C3
Riley Cl NG17 100 C3
Ring Leas NG12 188 A2
Ringrose Cl NG24 140 D8
Ringstead Cl NG2 185 C5
Ringstead Wlk NG5 161 B8
Ringwood S81 36 A6
Ringwood Ave NG18 102 C4
Ringwood Cres NG8 172 C5
Ringwood Rd NG13 177 C4
Rio Dr NG23 98 A2
Ripon Rd NG3 174 B5
Riseborough Wlk NG6 146 C1
Risegate NG12 187 F3
Riseholme Ave NG8 171 C3
Riseholme Rd DN21 24 F7
Rise Park Prim Sch NG5 146 F1
Rise Pk Rd NG5 146 E1
Rise The NG5 161 D3
Risley Ct DE7 157 F3
Risley Dr NG2 173 B2
Riste's Pl NG2 223 F2
Ritchie Cl NG12 188 A2
Ritson Cl NG3 223 F4
River Cl DN22 29 F1
Riverdale Rd NG9 183 C2
Rivergreen NG11 184 E3
Rivergreen Cl NG9 171 C2
Rivergreen Cres NG9 171 C2
River La
Misson DN10 4 C2
Retford DN22 39 E7
Riverleen Sch NG6 160 C8
River Maun Rec Ctr
NG18 102 D8
Rivermead
Cotgrave NG12 188 A3
Newark-on-T NG24 139 E6
River Rd NG4 174 E4
Riverside
Southwell NG25 121 F1
Whatton NG13 179 B4
Riverside App DN21 15 B1
Riverside Cl
Bottesford NG13 181 A3
Cuckney NG20 60 A3
Riverside Prim Sch NG2 173 B1
Riverside Rd
Beeston NG9 184 A3
Newark-on-T NG24 139 D5
Riverside Ret Pk NG11 185 A8
Riverside Way
Mansfield Woodhouse
NG19 88 D5
Nottingham NG2 173 B1
Riverside Wlk NG13 181 A3
River View
Market Warsop NG20 74 B5
Nottingham NG2 173 D1
Pye Bridge DE55 128 A6
Retford DN22 39 E3
Riverview Cotts DN10 4 C2
Riverway Gdns NG2 173 D2
Rivington Rd NG9 182 E2
Road No 1 NG4 174 F6
Road No 2 NG4 174 F5
Road No 3 NG4 175 A5
Road No 4 NG4 175 C5
Road No 5 NG4 175 B5
Road No 7 NG4 174 F6
Road No 8 NG4 174 F5
Roadwood La NG23 69 F8
Robbie Burns Rd NG5 161 C8
Robert Ave NG18 101 F5
Robert Dukeson Ave
NG24 125 B4
Robert Jones Inf Sch
NG21 118 A5
Robert Jones Jun Sch
NG21 118 A5
Robert Mellors Prim Sch
NG5 161 F8
Robert Miles Jun Sch
NG13 177 F4
Roberts Ave NG17 99 F2
Roberts Cl
Dunham on T NG22 54 A1
Kegworth DE74 203 D1
Robert Shaw Prim Sch
NG8 172 D6
Robert's La NG15 145 E7
Roberts St
Ilkeston DE7 170 A6
Nottingham NG2 173 E4
Roberts Yd NG9 184 A7
Robey Cl
Hucknall NG15 131 A1
Mansfield Woodhouse NG19 89 B1
Robey Dr NG16 143 F3
Robina Dr NG16 158 C8
Robin Down Cl NG18 102 D2
Robin Down La NG18 102 C2
Robinet Rd NG9 183 F5
Robinettes La NG16 158 D1
Robin Gr NG15 117 A1
Robin Hood Ave
Edwinstowe NG21 91 C8
Market Warsop NG20 74 C2
Robin Hood Cl NG16 143 F1
Robin Hood Doncaster/
Sheffield International
Airport DN10 3 B7
Robin Hood Dr NG15 145 E5
Robin Hood Ind Est 2
NG3 173 E5
Robin Hood Jun & Inf Sch
NG5 161 A6
Robin Hood Prim Sch
NG19 88 B4
Robin Hood Rd
Annesley Woodhouse
NG17 130 B8
Arnold NG5 147 B1
Blidworth NG21 118 B5
Robin Hood's Cave NG22 63 C2
Robin Hood St NG3 173 E5
Robin Hood Terr
Nottingham NG3 223 F3
Ravenshead NG15 117 B3
Robin Hood Way NG2 173 C2
Robinia Ct NG2 186 A5
Robin Mews LE11 220 A3
Robins Ct NG24 140 A8
Robinson Cl NG24 140 E8
Robinson Dr S80 35 E1
Robinson Gdns NG11 184 C1
Robinson Rd NG3 162 A2
Robin's Wood Rd NG8 172 B7
Rob Roy Ave NG7 222 B1
Rochdale Ct NG18 103 A5
Roche Cl NG5 162 C7
Rochester Ave NG4 175 A7
Rochester Cl
Long Eaton NG10 193 A7
Worksop S81 36 A7
Rochester Ct NG6 159 F6
Rochester Rd NG21 118 A8
Rochester Wlk NG7 184 F1
Rochford Ct NG12 186 C3
Rock Ct
Mansfield NG18 102 C7
Nottingham NG6 160 D3
Rock Dr NG7 222 C1
Rocket Cl NG16 159 A7
Rockford Ct NG9 170 E1
Rockford Rd NG5 160 F3
Rock Hill NG18 102 D6
Rock Hl Gd NG18 102 D6
Rockingham Gr NG13 177 C4
Rocklands The NG20 72 E4
Rockley Ave
Eastwood NG16 144 A1
Radcliffe on T NG12 175 F4
Rockley Cl
Clipstone NG21 90 A4
Hucknall NG15 145 C6
Rockleys View NG14 150 A2
Rockley Way NG20 72 E4
Rock St
Mansfield NG18 102 D6
Nottingham NG6 160 B8
Rock Valley NG18 102 C7
Rockwood Cl NG21 118 A5
Rockwood Wlk NG15 145 E6
Rodel Ct NG3 223 F4
Roden House Bsns Ctr
NG3 173 D5
Roden St NG3 173 E5
Roderick Ave NG17 115 B1
Roderick St NG6 160 D4
Rodery The NG18 102 E5
Rodney Rd NG2 186 A6
Rodney Way DE7 157 F3
Rodwell Cl NG8 172 C6
Roebuck Cl NG5 161 B8
Roebuck Dr NG18 102 B3
Roebuck Way S80 48 B8
Roecliffe NG2 185 E4
Roehampton Dr NG9 170 D2
Roe Hill NG14 149 C5
Roes La NG14 149 A7
Roewood Cl NG17 114 F7
Roewood La NG22 107 F2
Roger Cl NG17 100 F5
Roker Cl NG8 160 A1
Rolaine Cl NG19 88 C4
Roland Ave
Nottingham NG11 185 B7
Nuthall NG16 159 E4
Rolleston Cl NG15 145 D5
Rolleston Cres NG16 144 F1
Rolleston Dr
Arnold NG5 162 A7
Eastwood NG16 158 B8
Nottingham NG7 222 B1
Rolleston Sta NG25 137 F6
Roman Bank NG19 88 D3
Roman Bank La DN10 18 E6
Roman Dr NG6 160 E4
Romans Ct NG6 160 E2
Romilay Cl NG9 172 A1
Romney Ave NG8 171 D2
Romsey Pl NG19 101 D6
Rona Cl NG19 101 E5
Rona Ct NG6 160 E5
Ronald St NG7 222 B3
Rookery Gdns NG5 161 F8
Rookery La NG17 114 A8
Rookery The
Collingham NG23 98 A1
1 Mansfield NG18 102 A7
Rook's La DN10 6 E2
Rookwood Cl NG9 183 E6
Rookwood Cres NG15 145 D6
Rooley Ave NG17 100 C3
Rooley Dr NG17 100 C3
Roosa Cl NG6 159 F5
Roosevelt Ave NG10 193 C5
Roosevelt Rd NG17 101 B4
Rooth St NG18 102 B6
Ropery Rd DN21 15 B2
Ropewalk DE74 203 C2
Ropewalk Ind Ctr DE7 158 A1
Ropewalk The
Ilkeston DE7 158 A1
Newark-on-T NG24 140 B8
Nottingham NG1 223 D2
Southwell NG25 121 E1
Ropeway The NG17 114 E5
Rope Wlk LE12 205 D1
Ropsley Cres NG2 186 A8
Roscoe Ave NG5 147 E2
Roseacre NG9 184 A5
Rose Ash La NG5 161 B8
Rose Ave
Ilkeston DE7 157 E2
Retford DN22 40 A4
Rosebank Dr NG5 148 B1
Rosebay Av NG7 172 D8
Roseberry Ave NG2 173 E1
Roseberry Gdns NG15 146 C6
Roseberry St NG17 115 C4
Rosebery Hill NG18 102 C6
Rosebery St NG6 160 C3
Rose Cl NG3 173 D7
Rose Cottage Dr NG17 99 F2
Rose Cotts NG14 163 E5
Rosecroft Dr NG5 161 C6
Rose Ct NG10 182 B1
Rosedale S81 36 A8
Rosedale Cl NG10 193 B6
Rosedale Dr NG8 171 B4
Rosedale La NG15 116 F3
Rosedale Rd NG3 174 C6
Rosedale Way NG19 88 F2
Rose Farm Dr NG23 96 F8
Rosegarth Wlk NG6 160 D4
Rose Gr
Beeston NG9 184 B5
Keyworth NG12 197 F4
Rosegrove Ave NG5 147 F1
Rose Hill NG12 197 E3
Rosehill Cl LN1 57 A4
Rosehill Specl Sch NG3 173 E6
Rose La NG19 88 C4
Rose Lea DN22 39 D4
Roseleigh Ave NG3 162 B2
Rosemary Ave NG18 102 A8
Rosemary Cl 1 NG8 159 E1
Rosemary St NG18 102 A7
Rosemont Cl NG17 100 F6
Roseneath Ave NG5 146 E1
Rosetta Rd NG7 160 F1
Rosewall Ct NG5 162 B7
Roseway DN21 15 C1
Rosewood Cl
Carlton in L S81 25 D1
Newark-on-T NG24 125 B2
South Normanton DE55 113 B7
Rosewood Cres DE75 143 B2
Rosewood Dr NG17 115 C6
Rosewood Gdns
Nottingham NG6 159 F7
West Bridgford NG2 185 C3
Rosings Ct NG17 100 E1
Roslyn Ave NG4 162 E2
Ross Cl
Coddington NG24 126 B2
Lowdham NG14 150 E1
Rossell Dr NG9 182 E5
Rossendale DE7 157 E4
Rossett Cl NG2 186 D6
Rossetti Gdns S81 36 C3
Rossington Rd NG2 173 F5
Ross La NG4 163 C7
Rosslyn Dr
Hucknall NG15 146 C8
Rosslyn Dr *continued*
Nottingham NG8 160 A2
Rosslyn Pk Prim Sch
NG8 160 B1
Rosthwaite Cl NG2 186 C5
Roston Cl NG18 103 B5
Rothbury Ave NG9 170 D2
Rothbury Gr NG13 177 C5
Rotherham Baulk S81 25 C7
Rotherham Rd NG19 86 F8
Rothesay Ave NG7 222 B2
Rothley Ave NG3 173 F5
Rothwell Cl
Gainsborough DN21 24 E8
Nottingham NG11 185 A4
Roughs Wood La NG15 145 D4
Roulstone Cres LE12 205 E3
Roundhill Cl NG17 101 C1
Round Hill Prim Sch
NG9 183 F7
Roundwood Rd NG5 161 C7
Rowan Ave
Hathern LE12 213 A2
Ravenshead NG15 117 A1
Stapleford NG9 170 E2
Rowan Cl
Calverton NG14 148 D7
Kirkby in A NG17 114 F6
Mansfield NG19 88 D1
Rowan Cres S80 35 E1
Rowan Croft NG17 99 F4
Rowan Ct NG16 159 B6
Rowan Dr
Keyworth NG12 198 A2
Kirkby in A NG17 114 F6
Nottingham NG11 185 A4
Selston NG16 128 D6
Shirebrook NG20 72 D5
Rowan Gdns NG6 159 F7
Rowans The
2 Gainsborough DN21 15 F1
Saxilby LN1 56 F4
Rowan Way NG24 140 B5
Rowan Wlk NG3 174 A8
Rowe Gdns NG6 160 D6
Rowland Ave NG3 162 A2
Rowland Mews NG3 173 E7
Rowsley Ave NG10 193 A5
Rowsley Ct NG17 114 C8
Rowston Cl DN21 15 C2
Row The NG13 179 F6
Rowthorne La S44 86 B7
Roxton Ct NG16 158 F7
Royal Ave NG10 182 D1
Royal Cres S81 35 E6
Royal Ctr (Theatre Royal &
Royal Concert Hall)
NG1 223 E3
Royal Mews NG9 183 C3
Royal Oak Ct NG21 76 B2
Royal Oak Dr NG16 129 B7
Royal Way LE11 220 A6
Roy Ave NG9 184 B4
Royce Ave NG15 145 E4
Royds Cres S80 35 A5
Royland Rd LE11 220 A3
Royston Cl NG2 173 B1
Ruby Paddocks NG16 158 F5
Ruby Wy NG18 102 C5
Ruddington Ct 4 NG18 103 A2
Ruddington Framework
Knitters Mus NG11 196 C6
Ruddington La NG11 185 B5
Ruddington Rd NG18 103 A2
Ruddington Village Mus
NG11 196 C7
Rudge Cl NG8 171 F5
Rue de L'Yonne NG23 98 A2
Ruffles Ave NG5 162 B5
Rufford Abbey NG22 91 F6
Rufford Ave
Beeston NG9 183 A8
Carlton NG4 162 D2
Mansfield NG18 102 C7
Meden Vale NG20 74 F8
Newark-on-T NG24 139 F7
New Ollerton NG22 77 C4
Rainworth NG21 104 C1
Retford DN22 39 D3
Rufford Cl
Bilsthorpe NG22 106 A4
Hucknall NG15 146 C5
Sutton in A NG17 100 F5
Rufford Craft Ctr NG22 91 F6
Rufford Ct NG21 104 C1
Rufford Ctry Pk NG22 91 E6
Rufford Dr NG19 88 E3
Rufford Gr NG13 177 C4
Rufford Jun & Inf Sch
NG6 160 A7
Rufford La
Edwinstowe NG22 91 F8
Wellow NG22 92 B8
Rufford Rd
Edwinstowe NG21 91 C8
Long Eaton NG10 193 B4
Nottingham NG5 161 C3
Ruddington NG11 196 D7
Rufford St S80 47 B8
Rufford Way NG2 186 B6
Rufford Wlk 1 NG6 160 B7
Ruffs Dr NG15 145 E5
Rugby Cl NG5 160 E7
Rugby Rd
Rainworth NG21 118 A8
West Bridgford NG2 185 C5
Rugby Terr 17 NG7 172 F7
Rugeley Ave NG10 194 A7
Ruislip Cl NG16 158 E7
Runcie Cl NG12 187 F2
Runnymede Ct NG7 222 C3
Runswick Dr
Arnold NG5 161 F8
Nottingham NG8 172 B5
Runton Dr NG6 160 F4
Rupert Cres NG24 139 F7
Rupert Rd NG13 177 D4
Rupert St DE7 158 A1
Rushcliffe Arena NG2 185 D6
Rushcliffe Ave
Carlton NG4 174 D8
Radcliffe on T NG12 175 F3
Rushcliffe Ct NG6 160 D6
Rushcliffe Ctry Pk NG11 196 C5
Rushcliffe Gr LE12 205 E4
Rushcliffe L Ctr NG2 185 F4
Rushcliffe Rd NG15 145 E5
Rushcliffe Rise NG5 161 D5
Rushcliffe Sch NG2 185 F4
Rushes Sh Ctr The LE12 220 A4
Rushes The
Gotham NG11 195 B1
8 Loughborough LE12 220 B4
Mansfield Woodhouse
NG19 88 D5
Rushey Cl S80 36 B2
Rushford Dr NG8 171 D4
Rush Leys NG10 193 D5
Rushley View NG17 100 C1
Rushmere Wlk NG5 161 F5
Rushpool Ave NG19 88 D4
Rushpool Cl NG19 88 F2
Rushton Gdns NG3 173 F7
Rushworth Ave NG2 185 E8
Rushworth Cl NG3 173 E7
Rushy Cl NG8 171 D5
Ruskin Ave NG10 193 B5
Ruskin Cl NG5 161 D7
Ruskin Rd NG19 87 D1
Ruskin St DN21 24 D6
Russell Ave
Harworth DN11 8 F4
New Balderton NG24 140 B4
5 Nottingham NG8 172 A5
Russell Cres 6 NG8 172 A5
Russell Dr NG8 171 F5
Russell Gdns 5 NG9 183 C2
Russell Pl NG1 223 D3
Russell Rd NG7 172 F8
Russell St
Long Eaton NG10 182 D1
Loughborough LE11 220 C4
Nottingham NG7 222 C3
Sutton in A NG17 100 F3
Russet Ave NG4 174 F7
Russet Gr DN10 10 A7
Russey Cl NG14 150 E1
Russley Rd NG9 183 A8
Ruth Dr NG5 148 A1
Rutherford Ave NG18 102 E4
Ruthwell Gdns NG5 147 A2
Rutland NG17 115 D6
Rutland Ave
Beeston NG9 183 A2
Newark-on-T NG24 140 A6
Rutland Cl NG20 74 A4
Rutland Cres DN11 8 F5
Rutland Ct DE7 157 D1
Rutland Dr DN11 8 F5
Rutland Gr NG10 182 C5
Rutland House Sch NG3 173 C8
Rutland La NG13 181 B2
Rutland Rd
Bingham NG13 177 F5
Carlton NG4 162 D3
Retford DN22 40 B4
West Bridgford NG2 186 A8
Westwood NG16 128 C4
Rutland St
Ilkeston DE7 157 F2
1 Loughborough LE11 220 C3
Mansfield NG18 102 C5
Nottingham NG1 223 D2
Rutland Terr DE7 157 F2
Rydal Ave NG10 182 B2
Rydal Dr
Beeston NG9 183 D8
Hucknall NG15 145 F8
Worksop S81 35 E8
Rydale Gdns DN10 3 A1
Rydale Rd NG5 161 C5
Rydal Gdns NG2 186 A5
Rydal Gr NG6 160 E3
Ryder St NG6 160 D4
Rye Croft DN11 8 A8
Ryecroft St NG9 182 F8
Ryedale Ave NG18 103 A5
Ryehill Cl NG2 173 D2
Ryehill St NG2 173 D2
Ryeholme Cl LE12 205 F3
Ryeland Gdns NG2 173 C2
Ryemere Cl NG16 143 E2
Rye St NG7 160 F1
Rylands Cl NG9 184 B4
Rylands Jun Sch NG9 184 A4
Ryton Cl S81 18 B2
Ryton Ct 7 NG2 173 D1
Ryton Fields S81 18 B2
Ryton Pk Prim Sch S80 35 F2
Ryton Pl S80 35 F3
Ryton Sq NG8 160 B1
Ryton St S80 35 F3

S

Sacheverall Ave NG16... 113 D3
Sacred Heart Cath Prim Sch
LE11.................220 A1
Sacred Heart RC Prim Sch
NG4..................174 D7
Saddlers Cl NG19.......88 F1
Saddlers Yd NG12......197 E7
Saddleworth Ct NG3...223 E4
Sadler St NG19........101 F8
Saffron Gdns NG2.....173 B2
St Agnes Cl NG8.......171 D8
St Aidan's Ct NG6.....160 E4
St Albans Cl NG10.....193 E5
St Albans Ct NG5......147 B2
St Albans Mews NG6...160 D6
St Albans Rd
Arnold NG5...........161 E7
Bestwood Village NG6...146 E4
Nottingham NG6.......160 D7
St Albans St NG5.......35 D2
St Andrew Cl NG11....195 B1
St Andrews CE Prim Sch
NG17.................100 F6
St Andrews Cl NG6....160 C7
St Andrew's Cl NG15...146 A8
St Andrews Cres NG17..100 F6
St Andrews Ct NG6....160 D7
St Andrews Dr LN1......56 F4
St Andrew's Rd NG3...173 B7
St Andrew's Rise DE74..203 C1
St Andrews St
Kirkby in Ashfield NG17...115 B6
Sutton in A NG17......100 E6
St Andrew St NG18....102 C5
St Andrews Way DN22...39 E3
St Annes CE Prim Sch
S80..................35 D2
St Annes Cl S80........35 C3
St Annes Dr S80........35 C3
St Anne's La LE12......213 B6
St Annes Mews S80.....35 C3
St Annes View S80......35 C3
St Annes Way S80......35 C3
St Ann's Gdns NG3....173 E7
St Ann's Hill Rd NG3...173 C7
St Ann's Hill Rd NG3...173 C7
St Ann's St NG1.......223 E3
St Ann's Valley NG3...173 E7
St Ann's Way
Nottingham NG3.......223 E4
Shelton NG23.........168 C6
St Anns Well Inf Sch
NG3..................173 D7
St Anns Well Jun Sch
NG3..................173 F8
St Ann's Well Rd NG3...173 E6
St Anthony Ct NG7....172 E2
St Augustines Cl ❸ NG7...161 A1
St Augustine's Inf Sch
S81..................36 B4
St Augustine's Jun Sch
S81..................36 B4
St Augustines RC Prim Sch
NG3..................173 C8
St Austell Dr NG11....185 B6
St Austins Ct NG4.....174 F8
St Austins Dr NG4.....174 F8
St Bartholomew's Rd
NG3..................173 F7
St Botolphs Cl LN1.....57 B5
St Botolphs Gate LN1...57 A5
St Catherines Cl NG24...139 E7
St Catherines NG12...175 E2
St Catherine St NG18...102 C5
St Cecilia Gdns NG3...223 F4
St Chad's Cl NG18.....102 C3
St Chad's Rd NG3.....173 E5
St Christopher St ❾
NG2..................173 F4
St Clare's Gate NG24...140 A6
St Cuthbert's Rd ❶ NG3...173 E5
St Cuthbert St S80......35 F1
St David's Cl S81.......36 A6
St Edmund Campion Prim
Sch NG2.............186 A6
St Edmund's Ave NG19...88 C3
St Edmunds CE Prim Sch
NG19.................88 C3
St Edwards RC Prim Sch
NG3..................173 F7
St Edwin's Dr NG21.....76 A2
St Ervan Rd NG11.....185 B6
St Francis Hospl NG5...161 B5
St George's Ct NG15...146 A8
St George's Dr NG2...173 B2
St George's Ms LN1.....56 F4
St Georges Priory NG2...173 C2
St Giles Specl Sch NG22...39 C8
St Giles Way NG11....189 A4
St Giles' Way NG24....140 E4
St Helens Ave NG16....113 C3
St Helen's Cres
Burton Joyce NG14....163 F4
Trowell NG9...........170 C4
St Helen's Dr NG16....128 D7
St Helen's La NG16....163 E3
St Helen's La NG22....120 F2
St Helen's Rd
Retford DN22..........40 B4
West Bridgford NG2...185 F6
St Helen's St NG7.....222 C3

St James Ave DE7......170 A4
St James Ct NG10.....182 B3
St James' Dr NG16....143 D8
St James's Ct NG15...146 A8
St James's St
Nottingham NG1......223 D2
Stapleford NG9.......182 C6
St James's Terr NG9...182 D6
St James Terr NG1....223 D2
St John Baptist CE Prim Sch
NG4..................174 E6
St Johns CE Prim Sch
Stapleford NG9.......182 E7
Worksop S81...........35 E7
St John's Cl NG16....128 D1
St John's Cres NG15...146 C5
St Johns Ct NG4......174 D7
St Johns Ctr NG18....102 A7
St John's Dr DN22.....30 D4
St John's Pl ❶ NG18...102 A7
St John's Rd
Ilkeston DE7..........170 A7
Ruddington NG11.....196 C7
St John's St NG10.....193 D7
St John St
Mansfield NG18.......102 B7
Retford DN22..........39 F7
St John's Terr DN21....24 D7
St Josephs Prim Sch
DN22.................39 D7
St Joseph's RC Prim Sch
NG22..................77 E5
St Josephs Sch NG1...223 D3
St Jude's Ave NG3....161 E2
St Judes Way NG21...104 A1
St Laurence CE Prim Sch
NG10.................193 E6
St Laurence Cl NG10...193 E6
St Lawrence Bvd NG12...175 E2
St Leonard's Cl DN11....8 A7
St Leonard's Ct NG24...124 F1
St Leonard's Dr NG8...171 F4
St Leonards Way NG19...103 B8
St Leven Cl NG8.......171 D8
St Luke's CE Prim Sch
S80...................34 F8
St Luke's Cl NG2.....186 B5
St Luke's Cl ❻ NG3...173 E5
St Lukes Way DN22....53 A8
St Luke's Way NG14...175 F8
St Margaret Clitherow Cath
Prim Sch NG16.......161 C8
St Margarets Ave NG8...172 C8
St Margaret St NG18...102 C5
St Mark's Cl S81........35 F8
St Mark's La NG24....139 F8
St Mark's Pl NG24....139 F8
St Marks St NG3......223 F3
St Martin's Ave DN10...9 F7
St Martins Cl S81......18 B2
St Martin's Cl
Firbeck S81...........16 A6
Nottingham NG8......171 E8
St Martins Rd DN22....42 C8
St Martin's Rd NG8....171 E8
St Martin's Wlk S80....45 C5
St Mary & Martin Prim Sch
of S81................18 B2
St Mary's Ave NG4...162 E2
St Marys Cath Prim Sch
NG7..................172 F8
St Mary's CE Prim Sch
Edwinstowe NG21......76 A3
Nottingham NG6......160 C8
Tickhill DN11...........8 A7
St Mary's Church NG1...223 F2
St Mary's Cl NG9.....183 D1
St Mary's Cl
Arnold NG5...........147 F1
Bottesford NG13.....181 B3
❶ Loughborough LE11...220 A4
Lowdham NG14.......150 D2
St Mary's Cres
East Leake LE12.......205 F3
Ruddington NG11.....196 C7
Tickhill DN11...........8 A7
St Mary's Ct NG17....100 D4
St Mary's Dr NG21.....76 A2
St Mary's Gate
Nottingham NG1......223 F2
Tickhill DN11...........8 A7
St Mary's Gdns NG24...139 F5
St Mary's La NG13....181 B3
St Mary's Mews DN11...8 A7
St Mary's Pl NG1.....223 F2
St Marys Prim Sch ❶❸
LE11.................220 A4
St Marys Rd NG13....177 F5
St Mary's Rd
Sutton in A NG17....100 D3
Tickhill DN11...........8 A7
St Mary's Way NG15...146 A8
St Mary's Wlk NG16...128 D7
St Matthews CE Prim Sch
NG23..................81 E7
St Matthias Rd NG3...173 E6
St Mawes Ave NG11...185 B6
St Mellion Way ❸ NG17...114 F7
St Michaels Ave NG8...171 D8
St Michael's Ave NG4...162 E2
St Michael's Cl NG22...120 F1
St Michael's Dr DE55...113 A7
St Michael's Sq NG22...39 D8
St Michael's Way NG18...183 B8
St Michael's St NG17...101 A3

St Michael's View NG15..131 B1
St Nicholas Cl NG5....161 E7
St Nicholas St NG1....223 E2
St Patricks Cath Prim Sch
NG18.................185 B8
St Patricks RC Prim Sch
NG18.................103 A5
St Patrick's Rd
Hucknall NG15........145 F7
Nuthall NG16.........159 C6
St Paul's Ave NG7....172 F7
St Paul's Rd
Gainsborough DN21....15 B3
Worksop S80..........36 A2
St Paul's St ❶ NG8...172 D5
St Paul's Terr NG7....172 F7
St Peters Ave LE12....213 A1
St Peters Ave NG20....74 B6
St Peters CE Jun Sch
NG11.................196 D8
St Peters CE Prim Sch
East Bridgford NG13...165 C3
Farndon NG24.........139 A8
Gringley on the Hill DN10..12 E2
Mansfield NG18.......103 A8
St Peter's Church Wlk
NG1..................223 E2
St Peters Cl
East Stockwith DN21....7 E2
Farndon NG24.........138 F4
New Ollerton NG22....77 B4
St Peter's Cres NG11...196 C7
St Peters Dr NG21....104 A1
St Peter's Gate NG1...223 E2
St Peter's La DN22.....21 D5
St Peter's Ret Pk NG18..102 A6
St Peter's Sq NG1....223 E2
St Peter's St NG7.....222 A3
St Peter's Way NG18...102 C6
St Philip Neri RC Prim Sch
NG19.................102 A8
St Saviour's Cl DN22....40 A8
St Saviour's Gdns NG2...173 D2
St Stephen's Ave ❼ NG2..173 F4
St Stephen's Rd
Nottingham NG2......173 F4
Retford DN22..........40 B4
St Swithuns CE Prim Sch ❶
DN22..................39 F7
St Teresas RC Prim Sch
NG8..................172 A8
St Thomas' Ave NG17...115 B4
St Thomas Dr NG3....179 A5
St Vincent Cl NG10...193 E6
St Wilfreds Cl NG23...110 F2
St Wilfrids Dr NG17...114 D5
St Wilfrids
NG18.................148 E7
St Wilfrid's Sq NG14...148 F7
Salamander Cl NG4...162 D2
Salcey Dr NG9........170 D2
Salcombe Cir NG5....144 C1
Salcombe Cl NG4.....144 C1
Salcombe Cres NG11...196 D8
Salcombe Dr NG5.....147 D1
Salcombe Rd DN10.....9 F8
Salcombe Rd NG5....160 F3
Salford Gdns NG3....223 F3
Salisbury Ave LE12...205 F1
Salisbury Cl
Mansfield Woodhouse
NG19..................88 D4
Morton DN21..........15 B5
Salisbury Rd
Mansfield NG18.......101 E8
Newark-on-T NG24...139 F6
Salisbury Sq NG7.....222 A2
Salisbury St
Beeston NG9..........184 B7
Gainsborough DN21....15 C2
Long Eaton NG10.....193 E7
Loughborough LE11...220 C4
Nottingham NG7......222 A2
Sallie Bank La LN1......55 B4
Salmon Cl NG6........159 F7
Salmon La NG17......129 D7
Salop St NG5.........161 D7
Saltburn Rd NG8......172 A6
Salterford Ave NG14...148 F8
Salterford House Sch
NG14.................133 D5
Salterford La NG14...133 D5
Salterford Rd NG15...145 E5
Saltford Cl NG14......162 F2
Salt Hill S81............16 B5
Salthouse Ct NG9....184 A7
Salthouse La NG9....184 A8
Saltney Way NG11....185 A3
Salvin Cl NG12........189 A4
Sampson's La NG17....87 B3
Sampson St NG17....130 A8
Samson Ct NG11.....196 B8
Samuel Barlow Prim Sch
NG21..................90 A3
Samuel Cl NG19......101 F8
Samuel Way NG18....102 C8
Sandale Cl NG2.......186 C6
Sandalwood Cl NG18...103 B4
Sandalwood Dr NG17...115 C6
Sandays Cl NG2......173 C1
Sandbeck Cl DN10.....10 A8
Sandby Ct NG9.......183 C5
Sanders Ave NG18....102 E8
Sanders Cl NG21......104 A1
Sanderson Dr NG3....162 D6
Sanderson's Bank DN9...2 B3
Sandfield Ave NG15...132 B8
Sandfield Cl NG18....103 B4

Sandford Ctr NG7.....222 B2
Sandfield La NG22....78 B6
Sandfield Rd
Annesley Woodhouse
NG17.................129 F8
Arnold NG5...........161 F5
Beeston NG9.........182 E2
Nottingham NG7.....222 B2
Sandfield Way NG24...135 D3
Sandford Cl NG10....193 E7
Sandford Rd NG3.....162 A3
Sandgate NG9........171 D1
Sandgate Ave NG19...88 D4
Sandgate Rd NG19....88 D4
Sandhill Rd
Farndon NG24........139 A5
Selston NG16.........129 B3
Sandhills Cl NG24....124 E1
Sandhills Pk NG24....124 E1
Sandhill St S80.........35 E3
Sandhoes The NG22...119 C6
Sandhurst Ave NG18...102 C4
Sandhurst Dr
Beeston NG9.........183 C2
Ruddington NG11.....196 B6
Sandhurst Rd NG6....146 C1
Sandiacre Rd NG9....182 C6
Sand La
Besthorpe NG23.......97 F7
Broadholme NG23......70 E8
Spalford NG23..........83 A7
Torksey LN1............44 C2
Sandmartins S81......35 C7
Sandmartins Cl NG18...102 C5
Sandon St NG7.......161 A1
Sandown Rd
Beeston NG9.........182 F2
Mansfield NG18......103 B4
Sutton in A NG17....101 B3
Sandpiper Cl NG13....177 F3
Sandpiper Way NG7...222 A2
Sand Pit La LE14......211 C3
Sandringham Ave NG2...185 E8
Sandringham Cres
Nottingham NG8......171 C5
Worksop S81...........35 E6
Sandringham Ct
Harworth DN11..........9 A5
Mansfield Woodhouse NG19..88 B6
Sandringham Dr
Beeston NG9.........171 C1
Mansfield Woodhouse NG19..88 B6
Sandringham Pl NG15...146 B8
Sandringham Rd
Mansfield Woodhouse
NG19..................88 E5
❷ Nottingham NG2...173 F4
Retford DN22..........29 D1
Sandiacre NG10......182 B3
Sandrock Rd DN11......8 F5
Sands Cl NG4.........124 D6
Sandsfield La DN21...24 D6
Sandside NG12........187 F2
Sands The LE14.......211 D3
Sandstone Pl NG18...102 C5
Sandwell Cl NG10....193 A6
Sandwich Cl ❺ NG17...114 E7
Sandwood Cl DE55.....99 A3
Sandycliffe Cl NG19...88 F1
Sandyford Cl NG6....160 C3
Sandy La
Beeston NG9.........171 D1
Carlton NG12.........175 B2
Edwinstowe NG21.....91 B8
Gamston DN22.........50 F4
Hucknall NG15.......146 A7
Mansfield NG18......102 D7
Market Warsop NG20..74 B5
Oxton NG25..........134 C3
Ravenshead NG15....117 B3
Worksop S80..........35 D4
Sandymount LN1.......9 A5
Sandymount E DN11....9 A4
Sandymount W DN11...9 A4
Sanger Cl NG11......195 C8
Sanger Gdns NG11...195 C8
Sankey Dr NG6.......160 A7
Santon Cl NG19........80 A2
Santon Rd NG19........89 A2
Sapele Cl NG4........163 A2
Sapling Cl NG4.......140 C5
Sapphire Cl NG21....104 C1
Sapphire Dr NG17....115 C4
Sapphire St NG18....102 C5
Saracen Cl DN10.......24 F6
Saracen La DN10........9 F2
Saracen's Head Yd NG24..139 F8
Sargent Gdns ❶ NG3...173 F6
Sartfield Rd NG19......89 B2
Saskatoon Cl NG12...175 E2
Saucemere Dr NG24...139 F6
Saucers The NG13....178 E7
Saunby Cl NG5.......162 B7
Saundby Ave NG5......87 D1
Saundby Rd DN22......22 B8
Savage's Rd NG11....196 C8
Savages Row NG11...196 C8
Saversick La NG25....136 A8
Savile Rd NG2........105 F6
Savile St DN22........39 E6
Savile Way NG20......74 A4
Savile Rd
Arnold NG5...........161 F5
Sutton in A NG17....100 F6
Saville Cl NG5........118 B5
Saville St NG21.......118 C8
Saville Way NG20......74 A4
Sawley Dr NG18......103 B4

Saw Pit Ind Est DE55....99 C6
Saw Pit La DE55........99 B5
Sawyers Cl NG24.....140 B8
Saxby Dr NG18.......103 B4
Saxelby Gdns NG6....160 B8
Saxilby Rd
Saxilby LN1............57 A1
Skellingthorpe LN6....71 F8
Saxilby Sta LN1........57 A3
Saxondale Dr
Nottingham NG6.....160 C5
Radcliffe on T NG12...176 D3
Saxon Gn NG7........222 A1
Saxon Way
Cotgrave NG12......188 A3
Harworth DN11.........9 A3
Saxton Cl
Beeston NG9.........184 B6
Worksop S80...........35 D2
Scafell Way NG11....195 D7
Scalby Cl NG16.......143 D2
Scalford Dr NG8......172 C4
Scampton Rd S81......35 D8
Scampton Way NG22...62 A8
Scarborough Rd NG22...105 F6
Scarborough St NG3...223 F3
Scarbrough Cl DN11....8 A7
Scarcliffe Ctr NG17....100 F3
Scarcliffe La NG20.....72 C7
Scarcliffe St NG18....102 D6
Scarcliffe Terr NG20....59 A2
Scarfell Cl NG2.......186 C5
Scarf Wlk NG2........185 B7
Scargill Ave NG16....144 B1
Scargill Cl NG16......144 B1
Scargill Wlk NG16....143 F3
Scarle La LN6...........84 C3
Scarrington Ct ❶ NG18..103 A2
Scarrington Rd NG2...173 F1
Sceptre St NG5.......161 C2
School Ave NG15.....145 D4
School La
Newton DE55..........99 B3
Nottingham NG2......173 D1
School Hill NG15......130 D6
School House La DN10..13 F6
School La
Beckingham LN5.....142 D8
Beeston NG9.........183 C4
Bingham NG13.......177 E5
Caunton NG23.......109 B4
Claypole NG23......156 E7
Colston Bassett NG12...200 D7
Cuckney NG20.........60 A3
Eakring NG22..........92 E1
East Stoke NG23....153 C8
Farndon NG24........139 A4
Halam NG22...........121 A3
Harby LE14...........202 A3
Kirklington NG22....120 F7
Kneesall NG22.........93 F5
Long Clawson LE14...211 C3
Mansfield Woodhouse NG19..88 C3
North Scarle LN6......83 D2
Norwell NG23.........110 A8
Ollerton NG22..........77 B3
Rempstone LE12.....215 D5
South Normanton DE55..113 B4
Whatton NG13........179 B3
School Rd
Langold S81.............16 E3
Selston NG16.........129 A7
School St
Kirkby in A NG17.....115 B4
Loughborough LE11...220 B4
School View NG13....181 A2
School Wlk
Bawtry DN10............10 A7
Bestwood Village NG6...146 E4
School Woods Cl DE75...157 B6
Schrimshire's Rd DN22...32 A1
Science Rd NG7......172 D1
Scofton Cl S81.........35 C8
Scotholme Ave ❼ NG7...172 F8
Scotholme Prim Sch
NG7..................172 F8
Scot La DN10..........10 A3
Scotland Bank NG12...187 F3
Scotland Rd NG5.....160 F3
Scotswood Rd NG19...88 B6
Scott Ave NG9........184 A5
Scott Cl
Claypole NG23.......156 D7
Nottingham NG6.....159 F5
Worksop S81...........36 C4
Scotton Sq DN22......29 D1
Scott St DN21..........15 C1
Scotts Way NG17....115 B1
Scratta La S80.........34 C2
Scrimshire La LE12...187 E3
Script Dr NG6.........160 B8
Scrivelsby Gdns NG9...183 D4
Scrooby Rd
Bircotes DN11...........9 C4
Harworth DN11.........9 F3
Seaburn Rd NG9.....182 C2
Seaford Ave NG8.....172 B6
Seaford Way DE7....157 F5
Seaforth Sq NG19....101 D5
Seagrave Ave NG17...115 B1
Seagrave Prim Sch NG8..159 D2
Seagrave Rd NG8....159 D1
Seamer Rd NG16.....158 F2
Searby Rd NG17......101 C1
Searwood Ave NG17...114 C7

Seatallen Cl NG2 .... 186 C6
Seathwaite Cl NG2 ...... 186 D4
Seatoller Cl NG2 .... 186 C5
Seaton Cres NG8 .... 160 A1
Second Ave
  Beeston NG9 .... 184 C5
  Carlton, Gedling NG4 ....162 F1
  Carlton, Thorneywood
    NG4 .... 174 C8
  Clipstone NG21 ....90 A3
  Edwinstowe NG21 ....76 A2
  Mansfield NG21 .... 103 F2
  Mansfield Woodhouse NG19 89 A1
  Nottingham NG6 .... 160 B7
Sedgebrook Cl NG6 ..... 160 C3
Sedgebrook St NG19 ..... 88 E3
Sedgeley Rd NG12 ...... 186 D1
Sedgewood Gr NG11 .... 184 E3
Sedgeway Ave NG2 ..... 173 E5
Sedgmere NG2 ....39 D4
Sedgwick St
  Langley Mill NG16 ..... 143 B3
  Westwood NG16 .... 128 B3
Sedley Ave NG16 .... 159 C6
Seely Ave NG4 .... 148 E8
Seely Jun Sch NG5 ..... 161 C3
Seely Rd NG7 .... 222 C3
Sefton Ave NG9 .... 182 E8
Sefton Dr NG3 .... 161 D2
Selassie Ct NG8 .... 159 E2
Selbourne Ct 4 LE11 ... 220 C4
Selbourne St LE11 ..... 220 C4
Selby Cl NG9 .... 182 E3
Selby La NG12 .... 197 F2
Selby Rd
  Styrrup DN11............8 E2
  West Bridgford NG2 .... 185 F5
Selhurst Ct NG7 .... 172 F7
Selhurst St 5 NG2 ..... 172 F7
Selkirk Way 13 NG5 ... 161 B1
Sellars Ave NG1 .... 196 C6
Seller's Wood Dr NG6.. 160 A7
Seller's Wood Dr W NG6 159 F8
Sellers Wood Nature Reserve
  NG5 .... 159 E7
Selly Church Prim Sch
  NG5 .... 132 E2
Selsey Ct DN22 ....29 E1
Selside Ct NG9 .... 183 A4
Selston Bagthorpe Prim Sch
  NG16 .... 129 A4
Selston CE Inf Sch NG16 128 E6
Selston Dr NG8 .... 172 C3
Selston L Ctr NG16..... 128 F6
Selston Rd NG16 .... 128 B5
Selwyn Cl NG6 .... 160 E5
Selwyn St NG18 .... 102 E5
Sennen Ct DN22 ....29 E1
Serif Cl NG5 .... 161 B1
Serlby Rd NG16 .... 144 A3
Serlby Rise NG3 .... 173 F6
Serpentine Cl NG12 .... 176 D2
Seven Hills NG24 ...... 125 A3
Seven Oaks Cres NG4 .. 171 C1
Seven Oaks Rd DE7 .... 170 A1
Seventh Ave
  Beeston NG9 .... 184 C5
  Clipstone NG21 ....89 E2
  Mansfield NG19........ 103 A8
Severals NG9 .... 182 F7
Severn St NG6 .... 160 B7
Seward St 2 LE11 ..... 220 A3
Seymour Rd
  Eastwood NG16 .... 143 F1
  Hucknall NG15 .... 145 E5
  West Bridgford NG2 ... 186 B8
Seymour St NG3 .... 173 E6
SGCS Bsns Pk NG11 ... 184 A5
Shackleton Ct NG8 .... 159 D2
Shacklock Cl NG5...... 147 A2
Shadwell Gr NG12 ..... 175 E3
Shady La NG9 .... 183 D2
Shaftesbury Ave
  Burton Joyce NG14 .... 164 A5
  Long Eaton NG10 ..... 193 B4
  Mansfield NG19........ 87 E2
  Radcliffe on T NG12.... 176 E3
  Sandiacre NG10 .... 182 A5
Shaftesbury St 4 NG7 . 161 A1
Shaftesbury Way NG23...98 A1
Shakespeare Ave NG9...88 B4
Shakespeare Cl NG4 ... 174 E5
Shakespeare Rd NG16.. 158 C5
Shakespeare St
  Gainsborough DN21 .....24 D6
  Long Eaton NG10 ..... 182 D1
  Loughborough LE11 ... 220 B4
  New Balderton NG24... 140 B6
  Nottingham NG1 ...... 223 E3
  Worksop S81 ....36 B4
Shakespeare Villas NG1 . 223 E3
Shaldon Cl NG5....... 146 F1
Shale La NG14 .... 152 A8
Shandwick Cl NG5 .... 148 B1
Shanklin Dr NG8 ...... 172 D7
Shanwell Ct NG8 ...... 159 D2
Shardlow Way NG18 ... 103 B4
Sharnford Way NG9 ... 171 B3
Sharp Cl NG10 .... 193 C6
Sharpes Wy NG6....... 147 B5
Sharphill Rd NG2 ..... 186 B4
Sharpley Dr LE12 ..... 205 F3
Sharrard Cl NG14 ..... 129 A2
Sharrat Ct 8 NG18 ... 103 A2
Shaw Cres NG15 ...... 145 E4
Shaw Croft NG17 ..... 100 F5
Shaw Rd DN10...........12 F4
Shaw St E DE7........ 170 A6

Shaw St W DE7........ 170 A6
Shaw St
  Mansfield NG18....... 102 E7
  Ruddington NG11..... 196 C6
  Worksop S80 ....35 E3
Sheaf Pl S81 ....35 E7
Shearing Cl NG4 ...... 163 A1
Shearing Hill NG4 .... 163 A1
Sheepbridge La NG18.. 101 F5
Sheepfold La NG11 ... 196 C6
Sheepwalk La NG15.... 116 F2
Sheepwash La
  Sutton in A NG17....... 101 B2
  Tickhill DN11 ....8 E8
Sheet Stores Ind Est
  NG10 .... 193 D5
Sheffield Rd S81........18 A3
Shelby Cl NG7 .... 222 B8
Sheldon Cl NG10....... 182 B3
Sheldrake Rd NG24 ... 140 D8
Shelford Ave NG17.... 114 D6
Shelford Cl
  Beeston NG9 .... 183 D4
  Radcliffe on T NG12... 176 A4
Shelford Cres NG14 ... 164 A5
Shelford Dr NG13 ..... 177 D4
Shelford Hill
  Mansfield NG18....... 101 E6
  Radcliffe on T NG12... 176 C7
Shelford Rd
  Carlton NG4........... 162 D3
  Radcliffe on T NG12... 176 A5
Shelford Rise NG3 .... 174 A5
Shellburne Cl NG5 .... 160 E8
Shelley Ave
  Mansfield Woodhouse
    NG19................. 88 B4
  Nottingham NG11 .... 184 E3
Shelley Cl
  Balderton NG24 ...... 140 D3
  Hucknall NG15 .... 145 D6
  Nuthall NG16 .... 159 B6
Shelley Rd NG5 .... 161 D7
Shelley St S80 ....36 A3
Shelthorpe Ave LE11 .. 220 B1
Shelthorpe Prim Sch
  LE11................. 220 C1
Shelthorpe Rd LE11.... 220 B1
Shelton Ave
  Hucknall NG15....... 146 D4
  Newark-on-T NG24 ... 139 E5
Shelton Cl NG18 ...... 87 E1
Shelton Gdns NG11 ... 196 D7
Shelton Rd NG18 ..... 103 A2
Shelton St NG3 ...... 223 F4
Shenfield Gdns NG5 .. 146 D1
Shepard Cl NG6 ...... 159 F6
Shepherd's Ave S81....36 A5
Shepherds Cl NG24 ... 172 A7
Shepherd's Cl LE12 .. 213 C5
Shepherds Oak NG17 . 100 F6
Shepherd Specl Sch
  NG8 .... 171 F8
Shepherds Way NG17.. 101 B2
Shepherds Wood Dr
  NG8 .... 172 C7
Shepshed Rd LE12 .... 212 F1
Shepton Cl DE7....... 157 D3
Shepton Cres NG8 .... 160 B1
Sheraton Dr NG8 ..... 171 E3
Sherborne Rd
  Nottingham NG8 ..... 160 A1
  West Bridgford NG2 .. 185 F5
Sherbrook Ave NG18.. 103 A2
Sherbrook Cl NG14 ... 148 E8
Sherbrook Rd NG5.... 161 D6
Sherbrook Terr NG5... 161 D6
Sherbrook Way NG15.. 146 A3
Sheridan Cl NG24 .... 140 D5
Sheridan Ct NG9...... 170 F1
Sheridan Wy
  Hucknall NG15....... 146 A5
  Nottingham NG5 ..... 161 A3
Sheriff's Lodge The NG1.. 223 F1
Sheriffs Way NG2 .... 173 C2
Sheringham Cl NG8... 102 C5
Sheringham Dr NG18.. 102 C5
Sherman Dr NG9 ..... 183 C2
Sherriff's Lea NG9 ... 182 E2
Sherrington Cl NG11.. 195 C8
Sherwin Ave NG18 ... 103 A7
Sherwin Cl NG3 ..... 223 E4
Sherwin Gr NG7 ..... 222 A1
Sherwin Rd
  Nottingham NG7 ..... 222 A1
  Stapleford NG9 ...... 170 F1
  Stanton Hill NG17 ... 100 C5
Sherwin Wlk NG3 .... 223 E4
Sherwood Ave
  Blidworth NG21 ..... 118 C5
  Calverton NG14 ..... 148 D8
  Edwinstowe NG21.... 76 A2
  Newark-on-T NG24 .. 140 A8
  5 Nottingham NG5.. 161 A1
  Shirebrook NG20 .... 72 E4
Sherwood Cl NG18 ... 102 E7
Sherwood Cres S81 ... 18 A2
Sherwood Day Hospl
  NG5 .... 161 B4
Sherwood Dene 6 NG7 114 C1
Sherwood Dr
  New Ollerton NG22 ... 77 C4
  Shirebrook NG20 .... 72 E3
Sherwood Energy Village
  NG21................. 76 A3
Sherwood Forest Art & Craft
  Ctr NG21.............. 76 A3

Sherwood Forest Ctry Pk
  NG22 .... 76 A4
Sherwood Forest Farm Pk
  NG20 .... 89 F7
Sherwood Forest Fun Pk
  NG22 .... 76 B4
Sherwood Gr
  Bingham NG13....... 177 D4
  Calverton NG14 ..... 148 F8
Sherwood Hall Gdns
  NG18 .... 102 F8
Sherwood Hall Rd NG18. 102 E7
Sherwood Hall Sch & Sixth
  Form NG18........... 102 F7
Sherwood Heath Nature
  Reserve NG22........ 76 F4
Sherwood Jun Sch NG20. 74 B3
Sherwood Lodge Dr
  NG3 .... 132 C2
Sherwood Pines Forest Pk
  NG21 .... 90 E3
Sherwood Pk NG15 ... 129 F6
Sherwood Pl
  Annesley Woodhouse
    NG17............... 115 A1
  Clipstone NG21 ...... 90 B4
Sherwood Rd
  Harworth DN11....... 8 F5
  Rainworth NG21 ..... 104 B1
  Retford DN22........ 39 E3
  Sutton in A NG17.... 100 E1
  Worksop S80 .... 35 F4
Sherwood Rise
  Annesley Woodhouse
    NG17............... 115 A1
  Eastwood NG16 ..... 143 F1
  Mansfield Woodhouse NG19 88 A2
  Nottingham NG7 .... 173 B8
Sherwood St
  Annesley Woodhouse
    NG17............... 115 A1
  Hucknall NG15....... 146 C6
  Huthwaite NG17..... 99 F3
  Kirkby in A NG17.... 115 B4
  10 Mansfield NG18. 102 B6
  Mansfield Woodhouse NG19 88 B2
  Market Warsop NG20. 74 B3
  Newton DE55......... 99 B4
Sherwood Swimming Baths
  NG19 .... 88 B1
Sherwood Vale NG5.. 161 E3
Sherwood Way NG16.. 129 B7
Sherwood Wlk NG15.. 131 A2
Shetland Cl NG19..... 88 F1
Shilling Way NG10 ... 193 A7
Shilo Way NG16...... 158 B4
Shining Cliff Ct DN10 .. 9 F8
Shipley Cl DE7 ...... 157 D1
Shipley Ctry Pk DE75 . 157 A4
Shipley Rd NG8....... 159 F2
Shipley Rise NG4 .... 162 F3
Shipstone St
  Ilkeston DE7......... 170 B6
  3 Nottingham NG7.. 172 F8
Shirburn Ave NG18... 102 C8
Shirebrook Bsns Pk NG20 72 F2
Shirebrook Cl NG6.... 160 C3
Shirebrook Sta NG20.. 73 A4
Shire Cl S81.......... 36 B4
Shire La NG23, NG24.. 156 B7
Shireoaks Comm S81.. 34 F7
Shireoaks Ct 2 NG18.. 103 A2
Shireoaks Rd S80..... 35 B5
Shireoaks Row S81.... 34 E7
Shireoaks Sta S81 ... 34 E7
Shireoak Triangle Bsns Pk
  S81.................. 35 A7
Shires The
  Mansfield Woodhouse
    NG19............... 88 F1
  Sutton in A NG17.... 100 D1
Shirland Dr NG18 .... 103 B4
Shirley Dr NG5 ...... 162 B7
Shirley Rd NG3 ..... 173 C8
Shirley St NG10 ..... 193 A4
Shoreswood Cl 1 NG5. 161 B8
Shortcross Ave NG3... 161 F2
Short Hill NG1....... 223 F2
Short St
  Market Warsop NG20.. 74 B4
  Sutton in A NG17.... 101 A3
Short Wheatley La NG23 112 B5
Shortwood Ave NG15.. 145 F5
Shortwood Cl NG1.... 223 F1
Shortwood La NG22... 93 C8
Shorwell Rd NG3..... 174 C7
Shotton Dr NG5...... 148 A2
Shoulder of Mutton Hill
  NG17............... 115 B1
Shrewsbury Rd
  Bircotes DN11........ 9 B4
  Nottingham NG2 .... 174 A4
  Worksop S80 .... 36 B1
Shrewsbury View DN22.. 29 C1
Shrimpton Cl NG11... 196 D6
Shropshire Ave NG16. 128 C4
Sibcy La NG24....... 140 D3
Sibson Dr DE74...... 203 B2
Sibson Wlk NG14 ... 147 F2
Sibthorpe St NG18 .. 102 A5
Siddalls Dr NG17 ... 100 B3
Side Ley DE74....... 203 C2
Side Ley DE74....... 203 C3
Side Row NG24...... 140 B8
Sidings Rd NG17..... 115 C7
Sidings The

Sidings The continued
  Kimberley NG16...... 159 A6
  Saxilby LN1.......... 57 A3
Sidlaw Rise NG5...... 147 B2
Sidmouth Cl NG12 ... 197 E4
Sidney Rd NG9 ...... 183 E7
Sidney St
  Kimberley NG16...... 158 F6
  Long Eaton NG10 ... 193 D6
Sidsaph Hill DN10 ... 14 A5
Siena Gdns NG9 .... 184 A2
Sikorski Cl NG24 .... 124 F1
Silbury Cl NG11...... 195 D2
Silken Holme DE55 .. 113 B4
Silk St NG17......... 100 E1
Silver Birch Cl NG6.. 160 B4
Silver Hill Cl NG11.. 195 A8
Silverdale NG9 ..... 182 E5
Silverdale Ave NG19 . 88 B4
Silverdale Cl DN22... 29 C1
Silverdale Rd NG7 .. 172 C2
Silver Hill Cl NG8 .. 171 D6
Silverhill Cotts NG17.. 100 A8
Silverhill La NG17... 99 F8
Silverhow Cl NG2 ... 186 C6
Silver St
  Gainsborough DN21...24 C8
  Grasshorpe NG23.... 81 F4
  North Clifton NG23 .. 68 E5
  Retford DN22........ 39 D5
Silverwood Ave NG15. 117 A1
Silverwood Rd
  Beeston NG9 .... 183 E6
  Bottesford NG13..... 181 A2
Silvey Ave NG25..... 121 D2
Sime St S80.......... 35 E4
Simkin Ave NG3..... 162 A1
Simon Cl DN22....... 42 B1
Simone Gdns NG7 ... 184 E1
Simons Ct NG9 ..... 171 D1
Simpson Cl NG24.... 140 E3
Simpson Rd NG19.... 101 D7
Singleton Ave NG18.. 102 E8
Sir Edmund Hillary Prim Sch
  NG5 .... 148 E8
Sir John Sherbrooke Jun Sch
  NG14 .... 148 E8
Siskin Cl S81........ 35 C7
Sisley Ave NG9 ..... 182 E6
Sitwell Cl S81....... 36 B4
Sitwell Rd S81....... 36 C4
Six Hills La LE14 ... 219 A2
Sixth Ave
  Beeston NG9 .... 184 D6
  Clipstone NG21 ..... 89 E3
  Edwinstowe NG21.... 76 A1
  Mansfield NG19...... 103 A8
Skeavington's La DE7 . 157 E5
Skegby La NG17, NG19. 101 C6
Skegby Mount NG19 . 101 E5
Skegby Rd
  Annesley Woodhouse
    NG17............... 100 A1
  Huthwaite NG17..... 100 A3
  Normanton on T NG23. 81 C7
  Sutton in A NG17.... 101 A4
Skelwith Cl NG2..... 186 C5
Skerry Hill NG18.... 102 E7
Skerry La NG13...... 181 F1
Sketchley Ct 2 NG6. 160 A7
Sketchley St NG3.... 173 F6
Skiddaw Cl NG2..... 186 C6
Skipton Cl NG3 ..... 174 A5
Skipton Ct DE7...... 157 D3
Skirbeck Dr LN1..... 57 A3
Skithorne Rise NG14 . 164 D8
Skylark Cl NG13..... 177 F3
Skylark Dr NG6 ..... 160 D8
Skylarks Nature Reserve
  NG2 .... 175 A3
Slack's La NG13..... 152 B2
Slack Wlk S80....... 35 E1
Slade Cl DE55....... 113 B4
Slade Rd NG9....... 183 B5
Slaidburn Ave NG11.. 185 A5
Slake La NG24...... 124 E6
Slant La NG19...... 88 B4
Slater St NG17...... 100 F4
Slaughter House La
  NG24 .... 124 F1
Sleaford Rd
  Beckingham LN5 .... 142 D8
  Coddington NG24 ... 126 D2
  Newark-on-T NG24 .. 140 E3
Sleights La NG16 ... 113 C2
Sloan Dr NG9....... 171 B3
Sloane Ct NG11..... 185 C3
Slowthorne Gdns 2
  NG5 .... 161 D8
Smalley Cl NG16.... 129 A1
Small Farm Ctr NG13.. 202 E7
Small Gate NG18.... 102 E6
Small's Croft NG14.. 149 C4
Smeath La DN22..... 30 C4
Smeath Rd
  Retford DN22....... 30 A3
  Selston NG16....... 129 A2
Smedley Ave NG7.... 170 A7
Smedley Cl NG8..... 160 B2
Smedley's Ave NG10.. 182 B5
Smeeton St DE75.... 143 B1
Smite Cl NG13...... 179 A4
Smite La NG13...... 179 A4
Smith Cl NG13...... 143 A3
Smithfield Ave NG9.. 170 D4
Smiths Cl NG12..... 189 A4
Smithson Cl NG24... 140 E4
Smithson Dr NG8.... 171 E4
Smith Sq DN11....... 8 F4

Smith St
  Mansfield NG18...... 102 E6
  Newark-on-T NG24 .. 140 A8
Smithurst Rd NG16.. 158 B7
Smithy Cl NG11..... 184 D2
Smithy Cres NG5.... 161 F8
Smithy La LE12..... 212 A2
Smithy Row NG1.... 223 E2
Smithy View NG14 . 148 E7
Snaefell Ave NG19 .. 89 A2
Snape La DN11...... 9 A2
Snape Nook Ct NG6.. 159 F7
Snape Wood Prim Sch
  NG6 .... 160 A7
Snape Wood Rd NG6. 159 F7
Snead Ct NG5....... 147 A1
Sneinton Bvd NG2... 174 A4
Sneinton CE Prim Sch
  NG2 .... 173 F5
Sneinton Dale NG2 . 174 A5
Sneinton Hermitage
  .... 173 E3
Sneinton Hollows NG2. 173 F4
Sneinton Rd NG2 ... 173 E4
Snell Cl NG23....... 81 E1
Snipe Pk Rd DN11... 9 B4
Snowdon Cl 2 NG5.. 147 B1
Snowdon Rd NG23... 112 A8
Soarbank Cl NG16... 158 E7
Soar La
  Normanton on S LE12. 213 D3
  Sutton Bonington LE12. 212 F8
Sobers Gdns NG5.... 162 B8
Softwood Cl NG6.... 159 F7
Soloman Pk NG16... 158 B2
Soloman Rd NG16... 158 B2
Solway Cl NG9...... 183 C5
Somerby Ct NG9.... 171 B3
Somerby Rd DN21... 15 F1
Somerleyton Dr DE7.. 170 A4
Somersby Ct NG18.. 103 B5
Somersby Rd NG3... 161 E3
Somersby Rd NG5... 162 A5
Somerset Cl NG10... 194 A8
Somerton Ave NG11. 185 A4
Somerton Rd S81.... 35 C8
Songthrush Ave NG6. 160 D4
Sookholme Dr NG20. 72 F3
Sookholme La NG20.. 74 A3
Sookholme Rd
  Market Warsop NG20. 73 E1
  Shirebrook NG20.... 72 F3
Sophie Rd NG7...... 222 B4
Sorrel Dr NG13...... 177 C4
Soss La DN10........ 7 B2
Sotheby Ave NG17 .. 101 C1
Soudan Dr NG2..... 173 B1
Sough Rd DE55..... 113 B7
Southampton St NG3. 173 E6
South Ave
  Bawtry DN10........ 10 A1
  Radcliffe on T NG12.. 176 B3
  Rainworth NG21 .... 104 A1
  Shirebrook NG20.... 72 F3
  Worksop S80 .... 36 B1
South Cliffe NG24 .. 140 A8
Southchurch Dr NG7. 184 F2
Southcliffe Rd NG4.. 174 D7
South Cres
  Bottesford NG13.... 181 A1
  Clipstone NG21 ..... 90 A3
South Croft NG22... 51 F2
Southdale Dr NG4... 174 D7
Southdale Rd NG4... 174 D7
Southdene S81....... 36 A6
South Devon Ave NG3. 162 B2
South Dr NG22...... 105 F7
South End NG23..... 111 F7
Southern Ave NG24.. 139 F7
Southern Wood S80.. 46 E8
Southey St NG7..... 222 C4
Southfall Cl DN22... 19 B5
Southfield Rd DE55.. 113 C5
Southfield Ind Est S80. 45 A4
Southfield Rd S80... 45 A4
Southfields NG18.... 172 D6
Southfields NG10.... 193 D7
Southfields Ave NG17. 113 D4
Southfields Cl NG17.. 114 D1
Southfields Rise DN22. 42 C8
Southgate DN21..... 39 E3
Southgate Rd NG20.. 74 C5
Southglade Food Pk
  .... 160 E6
Southglade Jun & Inf Sch
  .... 161 E1
Southglade L Ctr NG5. 160 F7
Southglade Rd NG5. 160 F6
Southgore La DN22.. 42 D8
Southgreen Cl NG18. 102 E2
Southgreen Hill NG18. 102 E2
South La NG23...... 81 E5
Southlands Ave DN21. 15 E4
Southlands Dr DN21 .. 15 B4
Southlands Gdns NG4. 15 A4
Southlea Rd NG4.... 174 D7
Southmoor La LN1... 69 B7
South Moor Rd NG22. 50 B1
South Nottingham Coll
  .... 185 A1
Southolme DN21
  .... 24 D8

South Par
Bawtry DN10..............10 A6
Gainsborough DN21 ....24 F7
Nottingham NG1 ....223 E2
Saxilby LN1...............57 A4
Worksop S81..............36 A4
Southpark Ave NG18......102 F2
Southport Terr 4 NG7 ..172 E7
South Rd
Beeston NG9..............184 B4
Nottingham, Dunkirk NG7 .172 D2
Nottingham, The Park NG7 222 C1
West Bridgford NG2 ......185 E6
South Ridge Dr NG18 ....102 D3
South Scarle La NG6 ......83 D1
South Scarle Rd NG23 ....98 B2
South Sherwood St NG1 .223 E3
Southside NG5............162 C7
South Snape Cl NG6 ......159 F7
South St
Bole DN22 ....23 E2
Eastwood, Bailey Grove
 NG16..................143 E2
Eastwood, Giltbrook NG16 158 C8
Hucknall NG15...........146 A7
Long Eaton NG10.........193 E7
Loughborough LE11.......220 B3
Morton DN21..............36 A4
Normanton on T NG23.....81 E6
Retford DN22..............39 F6
South Normanton DE55...113 B6
South View
Austerfield DN10...........3 C1
Whitwell S80..............45 A5
Worksop S81..............35 F5
South View Dr DN22.......30 D3
Southview Gdns NG15....117 A2
South View Rd NG4........162 D1
Southwark Prim Sch
 NG6....................160 E3
Southwark St NG6 ....160 E3
Southwell Cl
East Leake LE12..........205 E1
Kirkby in A NG17..........115 A6
Worksop S80..............36 A2
Southwell La NG17........114 F6
Southwell La Ind Est
 NG17...................115 A7
Southwell L Ctr NG25 ...136 D7
Southwell Minster NG25 .136 E8
Southwell Rd
Farnsfield NG22...........120 A5
Kirklington NG22..........120 F7
Lowdham NG14............150 F2
Nottingham NG1 ....223 F2
Oxton NG25...............134 D4
Thurgarton NG14..........151 D8
Southwell Rd E
Mansfield NG21...........103 E2
Rainworth NG21..........118 B8
Southwell Rd W NG18....102 E5
South Wilford Endowed Prim
 Sch NG11...............185 B7
Southwold Dr NG8 ....172 C5
Southwold Prim Sch
 NG8....................172 D5
South Wolds Com Sch
 NG12...................197 E3
Southwood Ave NG17 ....100 D4
South Yorkshire Aviation
 Mus S81.................16 B7
Sovereign Gr NG10 ......193 B7
Sowter Ave NG17.........100 E4
Spa Cl NG17..............114 F8
Spafford Cl DN21.........44 D8
Spa La NG13.............180 B7
Spalding Rd NG3.........173 F5
Spalford La LN6...........83 D4
Spalford Rd LN6...........83 E5
Spalford Warren Nature
 Reserve LN6..............83 A5
Spang La NG17............99 F4
Spaniel Row NG1.........223 E2
Spa Ponds Nature Reserve
 NG19....................89 C4
Spa Rd DN22 ....39 F6
Sparken Cl S80...........46 E8
Sparken Dale S80.........46 E8
Sparrow Cl DN7...........170 A4
Sparrow Hill 6 LE11......220 B4
Sparrow La NG23.........68 B1
Spean Ct 4 NG8 ....172 A5
Spean Dr NG8...........172 B7
Speeds Pingle 1 LE11...220 A4
Speedwell La NG16.......158 E6
Speedwell Pl S80.........35 E4
Spencer Ave
Arnold NG3...............162 C5
Sandiacre NG10..........182 B6
Spencer Cl NG11.........196 B7
Spencer Cres NG9........182 F8
Spencer Dr NG16.........159 C6
Spencer St NG18.........102 A6
Sperry Cl NG16...........128 F6
Spey Cl NG15.............145 D3
Spicer Cl NG9............183 C2
Spicers Ct DN22..........39 F6
Spindle Gdns NG6........160 A7
Spindle View NG14.......148 F6
Spinney Cl
Cotgrave NG12...........187 F2
Kirkby in A NG17..........114 E6
Mansfield Woodhouse NG19 88 E6
Newark-on-T NG24.......139 E6

Spinney Cl continued
West Bridgford NG2 ......186 C4
Spinney Cres NG9........182 F3
Spinney Dr NG10.........182 C2
Spinneymead DN22 ......19 B5
Spinney Rd
Bingham NG13...........177 D4
Keyworth NG12..........197 E3
Long Eaton NG10.........182 C2
Spinney Rise NG9.........182 E3
Spinney The
Arnold NG5...............161 E4
Bestwood Village NG6....146 E5
Bulcote NG14............146 B5
Elston NG23.............153 D5
Farnsfield NG22...........119 E6
Mansfield NG18...........116 D7
Shirebrook NG20..........72 D3
Winthorpe NG24..........125 C5
Spinney Way NG11.......185 A4
Spinningdale NG5........162 B8
Spire Cl NG17............129 E8
Spire View NG13..........181 B3
Spitalfields S81...........18 B2
Spital Hill
Gainsborough DN21 .....15 D1
Retford DN22..............39 F7
Spital Rd S81.............18 B1
Spital Terr DN21 ....15 D1
Spondon St NG5..........161 C7
Sporton Cl DE55..........113 A7
Sporton La DE55.........113 B7
Spotlight Gall (Town Hall)
 NG4....................139 F8
Spray Cl NG4.............174 E5
Spridgeon Cl NG10 ......182 B2
Spright Cl NG24..........125 C6
Spring Cl NG16...........159 A7
Spring Ct NG22...........119 E7
Spring Dale Gdns NG9 ..170 D3
Springdale La NG13.......165 E2
Spring Dr NG24...........140 F2
Springfield DE74..........203 B1
Springfield Ave
Eastwood NG16..........144 A2
Long Eaton NG10.........193 F8
Sandiacre NG10..........182 B3
Shirebrook NG20..........72 E5
Springfield Cl
Cropwell Bishop NG12....189 B4
Gainsborough DN21 .....24 E8
Mansfield NG18...........103 A5
Springfield Ct NG9.......170 E1
Springfield Dr NG6.......159 F6
Springfield Gdn DE7......157 F2
Springfield Prim Sch
 NG6....................146 C1
Springfield Rd
Arnold NG5...............147 E1
Hucknall NG15...........145 D6
Retford DN22..............39 F8
Southwell NG25..........121 D2
Springfield Ret Pk NG6 .160 C8
Springfields NG5.........185 D6
Springfield Way NG16 ...115 D6
Spring Gdns
Bawtry DN10.............10 A8
Gainsborough DN21 .....24 D8
Newark-on-T NG24.......125 B2
Spring Gdn Terr DE7......157 F2
Spring Gn NG11..........195 E7
Springhead Ct NG6 ......160 A6
Spring Hill
Kimberley NG16..........158 F5
Mansfield Woodhouse NG19 88 B3
Southwell NG25..........136 F7
Whitwell S80..............45 A6
Springhill Cl NG6.........146 B1
Spring La
Arnold NG3...............162 E6
Balderton NG24..........140 F2
Flintham NG23...........166 F7
Lambley NG4............163 B6
Long Whatton LE12......212 C2
Shireoaks S80............34 F5
Sturton le S DN22........32 C4
Springland Farm Cotts
 NG16..................159 D6
Spring Mdw NG12........188 A3
Spring Moor NG1 ....174 D5
Spring Rd
Nottingham NG6.........160 C7
Sutton in A NG17.........100 E2
Springs Rd DN10..........4 D6
Spring St
Hucknall NG15...........146 A7
Whitwell S80..............45 A6
Spring Street Prim Sch
 NG15...................146 A7
Spring Terr NG16.........159 D5
Spring The NG10.........193 D5
Springthorpe Rd DN21 ...24 F8
Springwell St NG17 ....99 F2
Spring Wlk S80............35 E1
Springwood Gdns NG5...162 A6
Springwood View Cl
 NG17...................100 C3
Spruce Ave NG16.........128 D6
Spruce Ct S80.............35 B2
Spruce Gdns NG6.........160 A7
Spruce Gr
Hucknall NG15...........146 B4
Kirkby in A NG17..........115 C6
Sprydon Wlk NG11.......195 F7
Spur Cres S80............47 B8

Squares Dr NG6...........147 B5
Square The
Beeston NG9.............183 F6
Bestwood Village NG6....146 E4
Bottesford NG13 ....181 A3
Costock LE12.............206 C1
Gotham NG11............195 B1
Keyworth NG12..........197 E2
Nottingham NG8 ....171 E4
Rainworth NG21..........104 B1
Retford DN22..............39 E7
Squires Ave NG6..........160 B8
Squires Cl NG12 ....189 B4
Squires Croft NG21........90 C5
Squires La NG12 ....90 B6
Squires Way NG2........185 D6
Squirrel Way 3 LE11 ....220 A2
Stable Cl
East Bridgford NG13 .....165 D3
Worksop S81..............36 A7
Stacey Ave NG5..........160 F8
Stacey Rd NG12..........189 A8
Stadium Cl S81............35 C6
Stadium Ind Pk NG10 ...193 F8
Stafford Ave
New Balderton NG24.....140 C4
Nottingham NG6.........160 B6
Stafford Ct NG6...........159 F5
Staffords Acre DE74 .....203 C2
Stafford St
Long Eaton NG10.........193 F8
Mansfield NG19...........101 F8
Stagsden Cres NG8 ......171 C5
Staindale Dr NG8.........160 D1
Stainforth St NG19........88 C2
Stainmore Gr NG13......151 F8
Stainsborough Rd NG15..145 C6
Stainsbury Mill S44........85 D7
Stainsby Dr NG18........103 B2
Stainsby La NG17..........99 F2
Stamford Cl NG10.........193 E4
Stamford 4 NG5..........161 B8
Stamford St
Awsworth NG16..........158 C5
Eastwood NG16..........144 C1
2 Ilkeston DE7..........157 E1
Stamper Cres NG17......100 F6
Stanage Ct NG18.........103 B5
Stancliffe Ave NG6.......160 C7
Standard Hill NG1........223 D2
Standhill Ave NG4........174 B8
Standhill Inf Sch NG4 ...174 B7
Standhill Rd NG4.........174 B8
Stanesby Rise NG7.......184 E1
Stanford Gdns NG12.....125 F4
Stanford La NG11.........220 B6
Stanford Rd LE12.........213 F1
Stanford St NG1..........223 E2
Stanhome Sq NG2........185 D4
Stanhope Ave
Newark-on-T NG24.......125 C3
Nottingham NG5.........161 B1
Stanhope Cl NG2..........64 A2
Stanhope Cres
Newark-on-T NG24.......125 C3
Stoke Bardolph NG14....175 F7
Sturton le S DN22........32 C6
Stanhope Rd
Arnold NG5...............161 B8
Carlton NG4.............162 D3
Stanhope St
Ilkeston DE7.............170 A6
Long Eaton NG10.........193 D8
Nottingham NG1 ....223 F2
Stanhope Way NG13 .....177 E4
Staniland Ct 3 NG6......183 C2
Stanley Ave 5 NG7.......173 A8
Stanley Cl NG15..........117 A3
Stanley Dr NG9...........171 A1
Stanley La NG17..........85 D2
Stanley Pl NG1 ....223 D3
Stanley Rd
Mansfield NG18...........102 B8
Mansfield Woodhouse NG19 89 B1
Nottingham, Hyson Green
 NG7....................173 A8
Nottingham, Portchester
 NG3....................162 A1
West Bridgford NG2 ......185 F6
Stanley St
Gainsborough DN21 .....24 D6
Long Eaton NG10.........193 E7
Loughborough LE11.......220 B2
Newark-on-T NG24.......125 B1
Retford DN22..............40 A4
Stanley Terr NG24........140 B8
Stanmore Cl NG8.........159 E3
Stanmore Gdns NG5.....161 F6
Stannier Wy NG16........159 A7
Stansfield St NG7.........222 A3
Stanstead Ave
Nottingham NG5.........146 D1
Tollerton NG12...........186 D1
Stanthorne Cl NG11......185 A4
Stanton Cres NG17.......100 D3
Stanton Gate DE7.........170 C1
Stanton La NG12..........198 B2
Stanton Pl
Mansfield NG18...........102 A7
New Houghton NG19......86 F7
Stanton Rd NG10.........182 A7
Stanton St NG15..........86 F7
Stanton Vale Sch NG10..193 C7

Stanway Cl NG3..........174 C6
Stanwick Cl NG8.........171 E8
Stapleford La
Beeston NG9.............182 F3
Coddington NG24........126 D3
Stapleford Rd NG9.......170 D3
Staplehurst Dr NG5......161 A4
Staple La NG24..........140 C2
Staples St NG3...........161 E2
Stapleton Rd DE7.........157 E4
Starch Cl LE12...........205 E1
Starch La NG10..........182 C7
Stardust 4 NG23.........112 B7
Starion Cl 3 DE7.........157 E1
Station Hill NG19..........88 B3
Station La
Edwinstowe NG21 ....76 B1
Farnsfield NG22...........119 E7
Ironville NG16............128 A3
Old Dalby LE14..........218 F4
Station Rd
Awsworth NG16..........158 C5
Barnby Moor DN22 ....28 E5
Bawtry DN10.............10 A7
Beckingham DN10........23 C8
Beeston NG9.............184 A5
Bleasby NG14............151 F8
Bottesford NG13 ....181 C3
Burton Joyce NG14......163 F3
Carlton NG4.............174 F7
Clipstone NG21..........89 C2
Collingham NG23........112 A8
East Leake LE12..........205 D1
Edingley NG22...........120 E5
Fiskerton NG25, NG23...137 E4
Harby NG23..............70 C3
Heanor NG16............143 A2
Hucknall NG15...........146 B7
Ilkeston DE7.............157 E4
Kegworth DE74..........203 F2
Keyworth NG12..........197 E6
Kimberley NG16..........158 F6
Kingston-on-S LE12......204 A3
Langley Mill NG16.......143 B2
Long Eaton NG10.........193 F8
Lowdham NG14..........150 E1
Mansfield NG18...........102 B6
Misson DN10............39 F5
Newstead NG15..........130 E6
Nottingham NG6.........160 C6
Ollerton NG22............77 A3
Rainworth NG21..........118 A8
Ranskill DN22............19 B4
Retford DN22..............39 E5
Rolleston NG23..........138 A6
Sandiacre NG10..........182 C5
Scrooby DN10............10 A2
Selston NG16............113 E1
Shirebrook NG20..........72 E6
South Leverton DN22.....42 D8
Southwell NG25..........121 F1
Sturton le S DN22........32 C6
Sutton in A NG17.........101 B1
Sutton on T NG23.........96 E8
Thurgarton NG14..........151 D6
Torksey LN1..............44 B3
Upper Broughton LE14 ..218 C8
Walkeringham DN10 .....14 A5
Whitwell S80..............45 A5
Widmerpool NG12........208 E6
Station St
Bingham NG13...........177 F5
Cossall DE7..............158 A2
Kirkby in A NG17..........115 B5
Long Eaton NG10.........193 E7
6 Mansfield NG18.......102 B6
Misterton DN10...........7 A2
Nottingham NG2 ....223 F1
Sutton in A NG17.........100 F2
Station Terr
Hucknall NG15...........146 B7
Sutton in A NG17.........175 F3
Station View NG20........72 E3
Station View NG17........100 F7
Staunton Dr NG5.........161 C4
Staunton Hall NG13......169 B3
Staunton Rd NG24.......139 A4
Staveley Ct
Farndon NG24...........139 A4
1 Loughborough LE11...220 B5
Stavely Wy NG2..........186 C7
Staverton Rd NG8........171 E7
Staythorpe Rd
Averham NG23...........123 E1
Rolleston NG23..........138 C7
Steadfold Cl NG6.........160 B6
Steads Cl NG4............174 F7
Stedman Ave NG3........162 A8
Steeles Dr NG24.........140 E3
Steeles Way NG4........163 B7
Steeple Row 3 LE11......220 B4
Steeples The NG17.......129 E8
Steetley La
Rhodesia S80..............35 A4
Whitwell S80..............34 E4
Steinbeck Rd NG4.......174 C7
Stella Ave NG12..........197 D8
Stella Gr NG12...........197 D8

Stella St NG18...........102 B5
Stenton Cl NG25.........121 E2
Stepnall Hts NG22........77 E6
Stepney Ct NG8..........159 F1
Sterling Cl S81............35 D8
Sterling Dr NG24.........125 E1
Sterndale Rd NG10......193 B6
Sternthorpe Cl NG23.....81 E1
Steven Cl NG9............182 F4
Stevenholme Cres NG5..161 A6
Stevenson Cres NG17...102 A6
Stevenson Gdns NG11...196 D6
Stevenson Rd S81........36 B4
Stevens Rd NG10........182 A5
Stewart Cl S81............25 E6
Stewarton Cl NG5........148 B1
Stewart Rd S81............25 E6
Stiles Rd NG5............162 C6
Stillwell Gdns S81.........35 E7
Stinsford Cl 6 NG5......161 C8
Stinting La NG19..........88 E2
Stirling Ave
Bawtry DN10.............10 A8
Mansfield NG19...........101 E5
Stirling Cl DN21...........15 E2
Stirling Dr
Carlton in L S81...........25 E6
Newark-on-T NG24.......125 E2
Stirling Gdns NG9........183 B2
Stirling Gr
Kimberley NG16..........158 E7
Nottingham NG11........195 F8
Stirling Rd DN22..........39 D5
Stockdale Cl NG5........147 A2
Stockgill Cl NG2..........186 C6
Stockhill Cir NG8.........160 C2
Stockhill La NG6..........160 C2
Stocking La
Askham DN22.............51 E3
East Leake LE12..........205 D4
Stocks Fold
East Markham NG22......65 F7
Tuxford NG22.............66 F7
Stocks Rd NG16.........158 E7
Stock Well NG6...........160 B8
Stockwell Gate 8 NG18..102 B7
Stockwell La NG12.......216 C3
Stockwith Rd DN10 ......14 B8
Stodman Mews NG24 ...139 F8
Stodman St NG24........139 F8
Stoke Ave NG24..........139 C4
Stoke Ferry La NG14 ....164 A1
Stoke La
Burton Joyce NG14......163 F2
Stoke Bardolph NG14 ...175 D8
Stokes Ind Est NG18 ....101 E4
Stolle Cl NG5............162 C7
Stoneacre NG5...........160 B5
Stonebridge City Farm
 NG3....................173 E5
Stonebridge Cot Ind Est 8
 NG3....................173 E5
Stonebridge Dr LE12.....205 F2
Stonebridge La NG20.....74 A4
Stonebridge Rd NG20.....74 A4
Stone Bridge Rd NG3.....173 E5
Stonechurch View NG15..130 B8
Stone Cres NG19.........101 D7
Stone Cross La NG18....102 B8
Stonehaven Cl NG5......148 B1
Stonehills DE74..........203 C2
Stonehurst La LE12.......213 D3
Stone La DN22............31 D8
Stoneleigh Cl NG9........183 C5
Stone Leigh Cl NG18....102 E5
Stoneleigh St NG7........222 C3
Stonemasons Mews
Stone Mdws NG10.......193 E5
Stone Mill Grange NG20..74 C4
Stonepit Cl NG3..........161 F1
Stoney Bank NG14.......160 B5
Stoneycroft Rd NG6......160 E5
Stoneyford Rd NG17.....100 E4
Stoney Houghton Gdns
 NG6....................159 F8
Stoney La
Brinsley NG16...........143 D6
Selston NG16............128 E7
Trowell NG9..............170 B5
Stoney St
Beeston NG9.............183 F7
Nottingham NG1 ....223 F2
Sutton in A NG17.........101 A3
Stonish Hill NG22..........92 C1
Stoppard Cl DE7..........157 D2
Storcroft Rd DN22........40 A6
Storey Ave NG4...........174 F6
Stormont Cl DE55........113 B4
Stornoway Cl NG9........182 F8
Storth Ave NG15.........146 A6
Storthfield Way DE55 ...113 B4
Storth La DE55...........113 B4
Story Gdns NG5...........162 B5
Stotfield Rd NG8.........171 B5
Stourdale Cl NG10........193 A6
Stow Ct NG19.............88 E3
Stow Park Rd DN21.......44 D8
Strafford St DN21.........24 C6
Straight Mile DN22........38 D6
Strand The NG20.........183 D1
Stranraer Cl NG19.........88 C6

Stratford Cl NG4 . . . . .174 F5
Stratford Cres DN22 . . . . . . .39 D6
Stratford Rd NG2 . . . . .185 F7
Stratford St DE7 . . . . .157 F4
Strathavon Rd S81 . . . . .25 F6
Strathglen Cl NG16 . . . . . . .158 E7
Strathmore Cl NG15 . . . . . .145 E5
Strathmore Ct DN11 . . . . .9 A5
Strathmore Dr S81 . . . . .25 F6
Strathmore Rd NG15 . . . . . .148 B1
Strawberry Bank NG17 . . . . .99 E4
Strawberry Hall La NG24 125 E3
Strawberry Rd DN22 . . . . . . .40 A6
Strawberry Way NG19 . . . .103 B8
Straw's La NG13 . . . . .165 D3
Street La Rd DN22 . . . . .42 E8
Strelley La NG8 . . . . .171 B7
Strelley Rd NG8 . . . . .159 E1
Strelley St NG6 . . . . .160 B7
Striding Edge Cl NG10 . .182 B2
Stripe Rd DN11 . . . . .8 E8
Stripes View NG14 . . . . . . .148 F6
Strome Cl 8 NG2 . . . . .173 B2
Strome Ct 1 NG2 . . . . .173 C2
Stroud Ct NG13 . . . . .181 B3
Stroud's Cl LE14 . . . . .211 F8
Stuart Ave
  Mansfield NG18 . . . . .102 F8
  New Ollerton NG22 . . . . . . .77 D6
Stuart Cl NG5 . . . . .162 B8
Stuart St
  Mansfield NG18 . . . . .102 F8
  Sutton in A NG17 . . . . .100 E1
Stubbing La S80 . . . . .35 D3
Stubbins La NG25 . . . . .136 C4
Stubbins Wood NG20 . . . . . .72 E6
Stubbins Wood La NG20 . . .72 E5
Stubbin Wood Spec Sch
  NG20 . . . . .72 E6
Stubton Rd NG23 . . . . .156 F6
Studland Cl NG19 . . . . .88 D6
Studland Way NG2 . . . . . . .185 C5
Sturgate Wlk DN21 . . . . . . .24 F7
Sturgeon Ave NG11 . . . . . .184 F4
Sturton CE Prim Sch
  DN22 . . . . .32 D4
Sturton Rd
  Bole DN22 . . . . .23 D2
  North Leverton w H DN22 . .32 D1
  Saxilby LN1 . . . . .57 A7
  South Wheatley DN22 . . . . .31 E7
Sturton St NG7 . . . . .173 A8
Styring St NG9 . . . . .183 F6
Styrrup La DN11 . . . . .8 B1
Styrrup Rd DN11 . . . . .8 E3
Sudbury Ave
  Ilkeston DE7 . . . . .170 A7
  Sandiacre NG10 . . . . .182 B6
Sudbury Ct NG18 . . . . .103 B5
Sudbury Dr NG17 . . . . .99 F2
Sudbury Mews NG16 . . . . .143 E1
Suez St NG7 . . . . .160 F1
Suff La NG16 . . . . .113 C3
Suffolk Ave
  Beeston NG9 . . . . .184 C4
  Bircotes DN11 . . . . .9 D4
  Hucknall NG15 . . . . .145 C5
Suffolk Gr DN11 . . . . .9 C4
Suffolk Rd DN11 . . . . .9 C4
Sulby Cl NG19 . . . . .89 B2
Sullivan Cl NG3 . . . . .174 A6
Sumburgh Rd NG11 . . . . . .185 A1
Summercourt Dr NG15 . .116 F3
Summerfield Rd 11
  NG17 . . . . .114 E7
Summerfields Way DE7 .157 D3
Summerfields Way S
  DE7 . . . . .157 D2
Summergangs La DN21 . .24 D5
Summer Hill DN21 . . . . .15 E1
Summer Leys La NG2 . . . .223 F1
Summer's Rd NG24 . . . . . .125 A2
Summer Way NG12 . . . . . .175 E4
Summerwood La NG11 . .195 E7
Summit Cl NG17 . . . . .115 A4
Summit Dr NG20 . . . . .72 E4
Sunbeam St NG13 . . . . . . .179 B4
Sunbourne Ct NG7 . . . . . . .222 C4
Sunbury Gdns NG5 . . . . . .148 A1
Sunderland Gr NG8 . . . . . .159 D2
Sunderland Pl DN11 . . . . . . .8 B7
Sunderland St DN11 . . . . . . .8 B7
Sundown Adventureland
  DN22 . . . . .42 E3
Sundridge Pk Cl NG2 . . .185 C5
Sunfield Ave S81 . . . . .36 A4
Sunflower Cl NG20 . . . . . . .72 D3
Sunlea Cres NG9 . . . . .182 F5
Sunnindale Dr NG12 . . . . .186 E1
Sunningdale DN22 . . . . .39 D2
Sunningdale Cl 4 NG17 . .114 E7
Sunningdale Dr NG14 . . . .149 C5
Sunningdale Rd NG6 . . . . .160 E6
Sunninghill Dr NG11 . . . . .184 E3
Sunninghill Rise NG5 . . . .148 A1
Sunny Bank
  Mansfield NG18 . . . . .102 C3
  Newton DE55 . . . . .99 A5
  Worksop S81 . . . . .36 A4
Sunnydale Rd NG3 . . . . . .174 B6
Sunnymede S81 . . . . .36 A6
Sunnyside
  Farnsfield NG22 . . . . .119 F5
  Whitwell S80 . . . . .45 A6
  Worksop S81 . . . . .35 F6
Sunnyside Prim Sch
  NG9 . . . . .183 B6
Sunnyside Rd NG9 . . . . . .183 C6

Sunridge Ct NG3 . . . . .173 C8
Sunrise Ave NG5 . . . . .160 F5
Sunrise Hill Nature Reserve
  NG5 . . . . .161 A6
Superbowl 2000 NG18 . .102 B7
Surbiton Sq NG8 . . . . .160 B3
Surfleet Cl NG8 . . . . .171 C3
Surgery La NG21 . . . . .118 A4
Surgey's La NG5 . . . . .148 A2
Surrey Dr NG17 . . . . .101 F8
Susan Cl NG15 . . . . .131 B1
Susan Dr NG6 . . . . .160 D4
Sussex Way NG10 . . . . . . .182 B5
Sutherland Cl S81 . . . . .25 F8
Sutherland Dr NG2 . . . . . .186 A4
Sutherland House Prim Sch
  NG3 . . . . .174 B7
Sutherland House Sec Sch
  NG3 . . . . .161 C1
Sutherland Rd NG3 . . . . . .174 B7
Suthers Rd DE74 . . . . .203 C2
Sutton Ave NG24 . . . . .139 C5
Sutton Bonington Prim Sch
  LE12 . . . . .213 B6
Sutton Bonington Spinney &
  Mdws Nature Reserve
  LE12 . . . . .213 A7
Sutton Cl
  Sutton Bonington LE12 . .213 C6
  Sutton in A NG17 . . . . . . .101 A6
Sutton Ct NG16 . . . . .143 F2
Sutton Ctr Com Coll
  NG17 . . . . .100 F2
Sutton Cum Lound CE Prim
  Sch DN22 . . . . .29 A4
Sutton Gdns NG11 . . . . . .196 C6
Sutton La
  Granby NG13 . . . . .191 D6
  Retford DN22 . . . . .29 A1
Sutton L Ctr NG17 . . . . . . .100 F2
Sutton Mid La NG17 . . . . .114 F6
Sutton on Trent Prim Sch
  NG23 . . . . .97 A8
Sutton Parkway Sta
  NG17 . . . . .115 B8
Sutton Passeys Cres
  NG8 . . . . .172 B3
Sutton Pool Complex
  NG17 . . . . .100 C2
Sutton Rd
  Arnold NG5 . . . . .147 F2
  Beckingham LN5 . . . . . . .142 E6
  Huthwaite NG17 . . . . .99 F3
  Kegworth DE74 . . . . .203 C1
  Kirkby in A NG17 . . . . . . .114 E6
  Mansfield NG18 . . . . .101 C5
  Sutton in A NG17 . . . . . . .100 A3
Sutton Road Prim Sch
  NG18 . . . . .101 F6
Swab's La
  Cropwell Bishop NG12 . . .188 F1
  Owthorpe NG12 . . . . .199 F8
Swain's Ave NG3 . . . . .174 A6
Swaledale S81 . . . . .36 A7
Swaledale Cl NG8 . . . . . . .160 C1
Swales Cl DN22 . . . . .39 C8
Swallow Cl
  Mansfield NG18 . . . . .103 B4
  Nottingham NG6 . . . . . . .160 D3
Swallow Ct NG10 . . . . .7 A2
Swallow Dr
  Bingham NG13 . . . . .177 F3
  Claypole NG23 . . . . .156 D7
Swallow Gdns NG4 . . . . . .162 B1
Swallow Gr S81 . . . . .35 D7
Swallows Dr LE14 . . . . . . .202 F3
Swallow Wlk LE12 . . . . . . .213 A1
Swan Ct
  Sutton Bonington LE12 . .213 B6
  Worksop S81 . . . . .35 C7
Swan La NG19 . . . . .88 B3
Swan Mdw NG4 . . . . .174 F4
Swann Yd NG17 . . . . .99 F3
Swansdowne Dr NG7 . . . .184 F2
Swanson Ave NG17 . . . . . . .99 F3
Swans Quay DN22 . . . . . . .39 F5
Swan St
  Bawtry DN10 . . . . .10 A4
  Loughborough LE11 . . . . .220 B4
Swanwick Ave DN22 . . . . .72 F3
Sweeney Ct 3 NG5 . . . . . .161 A8
Sweet Leys Dr LE12 . . . . .205 E3
Sweet Leys Rd 7 NG2 . . .173 C1
Swenson Ave NG7 . . . . . . .222 A1
Swift Cl NG16 . . . . .143 F2
Swift's Cl LE12 . . . . .216 C3
Swifts Vw NG17 . . . . .114 F1
Swigert Cl NG6 . . . . .159 F5
Swildon Wlk NG5 . . . . .160 F8
Swinburne Cl NG4 . . . . . . .140 D5
Swinburne St 3 NG3 . . . .173 F6
Swinburne Way NG5 . . . .161 D7
Swinderby Cl
  Gateford S81 . . . . .35 C8
  Newark-on-T NG24 . . . . . .125 D1
Swinderby Rd
  Collingham NG23 . . . . . . .112 B8
  Eagle LN6 . . . . .84 D1
  North Scarle LN6 . . . . .83 E2
Swindon Cl NG16 . . . . .158 B7
Swinecote Rd NG21 . . . . . .76 B4
Swiney Way NG9 . . . . .183 A2
Swinfen Broun NG18 . . . .102 C3
Swingate NG16 . . . . .159 A5
Swinnow Rd NG16 . . . . .9 C4
Swinscoe Gdns NG5 . . . . .160 F8
Swinstead Cl NG8 . . . . . . .171 F6
Swinton Copse NG22 . . . .77 E6

Swinton Rise NG15 . . . . . .117 A2
Swish La NG22 . . . . .105 F8
Swithland Dr NG2 . . . . . . .185 E4
Swynford Cl LN1 . . . . .55 B4
Sycamore Ave
  Glapwell S44 . . . . .86 B8
  Kirkby in A NG17 . . . . . . .114 E6
Sycamore Cl
  Bingham NG13 . . . . .178 A4
  Hucknall NG15 . . . . .145 E5
  Newark-on-T NG24 . . . . . .139 D3
  Pinxton NG16 . . . . .113 D3
  Radcliffe on T NG12 . . . . .175 F2
  Rainworth NG21 . . . . .104 B1
  Selston NG16 . . . . .128 D7
  Worksop S81 . . . . .35 E1
Sycamore Cres
  Bawtry DN10 . . . . .9 F7
  Sandiacre NG10 . . . . .182 A7
Sycamore Ct 9 NG9 . . . . .184 A7
Sycamore Dr
  Gainsborough DN21 . . . . .15 E2
  Ilkeston DE7 . . . . .170 B7
Sycamore Gr NG18 . . . . . .102 F5
Sycamore Jun & Inf Sch
  NG3 . . . . .223 F4
Sycamore La NG21 . . . . . . .91 A2
Sycamore Millennium Ctr
  NG3 . . . . .173 D8
Sycamore Pl 2 NG3 . . . . .173 C8
Sycamore Rd
  Awsworth NG16 . . . . .158 C5
  Carlton in L S81 . . . . .25 E7
  East Leake LE12 . . . . .214 D8
  Long Eaton NG10 . . . . . . .193 C5
  Mansfield Woodhouse NG19 88 C5
  New Ollerton NG22 . . . . . .77 D4
Sycamore Rise NG6 . . . . .160 C7
Sycamore St NG20 . . . . . . .74 A6
Sycamores The
  Eastwood NG16 . . . . .143 E1
  South Normanton DE55 . .113 A5
Sydenham Ct 8 NG7 . . . .172 E2
Syderstone Wlk NG5 . . . .161 F6
Sydney Cl NG19 . . . . .88 C6
Sydney Gr NG12 . . . . .175 E3
Sydney Rd NG8 . . . . .172 B5
Sydney St NG24 . . . . .140 A7
Sydney Terr NG24 . . . . . . .140 A7
Syerston Rd NG18 . . . . . . .103 A2
Syerston Wy NG24 . . . . . .125 D1
Syke Rd NG5 . . . . .160 F8
Sykes La
  Balderton NG24 . . . . .140 D3
  Saxilby LN1 . . . . .56 E5
  Saxilby LN1 . . . . .56 F4
Sylvan Cres NG17 . . . . . . .101 A5
Sylvester St NG18 . . . . . . .101 F6
Synge Cl NG11 . . . . .195 C8
Sywell Cl NG17 . . . . .100 F5

T

Taft Ave NG10 . . . . .182 B6
Taft Leys Rd LE12 . . . . . . .205 F2
Talbot Cl NG12 . . . . .175 E3
Talbot Dr NG9 . . . . .170 D2
Talbot Rd
  Bircotes DN11 . . . . .9 B4
  Worksop S80 . . . . .36 A2
Talbot St
  Mansfield NG18 . . . . .102 B4
  Nottingham NG1 . . . . .223 D3
  Pinxton NG16 . . . . .113 C2
Tales of Robin Hood The
  NG1 . . . . .223 E2
Tall Gables NG22 . . . . .54 C1
Tamarix Cl NG4 . . . . .163 A2
Tambling Cl NG5 . . . . .162 B6
Tame Cl NG11 . . . . .184 E4
Tamworth Gr NG7 . . . . . . .184 F2
Tamworth Rd NG10 . . . . . .193 C5
Tanglewood LN6 . . . . .84 D3
Tangmere Cres NG8 . . . . .159 E1
Tanner's La LE12 . . . . .213 A1
Tannery Wharf NG24 . . . .139 E8
Tanwood Rd NG24 . . . . . .183 B1
Tanyard NG2 . . . . .79 E6
Tapton Pk 3 NG4 . . . . . . .103 B7
Tarbert Cl NG2 . . . . .173 B2
Target St NG7 . . . . .222 A3
Tarn Cl NG16 . . . . .143 B4
Tatham's La DE7 . . . . .157 E2
Tatmarsh LE11 . . . . .220 B5
Tattersall Wlk NG19 . . . . . .88 E4
Tattershall Dr
  Beeston NG9 . . . . .184 B7
  Nottingham NG7 . . . . .222 C2
Taunton Rd NG2 . . . . .185 F6
Taupo Dr NG15 . . . . .145 D5
Tavern Ave NG8 . . . . .160 B4
Tavistock Ave NG3 . . . . . .161 C1
Tavistock Cl NG15 . . . . . . .145 D5
Tavistock Dr NG3 . . . . .161 C1
Tavistock Rd NG2 . . . . . . .185 F6
Taylor Cl NG2 . . . . .174 A4
Taylor Cres
  Stapleford NG9 . . . . .182 E8
  Sutton in A NG17 . . . . . . .100 F1
Taylor's Cl NG18 . . . . .102 E8
Taylors Croft NG14 . . . . . .149 C4
Taylor St DE7 . . . . .157 F1
Teague Pl S80 . . . . .35 F2
Teak Cl NG3 . . . . .173 D7
Teal Ave NG16 . . . . .103 B4
Tealby Cl NG6 . . . . .159 F7
Tealby Wlk NG19 . . . . .88 E4

Teal Cl
  Carlton NG4 . . . . .175 B6
  Shirebrook NG20 . . . . .72 D3
Teal Ct S81 . . . . .35 D7
Teal Wharf 4 NG2 . . . . . .173 A2
Teasels The NG13 . . . . . . .177 D3
Technology Dr NG9 . . . . . .184 A5
Tedburn Dr NG18 . . . . . . .103 A2
Teddy's Farm Pk LN5 . . . .142 E8
Teesbrook Dr NG8 . . . . . .171 B4
Teesdale Ct NG9 . . . . .183 A4
Teesdale Rd
  Long Eaton NG10 . . . . . . .193 A6
  Nottingham NG5 . . . . . . .161 B2
Teignmouth Ave NG18 . .102 F5
Telford Dr
  Eastwood NG16 . . . . .144 B3
  Newark-on-T NG24 . . . . . .125 C3
Temperance La NG23 . . . .111 F8
Templar Rd NG9 . . . . .184 B6
Temple Cres NG16 . . . . . .159 D4
Temple Dr NG16 . . . . .159 E4
Templemans Way NG25 . .136 F8
Templemen Cl NG11 . . . .196 B7
Templeoak Dr NG8 . . . . . .171 D3
Tenbury Cres NG8 . . . . . . .160 C1
Tenby Gr S80 . . . . .36 A2
Tenby St NG24 . . . . .147 F2
Tennan La NG23 . . . . .166 A2
Tennis Ct Ind Est NG2 . . .174 A3
Tennis Dr NG7 . . . . .222 C2
Tennis Mews NG7 . . . . . . .222 C2
Tennyson Ave
  Carlton NG4 . . . . .162 F1
  Mansfield Woodhouse NG19 88 C2
Tennyson Ct NG15 . . . . . .145 D6
Tennyson Dr
  Beeston NG9 . . . . .183 D2
  Worksop S81 . . . . .36 C4
Tennyson Rd
  Arnold NG5 . . . . .161 E4
  Balderton NG24 . . . . .140 D4
Tennyson Sq NG16 . . . . . .158 C4
Tennyson St
  Gainsborough DN21 . . . . .15 C1
  Ilkeston DE7 . . . . .157 E3
  Kirkby in A NG17 . . . . . . .115 B4
  Mansfield NG18 . . . . .102 A7
  Nottingham NG7 . . . . .222 C4
Tenter Cl
  Long Eaton NG10 . . . . . . .193 D5
  Nottingham NG5 . . . . .161 B2
  Sutton Forest Side NG17 . .101 A3
Tenter La NG18 . . . . .102 A5
Tenters La NG22 . . . . .92 E1
Tenzing Wlk NG24 . . . . . . .140 E4
Terrace La NG19 . . . . .86 F5
Terrace Rd NG18 . . . . .102 C8
Terrace St NG7 . . . . .172 F7
Terrian Cres NG2 . . . . .185 F7
Terry Ave NG2 . . . . .125 B3
Terton Rd NG5 . . . . .160 F8
Tetford Wlk NG19 . . . . .88 E4
Tetney Wlk NG8 . . . . .172 A6
Tettenbury Rd NG5 . . . . . .160 F3
Teversal Ave
  Nottingham NG7 . . . . .222 B2
  Pleasleyhill NG19 . . . . .87 B4
Teversal Pastures Nature
  Reserve NG17 . . . . .100 E8
Teversal Visitor Ctr
  NG17 . . . . .100 B7
Tevery Cl NG9 . . . . .182 E8
Teviot Rd NG5 . . . . .160 F5
Tewkesbury Ave NG19 . . . .88 A2
Tewkesbury Cl NG2 . . . . . .186 A6
Tewkesbury Dr
  Kimberley NG16 . . . . .158 F2
  Nottingham NG6 . . . . . . .160 E4
Tewkesbury Rd NG10 . . . .193 E4
Thackeray Cl S81 . . . . .36 B4
Thackeray's La NG5 . . . . . .161 E5
Thackeray St NG7 . . . . . . .222 B3
Thales Dr NG5 . . . . .162 C7
Thames St NG6 . . . . .160 B7
Thane Rd NG9 . . . . .184 B6
Thaxted Cl NG8 . . . . .171 D6
Theaker Ave DN21 . . . . . . .15 F1
Theaker La DN10 . . . . .10 D5
Theatre Sq NG1 . . . . .223 D3
Thelda Ave NG12 . . . . .197 E3
Theresa Ct NG24 . . . . .140 D4
Thetford Cl NG5 . . . . .162 A6
Thickley Cl NG20 . . . . .72 F4
Thievesdale Ave S81 . . . . .35 F7
Thievesdale Cl S81 . . . . . . .36 A7
Third Ave
  Beeston NG9 . . . . .184 C6
  Carlton, Gedling NG4 . . . .162 F1
  Carlton, Thorneywood NG4 174 B8
  Clipstone NG21 . . . . .89 F3
  Edwinstowe NG21 . . . . . . .76 A1
  Mansfield NG21 . . . . .103 F2
  Mansfield Woodhouse NG19 89 A1
  Nottingham NG6 . . . . .160 C7
Thirlbeck NG12 . . . . .188 A1
Thirlmere NG2 . . . . .186 D5
Thirlmere Cl
  Long Eaton NG10 . . . . . . .182 B2
  Nottingham NG3 . . . . .173 F7
Thirlmere Rd NG10 . . . . . .182 B2
Thirston Cl NG19 . . . . .159 F7
Thistle Bank
  East Leake LE12 . . . . .205 E3
  Mansfield Woodhouse NG19 88 F4
Thistle Cl NG16 . . . . .143 B4
Thistledown Rd NG11 . . . .195 E7
Thistle Gn Cl DE75 . . . . . .143 B1

Thistle Rd DE7 . . . . .170 A4
Thomas Ave NG12 . . . . . . .176 C3
Thomas Cl NG3 . . . . .223 F4
Thomas Parkyn Cl NG11 .206 E7
Thomas Rd
  Kegworth DE74 . . . . .203 C1
  Newark-on-T NG24 . . . . . .140 F2
Thomas St DN22 . . . . .39 F5
Thompson Ave DN11 . . . . . .8 F4
Thompson Cl
  Beeston NG9 . . . . .183 C3
  East Leake LE12 . . . . .205 E2
Thompson Cres NG17 . . .100 F1
Thompson St NG16 . . . . . .143 B3
Thonock Cl DN1 . . . . .56 F4
Thonock Hill DN21 . . . . . . .15 D3
Thonock Rd DN21 . . . . .15 E5
Thoresby Ave
  Carlton NG4 . . . . .162 D2
  Edwinstowe NG21 . . . . . . .76 A3
  Kirkby in A NG17 . . . . . . .115 D4
  Newark-on-T NG24 . . . . . .140 A6
  Nottingham NG2 . . . . .173 F3
  Shirebrook NG20 . . . . .72 E4
Thoresby Cl
  Harworth DN11 . . . . .9 B5
  Meden Vale NG20 . . . . . . .74 D8
  Radcliffe on T NG12 . . . . .176 A4
Thoresby Cres NG17 . . . .100 C6
Thoresby Ct NG3 . . . . .173 D8
Thoresby Dale NG15 . . . .146 B7
Thoresby Gall (Pierrepont
  Art Gall) NG22 . . . . .62 D3
Thoresby Glade NG20 . . .106 A5
Thoresby Rd
  Beeston NG9 . . . . .171 C2
  Bingham NG13 . . . . .177 C4
  Long Eaton NG10 . . . . . . .193 C6
  Mansfield NG21 . . . . .103 F2
  Mansfield Woodhouse NG19 88 A3
Thoresby St
  3 Mansfield NG18 . . . . .102 A7
  10 Nottingham NG2 . . . . .173 E4
  Sutton in A NG17 . . . . . . .101 A4
Thoresby Way DN22 . . . . . .39 D2
Thoresland Ct NG5 . . . . . .146 F2
Thor Gdns NG5 . . . . .87 F1
Thorn Ave NG19 . . . . .87 F1
Thorn Bank DN9 . . . . .2 C8
Thornbury Dr NG19 . . . . . .101 D8
Thornbury Hill La S81 . . . .16 D8
Thornbury Way NG5 . . . . .160 F7
Thorncliffe Rd NG3 . . . . . .173 C3
Thorncliffe Rise NG3 . . . .173 C3
Thorndale Rd
  Calverton NG14 . . . . .148 F7
  Nottingham NG6 . . . . . . .160 C2
Thorndike Cl NG9 . . . . . . .184 B4
Thorndike Way DN22 . . . . .24 C7
Thorne Dr NG16 . . . . .158 B6
Thorne Rd DN10 . . . . .10 B8
Thorney Abbey Rd NG21 .118 B5
Thorney Ct 8 NG18 . . . . .103 A2
Thorney Hill NG3 . . . . .173 F7
Thorneywood Ave NG17 .129 C8
Thorneywood Mount
  NG3 . . . . .173 F7
Thorneywood Rd NG10 . .193 F8
Thorney St NG15 . . . . .146 B4
Thornfield Cl NG19 . . . . . .103 B8
Thornham Cres NG17 . . . .129 F8
Thornhill Cl NG9 . . . . .171 B2
Thornhill Dr
  Boughton NG22 . . . . .77 E5
  South Normanton DE55 . .113 B6
Thornhill La DN22 . . . . .33 C2
Thornhill Rd DN11 . . . . .8 E4
Thornley St 7 NG7 . . . . . .172 E7
Thornthwaite Cl NG2 . . . .186 C6
Thornton Ave NG5 . . . . . . .147 D1
Thornton Cl
  Mansfield NG18 . . . . .103 B6
  Nottingham NG8 . . . . .171 E4
Thornton Dale S81 . . . . . . .36 B7
Thornton Rd NG23 . . . . . .112 A8
Thorntons Cl NG12 . . . . . .188 A2
Thornton St
  Gainsborough DN21 . . . . .24 D7
  Sutton in A NG17 . . . . . . .100 F1
Thorn Tree Gdns NG16 . . .143 F4
Thorold Cl NG7 . . . . .184 E2
Thoroton Ave NG24 . . . . . .140 D3
Thoroton St NG7 . . . . .222 C3
Thoroughfare La NG23 . .125 D7
Thorpe Cl
  Coddington NG24 . . . . . . .126 B2
  Newark-on-T NG24 . . . . . .139 E4
  18 Nottingham NG5 . . . . .161 A8
  Stapleford NG9 . . . . .182 D7
Thorpe Cres NG3 . . . . .162 A1
Thorpe La
  Eagle LN6 . . . . .84 E2
  Shireoaks S80 . . . . .34 C6
Thorpelands Ave NG19 . . .88 E1
Thorpe Lea NG14 . . . . .165 A5
Thorpe Leys NG10 . . . . . .193 D5
Thorpe Rd
  Eastwood NG16 . . . . .143 F4
  Mansfield NG18 . . . . .103 A4
  Mattersey DN10 . . . . .20 B8
Thorpe St
  Askham DN22 . . . . .52 C7
  Ilkeston DE7 . . . . .157 E3
Thrapston Ave NG5 . . . . . .147 F2
Three Leys La DN22 . . . . . .32 D3

Three Tuns Rd NG16 .... 144 A2
Threlkeld Cl NG2 .... 186 C6
Thrumpton Ave NG10 .... 194 A2
Thrumpton Cl DN22 ...... 39 F4
Thrumpton Dr NG2 ...... 173 B1
Thrumpton Hall NG11 ... 194 B3
Thrumpton La DN22 ...... 39 F5
Thrumpton Prim Sch
DN22 .... 39 F4
Thurcaton Way DE55 ..... 99 A3
Thurgarton Ave ☒ NG2 . 173 F4
Thurgarton La NG14 ..... 151 E3
Thurgarton St NG2 ...... 173 F4
Thurgarton Sta NG14 .... 151 D6
Thurland St NG1 .... 223 E2
Thurlby Cl NG12 .... 189 A4
Thurlby Ct NG19 .... 88 E4
Thurlby La
Stanton-on-t-W NG12 . 198 C1
Widmerpool NG12 ...... 208 D8
Thurlby Rd DN21 .... 24 F8
Thurlestone Dr NG3 ..... 162 C6
Thurley Wlk NG18 ...... 103 B4
Thurloe Ct NG11 .... 185 C3
Thurman Dr NG12 .... 187 F3
Thurman St
Ilkeston DE7 .... 170 A6
Nottingham NG7 ...... 222 B4
Thursby Rd NG11 .... 184 E3
Thymus Wlk NG11 ...... 184 C1
Thyra Ct NG3 .... 161 E1
Thyra Gr
Beeston NG9 .... 184 A6
Nottingham NG3 ...... 161 D1
Tibshelf Rd NG17 .... 100 A7
Tibshelf Scis DE55 ..... 99 A7
Tickhill Castle NG19 ..... 8 A6
Tickhill Rd
Bawtry DN10 .... 9 F7
Harworth DN11 .... 8 E5
Tideswell Cl NG15 ...... 117 A3
Tideswell Ct NG18 ...... 102 D7
Tideworth Ct NG8 ...... 171 C6
Tilberthwaite Cl NG2 ... 186 C6
Tilbury Rise NG8 .... 160 B3
Tilford Gdns NG9 .... 182 E6
Till Bridge La DN21 ..... 44 F7
Tiln Ct DN22 .... 29 F1
Tiln La DN22 .... 29 F3
Tilstock Ct NG16 .... 159 A8
Timothy Rd NG22 .... 79 C3
Tindale Bank Rd DN10 ... 6 C7
Tinker La DN22 .... 27 F6
Tinker's La NG23 .... 97 F8
Tinkers Way NG7 .... 223 D1
Tinsley Cl NG23 .... 156 E6
Tinsley Rd NG16 .... 143 D1
Tintagel Gn NG7 .... 184 E1
Tintern Dr NG8 .... 160 E2
Tippings La NG22 ...... 119 F5
Tip Tree Cl NG16 .... 158 F7
Tiree Cl NG10 .... 170 D2
Tishbite St ☐ NG6 ..... 160 B7
Tissington Ave NG20 .... 74 C7
Tissington Cl ☒ NG7 ... 173 A8
Tissington Rd NG7 ..... 173 A8
Titchfield Ave
Mansfield Woodhouse
NG19 .... 88 D3
Sutton in A NG17 ...... 100 E2
Titchfield St
Hucknall NG15 .... 146 A4
Mansfield NG18 ...... 102 A8
Market Warsop NG20 ... 74 B3
Titchfield Terr NG15 .... 146 B7
Tithby Ct ☒ NG18 ..... 103 A2
Tithby Dr NG5 .... 161 D4
Tithby Rd
Bingham NG13 .... 177 E2
Cropwell Butler NG12 .. 189 C6
Tithe Barn Ct NG24 .... 125 A1
Tithe Gdns ☒ NG5 .... 147 A1
Tithe La NG14 .... 148 F7
Tithes La DN11 .... 8 A7
Tiverton Cl
Hucknall NG15 .... 145 D5
Nottingham NG8 ...... 160 B2
Toad La
Elston NG23 .... 153 E4
Epperstone NG14 ..... 150 A5
Laxton NG22 .... 79 B2
Tobias Cl NG5 .... 160 F8
Todd Cl NG11 .... 195 C8
Todd Ct NG11 .... 195 C8
Toft Cl NG12 .... 187 E2
Toft Rd NG9 .... 183 A3
Tokenhouse Yd NG1 .... 223 E2
Toll Bar Ave NG13 .... 181 A3
Tollerton Gn NG6 ..... 160 D5
Tollerton La NG12 ..... 186 E5
Tollerton Prim Sch
NG12 .... 186 A1
Tollhouse Hill NG1 ..... 223 D3
Tolney La NG24 .... 139 E7
Tom Blower Cl NG8 .... 172 A5
Tomlinson Ave NG11 ... 195 A1
Tom Otter's La NG23 ... 70 C8
Tom Wass Rd NG17 ... 114 E4
Tonbridge Mount NG8 .. 171 D2
Ton La NG14 .... 150 D2
Tooley St DN11 .... 24 D7
Toot Hill Comp Sch
NG13 .... 177 E4
Toothill La NG18 ...... 102 C7

Toothill Rd
Loughborough LE11 .... 220 B5
☒ Mansfield NG18 .... 102 B7
Topaz Gr NG18 .... 102 C5
Top Gn LE14 .... 210 A1
Top La NG19 .... 87 A1
Topliff Rd NG9 .... 183 C2
Top Pasture La DN22 ... 31 E8
Top Rd
Blidworth NG21 ...... 118 A2
Misson DN10 .... 4 D3
Ruddington NG11 ..... 196 C6
Thorney NG23 .... 69 F5
Top Row
Newark-on-T NG24 .... 140 C8
Westwood NG16 ..... 128 A5
Top Sandy La NG20 .... 74 C3
Top St
Askham NG22 .... 51 F2
Bawtry DN10 .... 10 A7
East Drayton DN22 .... 53 B3
Elston NG23 .... 153 D4
North Wheatley DN22 .. 31 D8
Rainworth NG21 ..... 104 B1
Top Valley Dr NG5 ..... 160 E8
Top Valley Sch NG5 .... 160 E8
Top Valley Way NG5 .... 160 E7
Topyard La DN22 ...... 30 D6
Torbay Cres NG5 ...... 161 B5
Torkard Dr NG5 .... 160 F8
Torksey Ave LN1 ...... 56 F4
Torksey Ferry Rd DN22 . 43 C2
Torksey Mews DN22 .... 39 D2
Torksey St DN22 ...... 43 A2
Torksey Wlk NG19 .... 88 E4
Tor La NG22 .... 77 A3
Torr St DN22 .... 24 D8
Torvill Dr NG8 .... 171 E5
Toston Dr NG8 .... 172 C4
Totland Dr NG8 ...... 160 D2
Totland Rd NG9 ...... 171 C2
Totley Cl NG6 .... 146 C2
Totnes Cl NG15 ...... 145 D6
Totnes Rd NG3 ...... 174 B5
Toton Banks Road Inf Sch
NG9 .... 182 F2
Toton Cl NG6 .... 160 D5
Toton La NG9 .... 182 E6
Tottle Gdns ☒ NG7 ... 172 C6
Tottle Rd NG11 ..... 185 A8
Tow Ct NG24 .... 139 A4
Tower Cres NG16 .... 159 A4
Tower St DN21 ..... 15 D1
Towe's Mount NG4 ... 174 E7
Towle St NG10 ..... 193 A4
Towlsons Croft NG6 .. 160 D3
Town End La NG23 .. 167 B8
Towngate DN10 .... 10 A7
Town La DE55 ..... 99 B3
Townroe Dr NG19 .. 101 D7
Townsend Ct NG5 .. 147 A1
Townside Cl NG10 .. 193 B4
Townside La DN22 .. 42 D3
Townside Rd DN22 .. 32 D1
Town St
Askham NG22 ...... 52 A3
Beeston NG9 ...... 183 B8
Claypole NG23 .... 156 D7
Clayworth DN22 ... 21 D5
Cottam DN22 ..... 43 D5
Grassthorpe NG23 .. 81 F4
Hawksworth NG13 .. 167 C3
Lound DN22 ..... 20 C1
Pinxton NG16 .... 113 E3
Sandiacre NG10 .. 182 B6
South Leverton DN22 .. 42 C7
Sutton DN22 ..... 28 F6
Treswell DN22 .... 42 B3
Town View NG16 .. 158 F7
Towpath LE11 ... 220 C5
Towson Ave NG16 .. 143 C2
Towson Field LE12 .. 205 E2
Towyn St ☒ NG5 .. 161 A7
Tracy Cl NG19 .... 171 D1
Trafalgar Rd
Beeston NG9 ...... 184 A4
Long Eaton NG10 .. 193 D6
Trafalgar Sq
Long Eaton NG10 .. 193 E7
Sutton in A NG17 ... 97 A8
Traffic St NG2 ...... 223 E1
Trafford Gdns ☐ NG8 . 172 D7
Tranby Gdns NG8 .. 171 F4
Tranker La S81 ..... 35 A6
Travell's Hill LE12 .. 214 A7
Travers Rd NG10 ... 182 A6
Treegarth Sq NG5 .. 147 B1
Tree View Cl NG5 .. 147 C1
Trefan Gdns NG5 .. 161 A7
Trelawn Cl ☐ NG5 .. 161 D2
Tremayne Rd NG8 .. 171 C5
Trenchard Cl NG13 . 177 C8
Trenchham Gdns NG14 . 163 D3
Trent Ave NG11 .... 196 C8
Trent Bridge
(Nottinghamshire Cty CC)
NG2 .... 173 E1
Trent Bsns Ctr NG10 . 182 C1
Trent Bvd NG2 ..... 174 A1
Trent Cl NG23 .... 110 F2
Trent Coll NG10 ... 193 C8
Trent Cres NG9 .. 183 E3
Trentdale Rd NG4 . 174 D6
Trent Dr NG15 ... 145 D3
Trentham Dr NG8 . 172 C7
Trentham Gdns NG8 . 172 C7

Trent La
Besthorpe NG23 ...... 97 E6
Burton Joyce NG14 .... 164 C4
East Bridgford NG13 ... 165 B4
Girton NG23 .... 82 E2
Kelham NG23 .... 124 B5
Long Eaton NG10 ..... 193 F5
Newark-on-T NG24 .... 125 A2
North Clifton NG23 ... 68 C5
Nottingham NG2 ..... 174 A3
South Clifton NG23 ... 68 D1
Trenton Cl NG9 ..... 171 A1
Trenton Dr NG10 .... 194 A8
Trent Port Rd DN21 ... 44 B8
Trent Rd
Beeston NG9 .... 184 B4
Nottingham NG2 .... 173 F4
Wellow NG22 .... 78 A4
Trentside NG14 .... 165 A4
Trentside N NG21 ... 173 E1
Trent S Ind Pk NG2 .. 174 A3
Trent St
Gainsborough DN21 .. 24 D7
Long Eaton NG10 ... 193 E8
Nottingham NG1 .... 223 F1
Retford DN22 ...... 40 A6
Worksop S80 ...... 35 E4
Trent Vale Inf Sch NG9 . 184 B4
Trent Valley View NG3 . 162 A1
Trent View DN21 .... 44 C8
Trentview Ct NG2 ... 173 F2
Trent View Gdns NG12 . 176 A5
Trent Way NG24 .... 125 B2
Trent Wlk NG19 .... 88 E4
Tressall Cl DE7 ..... 170 A8
Treswell Ct ☒ NG18 . 103 A2
Treswell Rd
Rampton DN22 ..... 42 F2
South Leverton DN22 . 42 C5
Treswell Wood Nature
Reserve DN22 ...... 41 E4
Trevelyan Rd NG2 ... 173 F1
Trevino Gdns ☒ NG5 . 147 A1
Trevone Ave NG9 ... 182 E6
Trevor Rd
Beeston NG9 ...... 183 F5
West Bridgford NG2 . 186 A6
Trevose Gdns NG5 .. 161 D3
Treyford Cl NG11 ... 185 A4
Triangle The DE7 ... 170 A6
Tricornia Dr NG6 ... 160 B4
Tring Vale NG5 .... 161 A4
Trinity Ave NG7 .... 222 B1
Trinity Cl DE7 ..... 157 E3
Trinity Cres
East Markham NG22 .. 66 B7
Lambley NG4 ..... 163 C7
Wymeswold LE12 .... 216 B3
Trinity Rd
Newark-on-T NG24 .... 140 A4
Retford DN22 ...... 29 D1
Southwell NG25 .... 136 C8
Trinity Sch NG8 .... 172 A8
Trinity Sq NG1 .... 223 E3
Trinity St
Gainsborough DN21 .. 24 D7
Loughborough LE11 .. 220 C3
Trinity Wlk NG1 .... 223 E3
Trinstead Way NG5 .. 161 C7
Triumph Cl NG22 ... 106 F8
Triumph Rd
Eakring NG22 ...... 106 E8
Nottingham NG7 .... 172 D4
Trivett Sq NG1 .... 223 F2
Troon Cl NG16 .... 158 E7
Trough La NG16 ... 158 F8
Trough Rd NG16 ... 159 A8
Troutbeck NG12 ... 188 A3
Troutbeck Cres NG9 . 183 C8
Trowell Ave
Ilkeston DE7 ...... 170 A5
Nottingham NG8 ... 171 B5
Trowell CE Prim Sch
NG9 .... 170 D4
Trowell Ct ☐ NG18 .. 103 A2
Trowell Gr
Long Eaton NG10 .. 182 C1
Stapleford NG9 ... 170 D2
Trowell La LE12 ... 213 E7
Trowell Pk Dr NG9 . 170 D2
Trowell Rd
Nottingham NG8 ... 171 D5
Stapleford NG9 ... 170 D2
True Lovers Wlk ☐ LE11 . 220 A3
Trueman St S81 .... 36 B5
Trueman Gdns NG5 . 162 B6
Trueman St DE7 ... 157 F4
Truman Cl NG3 ... 223 F4
Truman Dr NG15 .. 146 A6
Truman's Rd NG2 .. 173 D1
Truman St
Cossall DE7 ...... 158 A1
Kimberley NG16 ... 158 D7
Truro Cl LE12 .... 205 E1
Truro Cres NG7 ... 172 E7
Trusley Wlk NG19 .. 88 E4
Tryst The NG24 ... 125 A2
Tuckers Cl LE11 ... 220 C2
Tudor Ave NG18 .. 102 F8
Tudor Cl
Carlton NG4 ...... 174 E5
Long Eaton NG10 .. 182 E1
Newark-on-T NG24 . 140 B8
Trent Cres NG21 .. 118 A8

Tudor Dr
Mansfield NG18 ..... 102 C4
Morton DN21 .... 15 B4
Tudor Gr NG1 ...... 223 D4
Tudor Rd NG2 ...... 185 F7
Tudor Sq NG2 ..... 185 F7
Tudor St NG17 .... 100 E1
Tudsbury Terr NG17 . 101 A3
Tudwal Cl NG5 .... 161 A7
Tudwal Wlk ☒ NG5 . 161 A7
Tulip Ave NG3 .... 173 D2
Tulip Rd NG16 .... 158 B4
Tunnel Rd
Nottingham NG7 ... 222 C2
Retford DN22 ..... 39 E5
Tunstall Cres NG8 . 160 A1
Tunstall Dr NG5 .. 160 F4
Tunstall Rd NG5 .. 161 F4
Turnberry Cl NG9 .. 183 C6
Turnberry Ave ☒ NG17 . 114 E7
Turnberry Ct
Beeston NG9 ..... 183 C6
Ilkeston DE7 .... 157 C2
Turnberry Ct NG12 . 186 C3
Turnberry Rd NG6 . 160 D6
Turner Ave
Langley Mill NG16 .. 143 A3
Loughborough LE11 . 220 A2
Turner Ct NG9 .... 182 E6
Turner Dr
Eastwood NG16 ... 158 B7
Worksop S81 .... 35 F4
Turner Rd
Long Eaton NG10 .. 193 C4
Worksop S81 .... 35 F4
Turners Croft DN22 . 42 C8
Turner St NG15 .. 146 A7
Turneys Ct NG2 .. 173 E1
Turney St NG2 .. 173 D1
Turnley Rd DE55 . 113 C6
Turnpike La NG9 . 184 A8
Turnstone Cres NG18 . 103 C4
Turnstone Wharf ☐ NG7 . 172 F2
Turpin Ave NG4 .. 162 D3
Turpin Cl DN21 .. 15 C1
Turton Cl NG16 .. 143 A3
Turvey La LE12 .. 212 D2
Tuxford Ave NG20 . 74 E8
Tuxford Cl ☐ NG18 . 103 A2
Tuxford Prim Sch NG22 . 65 E2
Tuxford Rd
Boughton NG22 ... 77 C5
East Markham NG22 . 65 F5
Egmanton NG22 ... 79 A5
Normanton on T NG23 . 81 D6
Walesby NG22 .... 64 C2
Tuxford Sch NG22 . 66 A3
Tuxford Windmill NG22 . 65 E4
Twells Cl NG3 .... 173 F7
Twentylands Dr LE12 . 205 D1
Twin Oaks Dr NG17 . 100 C2
Twinyards Cl NG17 . 100 C1
Twitchell The
Beeston NG9 .... 183 E4
Newark-on-T NG24 . 139 E5
Sutton in A NG17 .. 100 F1
Two Acres S81 ... 18 B2
Twycross Rd NG5 . 161 B7
Twyford Gdns NG11 . 184 E4
Twyford La DN22 . 50 C3
Tyburn Cl NG5 .. 147 B1
Tylden Rd S80 .. 35 B5
Tylden Way S80 .. 35 B5
Tynedale Cl
Long Eaton NG10 .. 193 A6
Nottingham NG8 .. 160 D1
Tyne Gdns NG15 .. 145 D3

U

Ulldale Ct NG9 ...... 183 B4
Ullscarf Cl NG2 ..... 186 C5
Ullswater Cl NG4 ... 162 F2
Ullswater Cres NG9 . 183 D8
Ullswater Dr NG15 . 145 F7
Ulster Rd DN21 ... 15 D2
Underwood Ave DN22 . 19 B3
Underwood CE Prim Sch
NG16 .... 128 F1
Underwood Gdns S80 . 35 C3
Union Cl NG15 ... 131 A2
Union Rd NG3 ... 223 F3
Union St
Beeston NG9 .... 184 A6
Bingham NG13 .. 177 E4
Long Eaton NG10 . 193 E8
Loughborough LE11 . 220 A4
Mansfield NG18 .. 102 A7
Retford DN22 ... 39 F7
Selston NG16 ... 129 A7
Sutton in A NG17 . 100 F1
Unity Cess NG3 .. 162 C2
Unity Prim Sch NG7 . 222 C4
Unity Rd NG17 ... 115 B7
University Bvd NG7 . 184 C8
University of Nottingham
NG7 .... 172 D2
University of Nottingham
Department of Ag
Economics LE12 .. 213 B8
Unwin Rd NG17 ... 101 B3
Unwin St NG17 ... 100 A3
Upbrook Cl NG8 .. 171 F6
Upminster Dr
Arnold NG5 ..... 147 F1
Nuthall NG16 ... 159 D3

Upper Canaan NG11 ... 196 D8
Upper Coll St NG1 .... 223 D3
Upper Dunstead Rd
NG16 .... 143 B4
Upper Eldon St NG2 .. 173 E4
Upper Mexborough Rd
NG16 .... 129 A7
Upper Orch St NG9 .. 182 E7
Upper Parliament St
NG1 .... 223 E3
Upper Row NG22 ... 54 B2
Upper Wellington St
NG10 .... 182 C1
Uppingham Cres NG2 . 185 D5
Uppingham Gdns NG2 . 173 D2
Upton Cl DE75 .... 143 A1
Upton Dr NG5 .... 161 D5
Upton All Time Mus
NG25 .... 122 C1
Upton Hill NG22 ... 52 A4
Upton Mount NG19 . 87 C1
Upton Rd
Askham NG22 .... 52 A4
Southwell NG25 ... 122 A1
Upton Wlk DN21 .. 24 F7
Urban Rd NG17 ... 115 A5
Utile Gdns ☒ NG6 . 160 A7

V

Vale Ave NG20 .... 74 A4
Vale Cl
Aslockton NG13 ... 179 A4
Eastwood NG16 .. 144 B2
Mansfield NG18 .. 102 E4
Vale Cres N NG8 .. 172 D6
Vale Cres S NG8 .. 172 D6
Vale Dr NG20 .... 72 F2
Vale Gdns NG4 .. 174 D5
Valentine Ave NG16 . 128 E7
Vale Rd
Carlton NG4 .... 174 E5
Mansfield Woodhouse NG19 . 88 B4
Valeside Gdns NG4 . 174 E5
Vale The DE7 ... 157 E3
Valetta Rd NG5 .. 162 B7
Vale View NG23 .. 156 D1
Vallance St NG19 . 88 B4
Valley App NG22 . 105 F7
Valley Comp Sch S81 . 35 E5
Valley Dr NG16 .. 144 B1
Valley Farm Ct ☐ NG5 . 161 A8
Valley Gdns NG2 .. 186 C5
Valley La NG23 .. 169 D8
Valley Prospect NG24 . 139 D5
Valley Rd
Beeston NG9 .... 183 B5
Bilsthorpe NG22 .. 105 F7
Carlton NG4 .... 162 B1
Kimberley NG16 .. 158 D7
Nottingham NG5 .. 161 B4
Radcliffe on T NG12 . 176 A5
Shirebrook NG20 .. 72 E5
West Bridgford NG2 . 186 B5
Worksop S81 .... 35 E6
Valley View NG24 . 126 A1
Valley Vw NG18 .. 102 E4
Valmont Ave NG18 . 103 A6
Valmont Rd
Beeston NG9 .... 183 A7
Nottingham NG5 .. 161 A3
Vancouver Ave NG12 . 175 E2
Vanessa Dr DN21 . 15 C3
Vanguard Rd NG10 . 193 D5
Varden Ave NG9 .. 172 A1
Varney Rd NG11 .. 184 F3
Vaughan Ave
Bottesford NG13 .. 181 C2
Hucknall NG15 .. 131 C1
Vaughan Pl NG20 . 72 E6
Vaughan Rd NG9 . 183 A4
Vedonis Pk NG15 . 146 A5
Vellus Ct NG17 .. 101 B2
Ventnor Rise NG5 . 160 F4
Ventura Dr NG5 .. 146 C1
Venus Cl NG6 .... 160 E5
Verbena Cl NG5 .. 160 E5
Verbena Cl ☒ NG3 . 173 D7
Verder Gr NG5 .. 160 E6
Vere Ave NG17 ... 100 E5
Vere St NG6 ..... 160 B7
Verne Cl NG4 ... 174 C7
Verney St NG19 .. 86 F7
Verney Way NG19 . 86 F7
Vernon Ave
Beeston NG9 .... 183 F6
Nottingham NG15 .. 162 F1
Newark-on-T NG24 . 140 B8
Nottingham, Old Basford
NG6 .... 160 C2
Nottingham, Wilford NG11 . 185 B8
Ravenshead NG15 .. 116 F1
Retford DN22 ... 40 A4
Vernon Cres NG15 . 117 A1
Vernon Ct
Nuthall NG16 ... 159 F3
Shirebrook NG20 .. 73 A4
Vernon Dr NG16 .. 159 F3
Vernon Pk Dr NG6 . 160 D4
Vernon Pk Trad Est NG6 . 160 E3
Vernon Rd
Kirkby in A NG17 ... 114 F6
Nottingham NG6 .. 160 E6
Vernon St
Ilkeston DE7 ..... 157 F4
Newark-on-T NG24 . 140 A8
Nottingham NG1 .. 223 D3

Vernon St
Shirebrook NG20 . . . . .73 A4
Verona Ave NG4 . . . . .174 F6
Verona Ct NG18 . . . . .103 A3
Veronica Dr
Carlton NG4 . . . . .162 D1
Eastwood NG16 . . . . .158 C8
Veronica Wlk NG11 . . . . . .184 C1
Veronne Dr NG17 . . . . . . .101 A6
Versailles Gd NG15 . . . . . .146 A5
Vesper Ct NG18 . . . . .102 F8
Vessey Cl NG24 . . . . .124 C3
Vessey Rd S81 . . . . .35 E7
Vexation La NG22 . . . . .91 E7
Vicarage Ave DE7 . . . . . . .157 D4
Vicarage Cl
Collingham NG23 . . . . .98 A1
Nottingham, Old Basford
NG5 . . . . .160 F3
Nottingham, St Ann's NG3 . .223 E4
Shirebrook NG20 . . . . .72 E3
Vicarage Ct NG17 . . . . . . .100 E7
Vicarage Dr
Burton Joyce NG14 . . . . . . .163 E4
Clarborough DN22 . . . . .30 D5
Vicarage Gn NG12 . . . . . . .186 B3
Vicarage La
Beckingham DN10 . . . . .14 C2
Farnsfield NG22 . . . . .119 E6
Kneeton NG13 . . . . .151 F1
North Muskham NG23 . . . . .110 D4
Radcliffe on T NG12 . . . . . .175 E3
Ruddington NG11 . . . . .196 C7
Vicarage Rd NG25 . . . . . . .136 C8
Vicarage St
Beeston NG9 . . . . .183 E6
Ilkeston DE7 . . . . .157 D4
Vicarage Way NG17 . . . . .129 F8
Vicar La
Misson DN10 . . . . .4 C3
Tibshelf DE55 . . . . .99 A6
Vicars Ct NG21 . . . . .89 E2
Vicar's La DN22 . . . . .43 A2
Vicar's Wlk S80 . . . . .35 F2
Vicar Water Ctry Pk NG21 .89 E2
Vickers St NG3 . . . . .103 B7
Vickers St
Market Warsop NG20 . . . . . . .74 B4
Nottingham NG3 . . . . .173 D8
Vickers Way NG22 . . . . . .105 F7
Victor Cres NG10 . . . . . . .182 C4
Victoria Ave
Lowdham NG14 . . . . .150 E1
 Newark-on-T NG24 . . . . . .173 F4
Victoria Cl
Boughton NG22 . . . . .77 E5
Gainsborough DN21 . . . . . . .24 F6
Victoria Cres NG5 . . . . . . .161 D2
Victoria Ct
Ilkeston DE7 . . . . .157 E1
Mansfield NG18 . . . . .102 A5
Victoria Emb NG2 . . . . . . .185 D8
Victoria Gdns
 Newark-on-T NG24 . . . . . .140 A8
Watnall NG16 . . . . .145 A1
Victoria Gr NG15 . . . . .131 B1
Victoria L Ctr NG1 . . . . . .223 F3
Victoria Pk NG4 . . . . .175 B6
Victoria Pk L Ctr DE7 . . . .157 E2
Victoria Pk Way NG4 . . . .175 B6
Victoria Rd
Bingham NG13 . . . . .178 A5
Bunny NG11 . . . . .196 E1
Carlton NG4 . . . . .175 A6
Kirkby in A NG17 . . . . .114 F5
Nottingham NG5 . . . . .161 B3
Pinxton NG16 . . . . .113 D3
Retford DN22 . . . . .39 E6
Sandiacre NG10 . . . . .182 B5
Selston NG16 . . . . .129 A7
Shirebrook NG20 . . . . .72 F4
South Normanton DE55 . . . .113 A6
Stanton Hill NG17 . . . . . . .100 C6
Stapleford NG9 . . . . .182 D7
Sutton in A NG17 . . . . .100 E2
Victoria Terr DE55 . . . . . . .99 B7
Victor Terr NG5 . . . . .161 C2
Victory Cl
Kirkby in Ashfield NG17 . . .115 B6
Long Eaton NG10 . . . . .193 D5
Mansfield Woodhouse NG19 .89 A1
Victory Dr NG19 . . . . .88 F1
Victory Rd NG9 . . . . .184 A4
Village Cl
Farndon NG24 . . . . .139 B5
West Bridgford NG12 . . . . .186 B3
Village Farm Cl LE12 . . . . .204 F1
Village Rd
Normanton on S LE12 . . . . .213 D2
Nottingham NG11 . . . . .184 D2

Village St
Owthorpe NG12 . . . . .199 E7
West Bridgford NG12 . . . . .186 B3
Village Way NG24 . . . . . . .139 A5
Villa Rd
Keyworth NG12 . . . . .197 F4
Nottingham NG3 . . . . .173 C7
Villa St NG9 . . . . .183 F7
Villas The NG20 . . . . .59 A3
Villiers Rd
Arnold NG5 . . . . .161 D4
Mansfield NG18 . . . . .102 E7
West Bridgford NG2 . . . . . .186 A6
Vina Cooke Mus of Dolls &
Bygone Childhood
NG23 . . . . .110 F7
Vincent Ave NG9 . . . . .183 F5
Vincent Gdns ⑧ NG7 . . . .172 E7
Vine Cl NG13 . . . . .181 A1
Vine Cres NG10 . . . . .182 B6
Vine Farm Cl NG12 . . . . . .187 E3
Vine Rd DN11 . . . . .8 C7
Vines Cross NG8 . . . . .171 E2
Vine Terr NG15 . . . . .146 B7
Vine Tree Terr LE12 . . . . .215 C1
Vine Way NG18 . . . . .140 B8
Violet Ave NG16 . . . . .144 B1
Violet Cl
Nottingham NG6 . . . . .160 D3
Shirebrook NG20 . . . . .72 D3
Violet Hill NG18 . . . . .103 A8
Violet Rd
Carlton NG4 . . . . .162 D1
West Bridgford NG2 . . . . . .186 A8
Vista The NG9 . . . . .182 E5
Vivian Ave NG5 . . . . .173 B8
Vixen Cl NG24 . . . . .139 F4
Viyella Gd NG15 . . . . .130 F1
Voce Cl S81 . . . . .36 B6
Vulcan Cl NG6 . . . . .160 E4
Vulcan Pl S80 . . . . .35 F3
Vyse Dr NG10 . . . . .193 C6

W

Waddington Dr NG2 . . . . . .185 D4
Wade Ave DE7 . . . . .170 A7
Wade Cl NG18 . . . . .102 C3
Wades Ave NG7 . . . . .172 E8
Wadham Rd NG5 . . . . .161 E5
Wadhurst Gdns NG3 . . . . .223 F4
Wadhurst Gr NG8 . . . . . . .171 D2
Wadnal La NG23 . . . . .80 F3
Wadsworth Rd NG9 . . . . . .182 F8
Wagstaff La NG16 . . . . . . .128 B4
Wain Ct S81 . . . . .36 B7
Waingrove NG11 . . . . .185 A3
Wainwright Ave NG19 . . . .101 D8
Wakefield Ave NG12 . . . . .176 A4
Wakefield Croft DE7 . . . . .157 C3
Wakeling Cl NG25 . . . . . . .136 E8
Walbrook Cl NG8 . . . . .160 A3
Walcote Dr NG2 . . . . .186 B4
Walcot Gn NG11 . . . . .184 D1
Waldeck Rd NG5 . . . . .161 B1
Waldemar Gr NG9 . . . . . . .184 A6
Waldron Cl NG2 . . . . .173 D2
Walesby CE Prim Sch
NG22 . . . . .64 A2
Walesby Ct ⊡ NG18 . . . . . .103 A3
Walesby Dr NG17 . . . . .115 D5
Walesby La NG22 . . . . .77 C5
Walford Cl NG13 . . . . .181 A2
Walgrave Wlk ⓲ NG5 . . . .161 A7
Walkden St NG18 . . . . .102 B7
Walker Cl
Newark-on-T NG24 . . . . . . .140 A7
New Ollerton NG22 . . . . .77 C5
Walker Gr NG9 . . . . .182 E6
Walkeringham Prim Sch
DN10 . . . . .13 F6
Walkeringham Rd
Beckingham DN10 . . . . .14 B2
Gringley on t h DN10 . . . . . .13 A3
Walkerith Rd
Morton DN21 . . . . .15 A5
Walkerith DN10 . . . . .14 D8
Walkers Ave NG16 . . . . . . .143 E6
Walkers Cl
Bingham NG13 . . . . .177 E4
Mansfield Woodhouse NG19 89 B1
Walker Sq NG5 . . . . .160 E3
Walker St
Eastwood NG16 . . . . .144 A3
Nottingham NG2 . . . . .173 E4
Walkers Yd NG12 . . . . .175 F3
Walk Mill Dr NG15 . . . . . . .131 B1
Walks of Life Heritage Ctr
NG22 . . . . .66 A3
Walk The DN21 . . . . .24 F7
Wallace Ave NG4 . . . . .174 F7
Wallace Rd LE11 . . . . .220 A2
Wallan St NG7 . . . . .222 A4
Wallet St NG4 . . . . .175 A7
Wallett Ave NG9 . . . . .183 C8
Wallingbrook Rise S80 . . . .35 B3
Wallingwells La S81 . . . . . .25 A6
Wallis Rd NG18 . . . . .102 C7
Wallis St NG6 . . . . .160 E4
Wall St DN21 . . . . .24 D7
Walnut Ave
Shireoaks S81 . . . . .34 F7
Tickhill DN11 . . . . .8 A8
Walnut Cl
Aslockton NG13 . . . . .178 F5
Ilkeston DE7 . . . . .170 A7

Walnut Dr
Beeston NG9 . . . . .183 B8
Calverton NG14 . . . . .148 F8
Walnut Gr
Cotgrave NG12 . . . . .187 F3
East Bridgford NG13 . . . . . .165 C2
Radcliffe on T NG12 . . . . . .175 F3
Walnut Paddock LE14 . . . .202 B3
Walnut Rd NG13 . . . . .181 A2
Walnut Tree Cres NG19 . . . .89 D2
Walnut Tree Gdns NG6 . . .159 F7
Walnut Tree La NG13 . . . . .165 C2
Walsham Cl NG9 . . . . .183 C2
Walsingham Rd NG5 . . . . .162 B5
Walter Halls Prim Sch
NG3 . . . . .161 E2
Walter's Cl NG24 . . . . .139 A5
Walters Cres NG16 . . . . . . .128 D6
Walter St NG7 . . . . .222 C4
Waltham Cl
Balderton NG24 . . . . .140 D3
West Bridgford NG2 . . . . . .186 B6
Waltham La
Harby LE14 . . . . .202 B1
Long Clawson LE14 . . . . . . .211 E2
Waltham Rd NG15 . . . . . . .117 A2
Walton Ave NG3 . . . . .173 F5
Walton Cl NG19 . . . . .103 B8
Walton Cres NG4 . . . . .174 E7
Walton Dr
Keyworth NG12 . . . . .197 F3
Sutton in A NG17 . . . . .114 D8
Walton Rd NG5 . . . . .148 A1
Walton's La NG23 . . . . .110 E3
Walton St
Long Eaton NG10 . . . . .182 D1
Sutton in A NG17 . . . . .101 A3
Wandsck Cl NG7 . . . . .136 D8
Wansbeck Cl NG7 . . . . .222 C3
Wansford Ave NG5 . . . . . . .147 F1
Wanstead Way NG5 . . . . . .146 E1
Wapping La DN21 . . . . .44 C8
Warburton St NG24 . . . . . .125 A1
Ward Ave
Hucknall NG15 . . . . .130 F1
Nottingham NG5 . . . . .162 A3
Ward Cl NG5 . . . . .162 A8
Wardlow Rd DE7 . . . . .157 E3
Ward Pl NG18 . . . . .101 E6
Ward Rd NG21 . . . . .89 F4
Ward's End LE11 . . . . .220 B3
Ward St ⊡ NG7 . . . . .172 F8
Wareham Cl
Nottingham NG8 . . . . .160 A3
West Bridgford NG2 . . . . . .185 C5
Warkton Cl NG9 . . . . .183 C5
Warnadene Rd NG17 . . . . .114 E8
Warner Pl LE11 . . . . .220 C4
Warners La ⑨ LE11 . . . . . .220 B4
Warner St NG7 . . . . .222 A3
Warrands Cl NG25 . . . . . . .136 C8
Warren Ave
Annesley NG15 . . . .● . .130 C8
Nottingham NG5 . . . . .161 A2
Stapleford NG9 . . . . .182 D7
Warren Ave Extension
NG9 . . . . .182 D7
Warren Cl
Gainsborough DN21 . . . . . . .15 B2
 Sutton in Ashfield
NG17 . . . . .100 A2
Warren Dr NG19 . . . . .187 D7
Warrender Cl NG9 . . . . . . .171 C1
Warrener Gr NG5 . . . . .160 E8
Warrenhill Cl NG17 . . . . . . .161 C7
Warren La
Kegworth DE74 . . . . .193 B2
Long Eaton DE74 . . . . .203 B3
Warren Prim Sch NG5 . . . .147 A2
Warren Rd
Annesley Woodhouse
NG17 . . . . .115 B1
Hucknall NG15 . . . . .145 D5
Warren The NG12 . . . . .187 F2
Warren Way NG19 . . . . . . .103 C8
Warrington Rd NG6 . . . . . .160 C7
Warser Gate NG1 . . . . .223 E2
Warsop Cl NG8 . . . . .159 D2
Warsop La NG21 . . . . .117 F7
Warsop Rd NG19 . . . . .88 D3
Warton Ave NG3 . . . . .173 F8
Warwick Ave
Arnold NG5 . . . . .161 E5
Beeston NG9 . . . . .183 F7
Carlton in L S81 . . . . .25 F6
Warwick Cl
Kirkby in A NG17 . . . . .115 D5
Saxilby LN1 . . . . .57 A4
Warwick Dr
Mansfield NG18 . . . . .102 C7
Shipley DE7 . . . . .157 C3
Warwick Gdns NG12 . . . . .187 F1
Warwick Rd
Balderton NG24 . . . . .140 D4
Long Eaton NG10 . . . . .194 A4
Nottingham NG3 . . . . .161 D2
Wasdale Cl NG2 . . . . .186 C5
Washdyke La NG16 . . . . . . .158 F7
Washington Dr
Mansfield NG18 . . . . .101 F5
Stapleford NG9 . . . . .170 E1
Washington St DN21 . . . . . .24 D6
Wash Pit La NG12 . . . . . . .200 D8
Wasnidge Cl NG3 . . . . .223 F3
Wasnidge Wlk NG3 . . . . . .223 F4
Watchwood Gr NG14 . . . . .148 F8
Watcombe Cir NG5 . . . . . . .161 B1
Watcombe Rd NG5 . . . . . . .161 C1

Watendlath Cl NG2 . . . . . .186 C5
Waterdown Rd NG11 . . . . .184 D1
Waterford St NG6 . . . . .160 E3
Waterfront Ctry Pk DN10 . .7 C2
Waterfurrows La NG12 . . . .164 D1
Waterhouse La NG4 . . . . . .163 A2
Water La
Carlton in L S81 . . . . .26 A6
Long Clawson LE14 . . . . . . .211 E4
Mansfield NG19 . . . . .87 B3
Newark-on-T NG24 . . . . . . .124 F1
Oxton NG25 . . . . .134 B3
Radcliffe on T NG12 . . . . . .175 E3
Retford DN22 . . . . .39 E8
Shelford NG12 . . . . .164 D1
South Normanton DE55 . . . .113 B6
Tickhill DN11 . . . . .8 A8
Waterloo Cl DE55 . . . . .113 C8
Waterloo Cres NG7 . . . . . .222 C4
Waterloo La NG9 . . . . .170 F6
Waterloo Prom NG7 . . . . .222 C4
Waterloo Rd
Beeston NG9 . . . . .184 A5
Hucknall NG15 . . . . .131 A2
Nottingham NG7 . . . . .222 C4
Water Mdws S80 . . . . .35 D1
Water Mdws Swimming
Complex NG18 . . . . .102 C6
Watermeadow Cl NG19 . . . .88 C6
Watermeadows The
NG19 . . . . .193 B8
Water Orton Cl NG9 . . . . . .182 E3
Waterside Cl
 ② Loughborough LE11 . . .220 B5
Sandiacre NG10 . . . . .182 A5
West Bridgford NG2 . . . . . .186 C6
Waterside Gdns NG7 . . . . .172 E1
Waterslack Rd DN11 . . . . . . .9 B4
Waterson Cl NG18 . . . . . . .103 A4
Waterson Oaks NG18 . . . . .102 F4
Waterway St W NG2 . . . . .173 C2
Waterway St ⊡ NG2 . . . . . .173 D2
Waterway The NG10 . . . . .182 C4
Waterworks St DN21 . . . . . .24 D6
Watford Rd NG8 . . . . .160 B2
Watford St LE11 . . . . .220 B4
Watkin St NG3 . . . . .223 E4
Watnall Cres NG19 . . . . . . .101 E7
Watnall Rd
Hucknall NG15 . . . . .145 E4
Nuthall NG16 . . . . .159 C6
Watson Ave
Mansfield NG18 . . . . .102 C7
Nottingham NG3 . . . . .174 B6
Watson Rd
Ilkeston DE7 . . . . .157 C2
Worksop S80 . . . . .35 F2
Watson's La LE14 . . . . .202 B3
Watson St NG20 . . . . .74 B4
Wavell Cl S81 . . . . .35 D7
Wavell Cres DN10 . . . . .11 A1
Waveney Cl NG5 . . . . .162 A6
Waverley Ave
Beeston NG9 . . . . .184 A5
Carlton NG4 . . . . .162 E2
Waverley House PNEU Sch
NG7 . . . . .222 C4
Waverley Pl S80 . . . . .47 A8
Waverley Rd NG18 . . . . . . .102 B4
Waverley St
Long Eaton NG10 . . . . .193 D8
Nottingham NG7 . . . . .223 D4
Tibshelf DE55 . . . . .99 A7
Waverley Terr NG1 . . . . . .223 D3
Waverley Way S80 . . . . .47 A8
Waverly Cl NG17 . . . . .115 D5
Wayford Wlk ⑥ NG6 . . . . .160 B8
Wayne Cl NG2 . . . . .184 E1
Weardale Rd NG5 . . . . .161 B2
Wearmouth Gdns ⑤
NG5 . . . . .147 A1
Weaver Cl LE11 . . . . .220 B1
Weavers Cl LE12 . . . . .205 F3
Weaver's La NG15, NG16 . .129 F3
Weavers The NG24 . . . . . . .124 D6
Weaverthorpe Rd NG5 . . . .162 A5
Webb Rd NG8 . . . . .172 B7
Webster Ave NG16 . . . . . . .143 F1
Webster Cl NG21 . . . . .76 A2
Weedon Cl NG3 . . . . .174 A6
Weekday Cross NG1 . . . . . .223 E2
Weetman Ave NG20 . . . . . . .59 A1
Weetman Gdns ⓬ NG5 . . . .161 A8
Weighbridge Rd NG18 . . . .102 C6
Weightman Dr NG16 . . . . . .158 B7
Welbeck Ave
Carlton NG4 . . . . .162 D2
Newark-on-T NG24 . . . . . . .125 A1
Welbeck Cl
Nottingham NG3 . . . . .223 E4
Sutton in A NG17 . . . . .100 F5
Welbeck Dr NG21 . . . . .75 F2
Welbeck Gdns
Beeston NG9 . . . . .182 F3
Nottingham NG3 . . . . .162 A4
Welbeck Gr NG13 . . . . .177 C4
Welbeck Pl NG22 . . . . .66 A3
Welbeck Prim Sch NG2 . . .173 C2
Welbeck Rd
Harworth DN11 . . . . .9 A5
Long Eaton NG10 . . . . .182 C3
Mansfield Woodhouse NG19 88 E5
Radcliffe on T NG12 . . . . . .176 A4
Retford DN22 . . . . .39 E4
West Bridgford NG2 . . . . . .185 E8
Welbeck Sq NG17 . . . . .100 C6

Welbeck St
Creswell S80 . . . . .58 E8
Kirkby in A NG17 . . . . .115 C5
Mansfield NG18 . . . . .102 A7
Market Warsop NG20 . . . . . . .74 B4
Sutton in A NG17 . . . . .100 F2
Whitwell S80 . . . . .45 A6
Worksop S80 . . . . .35 F4
Welbeck Wlk NG3 . . . . .223 E4
Welby Ave NG7 . . . . .222 B2
Welch Ave NG9 . . . . .182 E8
Weldbank Cl NG9 . . . . .183 B4
Welfare Cl NG20 . . . . .72 E3
Welfitt Gr NG20 . . . . .59 B2
Welham Cres NG5 . . . . .162 A7
Welham Gr DN22 . . . . .40 A8
Welham Rd DN22 . . . . .40 A8
Welland Cl
Newark-on-T NG24 . . . . . . .125 B2
Worksop S80 . . . . .35 E7
Wellcroft Cl NG18 . . . . . . .101 F5
Wellesley Cl S81 . . . . .35 D8
Wellesley Cres NG8 . . . . . .159 D2
Well Fen La NG23 . . . . .156 D7
Wellin Cl NG12 . . . . .186 B3
Wellin La NG12 . . . . .186 B3
Wellington Cir NG1 . . . . . .223 D2
Wellington Cl NG20 . . . . . . .74 B3
Wellington Cres NG2 . . . . .185 F7
Wellington Gr DN10 . . . . . . .9 F8
Wellington Pl NG16 . . . . . .143 F2
Wellington Rd
Burton Joyce NG14 . . . . . . .164 A5
 Newark-on-T NG24 . . . . . .140 A8
Wellington Sq
Nottingham NG7 . . . . .222 C3
Retford DN22 . . . . .39 F7
Wellington St
Eastwood NG16 . . . . .143 F3
Gainsborough DN21 . . . . . . .24 D7
Long Eaton NG10 . . . . .182 C2
Loughborough LE11 . . . . . .220 C3
Nottingham NG3 . . . . .223 E4
Retford DN22 . . . . .39 F7
Stapleford NG9 . . . . .182 C6
Wellington Terr NG7 . . . . .222 C3
Wellington Villas NG7 . . . .222 C3
Wellin La NG12 . . . . .186 B3
Well La NG14 . . . . .210 A1
Wellow Cl NG17, NG19 . . . .101 D8
Wellow Gn NG22 . . . . .77 D1
Wellow House Sch NG22 . .77 D1
Wellow Rd
Eakring NG22 . . . . .92 E2
Wellow NG22 . . . . .77 C2
Wells Cl NG19 . . . . .88 D4
Wells Gdns NG3 . . . . .173 F6
Wells La DN22 . . . . .43 D5
Wellspring Dale NG9 . . . . .182 D5
Wells Rd Ctr Hospl NG3 . .161 F2
Wells Rd The NG3 . . . . .161 F1
Welshcroft Cl NG17 . . . . . .114 A6
Welstead Ave NG8 . . . . . . .160 B2
Welton Gdns NG6 . . . . .160 A8
Welwyn Ave NG18 . . . . .88 E4
Welwyn Rd NG8 . . . . .171 E5
Wembley Gdns NG9 . . . . . .171 B2
Wembley Rd
Arnold NG5 . . . . .162 B5
Langold S81 . . . . .16 F3
Wembley St DN21 . . . . .24 D8
Wemyss Gdns NG8 . . . . . . .172 D3
Wendling Gdns NG5 . . . . . .161 B8
Wendover Dr NG8 . . . . .160 B2
Wenham La NG17 . . . . .99 F4
Wenlock Cl NG16 . . . . .158 C8
Wenlock Dr NG2 . . . . .185 F5
Wensleydale Cl
Mansfield NG19 . . . . .88 E1
Nottingham NG8 . . . . .160 D1
Wensleydale Rd NG10 . . . .193 B6
Wensley Rd NG5 . . . . .161 E5
Wensor Ave NG9 . . . . .183 F8
Wentbridge Dr NG18 . . . . .103 A4
Wentworth Cl NG19 . . . . . . .88 F2
Wentworth Cnr NG24 . . . . .139 E5
Wentworth Croft DE55 . . .143 A3
Wentworth Ct NG16 . . . . . .158 E6
Wentworth Dr DN22 . . . . . . .39 D3
Wentworth Rd
Beeston NG9 . . . . .183 C6
Kirkby in A NG17 . . . . .114 E7
Wentworth St DE7 . . . . . . .158 A2
Wentworth Way NG12 . . . .186 C3
Wesleyan Chapel Wlk
NG9 . . . . .182 D7
Wesley Cl
Balderton NG24 . . . . .140 A3
Hathern LE12 . . . . .213 A1
Wesley Gr ⓰ NG5 . . . . . . .161 B1
Wesley Pl NG9 . . . . .182 E8
Wesley Rd DN22 . . . . .39 F7
Wesley St
Annesley Woodhouse
NG17 . . . . .130 A8
Ilkeston DE7 . . . . .157 E4
Langley Mill NG16 . . . . . . .143 C3
⓬ Nottingham NG5 . . . . . .161 B1
Wesley Way NG11 . . . . .196 D6
Wessex Cl S81 . . . . .36 A6
Wessex Rd S81 . . . . .36 A6
West Ave
Kirkby in A NG17 . . . . .115 C4

West Ave continued
Sandiacre NG10. . . . . .182 A6
Stapleford NG9. . . . . .182 E8
West Bridgford NG2 . . . . .185 E7
West Bank LN1 . . . . .56 F2
West Bank Ave NG18. . . . . . .102 B8
West Bank Link NG19 . . . . . . .88 B1
West Bank Lea NG19. . . . . .88 B1
West Bank Mews DE74. .203 C2
West Bank Wynd NG18. . .102 B8
Westbourne Cl
Retford DN22. . . . . .40 A6
Sutton in A NG17. . . . . .100 D3
Westbourne Rd
Selston NG16. . . . . .129 A2
Sutton in A NG17. . . . . .100 D3
Westbourne View NG17 . .100 D3
Westbrecks La DN22. . . . . . .43 A5
West Bridgford Inf Sch
NG2. . . . . .185 E7
West Bridgford Jun Sch
NG2. . . . . .185 F6
West Bridgford Sch The
NG2. . . . . .185 D5
Westbrook Ave NG15. . . . . .116 F3
West Brook La NG23. . . . . . .112 A6
West Burton Meadow Nature
Reserve DN22. . . . . .32 D7
West Burton Medieval
Village of DN22. . . . . .32 F7
Westbury Cl NG9 . . . . .183 C4
Westbury Rd NG5. . . . . .161 A2
Westbury Sch NG8. . . . . .171 E8
Westby La NG16 . . . . .158 D3
West Carr Rd DN22 . . . . .39 D6
West Cl NG12. . . . . .197 E2
Westcliffe Ave
Carlton NG4. . . . . .162 D3
Radcliffe on T NG12. . . . . . . .176 A4
West Cres
Beeston NG9. . . . . .184 B4
Kirkby in A NG17 . . . . .115 C4
Westcroft Dr LN1. . . . . .57 A5
Westcross Ave NG9 . . . . .182 E8
West Ct DN22. . . . . .39 D7
Westdale Ave NG17 . . . . .101 A5
Westdale Cl NG10. . . . . .193 A5
Westdale Cres NG4 . . . . .162 E1
Westdale Ct NG4 . . . . .162 D2
Westdale Jun Sch NG3. . . . .162 C3
Westdale La E NG4 . . . . .162 E1
Westdale La W NG3. . . . . .162 A3
Westdale Rd
Mansfield NG19. . . . . .88 B1
Westwood NG16 . . . . .128 C4
West Dr NG21 . . . . .76 A2
West End
Beeston NG9. . . . . .183 F5
Calverton NG14. . . . . .148 C2
Farndon NG24. . . . . .138 F4
Long Clawson LE14 . . . . .211 C3
Long Whatton LE12 . . . . .212 A4
Pinxton NG16. . . . . .113 C4
Sutton in A NG17. . . . . .100 E2
West End Arc NG1 . . . . .223 D2
West End Cl NG13 . . . . .181 A2
West End St NG9. . . . . .182 C5
Westerdale S81. . . . . .36 A8
Westerfield Way NG11 . . . .185 A5
Westerham Cl NG8 . . . . .171 D7
Westerham Rd NG11. . . . . . .196 B6
Westerlands NG9. . . . . .182 F6
Western Ave
Bingham NG13. . . . . .177 D5
Kirkby in A NG17 . . . . .115 B3
Mansfield NG18. . . . . .101 F5
Saxilby LN1 . . . . .56 F4
Western Bvd NG8 . . . . .172 D8
Western Fields NG11 . . . . . .196 B6
Western Gdns NG8. . . . . .172 D8
Western St NG1. . . . . .223 F3
Western Terr NG7 . . . . .222 C2
Western Wlk DN10. . . . . .10 A8
Westfield Cl
Mansfield NG19. . . . . .101 F8
Sutton in A NG17. . . . . .100 E2
Westfield Dr
Ilkeston DE7 . . . . .157 D2
Mansfield NG19. . . . . .101 E8
Worksop S81. . . . . .36 A5
Westfield La
Collingham NG23. . . . . .111 E8
Mansfield NG18, NG19 . . . . .101 E8
Woodborough NG14 . . . . . . .149 A4
Westfield Rd
Annesley Woodhouse
NG17. . . . . .115 B1
Bingham NG13. . . . . .177 D4
Retford DN22. . . . . .39 D6
Westfield Way NG24 . . . . . . .139 A4
West Furlong
Cotgrave NG12 . . . . .188 A2
Retford DN22. . . . . .39 D8
Westgate
Southwell NG25. . . . . .136 D8
Worksop S80. . . . . .35 E2
West Gate
Long Eaton NG10. . . . . .193 E6
 Mansfield NG18 . . . . .102 B7
Tickhill DN11. . . . . .8 A6
Westgate Ms NG25. . . . . . . .136 D8
Westgate St NG3 . . . . .173 E6
Westgate View S80. . . . . .35 E2

Westglade Jun & Inf Sch
NG5. . . . . .160 F8
West Gr Rd DN22 . . . . .39 F5
Westhay Ct NG8 . . . . .172 C5
West Hill
Mansfield NG18. . . . . .102 A8
Sutton in A NG17. . . . . .100 D6
West Hill Ave NG18 . . . . . . .102 B7
West Hill Pk NG19 . . . . .88 B3
West Hill Rd DN22 . . . . .39 D3
West Hill Wy NG18. . . . . .102 B7
Westholme Gdns NG8. . . . .172 C6
Westhorpe NG25. . . . . .136 C8
Westhorpe Ave NG5. . . . . . .173 F5
Westhorpe Dr NG10. . . . . . .193 C8
Westhorpe Mkt Pl NG25. .136 C8
West La
Edwinstowe NG21. . . . . .76 A2
Girton NG23. . . . . .82 E1
Westland Ave NG15. . . . . . . .145 D4
Westland Dr NG16 . . . . .113 C3
West Leake La NG11 . . . . . . .204 D5
West Leake Rd LE12 . . . . . . .205 C1
Westleigh NG19. . . . . .88 D6
Westleigh Rd NG8 . . . . .159 E2
Westminster Ave
Kirkby in A NG17 . . . . .115 C5
Stapleford NG10. . . . . .182 C5
Westminster Cl
Morton DN21. . . . . .15 B5
Nottingham NG3. . . . . .173 E7
Worksop S81. . . . . .36 A7
Westminster Dr NG12. . . . .176 E3
West Moor NG12. . . . . .174 D4
Westmoore Cl NG3. . . . . .162 A3
Westmoor La LN1. . . . . .55 D3
West Moor Rd DN10 . . . . . . .13 E6
Westmoreland Ct
NG5. . . . . .161 B1
Westmorland Ct DN11. . . . . .9 D4
Westmorland Dr S81. . . . . . .25 F8
West Nottinghamshire Coll
NG18. .102 C2
Weston Ave NG7 . . . . .173 A7
Weston Cl
Arnold NG5. . . . . .161 E4
Nottingham NG17. . . . . .115 C8
Weston La NG23. . . . . .81 D5
Weston Rd NG22,NG23 . . . .80 A6
Weston St DE75. . . . . .157 A8
West Pk L Ctr DE72 . . . . . . .193 B7
West Pk Pl DN22 . . . . .39 D6
Westray Cl NG9 . . . . .171 B3
West St
Arnold NG5. . . . . .161 E7
Harworth DN11. . . . . .9 A5
Hucknall NG15 . . . . .146 A7
Kimberley NG16. . . . . .159 A4
Langley Mill NG16 . . . . .143 B3
Misson DN10. . . . . .4 B2
Morton DN21. . . . . .15 B4
Nottingham NG2. . . . . .173 E4
Warsop Vale NG20 . . . . .73 D4
Whaley Thorns NG20. . . . . . . .59 A3
Worksop S80. . . . . .35 E2
West Terr
Hucknall NG15. . . . . .146 A7
 Ilkeston DE7. . . . . .157 F1
West Thorpe LE12. . . . . .217 C7
West View
Carlton in L S81. . . . . .25 F8
West Bridgford NG2 . . . . .185 D5
Westview Ct NG4 . . . . .174 F8
West View Rd NG4 . . . . .174 F8
Westville Dr NG15 . . . . .145 E4
Westville Gdns NG3. . . . . . . .173 D7
Westward Ave NG9. . . . . . . .184 A5
Westway
Cotgrave NG12 . . . . .187 F2
Worksop S80. . . . . .36 A7
West Wells La DN10. . . . . . . .12 E2
Westwick Rd NG8 . . . . .171 C5
Westwick St DE7 . . . . .170 A6
West Wlk
 Nottingham NG1. . . . . . .173 E4
Retford DN22. . . . . .39 C8
Westwood Dr S80. . . . . .35 B3
West Wood Est DN10. . . . . . . .9 F6
West Wood Jnf Sch NG16. .128 C4
Westwood Rd
Bircotes DN10. . . . . .9 F6
Nottingham NG2. . . . . .173 F4
Wetherby Cl
Kimberley NG16. . . . . .158 E7
Nottingham NG8. . . . . .160 B1
Wetherlam Cl NG2. . . . . .173 C2
Wetlands Waterfowl Reserve
DN22. . . . . .29 D7
Wetsyke La NG24 . . . . .140 E4
Whaddon Ct LE11. . . . . .220 C1
Whaley Bridge Cl NG18 . .103 C5
Whaley Comm S44. . . . . .58 D4
Whaley Rd NG20. . . . . .58 E2
Whaley Thorns Heritage Ctr
NG20. . . . . .59 A3
Whaley Thorns Prim Sch
NG20. . . . . .59 A3
Whardale Gdns NG18. . . . . .103 A5
Whardale Rd NG10. . . . . .193 A6
Wharfedale
Nottingham NG8 . . . . .172 B6
Worksop S81. . . . . .36 A7
Wharf La NG12 . . . . .175 E3
Wharf Rd
 Mansfield NG18. . . . . . . .102 B6
Misterton DN10. . . . . .6 F1

Wharf Rd continued
Nottingham NG7 . . . . .223 D1
Pinxton NG16. . . . . .113 D2
Retford DN22. . . . . .39 G6
Stanton Hill NG17 . . . . .100 C6
Wharf St DN10. . . . . .10 A7
Wharmby Ave NG19 . . . . . . .87 D3
Wharncliffe Rd
 Ilkeston DE7. . . . . .157 E1
Loughborough LE11. . . . . . . .220 C3
Retford DN22. . . . . .39 E4
Wharton St DN22 . . . . .40 A6
Whatton Gdns LE12 . . . . . . .212 E5
Whatton Ct NG18 . . . . .103 A3
Whatton Rd
Hathern LE12. . . . . .212 E2
Kegworth DE74. . . . . .203 C1
Whatton Rise NG5. . . . . .161 B4
Wheatacre Rd NG7 . . . . . . .184 F1
Wheat Cl NG8 . . . . .171 D5
Wheat Croft S81. . . . . .36 B7
Wheatcroft View NG11 . . .185 C3
Wheatfield Cres NG19. . . . . .88 E5
Wheatfield Dr DN11. . . . . .8 B3
Wheatfields Rd NG3 . . . . . .174 A7
Wheatfield Way NG17. . . . .100 F6
Wheatgrass Hall NG25,
NG23. .122 D4
Wheatgrass Rd NG9 . . . . . .183 B5
Wheatland Dr LE11 . . . . .220 C2
Wheatley Ave NG17. . . . . . .114 F5
Wheatley Cl
Mansfield Woodhouse
NG19. .88 F1
Ruddington NG11. . . . . .196 C5
Wheatley Dr NG4 . . . . .174 C7
Wheatley Gr NG9 . . . . .183 F4
Wheatley La NG23. . . . . .112 B4
Wheatley Rd
Clayworth DN22 . . . . .21 F3
Sturton le S DN22 . . . . .32 B6
Wheatsheaf Av NG4. . .125 B4
Wheatsheaf Ct NG14 . . . . . .163 F4
Wheeldale Cl NG8. . . . . .171 B4
Wheeldon St DN21. . . . . .24 D7
Wheeler Ave NG16. . . . . .144 B1
Wheeler Gate
Nottingham NG1. . . . . .223 E2
Selston NG16. . . . . .129 A2
Wheldon Ave NG4 . . . . .162 C2
Wheldon Sch The NG4 . . .162 C1
Whernside Rd NG5 . . . . .161 F5
Whetstone Cl NG8. . . . . .159 D3
Whickham St NG4 . . . . .173 D1
Whilton Cl NG17. . . . . .101 B5
Whimpton Medieval Village
of NG22. . . . . .67 A2
Whimsey Pk NG4 . . . . .174 E6
Whinbush La NG14. . . . . .133 D4
Whinfell Cl NG7 . . . . .184 F2
Whinlatter Dr NG2. . . . . . . .186 C6
Whinleys Rd DN22 . . . . .31 A2
Whinney Bank NG19. . . . . . .88 D4
Whinney Hill NG17. . . . . .101 A5
Whinney La NG22 . . . . .77 D5
Whinney Moor Cl DN22 . . .39 F5
Whinney Moor La DN22. . .39 F5
Whinney Moor Way DN22 . .39 F5
Whiston Cl NG5 . . . . .161 A6
Whitaker Cl DN22. . . . . .29 C1
Whitbread St NG7 . . . . .172 F8
Whitburn Rd NG9. . . . . .182 E3
Whitby Cl NG8. . . . . .171 B4
Whitby Cres NG5 . . . . .162 A5
Whitby Rd
Eastwood NG16 . . . . .144 A3
Harworth DN11. . . . . .9 A5
Whitchurch Cl NG5 . . . . .160 F8
Whitcombe Cl DN22 . . . . . . .40 A4
Whitcombe Gdns
NG5. . . . . .147 A1
White Ave S81. . . . . .16 E3
Whitebeam Gdns NG6. . . .159 F7
Whitechapel St NG6 . . . . . .160 D2
White Furrows NG12 . . . . . .187 E2
Whitegate LE11. . . . . .220 C5
Whitegate Prim Sch
NG11. .184 D1
Whitegates Further Ed Unit
S80. . . . . .35 F1
Whitegates Way NG17 . . . . .99 E2
Whitegate Vale NG11. . . . . .184 D1
Whitehall Cl DN22 . . . . .39 E6
Whitehall Gdns DN22 . . . . .39 F6
Whitehall Rd DN22. . . . . .39 F6
White Hart La NG23. . . . . . . .112 A8
White Hart St NG18. . . . . . .102 B6
White Hart St S80. . . . . .35 E1
Whitehead Cl DE7 . . . . .157 D2
Whitehead Dr NG16. . . . . . .143 D8
Whitehead La NG17. . . . . . . .100 F6
Whitehouse Ave LE11 . . . . .220 C2
White House Rd DN11 . . . . . . .9 F4
Whitehouses Rd DN22 . . . .40 A4
Whitelands NG12 . . . . .188 A2
White Lodge Gdns NG8 . .171 D7
Whitely Cl NG9 . . . . .182 E7
Whitemoor Ave NG8 . .172 D8
Whitemoor Ct NG8. . . . . .172 D8
Whitemoor La NG23 . . . . . . .112 A4
Whitemoor Prim Sch
NG8. . . . . .160 D1
Whitemoor Rd NG6 . . . . . . .160 D2
Whitemoss Cl NG8. . . . . .171 E3
White Post Farm Ctr The
NG22. .119 B7
White Rd NG5. . . . . .160 F3
White's Ave NG4 . . . . .174 B6

Whitestone Cl NG18 . . . . . .103 A3
Whitestub La NG22 . . . . . . .106 F5
Whites Wood La DN21 . . . . .24 E8
White's Wood La NG21. .24 E8
Whitewater Cl NG22 . . . . . . .77 C5
Whitewater La NG22 . . . . . . .77 C5
Whitewates Rd NG22. . . . . .77 C5
Whitewates La S81. . . . . .18 A5
Whitfield Cl NG11. . . . . .185 B6
Whitfield St NG24. . . . . .140 A7
Whiting Ave NG9 . . . . .182 F2
Whitney Cl NG19. . . . . .89 A1
Whitsun Dale S81. . . . . .36 B8
Whittaker Rd
Beeston NG9 . . . . .183 A3
Rainworth NG21 . . . . .118 A8
Whittier Rd NG2 . . . . .174 A3
Whittingham Cl NG3. . . . . .162 A3
Whittingham Rd NG3 . . . . .162 A3
Whittle Cl NG24 . . . . .125 C2
Whitton Cl
 Beeston NG9 . . . . .183 C2
 Nottingham NG5. . . . . . .147 B1
Ranskill DN22 . . . . .19 B4
Whitwell Cl NG8 . . . . .159 E1
Whitwell Prim Sch S80. . . .45 A5
Whitwell Rd
Nottingham NG8 . . . . .159 E1
Thorpe Salvin S80. . . . . .34 A4
Whitwell Sta S80. . . . . .45 A5
Whitworth Dr
Carlton NG4. . . . . .163 C2
Radcliffe on T NG12. . . . . . . .175 F2
Whitworth Rise NG5 . . . . . .160 F8
Whomsley Cl NG24. . . . . .140 D8
Whyburn La NG15 . . . . .145 D7
Whyburn Prim Sch NG15 .145 E8
Whyston Ct NG15. . . . . .145 C5
Wibberley Dr NG11. . . . . . . .196 B7
Wichnor Cl NG11 . . . . .184 E4
Wickens Wlk NG3. . . . . .173 E6
Wickerwood Dr NG17 . . . . .114 E6
Wicket Gr NG7. . . . . .222 A2
Wickstead Cl NG5 . . . . .161 F3
Widdowson Cl NG6 . . . . . . .159 F8
Widecombe La NG11. . . . . . .195 D8
Wide La
Hathern LE12. . . . . .213 A1
Wymeswold LE12. . . . . .217 C3
Wide St LE12 . . . . .213 A1
Widmerpool La LE12 . . . . . .217 D8
Widmerpool Rd NG12 . . . . .207 E3
Widmerpool St NG16. . . . . .113 C2
Wighay Rd NG15. . . . . .132 A5
Wigley Cl NG3 . . . . .173 E6
Wigman Rd NG8 . . . . .171 E7
Wigsley Rd
Harby NG23. . . . . .70 C2
North Scarle LN6. . . . . .83 D5
Wigthorpe La S81. . . . . .26 A4
Wigwam Gr NG15 . . . . .146 C7
Wigwam La NG15 . . . . .146 C7
Wilberforce Rd NG19 . . . . . .87 D2
Wilcox Ave NG15 . . . . .88 B5
Wilcox Dr NG16. . . . . .129 A1
Wilde Cres NG16. . . . . .129 A6
Wilden Cres NG7 . . . . .184 E2
Wildflower Gr NG17. . . . . . .100 D1
Wild Hill NG17. . . . . .99 E7
Wildman St NG7 . . . . .222 C4
Wildman Villas DN10. . . . . .14 B1
Wilford Cl NG24. . . . . .140 B8
Wilford Cres NG11 . . . . .196 C8
Wilford Cres E NG2 . . . . . . .173 D1
Wilford Cres W NG2. . . . . . .173 C1
Wilford Gr
Nottingham NG2 . . . . .173 C1
West Bridgford NG2 . . . . .185 D8
Wilford La NG2 . . . . .185 C2
Wilford Sports Complex
NG2. . . . . .185 D6
Wilford St NG2 . . . . .223 E1
Wilfred Ave NG24 . . . . .140 C4
Wilfrid Gr NG2 . . . . .185 E4
Wilhallow La NG16 . . . . .128 E2
Wilkins Gdns NG11. . . . . . . .184 C1
Wilkinson Ave NG9 . . . . . . .183 F6
Wilkinson Cl NG17 . . . . .87 A5
Wilkinson St NG7. . . . . .172 E8
Willand Ct DN22 . . . . .29 E1
Willaston Cl NG6 . . . . .160 C4
Willbert Rd NG5 . . . . .148 A1
Willerby Rd NG5. . . . . .162 A5
Willersley Dr NG2 . . . . .173 C2
Willesden Gr NG16 . . . . .159 D3
Willetts Ct NG17. . . . . .100 F1
Willey La NG16. . . . . .144 A8
William Ave NG16. . . . . .143 F2
William Booth Birthplace
Mus NG2. . . . . .173 E4
William Booth Inf Sch
NG2. . . . . .173 E4
William Booth Rd NG2 . . .174 A4
William Bradford Cl DN10 . .3 C1
William Cl NG4 . . . . .175 B8
William & Henry Mews
LN6. . . . . .84 C3
William Lilley Inf Sch
NG9. . . . . .182 D6
William Old Ct NG8 . . .172 A5
William Rd
Stapleford NG9 . . . . .182 D7
West Bridgford NG2 . . . . .185 E8

William Sharp Sch NG8 . .171 C7
Williams La NG22 . . . . .140 E2
Williamson St NG19. . . . . . .101 E7
Williams Rd NG9. . . . . .183 B3
Williams St S81. . . . . .16 E3
William St
Hucknall NG15. . . . . .146 A7
Long Eaton NG10. . . . . .182 C3
Loughborough LE11. . . . . . . .220 A3
Newark-on-T NG24 . . . . .140 A8
Saxilby LN1 . . . . .57 A3
Willingham Rd DN21. . . . . . .24 F2
Willis Rd NG24 . . . . .139 F6
Willoughby Ave
Long Eaton NG10. . . . . .182 C3
Nottingham NG7 . . . . .222 B2
Willoughby Chase DN21 . .24 E5
Willoughby Cl NG7. . . . . . . .184 B8
Willoughby Ct
 Mansfield NG18 . . . . . . .103 A2
Norwell NG23 . . . . .110 A8
Nottingham NG7 . . . . .222 B1
Willoughby Prim Sch
LE14. . . . . .217 C7
Willoughby Rd
West Bridgford NG2 . . . . .185 D8
Widmerpool NG12. . . . . .208 C3
Willoughby St
Beeston NG9 . . . . .184 A6
Cossall DE7 . . . . .158 A2
Gainsborough DN21. . . . . .24 D7
Nottingham NG7 . . . . .222 B1
Willoughby Way NG7. . . . . .64 B2
Willow Ave
Carlton in L S81. . . . . .25 C7
Carlton NG4. . . . . .175 A8
Hucknall NG15 . . . . .145 D4
Kirkby in A NG17 . . . . .114 E6
Long Eaton NG10. . . . . .182 C2
Mansfield Woodhouse NG19 .88 A3
Misterton DN10. . . . . .6 E2
Shirebrook NG20. . . . . .72 D5
Stapleford NG9. . . . . .182 E8
Willowbridge Cl DN22. . . . .39 E6
Willowbridge La NG17 . . .100 D2
Willow Brook NG2 . . . . .198 A2
Willowbrook Ct NG2. .173 C1
Willow Brook Prim Sch
NG12. .198 A2
Willow Cl
Burton Joyce NG14. . . . . .163 F5
East Leake NG11 . . . . .214 D8
Gainsborough DN21. . . . . .15 B3
Radcliffe on T NG12. . . . . . . .175 F2
Saxilby LN1 . . . . .57 B3
Selston NG16. . . . . .129 B7
South Normanton DE55. . . . .113 B5
Worksop S80. . . . . .35 C1
Willow Cres
Carlton NG4. . . . . .163 A2
Lambley NG4 . . . . .163 C7
Sutton in A NG17. . . . . .100 D3
Willow Ct NG16. . . . . .129 A1
Willowdene NG12. . . . . .188 A3
Willow Dr
Annesley Woodhouse
NG15. . . . . .129 F6
North Muskham NG23 . . . . . .110 E2
Willow Farm Prim Sch
NG4. . . . . .163 A2
Willow Gd NG17. . . . . .101 B2
Willow Hill Cl NG6 . . . . .160 A6
Willow Holt
Lowdham NG14 . . . . .150 C1
Retford DN22. . . . . .39 E3
Willow La
Carlton NG4. . . . . .163 A2
Langar NG13. . . . . .190 C2
Willow Pool La LE12 . . . . . .213 C5
Willow Rd
Bingham NG13. . . . . .178 A4
Carlton NG4. . . . . .175 A8
New Balderton NG24 . . . . . . .140 C5
Nottingham NG7 . . . . .172 E2
West Bridgford NG2 . . . . .185 E3
Willow Rise NG10. . . . . .182 B5
Willows The
Farndon NG24. . . . . .139 A4
Nottingham NG8 . . . . .172 A7
Pleasley NG19 . . . . .87 A6
Willow Tree Cl NG19 . . . . . . .89 D2
Willow Wong NG14 . . . . . . .163 F5
Will Scarlet Cl NG21 . . . . . .118 A4
Willwell Dr NG2 . . . . .185 C3
Wilmington Ct LE11. . . . . . . .220 C2
Wilmington Gdns NG5 . . . .161 D6
Wilmore Way NG19. . . . . . . .101 C5
Wilmot La NG9 . . . . .183 F5
Wilmot St
Ilkeston DE7 . . . . .157 E1
Long Eaton NG10. . . . . .193 A5
Wilne Ave NG10 . . . . .193 A4
Wilne Rd NG10 . . . . .193 A4
Wilsic Rd DN11 . . . . .8 F4
Wilson Ave NG17 . . . . .114 F5
Wilson Cl
Arnold NG5. . . . . .162 B5
Mattersey DN10 . . . . .20 A8
Wilson Rd NG16 . . . . .143 F1
Wilson's La NG25 . . . . .137 E4
Wilson St
Gainsborough DN21. . . . . .15 B1
Newark-on-T NG24 . . . . .124 F1
Pinxton NG16. . . . . .113 D3
Radmanthwaite NG19 . . . . . . .87 B3
Wilsthorpe Com Sch
NG10. .182 B1
Wilsthorpe Rd DE72. . . . . . .193 A8

Wilton Ave LE11 . . . . 220 C1
Wilton Pl DE7 . . . . 157 F1
Wilton Rd NG7. . . . . 222 A4
Wilton St
 5 Ilkeston DE7 . . . . .157 F1
 Nottingham NG6. . . . . .160 E4
Wilton Terr NG1 . . . . .160 E4
Wiltshire Ave NG16 . . . . . . .128 B4
Wilwell Farm Cutting Nature
 Reserve NG1. . . . . .185 B2
Wimbishthorpe Cl NG13. .181 A3
Wimbledon Dr NG1 . . . . . .159 E3
Wimbledon Rd NG5. . . . . . .161 A3
Wimborne Cl NG2 . . . . .185 C5
Wimbourne Rd NG7. . . . . . .222 B4
Wimpole Rd NG9 . . . . .171 D1
Winborne Cl NG19. . . . . . . .101 D6
Winchester Ave NG9 . . . . .183 E7
Winchester Cl
 East Leake LE12 . . . . .205 E1
 Mansfield NG18. . . . . .103 A3
 Worksop S81. . . . . .36 A7
Winchester Cres DE7 . . . .170 A8
Winchester Ct NG5 . . . . . . .161 E3
Winchester Dr NG16. . . . . .158 D6
Winchester St NG5. . . . . . .161 D2
Winchester Terr 7 NG5. .161 C3
Winchilsea Ave NG4 . . . . .140 A7
Windermere Ave DN11. . . . . 8 F4
Windermere Cl
 Carlton NG4. . . . . .162 F2
 West Bridgford NG2 . . . . . .186 C6
 Worksop S81. . . . . .35 E8
Windermere Gdns NG10. .182 B2
Windermere Rd
 Beeston NG9 . . . . .183 D8
 Hucknall NG15. . . . . .145 F7
 Long Eaton NG10. . . . . .182 A2
 Nottingham NG7 . . . . .173 A8
Windley Dr DE7. . . . . .157 D3
Windmill Ave NG15 . . . . . .146 A6
Windmill Cl NG3 . . . . .173 F5
Windmill Ct NG12. . . . . .197 F2
Windmill Gr NG15. . . . . .146 A6
Windmill Hill NG25 . . . . . . .134 C5
Windmill La
 Mansfield NG18. . . . . .102 C8
 Nottingham NG2 . . . . .173 F5
 Worksop S80. . . . . .47 B7
Windmill Rd LE11 . . . . .220 D3
Windmill Way DE74. . . . . . .203 B2
Windrush Cl NG9 . . . . .171 D1
Windsmoor Rd NG16 . . . . .143 D8
Windsor Ave
 Newark-on-T NG24 . . . . . . .139 E6
 Sutton in A NG17 . . . . .100 B3
Windsor Cl
 Collingham NG23. . . . . .112 A8
 Gringley on t H DN10 . . . . .12 E2
 Hucknall NG15. . . . . .146 B8
 Trowell NG9 . . . . .170 A5
Windsor Cres
 Arnold NG5. . . . . .162 B5
 Stapleford NG9 . . . . .182 E7
Windsor Ct
 Bingham NG13. . . . . .177 C4
 Newark-on-T NG24 . . . . 9 B5
 Sandiacre NG10. . . . . .182 B4
Windsor Dr NG20 . . . . .74 A4
Windsor Gdns
 Carlton in L S81. . . . . .25 E6
 Mansfield NG18. . . . . .102 D5
Windsor Rd
 Carlton in L S81. . . . . .25 E6
 Clipstone NG19 . . . . .89 D3
 Mansfield NG18. . . . . .102 D5
 Newark-on-T NG24 . . . . . . .139 E6
 Retford DN22. . . . . .29 C1
 Selston NG16. . . . . .129 A8
 Worksop S81. . . . . .35 D7
Windsor St
 Beeston NG9 . . . . .184 A6
 Stapleford NG9 . . . . .182 E7
Windyridge DN10 . . . . .11 C3
Windy Ridge NG20 . . . . .74 C3
Wing Alley NG1 . . . . .223 F2
Wingate Cl NG8 . . . . .171 F6
Wingbourne Wlk NG6. . . .146 C1
Wingfield Ave S81. . . . . .36 A6
Wingfield Dr
 Beeston NG9 . . . . .172 A1
 Ilkeston DE7 . . . . .157 D3
Wingfield Rd NG18. . . . . . .103 A4
Wings Dr NG15 . . . . .145 D3
Winifred Cres NG14. . . . . .163 F4
Winifred St
 Hucknall NG15. . . . . .146 B6
 Rhodesia S80. . . . . .35 A4
Winkburn La NG22. . . . . . . .121 E7
Winkburn Rd NG19 . . . . . .101 F7
Winnery Cl DN11. . . . . .8 A8
Winrow Gdns NG6 . . . . . . .160 C3
Winscale Ave NG5 . . . . . . .161 A8
Winscale Gdns 15 NG5. .161 A8
Winscombe Mount NG11.195 E7
Winsford Cl NG8. . . . . .160 B2
Winstanley Dr NG24. . . . . .140 E8
Winster Ave
 Carlton NG4. . . . . .162 D1
 Ravenshead NG15. . . . . . . .117 B3
Winster Cl NG9 . . . . .171 F1
Winster Gr S81. . . . . .35 F8
Winster Way NG18 . . . . . . .103 C5
Winston Cl
 Arnold NG3 . . . . .162 C5
 Stapleford NG9 . . . . .182 E8
Winston Ct NG24. . . . . .139 E5

Winston Dr NG23 . . . . .153 E4
Winston Gn DN10. . . . . .19 F8
Winston Gr DN22. . . . . .30 A1
Winterbank Cl NG17 . . . . .100 D1
Winterbeck Cl NG13 . . . . .181 A3
Winterbourne Dr NG9. . . .170 E1
Winter Closes NG16. . . . . .128 F1
Winterdale Cl NG24. . . . . .125 D1
Wintern Ct DN21. . . . . .24 D6
Winterton Cl NG5. . . . . . . .161 F6
Winterton Rise NG5. . . . . .161 F6
Winthorpe Prim Sch
 NG24. . . . . .125 D7
Winthorpe Rd
 Arnold NG5 . . . . .162 A7
 Gateford S81. . . . . .35 C8
 Newark-on-T NG24 . . . . . . .125 B7
Winthorpe St NG19 . . . . . .101 D6
Wintringham Cres NG5. .162 A5
Wire La DE55. . . . . .99 B3
Wisa Terr NG5. . . . . .161 D2
Wiseton Dr DN22. . . . . .21 C6
Wishford Ave NG7 . . . . . . .222 A1
Wisley Cl NG11 . . . . .185 C3
Wistow Cl NG8 . . . . .172 E8
Witch La NG23 . . . . .98 C2
Witham Cl NG24 . . . . .125 B2
Withern Rd NG8 . . . . .159 F1
Withorn Mews NG19 . . . . .101 E7
Witney Cl NG5. . . . . .160 E7
Wittering Rd NG10 . . . . . . .193 E5
Wiverton Rd
 Bingham NG13. . . . . .177 E4
 Nottingham NG7 . . . . .173 A8
Woburn Ave NG17 . . . . . . .115 C5
Woburn Cl NG2. . . . . .186 C4
Woburn Croft NG10. . . . . .182 A4
Woburn Gr DN22. . . . . .39 E3
Woburn La NG19. . . . . .87 C4
Woburn Pl NG19. . . . . .87 C4
Woburn Rd NG19 . . . . .87 C4
Woburn Rise NG5. . . . . . . .162 B5
Wodehouse Ave NG11. . . .195 B2
Wolds Dr NG12. . . . . .197 F3
Wolds Rise NG12. . . . . .197 F3
Wolfit Ave NG4 . . . . .140 E5
Wollacombe Cl NG3 . . . . .162 D5
Wollaton Ave NG4 . . . . . . .162 E2
Wollaton Cl NG18. . . . . .103 B7
Wollaton Cres NG6. . . . . . .183 E8
Wollaton Ct NG6. . . . . .160 E6
Wollaton Hall NG8 . . . . . . .172 A3
Wollaton Hall Dr NG8 . . .172 D3
Wollaton Paddocks NG8.171 C4
Wollaton Pk NG8 . . . . .171 F3
Wollaton Rd
 Beeston NG9 . . . . .183 E7
 Kirkby in A NG17 . . . . .115 C5
 Nottingham NG8 . . . . .172 D5
Wollaton Rise NG8. . . . . . .171 E4
Wollaton St NG1. . . . . .223 D3
Wollaton Vale NG8. . . . . . .171 E2
Wolseley Ct NG17. . . . . .100 F3
Wolsey Ave NG7 . . . . .222 B3
Wolsey Dr NG17 . . . . .115 B7
Wolsey Rd NG24 . . . . .125 B3
Wolsey Way 1 LE11 . . . . .220 C4
Wonderland Pleasure Pk
 NG22. . . . . .119 B7
Wong La DN11. . . . . .8 A8
Wood Ave
 Creswell S80. . . . . .58 C8
 Sandiacre NG10. . . . . .182 A5
Woodbank Dr NG8. . . . . . . .171 D2
Woodbeck Rise DN22. . . . . .39 E8
Woodborough La NG5. . . .148 C3
Woodborough Rd
 Mansfield NG18. . . . . .87 E1
 Nottingham NG3, NG1 . . . .161 E2
Woodbridge Ave NG11. . . .184 E3
Woodbridge Cl DE75. . . . .143 B1
Woodchurch Rd NG5. . . . .147 B1
Wood Cl NG18. . . . . .102 F8
Woodcoates Rd NG22. . . . . .67 B5
Wooden Beck Hill DN10. .13 C4
Wood End Dr NG15 . . . . . . .117 A2
Woodfield Rd
 Gainsborough DN21. . . . . . . 15 F1
 Nottingham NG8 . . . . .159 E1
 Pinxton NG16. . . . . .113 D4
Woodford Cl NG5. . . . . .146 E1
Woodford Rd
 Arnold NG5 . . . . .162 A5
 Hucknall NG15. . . . . .146 B6
Wood Gate LE11. . . . . .220 B3
Woodgate Ct NG7. . . . . . . .222 C3
Woodgate La
 Beckingham LN5 . . . . .142 E8
 Cotgrave NG12 . . . . .187 D3
Woodgate Rd LE12. . . . . . .214 C8
Woodhall Cl
 4 Kirkby in A NG17 . . . . .114 E7
 Mansfield NG18. . . . . .102 F8
Woodhall Cres LN1. . . . . . . .56 F4
Woodhall Gdns NG18. . . . .102 F8
Woodhall Gn DN22. . . . . . . .39 D2
Woodhall Rd NG8. . . . . .172 B5
Woodhead Cl NG21. . . . . . . .76 B1
Woodhedge Dr NG3. . . . . .174 A8
Wood Hill LE14 . . . . .218 E3
Woodhill Ave DN21. . . . . . . .15 E2
Woodhouse Ct NG23 . . . . . .98 A1
Woodhouse La
 Carlton in L S81. . . . . .26 A7
 Sutton in A NG17. . . . . .101 A7

Woodhouse Pl NG22 . . . . . .66 A2
Woodhouse Rd NG18. . . . .102 B8
Woodhouse St NG3. . . . . . .173 F5
Woodhouse Way NG16 . . .159 D3
Woodkirk Rd NG7. . . . . .184 F2
Wood La
 Barkestone-le-V NG13. . . . .192 C1
 Beckingham DN10 . . . . .23 B8
 Carlton NG4. . . . . .163 A2
 Creswell S80. . . . . .58 D8
 Egmanton NG22. . . . . .79 F5
 Gringley on t H DN10 . . . . .12 E3
 Grove DN22. . . . . .41 E4
 Hucknall NG15. . . . . .145 F7
 Kersall NG22. . . . . .94 A1
 Kingston-on-S NG11. . . . . .204 F7
 Market Warsop NG20 . . . . .73 F7
 North Wheatley DN22 . . . . .22 D1
 Shirebrook NG19 . . . . .72 E1
 South Scarle NG23 . . . . . . .98 E6
Woodland Ave
 Gainsborough DN21. . . . . . .15 B3
 Huthwaite NG17 . . . . .99 E4
 Ilkeston DE7 . . . . .157 D4
 Worksop S80. . . . . .36 B1
Woodland Cl
 Clipstone NG21 . . . . .90 B4
 Cotgrave NG12 . . . . .187 F2
 Farnsfield NG22. . . . . .120 A6
 Radcliffe on T NG12. . . . . .176 B3
Woodland Cres NG18 . . . .102 F4
Woodland Dr
 Mansfield NG18. . . . . .102 F4
 Nottingham NG3 . . . . .161 D2
 Nuthall NG16. . . . . .159 F4
 Southwell NG25. . . . . .121 D1
 Worksop S81. . . . . .35 E6
Woodland Gr
 Arnold NG5 . . . . .161 D4
 Beeston NG9 . . . . .183 D5
 Carlton NG4. . . . . .174 F6
 Mansfield Woodhouse NG19 88 C4
 Market Warsop NG20 . . . . .74 B4
Woodland Rd
 Mansfield NG18. . . . . .102 F8
 West Bridgford NG2 . . . . . .173 F1
Woodland Rise NG15. . . . .117 A2
Woodlands NG24 . . . . .125 D7
Woodlands Cl
 Newark-on-T NG24 . . . . . . .139 E6
 Wymeswold LE12. . . . . .216 C3
Woodlands Dr LE11 . . . . . .220 A2
Woodlands Farm Cl
 NG15. . . . . .145 D4
Woodlands Gr NG15 . . . . .145 D4
Woodlands Sch NG8 . . . . .172 A8
Woodlands The
 Blyth S81. . . . . .18 B6
 Mansfield NG18. . . . . .88 B1
 Nottingham NG6 . . . . .160 D5
 Whaley Thorns NG20 . . . . .59 A3
Woodlands Way NG17 . . . .100 C3
Woodland View
 Southwell NG25. . . . . .136 D8
 Whaley Thorns NG20 . . . . .59 A3
Woodland Way NG16. . . . .143 E2
Woodland Wlk NG17. . . . . .115 D5
Woodlane Gdns NG3 . . . . .173 F7
Woodley Sq NG6 . . . . .146 E2
Woodley St NG11 . . . . .196 C7
Wood Link NG6. . . . . .159 E7
Wood Nook Cl NG15. . . . . .128 F6
Woodpecker Cl NG13 . . . .177 F3
Woodpecker Dr NG21. . . . .118 B8
Woodrow Av NG8 . . . . .172 A8
Woodruff La NG22 . . . . . . .106 A5
Woodsend Cl NG14 . . . . . .163 F4
Woodsetts La S81 . . . . .25 A1
Woodsford Gr NG11. . . . . .184 D2
Woods Foundation CE Prim
 Sch NG14 . . . . .149 B4
Woods Hill NG17. . . . . .100 E3
Woodside
 Eastwood NG16. . . . . .143 E3
 Farnsfield NG22. . . . . .119 A6
 Retford DN22. . . . . .39 C8
 Sutton in A NG17 . . . . .100 E7
Woodside Ave
 Mansfield NG18. . . . . .102 D3
 Nuthall NG16. . . . . .159 B5
 Radcliffe on T NG12. . . . . .176 B3
Woodside Cres
 Ilkeston DE7 . . . . .157 D5
 Long Eaton NG10. . . . . .193 B8
Woodside Dr NG5. . . . . .161 D8
Woodside Rd
 Beeston, Chilwell NG9. . . . .183 B3
 Beeston NG9 . . . . .183 F8
 Burton Joyce NG14 . . . . . .163 D3
 Radcliffe on T NG12. . . . . .176 B3
 Ravenshead NG15 . . . . . . .116 F3
 Sandiacre NG10. . . . . .182 B5
 Shirebrook NG20. . . . . .72 E5
 Woodside View DN11. . . . . . .9 B4
Woods La NG14 . . . . .148 E7
Wood's La NG23 . . . . .153 A1
Wood St
 Arnold NG5 . . . . .161 F8
 Eastwood NG16. . . . . .143 F3
 Ilkeston DE7 . . . . .157 F1
 Mansfield NG18. . . . . .102 A7
 Market Warsop NG20 . . . . .74 B5
 Newark-on-T NG24 . . . . . . .140 B8
 Nottingham NG7 . . . . .222 C3
Woods Terr DN21. . . . . .15 C2
Woodstock Ave NG7 . . . . .222 A4

Woodstock Cl NG24. . . . . .140 C8
Woodstock Rd NG9. . . . . . .182 F3
Woodstock St NG15. . . . . .146 B6
Woodston Wlk NG5 . . . . . .148 A2
Woodthorpe Ave
 Arnold NG5. . . . . .161 E4
 Loughborough LE11. . . . . . .220 B1
Woodthorpe Ct NG5. . . . . .161 E3
Woodthorpe Dr NG3. . . . . .161 E3
Woodthorpe Gdns NG5. .161 F3
Woodthorpe Rd
 Loughborough LE11. . . . . . .220 B1
 Nottingham NG3 . . . . .161 F3
Woodview NG12 . . . . .188 A2
Wood View NG12. . . . . .186 B4
Woodview Bsns Ctr 15
 NG5 .147 A1
Woodville Rd NG3. . . . . . . .161 C3
Woodville Dr NG5. . . . . . . .161 C3
Woodville Rd 2 NG5. . . . .161 C3
Woodward St NG2. . . . . . . .173 D1
Woodwards The NG24. . . .140 C6
Woodyard La NG8 . . . . .172 A5
Wooliscroft Way DE7. . . . .157 C2
Woollaton St NG15. . . . . . .146 B7
Woolmer Rd NG2. . . . . .173 C1
Woolpack La NG1 . . . . .223 F2
Woolpack St DN22. . . . . . . .39 F7
Woolsington Cl NG8 . . . . .159 D2
Woolsthorpe Cl 2 NG8 . .172 A6
Wootton Cl
 East Leake LE12 . . . . .205 E2
 Nottingham NG8 . . . . .171 D7
Worcester Ave NG18 . . . . . .88 C6
Worcester Cl
 Lowdham NG14. . . . . .150 E1
 Worksop S80. . . . . .36 A7
Worcester Gdns NG5. . . . .161 E5
Worcester Mews NG19 . . .88 C4
Worcester Rd NG5. . . . . . . .161 E5
Wordsworth Ave
 Hucknall NG15. . . . . .145 D6
 Mansfield Woodhouse NG19 88 C4
 Sutton in A NG17 . . . . .101 A3
Wordsworth Dr NG24 . . . .140 D5
Wordsworth Rd
 Arnold NG5 . . . . .161 D7
 Awsworth NG16. . . . . .158 C4
 Nottingham NG7 . . . . .222 A4
 West Bridgford NG2 . . . . . .185 E6
Workhouse The NG25 . . . .122 A1
Worksop Coll S80. . . . . .47 E7
Worksop L Ctr S81. . . . . . . .35 E6
Worksop Mus S80. . . . . . . .35 F2
Worksop Priory CE Prim Sch
 S80. .35 F1
Worksop Rd
 Babworth DN22. . . . . .49 C7
 Blyth S81. . . . . .18 A2
 Cuckney NG20 . . . . .60 A4
 Edwinstowe NG21, NG22. .76 D5
 Nottingham NG3 . . . . .173 F5
 Whitwell S80 . . . . .45 A7
 Woodsetts S81 . . . . .25 A2
 Worksop Sta S80 . . . . .35 F4
Worrall Ave
 Arnold NG5 . . . . .161 F7
 Long Eaton NG10. . . . . .182 E1
Worsborough Cl NG18 . . .101 C4
Worthington Rd NG24. . . .140 E3
Worth St NG4. . . . . .174 E8
Wortley Ave NG9. . . . . .170 D3
Wortley Cl DE7 . . . . .170 A8
Wortley Hall Cl NG7 . . . . .172 C2
Wostruff La NG22 . . . . .106 A5
Wossock La LE12 . . . . .205 F1
Woulds Field NG12 . . . . . .187 F1
Wray Cl NG3 . . . . .173 E5
Wren Ct
 Long Eaton NG10. . . . . .193 A4
 Worksop S81. . . . . .35 C7
Wrenthorpe Vale NG11 . . .195 E8
Wrightson Cl NG17 . . . . . .101 B3
Wrights Orch NG12 . . . . . .197 E2
Wright St
 Carlton NG4. . . . . .175 A7
 Newark-on-T NG24 . . . . . . .140 A7
Wright Wilson St DN22. . . .39 F6
Wroot Rd DN9. . . . . .1 B6
Wroughton Ct NG16. . . . . .144 A2
Wroxham Dr NG8 . . . . .171 D2
Wycar Rd NG22. . . . . .106 A4
Wychwood Dr NG9. . . . . . .170 D2
Wychwood Rd NG13 . . . . .177 C4
Wycliffe Gr NG3 . . . . .161 E2
Wycliffe St NG7. . . . . .160 F1
Wycombe Cl NG11. . . . . . . .195 D8
Wye Gdns NG7 . . . . .172 D6
Wyggeston Rd NG13 . . . . .181 B2
Wykeham Rd NG5. . . . . . . .162 A5
Wyke La NG24 . . . . .138 F5
Wykes Ave NG4 . . . . .162 F2
Wymeswold CE Sch
 LE12. . . . . .216 C3
Wymeswold Ind Est
 LE12. . . . . .216 A1
Wymeswold Meadows Nature
 Reserve LE12 . . . . .216 C3
Wymeswold Rd
 Hoton LE12 . . . . .215 E2
 Rempstone LE12. . . . . .215 E5
 Wysall NG12 . . . . .207 C2
Wymondham Cl NG5. . . . .162 A6
Wynbreck Dr NG3. . . . . . . .197 F3
Wyndale Dr NG18 . . . . .103 A5
Wyndham Ct NG9 . . . . .183 B4

Wyndham Mews NG3 . . . .173 B7
Wyndings The NG5. . . . . . .161 F4
Wynhill Ct NG13 . . . . .177 C5
Wynlea Dr S81 . . . . .16 F6
Wyndale Dr NG5. . . . . .161 A3
Wynndale Prim Sch
 NG18 . . . . .103 A5
Wynward Cl DE7 . . . . .157 C3
Wynwood Cl NG9 . . . . .183 B2
Wynwood Rd NG9 . . . . . . .183 B1
Wysale Dr NG8 . . . . .159 E1
Wysall Cl NG19 . . . . .87 E1
Wysall La
 Keyworth NG12. . . . . .207 D7
 Wymeswold LE12. . . . . .216 D5
Wythburn Cl NG2 . . . . .186 C6
Wyton Cl NG5 . . . . .161 A5
Wyvelle Cres DE74. . . . . . .203 C3
Wyvern Ave NG10 . . . . . . .193 D6
Wyvern Cl NG16 . . . . .158 A8
Wyvern St NG7 . . . . .222 A3

Y

Yalding Dr NG8 . . . . .171 C4
Yalding Gdns NG8 . . . . . . .171 C4
Yarwell Cl NG3 . . . . .174 C7
Yatesbury Cres NG8. . . . . .171 E8
Yates Gdns 2 NG5. . . . . . .161 A8
Yellowhammer Dr S81. . . .35 D7
Yeoman Ave NG6 . . . . .146 F4
Yeoman Cl S80 . . . . .36 A4
Yeoman Park Specl Sch
 NG19. . . . . .88 C4
Yeomans Cl NG7. . . . . .222 C2
Yeovil Ct 8 NG18 . . . . . . .103 A2
Yew Barrow Cl NG2. . . . . .186 C5
Yew Cl
 East Leake LE12 . . . . .214 D8
 Nottingham NG5 . . . . .161 D2
Yewdale Cl
 Nottingham NG11 . . . . .195 D8
 West Bridgford NG2 . . . . . .186 C5
Yew Tree Ave
 5 Kirkby in A NG17 . . . . .114 F4
 Nottingham NG5 . . . . .161 C1
Yew Tree Cl
 New Ollerton NG22 . . . . . . .77 C5
 Radcliffe on T NG12. . . . . .175 D3
Yew Tree Dr
 Bawtry DN10. . . . . .9 F7
 Huthwaite NG17 . . . . .99 F2
 Shirebrook NG20. . . . . .72 D5
Yew Tree La
 Carlton NG4. . . . . .163 A2
 Nottingham NG11 . . . . .184 C2
Yew Tree Rd
 Elkesley DN22 . . . . .50 B4
 Hucknall NG15. . . . . .146 B4
 New Ollerton NG22 . . . . . . .77 C5
Yew Tree Way NG24 . . . . .125 F2
Yonge Cl NG12. . . . . .175 E2
York Ave
 Beeston NG9 . . . . .183 F4
 Sandiacre NG10. . . . . .182 A5
 Westwood NG16 . . . . .128 B4
York Cl
 Carlton NG4. . . . . .162 F2
 East Leake LE12 . . . . .205 D1
York Dr NG8 . . . . .159 D2
Yorke Dr NG24. . . . . .125 B3
Yorke St
 Hucknall NG15. . . . . .146 A7
 Mansfield Woodhouse NG19 88 B2
York Pl S81. . . . . .34 F7
York Rd
 Harworth DN11. . . . . .9 A4
 Long Eaton NG10. . . . . .182 D1
 Loughborough LE11. . . . . . .220 A3
 Shirebrook NG20. . . . . .72 E3
 Tickhill DN11. . . . . .8 B7
York St
 Carlton NG4. . . . . .175 A7
 East Markham NG22. . . . . . .65 F7
 Mansfield NG18. . . . . .102 A5
 Nottingham NG1 . . . . .223 E4
 Sutton in A NG17 . . . . .100 E3
York Terr
 Market Warsop NG20 . . . . .74 B4
 Misterton DN10. . . . . .7 A2
 Pinxton NG16. . . . . .113 C1
Young Cl NG6. . . . . .159 F5
Young Cres NG17 . . . . .101 B2
Youngs Av NG24 . . . . .140 E2
Youngs Cres NG24. . . . . . .125 E2
Yvonne Cres NG4 . . . . .174 F7

Z

Zouch Rd LE12 . . . . .213 A3
Zulla Rd NG3. . . . . .173 C8
Zulu Rd NG7. . . . . .160 F2

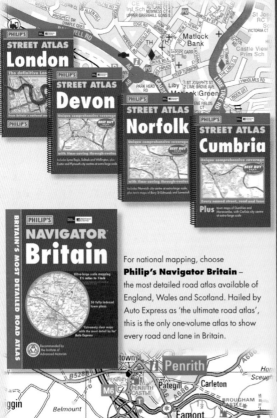